D0960573

Sticky Fingers

Sticky Fingers

The Life and Times of Jann Wenner and *Rolling Stone* Magazine

JOE HAGAN

ALFRED A. KNOPF
New York Toronto
2017

THIS IS A BORZOI BOOK
PUBLISHED BY ALFRED A. KNOPF

www.aaknopf.com

Knopf, Borzoi Books, and the colophon are registered trademarks of Penguin Random House LLC.

Library of Congress Cataloging-in-Publication Data
Names: Hagan, Joe, 1971– author.
Title: Sticky fingers : the life and times of Jann Wenner and
    Rolling stone magazine / Joe Hagan.
Description: First edition. | New York : Alfred A. Knopf, 2017.
Identifiers: LCCN 2017018102 (print) | LCCN 2017028387 (ebook) |
    ISBN 9781101874370 (hardcover) | ISBN 9781101874387 (ebook)
Subjects: LCSH: Wenner, Jann. | Editors—United States—Biography. |
    Publishers and publishing—United States—Biography. | Rolling stone
    (San Francisco, Calif.)
Classification: LCC Z473.W46 (ebook) | LCC Z473.W46 H34 2017 (print) |
    DDC 070.5/1092 [B]—dc23
LC record available at https://lccn.loc.gov/2017018102

Library and Archives Canada Cataloguing in Publication
Hagan, Joe, 1971– author.
    Sticky fingers : the life and times of Jann Wenner and
Rolling stone magazine / Joe Hagan.
Issued in print and electronic formats.
ISBN 978-0-345-81505-7
eBook ISBN 978-0-345-81507-1
    1. Wenner, Jann.   2. Publishers and publishing—United States—
Biography.   3. Editors—United States—Biography.   4. Rolling stone
(San Francisco, Calif.).   I. Title.
Z473.W46H34 2017   070.5'1092   C2017-903820-6

Jacket photograph of Jann Wenner, August 2, 1970.
Bettmann/Getty Images

Jacket design by Oliver Munday

Manufactured in the United States of America
First Edition

*This book is dedicated to Samantha Hunt
and our merry band, Rosa, Marie, and Juliet*

Can't you hear me knocking?

—*The Rolling Stones*

Contents

Sticky Fingers

Prologue: Get Back

John Lennon was in a movie theater, crying.

The image of Paul, singing from the rooftop in the final ten minutes, had set him off. Jann Wenner shifted in his seat. In the darkness of a tiny movie house in San Francisco, the Beatle, Wenner's hero, whose iconic spectacles and nose adorned the first issue of his rock-and-roll newspaper, *Rolling Stone,* had tears running down his cheeks as light flickered off his glasses. And next to him was Yoko Ono, the bête noire of Beatledom, raven hair shrouding her porcelain face, also weeping.

It was a Saturday afternoon in the spring of 1970, and John and Yoko and Jann and his wife, Jane Wenner, were watching the final scenes of *Let It Be,* the documentary about the Beatles' acrimonious last recording session. John and Yoko were deep into primal scream therapy, their emotions raw and close to the surface, and the image of a bearded Paul McCartney singing from the rooftop of Apple Records, against a cold London wind, was too much to bear.

Get back to where you once belonged . . .

For Wenner, the twenty-four-year-old boy wonder of the new rock press, who worshipped the Beatles as passionately as any kid in America, this was a dream, sitting here in the dark, wiping away his own tears at the twilight of the greatest band of all time, elbow to elbow with "the most famous person in the world, for God's sake."

"And it's just the four of us in the center of an empty theater," marveled Wenner, "all kind of huddled together, and John is crying his eyes out."

Lennon and Ono had driven up from Los Angeles to meet the San Francisco fanboy who had bottled the counterculture and now commanded 200,000 readers. Wenner received the couple like visiting royalty to his spanking-new offices on Third Street, the clatter of typewriters going silent as they walked through the cubbies of writers and editors, bushy-haired men in ties and Levi's who paused from parsing Captain Beefheart and Pete Townshend to gawk. Wenner's unabashed idol worship had so often embarrassed them—*starfucker,* they grumbled behind his back—but now here he was with an actual Beatle. And Yoko! Who could deny this? The hirsute supercouple were smaller than anybody imagined, but John Lennon still towered over Jann Wenner, who at five six so often found himself gazing up at his heroes like a boy vampire.

"I mean, it's everything you ever worshipped or cherished from afar," said Wenner. "You try and be as natural as possible because I don't think people want the worship and the 'gee whiz.' And you're just mainly curious and fascinated and hanging on to every word but also trying to be sociable, entertaining, and good company and not be groupie-ish and slavish."

Wenner guided them to his back office, past the plastic marijuana plant and the picture of Mickey Mouse shooting heroin, laboring to project the air of a self-possessed press baron inured to celebrity. He looked every bit the modish publisher, plump in his button-down oxford and blue jeans, shoulder-length hair fashionably styled, a True cigarette smoking in his fingers. Wenner personally moved the couple from the Hilton to the more upscale Huntington Hotel, in Nob Hill, and then took them sightseeing in Wenner's convertible Porsche, hoping to impress. "People like John Lennon," Wenner would say, "want to feel they are dealing with somebody important."

It worked, but maybe not for the reason he imagined: Yoko Ono's memory of the weekend would be Jane Wenner, Jann's wife, a chicly dressed waif with sculpted cheekbones and an insolent gaze. "I thought, how lucky is this man!" said Ono. "What did he do to get her?"

The women were crammed in the back of the Porsche, while Wenner and Lennon talked up front and Wenner drove through the hills where Ono once lived as a child in the 1930s with her Japanese immigrant parents, scions of imperial wealth. While he casually offered advice on promoting Lennon's promised "primal" album and inquired about their lifestyle in Los Angeles (Wenner recalled John and Yoko living in the mansion featured in *The Beverly Hillbillies*), Wenner found the proximity to John Fucking Lennon as intoxicating as a drug. Here was the selfsame Beatle who'd cracked open Wenner's world in 1964 when, on summer break from UC Berkeley, he first saw *A Hard Day's Night* in a Pasadena movie theater. The sly smile and scabrous wit had seemed to wink across the screen directly at him. Wenner even named his aborted novel for a Beatles lyric—"Now These Days Are Gone," a nostalgic, Holden Caulfield–at–Berkeley roman à clef. From the very first issue of *Rolling Stone,* Lennon was the lodestar: In his first editorial on November 9, 1967, Wenner declared that *Rolling Stone* was "not just about music, but also about the things and attitudes that the music embraces," proving his point with a cover image of Lennon from his role as Musketeer Gripweed in Richard Lester's absurdist antiwar comedy, *How I Won the War.* "Since 1965," wrote Wenner for an issue naming Lennon *Rolling Stone*'s "Man of the Year," a few months before John and Yoko's visit, "the Beatles have been the single dominant force in the new social thought and style for which the Sixties will forever be remembered, just as Charlie Chaplin was the public figure of the Twenties."

And so every moment with John Lennon felt like a story Wenner would tell for the rest of his life, a page of history he'd stepped into—indeed, that he would publish. Every detail of the weekend seemed charged with significance: the white sneakers dangling from Lennon's flight bag, the look of shock on the bellboy's face at the snobbish hotel when Lennon casually tossed him the bag. Over lunch, Wenner watched with awe and a certain satisfaction as Lennon savaged fans who approached him. "People would come up and ask him for an autograph, and he would just snarl, 'Go away!'" Wenner said.

When they got out to stretch their legs on Polk Street at four in the afternoon—the skies overcast, not a soul on the sidewalk—they chanced upon a little movie house showing a matinee of the Beatles film

Let It Be. Wenner figured John Lennon of all people had seen it, but he hadn't. Just as surprising, the woman selling tickets didn't recognize Lennon—another bearded hippie who looked like John Lennon—and none of the half a dozen people in the theater noticed that John and Yoko themselves had ducked in. "It was so emotional to see Paul up on the roof and singing," recounted Jane Wenner. "First of all, it was hard to believe John had never seen it before. And he was so taken aback."

An hour later, blinking in the evening light, Jann and Jane Wenner were crying, too. They began to hug, all four of them, on the sidewalk. "He's crying, she's crying, and we're just trying to hold on to ourselves," Wenner said. "You're there helping come to the emotional rescue of the Beatles."

But if this was the end of the Beatles, it was only the beginning for Jann Wenner. He was, after all, courting John Lennon for an exclusive interview in *Rolling Stone.* And before the weekend was over, Lennon would give Wenner a kind of promissory note in the form of an inscription inside a copy of Arthur Janov's book *The Primal Scream: Primal Therapy, the Cure for Neurosis:*

> Dear Jann,
> After many years of "searching"—tobacco, pot, acid, meditation, brown rice, you name it—I am finally on the road to freedom, i.e., being REAL + STRAIGHT.
> I hope this book helps you as much as [it did] for Yoko + me. I'll tell you the "True Story" when we're finished.
>
> Love, John + Yoko

•

ROLLING STONE CAUGHT FIRE as soon as it first appeared in November 1967. The fertile crescent of psychedelia, the Bay Area, was a firmament of names and places that were already becoming touchstones for a generation: Haight-Ashbury, the Grateful Dead and the Jefferson Airplane, Ken Kesey and the Merry Pranksters, Bill Graham and the Fillmore, the Hells Angels and the Black Panthers. Music was at the center of much of it, but it was bigger than music. It was an entire worldview in which young people had cornered the market on Truth with a capital *T.*

As John Lennon would articulate it for Wenner in *Rolling Stone:* "Rock and roll then was real, everything else was unreal." The original rock and roll that Elvis Presley built out of rural black blues had already been reduced and refined to (quite unreal) teen idols like Frankie Avalon and Ricky Nelson. Even the British Invasion, three years earlier, seemed brittle against the hammer blows of civil rights and the Vietnam War. The psychedelic counterculture of San Francisco promised a revolution, one immune to capitalist forces.

In those first days, Wenner was the star of his own magazine. For people who first got their hands on *Rolling Stone,* the editor with the Swedish-sounding name—or was Jann a girl? Not many knew (it was pronounced *Yahn*)—was their avatar in print, their gate-crasher at the Fillmore, a superfan as attuned to pot humor and art school nudity as they were, as versed in antiwar rhetoric, as hot to get his sticky fingers on a new Stones LP. *Rolling Stone* arrived on newsstands like a secret handshake: In a canny bit of salesmanship, Wenner offered a complimentary roach clip with every subscription, the "handy little device," each one lathed by his future brother-in-law, sculptor Bob Kingsbury.

Wenner was the fan he purported to be, but that was only one side of him. Though he walked in step with the counterculture, he was also a Kennedy-worshipping preppy whose thwarted ambition to attend Harvard had diverted him to Berkeley, a locus of left-wing radicalism where Wenner spent half his time with his nose pressed against the glass of high society. An inveterate social climber whom friends found so cocky as to be overbearing, Wenner crashed debutante balls and went on ski weekends to private resorts with rich and handsome friends who knew Kennedys and Hearsts. Keen to obscure his Jewishness, and his latent homosexuality, he chased after the sons and daughters of Old San Francisco—the children of local industry—as they migrated from the stolid precincts of Pacific Heights to pot-smogged Haight-Ashbury. Here was a breathtaking new freedom and opportunity, a world unhinged and made boundless by reality-smashing chemicals. "The freest generation this country has ever seen," marveled Ralph Gleason, the music critic for the *San Francisco Chronicle* and Wenner's mentor and co-founder in *Rolling Stone.* "No makeup, no bouffant hairdos, no button-down shirts and ties and no Brooks Brothers suits."

Wenner imbibed the new values—sex and drugs and rock and roll—but they were folded into a larger pattern of aspiration. He understood that along with the drugs and freedom there was fame, and also money. As a teenager, he attended a boarding school in Los Angeles that housed the offspring of Hollywood royalty, including Liza Minnelli, with whom he waltzed at a school dance. Their sparkling pedigrees offered Wenner solace from his broken home life. To fit in, he carefully monitored and organized his classmates in the school yearbook and won their allegiance with a rogue newspaper he invented to advertise his popularity and antagonize the faculty. Journalism was his VIP pass to everything he could hope to be.

To speak to the kids who understood that the revolution had arrived in 1967—to speak to the kids *who got it*—required a voice in the same register and cryptography as Bob Dylan's stoned telegrams, which Jann Wenner absorbed in lysergic waves with his head between two KLH speakers lying on his apartment floor in Berkeley. Wenner would later say he related to the Miss Lonely character in the seminal Dylan song "Like a Rolling Stone"—the female dilettante and object of scorn to whom Dylan is laying down his bitter education.

But Wenner was a quick study. He had an intuitive grasp of the most significant quality of the new rock audience: Unlike the one that fueled the British Invasion, it was largely male. For marketers, this new youth culture was uncharted territory, and Wenner was the pioneer. Until 1966, the primary outlets in America for the Beatles and the Rolling Stones were *16* and *Tiger Beat,* New York–based magazines for teenage girls who fetishized Paul and John and Mick and Keith as objects of romance and trivia. Wenner made it safe for boys to ogle their male idols as rapturously as any girl might by adding a healthy dose of intellectual pretense—a phenomenon that kicked into high gear with *Sgt. Pepper's Lonely Hearts Club Band,* released five months before *Rolling Stone* appeared. "If James Joyce played the electric guitar he would probably have made an album like *Sergeant Pepper's Lonely Hearts Club Band,*" wrote Wenner in a review pitched to *High Fidelity* magazine (and rejected as "pretentious guff").

In one sense, *Rolling Stone* was a natural reaction to *Sgt. Pepper's,* which signaled the emergence of full-length 33⅓ rpm albums as public statements to be fetishized and reckoned with—in effect, news from the youth front. The turning point was the Monterey International Pop Festival in June 1967, the convergence of new rock groups from London, New York, and Los Angeles for a media spectacle covered by every news outlet in America. It was arranged and produced by record men from Los Angeles and promoted by the erstwhile press secretary for the Beatles, who conscripted Jann Wenner to write publicity material. By courting the record men who knew next to nothing about what the San Francisco kids were doing and saying in private, Wenner was perfectly positioned as a go-between, connecting the counterculture of Haight-Ashbury—which every head in America now looked to for cues on LPs, politics, dope, and sexuality—and what was then known as the straight world. The two were already on a collision course, but Wenner, more than anyone else, catalyzed the process. "The business world, which was represented by the record companies, was just so old-fashioned and foreign," said Wenner. "They reluctantly came to rock and roll."

In creating *Rolling Stone*, Wenner borrowed heavily from a short-lived biweekly newspaper called *The Sunday Ramparts*, where Wenner worked until it ceased publication in June 1967. After Monterey, Wenner hustled up $7,500—the largest chunk from Jane's father, a Manhattan dentist—and simply recycled the defunct paper, an adjunct of *Ramparts* magazine, as his own. The printer didn't have to change the settings on the Goss Suburban press machine to spit out *Rolling Stone,* and Wenner even recycled the design and layout, a parody of stuffy British newspapers like *The Times* of London. The first issues had a primitive simplicity, but the clean lines and functional columns looked audacious next to underground papers like *Crawdaddy!* or the San Francisco *Oracle,* which defied convention with willfully amateurish layouts. By contrast, *Rolling Stone* was thoroughly commercial: The Fleet Street fonts and pin-striped lines of the original *Sunday Ramparts* were created by an advertising agency founded by Howard Gossage, a pal of Tom Wolfe and Marshall McLuhan who produced print ads for the Sierra Club and Rover cars. (The designer was a woman named Marget Larsen.)

It was this—the radical conventionality of *Rolling Stone*—that was Jann Wenner's most important innovation. When he stamped the whole package with a psychedelic logo designed by poster artist Rick

Griffin—the curled ligatures and looping serifs unmistakable signifiers of dope-peddling head shops on Haight-Ashbury—he instantly legitimized and mainstreamed the underground.

From the vantage of a swivel chair in a warehouse loft on Brannan Street, Wenner and his "little rock & roll newspaper from San Francisco" brought first-name intimacy to the scene. For the first issue, he simply drove across town to the Haight-Ashbury to interview the Grateful Dead in their living room and help publicize their arrest for pot possession. Keyboardist Ron "Pigpen" McKernan hoisted a rifle for the photo op—a triumph, a gleeful dare. "All the news that fits," Wenner put above his title, tweaking the East Coast's central journalistic institution. And his headlines declared it so: "A New Beatles Movie!"; "Eric Burdon Quits the Animals!"; "Jim Morrison Exposed!"; "John and Yoko Rock Toronto"; "Chicago 7: Youth on Trial"; "Paul McCartney Gets Back"; "Bob's Back!"

In 1967, it was still a radical idea to publish college-educated intellectuals like Jon Landau and Greil Marcus opining on James Brown or the Jefferson Airplane as if it were serious art, like jazz. "Though he didn't invent serious pop criticism, Jann was the one who popularized it," observed Mick Jagger, whose band had been playing to teenage girls for five years when *Rolling Stone* began. "There were magazines before, and criticism before, but the magazines were a bit fly-by-night and they weren't taken seriously. But this was a whole magazine about it that was dedicated to semi-serious criticism."

As far away as London, mods and rockers alike started passing *Rolling Stone* around. Suddenly Jagger knew Jann Wenner's name—the San Francisco kid with the chutzpah to name a magazine after his band and then trash his latest record. Bob Dylan was sent a letter from Wenner asking him to write a story for a new magazine named after his six-minute radio hit. Wenner printed every last utterance of Pete Townshend of the Who—an interview recorded at Wenner's apartment on Potrero Hill in the spring of 1968—as if it were an exclusive with God on the second day of creation. Twelve pages over two issues, some sixteen thousand words. Townshend loved it. And for eighteen-year-olds fretting over the draft and blowing pot smoke out their bedroom windows between sides of *The Who Sell Out,* Townshend's words were *the news.*

"Rock and roll is enormous," Townshend told Wenner. "It's one of the biggest musical events in history. It's equal to *the* classical music . . . You don't care what periods [the songs] were written in, what they mean, what they're about. It's the bloody explosion they create when you let the gun off. It's the event. That's what rock and roll is. That is why rock and roll is powerful."

The next week, *Time* magazine featured Spiro Agnew on the cover.

That somebody had dared—bothered, in the sentiment of the mainstream—to apply straight journalism to rock culture was a revelation. Eager for fame and legitimacy, the rockers were flattered. "I'll tell you what Jann did," said Keith Richards. "He put together a really good gang of writers, nice kids. Not afraid to go and ask questions. And turned something that could have just been a fan magazine into a real piece of journalism. That's what I think Jann did."

Five months after the Townshend interview, Wenner beat *Time* magazine on a story about the phenomenon of rock groupies, waving for the mainstream press to come have a peek at his collection of titillating nudes by taking out a full-page promotional ad in *The New York Times.*

It shouldn't be surprising that Wenner himself, roiling with unfiltered ambition, needed an editor. His girlfriend, Jane Schindelheim, a petite and neurotic creature of Manhattan, rolled her eyes at the dumpy San Francisco hippies living in squalor on the Haight. But when she met Jann Wenner while working as a receptionist at *Ramparts,* she had to marvel at his white-hot ambition, the naive charm and vulgarity of it, his brusque arrogance and childish whims, his casual betrayals and bullying force, the unembarrassed yen for work and excess. Somebody would surely have to look after this little barbarian whose lust for money, drugs, and sex threatened to outpace his razor intellect and turn him into Augustus Gloop falling into the chocolate river of the 1960s. She would become his wife and co-owner but also his compass and custodian, his style counselor and resident paranoid who fretted and plotted from behind the drapes. Her seductive beauty and chic tastes hedged against Wenner's extroversion and frequent obnoxiousness and became part of the formula for *Rolling Stone,* which was partly a social institution, a private club. She manicured Wenner's social life, offered succor to his biggest talents, and repaired relationships with people who felt burned by Wenner and his sometimes ruthless magazine. "She's the only one standing still in all these speedy lives," said photographer Annie Leibovitz, for whom Jane Wenner was a muse and steward in her early career. "I think [the Wenners] kind of understood that they were both attractive. Some people would be more attracted to Jane, and her personality, than to Jann and his."

The two were only intermittently attracted to each other, at least sexually. While Jann explored his sexuality with both men and women, Jane consoled herself with her own affairs—including dalliances with Leibovitz, whose intimacy with both Wenners completed a triangle of ambition and pleasure that lay at the creative heart of *Rolling Stone* in the 1970s. For all their ceaseless drift and constant coming apart, Jann and Jane always remained loyal to their cause, *Rolling Stone,* never tiring of each other, and it was a remarkably successful marriage, one that seemed to chart the culture as it shifted.

•

AFTER THE IDEALISM of Woodstock Nation was snuffed out at the infamous Altamont concert in December 1969, *Rolling Stone,* which had always had one foot in the world of commerce, was uniquely positioned to dominate the 1970s. With the record industry at his back, Wenner could annex new social worlds through journalism, fanning the ambitions of major American writers like Tom Wolfe and Hunter S. Thompson by offering their exploding-sandwich journalism as epic feasts for his stoned readers. Thompson, the single most important writer in the history of *Rolling Stone,* injected Wenner's magazine with a crucial piece of DNA—"gonzo" journalism, a form of performance-art writing, both uproarious and informed by deep reporting—that the Brahmins of the mainstream press could not ignore. Nor could they ignore the *Rolling Stone* readership who adored it. On the cult success of "Fear and Loathing in Las Vegas" in 1971, Wenner aimed his new star directly at the 1972 presidential campaign and hitched his magazine to quintessential youth candidate Senator George McGovern of South Dakota.

Thompson's book on the election—*Fear and Loathing: On the Campaign Trail '72*—made *Rolling Stone* the undisputed voice of the rock-and-roll generation.

As Tom Wolfe told *Rolling Stone* in 1987, youth culture was the most important thing to emerge from the 1960s, including Vietnam or civil rights. "Any of the big historical events of the Sixties are overshadowed by what young people did," he said. "And they did it because they had money. For the first time in the history of man, young people had the money, the personal freedom and the free time to build monuments and pleasure palaces to their own tastes."

Wenner, by birthright and inclination, was the ideal tastemaker to build those monuments. The raw material was rock and roll, but the primary building block was celebrity. And at its base, *Rolling Stone* was an expression of Wenner's pursuit of fame and power. He reinvented celebrity around youth culture, which equated confession and frank sexuality with integrity and authenticity. The post-1960s vision of celebrity meant that every printed word of John Lennon's unhappiness and anything Bob Dylan said or did now had the news primacy of a State of the Union address. It meant that Hunter Thompson could make every story he ever wrote, in essence, about himself. It also meant that climbing into bed with Mick Jagger was only worth doing if you had a Nikon handy. Self-image was the new aphrodisiac.

The 1970s was "the Me Decade," in Wolfe's famous coinage, defined by endless "remaking, remodeling, elevating, and polishing one's very self." This was a fundamentally Californian mandate, sprung from the halls of Berkeley and the hills of Hollywood, where a devotion to hedonism was baked into the West's culture of escapism and reinvention. That made Jann Wenner a walking bellwether, his own curiosities and desires a perfect editorial template for *Rolling Stone*. "He leads with his appetites—I take, I see, I have," said Art Garfunkel, a close friend in the 1970s.

From a lavishly appointed Victorian on California Street in San Francisco, Wenner and his wife hosted a rolling drug salon during the 1970s, mixing pleasure with *Rolling Stone* business with the stars of the moment, whether Michael Douglas or Jackson Browne or John Belushi. A core irony of *Rolling Stone* was that its founder celebrated every kind of personal liberty imaginable but his own. But his hidden homosexuality—and that of his chief photographer—nonetheless opened *Rolling Stone* to the currents of the decade, when androgyny and ambiguous sexuality were in vogue. Wenner understood innately the longing of young men who papered their bedrooms with posters of a shirtless Robert Plant. Being gay, said Wenner, "gave me a good and finer appreciation of the sexuality of the guys up there on the stage, and I could understand that in a way that other people didn't, to understand how sexual this whole thing was. All of rock and roll is sex, defined. I got it more. And I could see it; I was open to it. I was enjoying it. Much like the girls, and much like the guys who may not admit it, but it was really sexual."

Exploiting the talents of Annie Leibovitz, who was in love with his wife, Wenner could divine the homosexual subtext of a hetero rock culture through acts of image making, personally manning the turnstile to his distinct American moment—*Rolling Stone*'s cover. Leibovitz's nude photograph of teen idol David Cassidy on the cover in 1972— with a *Playboy*-inspired centerfold inside—was a signal moment, selling thousands of copies of *Rolling Stone* and establishing a new standard for self-exposure (and self-reinvention). It was also something Jann Wenner enjoyed looking at. Wenner turned the cover of *Rolling Stone* into a rock-and-roll confession box, with Paul Simon, George Harrison, Fleetwood Mac, James Taylor, Carly Simon, and Crosby, Stills, Nash, and Young all eager to climb inside the Oxford border and expose their dramas, and very often their flesh, so as to be sanctified by the essential *self-seriousness* of *Rolling Stone*. And as the cover became the prime sales pitch for selling records, and the prime sales pitch of Wenner's magazine, Wenner made *Rolling Stone* into a cultural event, adding vibrant colors (a rainbow border around a fedora-wearing Truman Capote), moody studio portraiture (Kris Kristofferson in shadow), winking humor (a Vargas girl riding a silver dildo for a Steely Dan profile), adventurous illustration (Daniel Ellsberg as a Roman bust), and liberal doses of insouciant sexuality whenever possible (Wenner commanded Annie Leibovitz to make Linda Ronstadt look like a "Tijuana whore").

None of this was exactly unique to *Rolling Stone*—art director George Lois pioneered pop irony at *Esquire;* Hugh Hefner liberated sexuality in *Playboy*—but *Rolling Stone* authenticated celebrity in a new way. Under Rick Griffin's banner, Wenner could place Dustin Hoffman, Jane Fonda, Bette Midler, Richard Pryor, George McGovern, and even John Denver in the same continuum as the Beatles, Bob Dylan, and the Rolling Stones. It was all prefigured by the cover of *Sgt. Pepper's*—a cavalcade of personalities and icons, seemingly disconnected but all flowing forth from a single fountain of youth.

And as the youth culture took over, Wenner built up a network of powerful co-conspirators: important writers and photographers (Tom Wolfe and Dick Avedon), ambitious record men and talent agents (David Geffen, Ahmet Ertegun), Hollywood executives and movie stars (Barry Diller, Richard Gere), Washington power brokers and politicians (Richard Goodwin, Ted Kennedy), and, his very favorites, the social matrons and celebrity icons in whose rarefied spheres gay men were welcome (Diane von Furstenberg and Jackie Onassis). This was a formula for Wenner's success. "The friendships I made with people, plus their desire to have publicity, plus the demonstrated integrity and value of *Rolling Stone,* it all was easy to do," said Wenner, hastening to add a last ingredient: "And my own charm."

The result was that from 1971 to 1977, Jann Wenner was the most important magazine editor in America, shepherding the generational plotlines of the 1960s into a rambling biweekly serial of rock-and-roll news, hard and outrageous (and impossibly long) journalism, left-wing political opinion, sexual liberation, and drugs—always drugs. It was a man's magazine, though women read it; it was a white magazine, though African Americans were fetishized in it; it was a left-wing magazine, though it was tempered by Wenner's devotion to the establishment. And the success of *Rolling Stone* would eventually make Wenner a full-blooded figure of that establishment. *Time* magazine named him one of the Top 200 "Faces for the Future" in America in 1974, among the youngest on the list at twenty-eight ("a brilliant, brash autocrat with an eye for lucrative markets and talented writers").

By the time Wenner moved his magazine to New York from San Francisco in 1977, rock and roll had become so mainstream—and profitable—it had already begun producing its own rebellion: punk. But with his lock hold on the music establishment, Wenner could navigate through cultural storms. *Rolling Stone* was a formula Wenner could recalibrate from year to year, absorbing, and exploiting, any new trend. While he recruited feisty new talents like Charles M. Young—a tall, lanky punk devotee they dubbed "the Reverend"—to cover the Sex Pistols, a band Wenner despised, Wenner could test his influence elsewhere, first in Washington, D.C., where he used his readership as a kind of youth lobby to expand his political influence, and then in Hollywood, where he tried mightily to reinvent himself as a movie producer while funneling favored movie stars to the cover of *Rolling Stone.* Indeed, *Fast Times at Ridgemont High,* the definitive youth movie of the 1980s, was launched partly because Wenner realized he knew nothing about what modern young people were doing and so sent reporter Cameron Crowe to find out.

When California Republican Ronald Reagan entered the White House in 1981, Wenner had so thoroughly stamped his times with the *Rolling Stone* worldview that he would arrive at the preppy green lawns of the new decade like a late Roman emperor, haloed by glittering friends and plump with self-satisfaction. His unembarrassed appetite for stardom and excess had made him an object of scorn and parody but also a rich man—and right on cue as his generation was embracing the "greed is good" ethos, wealth and power as their natural birthright. And he had proven that his original insight of 1967 was an abiding one: that the 1960s were, at bottom, a business. This didn't mean the original idealism was bogus—only that it was a thing you could stay tethered to through commerce, and specifically a subscription to *Rolling Stone.* For Wenner, idealism was never the enemy of money. "It was a false dichotomy," said Wenner. "Well, it's America! Rock and roll is America."

In the 1980s, rock and roll became an all-powerful institution—the opposite of revolutionary, except in the sense that Jann Wenner had turned the youth revolution into a spectacularly profitable enterprise. From there, Wenner went through all the baby-boomer stations of the cross, and made journalism out of them. He launched a parenting magazine when he had children (*Family Life*) and a men's magazine for his midlife crisis (*Men's Journal*). He would come out of the closet as a gay man in the spring of 1995, leaving Jane for a fashion designer named Matt Nye, when the vogue for coming out was in. By then, Wenner himself was interviewing sitting presidents, starting with Bill Clinton in 1993 and shuttling Bob Dylan in his private jet to the televised stage of the Rock and Roll Hall of Fame, an institution he helped found with Ahmet Ertegun of Atlantic Records and operated like his personal fiefdom. Jann Wenner cast himself as—and indeed was—the gatekeeper of the rock-and-roll story. That story was underwritten by the same market forces that produced classic rock radio stations, rock-and-roll-themed restaurants, and endless television and film revivals about the 1960s. Rock and roll sold beer and cars and clothes and watches and piles and piles of *Rolling Stone* magazines. At one point, *Rolling Stone* was throwing off $30 million a year in pure profit, making Jann Wenner a bona fide media baron of Manhattan.

It didn't necessarily make him beloved. In years to come, Jann Wenner's bold-faced contradictions would drive nearly everyone who knew him mad. But it was his schizophrenic nature—a polarity of vulnerability and rageful ambition—that drove the magazine. He was an antiwar liberal *and* a rapacious capitalist, naive *and* crafty, friend *and* enemy, straight *and* gay, editor *and* publisher. His mother would say of him, "I've always felt Jann was twelve years old going on seventy-five. He's certainly the most conservative member of our family."

Success would blunt Wenner's feel for the culture and sow the seeds of his decline. He missed the rise of MTV and hip-hop, and later the Internet, cultural revolutions he experienced like a well-heeled uncle squinting toward Manhattan from a ski slope in Sun Valley, where he began wintering in the 1990s. It was the prickly celebrity tabloid *Us Weekly*—his last successful invention, highly lucrative but culturally toxic—that would barricade his flagging rock magazine against the collapse of both the record and the print industries, and later the entire economy in 2008. The war-ravaged presidency of George W. Bush reanimated *Rolling Stone*'s once-righteous reputation as a left-wing voice, and the market crash of 2008 inspired one last star for Wenner's journalistic firmament: Matt Taibbi, the heir to Hunter S. Thompson, whose attacks on the banking industry almost single-handedly revived the reputation of late-period *Rolling Stone*.

This book is drawn from over a hundred hours of conversation with Jann Wenner, from the contents of his voluminous archive of letters, documents, recordings, and photography, and from 240 interviews with musicians, writers, publishers, friends, lovers, and current and former employees of *Rolling Stone*. Jann Wenner's life tells the story of a man and his generation. It is also a parable of the age of narcissism. Through image and word, Wenner was a principal architect of the rules of modern self-celebration—the "Me" in the Me Decade. The self-involvement of rock stars and celebrities became, eventually, something everyone could emulate. His advocacy of boundary-pushing journalism and the liberal verities of the Democratic Party was fundamental to the *Rolling Stone* formula, but above all he was a fame maker. Today the signifiers of fame—confession, preening self-regard, and blunt sexuality—are so built into modern media manners that few can even recall a time when they were novel. But the framework of American narcissism—from the permission to unload personal demons in public to the rise of the selfie—has its roots in Jann Wenner's pioneering magazine making. In the age of social media, calculated authenticity is the coin of the realm. And *Rolling Stone* helped define what authenticity meant, and well after it became decoupled from the 1960s idealisms that birthed it. That Wenner is the same age as President Donald J. Trump, whose ascent to power was built on celebrity, is perhaps no coincidence. Indeed, Wenner's oldest friends saw in Trump's personality, if not his politics, a striking likeness to the *Rolling Stone* founder—deeply narcissistic men for whom celebrity is the ultimate confirmation of existence. At one time, Jann S. Wenner wanted to be president, too.

His ex-wife, Jane, would say Jann lacked the "what-if" gene. From boyhood, he compulsively hoarded every document of his life, every newspaper clipping, letter, draft of a letter, envelope, postcard, pamphlet, press release, financial record, photograph, and telegram— because he believed he would one day be *important*. He seemed never to consider the possibility that *Rolling Stone* might fail. And why should he? If his appetite seemed bottomless, if he was "mad to live, mad to talk, mad to be saved, desirous of everything," as Jack Kerouac had it in *On the Road* (a book Kerouac nearly titled *Rock and Roll Road*), if he regularly spent more money than he had, made enemies of friends in record time, and consumed drugs like a Viking, Wenner figured it would simply work out, as if the bounty of the biggest, richest generation in the history of the planet, converging on Northern California in 1967, was a kind of manifest destiny, an endless wind at his back.

•

WHEN THE JOHN LENNON INTERVIEW APPEARED in *Rolling Stone,* published over two issues in January and February 1971 with cover portraits by Annie Leibovitz, Lennon's unvarnished honesty and hostility, and the sheer volume of his words, were the shattering end of the Beatles. But it established *Rolling Stone* at the center of the culture, making international news. Not incidentally, it also put Wenner's newspaper, which had been struggling financially, on a sound footing. But Wenner, as was his wont, could not stop there with Lennon. The interview, titled "Lennon Remembers," was simply too powerful. And so he proposed to publish the interview as a book. And though John Lennon strongly objected, Wenner published it anyway. Lennon was furious. "John took it so badly," Yoko Ono said. "It's not what the book says, or the interview, but the fact that Jann betrayed him . . . He took the money and not the friendship."

It was a signal moment for the young publisher. And it was also completely in character, for better and worse. The two never spoke again.

BOOK I

The Wunderkind

1

Atlantis

They fuck you up, your mum and dad.
—Philip Larkin, "This Be the Verse"

J ann Wenner stood inside a closet, tripping on LSD. A kitten purred outside the door. A young woman, sitting cross-legged, stroked the kitten and smiled mystically.

It was the spring of 1965, and Denise Kaufman, a dark-haired free spirit who played blues harmonica and wore tall velvet boots, had met Wenner a few hours before while sitting with friends at the Terrace, the outdoor café on the campus of the University of California at Berkeley. The sit-ins and protests of the Free Speech Movement, which pitted students against the university's administration over civil rights and the First Amendment, had focused the nation's attention on Berkeley in the preceding months and now dominated the talk. They all seemed to think they were making history, destinies colliding in nearby apartments and along Telegraph Avenue over joints and copies of Joseph Heller's *Catch-22*.

A couple of Kaufman's friends had shown up with a grinning preppy in a Brooks Brothers shirt. The brash fireplug of a boy declared he was going to take LSD for the first time and write a psychology paper about it. Kaufman's eyebrows went up. She'd heard of Jann Wenner before. Her parents, wealthy Jewish liberals from Palo Alto, were acquainted with his mother, Sim Wenner, whose racy dime novel Kaufman had furtively thumbed through as a teenager back in 1961. Kaufman also knew a society girl, the daughter of a British diplomat, who lost her virginity to a notorious Jann Wenner. "I was like, 'This is that guy,'" she recalled. "We were sitting next to each other, and he started talking about LSD."

For his class, Wenner had checked out library books about psychedelics, including *The Psychedelic Experience: A Manual Based on the "Tibetan Book of the Dead"* by Timothy Leary. The chemical compound lysergic acid diethylamide, discovered in 1938 by Swedish chemist Albert Hofmann, was still legal in California, but not for long. In the preceding months, people had been returning with tales of wild experiences with Ken Kesey, the author of *One Flew over the Cuckoo's Nest,* whose playful social experiment in a garishly painted 1939 International Harvester school bus was already taking shape on a ranch in nearby La Honda. LSD-25, Kesey's acolytes reported, plunged the user into a state of euphoric revelation, the unconscious mind emerging from the depths like a lost kingdom. In his 1968 best seller, *The Electric Kool-Aid Acid Test,* Tom Wolfe would quote a woman who inadvertently drank "electrified" Kool-Aid at an early Grateful Dead show:

> I stood close to the band and let the vibrations engulf me. They started in my toes and every inch of me was quivering with them . . . they made a journey through my nervous system (I remember picturing myself as one of the charts we had studied in biology which shows the nerve network), traveling each tiny path, finally reaching the top of my head, where they exploded in glorious patterns of color and line.

Wolfe would portray Kaufman, who joined Kesey's Merry Pranksters that summer, as Mary Microgram. And so Ms. Microgram had to laugh at Wenner's absurd proposal. "Well, you're not going to be able to write that paper!" she explained to Wenner. He would need a guide, she said. "How about you?" Wenner flirted.

On the way to his apartment on Carleton Street, they stopped by a dormitory and a friend's house to borrow a kitten and a stack of LPs, including a modal folk guitar album by Sandy Bull called *Inventions.*

When they got to Wenner's apartment, the living room was littered with beer bottles from a sorority party he'd thrown the night before. "We went into his room, and [he] took this acid," Kaufman recalled. "We were just talking, and the kitten was playing, and then the acid started to come on. I had the Sandy Bull music on, and he was like, 'Take that off, I can't stand it.'"

Freaking out, Wenner opened his closet door, stepped inside, closed the door, and stood by himself in a laundry basket full of starched shirts. "And I said, 'That's fine, if you need me, I'm here,'" said Kaufman. "He was in there for a long time."

•

RAINBOW ROAD.

That was the name the Wenner family gave the woody drive leading to their new house. In 1951, Edward Wenner, a stout man with dungarees hiked to his chest, bulldozed the grounds himself. His wife, Sim, a slim and attractive woman who wore her hair short, had paid $3,000 for the five acres, and Ed banged out a ranch-style dwelling with exposed beams and large windows, a flagstone fireplace, a playroom for the children with a tiled checkerboard on the floor, an office for his wife, a carport for their imported sports cars—her Alfa Romeo, his MG. A towering oak tree stood out front. It was their homemade version of the California dream, nestled in the base of a land preserve in rural San Rafael, eighteen miles north of San Francisco.

All this was paid for by Baby Formulas Inc., the business Ed Wenner came to California to create. At one time, he would claim his company fed 90 percent of the babies within a hundred miles of San Francisco. In 1946, Ed and Sim had arrived in San Francisco with a baby of their own, Jan Simon Wenner. For years to come, the son would look at 8-millimeter home movies of this life on Rainbow Road—his mother filming him as he hopped around the patio in a cowboy hat while his father dug a hole for the swimming pool—and craft a dewy vision of his childhood. "It was a pretty idyllic and archetypal childhood for that time," he said. "They came from the East Coast, out of the military, out to golden California to find postwar fame and fortune; I was the first child of the baby boom."

Wenner's early memories of childhood included baby bottles moving down the assembly line in his father's factory on Sacramento and Laurel and his mother playing *Moonlight Sonata* on the piano when he went to bed at night. There were weekends at Squaw Valley, near Tahoe, where his father taught him skiing, which became a lifelong passion for Jann Wenner. There were the dogs, Adlai and Estes, named after liberal Democrats Adlai Stevenson and Estes Kefauver. There was his mother writing on her Olivetti typewriter while listening to the Joe McCarthy hearings on the radio.

But Rainbow Road was as much an escape as an arrival. The Wenners' new son was born only a few months before they left New York, at Beth Israel Hospital in Manhattan at 12:25 p.m. on January 7, 1946. In Wenner's baby book, his mother, Sim, describes being startled by "the enormity of his nose" and reports his eyes as blue; Ed believed they were brown. (They were blue.) In a single stroke, Sim both blessed and cursed her son by naming him Jan, writing that his name referred to the Roman mythological figure Janus, a byword for betrayal and contradiction. "Two-headed," she wrote. "Gatekeeper of heaven." (As a teenager, Jan would add the *n* to his first name.)

Sim would describe the birth of her son as a time of intense loneliness: The bars on the hospital windows, she told Wenner in 1982, were all that kept them both alive. "I would have jumped," she said. Wenner's first pediatrician was Dr. Benjamin Spock, the progressive doctor and civil rights activist, who published the best-selling *Common Sense Book of Baby and Child Care* the same year Wenner was born. Sim, whose name was shorthand for her maiden name, Simmons, came from a well-off family who lived on the Upper West Side near Central Park. Her parents were first cousins. Sim's mother, Zillah, came to New York from Australia, where her parents were unsuccessful merchants. Sim's father, Maurice Simmons, grew up poor in New York, but he shone with ambition: After graduating from City College in Manhattan, he served in the army during the Spanish-American War and helped found the Jewish War Veterans of the United States of America. He became a judge in New York and gave the nominating speech for Al Smith's first run for office in the early twentieth century. Zillah, whom he married in 1919, ran an antiques store that sold silverware.

The Simmonses poured their immigrant hopes into their firstborn son, Robert, but the birth of their second child, a daughter, two years later, would mark the abrupt end of the marriage. A serial philanderer, Maurice had an affair with the family governess in a drama that actually made headlines: *The New York Times* reported that Zillah filed for divorce, the governess was arrested for physically attacking Zillah with a dog leash, and Maurice sued Zillah's sister-in-law for libel after she called him a "scoundrel." By the time Sim was born in 1922, Zillah was so bitter she couldn't bring herself to name her daughter. "She was 'baby girl something' for the longest time," said Wenner.

Sim's childhood was shadowed by Zillah's anger—her mother regularly threatened to throw herself out the window—and starting at age twelve, Sim was raised by her maternal grandmother, Kate Gilbert Symonds, with whom she often shared a bed. By the time she reached adolescence, Sim had developed a flinty independence and a desperation to escape her mother. Around 1940, a white knight presented himself: Edward Weiner, a stocky but sporting fellow she met on a ski trip to Stowe, Vermont.

Ed was raised by a single mother who immigrated to Boston from Russia with a penniless and ne'er-do-well husband. After Ed's father died of cirrhosis when Ed was five, he and his mother, Mary, and an older sister made their way to Brooklyn, where Mary changed the family name to Weiner to escape her past (the previous name was forgotten, as was her husband's name). Mary Weiner struggled with a lingerie business and tasked little Edward with helping women snap on their brassieres. Ed spent hours alone in the library, educating himself enough to start high school at thirteen. He came to hate his mother for reasons he couldn't discuss: He had watched her and his sister spread newspapers around the shop and burn their business down to collect the insurance money—an act that nearly killed the Italian fruit vendors who lived upstairs. As he would recall later, he and his mother stood on the street and watched it burn: "The fruit merchant came out and he said, 'You did this! You did this! You could have killed my baby!'"

His mother fainted. "After the fire," Ed later said, "the Italian family moved out and she used the insurance money to expand and buy new merchandise."

Though he spent years in denial, the event left Ed tortured with guilt. "I could have killed somebody," he confessed in a documentary made by Jann Wenner's sister Kate. "You don't know what that feels like."

"Cheating, lying—I thought that's the way life was," he admitted. "How could I be something people respected or admired? I'm going to be something that people will like. I'm going to make myself something."

One day, Ed stole money from his mother's cash register, she discovered it, they fought, he struck her, and she had him arrested. After a night in jail, Ed left home and never returned. "No matter what I did, I had to do something bigger, tougher, to prove myself," he said. "I had to compensate for being poor and growing up in the slums."

At the dawn of America's entrance into World War II, Ed's ambition was the antidote for Sim's desperation. After Ed enlisted in the air force, Sim joined a women's volunteer unit. And while on spring break from Hunter College, she flew to Alabama, where Ed was stationed, and they got married in an air base chapel in the spring of 1941.

At first, the couple lived apart. Sim was training as a supply officer at Radcliffe College in Cambridge when she discovered what she would call her "homosexual gene," having an affair with a fellow volunteer. The woman, nicknamed Smitty, asked Sim to run away with her to California. Sim confessed the affair to Ed, who was surprisingly understanding and offered to end the marriage. But Sim would say she wanted a "normal" life with children—not one living as a lesbian pariah—and went with Ed. To cement the decision, they decided to have a baby. In the spring of 1945, while Sim and Ed were furloughed in New York, they conceived Jann Wenner on a train trip to Chicago. After he was discharged from the air force, Ed became a traveling salesman of surplus mattresses for recycling into paper mulch. With Jan Simon Wenner in utero, they moved to Elmhurst, Queens.

Ed and Sim rejected Judaism, viewing the old-world culture as an embarrassing millstone. In Wenner's baby book, Sim wrote that "any religious ceremonies will be of his own choosing and not ours." For Ed Wenner, "the words 'Jew' and 'poor' were synonymous," Kate Wenner wrote in *Setting Fires,* a loose fictionalization of their father's history published in 2000. If they were going to reinvent themselves, they had to get away. Around the time Jann was born, Ed and Sim changed the family name to Wenner from Weiner. "The explanation was that he didn't want us as children teased," said Jann Wenner. But it also obscured the Jewish background that Ed resented.

In 1946, Ed dreamed up a business idea, inspired by a story he'd read in a magazine: The babies of British war brides, while on boats to America, had gotten sick from drinking unsterilized milk. "It hit me right then," Ed told *Newsweek* in 1961, "terminal sterilization had possibilities as a commercial venture." So in 1947, they put Jann Wenner in the back of their Dodge Coupe and drove west, part of a great postwar migration to California. "Of course," wrote Sim Wenner in a memoir published in 1960, "that's where any real pioneer headed in those days. It was the land of gold, a state littered with patio pools and producing parents."

After a period in the city, they settled north of San Francisco in Mill Valley, just over the Golden Gate Bridge, and Ed Wenner rented a former butcher's shop with a freezer, spending nights in a sleeping bag while he figured out how to sterilize and bottle formula. To sell the idea, he peddled a twenty-five-page "Mother's Guide" describing the benefits of formula but then shifted to bulk sales to Bay Area hospitals. Despite her skepticism, Sim's mother, Zillah, lent them money to expand, and Ed bought a green truck, had a stork stenciled on it, and began delivering formula.

The business boomed, and so did the Wenners. Sim became pregnant again not long after they moved to California and gave birth to Kate Wenner in 1947. Two years later, she had another girl, Martha. But as Ed became consumed with the business, Sim began to think of motherhood as both too much and not enough. When Jann Wenner was two, she began going to work as the office manager for Baby Formulas, leaving the kids at home with a series of African American nannies. Sim Wenner later maintained that her motherly remove made her son independent. He could scramble an egg when he was three years old, she claimed.

However it happened, what nobody could deny was that Jann Wenner was precocious in the extreme. Short and pudgy, with a prickly intelligence and a bracing self-confidence, he was kicked out of nearly every school he attended until the age of eleven. "A pain in the ass," his father said. He could be unpredictable and cruel. In third grade, he physically attacked the principal of his public school. A year-end review by his teacher characterized eight-year-old Jann as unusually intelligent but with a compulsion to violence. "In group situations he tries to dominate," his teacher wrote, "withdrawing when the group does not recognize his leadership. He attempts to make friends by teasing, which has recently resulted in fighting. Once he is involved in a fight or argument he becomes extremely angry and attacks, with every ounce of his rather considerable strength and energy, sometimes with any 'weapon' convenient to his hand."

When he was interviewed by a psychologist for his next potential school, Presidio Hill, near the Golden Gate Bridge, Wenner morphed into another child entirely—the charming little genius. "In light of this boys [sic] affable, pleasant, personal manner and his advanced social and mental maturity, it would seem that his school problem should be almost nil," said a school psychologist in 1954. "Most probably, his greatest difficulties will arise when teachers feel threatened by his very superior intelligence."

Wenner was kicked out of Presidio for pulling the keys out of the ignition of a school bus on a field trip.

Wenner said he felt isolated from the working-class people in San Rafael, few of whom were Jews, most of whom were less wealthy than the Wenners. But he was also desperate for attention from his absentee parents. Ed was a workaholic, once collapsing from a burst appendix because he refused to go to the hospital while waiting for a shipment of formula. Meanwhile, his mother made it a philosophical imperative to focus on herself and not her children. In her 1960 memoir, *Back Away from the Stove,* she codified her lack of attention into a child-rearing philosophy. "I missed a great deal of my children's childhood and they missed a great deal of me," she wrote. "My individual choice was to leave housewifery behind . . .

"I quit everything and concentrated on making enough money so that when the kids grew up we could have them psychoanalyzed," she continued. "Just because a lot of statistic-happy sadists want to make you miserable if you work by pointing to correlations, don't be taken in."

In its way, Sim's book foreshadowed *The Feminine Mystique,* published three years later by Betty Friedan. For Wenner, the product of his mother's pioneering philosophy, it simply meant he never saw his mother. "In grammar school, all the moms were around all the time, except our mom," he said. "We didn't have the conventional house, or home. They would travel away on the weekends, and even in the winter, on vacations, we would be shuttled off to the places we went for summer camp—long weekends with the people of the camp, in their houses."

Every summer, the Wenner children were sent to Camp Lagunitas, in Marin, run by a man named Ed Barbano, who Wenner told his parents was an alcoholic. His sister Martha Wenner described how the drunken camp leader veered off the road with a carful of kids until Jann Wenner grabbed the wheel to keep it righted. (The Grateful Dead would later hole up near Camp Lagunitas to write songs.)

Ed Wenner was hardly a source of comfort. Frustrated by his intemperate son, Ed frequently hit him. Kate said her brother would crawl out his bedroom window to hide from spankings. When Wenner threatened to run away from home, his mother put a can of creamed corn in a handkerchief tied to a stick, handed him a nickel, and said, "Here, take this, you'll need it."

While the Wenners sold themselves in magazine articles as baby experts, they tended to ignore their own children for more idealistic pursuits, namely politics. In the 1950s, Sim was involved in the California Democratic Council, a liberal wing of the Democratic Party, and befriended Democrat Alan Cranston, who later became a senator from California. On Rainbow Road, Ed and Sim socialized with two other couples, like-minded Democrats: the Roth family, who owned the Matson shipping company, and the Flaxes, who owned an art supply store in the city, enjoying cocktail parties around the patio and pool. Despite their parents' many failings, the Wenner kids were deeply influenced by their politics. The Wenners took their kids door to door around San Rafael for a Dollars for Democrats drive and once set up a hot dog stand so their mother could raise money for Guide Dogs for the Blind. In 1956, ten-year-old Jann Wenner met the Democratic presidential candidate Adlai Stevenson at the offices of the local Democratic committee that his mother headed.

But on the eve of the 1960s, the Wenners were cracking up. The business was creating a growing chasm between Ed and Sim. When he wasn't laboring to expand Baby Formulas, Ed spent endless hours in Freudian analysis; he loved hearing himself talk. Meanwhile, Sim was stirred by dreams of becoming a literary writer. They fought constantly, their screaming matches the central event of their children's young lives. "The money and the business took down my parents' marriage," said Martha. In the late 1950s, Sim began staying home to write a memoir, which doubled as a bitter attack on Ed, describing her regret at having devoted her time to the formula business, only to be ignored by her husband. "I'd much rather be crewing on a Tahiti-bound schooner, or selling nonobjective art on the Left Bank," she wrote. "Anything but business. I hated business."

As she embraced personal liberation, Jann got a brief but powerful close-up of the mother he idolized, imbibing her progressive opinions and ideas about literature or politics and basking in the glow of her increasingly eccentric personality. His mother primed him for an interest in writing. "She turned me on to E. B. White," he said. "And that was her background. She had been a magazine freelancer for a number of years."

•

WENNER'S JOURNALISTIC CAREER BEGAN at age eleven, when he joined two neighborhood kids who were producing a mimeographed newspaper. Wenner quickly shouldered them aside, renaming it *The Weekly Trumpet* (from *The All Around News*) and crowning himself editor in chief, which he made a stipulation if he was going to join. Wenner typed up news items about a neighbor "cracking open his skull" and getting stitches or earthquake damage to local pools and wrote editorials arguing, for instance, that kids who won prize money on TV quiz shows shouldn't have to pay taxes. He also asked his readers—all sixty-four of them—not to vote for a state legislator that his mother despised, asking, "Are you going to elect a man with racial prejudice, or are you not?" In the spring of 1957, he and his friends appeared on the front page of San Rafael's *Daily Independent Journal,* which reported that Wenner made $5.97 on subscriptions.

His sister Kate later recounted how Wenner conscripted her as a delivery girl, but she quit after he refused to give her a raise. When she threatened to start her own newspaper, Wenner replied, "Oh yeah? What are you gonna call it?"

She was flummoxed by his dare.

"He knew that without a name you had no concept and without a concept you had nothing," Kate said during a toast at Wenner's sixtieth birthday party. "Jann had the confidence to pull it off. It was as simple as that."

Wenner's confusion about his budding feelings for boys also started early. When he was twelve, Wenner was arrested at the local library for engaging in ambiguous horseplay with the son of a local sheriff, who told his father Wenner had harassed him. "It wasn't gay sex; it was roughhousing and goosing," said Wenner. "All of a sudden I ended up spending a day in juvenile hall."

According to his mother, this was why Wenner was sent to a coed boarding school in Los Angeles in 1958—because his father hoped the proximity to girls might cure him. Wenner said the incident was "misconstrued," and he had already been accepted to Chadwick School when he was arrested because his parents were getting divorced. When Sim's father, Maurice, died in Florida in 1958 after a long period of estrangement, the tension between Sim and Ed, over money, control of the company, and lack of love, came to a head. When Wenner flew home from Chadwick for Thanksgiving break, his father took him out to lunch and delivered the news of their separation. Wenner sobbed. "I lost my appetite and couldn't finish my food," he said.

In the divorce proceedings, Sim gave custody of Jann to his father and took the girls with her. It was a decisive blow to Wenner's sense of self. For years to come, Wenner would tell friends his parents fought over not who got to keep Jan Simon Wenner but who had to take him. His mother, Wenner said, once called her son "the worst child she had ever met."

Wenner began a campaign to get his parents back together. Sim told her son she wanted him to call only every other week to reduce her phone bills. "Your demand that Dad and I be something to each other that we're not, is basically a child's demand," she wrote to him in 1959, when Wenner was thirteen. "One stamps one's foot and says, 'Change the world and I will be all right!' and it's a nice comforting thought to have, but the world can't be changed, families can't be changed, mothers, fathers, sisters, brothers . . . There is only one thing that can be changed, or rather, only one thing that you can change, and that is yourself." ("Maternally yours," she signed the letter.)

As soon as she was able, Sim Wenner freed herself entirely from motherhood by sending Jann's sisters, Kate and Martha, away to boarding schools in Vermont and Colorado, respectively. The house on Rainbow Road was sold, and Ed Wenner moved to Southern California. Wenner would never forget his mother's parting words: "You're on your own, Buster Brown."

•

"I WAS UNHAPPY," Wenner wrote in an English paper about his first year at Chadwick School. "The year was miserable."

But he had arrived at the right place. A way station for the progeny of the wealthy and famous from Bel-Air and Hollywood, Chadwick was a progressive private school on the Palos Verdes Peninsula, nestled like a bucolic camp at the top of a shady hill. Founded in 1935 by Margaret and Joseph Chadwick, it enrolled fewer than four hundred students, with only fifty-two in Wenner's class. In his first year at Chadwick—or "Chad-suck," as he called it—Jann Wenner spent weekends sitting in his dormitory watching TV alone, a picture of his mother on his desk, sulking over the divorce. Ed had a new girlfriend, a nurse from South Texas named Dorothy, who recalled meeting Jann in a garage in San Francisco that year: A straw hat on his head, no shoes on his feet, he looked to her like Huckleberry Finn. She told Ed that his son would be famous one day because he "had the courage to be different."

For Wenner, Chadwick was, among other things, an education in celebrity. He was surrounded by the children of movie stars and famous directors: the offspring of actor Glenn Ford; the daughter of Jack Benny; the children of George Burns and Gracie Allen; and Yul Brynner's son, Rock, with whom Wenner roomed in ninth grade. In a letter to his mother, Wenner described waltzing with Liza Minnelli at a school dance. "Are the movie stars' kids the big shots in school?" she asked. "You sound impressed by them."

He was—*very*. He later claimed Minnelli was his first girlfriend at Chadwick and that they held hands for a week. "I would go home with friends on the weekends, and that was always great, to stay at someone's fabulous house in Beverly Hills," recalled Wenner. "It was the first time I saw these extremely big, extravagant houses. I stayed at Dean Martin's house; I was friends with the Martin girls."

Chadwick was accepting in a way his own home wasn't. He said being surrounded by wealth, and by Jews, made him feel more at ease. "I felt at home at last," he said. "They became my family."

With Wenner, there was a lot to accept. Bristling with insecurity, he regularly insulted the other students and teachers and gained a reputation as a prickly braggart. "He can be, and frequently is, extremely cruel to his classmates," reported one teacher, "and his actions show an alarming lack of integrity." His English instructor, Bill Holland, dubbed him Nox, for obnoxious, and the nickname stuck. "The obnoxiousness was very interesting," said Wenner's friend Bill Belding. "I originally attributed it to his being short, but looking back, it was his way of getting attention."

Wenner was advised by school counselors to tamp down his attacks. "I was not Mr. Popular at that point," said Wenner. "I didn't become popular until the tenth grade when I decided to work on it."

Wenner abused his teachers with impunity, starting with the adult head of his dormitory, a disciplinarian named John Simon. "Jann wanted to walk around barefooted; [Simon] wanted him to wear shoes," said Dorothy Wenner, the woman Ed Wenner would eventually marry in the 1960s. "He refused. They had a battle going on all the time. Every time the phone rang, I was nervous. He was always in trouble."

Once, Wenner cleaned his room to inspection standards but then hung closet hangers from the ceiling, claiming it was a piece of art inspired by the school's own philosophy of "self-expression." "It looked like a messy pile of shit in the middle of the room," recalled Andy Harmon, son of Sidney Harmon, who produced the 1958 film *God's Little Acre*. "And [Simon] got so angry, because everything was neat—the beds were made, we dusted, it was just 'self-expression.' Jann was going,

'I'm going to fuck you so bad that you aren't going to be able to retaliate.' And that was the way his mind worked." (For another infraction, Simon barred Wenner from going on the annual school ski trip, a stinging rebuke because Wenner considered himself the best skier in the school.)

But as people got to know him, they found Wenner strangely sophisticated for his age. Every morning he would open his box of Raisin Bran and count the number of raisins in the bowl, declaring the economy good or bad. "It was a revelation at that age, when I started school there, that one of my contemporaries could be that erudite and fascinating," said Terryl Stacy, formerly Kirschke, who went to school with Wenner and later to Berkeley.

•

IN 1961, Sim Wenner published a dime-store novel called *Daisy* about a group of swingers ("The Club") who lived in a Northern California suburb. "But one Saturday night they ran out of kicks—so someone jumped in the pool . . . with no clothes on," went the copy on the back flap. "From then on things were different."

The book was a thinly veiled roman à clef. The protagonist, Daisy, was the fill-in for Wenner's mother. Philip, the character who stands in for his father, "worked long days and played long nights, and if another woman was more sympathetic than his wife, well, he just wanted someone to talk to." Jann Wenner didn't have to scratch very hard to see beneath the surface: Here were the neighborhood families from San Rafael, with whom the Wenners had evidently been having affairs, if the book was to be believed. In one scene, Daisy gets pregnant and tries to have an illegal abortion, a procedure she recounts in excruciating detail:

> Soon she could feel the scraping inside of her and then chopping and she thought, Oh, my God, he's cutting it up. He's cutting up my baby! . . .

When Daisy starts bleeding profusely and is rushed to the hospital, the hapless husband believes she's miscarried his baby, not someone else's. In the very last sentence of the book, Daisy acts out her rage at Philip by raising a .22 rifle to his temple and pulling the trigger.

Wenner was horrified. After reading it, he wrote back to his mother, "The last paragraph was too much for me to bear psychologically. Your bitterness must be great, whether justifiable or not, but when so openly expressed as in the précis paragraph, you must have some idea of the effect on me."

In reality, Sim Wenner did have an abortion before the divorce. As columnist Herb Caen wrote of *Daisy* in the *Chronicle,* "definitely not for baby unless yours has a different formula than most."

After 1959, Wenner's mother parented him almost entirely through letters, updating him on the family business, calculating his allowance and debts, correcting his grammar, suggesting books to read, and even upbraiding him for his souvenirs from a field trip to Mexico ("A bull-whip and a switchblade knife are the weapons of a [pachuco] not a gentleman"). Wenner, feeling orphaned, wrote "Bastard" on a letter. But even as she drifted away, she was intent on conscripting her children in battles against their father, who once sued Sim to reduce child support. It was an attitude Wenner slowly absorbed and would last for years to come. "She turned us against him, me and my sister," Wenner said. "We didn't realize it at the time, but it was a constant, steady stream of picking away, a slow character assassination."

His sister Kate, after years of therapy, would maintain that Wenner and his sisters were deeply impacted by their mother's bitterness and cruelty—a view Wenner only partly subscribed to. "I came around to her point of view about how crazy our mother was," said Wenner. "My mother is, like, according to Katie, a classic narcissist.

"I escaped the impact of it," he insisted. "I mean, I went off on my way, fairly young, and just had this enormous success, which just overwhelmed all the need to be introspective, all the need to be insecure, it just vanished."

In eleventh grade, Wenner added an extra *n* to his own first name, making it Jann, inspired, he said, by a friend named Tedd. (His mother, a sometime fabulist, would tell a different story: Wenner was embarrassed when the school delivered his luggage to the girls' dormitory, believing "Jan" was a girl.) Wenner tried out other names as well, once asking people to call him George and printing up business cards that read "Jan G. Wenner." In 1961, when the surf craze hit Southern California beaches, Wenner saw surf guitar legend Dick Dale and started wearing huaraches. "He put a bleached streak in his hair," remembered Andy Harmon, "and my father, obviously, sensing something that ended up having some truth in it—'This is not something a man does'—went after Jann about it . . . He implied that Jann was gay."

In 1962, Wenner was nearly suspended from Chadwick for leaving campus without permission but was saved by the headmistress, Mrs. Chadwick, who admired his writing in her English class. Divining Wenner's troubles, she arranged for him to see a Beverly Hills psychiatrist and also directed him to the theater department, where Wenner starred in Christopher Marlowe's *Tragical History of the Life and Death of Doctor Faustus,* playing the title character who sells his soul to the devil in exchange for occult powers. Onstage, Wenner, as Faust, mused before Mephistopheles:

> *Shall I make spirits fetch me what I please,*
> *Resolve me of all ambiguities,*
> *Perform what desperate enterprise I will?*

He later played in *H.M.S. Pinafore* and became a lifelong fan of Gilbert and Sullivan.

Wenner's best friends were two boarders, Andy Harmon and Jamie Moran, the son of a social worker at Chadwick. Wenner and his pals identified as proto-beatniks, inspired by the Maynard Krebs character played by Bob Denver in *The Many Loves of Dobie Gillis* on CBS and humor magazines like *Mad,* intent on bucking the "bourgeoisie." While Wenner received middling grades, he gravitated to current events, keeping up with Kennedy and Nixon in the papers, writing a critical essay on the right-wing John Birch Society and another on the historic ramifications of the atom bomb. In keeping with his mother's quasi-socialist worldview, Wenner was an orthodox Adlai Stevenson liberal, aping his rhetoric in school papers and precociously imbibing books like *A Nation of Sheep,* a liberal critique of American foreign policy and the media by William Lederer, co-author of *The Ugly American.*

But Wenner was primarily distracted by the pecking order at Chadwick. Moran thought of Wenner as a kind of innocent hustler who admired creative people but was seduced by "the false glamour of celebrity." Even as he hung out with the bohemians, Wenner organized his calendar around popular kids in whose wealth and fame he found deep affirmation. "At Chadwick, he dressed in a fucking coat and tie," Harmon said. "He hung out with the preppies, which I couldn't bear . . . and was very attracted to power. I think he was attracted to my dad, because he had a reputation as a prominent filmmaker."

Even then, journalism synthesized Wenner's interests. In his junior year, he befriended Chadwick's publicist, Frank Quinlin, who assigned Wenner to cover sports for *The Mainsheet,* the school paper, and helped him get a weekly column in the local *Palos Verdes Peninsula News,* reporting the goings-on at Chadwick. Quinlin, known as Uncle Frank, also involved him in Chadwick's yearbook, *The Dolphin.* This gave Wenner access to the school's Graflex camera, and he used it like an all-access pass, snapping pictures in classrooms, study halls, and dormitories. It also gave Wenner access to a twenty-foot-long closet with a desk and a typewriter, dubbed Shaft Alley, over which Wenner put a sign reading MEMBERS ONLY. "I was the only person in the school who had an office," he said.

The yearbook was the perfect tool for social climbing. "His friends were mostly friends that would advance him socially at school," recalled his mother-in-law. "I remember he had made friends with this girl from Chadwick. She was able to give him a lot of money for the annual. Then I remember we were at the house one time and she called him. He was really abrupt with her. He was like, 'Why are you calling me? We don't have anything in common anymore.' And it was just awfully rough."

As graduation approached, Wenner set his sights on Harvard, Jack Kennedy's alma mater. His archrival at Chadwick, a handsome jock and class valedictorian named Dennis Landis, was also gunning for Harvard, while Wenner's friend Bill Belding applied to Yale. "I distinctly remember December of '62," recounted Belding. "Mrs. Chadwick came out and Jann and Dennis and I were talking in the rotunda. 'I have good news for you, Bill, you were admitted to Yale. And, Dennis, you were admitted to Harvard. And, Jann, you were not admitted to Harvard.'

"She handled that so badly, and I know Jann was devastated," he said. "Jann really, really wanted to go to Harvard and he didn't."

Instead, Wenner would be going to the University of California at Berkeley, where his mother had taken continuing education courses.

But Wenner found another way of pursuing his rivalry. His senior year, he devised an unorthodox plan to take over the student council and block Landis from becoming vice president. Instead of running for president himself, he created a slate of candidates on a so-called progressive platform, with swim champ Belding at the top of the ticket, an attractive girl named Cydny Rothe for secretary, and Wenner wedged in the middle as vice president. The Wenner sandwich worked: Advocating, along with a liberal agenda, for coffee for seniors, the progressives soundly defeated Landis, which Wenner ran as news across the front page of the premier issue of a rogue newspaper he'd recently founded, *The Sardine*. In his paper, Wenner described the campaign—his own—as one of "innovations and uniqueness." "Jann's whole reason for wanting to run for student body," said Belding, "was so he could become an insider and start an underground student newspaper . . . When he did *The Sardine*, he had the school at his feet."

With a title that spoofed the nautical themes of Chadwick, *The Sardine* published a gossip column called Random Notes, modeled on Herb Caen's "three dot" column in the *Chronicle*, using ellipses to separate news items. In the second issue, Wenner wrote a snide taxonomy of "poseurs" who adopted the surfer look—as he had done the year before. The school's main disciplinarian, Ed Ellis, shut down *The Sardine* after three issues, claiming it undermined school spirit (among other things, Wenner attacked the school for banning white Levi's). Regarding Wenner as egotistical, Ellis also tried unsuccessfully to remove Wenner as editor of the yearbook, but Margaret Chadwick intervened again. When the yearbook, *The Dolphin*, arrived in the spring of 1963, it was a fully formed Jann Wenner production, a blueprint for everything he would aspire to. "I designed the yearbook, layout, variety of pages, length and all the things," he wrote to his grandmother. "There are dozens of new things, innovations, and changes, all my ideas except one. I designed the cover, and picked out the class symbol, which I like very much, the whole think [*sic*] cost $6000, and we charged $6 per book, sold nearly 400 books, collected nearly 4500 in ads and patronage."

He also created a two-page spread to mock the faculty, featuring a photo of his friends posing as teachers and "reading books about how to get authority because they did not have any, with their cigarettes and their coffee cups."

On Wenner's personal page, he listed his accomplishments (skiing, sports statistician) and declared in his class quotation that "greatness knows itself"—a line spoken by Hotspur in Shakespeare's *Henry IV*.

In the back pages of the yearbook were irreverent photo montages that Wenner spent hours cutting and pasting together, including several images of shirtless boys horsing around in their dorm rooms. Wenner was keenly aware of his homosexual feelings, but he kept them concealed, not even telling the Beverly Hills therapist he was forced to see every week (his mother, perhaps attuned to Wenner's sexual confusion, complained that he was "manipulating" his therapist). Wenner said there were several teachers at Chadwick he believed were gay, including Bill Holland, the man who had dubbed Wenner "Nox." "He had a big friendship with a couple of cute guys in my dorm," he recalled. Another teacher took Wenner on a trip to Santa Barbara in a Corvette and put his hand on Wenner's knee, causing him to squirm. "I felt I was not being polite by moving over and getting away from him," he said.

Wenner clung to a girl he began dating his senior year, Susie Weigel, who was everything Wenner felt he should want: rich, blond, popular, Jewish, her father a federal judge in Northern California appointed by President Kennedy in 1962. Wenner impressed her with his literary interests—he co-edited a literary journal called *The Journey* with Andy Harmon—and gave her a John Donne love poem. But in other ways he treated her more like his acolyte than a girlfriend. Wenner returned her love letters with red grammatical corrections. Indeed, he tried editing her into an outline of his mother, noting she had the same initials as Sim Wenner and buying her replicas of his mother's clothes. Wenner was convinced he would marry Weigel once she graduated in 1964, a year after him. In Wenner's yearbook, Weigel wrote in floral cursive, "I love you very deeply, I honestly do. With all my love, forever and ever."

(Margaret Chadwick congratulated Wenner on the yearbook but also advised, "Stop and think first my impulsive friend.")

When Wenner and Weigel returned to San Francisco for the summer, Weigel served as Wenner's entrée to the small and provincial Bay Area society set, children of local industry and politics who mingled at lavish debutante balls. Wenner was enchanted by the Cotillion, the seasonal rite of house parties hosted by parents of young women and culminating in a grand ballroom party at the Sheraton-Palace Hotel in the winter. The swanning of the elite was closely monitored in the social pages of the *Chronicle,* complete with photo spreads and boldfaced captions, and Wenner read it religiously. "The wealth was on display, the booze, the big settings, young kids in black ties," said Wenner. "I was just dazzled by it."

Wenner was a quick study, absorbing the backgrounds of the local gentry. There was Ned Topham from the Spreckels sugar fortune; James Pike Jr., son of the famous Episcopalian bishop and civil rights spokesman; John Warnecke, son of John Carl Warnecke, the architect of the Kennedy memorial. A few, like Richard Black, whose father worked for the California energy company PG&E, traveled in the same social orbit as the Hearst family, and Black's stories of visiting the Hearst ranch in San Simeon were potent fuel for Wenner's imagination.

Meanwhile, Sim Wenner was living in Potrero Hill, at the time a largely black and industrial neighborhood that was becoming a bohemian enclave. After selling her share of the Baby Formulas business, she was socializing with a literary set at Berkeley, including beat writer Herbert Gold and artist and bullfighter Barnaby Conrad, and dating the Wenner family doctor, Sandor Burstein. Susie Weigel was fascinated by the unconventional divorcée but appalled by her lack of warmth for Jann. "She had three children and one bedroom," said Weigel, later Susan Pasternak. "I was so upset for Jann because there was no place for the kids. And Jann wasn't wanted by either [parent]."

Weigel, who went on to become a Manhattan psychoanalyst, had a simple, powerful theory of her boyfriend's psychology. "It was all about Sim Wenner," she said. "There was no room for anybody else except her. I think Jann internalized that. The only way he was going to have room for himself was to create himself."

Through an acquaintance of Sim's, Wenner was offered a job that summer as a traffic reporter at KNBR, the NBC affiliate, which required him to show up at 6:00 a.m. He didn't like the hours so instead took a job as a day laborer on a construction site. He quit after a week—"I didn't have the clothes for it," he said—and accepted the NBC job. He fetched coffee, memorized the traffic jargon, and dubbed himself the Traffic Eagle around the bureau. Wenner spent his free time at the Weigel family's retreat in Mill Valley, feeling at home with a Jewish family who had an "air of normalcy," he said. Wenner impressed Weigel's father, who told his daughter he believed Wenner would be famous, while Wenner labored to lose his virginity during secret makeout sessions with Susie in her bedroom. Weigel showed Wenner off to her friends, the brash young man with the oddly Swedish name and dashing grin who bragged a lot. They recognized the charm but also the grasping edge of his ambition. "When you're on the inside where we were," said Richard Black, "you can see faces pressed to the windows, and Jann was really determined."

Wenner opened a charge account at Brooks Brothers and had the pockets monogrammed on his button-down shirts, adopting the old-money look of William F. Buckley. That summer, Wenner bought a 1954 Jaguar XK120 for $120, hoping to fix it up himself and ferry his new friends around. When Weigel took him to pick it up, Wenner revved the engine and peeled off, leaving Weigel to frantically chase after him in her parents' car. "He drove so fast," she said. "So crazily fast. I was furious with him. It was so show-offy and made me so mad." After that, Judge Weigel forbade her to drive with Wenner.

The couple fought constantly. "He would annoy me to death," said Weigel. Wenner enjoyed access to her family compound until her father discovered them making out to a Johnny Mathis record.

In the fall of 1963, Wenner started classes at Berkeley, majoring in English literature with a minor in political science. A public school with twenty-six thousand students, Berkeley was a university at a crossroads. It was still an institution rooted in the 1950s, a factory producing graduates to plug into Eisenhower-era American capitalism. But a revolution was coming. In 1964, beatniks and Marxists were conspiring in local cafés to the sounds of Joan Baez and Bob Dylan while absorbing the literature of dissent from left-wing intellectuals like Eugene Burdick and Herbert Marcuse and North Beach cult heroes like Jack Kerouac and Lawrence Ferlinghetti. Wenner joined a student advocacy group called SLATE, run by two earnest young lefties named Phil and Joan Roos, who assigned Wenner to help edit student questionnaires for a tip sheet that rated professors called the *Slate Supplement to the General Catalog*. He took the most savage feedback from students and fashioned it into cheeky reviews tarring especially authoritarian professors. He remained an indifferent student—"it KEEPS ME OUT OF THE ARMY," he told his grandmother—but he manicured his social life with great care, throwing parties for debutante girls and getting himself invited to the Sugar Bowl, a resort near the Nevada border that was a premier skiing destination for wealthy families. Joan Roos became Wenner's surrogate mother, and he regularly showed up at her house for dinner and his favorite television program, *The Man from U.N.C.L.E.* Wenner became the associate editor of the *Slate Supplement* and bragged to the Rooses that he would one day be the head of NBC.

Despite the far-left politics of SLATE, Wenner remained a stalwart establishmentarian. This was made clear the day President John F. Kennedy was assassinated in Dallas, November 22, 1963, news of which Wenner heard over loudspeakers coming from the student union at Berkeley. "This strange cry of agony went around, as if people were in pain and bodies being tortured," he wrote of the moment. "I kind of slumped and bowed my head and cried." When Barry Baron, a society friend Wenner met through Susie Weigel, showed up at Wenner's apartment that evening, Wenner was conducting a private vigil, sitting cross-legged before two big candles, with tears in his eyes. "He took himself extremely seriously," said Baron.

Unlike Wenner, the SLATE crowd saw Kennedy as part of an imperialist conspiracy with ties to corrupt power. "The SLATE people were probably right, and had I been smarter, I would have agreed with them," said Wenner. But Kennedy's death, Wenner later said, was also the pivotal event that made the nascent counterculture possible.

"It all wouldn't have happened if Kennedy hadn't got killed," he told the British underground magazine *Oz* in 1969. "Everybody was still digging what was going on in that other scene. Kennedy made politics &

the whole thing very relevant because he was young, he was attractive, he was just plain beautiful you know & not ugly."

•

WENNER, like many young men, was focused on losing his virginity, though his reasons were more complex than some. He was troubled by his homosexual urges and thought that once he'd crossed that border, he'd be on the right path. When Susie Weigel came home for the holidays, she refused him sex. So Wenner pursued Weigel's best friend, whom he considered the most "in" of the society crowd. Over the holidays, Weigel's friend relieved Wenner of his outsider status. "I love you for what you have done for me," he told her in a letter. "I hope you feel the same way."

She didn't. After a weekend fending him off at the Sugar Bowl, she confessed the affair to Weigel, who was appalled and broke up with Wenner (and immediately took up with his best friend from Chadwick, Andy Harmon). Later, she saw Wenner crashing a deb party and was thoroughly disgusted. "I thought he was gross," she said. "It was so obnoxious. I actually wanted nothing to do with him."

In his journals, Wenner admonished himself for pursuing Weigel's friend, wondering what motivated him. "Is it her herself I want or is it what she represents?" he wrote. "There is something special, I can't grasp it, about the SF society which I want."

Weigel, he wrote, had offered the "normalcy" he craved, a normalcy that resolved the homosexual feelings that had plagued him "for the past five years." "Years of misery in which for all my time of happiness and joy were years of discontent," he said. "I met people at Sugar Bowl, SF socialites, who I wanted so much to be. I wanted security . . . so bad. Perhaps that is why I cling to Susie so much.

"In those weeks since this Sugar Bowl experience," he continued, "I have dropped more and more of my homosexuality which was never dominant but always present. I come more and more to what is called normal. But not completely. I don't know why."

At Sugar Bowl, Wenner also met a striking society boy named John Warnecke. He had all the qualities Wenner desired in friends: dashing good looks and a sterling pedigree, plus an appetite for experimentation, especially with drugs. Warnecke introduced Wenner to another friend, the square-jawed Ned Topham, whose family were fixtures of San Francisco since the nineteenth century. The three became fast pals, Warnecke and Topham admiring Wenner's scampish energy and independent spirit. Greil Marcus, a friend of Barry Baron's who met Wenner at Berkeley, was impressed that a freshman had his own apartment, let alone a Mose Allison LP on the stereo. "[I] went into this place and it was a bohemian student apartment like I had never seen before," said Marcus. "I was also struck by the fact that the *San Francisco Chronicle* two-page spread of this year's debutantes was pinned to the wall. So I thought, 'Whoa, interesting crosscurrents at work here.'"

As he social climbed, Wenner dated and slept with a series of debutantes, a relentless suitor battering away at his quarry. "In Jann's case a refusal is almost always a guarantee that he will pursue relentlessly," a former girlfriend wrote in a remembrance from 1966. He treated women strictly as social conquests. One of Wenner's roommates, Ted Hayward, recounted to writer Robert Draper how Wenner slept with the daughter of a British diplomat and used the sheet from their tryst as a tablecloth for a dinner party the next night, strategically placing her plate over a stain and giggling during the meal.

Wenner denied the incident occurred, claiming Hayward was only bitter about another incident: While they sought a third roommate to pay the rent for their pad, Wenner accused Hayward of scaring off candidates with his gay affectations. "Ted, let me do the roommate thinking," Wenner told him. "Everybody thinks you're gay."

"He was so hurt," said Wenner. "He never spoke civilly to me again. He was very flamboyant in his gestures."

But the woman in question confirmed that Wenner used the sheet as a tablecloth, as did Wenner's friend Robbie Leeds, who married her. "I found it to be in poor taste," he said. "It was embarrassing. It was their intimacy, and he made a big thing about it."

That summer, NBC made Wenner a gofer for the anchors of the NBC broadcast of the Republican National Convention, fetching coffee and Salem cigarettes for Chet Huntley and David Brinkley. As Barry Goldwater accepted the nomination of the party, Wenner inhaled the rarefied air of the eastern establishment, the big three TV networks, and the power brokers of party politics glad-handing in the hallways. His media credentials gave him a sense of privilege. "They are the rabble," he remembered saying to himself. "We are the pros."

The following month, Wenner drove to Newport Beach to see his father. Ed Wenner had started another branch of Baby Formulas Inc. in Anaheim, south of Los Angeles, this time partnered with Carnation. Jann Wenner went out with two boarding school friends to see a movie in Pasadena: *A Hard Day's Night,* the Richard Lester film depicting four long-haired lads running from ravenous female (and a few male) fans in a series of comic bits. In stylish black and white, the Beatles crashed through the screen, having more fun than anybody in human history. Ringo Starr parodied the media machine they were manipulating (Reporter: "Are you a mod or a rocker?" Ringo: "No, I'm a mocker"), and George narrowly escaped the clutches of a teen marketer who traded in "pimply hyperbole." There was Paul, the cute one, and John, the comic rebel, who was immediately Wenner's favorite.

Wenner had never been a die-hard music fan. His first record was a 45 of "Rock Around the Clock" by Bill Haley and the Comets. It didn't make a lasting impression. In high school, he was a fan of Paul Anka. "He is one of the two good singers that 'rock n' roll' has produced," Wenner wrote to his grandmother, "the other being Johnny Mathis, who I like a lot." Even the Mose Allison record was more fad than musical interest (everybody who met him in this period remembers him playing the same album). Jann Wenner missed the Beatles' iconic performance on *The Ed Sullivan Show,* but in *A Hard Day's Night* he saw young men who looked like himself, though infinitely more appealing. "They were young, fresh, and good-looking in that same sort of way Jack Kennedy was," he said. "These kids who are your age, who are so alive and upbeat and joyous and taking the piss out of everybody—man, that's how life should be."

His high school friend Susan Andrews, daughter of actor Dana Andrews (*The Best Years of Our Lives,* 1946), recalled driving to Los Angeles with Wenner in his VW Beetle, windows down and wind in their hair as Wenner shout-sang Beatles lyrics from the window. *Hey! You've got to hiiiide your love a-way . . .* Wenner was a committed mod, but he loved the rockers, too. Andrews's mother was confused when she got a credit card receipt for a tank of gas that Wenner had evidently signed "Mick Jagger."

The arrival of the Beatles and the Stones dovetailed with larger forces at work at Berkeley, where youth activists were challenging institutional power for the first time. In October 1964, a former student set up a table of civil rights literature in front of Berkeley's administration building, protesting the school's ban on political activism on campus. Jack Weinberg, who coined the phrase "Don't trust anyone over 30," was arrested by university police, prompting Mario Savio, a campus activist, to scale a police car and give a series of impassioned speeches on the First Amendment rights of students, sparking a thirty-two-hour protest. The fight between the students and the administration was national news, and Wenner dove headlong into the mix, attending protests and racing his audio recordings back to NBC News in time for the evening broadcasts. He positioned himself as the inside man. The day Savio gave his most stirring speech in December 1964, imploring activist students to put their "bodies upon the gears and upon the wheels, upon the levers, upon all the apparatus" of the "machine" of society, Wenner looked on from the steps as Joan Baez sang Bob Dylan's "With God on Our Side"—the first time he heard a Dylan song, he said. A few days later, Wenner would appear in AP photos chasing Savio up the stairs of Sproul Hall, boyish in a trench coat, tape recorder strapped to his chest.

Wenner was electrified and proud when a right-wing newspaper, citing his membership in SLATE, called him a communist sympathizer. "I was ID'd as a red," he said. But his true convictions lay with the "apparatus" of NBC News. When the police beat and arrested protesters at a sit-in at the Sheraton-Palace Hotel—the site of the Cotillion balls—Wenner had run away "before the busts went down." Indeed, Wenner rarely failed to mention his NBC job at parties, pushing the outer limits of his role there. The head of NBC News in Los Angeles accused him of misrepresenting himself to the administration at Berkeley, issuing an angry memo reminding the staff that "Jann Wenner is not a correspondent. He is not a reporter. He is not a field producer. He is a campus stringer."

But Wenner had already managed to capitalize on his position by publishing a long account of the Free Speech Movement from the point of view of a news stringer who sympathized with the students. He had briefly dated the daughter of Jack Vietor, heir to the Jell-O fortune, who published *San Francisco* magazine; Wenner convinced him to run his story about the protests. "He was the most ambitious person I've ever met," said Jane Kenner, whom Wenner dated that winter. "It was so clear, and he didn't care at all what kind of attention he got. He didn't care if it was negative or positive, as long as he got attention."

Wenner's love life was complicated by the arrival of a handsome young society man named James Pike Jr., son of the controversial Episcopalian bishop of California, James Albert Pike. A progressive civil rights advocate, Bishop Pike became famous for putting the images of Albert Einstein and John Glenn in stained glass in his Grace Cathedral in Nob Hill. The junior Pike attended the same deb balls as Wenner and also struggled with sexual confusion. Wenner said Pike was his first gay crush. For a time, they were constant pals, going on a road trip to Mexico to smuggle a kilo of marijuana back over the border in the car door, all the while tortured by their desires. "At that age, being gay wasn't an identity or an option," said Wenner. "The times that Jim and I came close to making that breakthrough, I don't think either of us knew there was a breakthrough to be made. We were running away from it, as much as we might have wanted it."

In a lightly fictionalized account of his life at Berkeley, Wenner would describe a character much like Pike getting an erection while the two wrestled in bed. Wenner was "afraid to tell him I love him," he wrote. "I wanted to make love to him." Their arrested romance did not go unobserved. Jane Kenner, who had also dated Pike, viewed Jann and Jim as rivals. "Very few people liked Jann," she wrote in 1966. "They envied him his job as campus reporter for NBC, and his aura of superiority was thought obnoxious. Jann and Jim each had several qualities that the other needed, and in turn they needed each other very much."

Friends whispered that Pike was impotent. Wenner had no such problem, but Kenner said "he received no pleasure from making love." Frightened by his own desires, Wenner insulted Pike at parties and paraded new girlfriends in front of him, as if to mock his sexual confusion. "It was about proving to himself that he was hetero," said Kenner. "He was trying to prove that to himself."

If his sexuality was unresolved, his ambition was not. Wenner published another story in *San Francisco* called "Marijuana, Who's Turned On?" Wenner tried pot for the first time in December 1964, around the time he bought *Beatles '65,* and fell over laughing at a jar of mustard in the refrigerator. He was an instant convert. "A close observer will tell you that 'nearly everyone is turning on,'" he wrote, sprinkling his story with anonymous stories from socialite friends at Berkeley and Stanford. "It is not unusual to come across madras-shirted students sitting beneath the house picture of a former U.S. president and 'blowing grass.' At least nine fraternities, including nearly all of the 'best houses,' have pledged 'potheads.'"

The story quoted the vice-principal of a local high school blaming the uptick in pot use on "too much money and too much freedom." Wenner, assuming an authority beyond his years, advised "a realistic and sensible approach" to legalization. (He edited out a concluding joke from the early draft: "Potheads, arise!") The story landed like a stink bomb among the matrons of Pacific Heights. Frances Moffat, society columnist at the *Chronicle,* accused Wenner of using the story to social climb. "The more serious article by Jann would have been improved if he hadn't been so busy making a point of his connections," she wrote. "In this case, his social connections, not the 'connection' of the marijuana user." ("I'm sure I was social climbing," said Wenner, "but not through that article.")

In the same story, Wenner cited a news item about a drug bust at Berkeley in February 1965. Five students were charged with possession of LSD. The ringleader, who was exonerated, would go on to become a drug-world legend: Augustus Owsley Stanley III, the Berkeley chemist whose powerful underground formulas blew the minds of every major figure in the brewing counterculture, including the Grateful Dead. As it turned out, Jann Wenner was among those trying to buy LSD from Owsley when the bust went down. He lost $125 and failed to try LSD. But not for long.

2

Are You Experienced?

Coincidences, trappings, costumes & climbing. These made me rich.
—fragment from "Now These Days Are Gone,"
an unpublished novel by Jann Wenner, 1966

When Jann Wenner emerged from the closet, he was crying. "His eyes were soft, and he had been weeping, and he just was beautiful," recounted Denise Kaufman, describing the day Wenner first tried LSD in the spring of 1965. Arms wrapped around his knees, Wenner asked her to put the Sandy Bull record back on. "And he just sat and listened," she said. "It was beautiful, and we listened and put the Beatles on. He was in the most beautiful state."

She said the moment marked a deep and abiding bond between her and Wenner, a cosmic understanding. Wenner would tell a version of the story in his lightly fictionalized memoir, "Now These Days Are Gone," which features a Berkeley student named Jim Whitman and his elusive muse Vicki (Denise Kaufman's middle name). The LSD scene includes the kitten, the LPs, and even the closet. The moment before he stepped inside, Wenner wrote, he had had a terrible vision:

I was fighting my father, hitting him, and then tearing him apart, ripping his flesh and pulling out his guts, but his guts were machinery, cogs and wheels, and pipes, and he lay there bloodied without blood, fleshy with metal.

It was a vision of Oedipal rage, prompting Wenner to climb into the womb of the closet.

Wenner was infatuated with his acid guide, Denise, the woman Ken Kesey later dubbed Mary Microgram. "Maybe it was the way Vicki did things, things girls weren't supposed to do," Wenner wrote in his novel. "Ride motorcycles, invite anyone on the street to parties, doing all those things and not just sitting around smoking cigarettes. She didn't even smoke."

She was also a distant cousin of Jann Wenner's through the Simmons family line, both of them tracing their roots to a Russian Jew named Isaac Szymonovsky. More important, she was, in the parlance of the times, "happening," the spirit of 1960s San Francisco made flesh. Jerry Garcia and Ron "Pigpen" McKernan, future members of the Grateful Dead, played at her high school graduation party in Palo Alto; she met Ken Kesey on a beach in Monterey and joined the Merry Pranksters, Ken Kesey's LSD explorers, riding alongside beat legend Neal Cassady on the painted school bus; she would form an all-female rock group called the Ace of Cups, who opened for both Jimi Hendrix and the Band. As important to Wenner, Kaufman was from a wealthy family who made their money in real estate. "She combined those two worlds so perfectly for me," said Wenner. "She was from a straight background, wealthy background, the proper background. The good Jewish girl, and the wild child thing. And that was perfect for me."

While acid transformed Kaufman from a folkie communist to a free-range child of the cosmos, Wenner's transformation was less clear. To Kaufman, his mother, Sim, seemed more turned on than he did. After moving to Hawaii, Sim morphed into a middle-aged bohemian who wore floor-length muumuus, usually nude underneath, and took up pot smoking and rediscovered her "homosexual gene." "I'm thinking, how did she get this straight son? She is so out there!" said Kaufman. "We ended up going to the Matrix together, the club in the Marina area, where Jefferson Airplane first played. Sim was kind of more in the groove of it than he was."

Wenner was embarrassed by his mother's libertine life, especially her pursuit of men his own age. She sashayed into the room and said whatever came to mind, usually something insulting or sexually provocative. When a friend brought her football player boyfriend to a party at Sim's apartment, Sim looked the guy up and down and said, "You're fucking him?" Wenner also recoiled at her increasingly "hip" lingo. "I had a terribly difficult time relating to that," he later said. "To have your mother say something like 'hey, man,' you know. It drives me nuts, her language."

In the summer of 1965, Sim's latest boyfriend convinced her to let Wenner use her house in Hawaii while she was stateside visiting Kate. Before he left, Wenner traded two tickets to see the Beatles for thirty hits of acid from Kaufman. (Wenner never saw the Beatles.) He spent a month in Kailua Kona, Hawaii, plucking out folk songs on an acoustic guitar that his sister Kate gave him for his birthday and exploring the effects of LSD while snorkeling over a local reef. When he returned to San Francisco, Wenner decided that Denise Kaufman was the answer to all his problems. Kaufman said she felt a "heart connection" with Wenner but no sexual spark, and she bristled at his relentless attempts to sleep with her. In a letter written from Esalen, the spiritual retreat in Big Sur, she told Wenner he was not "at ease" with himself. She wrote a garage-rock song about him called "Boy, What'll You Do Then," a feminist kiss-off to a jealous suitor.

> *You saw me out with your best friend*
> *And you can bet I'm gonna do it again*
> *But if I leave you*
> *Boy what will you do then?*
>
> *You say I must be true to you*
> *That's what you tell me*
> *Well, I say take me as I am, boy*
> *Or we're through—yeah, through!*

She printed a hundred copies of a 45 single, but they were stolen from a car, and the song never surfaced beyond San Francisco.

Wenner also tried forming a rock group, called the Helping Hand-Outs, with a spaced-out hippie named Scratch who lived on a mattress in North Beach. They disbanded after playing some strip clubs. Music was not exactly the focus. "With my hair as long as it is, if you didn't listen to my singing or playing, I look like a Beatle," he wrote to his grandmother.

Kaufman rebuffed Wenner's romantic entreaties but brought him along on her adventures, including a road trip to L.A. with Neal Cassady (who kept calling him "Jan," to Wenner's irritation) and the seminal event of the San Francisco rock boom, a psychedelic dance at the Longshoreman's Hall near the wharf featuring the Jefferson Airplane, the Charlatans, and the Great Society. "A Tribute to Dr. Strange," named for the Marvel Comics character, was conceived by a group of hippies who convinced Ralph Gleason, the aging *Chronicle* critic, to help promote the event in his column, On the Town. That night Wenner witnessed poet Allen Ginsberg lead a line of beaded dancers through colored lights that pulsed to clanging, psychotropic guitar playing and caterwauling vocals. Denise Kaufman, in a dress made from an American flag, briefly introduced Wenner to Gleason, who was hanging out with a record man from Capitol Records. The next day, Wenner flipped through the paper and reexperienced the event through the eyes of a veteran culture writer. Gleason would say he saw the 1960s come to life that night, documenting the costumed youths like butterflies pinned on a spreading board. "They all seemed to be cued into Frontier Days," he wrote in his 1969 book, *The Jefferson Airplane and the San Francisco Sound,* "and ranged from velvet Lotta Crabtree to Mining Camp Desperado, Jean Laffite leotards, I. Magnin Beatnik, Riverboat Gambler, India Import Exotic and Modified Motorcycle Rider Black Leather-and-Zippers alongside Buckskin Brown."

A personal friend and devotee of Duke Ellington's, Gleason none-theless called the Jefferson Airplane "one of the best bands ever." His advocacy got them an advance from RCA Victor for $25,000, an astonishing sum for a psychedelic rock group.

Turned on by Kaufman, Wenner now spent his weekends flopped out on the floor of John Warnecke's garden apartment on Telegraph

Hill, along with Ned Topham, listening to Bob Dylan's *Bringing It All Back Home* and the Byrds' *Mr. Tambourine Man* while tripping on Owsley Stanley's high-powered blotter acid. "We had costumes and toys," wrote Wenner in "Now These Days Are Gone." "Life was like a little kid. Instead of skip rope we played with pieces of cut glass from chandeliers. *Eye orgies.*" (One evening, Wenner had a druggy sexual encounter with Warnecke, which he recorded in an outline for his novel: "[Told] him I was thinking of a girl," he wrote, "a lie.") In his book, Wenner described dressing up in his own frontier costume—an Annapolis naval jacket, a cowboy hat, and a gold-handled walking stick—to see the Lovin' Spoonful with Denise Kaufman. While she mingled easily with "the sandaled spades and boys with funny glasses," Wenner felt awkward and out of place around the hippies. "The navy jacket was too hot," he wrote. "The collar rubbed on the back of my neck. People were standing around looking at each other. We danced to a few songs, but then she found other friends and danced with them without thought of tomorrow, like she was playing the drums. They stood and watched her and I was glad they saw me with her, but then they knew, they always knew."

•

THE IMAGE WAS TAKEN from the back of the $1 bill: a human eye inside a pyramid. It was a flyer posted around the Berkeley campus with the tantalizing question, "Can you pass the acid test?" Ken Kesey wanted to recruit local students for his LSD experiments with a large "happening" inside a Victorian mansion in downtown San Jose following a Rolling Stones concert at the Civic Auditorium in early December 1965. It was the first time Wenner saw the Stones. Mick Jagger swung a blue checkered jacket over his head, singing "(I Can't Get No) Satisfaction." Afterward, Wenner drove his VW downtown to press into the throng of acid-zonked students who vibrated to a very different rock band that chimed with involved psychedelic jams. Wenner approached the handsome guitar player in blue corduroy pants and velvet shirt to ask the name of the group. "The Grateful Dead," Bob Weir told him. Jerry Garcia later said it was their first show.

Early the next year, Jann Wenner walked into the offices of *The Daily Californian,* Berkeley's student paper, and pitched a weekly column on the rock and drug scene, which he wanted to write anonymously. A month before, Wenner had been roused from his bed at four in the morning by police officers searching for drugs and was arrested for possession of marijuana. Wenner spent the night in jail. "They missed the acid and the DMT, which I kept in the freezer compartment of the refrigerator," he said. Wenner believed he was fingered by a Berkeley student seeking revenge on Wenner for sleeping with his girlfriend. Wenner's lawyer got the charges dropped, arguing that the police had an improper search warrant. (The lawyer, Malcolm Burnstein, later employed a young Hillary Clinton as an intern.)

Wenner called his column Something's Happening and wrote under the pseudonym "Mr. Jones," the clueless, vaguely journalistic personage of Bob Dylan's "Ballad of a Thin Man," who walks into a room with a pencil in his hand and sees something happening but doesn't know what it is. But then again, who did? Across the Bay Area, student firebrands and stoned philosophers, biker outlaws and self-styled mystics, hipsters and poseurs alike commingled in a druggy renaissance of free expression that was remaking youth lifestyle, from the head shops of Haight Street to the bonfires of Stinson Beach. "The fact of the matter," Gleason wrote, "is that we are in a new age with a new religion and with new standards." In La Honda, an hour south of San Francisco, Ken Kesey was saying the same thing in country-cosmic aphorisms and into a microphone held by Tom Wolfe, who was documenting the lysergic bandwagoneers for a book, *The Electric Kool-Aid Acid Test.* "Everybody is going to be what they are," Kesey told him, "and whatever they are, there's not going to be anything to apologize about."

With Something's Happening, Wenner made himself the ultimate acid insider, Berkeley's window into the insular psychedelic rock scene. He judged the Trips Festival, a psychedelic rock happening inspired by Ken Kesey and organized by Bill Graham, a "flop," with "too many cops and too many undercover narcos." It was nonetheless significant, he said, because it rated reviews from "*Time, Life, Newsweek,* etc., and camera crews." (He blamed Graham for his "extreme uptightness," establishing a negative posture toward the rock promoter destined to last for years. In another column, he called Graham "a little man" who turned the dances into "money making schemes.")

Wenner also used his column to praise the Beatles and Bob Dylan and defend Mick Jagger against accusations that he was a "fag." "Girls aren't the only ones who adore Mick," he wrote. "When he gets married there will probably be more disappointed males than females."

In each column, Wenner turned his own friends into characters in an ongoing psychedelic serial that borrowed nonsense language from the Beatles' animated film, *Yellow Submarine*. Warnecke and Topham became Nowhere Man and Blue Nedd. "Nowhere Man and a bit of bored imagination," he wrote, "both at once, Nowhere, Neverwas, Notnow, Nottobe, World without End; People without names; Friends without Friendship."

The column ran alongside a photograph of "Mr. Jones": Jann Wenner in a fake beard and granny glasses and a harmonica around his neck. Another benefit of anonymity was that Wenner wanted to start an LSD business. He wrote a friend to say he had an investor on the hook—probably John Warnecke—who could front him $1,500, which they could earn back with sales of eighty-five thousand milligrams of LSD. "Since you would be doing the production work," he wrote to the friend, presumably a chemist, "and I would be distributing, which entails legal consequences, a fifty-fifty split seems thoroughly equitable."

The business didn't pan out, but Wenner advocated for legalization of LSD in his May 19, 1966, column, calling the drug "the closest we have come to a feasible manner in which men may reorient themselves around new pursuits and meanings." Unlike Mario Savio, who called Timothy Leary's "Turn on, tune in, drop out" motto an irresponsible slogan, Wenner saw LSD culture as virtuous precisely because it bypassed politics for an alternate reality. "Hippies, heads and other users of LSD are beyond any politics, let alone radical politics. Acid transcends politics," he wrote. "LSD users want no part of today's social structure. It's not just Vietnam and Alabama. These things are manifestations of a culture for which we don't care and don't support."

Over at NBC, Wenner was reporting stories about the fault line between the counterculture and the mainstream. "UC doctor says LSD is not harmful" went one of his reports. "Police arrest Bill Graham and kids at Fillmore auditorium" went another. And, "Long-haired boys banned at UC swimming pool."

Part of Wenner's job was driving a friend's motorcycle to the station at 2:00 a.m. to receive the dispatches from Asia and the East Coast. One night he was taking in the feed when he read an AP report from New York: James Pike Jr. had "shot himself to death in a drab, $5-a-day hotel room. Police said the 21-year-old youth fired two shots from the 30-30 range rifle. The first missed. The second ripped away the right side of his face and head."

Pike left a long and rambling note for loved ones, ending with "goodbye, goodbye." "There was no explanation for what motivated the youth," the report said, but Wenner knew better. He was crushed. Wenner mentioned Pike's death in his *Daily Californian* column with the glib remark that Pike had taken "a trip on the Suicide Express." In his veiled memoir, however, he described showing up at a debutante party after the news broke, disgusted by garish displays of sympathy from the socialites he felt didn't really know Pike. Wenner felt pangs of guilt for having shamed Pike about his sexuality. According to Wenner's Berkeley friend Robbie Leeds, Wenner confessed to him after Pike's death that he was a "latent homosexual." (Leeds said he kissed Wenner on the cheek and never told.) Wenner's mother, Sim, said she knew for sure that her son was gay when she saw his reaction to Pike's death. "I just saw Jann being broken up by it," she said.

Afterward, Pike's distraught father became unhinged, describing communiqués from poltergeists he believed were his son's ghost reaching out from the dead. In 1967, he tried summoning his son through a séance taped for TV and expanded on the phenomenon in a 1968 memoir called *The Other Side*. The book described his son's descent into drug experimentation but never mentioned his sexual confusion. Bishop Pike died the following year when he became lost in the Judaean Desert in Israel while trying to reexperience the life of Jesus Christ. In her essay on James Pike in *The White Album*, Joan Didion would write of Pike's restless pursuit of reinvention—his essential California-ness—as part of a time, the 1960s, when "no one at all seemed to have any memory or mooring, and in a way the Sixties were the years for which James Albert Pike was born."

·

ON THE WEEKEND of May 7, 1966, Jann Wenner was listening to the Grateful Dead perform "Midnight Hour" at the Harmon Gym at Berkeley when he noticed a man who looked like a Scotland Yard detective: deerstalker cap, curled mustache, pipe clenched in his teeth, and horn-rimmed glasses on his nose. It was Ralph Gleason, the music writer for the *San Francisco Chronicle*. Wenner introduced himself. "He said I know exactly who you are," Wenner recounted. "I've been reading your column."

Wenner was thrilled. Gleason was the patron saint of all that interested him, the senior statesman of the rock-and-roll scene, and a mentor to Kaufman, whose blues harmonica Gleason once heralded after witnessing her jam on the street in Berkeley. She spoke to Gleason almost daily and even told him about Wenner's acid trip in the closet. As the Dead played, Wenner and Gleason walked up to the loudspeakers on the stage and stuck their heads close to better hear Jerry Garcia's spidery guitar playing.

Gleason was the consummate hipster of San Francisco, a storied record collector and jazz writer who once published a magazine called *Jazz: A Quarterly of American Music* and helped co-found the Monterey Jazz Festival in 1958. His columns were syndicated in newspapers across the country, and his liner notes adorned the backs of classic jazz LPs. He first heard jazz on the radio in Chappaqua, New York, during a bout of the measles in the 1930s. He became obsessed and traveled the clubs of Fifty-Second Street with fellow record collectors who converged at the Commodore Music Shop and the Hot Record Society. "He knew Leonard Feather, Nat Hentoff, Jerry Wexler, John Hammond," said Wenner, "and after the war, he told me, he and [Gleason's wife] Jeanie brought ten pounds of pot in the trunk with them and moved out to San Francisco."

Gleason's eclectic passion, including New Orleans jazz at a time when it was deeply unhip, made him an outlier in the universe of jazz critics. But in San Francisco, his catholic taste was an advantage, and he became the city's quintessential music writer, interviewing Elvis Presley and Ray Charles on their swings through town. By 1966, he was a tie-wearing diabetic, forty-nine years old, who showed up at concerts with a chocolate bar in his coat pocket and hosted a local TV show called *Jazz Casual*. (The oft-told joke was that Gleason couldn't decide if he was composed of two twenty-four-year-olds, three sixteen-year-olds, or four twelve-year-olds.) Gleason was initially skeptical of Bob Dylan, panning his performance at the Monterey Folk Festival in 1963 ("I was deaf," he later said), but when he came around, he came around hard. In 1965, he arranged a press conference for Dylan on public television and invited the local press and bohemia, including Allen Ginsberg and Bill Graham. (*Rolling Stone* would later publish a transcript of the press conference as "The *Rolling Stone* Interview.")

Dylan was flattered by Gleason's attention. "I had heard that he had interviewed Hank Williams, which was impressive," said Dylan. "So there was a bit of a mystery to him. He wore a trench coat and horn-rimmed glasses and was the type of reporter you'd see around the Broadway area in New York. He wrote about jazz and folk music in the mainstream newspaper, so he was responsible for introducing me to a wider crowd, and his approval meant a lot."

Jann Wenner had grown up reading the *Chronicle* in San Rafael. The editor, Scott Newhall, was a jazz buff and confidant of Gleason's who called the *Chronicle* the country's only mainstream underground newspaper, turning against the Vietnam War and covering the beat and jazz culture of North Beach (Newhall and Gleason once interviewed Louis Armstrong while the jazz great sat on the toilet, part of his laxative-based health regimen). Gleason's column became the must-read report of the youth scene at Berkeley, and he was the rare public figure who advocated for the Free Speech Movement. But he also demanded obeisance from his acolytes, a hipster Socrates lording his knowledge of jazz over enthusiastic know-nothings. Wide-eyed Berkeley kids would gather in his study, surrounded by his piles of books and LPs, to listen to Gleason wax philosophic about the virtues of Duke Ellington or Lenny Bruce (who name checked Gleason in his routines). When Wenner told him he hated jazz, Gleason frog-marched him to a Wes Montgomery concert. "There *was* life before Jerry Garcia!" he would say.

"He wanted a newcomer on the scene to bow low to Ralph," recalled Michael Lydon, a *Newsweek* reporter who would go on to write for *Rolling Stone*. The potentate had new clothes, which some noticed. Greil Marcus said Gleason "wrote the same three columns, over and over again. I, like many people, got absolutely sick of reading these columns. First of all, it was all promotion. Promotion of the scene."

But Wenner followed Gleason around like a would-be son looking for an adoptive father. "I hadn't been in touch with my family for about three years," said Wenner, "and he and his wife and three kids, they had a house on Ashby Avenue, it was kind of an open scene to anybody looking for advice." Wenner became Gleason's most ardent devotee, reading his columns religiously and accompanying him to concerts. "We'd be reviewing the same things," said Wenner. "In far different ways; mine through the primrose glasses. We just kind of fell into a friendship. He became my mentor."

Gleason admired Wenner's zealous energy. He called him Janno and treated him like a precocious student in need of special guidance. And Wenner's devotion flattered Gleason. "Jann was the first writer (journalist) I had met who saw this whole mad world of pop music the way I did," Gleason wrote in *Rolling Stone* in 1972, "and who felt it had the kind of importance to all of our lives that, in the event, it turned out it did."

•

IN THE SPRING OF 1966, Wenner was hanging out with a handsome pal of John Warnecke's named Richard Black, a socialite turned bohemian who had just returned from traveling the world, including a three-month stint in London. To Wenner, Black seemed impossibly hip—well dressed, an LSD enthusiast, aspirations to work in television. They dropped acid together and lay in the middle of the street at the top of Telegraph Hill experiencing visions of "the explorers coming through the bay, and the moon is a giant lightbulb," Wenner recalled. Black planned on returning to London, along with his roommate, a sensitive and intensely intellectual writer named Jonathan Cott, who studied English literature at Berkeley. Wenner wanted to go. His grades at Berkeley were on an inverse trajectory with his drug taking, so Wenner dropped out to join them. "We did have the provision that we had things we were going to do, Jon and I, and we weren't going to babysit him," said Black.

Wenner arrived at Heathrow Airport in June 1966 with a guitar in one hand and a portable Olivetti in the other. He wore a porkpie hat. In his pocket was the phone number of Max Jones, editor of the *Melody Maker* and a friend of Ralph Gleason's to whom Wenner hoped to sell a story. Flush with excitement, Wenner took a taxi directly to Carnaby Street, where he gaped at the carnival of mods and rockers in velveteen coats and bell-bottoms wandering in and out of clothing shops. He wrote to Gleason that he saw Brian Jones of the Rolling Stones get out of a silver Rolls-Royce. He bought a pair of striped bell-bottoms and a flowered belt and rented a flat in Earl's Court. He hooked up with Black and went from party to party introducing himself as a rock writer from San Francisco, which lent him an aura of considerable cool. To earn spending money, he tried working as a wedding photographer and a folksinger in a café. "I played one solo gig at some restaurant, sitting in a corner for the evening," said Wenner, "and I'm sure I was boring; made 15 quid or so; that was the end of the professional career."

Wenner could not help but observe the open sensuality between men in London, a cultural femininity baked into British manners. "That was the period when homosexuality in England was not legalized, but it was decriminalized," Mick Jagger told Wenner in an interview in 1995. "It was part of a new freedom for men. It wasn't to do strictly with homosexuality, so much only, or androgynous, or whatever the noun is, but there was a freedom for men to dress as you please and act as you please and not conform to just one type."

The freedom was attractive to Wenner. "I had peace for my long hair," he wrote in his novel. "No men threatening me on the street, no crew-cut football players staring at me so frighteningly. The sexuality of it was intense." Richard Black picked up on Wenner's intensity during parties. "If there were gay people, I think he felt free to put his arm around me now and then," recalled Black. "We were at a party with Marianne Faithfull and a bunch of people. Somebody was under the impression that he was not only my friend but my lover. And I just was very totally heterosexual and trying to get laid every chance I could. So, he felt the dissonance."

At one point, Black was invited to a dinner party with Paul McCartney. Wenner, an unabashed devotee of mod in the mods-versus-rockers debate, implored Black to bring him. But the dinner was an intimate affair for couples, and Black's girlfriend had invited him. Wenner was wounded; afterward, he soured on both Black and London. Carnaby Street, "once so groovy," he wrote, was "commercialized to dreariness . . . a teenage scene."

Wenner looked up Max Jones, of the *Melody Maker,* and visited the offices on Fleet Street with a review of the new Beach Boys record. Though it was never published, Wenner was astonished to see a working newsroom populated with reporters smoking cigarettes and talking shop—a vision of order and professionalism amid the decadence of Carnaby. After a month of partying and interpersonal tumult—including an affair with a girl named Mandy who lived next door to him—he realized "the transient, ambiguous, do-little bohemian lifestyle wasn't for me." He feared he was wasting his life. The obvious solution, said Wenner, was "a conventional marriage with a good Jewish girl."

·

WHEN SIMON AND GARFUNKEL came to San Francisco to play the Community Theatre in Berkeley in May 1966, they made a special trip to Berkeley to meet Ralph Gleason, whose collection of Lenny Bruce recordings, bequeathed to him by Bruce himself, was highly prized samizdat. While Simon eagerly sampled the tapes, he met Denise Kaufman, Gleason's acolyte and Jann Wenner's "good Jewish girl" of choice. She offered to tour Simon around San Francisco and took him to an open mic at a folk café called Coffee and Confusion (where he played "The Sound of Silence") and then to meet the Grateful Dead in their communal three-story Victorian on Ashbury Street. Kaufman and Simon slept together at the apartment of Stewart Brand, founder of the *Whole Earth Catalog,* and Simon invited her to Anaheim to see him play the next weekend.

When Wenner heard about the affair, he seethed with jealousy, generating an animus against Paul Simon that lasted for years to come. In his pursuit of Kaufman, Wenner often told her parents that he intended to marry her, but Kaufman would roll her eyes. "I don't think so!" she moaned. "She loved me, but not like that," said Wenner. "Her mind was on these acid cowboys, and Hells Angels. She wanted the real authentic guys, the real deal. I thought I could get her."

The surest sign Kaufman didn't intend to marry Wenner was when she got pregnant by a member of the New Christy Minstrels. Wenner put her in touch with a doctor in Berkeley "who gave me the name of a doctor in Mexico who would do an abortion," Kaufman recalled. The procedure (performed on a washing machine in Tijuana) made Kaufman hemorrhage, and she went to an American doctor for help. The police showed up to file a report, and Wenner drove down from Berkeley to be with her. Kaufman was grateful, though later irritated when Wenner used the abortion fiasco to cast her as a troubled soul in need of his guidance. "I really can't believe your hypocrisy," she wrote to him. "You—who all year long wanted to sleep with me—trying to put me down for having had an abortion."

Wenner also accused her of corrupting him. "You say I got you going to the Fillmore on acid," she wrote. "It was you + John + Ned who did that, Mr. Jones—not me. Do you remember that or have you fantasized your own past[?]"

But in the summer of 1966, Kaufman's parents became so worried about her LSD use they had her institutionalized in the psychiatric ward at Mount Zion Hospital. Wenner offered a way forward: While in London, he proposed they give up drugs and rock and roll, get married, and move to Spain or Greece. Naturally, Kaufman figured the best way to meditate on the proposal was to take acid. "I was like, am I just ignoring the obvious?" she recalled. "Do I have this radar for attracting people who aren't truly loving, and here's someone who is? . . . I was questioning my own choices. When he said, let's do it, I said, okay."

Her acid revelation faded, however, when Wenner started planning the wedding ceremony with his mother. Kaufman gently applied the brakes, recommending they get to know each other better. Also, she wanted to come to London to take acid on Carnaby Street and buy some hip clothes before they went straight. In a panic, Wenner got the next flight back to New York and immediately got on a pay phone at Kennedy Airport to pressure Kaufman to marry him. When she said no, Wenner sobbed and fumbled with dimes, begging the operator to keep him connected. He threatened to commit suicide. "He told me he was going to kill himself," Kaufman recounted. "He was gonna do just what Jim [Pike] did; he got a hotel in New York and was gonna kill himself, unless I came there and married him."

Kaufman talked him down, after which Wenner's marriage fantasy collapsed. Plans thwarted, he accepted an invitation from Andy Harmon to stay at his family estate in Rye, New York, north of Manhattan. It was grand property with guesthouses and a tennis court moldering in neglect but still staffed with servants. Wenner brought a copy of the Beatles' *Revolver* from England, and they got stoned and listened to it as they mulled over their futures. Between tearful walks through the woods, a bereft Wenner harnessed his ambition for another project: the Great American Novel.

He started writing a book with the wistful title "Now These Days Are Gone," a story of his youth, which already seemed to Wenner worth enshrining in literature. An awkward blend of *On the Road* and *The Catcher in the Rye,* the book was Wenner's attempt to square the warring sides of his personality, his desire for a straight life with Kaufman with his hidden homosexuality, his love of high society with his love for rock and roll. In one scene, the Jim Pike character stumbles upon Wenner's open diary, where Wenner discusses their mutual attraction and concludes that "there are certain things that must be left unsaid and not openly recognized." When Pike confesses to seeing the journal, Wenner feels exposed and angry. "He had looked at Dorian Gray's portrait," he says. Alone in his "fortress on the fourth floor" in Berkeley, Wenner assesses his own personality and finds himself wanting:

> I knew lots of people but I had no friends. I slept with girls but I loved no one. I had invitations to deb parties. That seemed the most important thing. I was social, I knew debutantes, and I knew rich

people. I had worked so hard, I liked so many people I couldn't stand. A black leather address book with thin blue pages. With names of people with good addresses.

He resolved to move past his internal conflicts, finally be himself. But who was he? The only thing that bound Wenner's aimless, desperate life together was . . . rock and roll. He created a playlist of songs for citation in each chapter: the Rolling Stones, Bob Dylan, and the Beatles, the three-legged chair for his troubled soul. The final chapter of Wenner's book was to be called "The Rock and Roll Generation," a treatise on the magic that would set him free. But while he typed up the novel, Wenner received a letter from Ralph Gleason. He'd heard from Denise Kaufman about the aborted marriage, the suicide threat. He was worried. And there was a development back home. A job opening in San Francisco. Did Wenner want to write about rock and roll?

3

California Dreamin'

Are you going to let your emotional life be run by Time magazine?
—Allen Ginsberg, "America"

The day Jann Wenner strode into the offices of *Ramparts* magazine in North Beach, he wore a trench coat and sunglasses, a fedora cocked on his head. "He looked like he was from a Dashiell Hammett play or something," said Linda Kingsbury, the office girl Friday and Wenner's future sister-in-law. "I just thought, 'Who is this?'"

Wenner's fortunes began when *Ramparts,* a monthly founded by left-wing Catholics and edited by an eccentric Irish-Catholic newspaperman named Warren Hinckle, decided to launch a biweekly broadsheet in the fall of 1966 called *The Sunday Ramparts.* "The idea was to have *Sunday Ramparts* be irreverent in the style of the Manchester *Guardian* and the London *Times,*" Ralph Gleason later explained. "It'll look very stuffy but in actuality it would be outrageous."

Gleason, a member of *Ramparts'* editorial board, recommended Wenner as an editor and "rock and roll specialist," and Wenner immediately shelved his novel (which "didn't reveal any talent," he concluded) and moved back to San Francisco to help put out the first issue in October 1966.

Before he could start, however, there was a hurdle: He was reclassified as 1-A by the Selective Service System, making him available for the Vietnam draft. In 1966, the number of men sent to fight in Vietnam more than doubled to 385,000. Dr. Sandor Burstein, the Wenner family doctor (and his mother's ex-lover), declined to help him, so Wenner went to a Dr. Martin Hoffman on Telegraph Avenue in Berkeley. An advocate for gay rights who wrote the pioneering 1968 book *The Gay World: Male Homosexuality and the Social Creation of Evil,* Hoffman studied gay men around San Francisco and encouraged a "radical tolerance" for homosexuality. To help Wenner avoid the war, he diagnosed him with a "serious personality disorder . . . with its concomitant history of psychiatric treatment, suicidal ideation, homosexual and excessive heterosexual promiscuity, and heavy use of illegal drugs."

If the letter to the army draft board contained more than a kernel of truth, it also achieved its purpose: Like the rest of his friends in the society scene, Wenner avoided the most divisive and defining event of his generation. He did not know a single person who served in Vietnam. "The poor people went and fought the war," said Wenner. "No friends of mine died there. No people I went to high school with . . . No people from my college. My group of friends were wealthy enough to avoid the draft or they were 2-S deferred in college." (Only later did he learn that Bill Belding, class president at Chadwick, had become a Navy SEAL.)

Instead, Wenner would have a front-row seat to the rock-and-roll revolution, witnessing history from a desk at 301 Broadway, surrounded by folk cafés, seedy topless bars, drinking holes for sailors, and beat clubs like the hungry i, the same neighborhood where Ralph Gleason wore out his crepe-soled boots. "Ralph used to take me to Basin Street to see Ray Charles," recalled Wenner. "It was really at that epicenter of the post-beatnik hippie San Francisco . . . the melting pot of all that."

The same week Wenner started, a young woman stopped by his office to introduce herself. Jane Schindelheim, the resident "Xerox queen," sister of the secretary, couldn't help but notice the brash new editor bopping around like he owned the place. "I overheard Jann telling someone about Chadwick," recounted Jane. "So I went into his office, and he was reading the *Times.* He had all these Coca-Cola bottles lined up on the ledge. I said to him, 'Did you know John Muchmore?' And he said, 'Why?' and I said, 'My ex-boyfriend went to Chadwick.'"

Wenner brightened. Sure, he knew Muchmore—the only skier at Chadwick who had been better than him, he said. "I guess we're destined to get married," he told her, "because I just broke up with somebody."

A bold young man, she thought. Younger than Wenner by four months and shorter by an inch, Jane was a waifish girl-woman, narrow-hipped and flat-chested, tan-skinned and almond-eyed, with a casual chic gleaned from afternoons roaming Bloomingdale's as a Manhattan teenager. With her easy sophistication and vaguely Asian features (Wenner said it looked like somebody in her family had been raped by a Mongolian), she was exotic even in 1960s San Francisco. "She wasn't a hippie," said Wenner. "She was the Bloomingdale's girl. Just savvy . . . If she had an overcoat, it would be long, [with] clean lines, much more to the Jackie Onassis style."

"What I wasn't used to is the Grateful Dead," said Jane, "and people calling other people 'Mountain Girl.' That I wasn't used to."

Schindelheim grew up in Stuyvesant Town, the collection of high-rises along the East Side of New York City, her parents Eastern European Jews. Her father, Arthur, was from Austria-Hungary and wanted to be a lawyer but instead became a dentist because the schooling was quicker and the job more lucrative. Her mother Theresa's family was from Eastern Europe, but she was born in New York. Both were stiff teetotalers, conservative and remote, providing everything for their daughters but warmth. Domineering and status conscious, Theresa valued beauty and wealth and reminded her daughters, especially Linda, how they failed to measure up on a daily basis. She regarded Jane as a pretty bauble, "the beautiful one," said her sister, Linda. "And she was aware that that wasn't something she did; it was something she was born with. And that was a difficult thing."

Jane found solace in fashion and art, attending the High School of Music and Art in Harlem to study drawing. She wore black turtlenecks, smoked skinny joints, and drew moody portraits in charcoal and pencil evoking her inner torpor. She didn't smile easily, keeping friends guessing what lay behind her curtain of dark hair, offering her sly humor in small but tantalizing doses. A friend wrote a poem describing her as "plotting and scheming for nothing but the entertainment of it."

"She was always in a trench coat," recalled Peter Wolf, a classmate who later became the lead singer for the J. Geils Band. "Just reminded me of some babe that would have walked off a Godard movie. And she always wore the same black turtleneck, and these sandal shoes, she was quite stunning. Eyesight to the blind, as one might say. Just had an aura about her."

After graduating, Jane moved to Pittsburgh to study line drawing at Carnegie Tech. On her first day, she met the quietly handsome painter from California John Muchmore, and a heated romance ensued. Art drew them together. "She had an incredible line," Muchmore said of her drawing. "Speaking as a painter, there was an energy to it. It wasn't an even line. There was a pulse to it. An emotion to her line. So that her line drawings were very dynamic, very alive."

After a year and a half, Muchmore became disenchanted with school, they broke up, and a distraught Jane dropped out and flew west to visit her sister, Linda, who had moved to San Francisco. Jane figured she'd go back in two weeks.

While Wenner poured himself into his new job at *The Sunday Ramparts,* he enjoyed the company of the nice Jewish girl whose poise seemed a cut above, a sophisticated New Yorker who dismissed the fuzzy Bay Area hippiedom with a casual eye roll and regarded Wenner as the diamond in the local rough. After a few dates, Jann and Jane moved in together, mainly because Wenner needed a roommate to pay the rent at his mother's house. They began sleeping together, but neither was ready to commit. "It wasn't falling madly in love," Wenner said. "It wasn't love at first sight . . . I wanted a stable relationship, something to go home to."

They agreed they could see other people at first. "You can be free to do what you want; I'll do what I want," he recalled telling her. "We're not going to get that serious. [But] we were still fucking in the house."

Jane was both charmed and flummoxed by Wenner. He was in perpetual haste, but when he slowed down enough to pay attention to her, it opened her like a flower. "I remember one time he was running; he came to pick me up and was late from the plane," said Jane. "He had just bought this cake in the shape of a heart. That's when I think my feelings for him changed. He had a buttoned-up shirt over blue jeans. It was endearing."

But then off again he went.

•

AT *THE SUNDAY RAMPARTS,* Wenner wrote capsule reviews for the local film and theater listings, with a roving eye for the drug and sex flicks bubbling up from the underground, like the LSD exploitation film *Hallucination Generation* ("predictable, inaccurate") or *Underground Cinema 12,* "a potpourri of sexual revelry about an orgy, an intimate look at heterosexual stuff, a surrealistic glance or two and a 'sensitive' leer at homosexuality."

Typical was his review of the 1965 film *Sexus:* "The plot is a bore, but it contains a good sado-masochistic lesbian bit. Only for a joke at the Presidio."

For the rock listings, however, Wenner lavished wholly uncritical praise on the local scene like the junior-league Ralph Gleason that he was. Wenner touted San Francisco as having "two of the five or six top rock groups in the country." Local hero Steve Miller created "a musical ecstasy unusual in a blues group," and the Jefferson Airplane were "distinguished by an unusually professional manner, excellent original material and a unique tenor-alto sound." What he lacked in insight, he made up for with enthusiastic accessibility. While his Berkeley classmate Jonathan Cott, also at *The Sunday Ramparts,* was writing sophisticated criticism of avant-garde cinema ("Nowhere Man: A Clarification with Seven Propositions" was his review of *Blow-Up*), Wenner was glossing the revolution for the squares: Rock and roll, Wenner informed readers, was "noted for its heavy rhythms, pounding beat and loudness of approach, or, in a word, its sexuality." He named "(I Can't Get No) Satisfaction" by the Rolling Stones the best rock-and-roll song "ever done," though, he emphasized, the Beatles were the greatest band, and Dylan the greatest lyricist. His simple idea was already in evidence. "If [the songs] are about drugs, and more and more of them are, then that's what's happening with this generation," he wrote. "Rock and roll speaks for today's experiences. It is the poetry of youth."

Wenner interviewed Muddy Waters, who told Wenner that his favorite white rock-and-roll band was the Stones. "You know their name comes from a song I wrote," Waters said.

For new arrivals on the scene, Wenner was the travel guide to the renaissance in his backyard:

> Five to ten huge dance concerts take place every weekend, not just indoors, but often on the beaches and mountains. In addition, the big name tours, East Bay drag strip discotheques and smaller high school oriented shows flourish. This city loves that sound . . .
>
> . . . Avant-garde theater has been presented. Poster art comparable to that of Paris in the twenties has been nourished (one Family Dog poster bore the credo: "May the Baby Jesus Open Your Mind and Shut Your Mouth").

Wenner reserved his critical swipes for out-of-towners. Folksinger Tom Paxton of Chicago "left a feeling of pretentiousness much like Paul Simon's 'poetry.'" Wenner drove to Los Angeles for the express purpose of sniffing at the rival scene, disparaging the bands, mocking their clothes, and deriding their fraudulent fans ("two short haired boys in Macy's mod"). The two best L.A. groups, the Peanut Butter Conspiracy and Iron Butterfly, paled in comparison to any San Francisco band, he wrote, quoting Ellen Harmon, a co-founder of the Family Dog, calling L.A. "super uptight plastic America."

Meanwhile, his review of hometown favorites the Grateful Dead was so reverent Warner Bros. used it as a promotional tear sheet to sell the album. His article noted that Bob Weir was "from a social Atherton family" and that his jug band "played for his sister's debutante party this summer"; "noted jazz critic" Ralph Gleason had named Pigpen McKernan "one of the major bluesmen in America." "My tastes, and my music, were pretty mainstream," Wenner said. "I wasn't raised listening to the blues . . . I was not a deep musical person. I was a fan, and it spread out from there."

But San Francisco was no longer a secret beyond the Sierras. As boldfaced names of the youth revolution, like Tim Leary and Joan Baez, came to sample the scene, Wenner received them like a local diplomat.

Wenner had worshipped Leary as a righteous advocate of his favorite drug and was disappointed when he only wanted to eat a hamburger and drink beer in a bar. Wenner wrote a positive article nonetheless, titled "The Case for Dr. Leary."

In truth, Wenner was as interested in Leary's star power as in the content of his propaganda. After he met Joan Baez for lunch, getting her view on the rock revolution (she was ambivalent), he paraded her through the *Ramparts* offices to enjoy the effect of her celebrity. "I just remember everybody in the office gawked," said Wenner. "I was interested in watching the reaction of everybody. It lifted my stock."

Inside the *Ramparts* offices, Wenner kept his eye trained on Warren Hinckle, in whose profile Wenner could see an outline of his own future. A bon vivant and socialite, and heavy drinker, who wore expensive haberdashery and reveled in self-promotion, Hinckle made his name as a young journalist teasing a gay *Chronicle* columnist, "Count Marco," revealing that he'd been a hairdresser and hung out around public restrooms. Willfully eccentric, Hinckle owned a pet capuchin monkey named Henry Luce and wore an eye patch over one eye (lost in a childhood car accident). Hinckle was a gifted provocateur, drawing attention to *Ramparts* with searing covers like the image of a crucified Jesus Christ planted in a Vietnam battlefield. The magazine raked as much muck as possible, capturing the left-wing political tumult of mid-1960s San Francisco by hiring Eldridge Cleaver, a confessed rapist who was politically radicalized in a California prison and became a leader of the Black Panther Party, as a columnist. But Hinckle's main passion was controversy. For a feature on Hugh Hefner, Hinckle included a centerfold of Hefner smoking a pipe. The magazine was famously said to have "A Bomb in Every Issue," and Wenner watched, in early 1967, as *Ramparts* detonated the biggest bomb in its history: a story on the infiltration of student groups across the country by the Central Intelligence Agency, which ended up exposing, among others, pioneering feminist Gloria Steinem and her front work while a student at Harvard. As Hinckle muscled the story toward publication, the CIA tried to counter the report before *Ramparts* could print, but Hinckle beat it to the punch by taking out a one-page ad in *The New York Times* to break the story. The magazine's circulation doubled. Wenner clipped out newspaper stories about it and filed them away. "He transformed the magazine from a lefty, radical, Catholic magazine to a much more commercial, broader, muckraking publication," said Wenner. "It was a breakthrough magazine of its time. And in addition to the tough political, cultural writing, it was elegant . . . The mix was highly unusual. And that mix moved into *Rolling Stone*."

But a cultural divide now separated Hinckle's older twentysomethings, who drank liquor and aspired to New Left discourse, from Wenner's generation of younger twentysomethings, who smoked dope, wore denim, and embraced Bob Dylan. In truth, Wenner might have gone either way. He was devoted to rock and roll but was turned off by the hippie hair balls mobbing the Haight-Ashbury. After visiting Ken Kesey's ranch in La Honda with Warnecke, Wenner published a bracingly skeptical review of Kesey, who he felt had corrupted his would-be paramour, Denise Kaufman. He quoted at length a "noted writer in the Scene"—really just Wenner himself—criticizing Kesey as being on a "Christ Trip." Quoting himself "was a way of having an opinion but also doing objective journalism," Wenner said.

In early 1967, Warren Hinckle asked Ralph Gleason, the resident expert on the young, to write an essay on the hippies for *Ramparts* magazine. But without consulting Gleason, Hinckle decided to write and publish his own feature called "The Social History of the Hippies," which argued that they were lotus-eaters who avoided the difficult work of stewarding political change. (He later wrote in his memoir that he was sorry that he "dumped on [Gleason's] flower children without giving him a chance to defend the little fascists.")

Wenner might have agreed with Hinckle about hippies, but Gleason was so furious at the betrayal that he immediately resigned from the board of *Ramparts* and refused to set foot in the offices again. Wenner wasn't getting much love from Hinckle either: "Wenner was considerably frustrated by my oafish refusal to print his dope and rock stories in the magazine," Hinckle later wrote, "as I considered rock reporting as a state of the journalistic art on a level with Bengay ads."

And just as Hinckle and *Ramparts* pivoted away from Gleason and the counterculture, the magazine pulled the plug on its Sunday newspaper, leaving Jann Wenner without a job. Wenner and Gleason watched in dismay as the best outlet for journalism on the local counterculture disappeared. "Had it lasted a little longer," Gleason later said, "it would have been the biggest of all the underground papers."

•

"THE SUMMER OF LOVE" began as a marketing slogan, coined in the spring of 1967 by a consortium of San Francisco heads calling themselves the Council for the Summer of Love. The co-founder, Chet Helms, an impresario and band manager who was central to the San Francisco Sound (among other accomplishments, he'd helped discover Janis Joplin), held a press conference promising to lure 200,000 hippies to the city for a utopian reboot of the Haight-Ashbury. But Helms quickly lost control of the phrase when it was adopted by the eastern media as it prepared to descend on the Bay Area for a rock-and-roll event: the Monterey International Pop Festival.

The festival was planned, essentially, as a loss leader, fusing the values of the emergent counterculture with the marketing needs of the big record companies by creating a rock version of the Human Be-In, San Francisco's "gathering of the tribes" that telegraphed the concept of the hippie around the world. The architect Lou Adler, whose Dunhill Records was enriched by the success of the Mamas and the Papas, saw a chance for a major media event to showcase rock bands for the nascent industry. He struck a $400,000 deal with ABC-TV to finance and film the festival and he conscripted D. A. Pennebaker, who shot the vérité Bob Dylan documentary *Don't Look Back* in 1965, to film it. To promote the event, Adler produced a song written by John Phillips called "San Francisco (Be Sure to Wear Flowers in Your Hair)." Sung by Scott McKenzie, it became a No. 1 hit for Columbia Records on the eve of the festival. ("We all hated that song," said Wenner. "Hated it, hated it, hated it.")

While not altogether opposed to being sold, the San Francisco crowd was suspicious of those who were doing the selling. Ralph Gleason was the resident gatekeeper. To gain his support, the L.A. consortium needed to prove it wasn't out to exploit the psychedelic Eden for money and promise to showcase homegrown stars, especially Big Brother and the Holding Company, led by singer Janis Joplin. "I think we felt we were all in the center of something special," said Wenner. "As casual and informal and irresponsible as it was, it had a higher purpose. The LSD thing, the power of music. It was evangelical, in many ways. And I think that same impulse was there throughout the rock community. The Beatles felt it; the L.A. groups felt it. We were kind of purists. But San Francisco was seen as the epicenter of it all."

To broker peace, Adler and his business partner dispatched Derek Taylor, a waggish Brit who worked on and off as the press secretary for the Beatles. He argued that people would intuitively respect any event they paid money to get into. "Had it been free," recalled Bob Neuwirth, a friend of Bob Dylan's who was a consultant on the Pennebaker film, "you would have had every meatball in the Western Hemisphere." Here was a novel idea: putting up a fence and charging money for entrance to the great rock-and-roll love-in to give it *credibility*.

Wenner himself was a kind of junior broker of the deal. In a memoir published by Wenner in 1973, Derek Taylor would recall that most of the San Francisco people were skeptical of Adler and the hustlers from "the land of tinsel, false idols and broken promises"—except Jann Wenner, "who was most encouraging and quite (for him) honest."

Taylor conscripted Wenner as an informal consultant for the Monterey festival, soliciting his advice on converting Gleason and commissioning him to write an essay for the full-color catalog they intended to sell at the County Fairgrounds in Monterey. To overcome Gleason's resistance, Wenner recommended the festival promoters donate the profits to a well-selected charity. When Taylor suggested a rock-and-roll scholarship, Wenner unleashed a kind of manifesto about the meaning of the new culture. "It is a feeling, not skill, that makes the musician or writer," he wrote in a letter, "and the genesis of rock and roll is being young in the twentieth century.

"You have to think about what rock and roll is all about and decide from there," he continued, suggesting the "most obvious" cause was the legalization of marijuana. "The next best thing is aid to Vietnam," he wrote. (They didn't take his advice.)

As a postscript, Wenner threw in a little request: Could Taylor please send him free copies of all the Beach Boys records?

•

THE FIRST AMERICAN rock-and-roll magazine was invented in 1966 by an earnest Swarthmore College freshman named Paul Williams. *Crawdaddy!* was named for the club where the Rolling Stones first played, and the magazine—a mimeographed, collated sheet—billed itself as a no-frills publication of "rock and roll criticism" featuring "intelligent writing about pop music." From his perch on Broadway in San Francisco, Wenner noticed *Crawdaddy!* right away—and attacked it. In *The Sunday Ramparts,* he said the danger to the purity of rock and roll was "academics," citing a pretentious review of a Supremes record in *Crawdaddy!* as "completely contrary to the spirit of rock and roll. Unfortunately, some people take it seriously."

"Don't believe anything you read about rock and roll," Wenner wrote, "only what you see coming out of amplifiers."

But the idea for a West Coast rock magazine was already in the air, and Wenner was paying close attention. In San Francisco, two high school friends started a paper called the *Mojo Navigator Rock & Roll News* in August 1966. Wenner invited the editor, Greg Shaw, to the *Ramparts* offices to rap about rock music. That same spring, Wenner was approached by Chet Helms, who told Wenner he was germinating a hippie music magazine for distribution in record stores. To get started, Helms had a few hundred names and addresses for contestants in a radio contest put on by KFRC-FM, which would be the initial mailing list for the magazine. Helms also had a clever name for it: *Straight Arrow*. He asked Jann Wenner to be the editor.

While Helms went looking for money to launch *Straight Arrow*—he calculated a $200,000 budget—Wenner spent his afternoons looking for work, taking the civil service exam to apply to be a postal carrier, a popular hippie job, while writing a review of *Sgt. Pepper's* for *High Fidelity*. At one point, he was offered a position at Rogers & Cowan, the publicity firm, but turned it down, hoping for something related to rock and roll. He rummaged through Ralph Gleason's filing cabinets of newspaper and magazine clippings to put together proposals for both an anthology of rock criticism and a rock-and-roll encyclopedia. "It had to be something he would endorse," recalled Wenner. His pitch for a rock anthology was rejected by an editor in New York.

Maybe the best job was right under Jann Wenner's nose. He went to meetings with Chet Helms and drew up a prospectus and an organizational chart for *Straight Arrow,* which included the art director from the *Oracle,* Gabe Katz. At one point, the group talked of making a magazine shaped like an LP cover. "Since I was the guy who wrote for *Ramparts,* I was the one designated to put it together," said Wenner, "and the first beginnings of [*Rolling Stone*] stemmed from that . . . The notion of doing a rock magazine came square from that."

Wenner told a friend that the Chet Helms magazine "fell through because of the inability to get funds." But Helms came to believe Wenner had slunk away with his idea—as well as his list of radio contestants, which Wenner would use to solicit subscriptions and conduct a reader survey for the first issue of *Rolling Stone.* Wenner acknowledged that Helms felt betrayed, but "no one knew what they were doing. I knew virtually nothing, and they knew less."

"They were hippies," reasoned Jane Wenner. "They were supposed to raise the money, and they were just dragging their feet. You know? It was, like, never going anywhere."

Sometime in the spring of 1967, Wenner drove to Ralph Gleason's house on Ashby Avenue in Berkeley, plunked himself down in the study, and popped the idea. "Jann came over one day and said, 'How about a magazine?'" recounted Gleason. "Like the *Melody Maker* and the *Musical Express,* but an American one that would be different and better and would cover not just the records and the music but would cover the whole culture.

"And instantly that was the idea," Gleason said, "as soon as he said it we both agreed it was a hell of an idea. And that was it."

•

WHEN THE MONTEREY POP FESTIVAL opened in June, Jann Wenner arrived as both a consultant to the festival's PR man, Derek Taylor, and the would-be editor of a rock-and-roll magazine. He had written an essay for the festival's full-color catalog called "Rock & Roll Music," wherein he proclaimed that "rock and roll music has turned out to be more than just noise" and went on to make a case for its cultural ascendance. The public, he wrote, was coming around to the realization that this music was about *ambition*. "Brian Wilson spent 90 hours in the studio making 'Good Vibrations,'" he wrote. The Beatles were, "dare I say it, geniuses."

More than fifty thousand people showed up in Monterey to see the Byrds and the Mamas and the Papas from Los Angeles; Paul Simon and Art Garfunkel from New York; the Who and the Jimi Hendrix Experience from London. Local favorites the Grateful Dead and the Jefferson Airplane—along with Janis Joplin, whom Ralph Gleason had helped book, and the Steve Miller Blues Band, for whom Wenner advocated—played alongside Otis Redding from Memphis and the Indian sitar player Ravi Shankar. Taylor, who called the festival the "most outrageously ambitious event in the history of popular music," arranged a massive press pool, issuing a thousand press badges to reporters and photographers from the mainstream outlets of the East, including *Newsweek, The New York Times,* the Associated Press, and *Esquire,* plus every obscure underground paper in existence, "a flurry of hair and bearded and beaded literate hippies from Haight-Ashbury and Sunset Strip," as Taylor recalled. D. A. Pennebaker recorded the proceedings on 16-millimeter film. The last issue of *Mojo Navigator,* which ran out of money, reported that press cameras crackled throughout Ravi Shankar's set. The press area was so far beyond capacity Taylor likened it to "Buchenwald"; he was forced to issue new press passes to winnow the crowd the next day. "When John [Phillips] and I showed up on Friday morning," said Lou Adler, "the amount of worldwide and domestic press was unbelievable. A lot of it had to do with Derek Taylor and how he put it out there. That was the breakthrough."

As had been the fashion in the smaller world of San Francisco, Monterey was meant to be a microcosm of the whole culture. Outside the fairgrounds, hippies set up makeshift encampments that looked to Wenner more like "a medieval fair or an Indian religious holiday than a show. People camped out at night, danced until early morning on beaches . . . It is the music in which they find spiritual community." Inside, Wenner roamed backstage in his monogrammed Oxford and jeans, a Nikon camera looped around his neck, snapping pictures, including a shot of Brian Jones, whom he'd last seen emerging from a Rolls-Royce in London. Wenner summoned Jane to Monterey on the third day, and they slept in a house with the band Blue Cheer, friends of John Warnecke's. Jane shadowed him while he met Hendrix, and they sat near Brian Jones and Nico to watch Janis Joplin. "I was the girlfriend," said Jane.

Wenner the budding tastemaker studiously scribbled reviews in his notebook. His favorite guitar player was Mike Bloomfield of the Butterfield Blues Band, whom he called "superb," while Jimi Hendrix "lacks vocal style or smoothness, handles his guitar with agility and with minor drama; although not a master, his art is in his presence." (After Hendrix pretended to jack off with his guitar and then set it on fire during his epic performance of "Wild Thing," ABC chose not to air Pennebaker's film.) And Wenner continued to be unimpressed with Paul Simon, opining that his "primary talent is on the guitar and composing melodies for that instrument; he is not a lyricist." In his personal notes, Wenner lamented the absence of Muddy Waters, Chuck Berry, B. B. King, the Rolling Stones, Bob Dylan, and "the *sine qua non* of pop, the Beatles." "The festival was less than a complete artistic success," he wrote. "Poor judgment was the rule in the invitations to some artists and not to others."

His unpublished critiques notwithstanding, the festival was a watershed moment. As Mike Bloomfield told the crowd, according to a glowing press release Wenner helped draft with Derek Taylor, "This is our generation, we're all here together, to dig ourselves."

By the end of the weekend, Clive Davis, the Harvard-trained lawyer who was taking over CBS Records, had traded his white tennis sweater for an open-collared shirt and beads. He signed Janis Joplin and her band for an unheard-of $250,000.

•

THE MONTH AFTER the Monterey Pop Festival, a nineteen-year-old Welshman named Robin Gracey made his way to San Francisco on a Greyhound bus, rucksack on his shoulder, proverbial flower in his hair. The winsome lad wanted to experience this "Summer of Love" he'd been reading about in the papers, the siren song of the Doors' No. 1 hit "Light My Fire" curling through his imagination like hashish smoke.

Gracey had the easy manner of a naïf from the English countryside, oblivious to his own handsome looks, the casual mop of black hair, thick eyebrows, and easy smile. He met a beautiful Swiss woman on a stop in Winnipeg, Canada, and she gave him her number in San Francisco. When he settled in the Haight-Ashbury a week later, the woman invited him to a party north of the city, along the Russian River. It was the summer home of a prominent young man named John Warnecke. The woman, it turned out, was a nanny working for Jackie Kennedy, responsible for taking care of John junior and Caroline, ages six and nine. The senior Warnecke had an affair with the late president's widow, and her watercolor paintings now graced the walls of the Warnecke home—the same house where members of the Grateful Dead were showing up on a semi-regular basis to take drugs with the architect's wayward son. ("Phil the bass player roled [*sic*] a joint in a canoe while going down the river with the wind blowing," Warnecke wrote to Wenner in 1966.)

That day, Gracey and the nanny went canoeing on the river and returned to find two of Warnecke's friends hanging out: Jann Wenner and Jane Schindelheim. Recalled Gracey, "We were both swimming in the river below the house, almost certainly naked, and Jann was very ebullient and cheerful." Charmed by the nude young man with the British accent—who looked a little like Wenner and stood the same height, five six—Wenner invited Gracey to dinner in Potrero Hill the following week, where Jane's sister, Linda, was now living with them on Rhode Island Street. Jann and Jane were now a steady item. After Jane brought home a handsome doctor one night, Wenner became jealous and asked her to see him exclusively (it would not be the last time Jane used other men to try to get Wenner's attention). The relationship ran hot and cold, with Jane frustrated by Wenner's fickle desires and perpetual distraction. "Something tells me that your wants will always be three thousand miles away," she told him.

In truth, his wants were much closer. Wenner offered himself as Robin Gracey's all-access pass to the city. "He was my opportunity to go into Golden Gate Park, or see the Grateful Dead, or go to the Fillmore, and I saw Jim Morrison and the Doors," recounted Gracey.

Gracey wasn't gay, but Wenner's enthusiastic seduction seemed part of the woozy spectacle of San Francisco in 1967. At one point, Wenner stole a kiss behind a bush. "He was wooing me," said Gracey. "I felt on the one hand beguiled by it, charmed, and also somewhat frightened by it, I think. I think I probably lived under the philosophy that, you know, everything is experience." One afternoon, Wenner asked Gracey if he wanted to try LSD. "I have no idea how many hours we were actually high," Gracey said. "And I can remember being reluctant during this time, but knowing that, in a sense, I was actually in the vortex. A whirlpool, basically, and that it was going to happen. And it did."

They had sex at the Wenners' apartment in Potrero Hill, after which Wenner, on top of the world, took Gracey on a drive in his blue VW Beetle. "His driving on LSD seems a bit frightening," said Gracey. "I remember seeing visions of cars turning into sharks."

To that point, Wenner had had only tentative and unsatisfying flirtations with homosexuality. His tryst with Warnecke had been illicit and unformed, a happy accident on LSD. Despite the new age of freedom and self-expression, gay love was not part of the rock-and-roll menu, where "chicks" were the subject of 99 percent of the music. It was still taboo in the male-dominated hippie culture, too. Kenneth Anger's film *Scorpio Rising* featured gay bikers revving to the sound of Martha and the Vandellas and Mick Jagger preened like a drag queen, but it was part of the Shock of the New, theatrical titillation and subversion rather than a license for open liberation. But for Wenner, the Gracey affair was something deeper than a mere fling: He said it was his first bona fide homosexual romance. On the eve of the invention of *Rolling Stone,* Jann Wenner's Summer of Love was sanctified by a man.

But then there was Jane, his girlfriend. Her prettiness and sophistication—and her gender—were everything Wenner desired, in theory if not in actuality. She was the nice Jewish girl of his dreams, a cosmopolitan tastemaker to help articulate his ambitions, which, like Jane herself, were directed east. To keep faith with her would require secrets, a conception of truth and loyalty as fungible as Wenner's own sexuality. But Wenner was a natural at holding two conflicting realities apart, the compartments of his psyche as formalized as between the editor and the publisher of a newspaper. What was it his mother had written? *Janus. Two-headed.*

In late July, Gracey's head was still swimming from his LSD trip, his emotional life in turmoil as he prepared to return to England. While in San Francisco, he'd slept with two women and a man—including Jane's sister, Linda. Before he departed, Wenner drove to Haight-Ashbury to give Gracey a stack of rock LPs and a love letter he'd written. In it, Wenner dubbed them "water brothers," commemorating their nude swim with a reference to the polyamorous rite in Robert A. Heinlein's 1961 sci-fi book, *Stranger in a Strange Land* (a rite Wenner described in his rave review in *The Sunday Ramparts* as an "inter-personal baptism"). Wenner ended the letter with a lyric from a Bob Dylan song. It was a familiar line about a lost illusion—and a theft: "Ain't it hard when you discover that he really wasn't where it's at," he wrote, "after he took from you everything he could steal—how does it feel?"

•

HE NEEDED A NAME for his newspaper.

Jann Wenner had spent the summer of 1967 tossing around potential titles with Ralph Gleason, and for a while they settled on one: *New Times*. It was almost right, but not quite. Wenner proposed another: *The Electric Newspaper*. Gleason eyed his young charge and drew on his pipe.

That summer, Gleason was drafting an essay for *The American Scholar* that summed up his grandest ideas about the revolutionary impact of rock and roll. He quoted Nietzsche's *Birth of Tragedy* and R. H. Tawney's *Religion and the Rise of Capitalism* and opened with a quotation from Plato: "Forms and rhythms in music are never changed without producing changes in the most important political forms and ways."

The Beatles, he declared, were the genesis of a new age. Along with Dylan, that "tiny demon of a poet," the Dionysian energy of rock was destroying the old social forms and inventing a new value system around "the sacred importance of love and truth and beauty and interpersonal relationships." "They came at the proper moment of a spiritual cusp, as the Martian in Robert Heinlein's *Stranger in a Strange Land* calls a *cri-*

sis," he wrote. "This was, truly, a new generation—the first in America raised with music constantly in its ear, weaned on a transistor radio, involved with songs from its earliest moment of memory."

After Bob Dylan and the Beatles, he wrote, the record business "took another look at the music of the ponytail and chewing gum set, as Mitch Miller once called the teenage market, and realized there was one helluva lot of bread to be made there."

He titled the article "Like a Rolling Stone."

Rolling Stone! The nature of youth, gathering no moss. A Muddy Waters song, an age-old reference from the Bible. There was a popular band with that name and the six-minute radio hit by the generation's tiny demon. (Inspired by Gleason, Wenner had tried calling his rejected rock anthology "Like a Rolling Stone: Rock and Roll in the Sixties.")

Gleason blew out a little smoke: "How about *Rolling Stone?*"

4

Like a Rolling Stone

Here's something for you to turn the Beatles on with.
—letter from Jann Wenner to Derek Taylor, November 1967

A rt Garfunkel, of Simon and Garfunkel, offered an impersonation of the Jann Wenner he met in the early years of *Rolling Stone*. Standing up, he hunched his body forward, arms arched like a gunslinger. "I'm a business crab; my body is a little bent over," he said, curling forward in demonstration. "I am so full of *content* I have no time for elegance of the spine—that's for gentiles. I am all *content,* I got my envelopes in my hand, my sleeves are worked up—this is a workshop, man! This is not Hollywood; it's a *workshop*. I am *content*. I got my envelopes; I come out with a tempo. Thanks for the applause, but let's get right to it—

"And that's Jann. That's the Jann I first knew in San Francisco, always hunched over because the issues are too compelling, and too much fun, and there is stuff to be done."

His eagerness—Garfunkel called it "joy"—overflowed, seemed nearly to drown him. There was a Yiddish word for it: *shpilkes*—ants in the pants. If Jann Wenner had a tail, said writer Dotson Rader, it would always be wagging. Ralph Gleason would say Wenner's all-consuming devotion to his enterprise was like "some cat who had discovered a new way to split the atom."

With the name, the vision snapped into focus: *Rolling Stone,* the first mainstream paper for the rock-and-roll generation. Now everything that was ambiguous about Wenner's life was made clear: to become an editor and publisher, as big and important as Hugh Hefner—no, bigger than that. Henry Luce! William Randolph Hearst! Keeping such company made sense to Wenner, even if others rolled their eyes.

Who did this guy think he was? "Motherless, fatherless, sisterless, in the closet, starting a newspaper that nobody thought was going to go anywhere," said Jerry Hopkins, one of the first writers for *Rolling Stone.* "He was *out there.*"

Wenner reportedly said he started *Rolling Stone* to meet John Lennon. But it was just as true that he wanted to *be* John Lennon—as famous, as important, as talented in his sphere. After all, the best and the brightest of the baby-boom generation (a term not yet in common use in 1967) weren't necessarily going to Harvard or Yale anymore. They were dropping out and inventing a new generational order with the Beatles as their soundtrack. This was Jann Wenner's story line. "Jerry Garcia was as smart as anybody, as smart as a guy from Yale who was a clerk for a Supreme Court judge," Michael Lydon, the first staff employee of *Rolling Stone,* once explained. "That's really what created the opportunity for *Rolling Stone* magazine . . . the magazine caught on very fast because Jann had grasped the new vibration just when the old vibration was fading."

This was not obvious. "Professionalism"—a word Wenner now used with increasing frequency to describe his vision of *Rolling Stone*—was anathema to the average Levi's-wearing *freek.* It was an eastern establishment trope reeking of Eisenhower and the marketers of "pimply hyperbole" whom the Beatles mocked in *A Hard Day's Night.* It was "Moloch," as Allen Ginsberg wrote in his 1955 epic poem *Howl*— electricity and industry, the lifeblood of Wall Street and war profiteers. As Wenner assembled his newspaper in the fall of 1967, the Diggers of Haight-Ashbury, a group of communitarian radicals, were burning money on the streets and holding a funeral march for "the Death of [the] Hippie," whose demise they blamed on the media barbarians lured to San Francisco by the likes of Chet Helms and Derek Taylor. The

Diggers attacked the merchants of the new hipsterism—record stores and head shops—as "prettified monsters of moneylust."

But the barbarian had already found its way inside the gate. There was money to be made attacking Moloch, and after Monterey Pop, rock and roll was awash in it. The Jefferson Airplane, among the most passionate rock revolutionists, were already spending their advances from RCA Victor on fancy cars and swimming pools in L.A., a story Wenner put right on the cover of the first issue of *Rolling Stone*. "When they're not in the studios, they stay at a fabulous pink mansion which rents for $5,000 a month," Wenner reported. "The house has two swimming pools and a variety of recreational facilities."

The magazine was carefully positioned to be accessible to the American mainstream. "We didn't want to be a part of that hippie way of life," said Wenner. "We didn't want to be communal. We didn't want to have a hippie design. Our values were more traditional reporting. We wanted to be recognized by the establishment. Part of it was our own mission; part of it was what we were looking for, music. We wanted the music to be taken seriously. We wanted to be heard, we wanted the music to be heard, we wanted to change things."

But what did a twenty-year-old Berkeley dropout know about starting a business? Not much. Jane's sister, Linda, recalled seeing business books piled in Wenner's room on Potrero Hill that summer. But mainly he turned to Ralph Gleason, whose Rolodex overflowed with names of lawyers and press agents, record executives and music writers. Wise in the ways of newspapers, Gleason would point his finger and Wenner would go running: *Here's a law firm who can help you incorporate. Here's a writer from the* Melody Maker *in London. What about my friend in L.A.? He can write. Here's a record agent at A&M and a publicist at Columbia. Maybe this guy at Vanguard can help you get a few ads.*

From the start they discussed using the defunct *Sunday Ramparts* as the bones of the enterprise. The paper had been printed by Garrett Press, a union shop that produced newsletters like *The Hillsdale Merchandiser* and a union rag called *The Daily Worker*. "I was a veteran of the newspaper and magazine business at the point," recounted Gleason in 1973, "and Jann was not, and I suggested to him that many times a printer will give you free office space in his loft or storage area for you to put out your publication—if you're gonna print it at his press. And we talked Garrett Press into letting us do that and that's how we started off at Brannan Street. Upstairs in Garrett Press, in the corner."

It was located near a slaughterhouse. Most of the loft space was swallowed up by huge rolls of newsprint, Linotype machines, and a furnace that melted lead type and blew off an acrid stench. The walls were painted pink. The employees of Garrett Press were bemused by the hippie clientele who showed up that fall, long-haired, glassy-eyed, and snickering with private jokes. When Jane casually used the word "fuck" in mixed conversation, the burly union men were horrified. "My knee almost collapsed," said Dan Parker, a foreman at Garrett Press who wore a tie to work and would become an office manager at *Rolling Stone* for a decade. "I never heard a woman use the word 'fuck.' It was such an irrational thing for a woman to be saying."

He viewed Jann and Jane as typical hippies, their paper no different from the radical *Berkeley Barb*. But Wenner, he observed, "always walked like he was climbing a telephone pole. He was always walking like he was climbing."

Gleason sent Wenner a check for $300 to print a prototype of *Rolling Stone* and help sell advertising, including with it a postcard for *Jazz,* the defunct quarterly he once edited, wishing Wenner better luck than he had.

Wenner needed actual professionals to help build the professional enterprise he had in mind. At Monterey, he had run into Michael Lydon, a Yale graduate who worked for *Newsweek* but whose interests were increasingly countercultural. Over coffee at Enrico's, a North Beach café, Wenner asked him to help shepherd the first issue, offering him the job as his No. 2. Lydon agreed to work for him, in exchange for 200 shares in the company, while maintaining his *Newsweek* gig. Michael brought along his wife, Susan, who recalled in her 1993 memoir, *Take the Long Way Home,* that Wenner told them that his ambition "was to become the 'Henry Luce of the counterculture.'"

"He stood out in a crowd," recalled Michael Lydon, "for the drive and for the ambition and for [having] more going on than you might know right away—the wheels within wheels. You could look at the guy and [see] gears were moving in his head. He was thinking all the time."

Wenner assigned Lydon a story that Gleason suggested: an exposé on how the promoters of the Monterey Pop Festival, in particular Lou Adler, might have misappropriated the money.

A few months before, Wenner had met a freelance photographer named Baron Wolman at a panel discussion on rock and roll at Mills College featuring Ralph Gleason, Phil Spector, and Tom Donahue, the latter about to invent free-form FM radio in San Francisco at KMPX. Wenner told the impossibly old photographer, aged twenty-nine, about a new rock magazine he was cooking up, at the time the Chet Helms version. "I said, 'Wow, man, that sounds like a really good idea,'" recalled Wolman, who after a stint in the army had moved to California, married a ballet dancer, and ended up in Haight-Ashbury.

Savvy enough to understand the value of his own work, Wolman agreed to be the photographer of what was now *Rolling Stone* if he could own all his own negatives. Wenner agreed but also asked him if he had $10,000 to invest. "Baron, we are not countercultural," went Wenner's pitch. "We are not hippie. I'm in this to make a success and to make a lot of money. I know we can, and everything we do is gonna be professional; it won't be confused as something that isn't professional."

"That was when I began to realize he was very, very focused," said Wolman.

•

IF JANN WENNER WAS GOING to distinguish his paper from the corpus of *The Sunday Ramparts,* he needed a distinctive logo. He commissioned one by a psychedelic poster artist named Rick Griffin, who grew up down the hill from Chadwick in Palos Verdes and illustrated for *Surfer* magazine. The quasi-Victorian lettering that Griffin sketched out had the druggy wink of rolling-paper brands found in head shops. That same summer, Griffin illustrated a poster for an art show featuring a package of marijuana cigarettes and the words "Joint Show: A Rare Blend." As he was refashioning the fonts for *Rolling Stone*—with an *R* strikingly similar to the one in the *Ramparts* logo—Wenner became so impatient to get his hands on the drawing he went to Griffin's apartment and took the unfinished draft. "It was the second sketch," said Wenner. (Griffin later complained he was not paid for it, and Wenner wrote him a check for $5,000 in the early 1970s.)

Wenner's first expenditure was personalized stationery with Griffin's *Rolling Stone* logo on top. Gleason was furious. *What a waste!* But Wenner loved it, dreamed *into* it. A real newspaper! *Jann Wenner's* newspaper. Soon after, Wenner printed a hundred copies of a four-page dummy in the shape and layout of *The Sunday Ramparts,* with Griffin's logo hovering over a film still of John Lennon from *How I Won the War.* "Ralph and I have done it," he wrote to Jonathan Cott in London, "started a rock and roll newspaper called *Rolling Stone*. I hereby authorize you to be our feature writer in Merry Olde. Don't bother with the newsstand gossip as we already have *Melody Maker*. Instead, give us your impression of the scene and profiles or extensive interviews with the Beatles, the Stones, Andrew Loog Oldham, Peter Townshend, Donovan and such like that you can get to."

He offered him $25 a feature. Wenner didn't have the money to pay Cott, but he was hustling day and night, hitting up friends, relatives, friends of relatives, friends of friends. He went back to the old socialite crowd—Richard Black, Andy Harmon, Susan Andrews—with a rambling pitch about youth culture and rock and roll. A cross between the *Mojo Navigator* and *Seventeen* magazine, he told Harmon. "The *Mojo Navigator* sounded cool to me," said Harmon, "but *Seventeen*? Even then Jann had a sense of how to make a commercial enterprise."

Most people said no. But Joan Roos, the matriarch of SLATE, put in $1,000, and Wenner's mother wrote him a check, as did Wenner's stepmother, Dorothy, who gave him $500 under his father's name. (Wenner promised her she would make a million dollars and told her she now owned "page 18 and 23.") Gleason put up $1,500 for the first issue and agreed to write a column for *Rolling Stone,* which he titled Perspectives. In a contract Wenner formulated, he gave Gleason "50/50 veto power" over what went into the paper, making him his editorial equal. If they couldn't agree on a matter, Wenner proposed, "either party has the option of having the disputed matter printed in *Rolling Stone* under his byline."

Using Gleason's name as a reference, Wenner combed the Haight and North Beach asking for money from record stores and head shops to advertise in his new magazine, $100 for a full page. Tom Donahue's new free-form radio station signed up; promoter Bill Graham declined Wenner's offer to invest but bought ads for the first several issues at a discounted $25 a page. Wenner personally flew to Los Angeles to meet with record executives at A&M and Capitol, boldly promising he would displace *Billboard* magazine. ("*Rolling Stone* loves you," he ended his letter to A&M.) In person, his rambling spiel geysered forth as if it were all too exciting and self-evident to explain. But the thrust of it was the basis of his first editorial, wherein he described a newspaper "not just about music, but also about the things and attitudes that the music embraces." It was about "the magic that can set you free."

"To describe it any further would be difficult without sounding like bullshit," he concluded, "and bullshit is like gathering moss."

Jane Schindelheim never liked the name *Rolling Stone,* but she liked what *Rolling Stone* was doing to Jann Wenner. When he moved into the Garrett Press warehouse, he hired contractors to erect Sheetrock partitions for his own office and assigned Jane to decorate the headquarters for her little would-be press baron, a court from which Wenner could command his empire—seven tables manned by unpaid volunteers and some rented typewriters next to a loud and foul-smelling machine burning hot lead all day. By October, Wenner was still short the money he needed to get *Rolling Stone* off the ground. The Schindelheims of Manhattan had not yet met Jane's boyfriend, but received a letter describing how they could become a "limited liability partner" in his newspaper for the minimum investment of $2,000. There was, said Wenner, almost no chance of failure:

> The very least that can happen for any investor is approximately a 15% return on his or her money per year as well as equity in a going concern. The best that can happen is too fantastic to really talk about, but is roughly comparable to owning a very big and successful magazine on the financial order of *Playboy.*

Her parents liked the cut of this young man's jib. A nice Jewish boy with a business mind. They wrote the check, plus a little extra, and gave

Rolling Stone the financial push it needed. The money Dr. Schindelheim earned from yanking teeth and capping molars also gave their daughter an ownership stake in *Rolling Stone,* making her "secretary and director" of the start-up, which, in early October 1967, Wenner incorporated in the state of California under a name he liked quite a lot: Straight Arrow Publishers Inc.

Hey, it was *their* baby now. Unlike the do-nothing Chet Helms, with his long hair down to his Levi's, the clever and industrious Jann Wenner, who styled his hair in a pageboy, had managed to raise $7,500 in capital and make it all legal with lawyers. Clearly they were destined to be millionaires and Chet Helms was not. Many years later, while sitting in her vast estate in the Hamptons, on Long Island, Jane Wenner would recall walking into a little San Francisco shop to order an ice cream cone in the 1970s and behind the counter was Chet Helms taking her order. "He was smart enough to be at the right place at the right time, and he just couldn't do anything," she said. "There was something so sad to me about that moment for him."

•

JANN WENNER KNEW EXACTLY what he wanted: When the *Rolling Stone* telephone lines were installed at Garrett Press, he insisted they be answered by a woman because a woman's voice was "classy."

That fall, Jann Wenner and his girlfriend, Jane, and her sister, Linda, along with Michael and Susan Lydon and some volunteer hippies Wenner knew ("groupies," he called them), toiled to cobble together the first issue of *Rolling Stone.* Michael Lydon would show up after his shift at *Newsweek* and work into the night alongside Wenner, who worried every detail. It was hot in San Francisco, and Susan Lydon, pregnant and pouring sweat next to the furnace, wore a slip hiked up over her belly as she watched Wenner bound in and out. "Jann was maniacally driven, a natural speed freak," Susan Lydon wrote. "And to my great despair, he managed to involve Michael in most of his manic schemes, so that I had to be practically fainting or in tears before we could break for a meal."

Wenner spent as little money as possible, using *Newsweek*'s offices for long-distance phone calls and the offices of *Ramparts* to make

Xeroxes and lay out pages, courtesy of *Ramparts'* production director John Williams, whom Wenner listed on *Rolling Stone*'s masthead as the art director. "He was just so energetic and so enthusiastic and knew what he wanted and could talk anybody into doing anything," said Williams. "You just sort of wanted to help him.

"He offered me a hundred shares of stock for each issue. I was pasting up on some old flats that we had from another project, staying up until three in the morning, in between the *Ramparts* stuff . . . I didn't know if it was going to go anywhere or not. I didn't see how you could start a rock-and-roll magazine on newsprint and get anywhere."

If Wenner harbored any doubts, they were about his credibility as a rock critic. He loved the music, but he was realistic about his own ignorance, how it worked, what made it good or mediocre. What he needed was the authority of a brand-name critic to rival the bylines at *Crawdaddy!*, but the person he needed already worked for *Crawdaddy!* A student of history at Brandeis near Boston, Jon Landau was a twenty-year-old college hermit who was homebound with a painful intestinal disorder and spent his days listening to records and writing crisply pedantic essays on soul and R&B, which he typed up and sent to Paul Williams. Among the small pool of people who read rock criticism in 1967, he made a splash for a dissertation-like analysis of Motown and the Supremes called "A Whiter Shade of Black." Landau detested the San Francisco Sound, but Wenner didn't care about his R&B bias, only his respected byline, which was being followed with great interest by record executives at Atlantic and Elektra scrambling to discover new acts to replace the fading folk and jazz artists on their rosters. As it happened, Landau was a classmate of Andy Harmon's at Brandeis. In a pitch letter, Wenner shared his dream of turning *Rolling Stone* into a "very slick" magazine, describing the "youth market" he aimed to exploit and the competitors he aimed to vanquish, including the new full-color *Cheetah,* created by the publisher of *Weight Watchers;* the slickly turned-out *Eye* magazine, published by Hearst; and various others "proclaiming themselves mind blowing and turned on, hip and with it."

Landau admired Wenner's chutzpah. He had never been satisfied with the paltry money at *Crawdaddy!* and, to Wenner's chagrin, had started writing for *Eye*. (To supplement his income, Landau also developed a brisk business requesting multiple review copies of LPs and selling them to record stores.) Moreover, Landau didn't share Williams's aversion to negative, knives-out record reviews. He was an arrogant young man; he hated more records than he liked. This is precisely what appealed to Wenner, who wanted controversy in his paper. He didn't care if a review was "wordy or obscene, as long as it says something."

"Taste is the important thing," Wenner said, "and that is the premise of what we are doing."

Landau agreed to join *Rolling Stone* as Wenner's Boston correspondent, telling him he looked forward to "a long and mutually profitable relationship." If Landau was the high-flown critic Wenner needed, Wenner was for Landau a kind of walking, talking consensus of the new rock culture, the fat middle of youth opinion. "At that moment in time, Jann himself was a very pure distillation of the culture," Landau said. "He could ask himself, 'What do I like?' "

On October 18, 1967, Wenner gathered his exhausted staff of six next to the printing machine on Brannan Street as they watched the first issue of *Rolling Stone* roll off the conveyor belt of the Goss Suburban. They opened a bottle of champagne and drank from plastic cups. Only an hour before, Wenner had been typing a letter to Jonathan Cott asking him to get a Beatles interview for the next issue. A new Pink Floyd tape sat on Wenner's desk, awaiting review. Had Wenner breathed since Monterey? There was no time. But as he finally drew a breath, holding the first issue of *Rolling Stone* in his hands, he could not imagine anything better. "It's just so good," he said, and wept with joy.

5

Born to Run

An eighteen-year-old kid with a modified Beatles haircut and cuffed blue jeans was standing on the corner of Main Street in Freehold, New Jersey, dropping dimes in a pay phone. He was a guitarist in a rock-and-roll group that wore matching shirts and vests and played covers of "Twist and Shout" at the local drive-in and high school gymnasium. The kid's father was under-employed, and the family had no telephone in the house, forcing him to amble up to the newsstand to use the pay phone on the corner. In November 1967, he noticed a broadsheet folded in half and stamped with a druggy logo. On the front was a black-and-white photo of John Lennon wearing an army helmet, spectacles on his nose, lips set in a whistle.

Bruce Springsteen slapped twenty-five cents on the counter.

"I used to spend hours and hours on the phone outside the news-stand calling my girlfriends," he said. "You went in, and there it was. It reached out to my little town and said, 'You're not alone.'"

In the working-class town of Freehold, population 9,140, Spring-steen could count on one hand the number of local teens involved with rock and roll—most of them were in his band. "Maybe there was one or two other people you could talk to if you had something in com-mon," he said. "At that time, basically the rest of the world was against who you were becoming. You were young; you couldn't travel to San

Francisco. The most you could do was go to the [West] Village on the weekend, which Steve [Van Zandt] and I did, where we initially discovered this form of rock-and-roll writing. It initially came out in the form of *Crawdaddy!* magazine, which was sheetlike, this small printed sheet, and then *Rolling Stone*. These were your lifelines.

"You can't explain to someone today how unique and essential those things were to the fiber of your being in those days," he continued. "They were the only validating pieces of writing that somebody else out there was thinking about rock music the way you were. That was comforting."

The pages of *Rolling Stone* shaped Springsteen's idea of what a rock-and-roll star did, how to behave. Springsteen himself wouldn't appear in its pages for another four years—ironically, he would receive a rave review in Hearst's *Examiner* before that—but he would never forget that first issue. *Rolling Stone* opened to a full-page publicity shot of the wives of the Beatles, including Cynthia Lennon in a gold lamé dress, then flipped to a gossip column called Flashes, which reported that David Crosby had left the Byrds and *A Hard Day's Night* would be televised on NBC. Further on, Ralph Gleason opined on race in the record business, pointing out that Otis Redding sold more records than Frank Sinatra, and three pages later was "The Rolling Stone Interview" with Donovan, Wenner's homage to the *Playboy* interview, conducted by a friend of Gleason's in L.A. (Slotted into the bottom corner of page 11 was a little trade story reporting that Philco-Ford was spending $1 million to advertise a portable 45 player just as the full-length album renaissance was starting.)

Everything was in charmless black-and-white columns, blocked off with clean Oxford lines, stiff and workmanlike except for the rock-and-roll content—a no-frills *Daily Worker* for stoned rock fans. The whole thing had been begged, borrowed, recycled, and stolen: Chet Helms's idea and contestant list; Ralph Gleason's title and editorial philosophy; the newsprint and layout of *The Sunday Ramparts;* Jon Landau from *Crawdaddy!;* several stories from the *Melody Maker,* rewritten by Susan Lydon. *Ramparts* magazine had even published a cover image of John Lennon from *How I Won the War* the month before. But the seams of Wenner's Frankenstein's monster were fused together by his obsessive

mania and the newspaper's bold statement of purpose. The table of contents directed the reader to page 20, where "Jann Wenner reviews the
new records." He panned two out of the three albums, including Chuck
Berry's *Live at the Fillmore:* "If you judge the album by what's happening today, the judgment isn't very favorable." For his own opening gambit, Jon Landau dismissed the breakout Jimi Hendrix as having "inane"
lyrics and a "violent" artistic vision, which ran alongside a blurry photograph of Hendrix by Jann Wenner. In the arc of rock-and-roll history, many of these opinions would seem arbitrary and even wrong. But
who else was treating these strange records—the new Sopwith Camel
album—as matters of consequence?

As important, the clean look of *Rolling Stone*—the packaging—was
a revelation to rock fans used to squinting at the soupy, under-edited
prose of *Crawdaddy!* for the latest Bob Dylan exegesis. Newsprint,
which Wenner saw as merely pragmatic until he could afford to become
a "slick," gave *Rolling Stone* a street feel that made it more authentic
than a rock exploitation magazine like *Cheetah*. As Wenner told *Time*
magazine in 1969, "A lot of people ask why we're not psychedelic. But
that's the whole point. Psychedelic language and so-called hip language
is what the over-thirties think the kids want to see and hear. It's not.
What they respond to is somebody talking to them straight."

While Springsteen thumbed through his copy in Freehold, Jann
Wenner had no idea who was reading the forty thousand copies he
printed. As it later turned out, the distributor Miller Freeman left most
of the issues moldering in the warehouse and only six thousand copies
were sold. But a few reader letters trickled in, the first one from Sharon Miller of Los Angeles, who said, "We all dig *Rolling Stone*." By issue
No. 3, they heard from a representative of Stax Records in Memphis,
who declared, "Amen." By April 1968, Charlie Watts, the Stones' drummer, was writing to thank Jon Landau for the "nice things he said about
me personally," a coy reference to a critical slam of *Their Satanic Majesties Request* ("The rest of us, I'm sure, will try for the next one," said
Watts).

Wenner had one of his volunteers type up a survey to send out to the
KFRC contestant list, which generated a murky view into the nascent
"youth market" *Rolling Stone* was hitting—young men who bought and

listened to records, smoked pot, and avoided the Vietnam draft and regular work. One reader, for whom music was "the expression of the soul and mind," said his goal was to "drop out and distribute posters." Another described himself as "fanatically devoted to rock because it is the truth for a change," and another made an ornate psychedelic doodle to prove his point. "If I had to fill out the same questionnaire, it would probably sound the same," said Wenner. "I remember from our first surveys, the average reader was twenty-one, which is the age I was."

Wenner molded the results into a dubious report for advertisers, claiming that "seventy-three percent" of his readers were men and "95%" of the total readership" bought six records a month. After *Rolling Stone* debuted, Wenner got a letter from Jerry Wexler, the genius producer of Atlantic Records who recorded the soul albums of Aretha Franklin and Otis Redding. "First issue was strong," he wrote to Wenner, saying he admired Jon Landau but "believe[d] *Rolling Stone* needs a more specific orientation and point of view. For god's sake, avoid the groupie syndrome, and let's not be wide-eyed about the hashcapades or pot busts of the venerated. Need professionalism and detachment. Need identity."

Was *Rolling Stone* a trade paper, a critical journal, a teen rag like *16*? "What?" Wexler asked.

But Jann Wenner knew better than this fifty-year-old man did: It was all of the above.

•

WHEN GARRETT PRESS SPAT OUT the first issue of *Rolling Stone,* Jane Schindelheim's name was printed inside as the head of subscriptions. "BRAVO JANN WENNER!" she wrote to him. "ROLLING STONE LOOKS SMASHING!"

They were planning to move to a new apartment on Rhode Island Street in Potrero Hill, across the street from Jim Peterman of the Steve Miller Band. Jane was ready to become Jann's full-time partner in their ascendant enterprise. "Is there enough room in the kitchen for a table?" she asked, "and space for you and *Rolling Stone* and Chessai [her Lhasa apso] and me?

"I shall make it beautiful," she promised. "I will touch you soon my darlingest."

If she could catch him. If Wenner seemed manic before, the demands of his biweekly paper now spun him like a 45. Bands were forming and breaking up weekly, record deals getting made, albums recorded, drugs consumed, musicians busted, rock festivals mushrooming from Colorado to New Jersey. Stories and gossip bubbled to the surface: In the space of two weeks, Mick Jagger and Paul McCartney dreamed up a record label together, a new 50,000-watt FM station was coming to Los Angeles, members of the Lovin' Spoonful were cooperating with the police following a drug bust, and Jim Morrison was arrested for indecency in New Haven.

From the vantage of the loft on Brannan Street, Wenner looked out over a countercultural mecca that was quickly becoming a company town. Wenner, in his early column called Rock and Roll Music, defined and defended the local scene, which consisted of seven "indigenous" bands (the Grateful Dead, Big Brother and the Holding Company, the Jefferson Airplane, Moby Grape, Country Joe and the Fish, and Quicksilver Messenger Service) and was defined by long live shows with liquid light displays. A young economist named Michael Phillips, who was involved in inventing the MasterCard at Bank of California, predicted in the summer of 1968 that "the San Francisco Sound" would become a $6 million market by year's end and "increase the wealth of the city by $8 to $15 million." The Youngbloods, singers of the ubiquitous hit "Get Together," moved to San Francisco from New York and saw themselves as part of a crucial industry. "You feel like you're fulfilling a need," singer Jesse Colin Young told Rolling Stone, "like a garage mechanic."

Most of the record-selling business was elsewhere, a fact that actually gave Wenner a distinct advantage. Bands came through town on their tours and Wenner was their turnstile, giving them ink. "There was nothing else to do in San Francisco," Wenner said. "There were no record companies there. There was nothing else to do but shop and hang out, or hang out with me."

Steve Winwood of Traffic was the first rock star to visit the offices. "I showed him where all the lead type was," said Wenner, who called Winwood, in April 1968, "probably the major blues voice of his generation." To interview Hendrix, Wenner simply drove to his motel in Fisherman's Wharf and hit record on the tape machine. "Baron and I went out to his motel room and shot the shit," recalled Wenner. "We published it entirely as a quote."

It was Hendrix at his loopy best: "The Axis of the earth turns around and changes the face of the world and completely different civilizations come about or another age comes about. In other words, it changes the face of the earth and it only takes about ¼ of a day. Well, the same with love; if a cat falls in love, it might change his whole scene. *Axis, Bold as Love* . . . 1-2-3 rock around the clock."

Through people like Derek Taylor, who was training the Byrds and the Beach Boys about the media, Wenner tapped into a network of advocates who put his newspaper in all the right hands. "I used to read every word of every page of every issue," said David Crosby, who would soon form Crosby, Stills, and Nash. "It was the first one that wasn't a *Teen Scream* boy thing. It was the first one that was about *us,* that was about actual music, and we dug the shit out of it."

The artists came looking for him. Local heroes Steve Miller and Boz Scaggs took assignments to write stories and reviews for *Rolling Stone* ("Miller on the British Groups: Queer Bits in Underwear"). The manager of the Stooges in Detroit wrote asking for help booking gigs in San Francisco (Wenner suggested posting a free ad in his back pages). After Blood, Sweat, and Tears signed a lucrative contract with Columbia, Wenner assigned keyboardist Al Kooper to review the D. A. Pennebaker film of Monterey Pop, and two months later Wenner profiled Blood, Sweat, and Tears, calling them "the best thing to happen in rock and roll so far in 1968." When Lou Adler and John Phillips tried organizing a second Monterey Pop Festival and were met by local opposition, Wenner put them on the cover of *Rolling Stone* and called their opponents a "vicious" and "ugly collection of voyeuristic 'taxpayers.' " "They were going to the city council and the local swells to get a permit," he said. "I met them at the airport and I was with them as they stepped off the Lear jet." (The festival never happened, and *Rolling Stone* again turned on Adler, reporting that his accountant had embezzled $37,000 from the first festival. "[Wenner] was obsessed with the funds, and it went on for years," said Adler. "Truly years, almost every time he mentioned Monterey, 'Where's the money?' That's how I always thought of him. 'Where's the money?' He was definitely a pain in the ass." Adler insisted that all the money went to charity.)

Wenner seemed preternaturally certain in all things but his own writing powers. His failure to become a novelist still haunted him (he continued to rewrite and edit versions of "Now These Days Are Gone"), and at first his writing style had the generic feel of a student term paper. When in doubt, Wenner resorted to hippie patois, starting his cover story in issue No. 2, "Tina Turner is an incredible chick." When Otis Redding died in a plane crash in December 1967, Wenner asked Michael Lydon to write the obituary, but Lydon declined, saying Wenner needed to write it to establish his authority. "I said, no, Jann, you've got to do this," he said. "He wasn't confident in himself as a writer." ("Otis was the Crown Prince of Soul," wrote Wenner, "and now the Crown Prince is dead.")

Wenner improvised as he went. When John Williams left town for the holidays, Wenner was left to lay out the year-end issue for 1967 by himself—prompting a panicked call to Linda Schindelheim's boyfriend, Bob Kingsbury, a forty-three-year-old sculptor. "We're on deadline and I need you to help me put something together," he told Kingsbury, who was skiing in Tahoe. A graduate of the Swedish State School of Arts, Crafts, and Design in Stockholm, class of 1950, Kingsbury was a middle-aged bohemian and gifted artist with no experience in newspapers but a few novel ideas about arranging text and images. "He asked me if I thought I could be an art director," Kingsbury would later recount. "I went over to *Ramparts* one night to watch John Williams paste up 'til the wee hours of the morning. I watched him a couple of times. I figured it would just take me three days, every two weeks."

Wenner knew so little, even the most obvious suggestions were revelations—like Gleason's advice that he put an ad in *Rolling Stone* asking for record review submissions. It not only worked, it attracted writers who would become major figures of rock writing, like Leslie "Lester" Bangs, who sent in reviews from his mother's house near San Diego, and Jerry Hopkins, the future biographer of Elvis Presley and Jim Morrison. Hopkins was a sometime publicist and head-shop owner who sold *Rolling Stone* in L.A. He sent Wenner a story on seeing the Doors at the

Cheetah club in Santa Monica, and Wenner wrote him a check for $15. Soon after, Wenner showed up in L.A. wearing a suit and tie and asking to sleep on his couch while he went hustling for ad dollars from the record companies.

As advertising trickled in from Elektra and A&M, Wenner kept his paper glued together through Tom Sawyeresque exploitation. Kingsbury built his own drafting table and drawers for the lead type and was responsible for buying new desks and chairs every time an employee joined the newspaper. He also collected the reader mail and served as Wenner's personal handyman. When Jann and Jane complained that their power had gone out at home, Kingsbury came over and "changed the lightbulb and the lights went on," recalled Linda Kingsbury.

The Wenners now lived *Rolling Stone* twenty-four hours a day. They took the bus to Brannan Street in the afternoon and worked into the night, Wenner whacking away on an IBM Selectric, soliciting Dylan and Lennon for interviews and sending blue-sky letters to A&M and Columbia, trying to get distribution for *Rolling Stone* in record stores. Jane, in pigtails and overalls, tabulated the day's subscriptions, then went home to idle around the apartment or go shopping for furniture. If they got a dozen subscriptions in a day, it was cause for celebration, the uncorking of a bottle of wine or the smoking of a joint. The Springsteens of the world began writing letters to the editor. "At first it would be six or seven or eight [letters]," said Bob Kingsbury. "Then ten, fifteen, twenty, and pretty soon there's half a bag full of letters. And it just kept growing and growing. I couldn't do it anymore; I had to have someone else take over."

In April 1968, Wenner offered a weed dealer named Charlie Perry a job copyediting and managing the work flow at *Rolling Stone*. A Berkeley graduate, Perry was an eccentric drug adventurer, experimental cook, aspiring Arabic scholar, and former roommate of Augustus Owsley Stanley III's who heard about *Rolling Stone* through Jerrold Greenberg, a poet and junkie who wrote for the paper. Perry knew Wenner's byline from *Ramparts,* thinking this Jann person was "a pretty shrewd rock critic for a girl." He took the job because he figured "John Lennon knew something about LSD that he isn't putting in his songs and I thought if I met him I could ask him."

Perry, like everyone else, was excited by Wenner's creation, convinced it was something "brand new," though he still figured it would probably be dead in six months like every other fly-by-night paper that popped up at the Psychedelic Shop in the Haight. Wenner managed not to pay him for several months, which was fine with Perry until his dope trade dried up and he announced he was taking a job at the zoo. Wenner agreed to give him $40 a week. He would stay for ten years.

•

ON HIS FIRST TRIP to New York in 1968, Wenner slept on a couch in the West Twentieth Street apartment of Danny Fields, the A&R man for Elektra Records. Ironic and frank, Fields was the consummate scene maker and gossip of New York, one foot in the world of Andy Warhol, the other in teen pop magazines like *Hullabaloo* and *Datebook*. He followed with delight the young male quartets who pranced on stage and sang to the big beats. "Monks! Mark! Stones! Spoons!" went a typical headline on the cover of *16*, where Fields regularly published interviews. Fields joined Elektra in 1967 as a publicist and, after discovering the MC5 and Iggy Pop on the same weekend, became the "house freak," an after-hours talent scout. Most nights, Fields worked the back room at Max's Kansas City, Mickey Ruskin's nightclub, where rock and rollers began mingling with the Warhol crowd after Beatles manager Brian Epstein held a press conference there. Fields had hosted Pete Townshend of the Who in his apartment before Wenner showed up, plying him with drugs and groping him. "I enjoyed what he did, though I didn't let him actually fuck me," Townshend said in his 2012 memoir.

Fields was the Virgil to Wenner's Dante on a grand tour of the New York underground, which teemed with drugs and sexual adventure, groupies and bohemians. In Fields's orbit were a gaggle of the like-minded, including a beautiful blond photographer named Linda Eastman, daughter of an entertainment lawyer, who used her access to both photograph and pursue romantic tête-à-têtes with Mick Jagger and Jim Morrison. Eastman's best friend was Lillian Roxon, an Australian rock writer who published the *Rock Encyclopedia* in 1969 and whom *Rolling Stone* would later call "the Dorothy Parker of Max's Kansas City." In May 1968, Wenner put Eastman's portrait of Eric Clapton on the cover for an interview with Clapton that Wenner had conducted the previous summer—the first female photographer whose work appeared on the cover of *Rolling Stone*. From there, Wenner would regularly visit her apartment on East Eighty-Third Street to go through her portfolio for images. "That was how I came to hear of Jann," said Paul McCartney, whom Eastman met while on assignment in London for *Rolling Stone* and would marry in 1969, "as the sort of guy who was doing *Rolling Stone* and who picked photos from her little apartment."

Fields also introduced Wenner to Gloria Stavers, the forty-one-year-old editor of *16* magazine, a former model who looked like Katharine Hepburn and commanded four million teenage readers in America. When Wenner sent her a copy of *Rolling Stone,* Stavers welcomed the magazine as a "soul-brother in the fourth estate" and urged her readers to send a quarter to Brannan Street for a copy of *Rolling Stone.* (The Wenners used the coins that poured in to buy groceries.) Stavers received Wenner like a squire from the groovy West Coast kingdom. "They were excited to meet me," recalled Wenner. Over dinner with Fields, Stavers taught Wenner how to eat a lobster while wondering at his naïveté. As she would later recount to a friend, Wenner sat at her feet, looked around at the guests, and asked, "Is this a good party?"

Fields and Stavers taught Wenner some of the tricks of their trade. For one, Fields explained to him, he needed to treat the cover of his newspaper as the sales pitch—bold, eye-popping images of superstars were how magazines sold the wares. "I never, ever thought of that; it didn't occur to me," said Wenner. "If you're hip about media, it's obvious."

Stavers also pressed on him the importance of sexing up photos of young rockers by unbuttoning the top button of their pants before photographing them. These were experienced starfuckers, groupies, admirers, and they recognized Wenner as a fellow traveler, attuned to the provocative pleasures of boy rockers. "That's how you love the stars," observed Art Garfunkel, a staple of *Tiger Beat* and *16* at the time, along with Paul Simon. "You have to get under the pedestal and look up their pants, to praise the height of the star." (He called Wenner's lust for celebrity "erotic slavery.")

Wenner said he was not yet clued in to Fields's homosexuality or the gay culture hiding in plain sight at Max's. Instead, he chased whatever he could get. One night, he tried taking Linda Eastman home, but Lillian Roxon intervened. "Roxon was a nice girl, very witty, but dumpy looking," said Wenner. "She didn't want me to be with Linda, because Linda was *hers*."

Wenner said they went back to Eastman's apartment, but Roxon had skunked the mood. "Then, after failing to consummate what I thought was going to be a situation, we got along because she was a stone cold rock-and-roll fan," Wenner said of Eastman.

Wenner returned from his New York sojourns with an expansive sense of victory. He wrote to Baron Wolman that "Rolling Stone is distributed on every fucking newsstand in New York. I saw every important person in the music business, and they were most eager to see the man from Rolling Stone.

"When you get home," he said, "we'll just have to sit down and flatter the shit out of ourselves."

Afterward, Roxon wrote a short profile of Wenner for *Eye,* the hippie exploitation magazine published by Hearst and presided over by editorial director Helen Gurley Brown. In the article, Wenner told Roxon he was considering publishing naked pictures of rock stars. "I am giving the project serious consideration," he told Roxon. "After all, rock and roll is inescapably tied to sex."

Wenner wrote to Roxon to say he had received "nasty" letters about the profile, including one from a reader who asked, "What kind of man would publish pop stars in the nude?"

•

BOB KINGSBURY, twenty-five years older than his boss, described the twenty-three-year-old Jann Wenner as standing with hands on his hips, chest puffed out, athwart his kingdom like a tyrannical king. "I'd bring a layout and he'd look at it and throw it back at me and say, 'Do it over,' " said Kingsbury. "Well, I spent a long time on it, you know. And so I said, 'Why?' And he said, 'Because I said so.' "

"I was pushing fifty and he was pushing twenty-two," he said. "These are all kids. Twenty-three-year-olds. And if you've ever worked with a bunch of twenty-three-year-olds, you'll understand. But if you haven't, it's one of the most horrible—listen, every single one of them: '*I'm* an editor of *Rolling Stone!*' "

Wenner wrote long letters to Jon Landau and spent hours running up phone bills as they schemed and bragged about their newfound influence. ("What did Jon have to say?" Jane would ask Wenner after a marathon phone call. "Not much," he'd reply.) Landau was educating young Wenner about music, a subject that Wenner, as big a fan as he was, knew very little about. He took him to see the Four Tops in Boston and inspired him to interview Booker T. and the MGs. "I never had been exposed to the rhythm and blues until Jon turned me on to all that," he said. "I really learned at his knees. I was a San Francisco guy, just the basics."

In turn, Wenner was dropping Landau's name to recruit writers from rival publications, including Robert Christgau, a writer for *Esquire* who had cited Wenner in a feature on college dropouts shaping the rock world. In a May 1968 letter, Wenner ripped up a review Christgau submitted (for *Judy in Disguise with Glasses,* by John Fred and His Playboy Band), declaring himself the "EDITOR of Rolling Stone" and calling Christgau "Bobby Baby" as he attempted to school him on the finer points of rock reviewing. "The first page is all about Bob Christgau, *Esquire* reviewer, late of a college education, a man of renaissance tastes, elegant opinion, and high tone critic of 'secular music,'" scoffed Wenner. "I mean, baby, who cares? And is it true anyway?"

To rub it in, he declared Jon Landau "smarter than anybody." "Did you know he is majoring in medieavil [*sic*] history?" he asked. "You may think you don't have to know anything about music, but you are wrong. I can't tell you why. That's how wrong you are."

In a concluding twist, he granted that Christgau "could turn into one of the top rock and roll critics. I sincerely hope you do."

Indeed he would. The "Dean of American Rock Critics," as Christgau later called himself, told Wenner that he had the "worst case of San Francisco pompousness I've ever observed" and asked whether Wenner wrote all of his letters "while high." Christgau didn't write another review for *Rolling Stone* for decades. "I took out my animosity toward

New York–based critics and intellectualizers on him," said Wenner, "and alienated him early on and he never forgave."

Wenner had a fair-weather relationship to the "straight journalism" he aspired to. When Susan Lydon filed a film review that used the first person, Wenner tore it to pieces and stomped on it like a "crazed Rumpelstiltskin," she later recounted, telling her that the first person undermined journalistic objectivity. Meanwhile, Al Aronowitz, the rock journalist famous for introducing Dylan to the Beatles, excoriated Wenner for pasting whole paragraphs from a press release into his story on the Band. "Such use of press releases indicates that you are more interested in record company advertising than you are in honest reportage," he wrote.

Was *Rolling Stone* a newspaper, wondered Aronowitz, or "just your own personal ego trip"?

Wenner, for all his chutzpah, tended to avoid personal confrontation. In 1968, he published a fake letter to the editor disparaging a Landau review under the pseudonym "Kevin Altman." "I was disagreeing with something Jon Landau said, but I wouldn't say it to his face," he said.

But with *Rolling Stone* as his sword and shield, Wenner delighted in biting the hands that fed him. In the same issue he published his Clapton interview, and he tested his influence by running Jon Landau's critical assassination of Cream—"Clapton is a master of the blues clichés"—which Eric Clapton later said made him pass out and then disband the group. "The ring of truth just knocked me backward," Clapton would recount. "I was in a restaurant and I fainted. After I woke up, I immediately decided that it was the end of the band."

Not to be outdone, Wenner followed up with a slashing review of their album *Wheels of Fire,* saying, "Cream is good at a number of things; unfortunately, songwriting and recording are not among them." "Cream Breaks Up!" went the headline in the very next issue.

When the inevitable blowback from a record label came, Wenner would blame a writer or simply shrug. It was a cycle he was destined to repeat, fomenting controversy and then whistling past the ensuing storm: "I wrote a headline, 'Pig Pen to Meet Pope?'"—about a rock festival in Rome—"Bill Graham thought this was sensationalist. I just thought it was funny. But he thought it was terrible. Then he tried to ban me from the Fillmore." (Graham later caught Jann and Jane Wenner attending an Allman Brothers show.)

Some of Wenner's biases were merely petty and personal. After the song "Mrs. Robinson," from the soundtrack of *The Graduate,* made the success of Simon and Garfunkel too conspicuous to ignore, Wenner reported in his gossip column that they had made "an amazing comeback." Gleason, well aware of the personal history, called up Denise Kaufman to share a laugh about it. "Did you see *Rolling Stone?*" he asked and then read her the quote. "He had to say something," recalled Denise Kaufman, "but he had to justify why he hadn't written about them in all that time."

That spring, *Rolling Stone* panned Simon and Garfunkel's next album, *Bookends,* which also featured "Mrs. Robinson."

•

JANE SCHINDELHEIM WAS NOT FOND of work, preferring long afternoons on the couch or a languorous stroll through a department store, running her finger across an expensive Eames chair or pondering the appeal of an Oriental rug. And by the summer of 1968, she was tired of taking the public bus to work. She asked Jann to buy a car and not just any car but a Porsche. So Wenner borrowed $200 from Jane's sister, Linda, who figured they would use it to buy a sensible VW Bug. Instead, Wenner was raising money so he could buy a 1963 powder-blue Porsche 1600-N Cabriolet. "At first I was like, 'Well, that's outrageous,'" said Linda. "But then I thought, 'Well, why not? Why do you have to be stuck with a geeky car?'" Wenner said it would barely climb the hills of San Francisco, but he did pay to have it painted burgundy.

At the start, *Rolling Stone* was a family affair, with Linda briefly living with Jann and Jane, but the couple was moving up fast, relocating to an apartment on Rhode Island Street in Potrero Hill, an A-frame triplex with a rattan chair hanging from the ceiling, a sleeping loft, a Balinese-style bathroom, and a bowl of hash on the dining room table (the apartment belonged to David Buschman, co-founder of the outdoor equipment company Sierra Designs). For people their age, most of whom were still living on mattresses in communal circumstances, Jann and Jane were veritable sophisticates entertaining like upstart Medici. "Jann and Janie were closer to adults than the rest of us," said Ben Sidran, a jazz writer who met Wenner in London in 1968. "They were more plugged into society and the social scene."

Wenner regularly courted potential investors, offering Steve Miller a quarter of the company for $4,000 one night over dinner. Miller didn't bite. "I remember being really amazed when I got to his place because I was living in a funky old house in the Haight and driving around in an economy VW bus," Miller said. "Jann was driving a Porsche and living in this beautiful house, hip and zen, beautiful sound system . . . I thought he was smart as can be but too ambitious. I got the feeling he would sell me out in a second."

One day, two letters arrived from an old friend in London: Robin Gracey. One was for Linda Schindelheim and the other for Jann Wenner. Evidently suspicious, Jane asked Linda to boil a pot of water and steam open the seal on Wenner's letter, which revealed their secret love affair. "Jane discovered it one day in my files while I was away," recalled Wenner.

Wenner's gay affair was a bruising revelation for Jane, "terrifying and destroying," as Wenner described it later. He swore to her that his dalliance with Gracey was a one-off and proclaimed his commitment to her. "Once Jane [found out]," said Wenner, "I said, 'Look, I will stop. I will put an end to this.' And I did."

With his star rising in every other way, Wenner could not afford to lose Jane. There was her beauty and allure, of course, but also her calming effect on Wenner, the witty way she called Jann "Ya Ya" and casually punctured his ego at parties. Jane made Wenner palatable to people otherwise put off by his hyperactivity and forceful personality. She had a keen judgment, but she was not judgmental. Her feline presence, coy and ironic, invited confession and gave an impression of intimacy that Jann Wenner could not offer. There was also her caretaking eye. "Jann was always, in hiring, trying to bring in these people who were just horrible," said Laurel Gonsalves, a former secretary for the Steve Miller Band who went to work at *Rolling Stone* in 1969. "Just losers. Kind of like a bad judge of character. Jane was always spot-on."

One of her standards, it seemed, was whether a candidate was attracted to her. "When somebody was applying for a job there," recalled Charlie Perry, "she would flirt with them. On the basis of his reaction, she'd tell Jann whether to hire him or not. If they didn't react, she thought that was suspicious. If they reacted the wrong way, that was a no-no."

But there was also the little matter of her financial stake in *Rolling Stone,* the Schindelheim ownership of nearly half the company. Were Jane to leave Jann Wenner, *Rolling Stone* might fall into ownership dispute, threatening his control.

That summer, Jann and Jane stayed with *Rolling Stone*'s L.A. correspondent Jerry Hopkins, who was living in Laurel Canyon with his new wife and seemed to Wenner blissful and content. "When I came back from that trip, I was like, 'They are very happily married,'" said Wenner. "And all of my friends had said how much they liked Jane. People would come up to me and say, 'She's terrific, you should marry her.' I saw how happily married these two were, and I discussed that with Jane, and I said, 'Let's get married.'" (Hopkins would later divorce, move to Honolulu, and take up with a transsexual prostitute.)

After meeting him, Jane's parents were impressed by Wenner's ambition, especially her father, whose approval was important to Jane. Plagued by self-doubt, she clung to Wenner's promise of fidelity, even as she worried over the "un-ease that mocks at our relationship." In *Rolling Stone,* their mutual desires for wealth and status and the finer things in life came together. They saw themselves in each other, like a twin gazing into a gilt-framed mirror and experiencing an affectionate familiarity. Jane's devotion to Wenner could be seen as a kind of vicarious grandiosity. And wasn't that love? And so Jane agreed to marry Jann, but not without trepidation. "She said later she was really doubtful and dubious about that," recalled Wenner.

Wenner had his own apprehensions. By this time, Denise Kaufman had become close friends with Wenner's sister Martha, who had changed her name to Merlyn and was running a hippie day school in Marin County, living in teepees and teaching astrology and the *I Ching.* In the days leading up to his marriage, Wenner took Kaufman on a drive in his Porsche, and they parked in front of the Golden Gate Bridge. "It was pretty emotional," she said. "I was like, 'Are you really gonna do this?' and he was like, 'I don't know.' It was poignant."

On their wedding day, Jane cut Wenner's hair with a bowl, making him look like a little prince. He wore a bow tie, Jane a white linen dress. It was so casual that on the way to the ceremony at a synagogue next to the Fillmore, the Wenners ran into Bill Graham and invited him to attend. John Warnecke was the best man, and the piano player was Jim Peterman from the Steve Miller Band (whose playing Wenner characterized in *Rolling Stone* as "precise and heavy"). It was a quick ceremony before a rabbi, and afterward they went back to the Wenners' house and got stoned. None of their parents attended. Because Wenner's parents hated each other, Jane didn't invite her own parents, which she later regretted. Wenner's mother, who came out to her kids as a lesbian in the late 1960s, also made it clear she disliked Jane. For their wedding present, Sim gave them back her modest stock in *Rolling Stone,* "the cheapest thing she could get away with," said Wenner.

Nonetheless, Jane changed her last name to Wenner and removed her name from the *Rolling Stone* masthead so she could devote her time to being a homemaker, decorating their apartment on Rhode Island Street. Afterward, Jann wrote a four-page letter to Robin Gracey saying he was closing the book on their friendship, as painful as it was to him. According to Gracey, the letter ranged through Wenner's private desires and guilt as he tried justifying his decision. "He's kind of manufacturing his own security," Gracey recounted. "I think he was trying to say, 'Now I have a relationship with Janie, at another time I would have had one with you, and da-dee-da.'"

Wenner, said Gracey, told him that "he now has to put the letter in an envelope, seal it up, and get on with the life that he's really leading, which is a married life. But there's plenty else in the letter which suggests that things are not so secure as that."

"He was unsure whether he was gay or bisexual or which way he was," Gracey added.

(Gracey still possessed the letter, but Wenner asked him to keep it private because the contents would be "damaging," he said.)

For a honeymoon, the Wenners motored the Porsche to Tomales

Bay, fifty miles north of San Francisco, but when they arrived, they decided it was boring and returned to town. As it happened, British record producer Glyn Johns was in Los Angeles recording the first Steve Miller Band album, *Sailor,* and had invited Wenner to hang out. In a studio down the street, Johns would be helping the Rolling Stones mix a new record called *Beggars Banquet*. It would be Jann Wenner's first chance to meet Mick Jagger. Jann Wenner got on a plane and left Jane Wenner at home.

6

Sympathy for the Devil

When he first saw it, Mick Jagger was startled by the audacity of *Rolling Stone*—to name a newspaper after *his* band and not even put the Rolling Stones on the cover of the first issue? It was an affront that would stick with Jagger for the next fifty years. "Why did Jann call it that, when there was a band called that?" asked Jagger. "You could have thought something else, to be honest. I mean, I know it arised from a song name, but that's not really the point."

He continued, trying to discern Wenner's logic:

The song name, I wouldn't say, is very obscure, but it wasn't like the name of a *thing*. It was a song. Of course, there's no copyright for all these things—"Rolling Stone Ice Cream," go ahead. But it was a magazine about rock music. It wasn't quite the same as calling something ice cream. There's obviously a closer connection than that. It was obviously a very close connection. You could have called it *Beatles,* or spelled it slightly wrong, or something like that. Now, you think about it, it sounds ridiculous. But he could have done it. It's a backhanded compliment in one way, but it's also a very unoriginal title.

Keith Richards put it more succinctly: "We thought, 'What a thief!'"

From the start, there was confusion over the name. "Because *Rolling Stone* was brand-new," said Jerry Hopkins, "I was constantly saying to people, 'No, not the group, the *newspaper*.'"

Wenner once said he had no trouble getting the phone company to install his business lines on Brannan Street because they "thought we were the Rolling Stones." He benefited from the confusion, a fact not lost on Allen Klein, the band's manager, who immediately sent Wenner a cease-and-desist letter. "Your wrongful conduct constitutes, at the very least, a misappropriation of my clients' property rights in the name Rolling Stones for your own commercial benefit," wrote Klein's lawyer. "It is also a violation of my clients' copyright to the name 'Rolling Stones.'"

The lawyer demanded Wenner retract and destroy all copies of *Rolling Stone* or suffer "immediate legal action including an injunction and a suit for treble damages."

Wenner, whose friendship with Stones press secretary Jo Bergman had emboldened him to promise "an interview with Mick Jagger" in a *Rolling Stone* press release, began living in quiet terror. In November 1967, he wrote to Jagger directly, hoping to circumvent a lawsuit. "Greetings from San Francisco!" began the letter. "My feeling is that you haven't got any idea that this action has been taken on your behalf," he wrote. "'Cause it just doesn't seem like it's where you and the Stones are at."

Wenner asked Jagger to call him for an interview so *Rolling Stone* could publish something positive about the Rolling Stones. "That would be a groove," he said, "'cause we're all very interested in what's happening with everybody."

"It just looks like a great mistake," he concluded. "We love you."

Silence followed and Wenner squirmed, telling Bergman he was "very edgy" waiting for Jagger to exculpate him from legal action, which was "essential" if he were going to forge an advertising deal with Columbia Records. "We have to get this settled before it becomes out of sight," he wrote to her.

Stroking his chin from afar, Mick Jagger could not help but observe how the Beatles were using *Rolling Stone* as a handy promotional vehicle, with Wenner writing about them in the most reverent of terms. Indeed,

Jagger could use a guy like Jann Wenner in America, especially after his last album, *Their Satanic Majesties Request,* was so poorly received. Jon Landau ripped it in *Rolling Stone* as an insecure *Sgt. Pepper's* knockoff and declared the production and Jagger's lyrics "embarrassing." A full nine months and fourteen issues into the existence of *Rolling Stone* and the Rolling Stones had yet to appear on the cover, while their archrivals, the Beatles, had already appeared three times. If the lawsuit threat was a "great mistake," it was also a convenient bit of leverage, and if nothing else Mick Jagger liked leverage. "I don't think Mick lets anyone off the hook for anything," said Keith Richards. "He's never let anyone off the hook, once he's got one in."

That summer, Jagger learned that Wenner was hoping to start a British version of *Rolling Stone* in London. Jonathan Cott wrote to Wenner to report rumblings of legal hassles from the Stones if he attempted to publish in England. Bergman, the Stones' secretary, warned Cott that "the Stones might bring the legal thing out in the open here, since there is a *Rolling Stone* Magazine for the group, already here." It looked to Cott like a "bad scene."

Wenner had met Rolling Stones producer Glyn Johns through his neighbor Boz Scaggs, late of the Steve Miller Band, and over dinner one night in San Francisco asked him to invest in *Rolling Stone.* Johns declined but offered to broker a meeting with Jagger. The moment arrived when the Stones were mixing *Beggars Banquet* at Sunset Sound studios in Hollywood in the summer of 1968. Wenner arrived bristling with bonhomie, eager to win Jagger over for an interview and to broach the sticky issue of the *Rolling Stone* trademark. After Wenner scribbled detailed notes about the new album, Jagger invited him back to his rented house in Beverly Hills, where they listened to an acetate of the first album by the Band, *Music from Big Pink,* ate pizza, and talked business. Wenner was in heaven, basking in Jagger's luminous stardom. Jagger proposed that Wenner come to London to discuss the possibility of publishing the British version of *Rolling Stone,* with Mick Jagger as half owner.

Everything was falling into place: Jagger had already been toying with the idea of starting a magazine and now here was Jann Wenner, who already had a successful one named *Rolling Stone,* and was thereby poised under Jagger's thumb. "Jann and I thought it would be good to make one that was partly the same thing but would be localized in some way," Jagger said.

To show his appreciation, Wenner went back to San Francisco and wrote up a song-by-song preview of *Beggars Banquet* for *Rolling Stone,* comparing Jagger's lyrics to those of Bob Dylan and declaring it "the Stones' best record, without a doubt." Wenner's studious annotation of the album included the story behind the iconic "Sympathy for the Devil," the album's most "significant" song, with its famous reference to the Kennedys:

> The first version of the song—then called "The Devil Is My Name"—contained the lyric, "I shouted out, who killed Kennedy? After all it was you and me." The next day Bobby was shot. The second version of the song, the one which will be on the album, recorded the next day, had this line instead: "I shouted out, 'Who killed the Kennedys? After all it was you and me.'"

Wenner described Jagger as "a thin, modish Oscar Wilde figure" trailed by "bizarre" groupies whose "reaction to the famous—and in this case, almost what one could call the 'spiritually famous'—was as intense as ever." His presence, Wenner wrote, "caused wave-like spreading of recognition. He is still Mick Jagger."

What separated Jann Wenner from the other groupies, of course, was *Rolling Stone.* And the week of August 10, 1968, Wenner put Mick Jagger on the cover for the first time, the singer pouting and slithery in a tank top, a pair of headphones on his head. "The Return of the Rolling Stones," declared the headline.

•

THERE WAS A NARCOTIC FREEDOM to *Rolling Stone* as it charted the late 1960s, the primitive newsprint pages opening like a lotus flower, petal by petal, with revelations. The Beatles denounced the Maharishi. Dylan made a bunch of bootlegs in a basement. A blues-rock group called Fleetwood Mac was coming to America. And white people were finally learning how to be black. "They don't clap as well as a James Brown audience in the ghetto areas," wrote Ralph Gleason in June 1968, "but they clap a thousand times better than their parents did."

Wenner delighted in provocative photography celebrating liberated and alternative sexuality (mainly lesbianism) and published whole guides to buying and smoking marijuana, a habit so ubiquitous that a page 3 image of a boy smoking a joint shocked no one. There were poems by Richard Brautigan and Allen Ginsberg; stories on comic artist R. Crumb and pop artist Roy Lichtenstein; interviews with Miles Davis and Tiny Tim; premier LPs by new artists like Joni Mitchell ("A penny-yellow blonde with a vanilla voice") and Sly Stone ("The most adventurous soul music of 1968"). *Rolling Stone* recorded every tossed-off "um" and "uh" of Frank Zappa and Jim Morrison (including a long and pretentious poem Wenner reluctantly agreed to publish), every hiccup of John Lennon and Yoko Ono, which Jonathan Cott grokked for readers with the sensitivity of the Oxford scholar he had once hoped to be until *Rolling Stone* took over his life. Reviewing Lennon's first art show in London, Cott even transcribed the contents of the guest book, which included an insightful critique by the pioneering psychoanalyst Wilhelm Reich: "This armoring of the character is the basis of loneliness, helplessness, craving for authority, fear of responsibility, mystic longing, sexual misery, of impotent rebelliousness as well as of resignation of an unnatural and pathological type."

Even the advertisements were windows into the exotic American underworld of head shops, rock festivals, and free-form radio stations—Middle Eastern hookahs, a book by Carlos Castaneda, a three-day "Aquarian Exposition" in Woodstock, New York—all of it burbling up from the streets to be framed in Wenner's Oxford borders, made righteous by the *Rolling Stone* banner. "The moment I saw the logo and the layout, it just had this magnetism," recalled writer Timothy Crouse, who saw it at a kiosk in Harvard Square before coming to work at *Rolling Stone* in 1970. "That frame had a magic to it. That frame had a life to it."

The contrast between *Rolling Stone*'s straight design and the pot-tinged content inside was like "a circus," said David Dalton, who began at *Rolling Stone* in 1968 after writing for teen magazines in New York. "All the clowns and monkeys could jump around, but it was all contained in these Oxford lines."

Where else could you read, in a well-prepared newspaper, that a bunch of hippies climbed Mount Tamalpais, north of San Francisco, and had a pretty good time on acid? "No structure," wrote Mike Goodwin, who became *Rolling Stone*'s first film critic. "Never was any structure. Stephen said, 'Let's make it up to the mountain,' and The Class made it. Nothing to do but make it. Nothing to say but it's OK. Smoking dope and dropping acid in the sun. A hundred people singing to a guitar, 'I Shall Be Released,' softly. An energy bash at Mt. Tamalpais."

The newspaper was anchored by the loud sniffs and harrumphs of its bracing record reviews, written by college graduates who chin stroked and sneered as if they were parsing Picasso and not albums by the Steve Miller Band. Langdon Winner, a friend of Greil Marcus's from Berkeley, ripped the first album by Crosby, Stills, Nash, and Young, and Jon Landau reveled in casually ponderous dismissal, proclaiming Aretha Franklin's "Think" tied with "Chain of Fools" for "worst single" with "virtually no melody." But the actual opinions were not the most important thing; this was all the fine print of a *movement*, proof to readers that they were participating in a secret counterpower to the mass media. In *Rolling Stone,* they could finally hear themselves think aloud: Among Wenner's best ideas was to print highly opinionated reader letters, kids from Omaha and Miami sounding off with sarcasm and arch humor under the banner of "Correspondence, Love Letters & Advice."

- Let's face it: John and Yoko are embarrassing bores.
- Sitting up watching the chick across the street doing some nude exercises and trying to jerk off—but I didn't come until I read Paul Williams' review of the new Kinks album.
- I enjoyed your pipe article but was disappointed by your treatment of the bong.
- Many times I have seen your paper kill someone with paper and ink; it is always a very efficient job. And it is always justifiable homicide.
- You piss me off.

Jann Wenner at the Brannan Street offices of *Rolling Stone*, 1968.
(Baron Wolman)

Jann Wenner (center) with his sister Martha (left); his mother, Sim Wenner;
and his sister Kate (right) in the 1950s. *(Courtesy of Jann Wenner)*

Jann . . . Nox . . . Susie . . . ZTPC . . .
b. b. on the b. . . . greatness knows itself . . .
the Three Horsemen . . . P.E.? What's that?
. . . likes girls with a Weigel . . . me, V. P.? . . .
fiery young intellectual or damp young
vegetable . . . "the Sardine's canned" . . .
ask to see his lighter . . . "pray for June 19"
. . . intelligent, witty and perceptive.

Jann S. Wenner

Enrolled Five Years
Dolphin Editor-in-Chief '63
Student Body Vice President '63
Sardine Editor '63
Poetry Anthology Editor '62
Dolphin Junior Advisor '62
N.M.S. Finalist
N.E.D.T. Letter of Commendation '61, '62
Varsity Sports Statistician '60, '61, '62
Operetta Principal '62, '63
Shakespearean Festival '60, '61, '62, '63
Mainsheet Staff '61, '62, '63
Journey Staff '62
Scholastic Sports Association '60, '61, '62

"Please, get me out of here."

Wenner's page from
The Dolphin, Chadwick
School's yearbook, 1963.
(Courtesy of Chadwick School)

Mario Savio, leader of the Free Speech Movement, being led up the stairs by
police at the Greek Theatre at Berkeley—trailed by Jann Wenner, stringer
for NBC News, December 1964. *(Associated Press)*

Denise Kaufman, co-founder of and guitarist for the Ace of Cups and Wenner's girlfriend at Berkeley.
(Courtesy of Denise Kaufman)

Ralph Gleason, jazz critic and music columnist for the *San Francisco Chronicle*, at the Monterey Jazz Festival, 1969.
(Baron Wolman)

Wenner in his first *Rolling Stone* office on Brannan Street, early 1968.
(Baron Wolman)

Jann Wenner, 1969. *(Baron Wolman)*

Jane Schindelheim with Jann Wenner at their apartment in Potrero Hill, San Francisco, 1968. *(Baron Wolman)*

Robin Gracey at Oxford, 1969. *(Courtesy of Robin Gracey)*

Boz Scaggs and Wenner on Otis Redding's ranch near Macon, Georgia, May 1969. *(Stephen Paley/Getty)*

Writer and musician Ben Sidran with Wenner in London, 1969. *(Judy Sidran)*

Jann Wenner in his office at Brannan Street, 1969. *(Baron Wolman)*

Wenner in his new office at 625 Third Street in San Francisco, August 1970. *(Getty)*

Hunter S. Thompson during his campaign for county sheriff in Aspen, Colorado, 1970. *(David Hiser)*

Jann and Jane at their home on Ord Court, December 1970. *(Robert Altman)*

John and Yoko. Cover image by Annie Leibovitz, for the February 4, 1971, issue of *Rolling Stone*; part two of Wenner's post-Beatles interview. *(Courtesy of* Rolling Stone *magazine)*

Sandy Bull with his Turkish
oud in San Francisco, 1971.
(Baron Wolman)

Jann and Jane celebrate New Year's Eve with Max and Lynda Palevsky, 1973.
(Camilla McGrath)

The readers were people who knew every Dylan lyric, could give chapter and verse on every Stones controversy, *needed* things from the Beatles to get to the next day, had feelings as powerful as Landau or Greil Marcus, if not more powerful, and goddamn if they were going to stand by while *Rolling Stone* trashed John Mayall's Bluesbreakers. Jann Wenner had a tiger by the tail.

Even the problems could seem proof of the righteousness of *Rolling Stone*. When Columbia Records field-tested the sales power of *Rolling Stone* in record stores, it noted "consumer complaints with reference to their 'teeny-boppers' picking up the newspaper and being exposed to 'hard' language." The teenyboppers didn't mind. Indeed, they subscribed and got their free roach clip or free copy of the Grateful Dead's *Anthem of the Sun* (part of a deal Wenner struck with Warner Bros.) while their parents wrote in to demand, like Mrs. Marsha Ann Booth of Chagrin Falls, Ohio, that they "do not, and I mean *do not,* send *Rolling Stone* to my daughter . . . Keep it *under ground* and *bury it*. Never and I mean *never* send that thing to this address again. Trash! Trash! Trash!"—which Wenner published in full.

Inside the warehouse, as well, success had not bred happiness. There was a growing dissatisfaction with Wenner. Ralph Gleason was furious at him for letting *Rolling Stone* come out late and littered with errors ("We should never be in the situation, as we do in the Monkees story, discussing a facility like the Coliseum as being '24,000 or 30,000' when it is in fact around 16,000") and leaving behind a trail of angry and unpaid writers—including himself. In September 1968, Gleason tendered his resignation as vice president of Straight Arrow, saying he felt "seriously exploited" by Wenner, who had only paid him $35 since *Rolling Stone* began. He was further offended when Wenner offered to buy him out of his *Rolling Stone* stock for an offensively low sum. "Let's stop this charade," wrote Gleason. "I am totally out of sympathy with 1) the way you handle business affairs and 2) the way you handle personnel relations."

To placate Gleason, Wenner agreed to hire a new editor to run the newspaper—to "readjust" their relationship, said Wenner—while Wenner focused on expanding the business and procuring the big interviews. Gleason suggested a writer and editor he had met at San Francisco State named John Burks, a tall and prematurely crusty reporter who was now working for *Newsweek.* Burks told Gleason he thought *Rolling Stone,* while full of potential, "sucked," which Gleason relayed to Wenner with a certain relish. "I'm Jann Wenner from *Rolling Stone,*" Wenner said when he called Burks, "and I understand you think our magazine sucks." (He would hire critic Greil Marcus in the summer of 1969 with the same kind of come-on: "Hi, Greil? If you think the record review section is so terrible, why don't you edit it?")

Wenner quickly offered Burks a job as managing editor and asked when he could start, all before Burks had a chance to respond. "And I think my first words were 'What do you pay?'" said Burks. When he arrived at the Garrett Press offices, he saw the sunlight pouring through the large industrial windows and said to himself, "This beats the shit out of any underground paper I've ever seen." Burks hovered a foot higher than Wenner and had more interest in jazz than rock (he would be responsible for putting Miles Davis, Captain Beefheart, and Sun Ra on the cover of *Rolling Stone*), but he had a sturdy sense of newspapering protocol and a steady stream of story memos that he produced to the chug, chug, chug of the presses. "The whole place was rocking," said Burks. "It's not that you're hearing it; you're feeling it under your feet and in your seat. Can you beat this? I thought that was just wonderful."

Satisfied that Gleason was off his back, Jann Wenner flew to London to forge the deal with Mick Jagger.

•

"THE FIRST SIGN for me that Jann had audaciously grand ambitions," said Pete Townshend of the Who, "was his desire to create a U.K. version of *Rolling Stone.* He came to London on his first fact-finding mission, and we hung out together a couple of times."

In August of 1968, the Who had come to San Francisco to play the Fillmore, and afterward Wenner invited Townshend back to his apartment for an interview, which started at 2:00 a.m. and lasted until dawn. "There were no barriers," said Wenner. "There were no PR people, there were no security, there were no managers."

Townshend was trying to reposition the Who in the post-Monterey rock scene, because the mod incarnation of the band had been going out of vogue. He used Wenner as a kind of therapist and adviser—all on the record. "It was a tricky time for me, and I was surprised that Jann seemed to understand exactly where the Who would fit and would—if we were successful—prevail in a new self-created order," said Townshend. "I described my plan to complete *Tommy,* at that time a project around two-thirds completed."

Wenner asked him deceptively guileless questions, like "What is your life like today?" but as the conversation warmed, Townshend waxed philosophic on the power of rock and roll to upend society— and waxed and waxed and waxed. This would become a hallmark of Wenner's interview style, evincing naïveté to draw a subject out, and it often yielded results. Soon Wenner was asking him about the "tremendous sensuality" of rock, mentioning, among others, Mick Jagger, who Wenner noted was "tremendously involved in sexual things." Townshend described a Who concert as sex with the audience: "You've come your lot and the show's over."

The interview spanned two issues, with Townshend on the cover of *Rolling Stone* in September 1968, his patented guitar windmill gesture captured by Baron Wolman against a spotlight. Wenner noted that "nobody quite remembers exactly under what circumstances the interview concluded." The next day, Wenner drove him to the airport, and Townshend asked Wenner if he had spiked his drink with LSD. "I said no, not at all, why?" recalled Wenner. "He said he had some kind of experience, some kind of transcendent experience."

Townshend told writer David Dalton that Wenner had "completely taken me apart." (In the year-end wrap-up for 1969, *Rolling Stone* named *Tommy* the most overrated record of the year.)

A few months later, Wenner flew to London to meet with Jagger but first had dinner with Townshend. The guitarist picked him up in his gigantic Mercedes 600 and squired him to his Georgian house near the Thames. Townshend was struck with how quickly Wenner had embraced the role of press baron. "He seemed so much more worldly and grand than I remembered him," he said. "He assumed I would be comfortable with the scale of his business ambitions, and I suppose I was, but I remember feeling that he must have amassed a relative fortune fairly quickly."

He hadn't quite yet, but why wait? The next day, Townshend said, he and Wenner went to Olympic Studios to see the Rolling Stones record songs for a forthcoming album, *Let It Bleed*. They sat in the booth while the Stones played, both ogling Mick Jagger like feverish groupies. "It turned out that he, like me, harbored an adoration of Mick Jagger that was not entirely heterosexual," said Townshend.

Afterward, Wenner accompanied Jagger to his apartment in Chelsea, and they sat by a fireplace with a moose head over the mantel to discuss their joint venture. They hadn't gotten very far when Marianne Faithfull, Jagger's then lover, showed up after a bad day on the set of a film production of *Hamlet,* in which she played Ophelia. "She came home, hysterical and histrionic, and he had to comfort her and I left," recalled Wenner. (She would overdose on sleeping pills not long after.)

With a broad agreement from Jagger, Wenner returned to San Francisco and dove into the details of the joint venture, writing Jagger a series of excited letters and telegrams outlining his ideas for a British *Rolling Stone*. They would be fifty-fifty owners, he suggested, with Wenner in editorial control. He helpfully included a waiver for Jagger to sign absolving him of legal trouble from trademark infringement.

Not so fast, said Jagger. "For my part, I assumed that I would more or less have control of the [editorial] policy on this side of the Atlantic," Jagger wrote back, adding that the waiver "is not in any way valid, and even if I signed it, it means nothing. You can't expect me to waive all past or future rights to the name *Rolling Stone*—and waive to whom anyway."

They put the questions off to when Wenner returned to London in the spring. For now, Wenner would have to be satisfied that he was in business with Mick Jagger—wasn't that enough? Clearly, Jagger held the cards. For Jagger's first *Rolling Stone* interview in October 1968, Jonathan Cott shared a byline with an employee of the Rolling Stones, Sue Cox, who worked out of the band's Maddox Street office in London, where the interview was conducted ("It is not the most thorough and complete set of questions and answers," conceded the *Rolling Stone* introduction).

When he returned to London in March 1969, Jann Wenner was becoming a figure of notoriety in the underground press, in part because

of his impending deal with Jagger. *The Guardian* called him the Hugh
Hefner of pop, and Wenner boldly told *Oz,* the British counterculture
magazine edited by Richard Neville, "we're out to replace the *Melody
Maker* and all these shitty music publications." (*Oz* described Wenner
as looking "for all the world like an unusually hairy rugby player" with
the "cat-that-got-away-with-the-cream smile.")

That week, Wenner met with Prince Rupert Loewenstein, the
Bavarian aristocrat known as "Rupie the Groupie," who had taken over
management of the Stones' finances during Jagger's acrimonious split
with Allen Klein. Loewenstein was no less concerned about the trademark issue, telling Wenner he wanted *him* to sign a waiver giving *Jagger*
the rights to the name *Rolling Stone.* "I said, 'No, you can't own the name
Rolling Stone,'" recalled Wenner.

Regardless, Loewenstein said they were happy to go into business with Wenner, with Jagger as "chairman" of the joint venture they
decided to call the Trans-oceanic Comic Company Limited. Now Jann
Wenner was business partners with Mick Jagger. And the one person
Wenner thought to impress with his proximity to Jagger's "spiritual
fame" was his lost love from the summer of 1967, Robin Gracey. Married to Jane for less than eight months, Wenner continued to fantasize
about being with Gracey, who was now studying at the Oxford College of Technology. So he invited him to Olympic Studios in suburban
London, where the Stones were recording *Let It Bleed.* At nine o'clock
at night, Wenner and Gracey sat in the control booth with producer
Jimmy Miller and Stones bassist Bill Wyman, eating canapés and
watching a stoned-senseless Brian Jones fiddle about in a lonely corner of the cavernous studio. Jagger stood in a recording booth under
a microphone to sing to a backing track of the London Bach Choir as
Wenner and Gracey watched and listened in awe:

You can't always get what you wa-ant . . .

As the choir rose to a crescendo, Jagger started his famous howling,
"That scream was utterly riveting," Gracey said. "He was able to replicate it many times."

When the session ended at 4:00 a.m., the lovers filed into the back of Jagger's Rolls-Royce, a sleepy Jagger up front with his driver. The car dropped the couple off at the Londonderry House Hotel, and Wenner and Gracey walked into the glow of the lobby and up the elevator to Wenner's suite overlooking Hyde Park, Jagger's voice echoing in the night.

> *But if you try sometimes, you just might find—*
> *you get what you nee-eed!*

•

WHEN JANN WENNER GOT BACK from London, *Time* magazine published a profile of his rising rock publication, noting the eight-by-ten glossy of Mick Jagger on Wenner's wall and a book on his shelf titled "The Jann Wenner Method for Effective Operation of a Cool Newspaper," "which is blank, a gift from the bookbinder." What made *Rolling Stone* unique, Wenner told a *Time* reporter, was that it was authentic. "We never thought of filling a market," he said, "and we never created *Rolling Stone* toward anyone in particular."

That same month, *The Washington Post* published a story on *Rolling Stone* in which Wenner predicted the death of *Time* magazine—"because it's not going to make the change when the culture change comes."

But while Wenner plumped for his own cultural relevance, he had a little problem: He was broke. Wenner's trips to London and New York had sapped the company's meager coffers. Said Baron Wolman, "He had a credit card, and he stayed at the fanciest hotel, spent a fortune on clothes, custom-made clothes, came back, and we had no money. I said, 'Jann, we can't do this. We can't run a publication like that if you're not looking at a budget.' And he said, 'I'll do what I want, Baron.'

"If that's the case," continued Wolman, "I don't even want to be on the board of directors, because he's gonna do what he wants anyhow! It's just kind of fallen into a black hole."

When Wenner conceded he needed help, Wolman connected him with a local stockbroker named Charles Fracchia, who was married into an Old San Francisco family involved in the luxury department store I. Magnin & Company. Fracchia was a thirty-two-year-old father of three but fascinated with the counterculture buzzing around him. He put together a group of investors who forked over $10,000 in exchange for shares of *Rolling Stone* and drew up elaborate proposals envisioning a "multimedia entertainment/leisure operation," including a portfolio of magazines and an FM radio station. In truth, it was all an excuse for Fracchia to dabble in the earthly delights he was reading about in *Rolling Stone*. Wenner was happy to oblige: For their first "board meeting," Wenner invited him for breakfast on Rhode Island Street, and Jane scrambled marijuana into the eggs. "At end of meeting, I'm feeling really woozy," Fracchia recalled. "[Jann] starts laughing, 'Don't you know what she put in the scrambled egg?' That was my first drug hit."

Fracchia and Wenner agreed they needed to acquire more properties and expand the business, with Fracchia eager to take the company public and make a mint on the growing youth boom. In the spring of 1969, on his way back from London, Wenner met with the owner of *New York Scenes,* a somewhat seedy underground newspaper that covered drugs and orgies and that Fracchia saw as a natural property for Straight Arrow and bought the paper in exchange for 10 percent of *Rolling Stone* stock. In a matter of two months, Jann Wenner went from cash poor to operating three magazines—*Rolling Stone,* British *Rolling Stone,* and *New York Scenes.* Maybe this rock-and-roll empire thing would work out after all.

.

IN FEBRUARY 1969, Jann Wenner and Ralph Gleason went to San Quentin State Prison to see Johnny Cash perform for the inmates, a program recorded for an album on Columbia Records as *Johnny Cash at San Quentin*. Bob Dylan was embracing country music with the stripped-down *John Wesley Harding,* and Cash was performing Bob Dylan songs in concert, telling Wenner in May 1968 that country musicians "have been affected greatly by the sound of the Beatles and the lyric of Dylan."

On the next page was a full-page ad by Columbia Records, the label of both Dylan and Cash. *Rolling Stone*'s relationship to the "Columbia Rock Machine" had grown increasingly tight, starting with its first advertisement in issue No. 8. Clive Davis, having ascended to president of CBS Records, a subsidiary of Columbia, on the success of Janis Joplin and Blood, Sweat, and Tears, made *Rolling Stone* required reading for his staff as he moved the label past the square *Sing Along with Mitch* era. He viewed Wenner as an ally in building a new industry out of rock and roll, and he gave *Rolling Stone* its first steady advertising contract to keep the newspaper afloat. Wenner advertised the Columbia connection, sending out a PR letter to acquaint potential advertisers and distributors with "the approach and style with which we and Columbia Records feel reflects the changes in popular music of the last three years." Davis put *Rolling Stone* into record stores through Columbia's distribution system, which now accounted for 15 percent of the newspaper's single-copy sales. "It was no question that Jann had a vision," said Davis. "This was a whole new world for me that had opened up, post-Monterey."

In addition, Jann Wenner was using Columbia's offices in New York as a virtual bureau of *Rolling Stone*. In a letter to Bob Altshuler, the publicist for Columbia, Wenner thanked him for the "favors, the lunchs [*sic*], the tickets, and the use of your secretaries and offices. Someday we'll be buying the whold [*sic*] building, so keep it clean and in good shape."

The same month as the San Quentin concert, Wenner and Baron Wolman set up camp at Columbia to lay out a promotional ad for a story Wenner was sure would be a big hit: the "Groupies" issue, an exposé that featured snapshots of women Baron Wolman met backstage at the Fillmore. A few were nudes, with a provocative photo of two women kissing, tongues touching, which made Wenner sit up. The idea was far from novel—*Cheetah* had published a groupies issue in 1967—but timing was everything. When *Time* magazine tried to beat *Rolling Stone* with a groupies feature of its own, Wenner borrowed a play from the old carnival barker Warren Hinckle: He preempted *Time* with a full-page ad in *The New York Times,* asking, "When we tell what a Groupie is, will you really understand? This is the story only *Rolling Stone* can tell, because we are the musicians, we are the music, we are writing about ourselves." (Indeed, afterward a former *Rolling Stone* secretary named Henri Napier wrote in to point out that Wenner was the biggest groupie of them all. "Any reason he was left out?" she wrote.)

The ad cost *Rolling Stone* $7,000, but with Fracchia on the hook money was no object. The night before the ad appeared in the *Times,*

Wenner and Wolman ordered a bottle of champagne to their room at the five-star Warwick hotel and got drunk. "He was really excited," said Wolman. "I think the first issue [of the *Times*] comes out at, like, midnight, and we raced down to get the issue."

They taped up copies of the ad all over their hotel walls.

On the same trip, Wenner had dinner with Alan Rinzler, the "house hippie" at Macmillan Publishing, to discuss starting a *Rolling Stone* book division. Rinzler's wife was shocked when she looked out the apartment window and saw Wenner's ride: "There's a limousine out there! A black limousine!"

"We didn't know anyone who had a limousine at that time," said Rinzler. "A kid, with a limousine."

Fracchia was irked by Wenner's profligate spending. "I think Jann liked to live well," said Fracchia. "He had no other source of income other than what he could take out of the company." But for Wenner, the arrival of serious money was an inevitability—he was in *Time* magazine for Christ's sake—so whatever problems his personal spending created he believed to be temporary.

•

THE DAY NEIL ARMSTRONG SET FOOT on the moon, July 20, 1969, Jann Wenner was in London watching it on TV in a suite at the Londonderry Hotel, with his lover, Robin Gracey, by his side.

On his last trip to London, after hearing the Stones record, Wenner hired a large black Mercedes (like Pete Townshend's) to drive through the country to Gracey's school at Oxford, where the two caught the tail end of a Fairport Convention concert. At Gracey's house, they crawled up into the attic space where he kept their love letters in a bundle and made love. Perhaps Wenner could have not only what he needed but what he wanted, too. "There clearly was, from his point of view, sort of a possibility of a future together," Gracey said.

"He was my lover and mate," mused Wenner, though he said he felt pangs of guilt about Jane: "I felt bad and was sneaking around, and she kept wanting to come [to London] and I'd say no."

This time Wenner was in London to announce the launch of British *Rolling Stone* in a small press conference with Jagger. To crown the occasion, Wenner showed up wearing a blue velveteen suit and white Louis XVI shirt with ruffles that exploded from the sleeves, looking not unlike Brian Jones, who had been found dead in a swimming pool three weeks earlier (and eulogized by Greil Marcus in *Rolling Stone,* who said "Sympathy for the Devil" was his epitaph). Wenner had also grown a semi-handlebar mustache that wormed down both sides of his mouth. Having staked some of his own money on British *Rolling Stone,* Jagger insisted on hiring the editor, a young woman named Jane Nicholson, whose awe of Jagger tended to render her stammering and shaking with nerves. They set up an office in Hanover Square, where Wenner reminded the rambunctious staff during their first meeting that "we're not here to drink Mick's wine," prompting Jagger to correct him: "Hold it, that's exactly why we're here. To drink my wine."

Wenner could hardly argue. But it wasn't just the British edition over which Jagger now appeared to have control. David Dalton, Wenner's correspondent in London, reported to Wenner that *Rolling Stone* was, for all practical purposes, the same as the Rolling Stones Organization in England. Interviews with rock stars attached to big managers like Robert Stigwood, whose clients included the Bee Gees and Cream, could be arranged "only through the kind cooperation of Jane Nicholson," Jagger's chosen editor. Dalton described to Wenner how a *Rolling Stone* reporter had been barred from a recording session pending approval by Jagger's people. "We gathered very quickly that Jagger and Wenner had not really sorted out the terms of engagement too clearly," said Alan Marcuson, who was hired as the advertising manager and later became an editor.

Once British *Rolling Stone* launched in June 1969, with Pete Townshend on the cover, each new issue arrived in San Francisco like a fresh offense, a mutant version of Wenner's own *Rolling Stone,* trussed up with political diatribes, overly groovy prose, and egregious misspellings of rock star names on the cover. "There were two appalling incidents where we spelled Ray Davies's name wrong, and we called him 'Ray Davis' in a big headline," recalled Marcuson, "and then we spelled Bob Dylan's name wrong, 'Dillon' as I remember. As bad as it can fucking get, really. Wenner hit the roof, rightly so."

Wenner flew to London to try bringing order to the unruly staff, whose priority seemed to be enjoying Mick Jagger's wine as well as copious amounts of marijuana. "Wenner came over, and we had a very fractious, uncomfortable meeting with him," said Marcuson. "And he very quickly became the enemy of London *Rolling Stone*."

Jagger gave the staff carte blanche to ignore Wenner, which they were all too happy to do. "We said, 'Fuck it, the Stones are paying for this, we'll do whatever we like, he's not our boss,'" said Marcuson. After two months of frustration, Wenner sent a twelve-page letter to Jagger calling the British *Rolling Stone* "mediocre" and run with "unbelievable incompetence," reporting that he had fired one of Jagger's employees, Alan Reid, "Great Britain's leading male groupie." Citing his friend Pete Townshend, Wenner told Jagger that Reid had offended the members of the Small Faces ("or Humble Pie or whatever they're called") while interviewing them at their country cottage. Wenner insisted to Jagger that the British magazine come under the boot of the American *Rolling Stone*.

By this time, however, Jagger had lost interest entirely and flown to Australia to film an art-house outlaw movie called *Ned Kelly* (which *Rolling Stone* would later describe as "one of the most plodding, dull and pointless films in recent memory"). Meanwhile, Jagger's British *Rolling Stone* staff threw a record industry party in which the punch bowl was spiked with LSD and several attendees were hospitalized. One victim was Marc Bolan of T. Rex, who freaked out and locked himself in the bathroom until he was talked out by a gynecologist (and aspiring country music singer) who happened to be present. "I think that party was one of the big nails in the coffin," said Marcuson.

Wenner was desperate to pull the plug on British *Rolling Stone* but frightened by the prospect of letting Jagger down. "It took me a while to screw my courage up to do it, to write him a letter or call him," said Wenner. "I said this thing is awful, it's not working, they're spending your money at an incredible rate, and you're going to have nothing to show for it."

When Wenner announced to the British staff that the magazine was finished, his letter was immediately leaked to *The International Times,* an underground paper started out of the Indica Gallery in London, supported by Paul McCartney, which detailed the eviction of the "Stones staff" from their offices. For Wenner, it was a grand embarrassment, undermining the credibility of his paper and leaving a taste of bitter disappointment over Jagger's failure to uphold his end of the bargain. "I was upset and I said that to him," said Wenner. "There was never any reaction from Mick."

For Jagger, it was an expensive boondoggle, nothing more. "I didn't have that much money at that point," said Jagger, "because I was in all these disputes with Allen Klein." (Jagger felt Klein had ripped off the Stones.) Mick Jagger's staff implored the Stones' singer to reconsider shutting down British *Rolling Stone* and spent the next two weeks trying to commandeer the magazine from Wenner. The drama culminated in a long and heated telegram to Jagger explaining that it was the rock star's God-given right to use the name *Rolling Stone,* regardless of what Jann Wenner said. Marcuson remembered the precise date of the telegram they sent to Mick Jagger. It was the weekend of December 6, 1969, the eve of a free concert an hour south of the *Rolling Stone* offices: the Rolling Stones at Altamont Speedway.

•

GRINNING EAR TO EAR, Jann Wenner ogled the six naked men as they threw off their blue jeans and jumped into a cold creek in Macon, Georgia.

The Allman Brothers had just completed their first album under the guidance of Phil Walden, the onetime manager of Otis Redding and founder of Capricorn Records, who suggested an au naturel portrait for their first LP cover and maybe some *Rolling Stone* publicity shots. Wenner loved the idea. "Yeah, yeah! Do it! Do it! Do it!" he exclaimed. They all plopped into the water. "The guys weren't really into it," said photographer Stephen Paley, "but at that point they would do pretty much anything to get famous."

Paley took his clothes off in solidarity with the band while a fully clothed Wenner stood on the bank of the creek to snap photos of them all. One of the Paley images—Duane Allman, holding his hands over his crotch—would appear inside Boz Scaggs's first LP for Atlantic Records. Scaggs had just finished recording his solo album in Muscle Shoals, Alabama, with Allman on slide guitar and a rookie record producer in the booth: Jann Wenner.

By this time, the Wenners had become close friends with Scaggs, the laconic bluesman from Plano, Texas, and his new girlfriend, a stylish and beautiful socialite named Carmella Storniola from Seattle. Scaggs showed up in San Francisco after kicking around Europe playing blues covers. He was known as the "Bob Dylan of Sweden." After Scaggs's acrimonious split with Steve Miller, and Carmella's breakup with Dan Hicks (of the Hot Licks), the couple had moved next door to the Wenners and befriended Jane. As Scaggs would write in a draft of his liner notes, it happened "over Christmas and between neighborly exchanges of the odd cup of sugar and the even cup of scotch." This was the period of the record producer as auteur, the secret masterminds behind all the great albums. Jon Landau had temporarily left *Rolling Stone* to produce the next album by the MC5 for Jerry Wexler at Atlantic Records ("My first gig right now is learning how to be a producer," Landau would tell Wenner). Not to be outdone, Wenner sent Scaggs's demo tape to Wexler and suggested himself as producer. For Wexler, this was a fine trade: He had just started a new studio in Muscle Shoals and was getting reverent ink from *Rolling Stone*. "He loved Jon and he loved me and he really wanted to cultivate us and of course we were enamored of Jerry," said Wenner. "He had a Talmudic knowledge of music, and we didn't know what a shady character he was on the other side, how tough and poisonous."

Scaggs was eager to make an R&B album that sounded like Wexler's recordings of Wilson Pickett and Aretha Franklin, but he first wanted to investigate Wexler's new venture, Muscle Shoals Sound Studio, so Wenner gave Scaggs a *Rolling Stone* press card to pose as a reporter. "I was welcomed as a man of the press and given a grand tour and treated very nicely," Scaggs would recall. Wenner and Scaggs flew to Memphis in May 1969 and holed up in a motel, taking six days to record Scaggs's LP while Jane and Carmella flew to Acapulco on vacation. Scaggs wanted Duane Allman on his album, but Allman had moved to Georgia to start the Allman Brothers, so Wenner convinced Wexler to bring him back for one last Atlantic date. Wenner, of course, knew nothing about producing records. "But I'm just very confident," he said. "I knew what I liked. I said, 'Play it like this,' and I could reference a familiar record that everybody knew and I just knew how to manage things. And crazy enough, a little bit of dictating the girl singing parts to them."

Wenner said he conceived the twelve-minute blues jam, "Loan Me a Dime," with Allman on a long stretch of slide guitar. When the record was finished, Wenner promoted the track on San Francisco FM radio. "I called up the local DJs in San Francisco and brought them to Trident Studios and I got them all stoned," he said.

After the recording, Boz and Carmella moved to Macon, Georgia, to hang out with Walden and the Allmans. When the Wenners showed up for a visit, Scaggs's drinking was out of control, and they went on a terrifying drive down a country road until Jane Wenner insisted Carmella drive. She was also drunk, and the terror continued. The visit wasn't a total loss: In a letter to writer Stanley Booth, Wenner said he scored some coke from Duane Allman.

The Scaggs album, with a cover design by Bob Kingsbury, was a fine if mellow affair but not destined for success. The day after "Loan Me a Dime" was recorded, Wexler and Wenner had a screaming match on the phone over Wenner's expensive studio time, and Wexler told him to shut the session down. Wenner ignored him and kept recording. "I said, we're nearly done, I'm going to finish this up, I don't care what he has to say," said Wenner. "I think Jerry was more pissed off that we had made a really good record in a studio that he had failed to make a successful record in."

Consequently, Wexler didn't promote the record, it sold fewer than twenty thousand copies, and Atlantic dropped Scaggs from the label. It was a deep disappointment for Scaggs, who later told *Rolling Stone*, "I was kind of countin' on the album to sell or do somethin' big." Glyn Johns, who produced Scaggs's next album for Columbia, felt Wenner's arrogance nearly tanked Scaggs's career. "That might have been why Jann and I fell out in the end," he said. "He should never have risked Scaggs's career by presuming to produce."

Though *Rolling Stone* gave the album a perfectly nice review (assigned by Greil Marcus), it was buried at the bottom of page 33, wedged between reviews for the Beatles' *Abbey Road* and Miles Davis's

In a Silent Way, and didn't mention that the editor and publisher of *Rolling Stone* was the producer. Wenner told *The Village Voice* that he and Scaggs had a falling-out ("artistic temperament, all that stuff"), but the Scaggs/Wenner split was only a temporary hiccup. Scaggs had more to gain from Wenner than not, and Carmella was spending endless hours with Jane, shopping and decorating the Wenners' new apartment in the posh Ord Court neighborhood. For a while, the two women planned an interior decorating business, but Jane mainly curled up on the couch, stoned on downers, and complained to Carmella that Jann Wenner never paid attention to her. During one chat, Jane idly mentioned that Wenner was gay—as if it were only the third or fourth most depressing thing about her life.

The friendship with the Wenners would prove a thorny business. While Carmella was between houses and temporarily living in the Wenners' basement in 1971, *Rolling Stone* produced a feature on the Allman Brothers that revealed the story behind the band's instrumental jam "In Memory of Elizabeth Reed": While Scaggs was living in Macon with the band, Carmella was having an affair with Allmans' guitarist Dickey Betts. "Fuck," Duane Allman told *Rolling Stone* while snorting a pile of cocaine. "He wrote that fuckin' song after he fucked this chick on a fuckin' tombstone in a fuckin' cemetery in Macon. On a fuckin' *tombstone,* my man!" (The tombstone was Elizabeth Reed's.)

As Jane Wenner recalled, Carmella "always told Boz she was going there to look at the flowers, and whatever."

But it was too late; the story had already gone to press.

Wenner was the best man in Boz and Carmella's 1973 wedding in Aspen, Colorado—which made the Random Notes column and was attended by Hunter Thompson—but by then Scaggs had come to prefer the company of Jane over Jann. "Exquisite taste," he observed of her. "Jann's interest brought people in, but it was Jane who fascinated people. Always there, and funny, and sort of kept the party going when Jann's off on tangents. His is a frenetic energy; hers is more solid."

•

IF THE BOZ SCAGGS ALBUM didn't convert Jann Wenner into a record producer, it did presage his next big coup. When Wenner and Scaggs originally flew to New York to cut a deal with Atlantic, they shared a room at the Drake Hotel and were awakened one morning by a knock on the door. Wenner got up from his bed, still naked, to greet a small man wearing a sheepskin coat. It was Bob Dylan.

Dylan had been MIA since his mysterious motorcycle crash of 1966, and the race was on to see who would get an exclusive interview with the release of *Nashville Skyline,* which featured a duet with Johnny Cash. Wenner had filed a request with Columbia and written to Dylan directly, heartened after he received a phone message at the front desk of a New York hotel in September of 1968 from a "Mr. Dillon." "The big magazines that everybody read were *Time, Newsweek,* and *Life* magazine," said Dylan. "Maybe because they didn't review my records at those magazines, the Columbia people went to *Rolling Stone.*"

Dylan said Columbia arranged the interview, but he evidently wanted to suss Wenner out personally. Wenner would never forget Dylan's first handshake: limp and gripless, a cold fish in his hand. While they sat in the hotel room, he agreed to let Dylan approve the manuscript and edit it before publication, which would become standard operating procedure for Wenner's chosen stars. The interview took place eight months later, a Thursday afternoon in New York, "right around the corner from the funeral home where Judy Garland was being inspected by ten thousand people," Wenner wrote in his introduction to the interview in *Rolling Stone.* Dylan would only vaguely recall the interview, but he clearly remembered walking by the Garland funeral on his way to meet Wenner:

> I remember it because I had to wade through the crowd by the funeral home and I passed by Mickey Rooney up close. I always remembered seeing Mickey Rooney, but couldn't remember why or how . . . always thought it was something I might have dreamed. I couldn't imagine what I'd be doing there. Now I know. I was on my way to do an interview with *Rolling Stone* magazine.

Dylan could be forgiven for not remembering the interview. The only thing notable about it was that *Rolling Stone* had it—a fact that Wenner acknowledged, writing that "Bob was very cautious in everything he said." Evasive and snide, Dylan responded to questions with the contemptuous "Well, Jann, I'll tell you something . . ." and ". . . but you see, *Jann* . . ." When Wenner asked him about the meaning of "Leopard-Skin Pill-Box Hat," Dylan hemmed and hawed before saying, "Just a leopard skin pillbox. That's all."

Wenner tried unsuccessfully to get the master media manipulator to acknowledge his role as the voice of the generation. When Wenner asked about his "following," Dylan said, "You would probably know just as much about that as I would."

"The biggest revelation was that his voice was different because he had quit smoking," recalled Wenner. "I would ask him a question and he wouldn't answer and I'd look at him, and he'd look back, and it was kind of a stare down. And I thought surely he's gotta—but you couldn't break him."

A few *Rolling Stone* readers panned the Dylan interview, with one complaining that Dylan didn't "wanna say very much, that's for goddam sure. That's the sole conclusion one can draw from seven pages of a rap that is pure bullshit." In fact, Wenner probably told Dylan more than Dylan told Wenner. When Dylan said he wrote "Desolation Row" in the back of a taxicab, Wenner, in a portion of the interview he edited out, said taxicabs made him feel desolate, too: "When I first started coming here on business, I would come home at night and, like, be constipated and nervous and sweaty, and just generally . . . and I finally realized what it was—it was taxi cabs."

But Jann Wenner had what he needed: Bob Dylan's every "um" and "uh" and "well, Jann, lemme tell ya" in *Rolling Stone*, the mere presence of the generation's "tiny demon of a poet" ratifying the importance of his newspaper. While the critical foxes knew many things, Jann Wenner knew one big thing: that readers would never tire of hearing about Bob Dylan. He was too potent, too famous, too meaningful to too many people. Dylan could sneer all he wanted, mock his interviewers, and deny interpretations of his lyrics, but *Rolling Stone* was going to be his Boswell whether he acknowledged it or not—*and maybe precisely because he didn't acknowledge it*. "I don't remember a thing about the interview except that Wenner was likable and I thought he was a friendly person," Dylan said.

When asked about the impact of Jann Wenner and *Rolling Stone* on his legacy—twenty-five *Rolling Stone* covers, countless reviews and essays, studio portraits and tour books and an entire Bob Dylan anthology of interviews—Dylan echoed his coy and supercilious replies of 1969: "I have no idea. You'll have to ask him."

•

IN SEPTEMBER 1969, Mick Jagger returned from filming *Ned Kelly* to start the first Rolling Stones tour in almost three years. The band had been barred from working in the States because of drug busts, and they were returning to a brave new rock scene defined by the mammoth Woodstock festival, a media extravaganza that was filmed for a documentary and recorded for a triple LP. The Stones were feeling insecure, and competitive. So Jagger cooked up a sequel, a West Coast answer to Woodstock, this time in the hometown of his business partner Jann Wenner and featuring local heroes the Grateful Dead and the Jefferson Airplane. The first thing they did was hire a documentary film crew, Albert and David Maysles, to create a movie and promote their next album, *Let It Bleed,* in hopes of beating the Woodstock movie to the theaters in the spring of 1970. News of a free festival first leaked in November 1969, at the precise moment that British *Rolling Stone* was dissolving. "Yeah, there is going to be one," Richards told the *Los Angeles Free Press.* "But I don't want to say where or when right now. We've still got to get 'round the country and get things together. At the end, we'll get it all together and do the free show."

By December, the plans for a Stones movie were in place, but the festival itself was still in shambles. Jagger had called Wenner for help, desperate to secure a venue. "That's why Altamont became so charged," said Wenner. "Mick calls me and he wants to do this big concert."

Wenner gave Jagger the number of a local lawyer, Melvin Belli, who after a false start with the Sears Point Raceway (the owners demanded the film profits go toward Vietnamese orphans) arranged for the Stones to take over the Altamont Speedway and gamely posed for the Maysles brothers' cameras as he worked the phones, outfitted in a three-piece suit and garish tie. This was twenty-four hours before showtime.

Privately, Wenner was still smarting from the failed venture with

Jagger only a month before. When Wenner arrived at Brannan Street one afternoon to discover employees of the Stones using his private office to make phone calls, he yelled at his secretary for allowing them in. (The Rolling Stones ran up $140 in long-distance phone calls, and Wenner promptly forwarded them the bill.)

Even after the dissolution of British *Rolling Stone*, Jagger expected Wenner to remain his loyal scribe. Wenner put Jagger on the cover of *Rolling Stone* the month of the festival, headlined "The Stones Grand Finale." But there were signs of a creeping skepticism. Ralph Gleason excoriated the Stones in the *Chronicle*, complaining that their ticket prices were extortionary ("Can the Rolling Stones actually need all that money?"). This "free" concert looked to Gleason like a cynical ploy to make money off a movie, with San Francisco as the Stones' picturesque set. And indeed, Jagger was hard up for cash on the brink of the Stones' divorce from manager Allen Klein, not to mention the $40,000 Jagger had blown on British *Rolling Stone*. When *Rolling Stone* buttonholed him about why he wanted to spend $100,000 on a free concert, his flip reply was "Well, I wanted to do the whole tour for *free*, because, you know, I'm richer than the other fellas, and I can afford it.

"I'm just joking," he added.

Wenner had nearly joined the Grateful Dead's Jerry Garcia and Phil Lesh on a helicopter to the festival but opted out while still standing on the landing pad. Perhaps he'd seen enough of Jagger for one year. "The helicopter was crowded, and I had no plan to get home," he said. "I was a Stones fan, but I'd seen enough of them."

Altamont, as the Maysles film showed, was a gigantic mistake. That it represented the sudden and untimely death of Woodstock Nation is a truism that happens to be true: a precisely crafted Hieronymus Bosch mirror image of the heaven at Max Yasgur's farm, Altamont was a botched festival overrun by "every meatball in the Western Hemisphere," as Bob Neuwirth had warned of free concerts, and marred by violent fisticuffs and bad acid trips, including a man who declared he was pregnant and jumped off a nearby highway overpass. While drug-addled and seminude hippies desperately groped for pleasure, members of the Hells Angels, the hired "security" in wolf pelts and leather, swilled the $500 worth of beer the Stones gave them, beat concertgoers with pool sticks, and, finally, stabbed an eighteen-year-old black fan named Meredith Hunter to death while the Stones played "Under My Thumb" fifteen yards away.

In front of 300,000 shivering fans in an unlit and sprawling field at night, Jagger blithely advertised his diabolical reputation by performing "Sympathy for the Devil," which immediately set off a violent melee in front of the stage. "We always have something very funny happen when we start that number," he told the crowd, as if part of a script.

Fifteen minutes later, there was a dead man in front of him, which was not part of the script.

•

OVER THE WEEKEND of the concert, Wenner began hearing from his staff. Greil Marcus and John Burks were both sickened by the depravity they'd witnessed, and even more so after they read the headline in a San Francisco paper the following day, "300,000 Say It with Music," clearly pre-written without any eyewitness accounts. "Those of us who had been there were so dispirited," said Marcus, "both by what had happened—it was so awful, in so many ways—and then by the press coverage."

Before the murder took place, Marcus and Burks considered burying the story along with the rest of the press because the festival was so bleak. "I remember John [Burks] saying, 'This is so awful. Maybe we should not even cover it,'" said Marcus. "I said, 'Well, we have to cover it.' He said, 'Well, what if we just ran a column saying, "Stones Play Free Concert," and ran a couple of paragraphs.' I said, 'Yeah, that would probably be good.'"

But after the murder, there could be no denial. Burks called Wenner over the weekend demanding they "tell people what these fuckers did," but Wenner remained skeptical until Gleason called him from Berkeley and urged Wenner to face Jagger down. If *Rolling Stone* was a professional newspaper about rock and roll, the moment of truth was nigh. What did Jann Wenner really stand for? Was he a groupie or a fucking journalist? He told him to cover the Altamont disaster "like it was World War II."

The following week, Wenner, according to Greil Marcus, sat before his editors over lunch and declared, "We're gonna cover this story from top to bottom, and we're going to lay the blame."

"Everybody knew I was friends with Mick," said Wenner, "and everybody was walking around on tender toes, wondering is Jann going to let this happen. All our integrity was on the line with that. Me, in front of my staff, and me, in front of the world. And I just said, do it."

For Wenner, deciding to confront Altamont head-on was a moment of bravery, tinged though it was by the contretemps over British *Rolling Stone,* and not without Wenner's characteristic calculation. It was a risk worth taking. "I remember explicitly thinking this thought, that whatever we did, my relationship with Mick would survive," Wenner continued. "If it took a year or two to repair, it would take a year or two to repair . . . I had to be true to this."

Wenner deputized John Burks to stitch together the reportage of eleven different writers into a master story in the style of a *Newsweek* presidential campaign exposé. Even the record critics, like Lester Bangs and Greil Marcus, were conscripted into service. Marcus was tasked with the most difficult assignment of all: interviewing the family of the murder victim, Meredith Hunter. "So I did it," said Marcus. "I knocked on the door. I sat and talked for two hours with his sister. His mother was in the hospital. That was just a complete revelation for me."

Hunter's distraught sister told Marcus that the Stones were "responsible" for her brother's death: "They don't care, they don't care."

Wenner treated the events of Altamont like a personal betrayal. When he discovered that Hunter's family had never even been contacted by the Rolling Stones Organization, he wrote a personal check to the family for $500.

The conclusion of witnesses and local scenesters was that the Stones had hired the Hells Angels as extras in their grand cinematic homage to themselves and their expanding bank accounts. (After learning that the murder was captured on film, Universal Studios bid more than $1 million to release it, *Rolling Stone* later reported.) David Crosby, a staunch defender of the Hells Angels, told *Rolling Stone* he considered the concert "a grotesque ego trip" for the Stones. Burks, in his reporting, channeled the wrath of the Angels: "What an enormous thrill it would be for an Angel to kick Mick Jagger's teeth down his throat."

"Is Mick responsible for the killing?" ran a caption under a photo of Jagger, who was described in the story as a smug dandy in "a red velvet cape and red velvet cap," demanding "the best of hotels, limousines, cuisine."

As his story went to press, Wenner did try getting Jagger to respond, sending a telegram to Maddox Street in London. "There is no attempt to fix blame," he wrote to Jagger. "It was a cosmically preordained celebration for the end of the 60s."

But that was Wennerian obfuscation. Laying the blame *was* the point. With a dozen reporters at his back, notebooks bristling with incendiary quotations from every boldfaced rock name in San Francisco and L.A., Jann Wenner had to know he was baiting the hook for the former chairman of the Trans-oceanic Comic Company when he said, "We certainly don't blame you but your continued silence is making other people uptight and suspicious and I think if you will make a statement in *Rolling Stone* it will go a long way towards straightening matters up and putting people at ease."

Jagger didn't reply. But when the story was finished, it left zero doubt that *Rolling Stone* was "attempting to fix blame." "Altamont," said the story, "was the product of a diabolical egotism, high ineptitude, money manipulation, and, at base, a fundamental lack of concern for humanity."

Wenner had never betrayed his heroes quite like this before. He had slammed a record or two, angered a few record executives, made Eric Clapton faint. But through an alchemical mix of petty business grievance and self-preservation, Jann Wenner nailed Mick Jagger's hide to the wall with vindictive aplomb. For a generation of readers, the story of Altamont was the one printed in *Rolling Stone,* seared into history like a cattle brand held in Jann Wenner's grip.

•

FORTY-FIVE YEARS AFTER ALTAMONT, Mick Jagger was still aggrieved by *Rolling Stone*'s virtual crucifixion.

"The problem with having relationships with people in the press, it's like politicians in a way," he mused. "They name their magazine after you. And they become friends with you. But then when something happens and goes wrong, you feel that they should be more sympathetic. Sympathetic, meaning evenhanded. You don't expect them to take your side against the world, and stick up for you when you're wrong, but you expect to get a fair crack at the whip. And I'd obviously felt at that point that that didn't happen in this case."

For Jagger, the Altamont story was a betrayal by Jann Wenner; for everyone else, it was an inflection point for the youth culture. Afterward, Jerry Rubin, the antiwar radical of the Yippies (Youth International Party), wrote a letter to Ralph Gleason warning that *Rolling Stone* had a choice to make, lest it be lumped in with the capitalist record companies that, in addition to selling records, sold "electronic equipment to help kill Vietnamese kids." "The connection between the company's advertising and the way Jann Wenner feeds his kids and keeps a roof over his head is not just 'incidental'!" he wrote. "*Rolling Stone* magazine has a vested interest in the business of rock music."

He urged *Rolling Stone* to acknowledge that "the trip is over." (Rubin also admitted he was angry that *Rolling Stone* didn't print his writings.)

As the media narrative calcified around the idea of Altamont as the death of the 1960s—with the murder weapon in Mick Jagger's hand— the "visibly shaken" singer told Ralph Gleason, who was reporting on Altamont for *Esquire*, "If Jesus had been there, he would have been crucified."

Rolling Stone continued to chew over the story for months on end. By spring, the Stones' own tour manager, Sam Cutler, his back against the ropes, was pointing the finger at Jagger, his barbed quotation printed big and bold on the inside cover of *Rolling Stone:* "The Stones Have Not Acted Honorably."

On February 25, 1970, Jagger finally responded to Wenner's queries with a civil if curt retort:

DEAR JANN YOU WANT TO ASK ME MANY
QUESTIONS ABOUT ALTAMONT WHICH I WOULD
NORMALLY BE ONLY TOO PLEASED TO ANSWER
AND HAVE INDEED ANSWERED TO MANY OTHER
PEOPLE STOP HOWEVER UNFORTUNATELY
RIGHTLY OR WRONGLY WE NO LONGER TRUST

YOU TO QUOTE US FULLY OR IN CONTEXT STOP
I HOPE OUR FRIENDSHIP CAN FLOURISH AGAIN
SOME DAY.

M

Almost immediately, Wenner began secretly campaigning to repair the relationship. After all, he couldn't very well publish a newspaper called *Rolling Stone* and not have the Rolling Stones in it. There was also the matter of the unresolved trademark issue.

As it happens, the Stones had hired a friend of Wenner's to act as a publicist: Marshall Chess, the son of Leonard Chess, founder of the vaunted Chicago blues label of Muddy Waters and Howlin' Wolf. Chess was record business royalty. Both Ahmet Ertegun and Jerry Wexler of Atlantic Records were at Marshall's bar mitzvah, and his father and uncle, who first recorded Chuck Berry, had invited the Stones to meet the blues legends and record an album at Chess in 1964, inspiring the Stones' instrumental "2120 South Michigan Avenue." In 1968, the Wenners had met Chess on a train trip east as they passed through Chicago (Chess said it was the first time the blues label ever paid for a limousine to pick somebody up). The meeting was something of a patch-up: Chess had pulled advertising from *Rolling Stone* over a bad review of Chess's first record for his father's label, Muddy Waters's notorious psychedelic record, *Electric Mud*. They became fast friends, two "workaholic Jews" with a taste for the high life. The next year, however, Chess's father sold the label and then died suddenly, a disinheritance that left Marshall with nothing but his name. Wenner gave him the number for Arthur Janov, and Chess started primal screaming. For a while, he planned to start his own label, beginning with Wenner's friend Boz Scaggs. Instead, Chess arranged to meet Jagger in London and help launch a new independent label, Rolling Stones Records, which would be distributed by Atlantic. To help Chess gain Jagger's trust, Wenner agreed to publish an obliging item in Random Notes, after which Chess, the president of the Stones' new label, thanked him and promised "the first detailed story about the Rolling Stones' new ventures. Give my love to Janie."

Wenner's reading of Mick Jagger was accurate: He was nothing if not pragmatic. Asked why he trusted Wenner again after the Altamont story, Jagger said, "It's not the trust, or distrust. They have an agenda and you have an agenda. It might not meet." Their agendas, of course, were destined to meet again and again. Jagger was a budding film star and entrepreneur. While *Rolling Stone* flogged him over Altamont, Jagger was dreaming up ideas like selling Rolling Stones albums on magazine newsstands, starting with the soundtrack to Altamont.

The truce finally came in the late summer of 1970 with the arrival of Mick Jagger's film acting debut in *Performance,* in which he played a bisexual former rock star named Turner, his hair slicked back like a mobster. In a memo, John Burks reported to Wenner the "big news" from *Rolling Stone*'s New York bureau: "Mick's extending a token of reconciliation in your direction. Namely, he wants you, of all people, to see *Performance* before anyone else in the Western world."

Wenner promptly put Mick Jagger on the cover of *Rolling Stone* in September 1970, a black-and-white film still from *Performance,* Jagger's lips hand-painted pink by Bob Kingsbury. Wenner's staff was outraged that he bent his knee to the man *Rolling Stone* virtually implicated in a local murder. The rapprochement was especially upsetting because Wenner had canceled plans for an ambitious book on Altamont by John Burks and Greil Marcus (which Burks had hoped to title *Please Allow Me to Introduce Myself* and which was later translated and published as a paperback in Germany). Instead, Wenner was proposing to Marshall Chess that they publish a Rolling Stones lyrics book designed by a talented refugee from British *Rolling Stone,* Jon Goodchild. However hypocritical he appeared, Wenner wasn't interested in further alienating Jagger. It was an astute business decision. Mick Jagger would be the most important and iconic face in *Rolling Stone*'s history, appearing on more *Rolling Stone* covers than any other artist (thirty-one times), always a consistently high seller. Jagger benefited, of course—years of being mythologized and glamorized by the best writers and photographers in the country, with Wenner's personal guarantee of editorial control over his own image in a magazine conveniently named *Rolling Stone.* Marshall Chess, who spent much of the 1970s with the Stones, said Wenner fawned over Jagger like any female groupie he'd ever known. Jagger "knew he had him wrapped around his finger," said Chess, who speculated, as many would, that the two slept together. (Asked about this, Wenner laughed and said, "I neither confirm nor deny.") When Jagger brought up Wenner's name, said Chess, it was always with a dismissive wave of the royal hand: "He'll do whatever I want."

But as Wenner became more successful, it would become less clear who was getting the better of whom, the star or the starfucker, the rocker or his groupie. After a time, Mick Jagger came to feel exploited by Wenner. "They liked each other; they didn't like each other," recalled Diane von Furstenberg, the fashion designer and entrepreneur who befriended both men in the early 1970s. "Mick always thought that Jann took advantage of him."

When the Stones returned to San Francisco in 1972, Jagger and Wenner could share a laugh and some dope and rarely mention the little Altamont debacle. Why make things unpleasant? They could even put off the trademark issue—for now. In the cosseted back rooms of the rock-and-roll business, where ambition and self-interest casually tangled in stoned grins and idle flattery, this sort of thing was simply called being "friends." "They're very similar people," observed Keith Richards. "They're both very guarded creatures. You wonder if there's anything worth guarding."

Bridge over Troubled Water

It's God that's dead, not Paul McCartney.
—Ralph Gleason, November 1969

B y early 1970, Jann Wenner was receiving regular assessments of his karma from a self-described "occultist and nature-mystic" named Ambrose Hollingworth, whom Wenner assigned to write an astrology column for *Rolling Stone* in May 1969. A close friend of his sister Merlyn—and the former manager of Denise Kaufman's group, the Ace of Cups—the wheelchair-bound Hollingworth wrote to Wenner in 1970 to say that his horoscope "shows no danger and a general time to get rich."

That March, Wenner gave a talk at Stanford University, where he explained to students how he became "a successful businessman at the age of twenty-four." After some musings on fortune and luck, Wenner finally chalked it up to the stars:

Astrologically, I'm a Capricorn. So that helps that *Rolling Stone* is a Libra and it's got a grand [trine] in certain aspects. And I think it was just right for the time. It's not that I'm a great businessman because I'm not. I mean, I have learned to be. After doing it for two and a half years and after hassling with all these people, distributors, writers, and whatever, it may be that I have learned to hassle good and I can hassle now with the best of them. So that's helping us now and we can start to clean up.

The "cleanup" included moving the magazine's offices to handsome new digs at 625 Third Street, next to the MJB Coffee Company building near the harbor, rented to him by the wife of a *Rolling Stone* investor named Ed Berkowitz. A four-story elevator ride opened to a large, airy space with exposed-brick walls, wooden beams, and large industrial windows overlooking a parking lot, which included an executive space for Wenner's Porsche. Wenner poured himself into the interior design, picking out the $400 rugs and hiring contractors to build and rebuild partitions to his specs, positioning his private office like a royal chamber at the end of a long hallway. Amid the posters of Jagger and Lennon were a new switchboard telephone system, new Xerox and telex machines, a postage machine, and new IBM Selectric typewriters. Some of the staff were already sighing over the loss of Brannan Street, as if a golden age had passed in two years. An underground newspaper reporter, expecting to see longhairs smoking dope in a shambling hippie den, sniffed that it looked as "icily functional as IBM and moved more by mammon than music."

Certainly the whole thing would require quite a lot more mammon: On top of $15,000 for upgrading and remodeling the offices, *Rolling Stone* had gone from a free space above Garrett Press to $6,000 a month in rent. In a diary-like editorial in late 1969, Wenner explained to readers that *Rolling Stone* had turned a corner. British *Rolling Stone* and *New York Scenes,* which Wenner shuttered within six months, had both failed because Wenner had "leapt before looking," taking his eye off the prize, "the thing it turns out we're best at . . . *Rolling Stone* and rock and roll music." *Rolling Stone* was now "wailing along at a nice little clip," he wrote, while "this country is also wailing along at a nice little clip on the road to destruction."

But while *Rolling Stone* was on the move, the crossroads that Jerry Rubin had warned about were fast approaching. Altamont exploded Wenner's 1960s, leaving jagged fragments and editorial turmoil. The Vietnam War was at a bloody apex, and rock and roll no longer lit the way against the encroaching darkness. The top radio hits of 1970 were the velvety downers "Bridge over Troubled Water" by Simon and Garfunkel and "(They Long to Be) Close to You" by the Carpenters. The Beatles were breaking up, as Wenner seemed to have predicted in his long review of *The White Album* in late 1968 when he said it sounded like a record by four different solo artists (an idea he borrowed from writer David Dalton, who was embedded at Apple Records in London and scoring hashish for George Harrison). As John and Yoko became increasingly messianic, appearing on the cover of *Rolling Stone* with a white dove in February 1970, McCartney was preparing a solo album, complete with liner notes trashing his former writing partner. "John and Yoko in one corner," wrote Wenner in May 1970, "Paul and Linda McCartney in the other." (Wenner compared it to a lovers' breakup.) Increasingly, the music was going inward, dark, and solitary—the moody introspection of Joni Mitchell and Graham Nash in Laurel Canyon, four hundred miles south, and the working-class primitivism of hard rock, Led Zeppelin, and Black Sabbath, which Wenner personally detested.

Wenner attempted to treat the dour climate as a business opportunity. When a student named Stephanie Mills became a cause célèbre for her college graduation speech declaring she would save the earth by not having a baby, Wenner appointed her the editor of a new ecology magazine called *Earth Times* in early 1970, putting a young journalist named Jon Carroll in charge of it. The first issue, which looked and felt like *Rolling Stone,* featured a story on the environmental sins of Standard Oil (featuring a cover illustration of a dying Superman declaring, "Stop the *deadly pollution* or no one on Earth will be *left alive!*"). Ralph Gleason shook his head, calling the newspaper "The Grave Digger's Special." "Every news spread is more gloomy than the one before," he'd say, "like a trip to the funeral parlor."

Inside *Rolling Stone,* the news became even bleaker. Wenner spent $30,000 on an advertising campaign in March 1970 to promote a *Rolling Stone* subscription coupon in ten metro newspapers, hoping to goose readership, just as the U.S. Postal Service went on strike, freezing the mail system and killing the subscription offer dead.

The following month, Wenner received notice from his distributor claiming *Rolling Stone* had sold poorly on the newsstands and Straight

Arrow owed tens of thousands of dollars in unrecouped advances. The distributor had encouraged Wenner to print up 400,000 copies of each issue and paid him advances on a percent of sales. Wenner's cut of the revenue was dreadfully low, only 40 percent of every issue sold, so he had to sell a lot of newspapers to earn back the sizable advance. The bottom line: With the overhead from his brand-new offices, the failed ad campaign, and a large debt to the distributor, Jann Wenner was $200,000 in the hole. "It was a shocking day," Wenner said.

Another shock was on its way. On May 4, 1970, four students at Kent State University were gunned down in a hail of sixty-seven shots by the Ohio National Guard, their young blood running in pools on campus sidewalks. Even after Altamont, it was an event that *Rolling Stone*'s vision of a youth culture built around rock and roll couldn't fully process, and it pushed the struggling magazine toward a reckoning.

•

WENNER'S BELIEFS about the relation between rock and roll and the fires burning in the culture were at the core of *Rolling Stone*'s problems. Ever since he snuck out of the Sheraton-Palace Hotel sit-in of 1964 to avoid a beating by police, his relationship to radical politics had been a cautious one. Advocating for drugs and sex was all well and good, but fomenting revolution, especially when a revolution seemed so real, was quite another. In 1968, the escalating gloom of Vietnam and the assassinations of Martin Luther King Jr. and Bobby Kennedy splintered the left. In the run-up to the Democratic National Convention in Chicago, southern Democrats were in a tense standoff with the antiwar vote, with student factions of the New Left proposing to tear down the whole system before pulling a lever for Democratic nominee Hubert Humphrey, who was promising to send 13,500 more troops overseas.

Abbie Hoffman and Jerry Rubin, the provocateurs of the Yippies, saw rock and roll as a powerful propaganda tool in a bigger struggle. They proposed to counter the Chicago convention with a rock concert called the Festival of Life, which would feature Bob Dylan, the Byrds, the Who, and other artists for "our own revolutionary youth culture," which Hoffman said would "fuck the system." Hoffman and Rubin, former students at Berkeley (or "School for Advanced Toilet Training" as

Rubin called it), were as ambitious and full of unvarnished chutzpah as Jann Wenner; none of the bands they advertised had yet agreed to participate. And whereas Wenner's idea of politics was John Lennon and Yoko Ono staging concerts and bed-ins to the chants of "Give Peace a Chance," Hoffman proposed dropping LSD in the water supply in Chicago and burning draft cards in the streets ("We will burn Chicago to the ground! We will fuck on the beaches!"), which prompted Chicago's mayor, Richard Daley, to prepare a crushing police presence to defend the sanctity of the convention against long-haired radicals.

Wenner was cynical about politics and often oddly tone-deaf. In *Rolling Stone,* he wrote that Martin Luther King Jr.'s death, "shattering though this tragedy was . . . meant little or nothing to the majority of the American people." Wenner made clear just which side he was on after a thwarted antiwar demonstration by the Yippies in Grand Central Station in New York. He attacked Hoffman in *Rolling Stone,* claiming he was exploiting rock and roll for his own power trip. Warning readers to stay away from the Chicago convention, he accused the Yips of "recklessness" and a "thorough lack of moral compunction," comparing Hoffman and Jerry Rubin to another bogus leader he'd known: Chet Helms, of the Council for the Summer of Love, who had promised a hippie revolution in 1967, only to become a "patent joke."

"I thought this was a crock of fucking shit," said Wenner of the Yip Fest. "I did not like Jerry [Rubin] and his ethics. And I knew from talking to musicians no musicians were thinking of going; [Hoffman and Rubin] were just lying to everybody. And, very much against the conventional wisdom—and the cool, hip, party line, very un-PC—I attacked it." (Wenner titled his op-ed "Musicians Reject New Political Exploiters.")

Wenner was right about the rock and rollers. On August 28, when police beat up students and protesters in the streets, the only artists to support the Yippies were folkie Phil Ochs and the MC5, leaders of the Hoffman-approved White Panther Party, whose rallying cry on their Elektra Records debut was, "KICK OUT THE JAMS, MOTHERFUCKER!" Wenner credited *Rolling Stone*—mostly himself—with squelching Hoffman's plans. "This chilled any big festival," Wenner said. "For us and our world, it was taking on a serious political issue and controversy." (Lester Bangs, who savaged MC5's album in *Rolling Stone,* agreed with Wenner, writing in an open letter to their "apologists," "Friends, the MC-5 don't know shit about rock and roll. But compared to their political acumen, their understanding of rock is truly prolific.")

Consequently, Hoffman would call Wenner "the Benedict Arnold of the Sixties," a traitor to the political cause. And he wasn't alone: Hunter Thompson, radicalized by Chicago after witnessing brutal street beatings, would recall with disgust that Wenner told "all *Rolling Stone* readers—all 750 of them—to stay away from Chicago, it's all bullshit."

But if Wenner disapproved of the revolution, he also saw that it made for great copy, and he was willing to shift with the climate. For the trial of the Chicago Seven, in which Hoffman and Rubin faced charges of inciting violence, *Rolling Stone* published an incisive essay by *Ramparts* writer Gene Marine, the newspaper's first truly great piece of journalism, which attempted to correct the press perception that the student protesters were violent—in essence, defending Hoffman and his "co-conspirators." Wenner took out a full-page ad in the *Times* to sell the story, saying, "*Our* reporter says the Chicago defendants were mostly patient, reasonable and quiet . . . the day to day goings on were not really about what happened in Chicago at all. They were about hair, dope, sex, dirty words, that kind of thing. Misbehavior. And that a whole generation could go to jail in the same kind of trial." (In truth, Gene Marine was originally in Chicago on assignment for *Ramparts,* not *Rolling Stone,* but Wenner nonetheless encouraged the public to contribute to their defense fund.)

Wenner made another feint back to the radical left in the spring of 1969, publishing an incendiary cover image of a helmeted police officer with a baton on the bloody head of a protester, with the cover line "American Revolution 1969." Goddard Lieberson, the president of Columbia Records, wrote to Wenner to voice his disapproval of any such revolution, describing it as "moving like an uncontrolled blob in an old-fashioned horror movie with no apparent program, or direction[,] and using, for the most part, the methods of the people they are fighting against." Wenner agreed with him but he was walking a fine line: When the Isla Vista, California, branch of the Bank of America was looted and burned down by antiwar radicals in February 1970, Wenner offered to run an open letter from leftist sympathizers in the *Chronicle* as long as they didn't tell anybody who paid for it (the paper refused to publish it anyway). Greil Marcus said Wenner chastised him for putting his money in the Bank of America. But on May 14, 1970, *Rolling Stone* published an item in Random Notes saying the FBI had come by the offices asking if anyone had seen the exiled Lawrence "Pun" Plamondon, the information officer of the White Panther Party who was on the lam for bombing a CIA office. "If you should see him, get in touch," Wenner's newspaper said, and published a photograph purporting to be the fugitive Plamondon ("Pun is accused of doing something awful").

Before the student killings, Wenner had told *Oz* magazine that "there is yet to be anyone killed at a college demonstration. When it happens we're talking about revolution; now we're not." But now *we were*. And when two black students were gunned down at Jackson State in Mississippi eleven days after Kent State, the moral line was stark: *Rolling Stone* could be a newspaper devoted to the life-and-death concerns of American youth or a newspaper for the Lovin' Spoonful. In June 1970, while Wenner was in New York sweating over his imminent financial collapse, John Burks and the staff of *Rolling Stone* made the decision for him, assembling a very different newspaper from the one they'd been publishing. The cover featured student protesters waving a peace flag, an image taken by first-time freelancer Annie Leibovitz, with a cover line tweaking a notorious Nixon line justifying America's involvement in the war: "On America 1970: A Pitiful Helpless Giant." Inside was "The Rolling Stone Top 40," a timeline of protest news from the revolutionary front (January 15: "A former Army officer reveals that the Army has 1,000 agents working in 300 offices in U.S. just keeping tabs on protestors"). A *Rolling Stone* reporter interviewed protesters who spoke with Richard Nixon one strange night when he walked out of the White House at 4:00 a.m., perceptibly drunk, to try reasoning with the youth activists about Vietnam. On page 28, a two-page poem by Allen Ginsberg, titled "Friday the Thirteenth," enjambed 120 lines of tear-gas-smoking rage. At this point, even the record companies recognized the need to meet the moment, with Jac Holzman at Elektra buying a full-page ad declaring solidarity with the kids, but also steering the conversation back to Jann Wenner's point of view, that "the music of our time is perhaps the only medium through which we can come to recognize and understand these ideas and feelings."

The issue of *Rolling Stone* was a landmark of 1970 and, according to every staffer available to be interviewed, assembled entirely without Jann Wenner. "This all happened with Jann gone," said Greil Marcus. "It had been done without his involvement. And it also was more blatantly political than any *Rolling Stone* issue had been before. And it seemed like it was about to launch the magazine in a completely different direction."

"It was literally a life-and-death matter for our generation," said John Burks, "and if we hadn't moved on it right away, we'd have lost the moment."

Wenner, however, insists that he not only participated in the issue, despite his physical absence, *but had actually conceived it.* "That was all my idea," Wenner told me. "The headline was my headline. I got Ginsberg to write the poem, which was the centerpiece of the whole thing!"

He also said he sent the reporter John Morthland to interview the activists in Washington, "which," he added, "I thought was particularly inspired."

Nobody would remember it this way. John Burks said he tried telephoning Wenner repeatedly while the issue was being assembled and he never found him. Morthland said he never spoke to Wenner about the Washington assignment. In the fog of *Rolling Stone* in June 1970, Jann Wenner was MIA.

•

THE NEXT MONTH, Jann Wenner was being accompanied by a *New York* magazine reporter while he met with advertising executives from Doyle Dane Bernbach, the firm behind the classic "Think Small" Volkswagen ads, which featured the VW Beetle against a stark white background. Wenner was always flipping through *Life* and *Time* magazines looking for "hippie-looking" car ads that might help *Rolling Stone* crack the lucrative Detroit advertising market and "confer status" on his newspaper.

As the reporter scribbled in his notebook, Wenner chewed his nails and pulled on a True cigarette. "What would convince you to take an off-the-wall chance with a little publication like ours?" Wenner asked, urging them to talk to "the guys with long hair up in the media department" of the ad agency.

The skeptical executive replied, "Some of the biggest squares I know have long hair."

The "Pitiful Helpless Giant" issue had only recently been on the stands. Wenner's pitch was rejected. Next, Wenner tried landing himself as a guest on *The Dick Cavett Show,* but he struggled to explain to the show's screener why he was relevant and TV-worthy. "How would you describe the philosophy of *Rolling Stone?*" the woman asked.

After some hesitation, Wenner said, "What we're faced with in this country is the yawning gap between two cultures. There's Old America and there's New America. We're just a publication for the New America."

Sensing skepticism, Wenner suggested she ask him "how it feels to be a member of the establishment. I have an answer all figured out." The woman eyed Wenner's pin-striped suit and said he looked "like one of the elite [*sic*] corps of impudent snobs" (Spiro Agnew's term for the liberal elites). When Wenner said he could talk about "why the underground press is so awful," the screener looked surprised: "You mean, you don't consider yourself part of the underground press?"

Wenner didn't get the booking.

And in truth, the magazine's trajectory had never looked so dire. British *Rolling Stone* was a flop, *New York Scenes* was dead, and Wenner pulled the plug on *Earth Times* after four issues. Critics began to whisper that maybe Wenner had only one good idea, *Rolling Stone.* Nothing haunted Wenner more than this—that he was a guy who got lucky once, a grinning fool who wore velvet suits and fawned over Mick Jagger as he clung to a moment quickly disintegrating like the last traces of a fireworks display. In a photograph for *New York,* Wenner smiled wanly under a drooping mustache, looking afraid and washed out—the spiritual portrait of 1970. "What you've seen today," Wenner told the reporter, "just isn't the real me."

Then he climbed into a limousine and drove away.

If Wenner's involvement in the "Pitiful Helpless Giant" issue was remembered only by Wenner, it was because he was so often doing this: hustling to keep his newspaper alive. While he hustled, he ceded the newspaper's editorial to John Burks, who once published a twelve-page survey of the underground press that clocked in at thirty-one thousand words—not a one that Jann Wenner read. Even when Wenner was in San Francisco, he holed up in his private office at the end of the long hallway that the staff dubbed "the bowling alley" and did God knows what. To his staff of fifty, Wenner seemed like a dervish, arriving late and often too stoned to function. In July 1970, he gave an interview in which he said, "We try to do all kinds of news. Psychic news is as important as hard fact because it's fact, too."

"Jann was like water dropped on a hot, greasy frying pan," said Jerry Hopkins. "He was all over the place."

But the prospect of bankruptcy arrived like a sobering slap. Back in his office, Wenner paced, unkempt and sallow-skinned, tears welling in his eyes, smoking cigarette after cigarette. He wondered if he might extract himself from his predicament by selling *Rolling Stone* to Hugh Hefner at *Playboy,* who had shown some interest. Pennfield Jensen, an assistant editor at the defunct *Earth Times,* later told *West,* the magazine of the *Los Angeles Times,* that Wenner had acted as if he were "omnipotent" until he ran out of money. "Then he was broke, everyone was clamoring for money and saying, 'Jann, you're a dirty rat!' His fantasies collapsed, and he was saying, 'No! It isn't true! I didn't mean this to happen!' "

As in many a fall, hubris had played a large role—along with Wenner's drug-addled management style. In the midst of all this, Wenner had been attempting yet another expansion of his empire, a book publishing company. Wenner realized he had a gold mine in the copyrights from stories in *Rolling Stone,* which he made sure writers signed over to him in their contracts. He envisioned anthologies and underground how-to manuals, secret histories and political diatribes. The Manhattan publisher Random House was already collating stories from the underground press for hardcover titles like *The Age of Rock* and *The Age of Rock 2.* Wenner had started discussing a book division with editor Alan Rinzler, the "house freak" at Macmillan Publishing in New York who wore John Lennon spectacles and his hair in an Afro (a "Jewfro" in later parlance). Rinzler made his name publishing Dee Brown's *Bury My Heart at Wounded Knee.*

In late 1969, Wenner offered him a job as the No. 2 man in the company, with a salary of $28,000, a company car, and 150,000 stock options. Wenner stated plainly that Straight Arrow would go public and they would become millionaires. While getting high one night, they would laugh about their mutual belief in something they called the "cosmic giggle," a stoner koan that so pleased Wenner that he stuck it on the masthead. Rinzler agreed to work with Wenner and move his family west in the summer of 1970, but after he was hired he discovered Wenner had not only hired another man for the same job—Jeffrey Steinberg, a stoner who got rich selling reprints of the 1922 Sears, Roebuck Catalog—but that Straight Arrow was out of money. "I was kind of upset at that, but we dug in," Rinzler said. (Wenner made Steinberg the head of a *Rolling Stone* business office in New York that was started with a $25,000 loan procured by Steinberg.)

Ralph Gleason, who retired from the *Chronicle* in 1970, would remark that the proof that *Rolling Stone* was a great idea was that it survived Wenner's management. Though he tended to look on Wenner with a paternal sigh, he recognized that Wenner was in real trouble. It was Gleason, Wenner said, who pointed him to the record labels; perhaps they could be convinced to help bail Wenner out of his financial woes. Wenner first approached Jac Holzman of Elektra and explained his situation. "I'd say, 'Look, we're down to the wire here,'" recounted Wenner, "'and I need an advance of money, give me some money, I need money in the bank.'"

Wenner had met Holzman at a record conference in Las Vegas in late 1968, after which they'd flown to Aspen to ski and spent an evening listening to *The White Album* while playing highly competitive games of Monopoly ("He'd get pissed off when I beat him," said Wenner). Holzman became a strong financial booster of *Rolling Stone,* and Wenner put his artists, the Doors and the MC5, on the cover. Along with Clive Davis of CBS, who gave *Rolling Stone* more than $30,000 in advance advertising and some free business consultation, Holzman agreed to help Wenner by explaining his situation to Steve Ross, the operator of a successful chain of funeral parlors and parking lots who was rolling up the independent record labels under his corporate umbrella Kinney National Services, Inc. (later renamed Warner Communications). Holzman was about to sell Elektra to Ross for $10 million and, it so happened, Ross owned Independent News, the magazine distributor with which Wenner was having his financial Waterloo. Independent agreed to cut Wenner a check for $100,000 if he signed a seven-year extension that locked in 60 percent of the newsstand revenue. In effect, Ross probably figured he was rolling up *Rolling Stone* along with Elektra, Atlantic Records, and Warner Bros.-Seven Arts. Wenner later said he took the check but carefully avoided signing the contract, believing he was getting away scot-free. "I walked out of there with a hundred grand," Wenner recounted in 1976, "and then Clive and Jac each advanced me something like $25,000 or $35,000 . . . which was both sweet of them and also very smart of them. I mean, shit, supposing they lost $50,000, supposing it didn't work and they lost it, big fucking deal. On the other hand, I'll always be indebted to those two guys." (Wenner said Gil Friesen of A&M weighed in with another $30,000.)

Wenner would say he raised $200,000 in two weeks "without tying ourselves to anybody." But what it looked like in the underground press—and to staffers at *Rolling Stone*—was that Jann Wenner had just sold his newspaper to the record companies while their readers were being shot dead in the streets of America.

•

EARLIER THAT YEAR, an ambitious writer (and ardent opportunist) named Hunter S. Thompson wrote to congratulate Jann Wenner: "Your Altamont coverage comes close to being the best journalism I can remember reading, by anybody." Wenner replied that he was submitting the Altamont piece for a Pulitzer and offered to publish Thompson in *Rolling Stone*.

Thus began a correspondence that would alter the course of *Rolling Stone*'s future, though not for several months to come. Despite rising tensions at Third Street over Wenner's ethical turpitude, the Altamont exposé had given everyone at *Rolling Stone* a shot of ambition. In crucifying Mick Jagger, Wenner had gained a new level of journalistic credibility. The sales sheets for advertisers now said *Rolling Stone* offered the "finest journalism," which "attracts youth at a rate unprecedented by any recent publication."

As the 1960s kept ending, the next installment was the arrest of Charles Manson and four of his followers for the horrific murder of five people, including actress Sharon Tate, wife of Roman Polanski, at a luxury mansion north of Beverly Hills. When Manson's trial began in 1970, Wenner leaped at the story with an idea for the headline: "Charles Manson Is Innocent!"

Wenner's headline was less insane than it sounds to modern ears. Manson was already an object of media obsession, a former Haight-Ashbury denizen who drifted to L.A. and collected hippie acolytes for LSD orgies and quasi-biblical prophecies. While the straight world viewed him as a monster, much of Wenner's audience saw him, at least hypothetically, as one of their own. The underground press of Los Angeles, including the *Free Press,* cast him as the victim of a hippie-hating media. Manson was a rock-and-roll hanger-on. Wenner was convinced of Manson's innocence by his own writer David Dalton, who had lived for a time with Dennis Wilson of the Beach Boys, a Manson believer. "I'd go out driving in the desert with Dennis, and he'd say things to me like 'Charlie's really cosmic, man.'"

Wilson told Dalton that Manson heard coded messages in the Beatles' *White Album,* especially the lyrics of the McCartney vocal "Helter Skelter." Dalton had helped Wenner review *The White Album,* so he knew Manson wasn't the only one confused by it. When Dalton asked an L.A. district attorney why he thought Manson was guilty, the lawyer said, "They're trash, they eat out of dumpsters, they have orgies, they smoke pot."

"Yeah," said Dalton. "That's what everybody I know does."

Wenner paired Dalton with a new hire at *Rolling Stone,* a former *Los Angeles Times* writer named David Felton who was part of the Pulitzer Prize–winning team that covered the Watts riots in 1965. A talented comic mind with a blond nimbus of hair and a brush mustache, Felton was assigned a report on the Summer of Love and produced a three-act play, which the *Los Angeles Times* published. But then he developed a speed habit, grew a long beard, and fell apart. (Colleagues famously dubbed him "the Stonecutter" because he was so slow to finish a story.) Felton was skeptical of Manson, but he and Dalton managed to gain access to the murderer—who had his head shaved and looked like a menacing hillbilly—because Manson thought it would be good for his music career. At the time of the interview, David Dalton was actually living on Manson's ranch.

Meanwhile, a lawyer in the DA's office, believing he was doing a favor for a friend of Felton's at the *Los Angeles Times* and that this hippie rag from San Francisco was a benign nonentity, brought Felton and Dalton into the office to show them the crime scene photos of the butchered bodies of Manson victims—including a man with the word *war* etched in his stomach with a fork. Dalton blanched when he saw the words "Healter [*sic*] Skelter" painted in blood on a refrigerator, instantly recalling what Dennis Wilson told him about the coded instructions Manson heard in the Beatles songs. "It must have been the most horrifying moment of my life," said Dalton. "It was the end of the whole hippie culture."

Jann Wenner changed the headline.

When the time came to write the story, Felton and Dalton were at each other's throats and couldn't agree on who would write it. They fought and wrote nothing until Wenner brought them both into the conference room on Third Street and got them stoned and assigned Felton to write it, with Dalton as the second byline.

Felton turned the Manson story into an elegy for the end of an era—"a disturbing sign of the times." Both Manson and his lawyers and the DA who had shown them the crime photos were infuriated by the story, viewing it as a betrayal. Dalton never forgave Wenner for letting Felton write the story, but Wenner didn't care; along with the Altamont exposé, "Charles Manson: The Incredible Story of the Most Dangerous Man Alive" earned *Rolling Stone* a National Magazine Award for the year 1970.

"*Rolling Stone* ran two reports dumping on the rock-and-roll scene and the counterculture," said Wenner. "Therefore the establishment was saying, 'Hey, give them the award!'"

•

THE 1960S WERE OVER. The 1960s would never end.

If Jann Wenner had only one great idea, it was an idea with stay-ing power: that the 1960s—"the Sixties"—was a mythic time that would be endlessly glorified and fetishized by his generation in records and books, TV shows and films, T-shirts and posters, for years to come, for ever and ever, amen. The 1960s, with all its passion and idealism, was, at its sacred core, a *business*. Mick Jagger understood. So did Jerry Garcia of the Grateful Dead. So did Bill Graham, the thick-browed Holocaust refugee turned rock promoter who was regularly demonized as a "profi-teer" in Wenner's newspaper. Wenner and Graham had fought pitched battles over *Rolling Stone*'s coverage of him, which was almost entirely negative. Wenner said Graham once confessed to him that "he'd collect a ticket at the door, and resell the ticket, so he didn't have to report all his income to the IRS"—a fact that made Bill Graham all too famil-iar to Wenner. When writer Tim Cahill tried talking to Graham for a story on the closing of the Fillmore in 1972, Graham growled, "Let me tell you something about the dishonest, slimy little paper you work for, mister, and that . . . evil . . . slimy little *cunt,* your editor. There are only a few people I'd like to take out to the street and kick the shit out of, so you tell him for me, mister, you tell that clever little creep who makes his living calling honest businessmen capitalist rip-off pigs—"

"We never called you that," replied Cahill.

"Read your magazine, mister."

After the story appeared, Graham threatened to kill Wenner and showed up at Third Street for a five-hour confrontation in which he bellowed and cursed over every line of the story. Wenner tried soothing him by saying he was a fellow capitalist and didn't begrudge him the money.

After Wenner put Mick Jagger on the cover of *Rolling Stone* in Sep-tember 1970, Wenner faced a staff revolt led by John Burks, who had been butting heads with Wenner for over a year. "Every time I left the office, John Burks would get some fucking revolution going on among the editors," said Wenner. "Every time I go away, I get a call from Char-lie Perry or Ben [Fong-Torres] saying, 'You better come back here; there's trouble brewing.'" Among other things, the insurrectionists wanted more oversight of Wenner's editorial decisions and more "independence" for the reviews department. Wenner had long fiddled with the reviews, tweaking them for personal and business reasons. "In the early days, Jann would sometimes put addenda into bylined articles and reviews without requesting permission from the writers," Charlie Perry said in 1971. "I knew nothing about journalism when I came here, but even I thought it was a bit funny at the time."

When Marcus slashed Bob Dylan's *Self Portrait* LP ("What is this shit?"), Wenner was so furious he had a more positive review drawn up and printed in a subsequent issue. Didn't Marcus understand that Clive Davis of Columbia had just forked over thirty grand to save *Rolling Stone* from dissolution? And that Bob Dylan was on Columbia Records? And that Bob Dylan was . . . Bob Dylan? (Dylan himself said no *Rolling Stone* critic "would have any idea of my motives for releasing a record like that, so they really wouldn't have been able to make an honest interpretation of what they were hearing.")

As news of Wenner's record company bailout slowly seeped into the office chatter, cries of conspiracy followed: John Burks said he learned from a business-side staffer at *Rolling Stone* that Wenner had intended for a female folksinger on Columbia, most likely Laura Nyro, to appear on the "Pitiful Helpless Giant" cover, evidence to him that Wenner had promised the cover of *Rolling Stone* to Clive Davis.

This fit into a larger conspiracy bubbling up from the underground. In late 1969, Columbia—whose suited executives were indistinguishable from IBM men—ran an ad campaign called "But the Man Can't Bust Our Music," imploring rock fans to reject the establishment by purchasing records from Columbia, the label of Andy Williams and Mitch Miller. The underground press responded with acid mockery, and Clive Davis responded by pulling advertising from the underground press. Research, he claimed, showed they didn't sell records anyway. But Davis continued to advertise in *Rolling Stone,* which reported the fracas over the ad as a lightly critical news story. *Rolling Stone* had by far the most evenhanded coverage, but Davis still wrote in to complain that the story was "misleading" because it implied retaliation against underground papers. Rumors swirled that the U.S. government had leaned on the record companies to defund the antiwar press. Top executives at CBS, Columbia's parent company, had cooperative ties to the CIA, but nothing was ever proved. In the letters column, Davis said *Rolling Stone* made the cut because it was "good for music . . . wrapped up in it, sensitive to it, involved and concerned about it."

To regain the faith of his staff, Wenner tried creating an editorial board featuring himself, John Burks, Ralph Gleason, and Greil Marcus. They would cooperate and collaborate, a checks and balances system. But the meetings devolved into group bitch sessions about the intransigence of Jann Wenner. "I remember my wife saying at one point, 'How long do you think Jann is going to want to have people meet with him every week to tell him all the things he's doing wrong?'" recalled Marcus. "And I said, 'Hm, now that you've put it that way, I'm not sure how long.' 'Cause that's all we were doing, pretty much."

"The final straw," recalled Wenner, "was I wanted to publish this picture of Dylan, who was getting an honorary degree from Princeton. And they thought, 'Oh no, that's not news.' Well, to me it was fucking news. Bob Dylan, the most important writer of the twentieth century, was a rock star, getting an honorary degree from Princeton. In [1970], this was pretty revolutionary. There was no recognition of rock and roll.

"Our core mission was the purpose of the music," he said. "I didn't like their particular politics, and I wanted to do what I wanted to do, which was about music."

Jann Wenner recognized, correctly, that rock and roll and the counterculture were getting a divorce—rock and roll on one side, revolution on the other. But his draft-age staff was disenchanted with rock music just as Wenner was underlining his commitment to it. Wenner once tried reclaiming his newspaper by calling an all-hands meeting in which he pumped his fists to a Beatles song to reemphasize the mission: *Get back, get back to where you once belonged . . .* Wenner reminded them that *Rolling Stone* was his baby, not an outpost for revolution. And later, he would argue that rock and roll was the true expression of his generation, that the poetry of Bob Dylan eclipsed politics, radical or otherwise. This was Ralph Gleason's point of view as well—poetry over politics. History would tell. But for the moment, Wenner had made up his mind. And by December 1970, all but a dozen employees of *Rolling Stone* either were fired or had left in disgust, starting with John Burks. Said Greil Marcus, "I didn't speak to Jann for five years."

Consequently, a story line gelled in the underground press: Jann Wenner was the man who sold out the revolution for dirty record money. "Kent State and Cambodia have concerned more of us, and in a more vital way, than the latest news on Paul McCartney," Burks said in 1970. "What's going to happen now, I think, is the trivialization of *Rolling Stone*—and that just makes me very sad."

On a brick wall next to the office elevator on Third Street, somebody had scrawled a crude bit of graffito: "Smash 'Hip' Capitalism." Paul Scanlon, who had been reading *Rolling Stone* since a stint in the army in the late 1960s, was thrilled to be hired as an editor in December 1970 but also spooked by the skeleton crew he found when he showed up. "There was nobody," he said. "It was decimated. You could smell it in the air; there was death in the air."

As one ex-staffer said after he left, "It was the only case of a ship jumping a sinking rat." Richard Neville, the editor of *Oz* in London, noted that Wenner "becomes at times so engrossed by the battle of being a Success that the battle of being human is ignored." Looking back, Jann Wenner said he didn't care. "It never bothered me," he said. "I didn't give a fuck. I knew what I was doing, and I knew I was right about it."

Indeed, after the trials of 1970—"Jesus, what a year!" declared Gleason in his December column—Jann Wenner felt liberated. He would regain control of his paper, move out of his isolated back office and out among the editorial ranks, commit himself to becoming a real editor, rebuild the staff of *Rolling Stone,* and forge ahead. "He went through this depressed period where he seemed almost a little brother to me," said Rinzler, a man who would one day come to despise Wenner, "but he very quickly recovered and became like a master of the universe. He took on the power of authority, he embraced it with zeal, and self-reinvention. He buried a lot of problems, like being gay."

Wenner rightfully pointed out that his former staffers didn't go off to start revolutionary publications after *Rolling Stone.* In fact, Burks joined the disaffected Baron Wolman in a hippie fashion magazine called *Rags,* which published unflattering gossip about Wenner before folding after a few issues. The leftover *Rolling Stone* staffers expressed fatalism about the upheaval. "Well, Jann was building a *corporation*," a staff writer told *The Village Voice*. "Love it or leave it, right?"

"A lot of people say he's an asshole and blah, blah, blah," said Wenner's secretary, Gretchen Horton. "But that's not as important as the paper itself, which is strong enough now to take on any kind of a disaster."

Wenner had, in fact, cast off the youth revolution, such as it was. But it wasn't exactly a betrayal, because he had never subscribed to its political tenets in the first place. And he'd survived; to Wenner, that was what mattered. As Pete Townshend observed, "It was clear to me that Jann, like myself, was growing up in a world surrounded by people who were often out of their minds on drugs, and equally out of their minds on conspiracy theories and rhetoric. All we had to do was enjoy the company and carefully steer the journey, and we might survive; standing on a pile of corpses perhaps, but having survived."

By the end of 1970, Wenner had all the ingredients for a new era of *Rolling Stone:* the financial backing of the American record industry; two reel-to-reel tapes of John Lennon spilling his guts about the Beatles; two budding superstars in photographer Annie Leibovitz and writer Hunter S. Thompson; a new book publishing division called Straight Arrow Books, which would launch with *The Connoisseur's Handbook of Marijuana;* and last—and far from least—a new investor on the hook, Max Palevsky, chairman of the Xerox Corporation, a multimillionaire prepared to dump hundreds of thousands of dollars into *Rolling Stone* in 1971.

Wenner embraced the image of himself as a sellout and a generational traitor. He published in-jokes in *Rolling Stone* that eagled-eyed readers would understand: In the year-end roundup called "It Happened in 1970," he included a list of the names of exiled staffers ("Free All Editorial Prisoners," he declared, listing Burks and Marcus) and mocked rumors of *Rolling Stone*'s corruption with a quiz called "Conspiracy Theory of the Year":

Rolling Stone is really owned by (pick two) (a) Playboy (b) Kinney (c) Xerox (d) the Mafia.

To live to print another day—*that* proved you were right, not some phony revolution. Abbie Hoffman couldn't keep a newspaper running if his life depended on it! And rock and roll was here to stay. And now Jann Wenner—friend of Mick Jagger's, pal of John Lennon's—could drive his Porsche up through the lush and winding hills of Ord Court in San Francisco, fling open the door, pour himself a glass of scotch, turn on the KLH Model 20 high-fidelity stereo, lay the needle on a complimentary slab of *Let It Bleed,* and declare victory. A street-fighting man indeed.

Except there was a little wrinkle—an unsettling quiet in the house. Wenner's two pet doves, Christmas presents from Gil Friesen of A&M Records, rustled nervously in their cage. As Janis Joplin was turning heroin blue in a cheap motel and Jimi Hendrix was choking to death in a final haze, Wenner's wife, Jane, half owner of *Rolling Stone,* had left him for another man.

BOOK II

The 1970s

8

Temptation Eyes

Nineteen seventy was a hinge year in the history of *Rolling Stone,* the precarious leap from the revolutionary 1960s to the commercialized 1970s. After Altamont and Kent State, the rock-and-roll industry that powered *Rolling Stone* had begun decoupling from the counterculture. And once again, it was John Lennon who was going to help Jann Wenner make the transition.

The timing of the Wenners' relationship with Lennon had been fortuitous from the start. Lennon met Yoko Ono during an art exhibition at Indica Books and Gallery in London precisely one year, to the week, before *Rolling Stone* published its first issue. The emergence of a credible and well-read American rock-and-roll newspaper (highly coveted copies of which were already being passed around in London by early 1968) tracked precisely with the erosion of the Beatles. Lennon wanted to wrest control of his media image from the tyranny of the mop-top machine, and he saw *Rolling Stone* as an opportunity; indeed, in his legendary petulance, Lennon felt *Rolling Stone* owed him something. He was rankled, said Ono, that Wenner had evidently named his magazine after the rival Rolling Stones. "*Rolling Stone* decided that they were going to call the magazine *Rolling Stone* because of their respect for Mick Jagger, which didn't make John happy," said Ono. "Because of that, John wanted to get something."

It wasn't exactly true—the Bob Dylan song was the actual inspiration—but Wenner was only too happy to serve. "We were a full forum for John and Yoko," he said. "Anything they said, we printed."

It began when Capitol Records rejected John and Yoko's infamous *Two Virgins* album cover of the couple naked and holding hands against a white background. Encouraged by Ralph Gleason, Wenner sent a telegram to Derek Taylor, the Beatles' press secretary in London, asking to publish it for the one-year anniversary of *Rolling Stone*. Wenner led Lennon to believe it would save his newspaper from financial ruin, and Lennon liked being the savior. Wenner underscored their likeness to Adam and Eve with a quotation from the Bible: "And they were both naked, the man and his wife, and they were not ashamed."

"That was the start of our relationship," Wenner said, "and having done that, we burnished our trust. They loved it. They loved publicity and media."

The impact on *Rolling Stone*'s fortunes was immediate: The "Two Virgins" cover made national news and doubled Wenner's sales. "This was our first experience with controversy," Wenner said. "We sold out and we reprinted the issue for another, like, twenty thousand copies."

"The point of this," Wenner wrote in his next editorial, "is, print a famous foreskin and the world will beat a path to your door."

For Wenner, controversy was the point of any story. And Lennon got the intended results, too: The other Beatles were pissed off by the "Two Virgins" cover, which put the band on notice that Lennon was carving out a new path with his girlfriend. "George [Harrison] was going, 'What is this thing?'" recalled Ono. "Paul was very forward. He said, 'Don't do this!' . . . And John loved it."

Before long, Wenner was invited to Lennon's British country estate in Ascot, though Lennon was too paranoid to come downstairs and meet him. Ono assured him over a cup of tea that Lennon would meet him someday. Jonathan Cott, *Rolling Stone*'s London correspondent, befriended Ono and mailed Wenner the latest doodles and poetry from the couple, plus regular reports on their activities. Ono appeared to be managing Lennon's affairs, filing regular demands of Wenner. In January 1969, she offered *Rolling Stone* a calendar she had created—for a fee, and leaving her the rights to sell it in Europe and Japan. "She wants to know *soon,* and what you'd be willing to pay her for it," wrote Cott.

"Yoko certainly seems to be anxious to make as much money and publicity as possible in the current situation," Wenner replied.

And so was Wenner. Throughout the early years of *Rolling Stone,* he was happy to run Lennon's unedited missives on macrobiotics and rock festival controversies, and he worked hand in glove with Derek Taylor to make Apple Records a de facto bureau for *Rolling Stone,* publishing the PR man's own essay about the Beatles, who in turn gave *Rolling Stone* intimate previews of Beatles albums and supplied Wenner with advertising dollars. (Later, a *Rolling Stone* editor learned that Beatles manager Allen Klein had "laundered and pre-digested" much of what Lennon sent to Wenner's paper, editing him for libel.) *Rolling Stone* would become a convenient partner for John and Yoko to create their own narrative—and a formula for Wenner's success.

While all this was happening, Paul McCartney and his wife, Linda, kept their distance from Wenner, who McCartney always contended was inspired to create *Rolling Stone* after coming to London in 1966 and seeing *The International Times,* the underground broadsheet based in the Indica bookshop that McCartney helped finance. "My feeling is that Jann came over then, saw this, and one thing or another, thought, 'Great, gotta do the American version,'" said McCartney. "I've said this to him, and he doesn't admit it."

Consequently, he gave Wenner only a perfunctory interview in 1970, a preview of a pre-written press release he was putting inside promotional copies of his first solo album—a Q&A with barbed attacks on Lennon. Wenner was obsessed with this feud. When critic Langdon Winner turned in a review of McCartney's solo record, Wenner argued that it should be rewritten to elucidate the coded attacks on Lennon. "This album is a political statement," he argued, according to Greil Marcus. "This album is a weapon. This album is part of a feud. All of this has to be taken into account."

The revised review declared McCartney's genial songs of family contentment fraudulent, his PR attacks on Lennon "tawdry propaganda," and his music "distinctly second rate" compared with the Beatles'. (Given that Wenner was so close to Lennon at the time, Marcus said, "maybe John is the shadow editor here, and Langdon and I are not aware of that. Nevertheless, that's not how it felt.")

After the bloodletting of 1970, Wenner needed a major victory, an editorial coup to reclaim the high ground for *Rolling Stone*. The exclusive John Lennon interview offered one. Photographer Annie Leibovitz, who had begun freelancing a few months earlier, saw a chance for her own coup and appealed to Wenner's newfound interest in pinching pennies by offering to fly to New York on student plane fare and sleep on couches—if she could photograph John Lennon for the cover. "I knew it was really important to him," said Leibovitz. "I knew he was nervous. I knew he was really nervous."

Wenner agreed, as long as he could own the negatives.

The John Lennon interview took place at the midtown Manhattan law offices of Allen Klein. McCartney had broken with Klein (for whom he wrote the couplet "You never give me your money / You only give me your funny paper") and was suing his bandmates to get out of the contract Klein hammered out with Lennon. Wenner had previously suggested in a letter that Lennon fire Klein for malpractice: "Your Libra balance can't make up your mind and [you] place trust in untrustworthy people." Gruff and controlling, Klein insisted on making his own recording for insurance as Yoko sat by Lennon's side. At the start of the recording, you hear Lennon tell Wenner, "Don't be shy," to which Wenner lobs tentative, simplistic questions ("How would you rate yourself as a guitarist?"). From there, Wenner got more than he ever imagined back in the movie theater in San Francisco, when they all wept watching *Let It Be*. Lennon raced past him, unloading personal demons, revising Beatles history, settling scores, trashing the Beatles as "nothing" and Paul McCartney's first solo album as "rubbish." Being in the Beatles, he told Wenner, "was awful, it was fuckin' humiliation. One has to completely humiliate oneself to be what the Beatles were, and that's what I resent."

This was Lennon's way of divorcing himself from the Beatles while working through the emotions that primal screaming had unearthed and defending Yoko Ono against his bandmates. The other Beatles "despised her," he said, and Capitol Records had dismissed Lennon's work with Yoko because "they thought that I was just an idiot pissing about with a Japanese broad."

"Why should she take that kind of shit from those people?" he told

Wenner. "They were writing about her looking miserable in the *Let It Be* film, but you sit through 60 sessions with the most bigheaded, uptight people on earth and see what it's fuckin' like, and be insulted."

And now he was in a face-off with McCartney and determined to win. When Wenner asked why he hired Allen Klein against McCartney's wishes, Lennon said, "That's what leaders do . . .

"Maneuvering is what it is, let's not be coy about it," he went on. "It is a deliberate and thought-out maneuver of how to get a situation the way we want it. That's how life's about, isn't it, is it not?"

Sitting by his side, Ono offered corrections and amplifications. When Lennon proclaimed *Sgt. Pepper's* the "peak" of the Beatles output, Ono chimed in:

YOKO: But this new album of John's is the real peak, that's higher than any other thing he has done.
JOHN: Thank you, dear.
WENNER: Do you think it is?
JOHN: Yeah, sure. I think it's "Sergeant Lennon."

Being in the Beatles, Ono added, "was like cutting [Lennon] down to a smaller size than he is."

Emboldened by Lennon's honesty, Wenner inquired about Lennon's holiday trip to Barcelona with Beatles manager Brian Epstein in 1963, the site of a rumored gay liaison. Grappling with his own sexuality, Wenner had more than a passing interest in the story. "We didn't have an affair though," Lennon told him. "If somebody is going to manage me, I want to know them inside out. He told me he was a fag."

That week, Leibovitz was scheduled to photograph Lennon at a West Side studio where John and Yoko were making an art film called *Up Your Legs Forever*. The couple sat in directors' chairs with a 16-millimeter camera and filmed 331 nude friends and associates from the waist down. "We wanted to show we have peaceful legs," Yoko told *Rolling Stone*. "And legs are peaceful." One by one, their pale, hairy bodies stood like artist's models on a platform while the couple chatted amiably with them, camera rolling. Jann Wenner showed up in the afternoon with Tom Wolfe, who was outfitted in his white fedora, three-piece suit, and spats. "Tom," recalled Wenner, "wasn't going to do this at all."

Wenner wanted to participate—these were his people, after all—but he had his limits. Among Leibovitz's photos from that day is the image of Jann Wenner smiling in his blue oxford shirt, pale legs exposed, but still wearing his white briefs. "No matter if I published them naked," Wenner said of John and Yoko. "I'm not taking my pants off."

•

THE "LENNON REMEMBERS" INTERVIEW buoyed *Rolling Stone*'s national presence like nothing before it. Archconservative William F. Buckley devoted a newspaper column to it, dubbing the interview "How I Wrecked My Own Life, and Can Help Wreck Yours," describing *Rolling Stone* as "endless copy about other rock groups, classified advertising for abortion seekers, and home-growing advice for marijuana users, plus a great deal that is inscrutable except to high-honor students in the sub-culture."

In the printed interview, Wenner left in evidence of his own relationship with Lennon, including his advice to Lennon not to buy a billboard in Los Angeles declaring his commitment to Arthur Janov. "You were right to tell me to forget the advert," Lennon said, "and that is why I don't even want to talk about it too much." (As it happened, Wenner was about to publish a profile of Janov that ripped him as a charlatan.)

Wenner was delighted by his coup and his new friendship. But characteristically, he didn't stop there, and it cost him dearly.

Before the Lennon interview was published, Wenner told Alan Rinzler that "Lennon Remembers" might make a great book and that Rinzler should "put it up for bids" once the interview was published. But there was one little problem: John Lennon had specifically said he didn't want the interview published anywhere but *Rolling Stone*. In fact, Lennon told Wenner that he *owned* the interview. And Wenner had agreed. Rinzler waved away the promise, unmoved by Wenner's handshake deal. He told Wenner that the book was a surefire moneymaker for the 1971 holiday season, mentioning a publisher that would offer big money for the book rights.

John Lennon had every expectation that Wenner would submit to his demands. That had always been the deal: When Lennon said jump, Wenner said how many column inches. Wenner allowed Lennon to read and edit the transcript of the interview before it was published in *Rolling Stone*. And Lennon rewarded his superfan with goodies, like a cache of original ink drawings, which included a sketch of Yoko Ono with her legs spread and came in a white vinyl carrying case. But when Wenner tested the bounds of the partnership by forwarding Rinzler's letter about a publishing advance, Lennon chided him for "jumpin' da gun." "I don't think you should have approached publishers," he wrote to him.

But Wenner kept pressing. In April 1971, he flew to England and drove to Lennon's estate in Ascot to try developing the book idea with Lennon. But when he arrived, the couple had flown to Spain, evading him. Lennon quickly made clear that he wouldn't do the book, writing on the stationery of a Spanish hotel that he was "not interested at all really, so that's that." For Lennon, the damage was done. "At the time it was a big triumph and he was happy he did it," said Wenner, "but then he expressed his regrets by not wanting to see it circulate further."

Wenner's interests, however, now diverged from his idol's. He went ahead and published *Lennon Remembers* in the fall of 1971, collecting $40,000 from a publisher. The interview, he reasoned to Lennon's angry lawyer, was "a traditional journalistic property," and *Rolling Stone* was a journalistic enterprise—so that's that.

Lennon was apoplectic. "By then, we felt that Jann was our ally, and we could trust him, so John had a big surprise," said Yoko Ono. "There was a phone call from Jann to our hotel room. He said something like 'We're putting out this book, and I'm gonna send you six copies.' So John just hung up on him. He was furious." (Wenner sent Lennon a copy inscribed, "Without you, this book could never have been done.")

In a letter to Lennon, Wenner described a phone exchange of "some fairly harsh words and bad thoughts of each other," which Wenner said were "probably an inevitable result of the various karma that went with the interview."

Hoping to smooth things out, Wenner invited Lennon to a "quiet dinner at my house" with Ralph Gleason and Jerry Garcia of the Grateful Dead. To which Lennon responded with a scorching letter to the editor in late November 1971:

As your company was failing (again), and as a special favor (Two Virgins was first), I gave you an interview, which was to run one time only, with all rights belonging to me. You saw fit to publish a book of my work, without my consent—in fact, against my wishes, having told you many times on the phone, and in writing, that I did not want a book, an album or anything else made from it.

Wenner sent Lennon a telegram asking if they could discuss the matter further. "Print the letter," replied Lennon, "then we'll talk." Wenner never printed the letter, and Jann Wenner and John Lennon never saw each other again. "I remember just feeling sick to the stomach," Wenner said. "Kind of feeling, 'You've betrayed him.' You feel guilty. Someone you cherish, enormously, and revere, tells you you're an asshole. I felt terrible about it for months."

"That was one of the biggest mistakes I made," Wenner said. "I chose the money over the friendship."

The friendship, of course, *was* money: Apple Records pulled all of its advertising from *Rolling Stone*. And soon after, John Lennon agreed to help support a new magazine called *SunDance,* founded by two politically radical journalists in San Francisco, in hopes of driving Jann Wenner out of business. But by the time *Lennon Remembers* (or "Lennon Regrets," as Lennon called it thereafter) appeared in print, published by Wenner's new Straight Arrow Books, Jann Wenner no longer needed John Lennon.

·

CIGARETTE SMOKE SNAKED around the stranger's mirrored sunglasses. The editor of *Rolling Stone* could see himself in twinned reflection: shaggy hair, drooping mustache, bewildered look in his eyes.

Hunter Thompson cracked a thin-lipped smile.

It was a Saturday afternoon in July 1970, and two things were eating at Jann Wenner: money woes and a growing staff revolt. But if Thompson needed Wenner's undivided attention, here was a way to get it: ambling into the offices of *Rolling Stone* wearing a red Bermuda shirt and knee-high athletic socks, a pair of shades locked on his nose and a

wig cocked unevenly on his head. He mumble-grumbled like a character actor from a Bogart movie, an FDR cigarette holder clenched in his
jaw as he pulled one strange artifact after another from a leather satchel
under his arm: flashlights, whiskey, corkscrews, flares. He drank from
a six-pack of Coors, aluminum can still in the plastic ring.

Beneath the wig, Thompson's skull was freshly shaven, a campaign
stunt for his race for county sheriff in Aspen, Colorado, on the so-called
Freak Power ticket, a political party he and his drinking buddies cooked
up in a watering hole called the Jerome. Thompson told the strange tale
of his friend Joe Edwards, a member of something called the Woody
Creek Rod and Gun Club, who had very nearly won the Aspen mayoral
race on behalf of the Freaks, made up of local ski bums and bohemians,
including Thompson's gun-toting lawyer John Clancy. Thompson's rap
was in a lingo neither Wenner nor his accompanying editor, John Lombardi, could quite understand: "Fun Hogs." "Greed Heads." "Fat City."
"Pigfuckers." "He was inventing vocabulary," recalled Lombardi in an
interview with Peter Whitmer in 1990. "You could see the seeds of the
writing style."

Asked years later of his impression of Wenner in that first meeting,
Thompson snickered and said, "A troll of some kind." Wenner wasn't
instantly convinced either. As Thompson ranted on about his Freak
campaign, Wenner sank lower and lower in his oversized rattan-backed
chair until his nose was nearly below his desk. When Thompson got up
to go to the bathroom, Wenner shook his head: "I know I'm supposed
to be the youth representative in the culture, but what the fuck is *that*?"

"Jann was somewhat taken aback," Thompson would recall.

Thompson's performance went on for three hours until Wenner,
exhausted, said he had to go home. Only later would he understand that
he was a mark, Thompson conning him with what Thompson himself
called his "flagrantly cranked-up act." "He knows full well what the
effect is," said Wenner.

It was odd that Thompson and Wenner hadn't met. Thompson had
lived a parallel life in San Francisco, showing up in 1964 to work as a
freelance newspaper correspondent, befriending Ralph Gleason, gob-
bling LSD, falling for the Jefferson Airplane, and motoring around Big

Sur with the Hells Angels. Thompson would claim in a letter that he saw the Jefferson Airplane at the Matrix in September 1965 and called Gleason the next day to urge him to go hear them—which, if true, means Thompson set off the domino effect that led to the Jefferson Airplane getting a $25,000 record deal with RCA and thus the entire San Francisco rock-and-roll boom. It was true that Thompson arranged for the Hells Angels to motor into Ken Kesey's ranch in August 1965, catalyzing the official if uneasy merger of the acidheads and biker hoods, with Hells Angels tripping on LSD as Bob Dylan sang "Mr. Tambourine Man" from speakers wired into the trees. Allen Ginsberg celebrated the affair with a poem, and Thompson offered tape recordings of his fireside chats with the Angels to Tom Wolfe for use in *The Electric Kool-Aid Acid Test*.

But Thompson, at thirty-three, was as unlike the twenty-four-year-old Wenner as a man could get—a tall and athletic southern squire from Louisville, Kentucky, a high school petty criminal and charming rogue with a razor intellect and a penchant for drink and provocative confrontation. In letters to friends and editors, he developed the art of the mock-insulting friendship—"You worthless, acid-sucking piece of illiterate shit!"—and had the kind of thorny ambition you read about in books, particularly those of Norman Mailer and Jack Kerouac, macho hero-writers he admired and emulated. By 1970, he'd already worked as a sportswriter in Puerto Rico, befriending novelist William Kennedy while attempting to tap out a Great American Novel of his own (what would eventually become *The Rum Diary*). While working at *The Sunday Ramparts,* Wenner came across Thompson's first book of journalism, *Hell's Angels: The Strange and Terrible Saga of the Outlaw Motorcycle Gangs* from 1966, which chronicled Thompson's yearlong travels with the biker gang as they raped and pillaged Northern California, terrorizing, most of all, the straight press, who imagined them as roving homosexuals and rapists, "brawling Satyrs, ready to make congress with any living thing." Thompson emerged as a self-styled antihero journalist willing to get the true story of the Angels' mores and codes (including gang rapes), rewarded for his efforts with a beating by one of the bikers before making a narrow escape in his car while "spitting blood on the dashboard." Reviewing the book in 1968, *Rolling Stone* said the story was well executed, if sensationalist, "straight out of the men's magazines whose covers invariably picture sex-starved S.S. officers preparing to defile American beauties in various stages of undress."

Wenner initially tried assigning Thompson an obituary for a Hells Angel who had helped Thompson escape his thumping, but he was more taken with the "Freak Power" story, with its platform of converting the former mining town of Aspen into an idyllic grassland for hippie bacchanals, including plans to legalize marijuana, put dishonest drug dealers in stockades, and rename it "Fat City" to ward off developers. Thompson, their belligerent mascot, put an image into Wenner's mind: If his Freaks could win both the sheriff's race *and* the county commissioner contests in 1970, they could seize real power, and wouldn't *that* be a gas. "My sheriff's gig is just a small part of the overall plot," wrote Thompson, "which amounts to a sort of Freak Power takeover bid."

A plot. A takeover. It was a revolution Wenner could get behind, what with its faint echoes of his class takeover at Chadwick in 1963. He even upped the ante, telling Thompson "your story in R.S. should be part of the larger effort to get everyone to register for 1972." Indeed, that summer Senator Ted Kennedy of Massachusetts was pushing through an amendment to lower the voting age to eighteen from twenty-one (ratified by Richard Nixon in 1971), making the youth vote consequential as never before, an opening for *Rolling Stone,* the bible of the rock-and-roll young, at a time when Wenner was being lambasted as a turncoat and capitalist sympathizer. Thompson, of course, had got religion after Chicago 1968. While Wenner warned people away from the Democratic convention, Thompson bore witness. "I saw people beaten so badly in the street that I couldn't talk about it for two weeks without breaking into tears," he said. "I was very, very shaken. If that's what the fuckers want, if that's how they want to play politics, then we'll give them politics."

Thompson's first story for *Rolling Stone* was "The Battle of Aspen," a solipsistic essay on the 1969 mayoral race of proto–Freak Power candidate Joe Edwards, who employed Thompson as his campaign manager and lost by a mere six votes, prompting Thompson to run for sheriff against an incumbent Republican. That story would arrive long past deadline, however, because Thompson had another assignment covering the Kentucky Derby for Warren Hinckle's new magazine, *Scanlan's Monthly,* the unofficial continuation of *Ramparts.* On Hinckle's dime, Thompson was trying out an entirely new style of writing, a delirious, quasi-fictional hallucination starring Hunter S. Thompson and Welsh illustrator Ralph Steadman, whose ghoulish ink-splatter grotesques were unlike anything in American magazines at the time. Instead of polite reportage on a hallowed sporting event, Thompson and Steadman would down bourbon at the club and paint the whole Grand Guignol from bar stools. The coup de grâce in "The Kentucky Derby Is Decadent and Depraved" is reporter Hunter Thompson seeing himself in the mirror the day after the race:

> For a confused instant I thought that Ralph had brought somebody with him—a model for that one special face we'd been looking for. There he was, by God—a puffy, drink-ravaged, disease-ridden caricature . . . like an awful cartoon version of an old snapshot in some once-proud mother's family photo album. It was the face we'd been looking for—and it was, of course, my own. Horrible, horrible . . .

According to Wenner, Thompson simply filed a bunch of loose-leaf notes to *Scanlan's* that Warren Hinckle stitched together into a coherent story. "He didn't actually get Hunter to write the piece," he said. Nonetheless, it was a major epiphany for Thompson, who likened the feeling of freedom he experienced to "falling down an elevator shaft and landing in a pool of mermaids." Thompson was so pleased with what he'd done with Steadman that there was talk of a Thompson-Steadman report, an entire publication that would attack the country's institutions and "shit on everything" with this new method, which a friend of Thompson's dubbed "gonzo," a nonsensical word that Thompson used because he liked how it sounded. They would take on Mardi Gras, the Masters golf tournament, the Super Bowl, and New Year's Eve in Times Square and package the stories under the theme of the American Dream. But Thompson's run with Hinckle ended as soon as it began. When Thompson learned that *Scanlan's* was going out of business, he and Steadman decided to turn a report on the America's Cup in Newport, Rhode Island, into a kind of Hail Mary stunt, eating psilocybin mushrooms and floating a boat alongside a sailing yacht to try spray painting "Fuck the Pope" on the bow. They were discovered and chased out of town. The story—if it was even true—was never published.

The crashing of *Scanlan's* meant that Wenner had a clear path to Thompson, complete with the Thompson-Steadman concept. Wenner leaped at the opportunity: In August 1970, he and Jane, gunning to recruit Thompson, came driving up the dirt path to Thompson's cabin in Woody Creek, Colorado, both tweaking on speed after driving seventeen hours straight from 38 Ord Court. "We were trying to take a rest in the car," said Jane. "I said, thank God for drugs."

Thompson and his wife gave the Wenners the grand tour—the Hotel Jerome and his gun collection and menacing Doberman pinschers— and for a week Wenner and Thompson, lubricated with dope and acid, plotted their future together. (The first idea was to send Thompson to Vietnam.) Thompson had a bottomless need for attention, and who better than Jann Wenner to provide it, what with his upward-looking thousand-watt grin and wide-screen ambitions? Together, they were an amusing sight, the ambling beanpole with cigarette holder akimbo and the squat pole climber Jann Wenner. "They looked like Laurel and Hardy," said Ralph Steadman. "'Another fine mess, Jann. Fuck you, Jann.' He treated everybody like that a bit."

Thompson, of course, painted the whole affair as a Faustian bargain, but one in which Mephistopheles—Jann Wenner—would ultimately lose. He made a "solemn promise to sell his soul to *Rolling Stone* and then with a twinkle in his eye buy it back," Steadman recalled later. "'Fuck them, Ralph! Even the devil has to pay!! I have tapped into a rich, greedy vein, and I will milk it like a terminal heroin addict.'"

But while Thompson was using Wenner, he acknowledged the excellence of the instrument. Thompson saw Wenner's ambition as the perfect analogue of his own. "What a fuckin' editor," he told Steadman. "He's crazy, but he's got a dream. He wants to be a big editor, like . . . Hugh Hefner." Indeed, this was a rare and "cosmically preordained" marriage: Thompson needed ample attention and freedom, Wenner a new blueprint for *Rolling Stone*. "I wasn't consciously looking for Hunter to be the next big thing," said Wenner. "We sparked as we saw each other as kindred spirits."

Thompson and Wenner were both cynics—different species, same genus. They were both children of the 1960s who didn't fully believe in revolution, both of them voyeurs, hedonists, and gleeful substance abusers. And they were both users of other people, which bound them in balanced symbiosis, each certain he was getting the better of the other.

Hinckle would remain embittered toward Wenner for years to come. "He inherited Hunter, and he fell into it very luckily," said Hinckle, "because the *Stone* was a piece of shit. It was just there to sell records." ("I think part of what led to Hinckle's bitterness toward me was that Hunter became mine," said Wenner. "I got all the glory.")

The reinvention of *Rolling Stone* around Hunter Thompson would be nearly as important as the invention of the newspaper itself. Had Thompson never come along, *Rolling Stone* might have survived as a rock-and-roll trade paper, but instead it was about to become the most adventurous and ambitious newspaper-cum-magazine of the 1970s, Thompson imbuing Rick Griffin's Summer of Love logo with a new sensibility. For the next several years, Wenner's identity would be wrapped up in the image he saw in Thompson's warped aviators—the sunglasses that Thompson would call, in the most famous piece of writing he would ever publish in *Rolling Stone,* "Sandy Bull's Saigon-mirror shades."

•

WHILE *ROLLING STONE* WAS expanding and collapsing (and expanding again) in 1970, Jann left Jane Wenner home at 38 Ord Court to entertain herself in any way she could. David Felton remembered driving around with the Wenners in late 1970: "He's talking about stuff with me and says to Janie, 'What did you do today?' And then he's talking to me some more, and then he goes to Janie, 'So, what did you do today?' Like he hadn't even heard her. I thought, 'Oh, this is not good.'"

While Jann ping-ponged, Jane suffered bouts of pronounced ennui, popping downers and surrounding herself with stray animals and stray men. "She was always kind of attracted to these poor souls," said Laurel Gonsalves, who started at *Rolling Stone* in 1969. "Damaged people."

Few fit the bill as well as Sandy Bull, an experimental folk guitar player who showed up in San Francisco in 1963 and proceeded to develop a $1,000-a-week heroin habit. Bull was already a cult figure back in the Boston folk scene for his ability to play Bach on a banjo and for a Middle Eastern–tinged guitar style (the same snake-eyed pluckings that sent Jann Wenner into the closet during his first acid trip). Bull's addiction was legend. While at *The Sunday Ramparts*, Wenner had described seeing him in New York, wandering the stage in a daze. "Bright lights," Bull said, "make you forget where you are."

In 1969, Bull was arrested for attempting to rob a pharmacy and sent to Mendocino State Hospital to clean up. When he was discharged, he returned to San Francisco and met the Wenners. Both of them were instantly smitten. "He would walk into a room, and the girls would just go wet between the ears," said Bob Neuwirth, Bob Dylan's right-hand man on his 1966 tour and Bull's best friend at the time. Bull had the easy manner of a Manhattan blue blood, which, it so happened, he was. As the Wenners discovered, Bull was the heir to a banking fortune left by his great-grandfather, who helped found a bank that was merged into Chase Manhattan. Bull's father had been the editor of *Town & Country* magazine, and his mother, Daphne van Beuren Bayne, was an eccentric jazz harp player, twice divorced, who still held regular salons in her apartment on East Sixty-First Street starring a revolving cast of luminaries like Vincent Price, James Thurber, Jim Hall, and Charles Mingus. She collected animals, including a pet armadillo and a parrot that could whistle a perfect triad. "She had all these birds flying around the house," recalled Jane Wenner. "I think [Bull] became a junkie because his father used to collect butterflies and he became obsessed with needles."

In April 1970, Wenner assigned a story on Bull to writer Ben Fong-Torres, who described him as a "tanned, lanky figure who hides his almost Oriental eyes behind a pair of tinted rimless glasses" and whose arms were covered in heroin tracks. The story was titled "Sandy Bull, I Thought He Was Dead."

Jane Wenner played Bull's albums endlessly for friends, but she also liked his looks and money. "He was a junkie, but he was a rich junkie," she said. "Sandy used to say, 'How many druggies could afford to put Cadillacs up their arm?'" Jann Wenner also took an interest, especially after learning that Alexander "Sandy" Bull had begun accessing his trust fund again after rehab. Wenner started advising Bull on legal problems with an ex-girlfriend, acting as an agent in some of his business affairs, and buying him a wah-wah pedal for his guitar. As it happened, Bull appeared in *Rolling Stone* the same month Wenner hit a financial wall and was desperate for cash. Jann Wenner asked Bull to loan him $20,000 to help shore up the newspaper in the spring of 1970, and Bull agreed. As Wenner recalled, the bankers at Chase Manhattan took a dim view of him when he came to cash the check. "Here's someone showing up to get his money," said Wenner, "and I had to convince them that I was legit and . . . not just buying junk for him."

Bull loaned Wenner the money because he was in love with Jane. In August 1970, Bull and the Wenners all went to London together, but Jane and Sandy traveled separately on a French ocean liner. They attended the wedding of a *Rolling Stone* writer named Jan Hodenfield, where Wenner asked Hodenfield to help score Bull some smack (later, Bull vomited over the second-floor banister at the Hodenfields' country house). From there, Bull and the Wenners went to Europe together, driving through the Pyrenees and taking a boat to Ibiza, the bohemian enclave off the coast of Spain where naked hippies wandered the beaches on mescaline. They were on the island for a week when Wenner got a call from home: Jimi Hendrix was dead, choking on his own vomit after taking too many pills. Wenner returned to London to oversee the obituary in *Rolling Stone,* waving good-bye to Jane and Sandy at a boat launch. "In the back of my mind, I figured something was going on, but I wasn't worrying about it too much," said Wenner.

Wenner would concede that he virtually threw Jane into Bull's arms. And he found time for casual disloyalties of his own. While in London, he'd had an affair with a friend of Jane's, with Jane pounding on Wenner's hotel door and yelling for him to come out while they scrambled around inside. Their parting in Ibiza had been an uncertain one. Wenner was remote, Jane increasingly attached to Bull. As Jane and Sandy boarded a boat in Piraeus, Greece, and continued to Istanbul, Jane wrote to Wenner to report that Bull was keeping her in good company during her depression over the state of their marriage. In Turkey, she bought Bull a new oud. She also reported seeing *Rolling Stone* on a newsstand in Genoa: Janis Joplin, dead at age twenty-seven from a heroin overdose. "Her lips were bloody when they turned her over," reported *Rolling Stone,* "and her nose was broken. She had $4.50 clutched in one hand."

Everything was falling apart—the 1960s, rock and roll, the Wenners' marriage. When Wenner gave Jane an ultimatum over the phone—come back from Europe or don't ever come back—she returned to San Francisco. But Jane had fallen for Sandy. She packed her bags, and the Lhasa apso, and took a train to New York to live with Bull, moving in with his mother on East Sixty-First Street, surrounded by birds and harps and butterflies and needles.

.

JANN WENNER HAD BEEN roping in rich dilettantes since the stockbroker Charles Fracchia poured good money after bad into Straight Arrow back in 1969. During Wenner's scramble for money in 1970, his former moneymen connected him with Arthur Rock, a pioneering venture capitalist who became fabulously rich financing the Intel Corporation. In the late 1970s, he would become a pivotal board member on Steve Jobs's young computer company, Apple. After Tom Wolfe published "Radical Chic" in *New York* magazine—depicting composer Leonard Bernstein and his socialite friends hosting Black Panthers in a luxe Upper East Side apartment—Alan Rinzler, acting as Wenner's right arm, was bringing marijuana and a black hipster to a dinner party hosted by Rock and his wife. As he reported back to Wenner in a memo, "Arthur said very loudly to the assembled gathering of business executives and their Palm Beach tanned wives: 'Alan, you have the dope.'" Thus summoned, Rinzler passed a joint around to the attendees, including a campaign manager for New York's mayor, John Lindsay. Afterward, he wrote, a woman with a "voice that sounded like money" asked for Rinzler's autograph for her daughter, thinking he was in the Rolling Stones.

Wenner initially went to Rock thinking he might sell *Rolling Stone.* The financial situation was so dire in 1970 that Wenner and Rinzler had considered filing for Chapter 11 bankruptcy. "At that time, there was nobody there who had any knowledge of running a company, or doing business," said Rinzler. "There were no grownups. It was just me and Jann."

Rock and a new associate named Dick Kramlich advised Wenner to pare back his operation and refocus instead of selling. While Rock was in Aspen skiing, Wenner introduced him to Hunter Thompson at a restaurant called the Paragon, which allowed customers to bring in their own meat for grilling. Prepared to shock, Thompson arrived with a mysterious bag and pulled out an unidentifiable maggot-filled carcass. "I was cracking the fuck up," said Wenner. "'Man, Hunter, you're crazy, what is this, disgusting' . . . Arthur was really white at the sight of it."

Rolling Stone wasn't the kind of investment Rock was looking for, but he had a friend who might enjoy this: Max Palevsky. In 1969, Rock's venture capital fund midwifed the sale of Palevsky's computer company, Scientific Data Systems (SDS), to the Xerox Corporation for the then-unheard-of sum of $900 million. The deal was one of the worst acquisitions in Xerox history (SDS was shuttered after six years), but it made the mathematician from Chicago, with a PhD in philosophy from Berkeley, an instant multimillionaire. Having started the company with $20,000, he personally netted more than $90 million and became the chairman of the board at Xerox. Flush with money and access, the engineer bought a mansion in Bel-Air and invested in a film company called Cinema V, which went on to produce the Oscar-winning 1972 documentary, *Marjoe,* about a religious swindler. In the late 1960s, Palevsky wore a hairpiece and a cravat and was at that moment dumping his second wife for a third. *Rolling Stone* seemed like a natural fit. "Max just loved us," said Rinzler. "He loved Jann, especially."

Palevsky saw a bit of himself in Wenner—Jewish, shrewd, ambitious—but he also liked the Wenners' access to large quantities of marijuana. "He wanted to get some dope, so we bought a half a kilo for him," recalled Wenner, who said he put it inside a felt hat from Brooks Brothers with a press card on the brim. "He got so paranoid about it that he left it on the plane. This was obviously not a business venture for him."

The source of the dope was Wenner's advertising manager, Laurel

Gonsalves, an auburn-haired stoner and former secretary for the Steve Miller Band who was funneling pot from Mexico through a hanger-on in Miller's band (Wenner often directed friends to Gonsalves, including Art Garfunkel). Gonsalves herself had become tied to the Wenners by investing $10,000 into Straight Arrow, which made her, in addition to their top drug connection, one of the larger stockholders in Straight Arrow. In 1971, the chairman of the Xerox Corporation sent a check to Gonsalves for $1,000 to keep him in the latest supply. "I appreciate your always being there—like a trusty doctor," Palevsky told her. (In 1971, when Gonsalves got busted sneaking coke and pot over the Mexican border, Palevsky sent his lawyer to bail her out.)

Wenner has said that by the time Palevsky showed up, he had shored up the finances of *Rolling Stone*. He didn't need the money, but he was happy to have a willing benefactor, especially one who owned several lavish homes, including a modernist showpiece in Palm Springs designed by L.A. architect Craig Ellwood, and a luxury suite at the Sherry-Netherland in Manhattan overlooking Central Park, a place Palevsky told people he bought because he enjoyed the raspberry soufflé from the kitchen. But Palevsky, no rube, had been duly informed that Wenner had a spending problem. His idea was to put a harness on his young charge by tying his hefty investment of $200,000 to a cost-control formula. If Wenner spent too much, Palevsky's shares in Straight Arrow would be worth more, thus incentivizing thrift. In Palevsky's mind, this essentially gave him control over the *Rolling Stone* checkbook. The deal was finalized in late November 1970, the three-year anniversary of *Rolling Stone*. And almost immediately Palevsky began advertising at cocktail parties—and later in the press—that he had just saved *Rolling Stone* from bankruptcy. (At this point, Wenner was in such disarray that he had skipped an issue of *Rolling Stone* and for the three-year anniversary just reprinted his original editorial of 1967.)

For a while, Wenner didn't mind allowing Palevsky the illusion that he was in control of *Rolling Stone*. In Palevsky, he saw new horizons, entrée to a fabulous world of jet setting the likes of which the Wenners had never seen. "I think Jann really looked up to Max as a beacon," said Dick Kramlich. "The kind of guy he would try to emulate in some ways. He saw his life as being filled with dynamism."

•

BY THE SPRING OF 1971, Jann Wenner was using Max Palevsky's suite at the Sherry-Netherland as his base of operations in New York. While Jane idled at Daphne van Beuren Bayne's nearby apartment, nursing her junkie boyfriend and getting heavily into pills, Wenner was taking a limousine downtown at night to mingle in the chicly decadent back room of Max's Kansas City. While sitting at a booth one night with Penny Arcade, the transsexual performance artist; Gerard Malanga, the Warhol collaborator who made a notorious nude photograph of Iggy Pop; and twenty-four-year-old singer Patti Smith (who reviewed a Todd Rundgren album in *Rolling Stone* in August 1971), Wenner spied his old friend Danny Fields across the room, sitting with a handsome and available young man named Tony Pinck. Wenner introduced himself and whispered to Pinck to meet him back at the Sherry-Netherland.

Pinck was a sixteen-year-old from Cambridge whose mother was a dean of the Harvard Business School. Handsome and confused, he'd hitchhiked to New York, got picked up on Park Avenue, and became a hanger-on in the Warhol scene, surviving by dealing coke and trading on his own sexual availability (Tennessee Williams once paid him $100 just to sleep next to him: "I was up listening to him snore all night," said Pinck). After Pinck spent the night with Wenner at the Sherry-Netherland (Wenner kissed him good-bye on the corner of Fifty-Third Street), Pinck circled back to Danny Fields's apartment on Twentieth Street and divulged every sordid detail of the affair as Fields rolled a tape recorder.

At the time, tape-recording party talk was all the rage. As Lillian Roxon reported in the spring of 1971, her friends were all "carefully saving and filing their cassettes for the great day when they can be released as 'social history.'" Fields was accumulating hundreds of hours of conversations ("I tape everything," he told Roxon), including an hour of Tony Pinck describing his tryst with Wenner, down to the fine details of the interior of Palevsky's suite ("Mirrors, all over," said Pinck). With the J. Geils Band's first album playing in the background, Fields can be heard calling up Lisa Robinson, a rock writer for the *New York Post*, to gush about the news. "Oh, that's so fabulous," Robinson says of the Wenner revelation. A hiss of gossip ensues, in thick New York accents.

ROBINSON: Did he find out any fabulous secrets?

FIELDS: Well, he uses Braggi deodorant and cologne. And he has two hair dryers.

ROBINSON: What's his wife—

FIELDS: His wife is a beautiful little girl.

ROBINSON: Oh, I know that. But I mean, is she living with Sandy Bull?

FIELDS: I guess.

ROBINSON: Are they getting divorced?

FIELDS: I don't know.

Fields labeled the tape "Pinck on Wenner," and it quickly became a hot item of gossip—including with the staff of *Rolling Stone*'s New York bureau. Danny Fields regarded Wenner as a font of endless dish. "He's such an absurd prick and I love him so much," he cooed to Robinson. "I really like getting off on him. I really like putting him down."

A writer working for Andy Warhol's new *Inter/View* magazine drew up an item about the tape's existence, but the editor, Glenn O'Brien, declined to run it. Instead, a pugnacious publisher named Al Goldstein, who ran an underground porn magazine called *Screw,* released it under the headline "Repression in the Underground."

The "alleged" tape recording that Danny Fields possesses concerning Tony Pink [*sic*] and the publisher of a famous rock journal would probably lead to a "contract" being put out on Tony if the "alleged" scurrilous remarks fell into the hands of said publisher.

Writer Timothy Ferris, who began as the New York editor for *Rolling Stone* in August 1971, remembered Wenner arriving at the office in a panic over the possibility of a blackmail scheme. None existed— yet—but the efficacy of Wenner's paranoia was borne out: Jane Wenner eventually learned of Tony Pinck, further complicating their fragile marriage. Jann and Jane were separated for much of 1971, and the Tony

Pinck incident was the capstone of a year in which Wenner dabbled in homosexual affairs. In January, Wenner and Robin Gracey had broken up in a bittersweet parting that Gracey eulogized in a song he wrote called "Jet Lag."

Now four years of acting out your fantasies and dreams
Is getting pretty hard to take,
Especially when you've locked yourself in
And I do it just for your sake.

You parody my actions and you smile at my words
But you go on asking for more,
And when I reach for the answer
You say, "I love you," and make for the door.

(Gracey would marry a woman and become an educator and garden designer. He said of Wenner, "I am pleased to think that I have a different perspective on Jann than many others. I can ascribe to him tenderness, thoughtfulness, care, tact, and love.")

Meanwhile, Max Palevsky had agreed to finance a documentary project Wenner wanted to make about a theater troupe of radical drag queens called the Cockettes, led by a gay dancer who called himself Hibiscus. "I made it with the conscious decision not to betray too much interest in it," said Wenner. "Yet, enjoying it . . . it was an outrageous hippie drag show, but it was very musical."

The movie fell apart, and Wenner became more interested in one of the troupe's other stars, a cross-dressing African American singer named Sylvester, who told Wenner he was a cousin of Billie Holiday's. Wenner offered to produce Sylvester's record for A&M and recorded six tracks for an album, tentatively titled *God Bless the Child*. Gil Friesen of A&M, however, hadn't officially sanctioned the idea and was alarmed when Wenner ran up a $15,000 recording bill. When he asked Wenner to repay him, Wenner convinced Friesen that A&M could make the money back on Sylvester's cover of the Carpenters' "Superstar." (It was never released.)

In early 1971, Wenner read a novel called *Gov't Inspected Meat and*

Other Fun Summer Things, the story of a male prostitute by a New York writer named Dotson Rader. Wenner invited Rader to the Sherry-Netherland for a meeting, ostensibly to talk about writing for *Rolling Stone.* When Rader showed up, Wenner was pacing back and forth, stoned, and retreating every few minutes to the living room to watch a beauty contest on TV. "It was like trying to hold a conversation with a tennis ball," Rader said. "He kept bouncing back and forth."

Wenner seemed tortured, struggling with his sexuality, with money, with his broken marriage to Jane. "He was unhappy," Rader said. "He was vulnerable and he was lost. He had come to a country where he didn't have the map."

"It's not like the closet he was in didn't have a door," Rader observed, "but it was a very, very, very thick door, and he was very afraid of being publicly revealed."

After an awkward liaison, Wenner assigned Rader a story on Joe Dallesandro, the jaded hunk of Warhol's 1968 underground film *Flesh,* whose crotch was rumored to be the one on the cover of the Rolling Stones' *Sticky Fingers* album and for whom Lou Reed wrote the line "Little Joe never once gave it away" in "Walk on the Wild Side." In April 1971, Dallesandro appeared shirtless and holding his infant son on the cover of *Rolling Stone,* a black-and-white portrait by Annie Leibovitz. The story was far from sweet. Rader referred to Dallesandro as "faggot bait" and detailed his role in an underground porn film for which he was paid $50: "He is 17 years old, dressed like a cowboy, bikeboy, and he undresses quickly, and then does calisthenics, sit-ups, push-ups, running-in-place, his penis bobbing like a shuttlecock."

Rader was Wenner's correspondent in the gay culture he was flirting with, cataloging the "celebrities, freaks, drag queens, street hustlers, pretty boys out-of-luck, parasites and poets" at Andy Warhol's Factory, from Candy Darling and Lou Reed to the rotisserie of hangers-on like Peter and Jane Fonda, Hedy Lamarr, Jon Voight, Jean Shrimpton, and Larry Rivers. "It is also where you are most likely to find Joe Dallesandro on any given afternoon," wrote Rader, "sitting at one of the glass desks in the front room, or by the eight-foot-high Campbell Soup can reading movie magazines, or remaining at a distance, unapproachable, silently watching the people come and go."

In the post-Altamont phase, the Weimar tint of nighttime Manhattan, driven by abundant cocaine and speed, filled with narcotic and sexual adventurers, was an essential scene, even if its rock and rollers, like the Velvet Underground, tended to attract smaller audiences. Critic Lester Bangs tried mightily to convince *Rolling Stone* that the Velvet Underground were important, but failed. "Why has *Rolling Stone* never done a feature article on the Velvet Underground?" he asked in a letter. "Just what the fuck is going on?"

Even as Wenner sampled this underground, he was frightened by it. Fields and his gossips considered Wenner a Johnny-come-lately, his newspaper a threat to their livelihoods. Fields gleefully played the Tony Pinck tape for friends. This was a threat not only to Wenner's marriage but also to his relationship with his business partners and his writers, especially the new *Rolling Stone* star, Hunter Thompson. Thompson's then wife, Sandy, married to him from 1963 to 1979, said Thompson was a virulent homophobe. In the mid-1960s, while working as a security guard at Esalen, the spiritual retreat in Big Sur, Thompson enjoyed visiting the hot springs at night with a billy club and a dog on a chain to scare off gay men. "Would it look good if he were working for a gay editor?" said Sandy Thompson. "And did this gay editor have something for him? That would not be acceptable and would be hard to deal with." (Thompson was estranged from his gay younger brother Jim until 1993, when he was dying of AIDS.)

As the covers of *Rolling Stone* went from John Lennon to James Taylor to Bob Dylan to Muhammad Ali in the spring of 1971, Wenner became burned out and depressed, seemingly wagged to death by his own tail. What was clear was that Jane Wenner was his own Oxford rule, a border containing his woolly energies and divining his desires and thoughts when he himself could not. Without her, he was a puddle. Ralph Gleason worried for him, telling Wenner to take a leave of absence, maybe hang out with Mick Jagger in Cannes, leave the newspaper to managing editor Paul Scanlon for a while. "Just fucking treat yourself kindly," he advised. "Crucifixs [*sic*] are a drag."

The marriage of Jann and Jane had never been a conventional love. It was not so much sex that Jane craved from Jann Wenner as the thrust of his ambition; from Jane, Wenner craved security and perhaps . . . permission. She gave him cover, enabled him to pass as one of the boys he so desperately wanted to be, and indeed needed to be for the *Rolling Stone* enterprise to succeed. In letters, it's clear she seemed to genuinely adore him. And who else loved Jann Wenner but his co-owner in the only thing he really cared about, *Rolling Stone?* "If you saw an aerial view of a football field, and there's like eighty thousand people, and there's two people that are meant for each other, that's Jann and Jane," said Laurel Gonsalves.

And then there was the not-insignificant matter of Jane's shares in Straight Arrow. Along with her brother-in-law, Bob Kingsbury, whose name was listed directly below Wenner's on the masthead, the Schindelheims of Manhattan held a large stake in *Rolling Stone.* Jann Wenner wanted Jane back, but he also *needed* her back if he was going to maintain the business he'd just spent the whole of 1970 trying to save. "Jann wanted to put her photo on the cover of *Rolling Stone* with the headline 'Janie, Come Back,'" recalled Charlie Perry. "He was very distraught. He wanted her back."

While Jane lived with Sandy Bull, she wrote to Wenner regularly to chronicle her pill consumption, therapy visits, and conflicted feelings about being "Mrs. Rolling Stone." She loved Wenner, but she was *in love* with her rich junkie. She suggested a legal separation. But when Wenner mentioned divorce, she panicked. She felt like a "great Hollywood tragedy."

For help, Jann Wenner turned to an unlikely mediator: Hunter Thompson. Jane and Hunter were smitten with each other from the start, natural flirts with an easy chemistry. "Hunter worshipped Jane," said Wenner, "because Jane was funny and flirtatious and Hunter was a professional flirt and lady killer. He was a southern gentleman and could turn on the charm." (Both Jann Wenner and Thompson's wife, Sandy, wondered if a romance occurred; Jane said none did.)

In September 1971, Wenner asked Thompson to go see Jane and convince her to come back to San Francisco. In a recorded phone conversation, Thompson told Wenner he had recently seen Jane, who told Thompson she was "absolutely certain" that she needed Bull and that Bull needed her, while Wenner treated her like an "accessory and as handy sometimes, but most of the times [as] kind of in the way."

Thompson reluctantly agreed to help, suggesting his own moral inadequacies and the "subtle" nature of the Wenners' marital woes didn't exactly make him ideal for the job.

> THOMPSON: If you were involved with eight women in San Francisco, that might be—I could at least talk about something like that, but it seems more subtle from what I know about it, and here I am, running around, you know, completely involved in whatever I am doing. So I am a hell of a model for anyone . . . well, fuck, she may hear what I have to say . . .
> WENNER: Okay, anything you can do to get her back to San Francisco.

Soon after, Thompson met Jane and Sandy at Max's Kansas City for drinks and reported back: It didn't look good. "I wasn't aware of the seriousness of her relationship with Sandy," he said. "This put me a bit on edge + made me think seriously for about 4 hours up here in my suite"—and here Thompson digresses for a page and a half to describe the plush hotel accommodations at Delmonico's, where "they treated me like Winston Churchill," before returning to the matter at hand—"Her relationship with Sandy seems hung on a 13 or 14 yr old level, complicated by all the obvious 30 yr old problems—+ I get the feeling that nothing except bad shit + doom can come of it.

"I can't even pretend to understand your relationship with her," Thompson continued, "but if it's important to you I think you should tell her you want her back *now*." (Jane wrote to Jann about the same meeting, calling Thompson "one of the most special people in the world" and noting that he seemed like a first-class alcoholic.)

At that, Wenner began drafting a series of tortured confessions to Jane about his insensitivity and lies, lamenting their mutual infidelities, his affair with Robin, her affair with Sandy, the feelings of guilt and resentment between them. He was Rhett Butler, he declared, and she was Scarlett O'Hara. They once agreed that they could sleep with other people as long as they didn't tell, but Wenner had gone too far, loved too little, and *Rolling Stone* had taken its toll. "But I did do those things, did hate you in my eyes, did throw you into the arms of yet another man," he wrote. "Been unfaithful and untruthful, watched our love-birds pick each other to death, and somehow let you become weaker and unhealthier in our own house, by my own hand."

He promised to quit *Rolling Stone* in October 1972, "and if you want, well before." "I'd like to continue at *Rolling Stone*," he said, "but not at that cost, not at the cost of losing you and my own humanity. I hope to God that neither of those have happened."

Wenner wrote six long letters in all. It's unclear whether he ever sent them, but after several phone calls he finally told Jane he couldn't take it anymore.

Jane enjoyed the attention. She felt as if she were just getting to know Jann Wenner for the first time. "Jann is breathing," she told a confidante. "Now—only five years later."

•

"I HAVE NEWS for you," said Jane Wenner. "It was like that whole part of our lives was 'Fear and Loathing.'"

While the co-owners of *Rolling Stone* suffered and cried and the fate of *Rolling Stone* hung precariously in the marital balance, Hunter Thompson was punching out the first lines of a masterpiece in a motel in Los Angeles. Assigned to cover the political aftermath of the murder of Chicano reporter Ruben Salazar, who was killed by the Los Angeles Police Department, Thompson avoided his deadline by toying with another story. He cranked up the Rolling Stones' *Get Yer Ya-Ya's Out!* and began describing a druggy misadventure with Oscar Zeta Acosta, the larger-than-life lawyer and Chicano activist who represented Salazar. Thompson brought Acosta with him to a motorcycle race in the desert outside Las Vegas that he was covering for *Sports Illustrated* (a piece that would be rejected, said Thompson, with extreme prejudice). Out of the blue, an excited Thompson showed up at David Felton's house in Pasadena with the germ of what would become *Fear and Loathing in Las Vegas*. Felton, the L.A. correspondent for *Rolling Stone,* had never met Thompson. "He said, 'Listen to this,'" recalled Felton. "He knew he had something."

Thompson needed more narrative thread to work with, and Felton suggested it might be funny if he and Acosta went back to Nevada to

cover a convention he'd read about: the National District Attorneys'
Conference on Narcotics and Dangerous Drugs, which took place in
the Mint hotel in Vegas. *Eureka!* As Thompson would write in *Fear and
Loathing,*

> But this time our very presence would be an outrage. We would be
> attending the conference under false pretenses and dealing, from
> the start, with a crowd that was convened for the stated purpose of
> putting people like us in jail. We were the Menace—not in disguise,
> but stone-obvious drug abusers, with a flagrantly cranked-up act
> that we intended to push all the way to the limit . . . not to prove any
> final, sociological point, and not even as conscious mockery: It was
> mainly a matter of life-style, a sense of obligation and even duty. If
> the Pigs were gathering in Vegas for a Top-Level drug conference,
> we felt the drug culture should be represented.

For this, of course, they would need a handsome expense account
and a convertible Cadillac. Wenner reluctantly agreed when Thompson told him the American Dream couldn't be discovered in a VW
Bug. With a reel-to-reel tape recorder rolling, Thompson and Acosta
sampled from a bag of narcotics—"two bags of grass, seventy-five pel-
lets of mescaline, five sheets of high-powered blotter acid, a saltshaker
half-full of cocaine, and a whole galaxy of multi-colored uppers, downers, screamers, laughers"—while maxing out a *Rolling Stone* American
Express card and courting mental breakdown in a hotel room. Afterward, Thompson holed up in the Wenners' basement on Ord Court,
bashing out fifteen-odd pages of the new opus, which channeled monologues and conversations from the tape recordings and relied heavily
on the persona and eccentric vocabulary of Oscar Acosta, the real-life
attorney whom Thompson now cast as a three-hundred-pound Samoan
named Dr. Gonzo: "We were somewhere around Barstow on the edge
of the desert when the drugs took hold."

"I remember Hunter asking, 'Do you want me to keep going?'"
recalled Wenner. "'This has gotten me more excited than anything I've
ever written.'"

Wenner showed the pages around the offices of *Rolling Stone* to make sure he wasn't crazy. A new freelancer from Texas named Chet Flippo saw the original manuscript and howled with laughter: This was it. "As I started reading the now-famous first sentences, I felt a crackle of electricity in the air," Flippo wrote later. "'This is going to change everything,' Jann told me. I'm not generally a big believer in dramatic moments outside of movies but that was a genuine dramatic moment."

Wenner told Thompson to "keep going," but he also told him to finish his other story first. "Strange Rumblings in Aztlan," which suggested a racist cover-up of Ruben Salazar's murder by L.A. law enforcement, was Thompson's second story for *Rolling Stone* and the last semi-conventional piece of reporting he would write. Wenner said that unlike Thompson's other "gonzo" writings, before and after, *Fear and Loathing* arrived fully formed, requiring little editing from Wenner. (Later, Oscar Acosta would threaten to sue Thompson not only for stealing his likeness in *Fear and Loathing* but for lifting his ideas, lingo, and humor as his own; Wenner agreed to give Acosta a book deal, resulting in *The Autobiography of a Brown Buffalo,* published by Straight Arrow Books.)

Thompson knew it was good, too. Before he published it in *Rolling Stone,* he managed to get a $12,500 book deal from Random House, news of which he shared with Wenner in the September 1971 phone call, a couple of weeks before the first installment was published in *Rolling Stone.*

> WENNER: You are going to get twelve-five from Random House.
> THOMPSON: Well, not all. Not, like, a check for it.
> WENNER: Yeah, but wow.
> THOMPSON: I should have told you two-fifty [for the *Rolling Stone* version of "Fear and Loathing in Las Vegas"]. Two hundred and fifty dollars.
> WENNER: You are getting four from us . . .
> THOMPSON: Well, it *is* a masterpiece.
> WENNER: Those expenses—

And here Wenner stopped short, for he instantly saw that he was going to make Thompson pay for his formidable expenses from Las

Vegas with his book advance instead of relying on Wenner's money, which was now tied to Max Palevsky's investment. Wenner had hoped Thompson would publish the book with Straight Arrow Books, and Thompson had tried expensing a laundry list of drugs, alcohol, and even weapons paraphernalia to *Rolling Stone*. This was the opening salvo in a years-long war between Thompson and Wenner over money.

WENNER:—that is great, Hunter . . . that is great.

But the money from Random House was the affirmation Thompson and Wenner needed. The *Rolling Stone* editor was thrilled by Thompson's anarchic theater and became a gleeful participant. Thompson looped Wenner in on grand pranks he was planning, including getting a pal inside ABC-TV to air a fake news report. Thompson had nearly managed to air a script he'd written on a deadly riot in California, but the insider chickened out. "Oh, that's a great scheme," Wenner said, suggesting they get some video cameras and make their own fake footage for a second try.

At the time, Wenner was having Thompson work on the "American Dream" section of his piece, the moment of revelation in Thompson's works they would come to refer to as "the Wisdom," the most eloquent and powerful scene of the story, which encapsulated the entire mood of the rock-and-roll generation in 1971, the great splintering of the 1960s into a Nixonian malaise. The germ of it had come from the tapes Thompson and Oscar made while high on acid:

Strange memories on this nervous night in Las Vegas. Five years later? Six? It seems like a lifetime, or at least a Main Era—the kind of peak that never comes again. San Francisco in the middle sixties was a very special place and time to be a part of. Maybe it meant something. Maybe not, in the long run . . . but no explanation, no mix of words or music or memories can touch that sense of knowing that you were there and alive in that corner of time and the world. Whatever it meant . . .

History is hard to know. Because of all the hired bullshit, but even without being sure of "history," it seems entirely reasonable to think that every now and then the energy of a whole generation comes to a head in a long fine flash, for reasons that nobody really understands at the time—and which never explain, in retrospect, what actually happened.

If Jann Wenner needed a mission statement and defining premise for *Rolling Stone,* he could not have done any better than this. Not only did it seem "entirely reasonable" that the 1960s were a "Main Era"; Wenner now had the poet laureate of "hired bullshit" to make sure the spirit of the 1960s kept rampaging across America, right inside the pages of *Rolling Stone.* With Wenner as his producer, *Rolling Stone* would make Hunter S. Thompson the star of his own movie, the character Raoul Duke, the made-up byline with which Thompson transformed himself into the most important cult journalist of his time.

Thompson brought something to *Rolling Stone* that Wenner had never quite perfected on his own: satire. Though the newspaper traded in nudge-wink self-awareness about drugs and sex, it had never managed the acidic morality embedded in Thompson's humor, the post-Altamont hangover incarnated as a comic Philip Marlowe inhaling ether as he slouched toward Bethlehem. As the critic John Leonard would later write, "Thompson, compulsive innocent, is higher on morality than anything else he smokes or drops."

"Fear and Loathing" was published in November 1971, alongside news that Duane Allman had died in a motorcycle crash. The response was not an immediate spike in newsstand sales (the Random House book would only sell eighteen thousand copies in hardcover in 1972). But numbers were a minor part of the story. Wenner's readers were gobsmacked by Raoul Duke, as if someone had spoken what everyone was thinking down to the exclamation points and ellipses. "I bought a paperback of *Las Vegas* while traveling with my girlfriend in England," recalled Garry Trudeau, who would later parody Hunter Thompson as "Uncle Duke" in his syndicated comic strip, *Doonesbury,* "and we stayed up all night howling over it. I would devour a few pages, then tear them out of the book and hand them to her. Neither of us had ever read anything remotely like it."

A *Rolling Stone* reader from San Diego, writing in late 1971, pro-

claimed the story "an artifact of certain times" and said he was "anticipating an overwhelming response from blown out, latter-day 'youth
culture' refugees."

Jann Wenner was anticipating it, too.

•

ON THE EVE of the first installment of "Fear and Loathing" in *Rolling
Stone*, Sandy Bull nearly overdosed on heroin, and Jane Wenner rushed
him to a hospital in Manhattan. Whereas she used to take Wenner's
Porsche into the shop for repairs, she wrote to Hunter Thompson,
she was now taking Sandy Bull to the hospital for overdoses. In October, Jann Wenner showed up in New York to take Jane Wenner back.
Wenner pleaded. Jane worked her neuroses like a rosary. Bull declared
his love and, according to Jann Wenner, offered to forgive the $20,000
loan if Wenner would let Jane go. "He offered to let me have the money
if he could have Jane," said Wenner.

Bull figured he knew what Wenner was really after and it was
money, not Jane. Wenner said he declined Bull's offer, but he did agree
to a rather large concession: Bull could return to San Francisco and live
with them for a while. They all moved into 38 Ord Court. "I thought,
wow, this is a guy that really wants to hang on to his wife," recalled Tim
Ferris. "Personally, a girlfriend of mine pulls something like that—'Tell
me where you want me to send your bag.'"

Jane said the arrangement "suited me, it suited Jann; he was busy
working or whatever."

But it didn't suit them particularly well. In December 1971, *Rolling
Stone*'s London bureau chief, Andrew Bailey, traveled to San Francisco
to stay with the Wenners for a month. "They bitched at each other the
entire time," said Bailey. "It wasn't comfortable at all."

The Wenner home was an exotic menagerie, to be sure: Jann
Wenner smoking a joint as he drove the Mercedes to Third Street after
he rolled from bed after lunch; Jane Wenner, distant and morose in her
pharmaceutical haze; Sandy Bull wandering around like a junkie ghost,
noodling on his guitar at top volume in the garage; Hunter Thompson,
boorish and drunk, staying up all night and disappearing during the
day. "I fell into dreamland there," said Bailey, who also fell into bed

with another houseguest, Diane Chess, wife of Marshall. "It felt like it was almost expected and arranged. If you turned up and there weren't enough beds, people got in bed with each other. It was delightful." (He was nicknamed Bedroom Bailey.)

Some *Rolling Stone* staffers thought they saw a love triangle in the trio of Jann, Jane, and Sandy. Wenner was curious about group sex. In 1970, while David Dalton was living with two women—one of whom was his wife in a church where LSD was the marital sacrament ("my acid bride," Dalton called her, the daughter of Jackie Kennedy's lawyer), the other his future wife, Susann—Wenner rang to ask if they would be interested in a foursome. Dalton said lots of people called with this request, including, he claimed, Brian Wilson of the Beach Boys. Dalton replied that it was untenable because the women weren't interested: "Like, no, they're fighting about where to hang the frying pan."

Wenner paid off Bull's loan in November 1971 and supported him when he expended his monthly trust-fund allowance on smack. The Bull arrangement went on well into 1972. Wenner said that at one point Jane encouraged him to take a trip to Mexico with Bull. But after two days, he decided he could no longer abide having his wife's lover hanging around. "I remember coming back from Puerto Vallarta early and just confronting Jane on it and saying, 'I've had it,'" he said, describing how he screamed at her and angrily smashed a chair. (Jane said she didn't recall any of this.)

In 1972, Bull moved out and made an excellent album on Vanguard Records called *Demolition Derby*. It was not reviewed by *Rolling Stone*. The breakup was not an easy one.

Q: Was there anybody that you were ever in love with?
JANE: Sandy.

From the outside, nobody could quite understand why Jann and Jane had stayed together. "Everybody knew that she owned half the company, and everybody assumed therefore that that was the leash," said Bailey. Perhaps. Wenner said he and Jane went into therapy to repair their marriage, but over time they also developed an unspoken arrangement: They were both free to take new lovers as long as the other didn't learn about it—no more Tony Pincks in the gossips. As long as they remained committed to the partnership—to *Rolling Stone*—then all was forgiven. Maybe this could work. "I was a better partner for her," reasoned Wenner. "Her life was more suited with me than . . . this guy who is fucked-up and a junkie and had all these problems in New York. I represented the much more serious Jewish prince guy than he did. Our marriage was much more suitable, as crazy as it was."

"My future was with Jane doing *Rolling Stone,*" he added. "We did love each other. Still do. In that fortuitous way, bumped into somebody you're going to spend the rest of your life with, and brother and sister as well as husband and—you know, all the things."

•

MAX PALEVSKY FLOATED across the patio of his glassy Palm Springs home in a floor-length paisley caftan looking like a bald Roman emperor in a golden desert light. A black butler in a white uniform walked around the turquoise pool with drinks as Jann and Jane Wenner bobbed their feet in the T-shaped hot tub next to an angular steel sculpture by Alexander Calder.

Somewhere across the desert, Hunter Thompson was rumbling toward them in a rented Cadillac.

In early November, Jane showed up as Wenner's wife for the first time in months. To celebrate, Wenner proposed a weekend retreat at Palevsky's pad and Palevsky agreed, happy to engage with the staff he'd paid $200,000 to have in his orbit. The editors had started calling Palevsky "Max-a-billion." "You couldn't ever look at Max without seeing dollar signs," said Laurel Gonsalves. Nor could Hunter Thompson. "Hunter became enchanted with the idea of 'Max the billionaire,'" Wenner said.

The first installment of "Fear and Loathing" had just hit the newsstands, and the attendees—Palevsky and his next wife, Lynda; Ben Fong-Torres and his fiancée, Dianne; Bob and Linda Kingsbury; Laurel Gonsalves; Alan Rinzler; and the Wenners—held their breath waiting for Thompson to show up, the conquering hero. They set up a canister of nitrous oxide by the pool and sucked the gas from a clear tube as they swam by. Wenner and Rinzler talked business with Palevsky, discussing, among other things, the idea of taking *Rolling Stone* public, which it was agreed was a natural part of their investment plan.

After getting lost in the desert, Thompson finally showed up on Sunday afternoon. Almost immediately, he went about dosing the attendees with an unidentified drug. "Hey, I've got some of this great stuff," Thompson told Palevsky. "I don't know what it is, who knows, it might be poison, but I think we should all take it tonight."

While he claimed not to know what it was, he convinced Jane Wenner it was his last hit of high-quality LSD. "Hunter came around and said, 'Jane, do you want to try this acid?'" recounted Jane Wenner, "and I said no. And then he said, 'But listen, I only have this one tab left . . . there's only one left. Do you want it?' So I took it and I thought, 'This is pretty groovy.'

"And then I looked at my watch," she said, "and thought, 'Only twenty minutes have passed? I have another seven hours of this?' They called us to dinner and this butler brought out this big platter of roast beef or prime rib"—it was duck with red cherry sauce—"and the blood was dripping and I thought, 'This is so horrible; it's really moving.' Then I looked around and everybody was stoned. So Hunter had sandbagged everybody!

"I only remember that I wanted it to be over," she said. "I hated acid."

"Hunter didn't tell us what he was giving us; we all just took it," recalled Rinzler. "We were watching this film Max had brought in that he thought was pretty cool, a 19-millimeter projected film, made by Les Blank, a documentary or something. It was a good film, but none of us could pay attention. I remember the film ran out and was flopping around, and everyone was just sitting around completely zonked. Everyone except Hunter, who was sort of cavorting."

As it turned out, Hunter hadn't taken anything, preferring to watch the others deteriorate for his own amusement. A psychedelic rookie, Palevsky spiraled into a panic attack, fearing he was having a cardiac event, and stumbled into the bathroom to find a tranquilizer to bring himself down. Meanwhile, Thompson fumbled with a box of Roman candles and set them off across the pool, cackling and slapping his sides with laughter as the group groped around the patio. Rinzler climbed into Palevsky's Bentley and drove into the desert, where he got down on the ground and listened to the ants.

Nobody remembers what Jann Wenner was doing, including Jann Wenner. But the next day, Palevsky managed to laugh off the whole affair, though he felt he'd peered into the dark heart of Hunter Thompson, the quasi-sociopathic prankster. "Hunter had a very nasty streak to him," said his then wife, Lynda Palevsky.

Afterward, Wenner had a diploma printed, signed by the staff, declaring Palevsky had survived the "First Annual Serious Palm Springs Endurance Run" at the "Palm Springs Proving Grounds." "It is testimony that we all made it through that night," Palevsky later said. "I call it the 'Proclamation of Survival.'"

"Palm Springs was great," Wenner wrote to him afterward. "Beyond just the fun, it really seems to have welded a spirit and a team together. Your advice and questions, as usual, were stunning."

·

WHILE HE WAS hazing Max Palevsky in Palm Springs, Hunter Thompson became fixated on a piece of equipment in Palevsky's study: a protofax machine, made by the Xerox Corporation, that could instantly transmit documents from one machine to another over phone lines. Thompson asked Wenner to get him one so he could file his stories on time for deadline, and not a minute sooner. Wenner agreed to install a line between *Rolling Stone* and Thompson's new apartment in Washington, D.C., which Thompson dubbed the Mojo Wire. This would be the fabled hot link between himself and *Rolling Stone* as Thompson and Wenner aimed their sights on the 1972 presidential campaign.

The idea to cover the campaign had been in the works since the previous summer. Putting aside the Vietnam assignment, Wenner plotted instead to get Thompson press credentials for the White House while haggling over Thompson's expenses for moving him and his family to the capital. In Max Palevsky, *Rolling Stone* now had entrée to Washington power. A lifelong Democrat, Palevsky had been inside the convention hall in Chicago in 1968, roaming the floor with his friend Frank Mankiewicz, a Democratic political adviser, both guests of Senator

George McGovern of South Dakota, whom they were urging to run for president. The idea was to harness the newly empowered youth vote to take on Richard Nixon on an antiwar platform. Palevsky offered to be his lead financial backer, staking him $300,000. For Wenner and Thompson, the path forward seemed clear: *Rolling Stone* could serve as the journalistic wing of the McGovern campaign, with Thompson stirring the shit with his patented Fear and Loathing. Thompson was game but also wanted the approval of the *Rolling Stone* staff, or at least their dramatic reaction when Jann Wenner presented him as the superstar of 1972. "What he wants is for everybody to sign on and go, 'Yeah, we love you!'" recalled Wenner. "Of course, Hunter's made up his mind and he's done. What Ben Fong-Torres says is not going to change anybody's mind."

For the end of 1971, Wenner planned a grand editorial powwow to be held at Esalen. It was the sort of hallowed hippie ground where the owner yelled at guests for drinking beer instead of smoking pot. Thompson showed up with a red police light on top of a white 1971 Mustang, prepared to consume copious amounts of beer, in addition to the drugs he brought with him. It was at Esalen that every staffer at *Rolling Stone* would begin collecting his mythic stories of Hunter S. Thompson, pocketing them like gems in black velvet to pull out for buffing and re-buffing over the years. As Felton told writer Timothy Crouse on the way to the conference, "Don't worry, if we run out of drugs, we can all suck on Hunter."

For others, it was a surprise to find that the author of "Fear and Loathing" was less a deranged wild man than a mild-mannered, almost shy jock whose voice sounded like Fred MacMurray, the actor who played the father in the 1960s sitcom *My Three Sons*. "Hunter had this act that he put on, this drug-addled bullshit," said Robin Green, among the first women Wenner hired as a writer at *Rolling Stone*.

As Wenner attempted to treat the conference as Serious Business, Thompson wore a surgeon's scrubs and pretended to inject rum into his stomach using a fake syringe, sending the staff into convulsions of shock and laughter. "Everybody was poking the elephant with the stick," said writer Robert Greenfield, who'd flown in from London to attend. "They were all standing around waiting for Hunter to do something."

When Wenner finally managed to call the staff to order, he announced that *Rolling Stone* would cover the 1972 presidential campaign, with Thompson as the Washington correspondent filing regular columns. The idea of getting so deeply involved with mainstream politics was almost universally disliked by the staff, but no one was prepared to oppose Hunter S. Thompson. When Wenner asked who wanted to be Thompson's assistant in Washington, D.C., only one hand went up— actually, two, both of them belonging to Timothy Crouse. Crouse joined *Rolling Stone* in 1970 as a correspondent on the Boston music scene, but Wenner never cottoned to him, resentful of his Harvard pedigree and storied family (his father helped write *The Sound of Music*). But Wenner was starry-eyed over Thompson, prepared to give him the earth, moon, and stars. "I think it would be fair to say 'in love,'" said Crouse. "That's what I saw. Jann really worshipped Hunter."

With the plan established, the party could now begin. Hunter Thompson, Annie Leibovitz, David Felton, and Robin Green hopped into Thompson's Mustang to zip up the coast for liquor. On their way back, they were pulled over by the California Highway Patrol. They had marijuana and acid on them. "I knew I was going to jail," said Felton. "And Hunter said to Annie, 'You better shoot this.'"

That night, Thompson tried the confrontational approach to disarming police that he described in *Fear and Loathing,* performing a stunt he claimed never to be able to replicate: Asking the officer whether an intoxicated man could do *this,* he flipped his sunglasses off the back of his head and quickly caught them behind his back. "That should count for something, shouldn't it?" he said.

Leibovitz snapped a photo and the cop let them go. The future of Wenner's newspaper was saved in a single stroke.

That night, Wenner and his staff draped themselves around the mineral pools, drinking beer. "This is like an old porn movie," Thompson growled. Only three women were invited to the retreat: Jane Wenner, Annie Leibovitz, and Robin Green, who was David Felton's girlfriend. "Hunter looked like a Greek god," recalled Green. "Jann looked very handsome and beautiful that night, and I remember wanting to take a walk with him. Jane was there. And she did not look beautiful. She looked very unhappy. She was not a happy woman."

As the sun faded over the Pacific Ocean, Annie Leibovitz stood apart from the staff, nude save for a 35-millimeter camera, and called out for Wenner and his men to stand for a portrait. Naked, they stood in silhouette against the dying lights of 1971, their bare asses against the encroaching darkness of the decade.

Click.

9

Sticky Fingers

I n 1971, Jann Wenner heard a delectable rumor: David Cassidy, the fresh-faced twenty-one-year-old heartthrob who played the eldest brother in ABC-TV's *Partridge Family,* was desperate to break out of his teenybopper career. So Wenner went on a months-long campaign to court Cassidy for *Rolling Stone,* offering a surefire way to wreck his image. "They sent me limousines; they put me up in the Plaza hotel," Cassidy later recalled. "They spent months trying to get me to do a cover."

When Wenner convinced Cassidy to cooperate, he assigned the story to Danny Fields, who was thoroughly smitten with the sweetly grinning idol. When Fields filed a story in the fall of 1971, Wenner initially praised it in letters. But later he told Fields the piece was too fawning, and he reassigned it to Robin Green, who was getting a reputation for taking a sharp scalpel to her subjects. (Another reason Wenner might have canceled Fields's assignment was the sudden emergence of the "Pinck on Wenner" tape at a time when he was getting back with Jane; Fields never had a byline in *Rolling Stone.*)

While Green was on the story, Wenner went to New York to meet Cassidy and his entourage at the Plaza. That afternoon, Wenner invited Green back to the Sherry-Netherland, and when she got there, Wenner was stoned on Quaaludes and in the mood for sex. "There wasn't a lot of chitchat," Green said. She would write one of the classic *Rolling Stone* profiles, depicting the cosseted teen idol, stoned on pot, watching an episode of his own TV show: "Watch, here's where I do my pouting shtick. I always have to do one of these things." But it was the photograph by Annie Leibovitz that would go thermonuclear: David Cassidy naked on his back, arms behind his head, a look of dreamy postcoital satisfaction on his face. Danny Fields said he gave Cassidy his first snort of cocaine moments before he dropped the heartthrob off with Leibovitz. Recalled Wenner, "When Annie brought that back, it was like, 'Oh my God, if you cut it here and it's just a little bit of pubic hair, and he's naked, it's like a *Playboy* Bunny. It's unbelievable, you get a teen star to do that? It's huge. That was something very special that only Annie could have done."

Wenner immediately set about publicizing the picture of the "darling of the bubble-gum set," issuing a press release saying, "Burt Reynolds did it for *Cosmopolitan*. Now David Cassidy is doing it for *Rolling Stone*."

At first, Leibovitz was startled by Wenner's salacious salesmanship. "This makes me feel rotten," she wrote to him in a memo. Wenner not only put it on the cover of *Rolling Stone*—titled "Naked Lunch Box: The Business of David Cassidy," alongside a William Burroughs interview—but also included a pullout centerfold of Cassidy in imitation of *Playboy*. For Wenner, the gambit worked: As *Rolling Stone* reported later, Woody's Adult Books of Hollywood rush ordered a thousand copies as Cassidy's mother flew to Mexico to escape the press glare. "Jann Wenner told me years later that until John Lennon died and he was on the cover that week, it was the biggest-selling, the fastest-selling issue," Cassidy said.

The results were more than Cassidy bargained for. For the next year, young fans would wave the poster in the air at his concerts. "It pissed a lot of people off," recalled Cassidy. "It pissed Coca-Cola off, it pissed Columbia Pictures off, it pissed my manager off, it pissed everybody who was really profiting from the business of David Cassidy off."

At least one part of the story was tabloid froth: Annie Leibovitz's original uncut photo never actually showed David Cassidy's full plumage. "I wasn't interested in the penis," she said.

Annie Leibovitz showed up at 625 Third Street in the spring of 1970 with a portfolio of photographs from a war protest at the People's Park in Berkeley the day before, including an image of Allen Ginsberg smoking a joint. At the time, Bob Kingsbury, the art director, was regularly publishing the work of unpaid student photographers on page 3, and Leibovitz's boyfriend urged the twenty-year-old to take her pictures to *Rolling Stone*. Leibovitz's timing was fortuitous: Kingsbury and Jon Goodchild were just then stewing over what to do about the "Pitiful Helpless Giant" issue. In the lobby, reported Goodchild, was a young woman with pictures she'd developed overnight. Her fingertips were still brown from an all-night session with film-developing chemicals. "And so Annie came dilly-bopping in," said Kingsbury, "and it wasn't so much the photography was brilliant; it was the printing quality of those prints that was amazing."

"They were impressed, I think, that it was just shot the day before and they had it," said Leibovitz.

The image of student protesters waving a big peace flag was her first cover image for *Rolling Stone*. Leibovitz's arrival was fortuitous in other ways as well: Baron Wolman, who'd been the staff photographer from the beginning, was fed up with Wenner and increasingly interested in running his own magazine. "I think Baron just wanted to be Jann and there wasn't going to be room for two Janns at this place," said Leibovitz.

One of six children born to an air force family, Leibovitz spent her young life traveling from Alaska to Texas to Maryland. After graduating from high school, she moved to the Bay Area in the fall of 1967 to study painting at the San Francisco Art Institute (inspired, she said, by an image of the bay on the catalog). She was a naive suburban girl who found the wild-haired hippie scene in Haight-Ashbury scary, but after discovering photography on a family trip to Japan, she shifted focus and devoted herself to the street style of Robert Frank and Henri Cartier-Bresson. She planned on becoming a teacher. When she moved to Israel in 1969 to live on a kibbutz and photograph the communal lifestyle, her boyfriend, Christopher Springmann, a freelance photographer for the *Chronicle*, mailed her issues of *Rolling Stone*, which were passed around like missives from the countercultural front. "I read every single line," she said. "It gave me all the information about what was going on in

San Francisco and that world back there, and I just had a dream about maybe one day I would work for them."

Six feet tall, large boned, shaggy, braless, wearing Coke-bottle glasses—Tom Wolfe said she looked like Barbra Streisand elongated by French expressionist Bernard Buffet—Leibovitz obscured her imposing, awkward presence by having a Nikon perpetually latched to her face, a camera so ubiquitous she sometimes wore it to bed, earning her the nickname Natasha Nikon. After the peace flag cover, she began to shoot regularly for *Rolling Stone,* freelance at first. She had little interest in rock and roll, but the work exposed her to the new lifestyle, like members of the Jefferson Airplane lying on a water bed smoking joints while Ben Fong-Torres asked them about their latest album.

In her first year at *Rolling Stone,* she said, the rock stars did the work for her. When she arrived to shoot Rod Stewart for the December 1970 issue, he opened his legs in a sensual come-on and she clicked the camera. The John Lennon cover image was a light-meter reading on his face that Wenner selected against her protests. What Wenner and Kingsbury liked was her obsessive and all-consuming work ethic. Soon enough, she was a virtual slave to their biweekly schedule. A memo of her assignments from 1971 reads like a countercultural marathon: Art Garfunkel, Santana, the Stones, Ahmet Ertegun of Atlantic, Dick Cavett, Dr. Hook, Grand Funk Railroad, Sonny and Cher, Chicago, Stephen Stills, Delaney and Bonnie, Procol Harum. "This is just a tentative list," she concluded.

Her intensity was her talent. She seemed to wear down her subjects, even beguile them with her desperate, anxiety-riddled snapping as she consumed roll after roll of film. The attention of a female with a camera was a powerful aphrodisiac for a male rock star, especially a guy wanting to be in *Rolling Stone.* They felt a certain obligation to help this shambling wreck sent over by Jann Wenner and often the desire to sleep with the vulnerable girl who showered them with Kodak film and gamely removed her own clothes. As Wenner described the Leibovitz working method, "You feel you're in the presence of some deeply crazy person and you're trying to reach out and help her. And I think she does that same thing when she's shooting; she makes you feel she's helpless and in trouble and now you're going out of your way to bend over backward and help her. And other times, she can be completely steely about shit. Be an immovable object on subjects."

The David Cassidy image was transformative in her relations with her subjects. It now served as a bit of leverage: If a teen idol would disrobe for her, why not Peter Fonda? "She could intimidate people into getting naked," said Robin Green, "because it would be uncool not to. It was practiced."

This, of course, was exactly what Wenner wanted, the Gloria Stavers maxim—unbutton the top button—writ large. Hadn't Wenner wanted them all naked back in 1968? It was a fusion of the countercultural imperative to liberate oneself and good old-fashioned show business. They were selling intimacy, the photographs getting closer to the subjects than an article ever could. "Annie and I were on the same page," said Wenner. "Taking their clothes off, that was the big thing . . . and provocative. Making our name."

As she wrote in an autobiographical essay for *Shooting Stars,* a book of rock photography published by Straight Arrow Books in 1973, photography and sexual desire were the same. "When I say I want to photograph someone," she wrote, "what it really means is that I'd like to know them—fuck them, know them, be their friend, it's a way in. To know them is to photograph them." (Wenner edited out some of this for the book.)

After shooting Jerry Garcia for the cover of the hundredth issue of *Rolling Stone,* a languorous image of the Grateful Dead guitarist lying on the beach with his eyes closed, she tried pursuing him romantically, looking for any excuse to visit him. "She was in love with him," said Robin Green, who accompanied her on one of her trips. In the 1970s, her liaisons with *Rolling Stone* cover boys became a running comedy around Third Street.

If she lacked boundaries, Leibovitz said she felt naive and overwhelmed by her constant work. "It was really a survival thing; you just get placed in these places," she said, "and the volume of what I witnessed and saw and photographed began to create me."

As a female photographer hovering on the edges of the scene, anonymity was her power, and she soon became Wenner's best source for gossip. While photographing Ike Turner, she saw more than the writer

Ben Fong-Torres ever did. "He had an Aladdin's lamp, filled to the top with white powder," she recalled. "He said, 'Do you know what this is?' That was in that house in Palo Alto. He had cameras in every room to watch people having sex."

When the story came out, Ike Turner threatened to break the limbs of both Jann Wenner and Ben Fong-Torres. "Annie, I trusted you!" he screamed at Leibovitz on the phone.

But her output came with a price tag. Wenner was continually frustrated by Leibovitz's inability to manage herself, her penchant for expending endless rolls of film for a simple head shot or losing expensive camera equipment on a shoot. She was known to abandon a rental car at the airport if it meant getting to the church on time ("Nothing was cheap about Annie," said Kingsbury). A blur of drugs and overwork made Leibovitz notoriously spaced-out: When she parked her car at the wedding of Bob Kingsbury and Linda Schindelheim, she left the emergency brake off and it rolled down a hill ("We were all stoned and watched it in slow motion," said Linda). When she wasn't spaced-out, she was temperamental. Bruce Mann, a lawyer brought to *Rolling Stone* by Arthur Rock, recalled Leibovitz as a chief liability: "She threw a camera on the pavement and broke it at a time when the company was very concerned about money." Wenner found himself constantly browbeating Leibovitz over scheduling and expenses, giving her loans (with interest), and forcing her to adhere to a calendar. "I'll be watching!" he warned in a memo. (Eventually, they took her credit card away and just gave her envelopes full of cash.)

By 1972, Wenner had the idea to put Leibovitz together with his wife, Jane. Maybe Jane, with her chic tastes and abundant free time, could housebreak Leibovitz while he focused on his other star, Hunter Thompson. "When she first came into my life, in the office, I found her totally annoying," said Jane. "Then we became very good friends. Annie was obsessed; she was always there, big, awkward."

"I didn't take it seriously to begin with," said Leibovitz. "I really had enough to do. With all that was going on in my life, I had enough to do. I really did it for Jann."

When she first began padding around the Wenners' home at 38 Ord Court, Leibovitz could hardly believe their sophistication. "It was certainly entering a world that was way over my head," she said. "Jane was very sophisticated. I remember she was moving a lot of furniture around. I never thought about furniture in a house, and I never thought about architecture, and to this day my foundation for architecture and interest in furniture and design comes from those days with her. I learned a lot about it."

If Leibovitz was yet aware of her homosexuality, she didn't let on, but then here was Jane Wenner, this lovely Siamese cat of a woman whose menagerie of neuroses and prescription-pill melancholy was a kind of intimacy of its own. The moment Annie Leibovitz lifted her Nikon to Jane, Jane gazed into her lens with the magnetic sensuality of a silent film star. The camera loved her. And soon, so would Annie Leibovitz.

•

JANN WENNER AND TRUMAN CAPOTE walked into a gay bar. It was March of 1973, and Wenner had spent the day in Palm Springs interviewing Capote over lunch at Don the Beachcomber's, a tiki bar on North Palm Canyon Drive. Capote suggested they go out for the night. Acting as arm candy and social cover, Wenner was astonished when they were received like royalty at Oil Can Harry's. "The seas parted for Truman," said Wenner. "At the time he was a big celebrity. Always appearing on Carson, with that high squeaky voice, so he's the biggest thing in gay culture. To accompany him to this place was—whoa!"

Wenner had never been to a gay bar and was unprepared for the sight of a roomful of like-minded men. It frightened him. ("It was weird," said Wenner. "It was all guys.") At 2:00 a.m., they were driving back to Capote's house when the car broke down on the side of the road, forcing them to walk to a nearby gas station to call for help. Capote had only recently been on assignment for *Rolling Stone,* covering the 1972 Rolling Stones tour. Or rather, failing to cover it. Capote was now an alcoholic socialite who hadn't written much since the publication of *In Cold Blood* in 1965. Herb Caen chronicled his industrious life as an accoutrement to European jet-setters and American media moguls like William Paley of CBS. While Capote was in San Francisco participating in a documentary on Bobby Beausoleil, a Manson family member who went to prison for murder (and who Capote believed was gay), he was introduced to Wenner by the movie's producer, a New York socialite named Mary "Piedy" Gimbel, an heiress to the Gimbels department store fortune. Wenner invited Capote to lunch with his top editors, and when Capote showed up, dressed in a sailor suit, Wenner proceeded to shake him down for story ideas. Recalled *Rolling Stone* writer Michael Rogers, "Jann says to Truman, 'Tell me the three great stories that you'd love to write.' Truman said, 'Jann, I don't talk that way for fun, I only talk that way for money.'" ("Jann knew it was embarrassing, he just didn't care," said David Felton.)

Truman Capote would later say Wenner "thinks like a water moccasin." Indeed, Wenner stole away with one observation: Truman Capote was fascinated by Mick Jagger. As it happened, the Stones were preparing a massive tour of America, which they advertised as the biggest and most expensive in the history of rock and roll.

By now, Wenner and Jagger were a hand-in-glove operation. Whatever the Stones were pushing, Wenner funneled straight into the pages of *Rolling Stone*. Readers could follow Jagger's exploits like a bouncing ball from issue to issue: "Mr. and Mrs. Mick Jagger are expecting. The baby is set to debut in October"; "There's a good chance that by the time you read this it'll be Mick and Bianca Jagger. Well, why not?" In a recorded phone conversation from January 1972, as Marshall Chess prepared to patch Wenner through to Mick Jagger, who was in Sunset Sound studios in L.A., Wenner played the role of court stenographer.

CHESS: Okay, I'm going to get Mick.

WENNER: What do you suggest I ask?

CHESS: Anything you want, man! This is your chance!

WENNER: I can't think of anything to ask.

CHESS: Oh, you can't? You must have done too much coke, man.

WENNER: What should I ask?

CHESS: What should you ask him? Ask him about the new album.

WENNER: *Jamming with Edward!* or the new one?

CHESS: Both. But with *Jamming with Edward!*, I've got to sell some records, straight on top, so ask him about that one. I'll get'm.

Wenner tried trading gossip with Jagger, telling how Keith Moon of the Who had collapsed during a concert in San Francisco, prompting Wenner to call in Sandor Burstein for a special injection. Bored, Jagger turned to the business at hand. "I was supposed to tell you something about *Jamming with Edward!*," he said. "It's just this jam album with Ry Cooder and Nicky Hopkins."

Agreeing to write it up, Wenner cajoled Jagger for a full interview, promising that together they could "have it transcribed and look at it and then finish it up while you're back here on tour and then put it out afterward. You know, wait, and handle it cool."

Wenner piped Jagger's info into the February issue of *Rolling Stone,* along with news of the tour and the latest Stones recording made in the South of France, *Exile on Main St.* "The words are simple, it's less . . . pretentious [than *Sticky Fingers*]," said Jagger. "I think you'll get off on it." (Jon Landau had trashed *Sticky Fingers* as suffering "from its own self-defeating, calculating nature. Its moments of openness and feeling are too few; its moments when I know I should be enjoying it but am not, too great.")

At that point, Robert Greenfield was the man on the Stones beat, covering the 1971 tour, with a specialty in reproducing Jagger's limey patois ("'Ere, wot's the law doin' 'ere? Come to arrest us all, have you? Oy, you you, oy"). He even captured for *Rolling Stone* the very moment Jagger read Lenny Kaye's review of *Exile on Main St.* while lounging at the Playboy Mansion and drinking from a bottle of Lafite-Rothschild 1961 (he was nonplussed). It was Greenfield who suggested to Wenner they cover the 1972 tour—fifty-one dates in thirty-two cities over eight weeks—like a military campaign. "What this means is that the piece will be journalistic rather than fiction," he told Wenner. "It will not be a personality piece on the Stones but a report on the effect of what they do."

Wenner agreed to the idea, though only because Marshall Chess liked Greenfield and agreed to have the Stones pay for his airfare and lodging. "*Rolling Stone* didn't pay a dime of the expenses," said Greenfield. Wenner assigned Annie Leibovitz to accompany him. Leibovitz immediately fell under Jagger's spell, writing that he was the most elusive of her photographic muses, overwhelming her with sexual power.

Laurel Gonsalves.
(Camilla McGrath)

Tony Pinck and
Danny Fields at Max's
Kansas City, 1971.
(Anton Perich)

Wenner, with nitrous
oxide tube, and Alan
Rinzler at the Palevskys'
Palm Springs home,
November, 1971.
(Dianne Sweet Fong-Torres)

Jann Wenner. *(Courtesy of Jann Wenner)*

Hunter S. Thompson. *(Courtesy of Jann Wenner)*

Jane Wenner. *(Courtesy of Jann Wenner)*

Annie Leibovitz. *(Courtesy of Jann Wenner)*

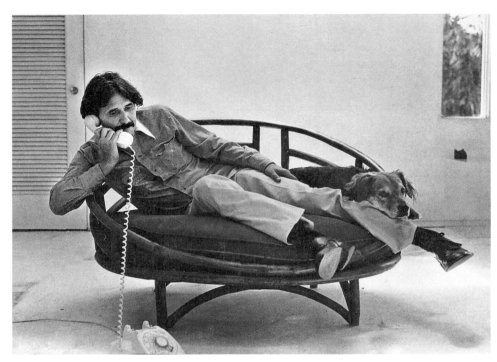

Earl McGrath with his dog, Jiminy, in Los Angeles, 1974. *(Camilla McGrath)*

Jann and Earl McGrath.
(Camilla McGrath)

Wenner (bottom left) aboard a cruising boat in 1974 with Camilla and Earl McGrath (bottom right). Seated next to Wenner is Daniel Filipacchi, the French publisher with whom he would try to revive *Look* magazine in 1979. *(Courtesy of the Camilla and Earl McGrath Foundation)*

Jann Wenner, Los Angeles, 1974. *(Camilla McGrath)*

Diane and Egon von Furstenberg, 1973.
(Ron Galella/Getty)

Annie Leibovitz, Los Angeles, 1974.
(Camilla McGrath)

Jane Wenner and Diane Chess,
1974. *(Camilla McGrath)*

Diane Chess
(bottom left),
Jane Wenner,
Earl McGrath, and
Annie Leibovitz
in Barbados, 1974.
(Camilla McGrath)

Earl McGrath (foreground) with (clockwise) Camilla, Daniel Filipacchi, Mick
Jagger, unidentified man, and Ahmet Ertegun (holding child) at the Villa
Reale di Marlia, Italy, 1974. *(Courtesy of the Camilla and Earl McGrath Foundation)*

Mick Jagger, *Rolling Stone,* September 11, 1975. Photograph by Annie Leibovitz. *(Courtesy of* Rolling Stone *magazine)*

Mick Jagger and Keith Richards. Portrait by Annie Leibovitz. *Rolling Stone,* July 17, 1975. *(Courtesy of* Rolling Stone *magazine)*

Mick Jagger and Annie Leibovitz, 1975. *(Christopher Simon Sykes/Getty)*

"Jagger is a master craftsman, and a fucking sexy little devil and he knows he has me," she wrote. "All it is is a sexual tension. It drives me insane. He's the only one who does that to me. And that means he can have that much control over me."

While Greenfield was on tour, Wenner was pushing to get Truman Capote to cover the tour instead, proposing he join forces with photographer Peter Beard and his then girlfriend, Lee Radziwill, the socialite sister of Jackie Onassis ("Classic fag hag," said Wenner). They were all card-carrying members of New York's café society, perfect for the collision of socialite ennui and rock-and-roll decadence being husbanded by Ahmet Ertegun, the gentleman hipster of Atlantic Records who ran in the same Manhattan circles as Capote and whose wife, Mica, was an interior decorator aspiring to Park Avenue respectability. Even if Capote could no longer write, Wenner thought Jagger might finally move him to return to the typewriter. The tour was half over when Capote finally capitulated, prompting Wenner to tear up Greenfield's monster story. "I write this huge piece that Jann has sworn on a stack of Bibles is going to run," said Greenfield, which instead "gets slashed to ribbons for captions for Annie's photos." (He quit *Rolling Stone* and afterward was offered a publishing contract to write an entire book on the Stones tour, which became *S.T.P.: A Journey Through America with the Rolling Stones*.)

In late June, Capote, Beard, and Radziwill joined the Stones' bloated wagon train in Kansas City, which now included writer Terry Southern and photographer Robert Frank, who shot the cover images for *Exile on Main St.* and was making a sordid (and legendary) documentary called *Cocksucker Blues*. In New Orleans, Capote held court at a fabulous dinner featuring the entire entourage, hosted by Ahmet Ertegun and attended by Annie Leibovitz. "He loved it; he was in socialite heaven," said Greenfield, who remained on the tour, even though he had quit *Rolling Stone*.

Predictably, Capote only turned in a few pages of digressive and unpublishable rambling about his dislike for the Stones, and especially their publicist Marshall Chess. "He talked about my fat thighs rubbing together," recalled Chess, who said Capote's infatuation with the Stones' saxophone player Bobby Keys set off homophobic alarms with the macho gang led by Keith Richards. "Truman Capote was, like, infatuated with Bobby Keys, who was the last thing from gay," said Chess. "So we all went and pissed on Truman's hotel room door."

When Capote joined them on the tour plane afterward, he was crying. "I didn't think much of Truman," said Richards. "I did wonder how much Jann was paying him. I just thought it was miscasting."

With Greenfield gone, Timothy Ferris was called in for a rich and gossipy report on the tour's finale, a five-hundred-person bash at the St. Regis hotel in Manhattan for Mick Jagger's twenty-ninth birthday party, dreamed up by Ahmet Ertegun. As Bob Dylan posed with Zsa Zsa Gabor, Jagger swanned among high society matrons and media luminaries like Dick Cavett and Woody Allen as four Harlem tap dancers did a racist minstrel act and a stripper in pasties sprang from a multilayered birthday cake. Count Basie played from the stage. "What are Zsa Zsa Gabor and George Plimpton and all these other society freeloaders doing at a party for Mick Jagger?" wondered the *New York Times* social columnist in *Rolling Stone*. "If the Rolling Stones are the latest mind-fuck for the Truman Capote crowd, what does that say about the Rolling Stones?"

To salvage the Capote assignment, Wenner borrowed an idea from Andy Warhol, whose *Inter/View* magazine, which focused on underground film, had begun publishing long transcripts of catty conversations between filmmakers and art world mavens. Warhol could interview Capote about Mick Jagger, and Wenner could publish the resulting transcript as an "audio documentary." As it happened, Wenner had tried buying *Inter/View* from Warhol, telling a reporter in 1973, "I'm very interested in the rich and beautiful people." But he offered so little money that Warhol laughed at him, according to Glenn O'Brien, who edited *Inter/View* and later went to work for *Rolling Stone*. In this same period, Wenner acquired ten silk-screen portraits of Mao Tse-tung from Warhol for $3,000. After Warhol agreed to the project, Wenner stage directed him with pre-written questions ("Jann wanted to know your problem with writing the article," Warhol told Capote) and then followed up by flying to Palm Springs to round out the story with more on-point material. "Sunday with Mr. C" appeared in 1973 with a cover image by Leibovitz of Capote in a fedora with a colorful scarf draped around his neck ("To hide all his chins," said Wenner). Dripping with gossip, the two "Elder Vampires" (as filmmaker Kenneth Anger later described them in *Rolling Stone*) discuss everything from Capote's dermatologist (Dr. Orentreich could make a person "look like Venus DeMilo") to transsexuals ("All I can tell you is," said Warhol, "don't get involved with drag queens. It's trouble").

For a pull quote, Wenner highlighted this Capote gem: "I can't count five important people in media who aren't Jewish."

Capote told Warhol he couldn't write the article because Jagger was boring. "I mean, he's a highly trained performer, and on the other hand, he's a businessman *par excellence*," he said, "and the whole thing is perfectly obvious, and so it had no mystery to it. That was my problem . . . since there was nothing to 'find out,' I just couldn't be bothered writing it."

Andy Warhol, too, found the Stones creatively uninteresting and obnoxious to their fans, summing up their attitude as "Who the fuck cares about them?" But for readers of *Rolling Stone,* this was astonishing exotica, the kind of unmediated tattle that would ruin everyone involved had it been published in a later, less freewheeling age. At one point, Capote describes the tour doctor recruiting thirteen- and fourteen-year-old girls for sex play on the tour plane, with one such incident allegedly filmed for posterity by Robert Frank. Capote: "The one I remember the most was a girl who said she'd come to the Rolling Stones thing to get a story for her high school newspaper, and wasn't this wonderful how she'd met Dr. Feelgood and got backstage . . . Robert Frank got out all of his lights, the plane was flying along and there was Dr. Feelgood screwing this girl in every conceivable position while Robert Frank was filming, and as the plane was flying back to Washington it was flying at some really strange angle. And the stewardess kept saying, 'Would you please mind moving forward?'" (Robert Greenfield insisted this never happened: "There was no fact-checking.")

Capote also offered his interpretation of the 1972 hit single by Paul Simon, "Me and Julio Down by the Schoolyard," which he believed was Simon's not-so-veiled reference to a gay lover. "He and Julio are great friends," said Capote. "One day, Julio's parents find out that he, Julio, is having an affair with Paul Simon."

Mick Jagger had been agreeable to the Capote experiment from the start, staying with him in his house in Montauk and believing it was all good for a laugh. But afterward he felt Wenner's grandiose idea had once again made the Stones objects of ridicule. Truman went on *The Tonight Show* with Johnny Carson and repeatedly called the band "the Beatles" while complaining that the tour had been a bore.

"The Stones, right?" corrected Carson.

•

IN 1972, Hunter Thompson was Jann Wenner's de facto partner in *Rolling Stone,* an editorial adviser and co-conspirator, the man with whom Wenner confided his biggest aspirations and looked to for consultation on writers and stories as well as business affairs. Wenner hired a friend of Thompson's from Kentucky, Porter Bibb, to take over as publisher in 1972; christened the conference room at *Rolling Stone* the Raoul Duke Room; and gave Thompson the ironic title "Sports Editor" in the masthead, an homage to Thompson's legacy as a sportswriter. Wenner moved Thompson and his wife and son, and also his two Doberman pinschers, to Washington, D.C., from Woody Creek, Colorado, to write his biweekly column for *Rolling Stone,* to be called Fear and Loathing in Washington. Through Max Palevsky, the chairman of the board of *Rolling Stone* and top donor to the George McGovern campaign, they would have easy access to their chosen candidate, allowing Wenner and Thompson to ride herd on the most important election of their young lives, with *Rolling Stone* deeply embedded in McGovern's inner circle and Thompson their unofficial rodeo clown in the press. McGovern's strident antiwar position and promise to legalize pot made him the long-shot candidate of 1972 but also the great liberal hope of the rock-and-roll celebrity class, chief among them Warren Beatty, with whom Wenner tried coordinating on a fund-raising concert in San Francisco. The attack line opponents used against McGovern was the very reason they loved him: the "Amnesty, Abortion, and Acid" candidate. Wenner became the point man for music industry contributors like Jac Holzman of Elektra, and he wrote to Bob Dylan to encourage him to support McGovern and perform a benefit concert. "If you like I can set up a private meeting between you and Senator McGovern in New York," said Wenner. (Dylan didn't respond.)

Wenner and Thompson, in the spirit of the McGovern campaign, got stoned before they met with his chief political strategist, Frank Mankiewicz, in early 1972, stifling giggles as he outlined the campaign playbook for them in advance—an insider's blueprint for Thompson's *Rolling Stone* columns, which he would file regularly for the next several months. Thompson was the perfect representative for *Rolling Stone,* a publication mostly off the radar of the stodgy and aged press corps, which regarded McGovern as a flake and *Rolling Stone* as a fan magazine for a band they didn't particularly like. As Timothy Crouse wrote in *The Boys on the Bus,* his definitive account of the press pack that followed the election (a book idea Thompson gave him), few even knew what *Rolling Stone* was until Hunter Thompson came ambling along in his golf shirt and sun visor, FDR cigarette holder wagging up and down in his mouth:

> Rolling Stones? Is that the fan magazine of the rock group? Nobody on the campaign trail had ever heard of the magazine back in January of 1972, and it was not an easy publication to define in one or two sentences. The *Time* magazine of the Counter Culture? Well, not exactly. An underground rag? . . . *Rolling Stone*'s young founder and editor saw himself as the Charles Foster Kane of the seventies; it was his dream that *Rolling Stone* would muster the gigantic, newly enfranchised Youth Vote and throw it to the best man. Things did not exactly shape up that way, but fortunately the editor had the wit to hire Hunter Thompson as political correspondent.

That summer, Random House published *Fear and Loathing in Las Vegas,* which was passed around by political reporters from major newspapers as a primer on this mumbling interloper who was making bets with *Washington Post* columnist David Broder and smoking pot with younger reporters from the big-league papers. Thompson, as he had in Vegas, observed presidential politics like a man standing horrified and bemused before a horde of entrenched stenographers trailing politicians like George Wallace ("a charlatan") and Hubert Humphrey ("a gutless old ward-heeler who should be put in a . . . bottle and sent out with the Japanese Current"). His Gonzo style cleaved open the reality with doses of hysterical fiction: No, Democratic candidate and establishment favorite Edmund Muskie of Maine had not secretly eaten an obscure psychedelic called ibogaine, as Thompson rumored in *Rolling Stone;* it was only a parody of his odd behavior on the campaign trail. Mankiewicz famously called his reportage "the most accurate and least factual" of the 1972 campaign. As Thompson's fame rose, Wenner made *Rolling Stone* a full adjunct of the McGovern campaign, printing his campaign schedule in the paper. In turn, McGovern invited Thompson to swim laps with him in Max Palevsky's pool in Bel-Air to discuss strategy, while an infuriated press stood outside waiting for a quote. Wenner, who lunched with McGovern that same day, published a photograph of McGovern in the pool, Palevsky lying on a deck chair in the background, toupee locked on his head. The McGovern high command read Thompson's columns, laughing uproariously to hear Mankiewicz described as a "scurvy, rumpled, treacherous little bastard" or Thompson's satirical footnote explaining that he had actually invented the Xerox fax machine before Palevsky stole the patent. "He got to see things that most reporters didn't because it was understood he wasn't a normal political reporter," said Pat Caddell, a polling wunderkind from Harvard who became part of *Rolling Stone*'s druggie entourage and published a long and wonky election essay in the newspaper. "It was symbiotic. We were all on a political magical mystery tour."

Wenner put McGovern on the cover in June 1972 and endorsed him with a one-page editorial, highlighting his liberal views on pot and proclaiming him "the best presidential candidate since Franklin D. Roosevelt. Such men do not come often, and without our support and our votes, they never come again."

But Thompson's column, as popular as it was, was also a management nightmare for Jann Wenner, who monitored Thompson's metastasizing expense account and played the role of a mustache-twirling bean counter while urging Thompson to meet his deadlines. Thompson made it all part of his misanthropic narrative. Every two weeks, Thompson's columns came in on the Mojo Wire, which spat out pages of curled, waxen fax paper, each page labeled with letters and numbers, like a puzzle Wenner and his crew were tasked with putting together (Wenner so hated the feel of the wax paper he had every page retyped before he'd read them). As Thompson described it in his you-are-there *Rolling Stone* column, "I can hear the Mojo Wire humming frantically across the room. Crouse is stuffing page after page of gibberish into it . . . The pressure is building up. The copy no longer makes sense. Huge chunks are either missing or too scrambled to follow from one sentence to another. Crouse just fed two consecutive pages into the machine upside-down, provoking a burst of angry yelling from whoever is operating the receiver out there on the Coast."

Wenner and his editors laid the pages out on the floor on Third Street, Wenner stroking his chin and declaring, "This sounds like an opener . . . this reads like the middle . . ." until a column was finally stitched together as the morning light poured into the windows. As Thompson bitched about his distressed psychological state or his fruitless attempt to track down a secondhand rumor he picked up in a strip club on La Cienega Boulevard in Los Angeles, he made every hiccup of his adventures on the trail part of the story so readers could follow him like a detective in a crime caper, the murder suspect almost always Thompson's bête noire, Richard Nixon. His columns reportedly generated five hundred letters a week from *Rolling Stone* readers. For the Democratic convention in Miami Beach, where McGovern was nominated, Wenner devised a plan to ship a thousand complimentary issues of *Rolling Stone* and print up a flyer with Hunter Thompson's funniest quotations and a subscription coupon inside, all of it to be distributed by McGovern volunteers. On the eve of the convention, however, Palevsky broke with McGovern over a dispute with his finance chairman and pulled out of the campaign, leaving Thompson and Wenner demoralized and adrift. When Thompson finished his reporting (taking McGovern's speedboat to the convention hall "was the only thing I did all week that I actually enjoyed," he wrote), he and Wenner sat among the California delegation and inhaled amyl nitrite, the signs and horns blurring into the bright lights. McGovern didn't give his acceptance speech until after midnight, when "anybody still glued to the tube . . . is probably too stoned or twisted to recognize McGovern anyway." The McGovern fantasy died eighteen days later when his vice presidential pick, Senator Tom Eagleton of Missouri, admitted he had received shock treatment for depression in the 1960s and forced McGovern to drop him from the ticket. A distraught Thompson asked Wenner to run a free ad for McGovern every week until the election, but Wenner refused. Those pages cost two grand!

By this time, Thompson was running on fumes, his life in shambles. Earlier that spring, Thompson's wife, Sandy, had lost a premature baby boy at seven months. But Thompson barely had time to be shattered: Sandy took a taxi home alone, and Thompson continued to stew over deadlines and internecine campaign details, getting deeper and deeper into drugs and alcohol and missing columns. (Timothy Crouse filled in, giving him the opening he needed to establish his own name.) During the California primary, Thompson took a long drive up the coast on a Vincent Black Shadow motorcycle with a "McGovern for President" sticker on the handlebars, writing in *Rolling Stone* that "my brain is turning to wax and bad flab; impotence looms; my fingernails are growing at a fantastic rate of speed."

He wasn't joking. After McGovern lost to Nixon in a landslide, what was left was a large pile of expenses and a deadline for a campaign book Thompson was under contract to write for Straight Arrow. After the Republican National Convention, Wenner, reading the writing on the wall, refused to pay for his air travel any longer and canceled his company credit card, signaling that *Rolling Stone* was finished with the election. Wenner demanded Thompson pay him back for $363.39 in shirts and slacks Thompson charged to *Rolling Stone* during the Republican convention and complete his book. Wenner also wanted him to take on more assignments.

In the backwash of Election Day, Thompson was aggrieved: McGovern had lost, but somehow Jann Wenner had won. Thompson's fame had injected *Rolling Stone* directly into the national conversation, cracking the door for *Rolling Stone* in the corridors of Washington, D.C. As Wenner boasted soon after, *Rolling Stone* was the "paper of record" for the 1972 campaign, more so than *The New York Times*. Thompson felt exploited. He wrote Wenner a letter of resignation and demanded he remove "Raoul Duke" from the masthead. He would finish the book, but damned if he was going to let Wenner dine out on his success, which was so hard won and had ended so sourly. Thompson wanted independence from Wenner, freedom to write for *Playboy* and other publications, proclaiming he would only work freelance from then on out. Draw up a contract, Thompson told Wenner, who promised Thompson whatever he wanted—except taking his name off the masthead.

Thompson was infuriated. They didn't speak for months.

10

California

I n the summer of 1971, Joni Mitchell released the seminal song "California" from her fourth album, *Blue,* wherein she finds herself in Europe surrounded by "pretty people" who were "reading *Rolling Stone,* reading *Vogue.*" Plucking a dulcimer and ululating, a luminous goddess of the 1970s, she pined for California and promised to return once her skin turned brown. Mitchell's poetic juxtaposition of *Rolling Stone* and *Vogue* was telling, capturing the glint of celebrity and self-regard that now animated the youth culture, where Warren Beatty and Jack Nicholson were the enfants terribles of Hollywood and Mitchell's friends and lovers from Laurel Canyon, managed by David Geffen, the new Rasputin of 1970s rock, jostled for space in the pages of *Rolling Stone.*

Geffen, a striver from Borough Park, Brooklyn, famously started out in the mail room at the William Morris Agency and became a twenty-seven-year-old millionaire managing L.A. superstars Jackson Browne, the Eagles, Joni Mitchell, and Crosby, Stills, Nash, and Young. Though Wenner's first memory of Geffen was meeting him in the early 1970s during a hospital visit to Neil Young, Geffen said he'd known Jann Wenner since the late 1960s through mutual partners. ("If you're gay," said Geffen, "it's a small world.") They once went to a concert where Wenner tried plying Geffen with speed, but Geffen balked, telling Grover Lewis he found Wenner's offer "absolutely shocking." As he'd been doing since 1967, Jann Wenner made puncturing Los Angeles egos a staple of his San Francisco newspaper. *Rolling Stone* panned *Déjà Vu* by Crosby, Stills, Nash, and Young as "too sweet, too soothing, too perfect, and too good to be true," backhanding them as a careerist supergroup who valued fame over art. Neil Young's *After the Gold Rush* was regarded by *Rolling Stone* as "uniformly dull," and 1972's *Harvest* critiqued as a weak follow-up to *After the Gold Rush.* Wenner splashed David Crosby on the cover in 1970 with a picture of him bugging his eyes like Charles Manson (which Crosby hated), and even his first solo record from 1971, *If I Could Only Remember My Name,* recorded in San Francisco with members of the Grateful Dead and the Jefferson Airplane, was met with a sneer from Lester Bangs, who called it "a perfect aural aid to digestion when you're having guests over for dinner." ("Did it hurt my feelings? Yes, it really fucking did," said Crosby.)

Joni Mitchell, who was living in David Geffen's guesthouse in Beverly Hills, expressed ambivalence about her rock-and-roll fame. "Inside I'm thinking, 'You're phony. You're being a star,'" she said in a quotation *Rolling Stone* put under her unsmiling photograph. (She also mused on photography as a kind of rape.) After she released "California," *Rolling Stone* published an infamous two-page chart called "Hollywood's Hot 100," annotating the internecine relationships of the Los Angeles "haute monde," from A&M's "Aristocrats" (Gil Friesen and Herb Alpert) to the singers and sidemen, including the CSNY "Bachelors," with Joni Mitchell at the center of it all, her name printed inside a lipstick stain and surrounded by arrows suggesting she'd slept with David Crosby, James Taylor, and Stephen Stills. "We heard about that right away," recalled Charlie Perry. "I was told, 'Why do this to Joni? She's just looking for love like all of us.'"

The call Perry was referring to was almost certainly from Geffen. "That was an outrageous thing," recalled Geffen. "It was something expected more of a gossip magazine than [what] *Rolling Stone* would be. She was very offended."

The chart had no attribution or byline but was created by Jerry Hopkins, Wenner's L.A. correspondent, who said he initially drew it up as a joke. It was Jann Wenner, he claimed, who insisted on publishing it in February 1972. "I was horrified," Hopkins said, "but not nearly so much as Joni was. I am grateful only that my name was not attached." ("Joni . . . if you see this, I'm sorry," said Hopkins.)

Joni Mitchell didn't speak to *Rolling Stone* for seven years. Jackson Browne was dating her at the time and recalled her fury and his own: "I thought, 'What the fuck happened to our magazine? What happened to our generation's voice?'" After it appeared, Wenner went backstage at a Mitchell concert, evidently high and seemingly oblivious to her fury over the article. "He couldn't actually tell that Joni was livid that he was there," said Browne. "Did he even read the magazine?"

(Later, Browne broke up with Mitchell, sending her into a near-suicidal depression and inspiring the song "Car on a Hill," from 1974's *Court and Spark,* which also includes a song about David Geffen, "Free Man in Paris." Reviewing the album, Jon Landau observed that Mitchell "has composed few songs of unambivalent feeling.")

Wenner often blamed his writers for negative stories and reviews. But the Mitchell backhand was not a mistake: *Rolling Stone* doubled down by naming her "Old Lady of the Year" in 1972 "for her friendships with David Crosby, Steve Stills, Graham Nash, Neil Young, James Taylor, et al." And all this antagonism toward the Los Angeles scene flowed directly from Jann Wenner, who saw these richly egoed rockers as fair game for his newly muscular journalistic enterprise. His pointed tool for raking muck was Ben Fong-Torres, whom Wenner referred to as "the inscrutable Oriental." Fong-Torres was a first-generation Chinese American; his father immigrated to San Francisco as a Filipino national using the fake name Ricardo Torres, thus Fong-Torres. After freelancing for *Rolling Stone* in the late 1960s, Fong-Torres quit his job producing an employee magazine for the local telephone company and became Wenner's full-time workhorse in 1969, churning out reams of Random Notes gossip. His first story as a staffer was an interview with Joni Mitchell. Among the few *Rolling Stone* employees to study journalism in college, he described his approach in the introduction to the second volume of *The "Rolling Stone" Interviews:* "I know to do research beforehand, to be friendly during the warm-up ('I heard your new album just yesterday.' Pause, shaking head slowly. 'Whew!'), to take notes and keep the recorder going while maintaining contact and, afterwards, to make no promises."

Fong-Torres's journalism didn't respect many boundaries, as Jackson Browne soon found out. Wenner was introduced to Browne by Danny Fields in the offices of Elektra in the late 1960s, and he first appeared in *Rolling Stone* in 1970, name checked by David Crosby as "one of probably the ten best songwriters around." Browne's first *Rolling Stone* cover, when he was twenty-five, featured him cradling his baby son, Ethan, in his arms, an echo of the Joe Dallesandro cover. Wenner assigned the story to a sixteen-year-old reporter named Cameron Crowe, who lived at home with his mother in San Diego. Browne remembered him as enthusiastic and sweet, a guileless fan scribbling notes, but afterward Crowe's editor, Ben Fong-Torres, called Browne to ask for more material. "They sent Ben Fong-Torres to my house to interview me, to touch it up, to beef it up," Browne said. "And it was the same day that Annie came to shoot me. I went to the store, and Ben Fong-Torres went into my house alone. He literally came into my bedroom . . . he wandered through the whole house, he described the contents of the house, he wrote down shit that I had in my fucking notebook. I felt so violated. Like, I'm going to kill this guy. I'm gonna walk to San Francisco and walk across the fucking floor and deck this motherfucker."

The story, which had Cameron Crowe's name on it, said Browne had "pollinated every virgin in Southern California" and was currently working on a new song, the lyrics of which Fong-Torres copied directly from Browne's open notebook: "In my early years I hid my tears / And passed my days alone / Adrift on an ocean of loneliness / My dreams like nets were thrown."

David Geffen told Fong-Torres he was becoming *Rolling Stone*'s own Rona Barrett, the glamorous Hollywood gossip columnist famous for her dishy (and sometimes vicious) reports. "I just read your latest bit of bullshit," Geffen told him in 1974. "Congratulations . . . you finally made the small time."

Jann Wenner, of course, was delighted. That same year, he began setting names in boldface in Random Notes to make it more like a classic gossip column and experimented with another column called Social Notes, written by Glenn O'Brien, with fine detail on fashion ("Yoko Ono wore a black cape, black boots and black hot pants") and who was sleeping with whom ("Romance Rumors: Andy Warhol and Paulette Goddard; Liza Minnelli and *Pippin* star Ben Vereen; Faye Dunaway and/or Peter Wolf and/or Jack Nicholson and/or Roman Polanski"). A writer billed as "Our Society Editor" (in this case, Tim Ferris) produced near-hourly coverage of John and Yoko in New York in 1971, and the same byline covered the wedding of Mick and Bianca Jagger in St. Tropez, publishing the entire guest list. "I don't want to be married in a fishbowl," said Jagger in a caption below an image of the couple at the altar. Meanwhile, Annie Leibovitz provided party pictures that would make pioneering 1970s paparazzo Ron Galella proud, including a layout of an Elton John after party in Los Angeles with a caption that said, "Hey, campers, here's something new, a whole bunch of little pictures to look at without having to read hardly anything—like on television!"

Wenner was, in effect, reframing rock and roll as a celebrity culture like any before it. It wasn't a movement, or a youth culture anymore, let alone a revolution. This was the age of *personalities,* just as the cover of *Sgt. Pepper's* had portended. Mainstream magazines like *Time* and *Newsweek* ran small sections called "Transition" and "Newsmakers" to highlight the famous and important, but boldfaced names were now the *medium* of rock and roll and thus the message of *Rolling Stone.* Everyone wanted to be famous, even the L.A. record executives who were counting the cash behind the scenes. "We are artists!" declared Joe Smith, the head of Warner Bros., in a 1971 interview with Wenner, who shook Smith down for every last detail of the record business, from the losses the label took on the Grateful Dead to rumors that Steve Ross, head of Warner Communications, was connected to the Mafia. (He wasn't, said Smith.) Smith hated the story, and Wenner reprinted it in a *Rolling Stone* anthology.

David Geffen often dismissed *Rolling Stone* as a mere vanity page for his rock stars; it didn't affect record sales, he insisted, so who cares? But that didn't mean David Geffen didn't want his own ink. He put a picture of himself in the gatefold of David Crosby's solo album, a wet shirt stuck to his body and a rose in his teeth. In 1973, he asked Jann Wenner to profile him in *Rolling Stone,* but Wenner told him he didn't want to alienate Clive Davis of CBS, with whom Geffen had warred over Laura Nyro and who was still angry at Wenner about a "hatchet job" on Neil Diamond, telegraphing his unhappiness by temporarily pulling Columbia's advertising. Geffen said he understood Wenner's dilemma, but he became less understanding when he got a call from Ben Fong-Torres asking for a quotation for another profile— of Clive Davis. "I said, '*What?*'" Geffen later recounted. "Fuckin' Jann Wenner."

Geffen wrote a scathing letter to Wenner, calling him dishonest and weak and demanding an explanation "upon your return from Paris." But David Geffen didn't have to worry: Before any story appeared, Clive Davis was fired from CBS for allegedly charging his son's $20,000 bar mitzvah to the company expense account.

•

WHILE WENNER'S PAPER WAS raking muck in Los Angeles, his wife was regularly accompanying Annie Leibovitz there on *Rolling Stone* assignments, cruising down the Pacific Coast Highway in Leibovitz's cream-colored 1963 convertible Porsche 356 C. Leibovitz had so many speeding tickets she'd lost her license, "but because I hadn't admitted guilt," she said, "they couldn't take me to jail. So I'd drive down to L.A., and say, 'I already lost my license; I'll drive a hundred miles per hour.'"

She made a series of Polaroids of the policemen who pulled her over, the collection of which she eventually gave to Jane.

In L.A., the two luxuriated in Palevsky's L.A. and Palm Springs homes or curled up in an apartment on North Robertson Boulevard owned by Earl McGrath, a bohemian man-about-town married to an Italian heiress, Countess Camilla Pecci-Blunt, a descendant of Pope Leo XIII. Though McGrath had the title of vice president at Atlantic Records, he was more like a glorified manservant to label president Ahmet Ertegun, who was amused when McGrath pretended to be the butler and took his coat at a party in the early 1960s. "Earl is to the rock-and-roll business what surfing is to Kansas," said David Geffen. "He was a friend of Ahmet's."

With a prankish wit and elfin smile, he mainly focused on cultivating a salon of artists, celebrities, and hip hangers-on amid his growing collection of modern art. To be with McGrath in his garden courtyard in West Hollywood in the 1970s was to chance an encounter with Cy Twombly or Anjelica Huston or Christopher Isherwood. He employed a handsome young carpenter named Harrison Ford who hung around for months getting stoned while his projects languished. For laughs, McGrath would blow pot into the ear of his pet beagle, Jiminy, or dramatically announce a magic trick in which he would pull a tablecloth out from under the dishware, only to yank everything onto the floor and break all the dishes. He once planted a story in the Hollywood trades about the bizarre alter ego of Diane Chess, wife of Marshall, who would prank call Ahmet Ertegun and Paul Simon pretending to be a tough guy named Alfred while McGrath and the Wenners listened in on a separate phone line, stifling laughs.

Though happily married, McGrath, like Wenner, was happy to play both sides, often traveling to Europe with British producer and manager Robert Stigwood, a fabled member of the "Pink Mafia" of gay record men in 1960s London who discovered and managed the Bee Gees. "I was pretending to my wife I was looking for a job in the music business," said McGrath.

Consequently, McGrath became part of the *Rolling Stone* inner circle, introducing the Wenners to the Important and the Beautiful, including Joan Didion (who dedicated *The White Album* to McGrath) and Francois de Menil, heir to the Schlumberger oil fortune. While working at Atlantic Records, McGrath conspired with Jann Wenner and the Robert Stigwood Organisation to produce a *Rolling Stone* television program for the magazine's fifth anniversary, bringing in a young comedy writer named Lorne Michaels, who was working for Lily Tomlin's comedy special on CBS (Tomlin appeared with Richard Pryor on the cover of *Rolling Stone* in 1974). The idea evolved into a twice-monthly music program with a comic sensibility, but it never panned out, and later McGrath came to feel Michaels ran off with the idea and invented *Saturday Night Live* on NBC. "I felt kind of used," said McGrath.

What McGrath was really doing for the Wenners was housebreaking them for the jet set. The painter Brice Marden, part of McGrath's art world orbit, said, "Earl taught the Wenners how to be rich." And the bond was further tightened by Annie Leibovitz, with whom McGrath had a yearlong affair. "He was so handsome, so seductive," said Leibovitz. "This was another world for me. You have to imagine, I'm walking into these worlds and I photograph them." ("In a way, I thought she was using me, too," said McGrath. "She knew I was a very good friend of the Wenners.")

Another luminary in the McGrath orbit was Eve Babitz, a legendary chronicler of 1970s Los Angeles and the LP designer for Buffalo Springfield. Famous for a photograph of herself nude and playing chess with Marcel Duchamp, Babitz lived for a time in San Francisco with *Rolling Stone* editor Grover Lewis, who published her seminal essay "The Sheik," a diary-like chronicle of growing up in Hollywood amid a new generation raised on the golden nectar of California, "where statistically the children grow taller, have better teeth, and are stronger than anywhere else in the country. When they reach the age of 15 and their beauty arrives, it's very exciting—like coming into an inheritance and, as with inheritances, it's fun to be around when they first come into the money and watch how they spend it and on what."

It was Babitz who first invited Annie Leibovitz to hang out at McGrath's, and along came Jane Wenner, whom Babitz captured with scalpel-like precision in a short story called "Bad Day at Palm Springs," published in 1974. A tale of torpid glamour and lush ennui among a small coterie of L.A. scenesters, it featured a thinly veiled Laurel Gonsalves and Paul Ruscha, brother of artist Ed Ruscha, and cast Jane Wenner as Nikki, a woman with "something tragic and theatrical about her" who suffered migraines while luxuriating unhappily at a Palm Springs house "fit for a king, or a child—it was a perfect human dwelling with no extras, all plain surfaces and simple" (it was, unmistakably, Max Palevsky's house).

In spite of her girlish posture and quaint baby-colored dress she looked oddly ominous. Her skull, her cheekbones, the brutal cut to her mouth all were Egyptian and timeless. Her skin was the tone of the desert, no traces of rose, neutral. And just as you thought she was a complete reptile in doll's clothes, she'd raise her eyes and there was that most wonderful surprise—her eyes were warmly golden near the pupil and became violet at the iris's edge.

After a weekend of Valium-tinged malaise, Babitz called Jane to apologize for the depressing weekend, paranoid that Jane's quiet sulking behind extra-large sunglasses meant she had a bad time. To Babitz's surprise, Jane is relieved to hear from her: "I thought you guys all hated me."

•

IN HER SHORT STORY, Eve Babitz made Jann Wenner a lawyer named Saul Kroenberg. After meeting Wenner's wife in real life, Babitz said she felt sorry for him. "He was a guy who should have had fun," she said. "But I guess marrying Janie Wenner kind of crimped his style. I don't know why he married her."

Babitz said Jann Wenner wanted her help getting into the movie business, perhaps inspired by his newest friend, the actor Michael Douglas. The son of movie legend Kirk Douglas first appeared in *Rolling Stone* for a montage of Annie Leibovitz party shots taken backstage at a Grateful Dead concert, sitting next to his pal Jimmy Webb, writer of ornate countripolitan hits like Glen Campbell's "By the Time I Get to Phoenix." Webb was Douglas's houseguest while the twenty-eight-year-old actor shot a TV show called *The Streets of San Francisco,* a classic tutor-tyro cop show on ABC starring Karl Malden. Herb Caen sniped about the invasion of their fair city by the barbarians of Tinseltown, but Wenner was dazzled and found his way onto the set and invited Douglas back to *Rolling Stone.* They immediately hit it off over lines of cocaine, two former prep school toffs who thought of themselves as "bad boys" and recognized the glinting edge on the other's ambition. (Wenner also thought he was pretty cute.) Soon enough Douglas was a regular guest of the Wenners' at Ord Court. "His home was open, with Jane, and the intimate relationship with Annie, that communal feeling that came out of the '60s that still existed," as Douglas described it.

Cocaine had arrived in Jann Wenner's world in 1971, around the time *Rolling Stone* published a long explainer called "Cocaine: A Flash in the Pan, a Pain in the Nose," by Jerry Hopkins. In the first few paragraphs, Hopkins quoted a Hollywood doctor warning of the deleterious effects he observed in "cocaine casualties in the music industry," including "restlessness, excitability, hallucinations, rapid heartbeat, dilated pupils, chills or fever, sensory aberrations—the inability to feel heat or cold, abdominal pain, vomiting, numbness or muscle spasms, followed by depressed and irregular respiration, convulsions, coma and circulatory failure."

If Jann Wenner read this, he certainly didn't take it seriously. Instead, he was taking to cocaine like an Irish poet to rhyme. In 1972, Douglas started coming by Wenner's office with blow he scored from photographer Jim Marshall or stuff he was gifted from his new pals in the San Francisco Police Department, whom Douglas was glamorizing on network television. "The narcotics officers were known to off-load some of the evidence," said Douglas.

Unlike psychedelics, which inspired cosmic oneness with other people, cocaine inspired feelings of acute exclusivity, separating the cocaine haves from the cocaine have-nots and lasting as long as one could afford to maintain the sensation of keyed-up exaltation—in other words, the ideal drug for Jann Wenner. Wenner first tried it at a Las Vegas record business convention in 1969 when Bob Krasnow of Buddah Records (who discovered Captain Beefheart) gave him a snort. He wasn't immediately impressed. Then Laurel Gonsalves showed up with the supply, and Wenner was off to the races.

Coke eventually distorted all facets of Wenner's life. His staff began to notice, starting in 1972. During the thirty-six-hour rush to close an issue, Wenner began conducting what staffers would come to refer to as "cocaine edits" on stories and covers, slashing them up during weekend frenzies. Office manager Dan Parker, who delivered some layouts to the Wenners' house in the early 1970s, recalled Wenner sitting with a powder-filled goblet by his side. "I would guess a pound at least of cocaine," he said. "I said, 'No thanks, I've got a lot of things to get done.'"

Errors began multiplying in *Rolling Stone,* infuriating writers like Joe Eszterhas, a street-smart newspaper reporter from Cleveland who avoided Wenner's intemperate hand by turning in thirty-thousand-word exposés at the very last minute so there was no time to edit them, which invariably led to more errors and mistakes. Eventually, Wenner was confronted by his staff in a tense meeting in the Raoul Duke Room. "We complained about the coke," recounted Charlie Perry. "Jann said that Paul Scanlon had been urging him to come to the meeting sober, and to come clean about the coke. Joe Eszterhas took a buck knife out of his pocket and put it on the table, which was something he did when he was gonna disagree with Jann. And he started laying into him about his coke-fueled mistakes and wanted to know what guarantee there was gonna be that this wasn't gonna happen in the future, and Jann gradually crumpled, and then he reached into his pocket and took out a packet of cigarettes and removed a cigarette from which tobacco had been removed and filled with coke, and he poured it out and snorted it.

"It was a sad, sad moment, it really was," said Perry.

But cocaine, for all its downsides, was also the magnet and bonding agent for the kinds of people Wenner wanted around him. It was the lingua franca of countercultural risk—breaking the law on a daily basis, testing the boundaries of discretion. It was also a service he could provide his subjects as he herded them into *Rolling Stone*'s pages. "Although there were periods of time where they were destructive, Jann got a tremendous amount out of his drug experiences," said Jon Landau. "Maybe one of them was Hunter. He could understand Hunter; they were talking the same language. That in and of itself was one of the most important things that happened to *Rolling Stone*." (By 1974, Joe Eszterhas was no longer complaining, snorting cocaine through Wenner's $100 bill to power through a deadline.)

Wenner's coke use became so blatant that he snorted some while a reporter for the *Columbia Journalism Review* sat across from him. "I hope this doesn't start making me yak," he told him. Wenner later tried passing it off as a joke—it wasn't real, he said—and blamed his publicist for letting the reporter write the scene into a generally scathing profile. "He was pissed off at me," said Bryn Bridenthal. (As was his custom, Wenner scrawled corrections and exclamatory insults all over the profile and gave it back to Bridenthal.)

Quite a few of the symptoms described by the doctor quoted in

Rolling Stone became evident in Jann Wenner, including heightened paranoia. He had an acute suspicion that his phone was being tapped, possibly by gossip columnist Herb Caen, and asked Max Palevsky for help. At least some of this paranoia was warranted: After Joe Eszterhas published "Nark" in 1972, about corrupt undercover cops framing drug users, unmarked packages of pot and cocaine began arriving in the mail from grateful *Rolling Stone* readers. Afterward, Wenner banned pot smoking in the office and washed off the drawing of a coke spoon a staffer had painted on his parking space.

11

The Cover of the *Rolling Stone*

In 1974, novelist Ken Kesey, the godfather of the San Francisco Acid Tests, was scheduled to pick Jann Wenner up at the airport in Portland, Oregon, where they planned on interviewing the governor of Oregon, Tom McCall, an environmental and drug-law progressive whose administration organized the first state-sponsored rock concert. But when Wenner got off the plane, Kesey gave him a quizzical look. "You don't look like what I thought you'd look like," he said.

"What do you mean?" Wenner asked.

"I thought you'd be tall and blond," he replied, "the way you looked in the comic book."

Wenner had appeared in an issue of Marvel's *Daredevil* in June 1973, issue No. 100, depicted as a curiously tall and blond figure who scores an interview with the masked superhero for *Rolling Stone*. "I didn't think the counterculture was interested in anybody who works with the police," says Daredevil, floating above him.

The image of Wenner as a dashing Aryan was indeed comic. Glamour, someone once wrote, required looking like you didn't work. By that definition, Wenner would never be glamorous. The stiff keys on his beige IBM Selectric typewriter required him to bash down so hard that, from his office, Wenner's never-ending letter writing, his tireless scheming, sounded like an act of violence echoing down the hallways, a rhythmic clacking of ambition and need. His fingers punched bold-faced names into his beloved letterhead with the zeal of a boxer: Dear Tom Wolfe, Dear Mick Jagger, Dear Norman Mailer, Dear Truman Capote, Dear Tim Leary. The names piled up like cigarettes in his ashtray. The bolder the name, the bigger the dopamine kick, the bigger Jann Wenner's desire to stamp them into his yearbook, *Rolling Stone*.

"This sounds weird," said Timothy Crouse, "but I would swear that I sometimes used to see purple clouds around his eyes, a kind of effluvium. It was like this gas that was swirling around them because he was so hungry for everything he looked at. There are people who look at things to understand them, and people who look at things because they have to have them. With Jann, it seemed to be about desire, or greed, or a lust for power."

In person, Wenner's words were often lost in a jumble of "ums" and "you knows" and "blah, blah, blahs," but in letters Wenner could articulate his thoughts with precision: In late 1971, he wrote a letter to Arthur Ochs Sulzberger, the publisher of *The New York Times,* crystallizing his ambitions in an urgent plea for coverage by the paper of record. "We are in a key and strategic transition now in the way the 'outside world' views us," he wrote. "Are we some temporal 'Woodstock Nation' sheet or a serious and worthy new kind of publication that will be around for some time to come?"

Wenner intended to answer his own question. With Jane back at Ord Court, he returned to breathing *Rolling Stone* 24/7. "Razzle-dazzle, night and day, coast to coast," as Alan Rinzler would later say of these days. "We were exploding sparks of amphetamine energy, bolts of manic lightning striking down every obstacle in our path." Marshall Chess recalled waking up in the middle of the night as a houseguest to find Jann preparing to go into the office in pajamas and robe. There was too much fun! On Third Street, stars like Elton John, Bette Midler, and Al Green drifted in and out. During his visit, Green dramatically brushed off Wenner's chair for a TV camera. "I was intimidated by Jann," said Elton John, who met Wenner at *Rolling Stone* in 1971 after appearing on the cover, "not because he was a nasty or snobbish person, but because he founded something so great . . . like someone who formed *The Washington Post* or whatever."

His mother started calling him Citizen Wenner, after *Citizen Kane,* the 1941 Orson Welles film based on the life of William Randolph Hearst. She used it pejoratively, as did writers like Grover Lewis, who hated Wenner. But Wenner embraced it. David Obst, the book agent who came to represent Bob Woodward and Carl Bernstein, recalled Jane Wenner screening *Citizen Kane* for Jann's birthday one year. "I remember he literally couldn't sit down," recalled Obst. "This had to be his umpteenth screening of it. He would just get so excited, and his empathy with the Kane character and what he was going through, not on the sexual side, but on the business side, was palpable."

Inspiring satire is a clear sign of success, and by this measure *Rolling Stone* had fully arrived. In Las Vegas, actress Mitzi Gaynor of *South Pacific* fame now included a *Rolling Stone* parody in her song and dance act ("It's a very versatile magazine: you can either read it or smoke it"), and Dr. Hook and the Medicine Show, a rowdy southern-tinged band on Columbia Records, recorded a virtual advertisement for the newspaper, "The Cover of the Rolling Stone," written by Shel Silverstein. It reached No. 6 on the pop charts, and *Rolling Stone* put a comic illustration of the band on the cover in March 1973 (Wenner later tried policing the use of the song for copyright abuse). There were also published parodies of *Rolling Stone*—"Rolling Drone"—that made fun of the newspaper's self-seriousness and endless nostalgia for the Summer of Love. But herein was Wenner's power: There was simply too much heaven behind the gates of the 1960s and 1970s. In his fourth-anniversary editorial, Wenner dispensed with any pretentions to countercultural purity, proclaiming *Rolling Stone* free from anybody's agenda but its own and embracing the true calling of his newspaper: making money. "If you're doing public art and communication in America—if you even live here—you're dealing with money, and you're in business . . . As long as there are printing bills to pay, writers who want to earn a living by their craft, people who pay for their groceries, want to raise children and have their own homes, *Rolling Stone* will be a capitalist operation."

Wenner wasn't a very good capitalist yet. Instead, he was a serial recruiter of capitalists, discovering publishers and businessmen who could advance *Rolling Stone*'s fortunes and teach Wenner a new trick—before Wenner hired somebody to squeeze them out and continue his march to the next hill. In 1971, Wenner hired a childhood friend of Hunter Thompson's named Porter Bibb, a Louisville bon vivant who had helped produce the film *Gimme Shelter* with the Maysles brothers. Bibb, who favored Gucci loafers, painted extravagant visions of a hippie empire for Wenner, including a syndicated *Rolling Stone* radio show, a *Rolling Stone* record club, closed-circuit TV concert deals with Pepsi, and even a *Rolling Stone* insurance policy ("a guaranteed sure-fire money maker"). Wenner put him on the masthead as "Porter Bigg" and waited for the cash to roll in. Within a year, Bibb's expense account swamped his fantasies as he tried and failed to get Wenner to invest in the business, and eventually Wenner fired him. Only the *Rolling Stone Radio Hour* materialized—until Wenner clashed with the man Bibb hired to run it, Bob Meyrowitz, who left to start the syndicated radio program the *King Biscuit Flower Hour*. "He was very upset, and he ended up suing Jann for breach of contract," recalled Bibb.

Until 1974, Wenner's capitalist operation ebbed and flowed with the fortunes of record companies that bailed him out in 1970. Three-quarters of the ads still came from record companies and stereo manufacturers, which floated in with minimal effort: Laurel Gonsalves, who kept scales on her desk for weighing pot and cocaine, was more like the newspaper's conscience than an ad saleswoman, policing for cigarettes, alcohol, and pornography while drawing up ethical guides showing why she rejected companies like Hi-Fashion Water Beds, whose ads used "women as sex objects, in the fashion of *Playboy*." (She was also meticulous about accredited abortion referral agencies and ran Planned Parenthood ads for free.) But her attempts to get the big-league ads that Jann Wenner wanted in *Rolling Stone*—Porsche, Audi, Jeep, Kodak, Polaroid, Gillette, and TWA—were all but hopeless. In part this was because Gonsalves rarely ventured outside the office but also because she hired salespeople who looked like cast members from *Hair* and who rolled into the office after lunch.

In 1972, Wenner commissioned the corporate accounting firm Dun & Bradstreet to value the company, which it put at a relatively paltry $424,920. But profitability was up for the first time in three years, and a "planned expansion" promised more. The architect of the expansion was Wenner's next business partner, a large-bodied and sharp-tongued

Boston Irishman named Larry Durocher who was a close friend and mentor to Jon Landau and had helped salvage the Boston alt-weekly *Phoenix*. Durocher became *Rolling Stone*'s publisher, extracted Wenner from his contract with Independent News, and negotiated a new deal that put *Rolling Stone* next to *Time* and *Newsweek* on the newsstands. Durocher also plotted an important upgrade: By changing the size and shape of *Rolling Stone*—making it a large, folded tabloid—they could accommodate more pages, publish better color images, and charge advertisers $4,000 for a page.

Before Durocher was fired in 1974, Wenner recruited Tom Baker, a straitlaced business consultant who had success with a chain of California convenience stores called Short Stop. Tasked with streamlining *Rolling Stone*'s finances, Baker replaced Wenner's longtime business manager, Hank Torgrimson (who didn't wear shoes and still included astrological signs on employee forms), and installed basic financial systems at *Rolling Stone,* which helped Straight Arrow go from break-even to "pleasantly profitable," as Wenner put it in 1973 when he claimed in the press that *Rolling Stone* earned $430,000 in profit on $5 million in revenue. (In truth, it was probably half that, which was still pretty good.)

Before Wenner fired Baker in 1975, his most important business partner of the 1970s entered the picture, a thirty-year-old salesman named Joe Armstrong. A tall, lean Texan with a flop of sandy-brown hair, Armstrong wore three-piece suits and had an aw-shucks accent to go with his wide, pleasing smile. His ambition fizzed like a glass of champagne: He had a journalism degree from Trinity and a law degree from the University of Texas. After escaping the conservative confines of Texas for the bright lights of New York City, he first tried working on Wall Street before leaping to magazines, becoming assistant publisher at *Family Week*. Wenner discovered Armstrong through a grand old advertising man named Whit Hobbs, a consultant to *The New Yorker* whom Wenner hired to try getting the same ads in *Rolling Stone*. Though he didn't look like one, Armstrong was a *Rolling Stone* devotee. But he saw the advertising materials *Rolling Stone* was circulating—a cartoon hippie flying through the air and the words "Our readers like to fly, too. Especially on planes"—and knew what he had to do: deliver

an image and a message that the suits on Madison Avenue could understand. Surely they could get all those blue-chip ads Wenner had been
clipping from *Newsweek,* but *Rolling Stone* would need a makeover—a
new image in brochures, mailers, and posters. He would need to recruit
a new ad sales team, none with long hair or tank tops or drug scales
on their desks, all with pressed clothes and fresh-faced smiles, able to
hold the hands of old admen who listened to Ray Conniff and explain
how a magazine featuring "naked hippies" and actor Paul Newman saying "fuck" in print was conducive to car and liquor sales. And above
all, these straitlaced salespeople had to love *Rolling Stone* as much as
Joe Armstrong did. "I could really only sell something I believed in,"
said Armstrong. "When I got to *Rolling Stone,* I only hired magazine
salespeople that loved the magazine, so it took me a looong time to find
people. This was rare for ad sales people, anywhere."

Jann Wenner met Joe Armstrong in a diner on Third Avenue in New
York and listened to his pitch—the courtly manner, the gushing enthusiasm, the fluttering eyelashes. Wenner had never met somebody who
seemed to love his newspaper as much as he did. A business romance.
And out of the blue, Wenner made a strange request of the charming
Texan. "He wanted to see everything in my billfold," recalled Armstrong. "I said, 'Well, I'd like to see yours.'"

•

IF JANN WENNER WAS not yet a great capitalist, the alchemy of his
appetites and the fertile culture was making him a great editor in chief.
The youth movement in the 1960s seemed to be essentially unitary, but
as it shattered, its fragments proved to be even more journalistically
interesting, and *Rolling Stone* was perfectly positioned to sweep them
up. Here was the premier interview with David Bowie, the androgynous spaceman from England, and an exposé on astronauts by Tom
Wolfe. Here was Tim Cahill infiltrating a Christian cult in Hollywood
and Grover Lewis infiltrating the set of *The Getaway* in 1972, headlined
"Why Did Sam Peckinpah Tell Steve McQueen to Belt This Actress
in the Face? See Page 40" (it was Sally Struthers from *All in the Family*). Here was beat legend William Burroughs on Scientology, Eldridge
Cleaver on Timothy Leary ("He has blown his mind on acid"), Lester

Bangs on the death of Jack Kerouac, Jonathan Cott interviewing Stock-hausen. How deep the well! How endless the smorgasbord! Woody Allen explained his 1971 comedy, *Bananas* ("The film is about the lack of substance in my movie"), and a group of media revolutionaries called TOTAL ACCESS explained the future: "When my fuckin' revolution comes, everybody in the world's gonna be on television all the time." In a time of such ferment, *Rolling Stone* readers expected literary excess and a certain overripeness, and they often got it. Here is how the Nick Tosches review of Black Sabbath's *Paranoid* began:

> A young girl's voice. She is dressed in a nun's habit. The boy turns and faces her. She proffers a chalice of cervical exudate and he drinks from it. She gets down on her knees and elbows, *como peros,* and tosses the nun's hem above her posterior. On each naked but-tock is the scrawled sign of Ashirikas; "Fuck me, Rolf." The boy whips out a 10" personal vibrator, adorned in waterproof acrylics with the image of the Nazarene. He intones the words *"nuk Khensu tenten nebu"* and approaches her intendent fundament . . . imple-tion . . . across the room the fresh corpse of an illegitimate hippie baby is dis-impaled from a ceremonial sword of Baphomet.

The album was pretty good, too.

Jann Wenner was romping through this new anything-goes culture, publishing a gleefully smirking profile of Tricia Nixon, daughter of the president; putting nine-year-old Tatum O'Neal, daughter of actor Ryan, on the cover on the occasion of her role in *Paper Moon* ("The Portrait of an Artist as a Little Girl"); and publishing an illustrated pinup of Olympic swimmer Mark Spitz wearing a leopard-skin bikini and licking his lips in a salacious come-on ("That was very gay," said Wenner). Perhaps it was true that "greatness knows itself," but Wenner wasn't so much interested in knowing himself as in imbibing the "great-ness" of everything and everyone else around him. Wenner looked east to the successful magazines of Manhattan publishing—*Esquire* and *New York,* the Medici of the New Journalism—and vowed to best them on their own turf by publishing the greatest work by the greatest writers. Unlike Hugh Hefner of *Playboy,* whom Wenner criticized for paying top dollar for big-name writers only to get second-rate work, he would get first-rate work by the best writers. "That was my attitude to everybody: 'I only want your best stuff,'" said Wenner. "Hefner got into that habit; he would take name writers with throwaway pieces."

And if Hugh Hefner didn't hear him clearly, *Rolling Stone* published a sharp takedown of the *Playboy* founder in 1973 by British muckraker Anthony Haden-Guest. Afterward, a publicist for Hefner slammed "The Pubic Hair Papers" as inaccurate and unfair and complained about "Little Offal Annie [Leibovitz]," whom they had allowed to intrude on "Mr. Hefner's privacy," only to be rewarded with "unflattering" images. *Touché!*

But nothing proved Wenner's point more than publishing Tom Wolfe, whom Wenner convinced, after a few false starts, to take on the American space program on the occasion of the last Apollo launch in 1972. To Wolfe, Jann Wenner was the sort of character he might have written about had Wenner not been working for years to get Wolfe into his newspaper. "There was something really innocent about Jann," said Wolfe. "He was very open."

Wenner had paid a visit to Wolfe in 1968 while Wolfe was in San Francisco researching *Radical Chic & Mau-Mauing the Flak Catchers,* his reportage and essays on the counterculture, in an effort to get Wolfe to admit he really did take LSD while reporting *The Electric Kool-Aid Acid Test* (Wolfe denied it but later admitted in *Rolling Stone,* in 1980, he tried it once: "It scared the hell out of me. It was like tying yourself to a railroad track to see how big the train is").

Wolfe's arrival at *Rolling Stone* was prefigured by Wenner's own impersonation of him. For a report from a record convention at the Riviera Hotel in Las Vegas, titled "The Blind Leading the Deaf Through a Desert," Wenner quoted and name checked his new idol ("Tom Wolfe, you were right!") and composed a detailed, Wolfe-like cataloging of the record men he saw there, with their "carefully trimmed reddish sideburns, yellow-tinted sunglasses in the wide-lens, gold-wire rim fashion, moccasins and/or buckskin jackets with fringes, all of it so neatly done."

But, never satisfied with his own writing, he pursued the real thing. In late 1969, he had asked Wolfe to write a profile of Jimi Hendrix. Wolfe demurred, but he was taken by Wenner's fanboyish enthusiasm and outrageous confidence. After Wenner took him on a ride in his limousine with tinted windows and a bandannaed hippie for a driver, it was clear Wenner wasn't one of the freaks Wolfe had written about in *The Electric Kool-Aid Acid Test*. "I think he always had his head on his shoulders," Wolfe said. "I don't know how many chemicals he took, but I'm sure he took his share. But he really did not act off the wall. He wasn't far out; he always seemed like he knew what he was doing."

Wolfe's first project for Wenner was covering a record convention in Miami in 1970. Wenner accompanied him to the meeting of the National Association of Recording Merchandisers, trying to sell advertising pages while Wolfe observed the scene—and promptly decided against writing about it after seeing how little any of it was about music. "Their interest is how many square feet of department store space you can sell," he said.

Wolfe came back with a story pitch about *Jesus Christ Superstar* and the "Third Great Awakening" of religious fervor among hippies (an idea that never materialized in *Rolling Stone* but later became "The 'Me' Decade," published by *New York* magazine in 1976). In the introduction to "Post-orbital Remorse: The Brotherhood of the Right Stuff," Wenner wrote that Wolfe came to him with the idea. "I went down to the Kennedy Space Center in 1969, for the launch of Apollo," said Wolfe. "So I was interested in that and decided to move forward with it."

But it became a full *Rolling Stone* production, with staffers mailing out form letters to the astronauts to campaign for Wolfe's access. When Wolfe went to Cape Canaveral for the launch in December 1972, he was accompanied by Annie Leibovitz and met by another space gawker, Atlantic Records chief Ahmet Ertegun. Wenner teased the story in advance, writing in *Rolling Stone* on the eve of the launch, "The Mojo Wire will be humming from the Eastern seaboard tonight, and our thoughts are with you, Tom."

The story extended over four issues, seventeen pages on the lives of test pilots who subjected themselves and their long-suffering families to the terrible pressures of piloting experimental planes and spacecraft. According to Wenner, the talkative first-person opener of the story was an homage to Hunter Thompson, whom Wolfe first met in Manhattan over lunch at the Brazilian Coffee House on West Forty-Sixth Street. In usual form, Thompson brought a mysterious object with him. "He said, 'I have something in this bag that could clear out this place in fifteen seconds,'" recalled Wolfe. "'Here, I'll show you.' I said, 'You don't have to show me,' and he took the thing out. It was like a little can of shaving cream. He pressed the top, and there was a piercing sound."

It was a marine air horn. "I was surprised I had any hearing left," said Wolfe.

It would take Wolfe several years to turn his NASA exposé into the 1979 best seller *The Right Stuff,* by which time Wolfe felt the stuff that appeared in *Rolling Stone* was not quite right. "Jann seemed to like it more than I did," Wolfe said. (When Wenner asked for minor changes on a draft, Wolfe had said, "Oh, come on, Jann, just say it's shit!") Nonetheless, he credited Wenner with getting him started on a story that would define his career. And the effect of Tom Wolfe on *Rolling Stone* was bigger than the story itself. Wolfe's fame—he was a regular guest of Dick Cavett's on ABC—made Wenner's newspaper the center of gravity for New Journalism at the movement's high-water mark. Wenner managed to recruit Wolfe from editor Clay Felker at *New York,* who had belittled and intimidated Wenner at a dinner party four years earlier. Felker, a veteran of *Esquire* and the *New York Herald Tribune* who'd founded *New York* magazine, along with Milton Glaser, in April 1968, was every bit as ambitious as Wenner and had been publishing Tom Wolfe for years. Wenner hung a quotation from Felker over his desk that read, "Where is it written that Jann Wenner should inherit the earth?" (Later, Felker acknowledged that Wenner had "one of the best journalistic antennas in the United States. He has an incredible sense of knowing what's going to be hot. Whenever things change, he's there.")

In competition with ad-rich super magazines like *Playboy* and *Esquire,* Wenner survived by being an inveterate cheapskate. He once asked writers to use three-minute egg timers to make long-distance calls, and he made the staff send him cost-saving memos with signed promises to pare back expenses. He drove by the offices late at night to make sure the lights were all off. But mainly he saved money by regularly underpaying writers. As Wenner joked to a group of students in 1973, "The better they are, the less we pay them." In some cases, this was literally true: When Norman Mailer agreed to publish an open letter to Truman Capote in *Rolling Stone* in 1973—a rebuttal to Capote's comments about him in the Warhol interview—Wenner declined to pay Mailer, arguing that his literary bon mot was, after all, just a letter. "It's not a matter of the rates[,] which I'd certainly be willing to stretch to our outer limits for your work," he wrote, "it's just that I felt in view of its nature as a letter, it would simply be inappropriate." ("Since I can't afford your rates," Mailer replied, "you get it for nothing.")

For years, Wenner would go through the assignment lists for writers and lop off a few hundred dollars from their promised fees, leaving his editors to apologize or grovel. Wenner's secretary revealed the practice to Michael Rogers. "I said, 'You're kidding,'" recalled Rogers. "She said, 'No, he does that every two weeks.' So I complained about that, until we got the right amount of money." (Rogers's first story was published not only without payment but without his knowledge.)

What Jann Wenner had instead of money was a come-on like no other. He would sit in his oversized chair, a man-child with twinkling blue eyes, and charm a writer with visions of endless freedom and literary fame inside his Oxford-bordered playground. "I covered the motorcycle races on the Isle of Man and spent a week with Tim Leary, who was then in exile (following his escape from a California jail) in Switzerland," recalled Jerry Hopkins. "Jann also paid for a journey to Kenya and South Africa, where I wrote stories about a hippie colony."

When Jonathan Cott asked to fly to Zurich and interview Marie-Louise von Franz, a disciple of Carl Jung's, Wenner didn't know who she was but said sure. Writer Robert Palmer was accompanying Wenner shopping when Palmer began telling him about the ecstatic Jajouka musicians in the desert of Morocco. Wenner offered him $500 to go and write about it. "I agreed instantly," Palmer later wrote, "right before Jann shelled out several thou for a Persian rug without batting an eye." Occasionally, this method backfired, like the time Wenner bought a customized van for a writer going on a reporting trip to Mexico and never heard from him again.

In those years, Wenner's deputies, the two poles of his editorial psyche, were Paul Scanlon, the mustachioed former *Wall Street Journal* writer with a nose for talent and hard drink, and David Felton, the gifted experimentalist with Harpo Marx hair whose love of nitrous oxide was matched only by his loathing of a deadline but who dreamed up novel ideas—like a participatory journalism project to publish first-person stories by readers in 1972 (including a moving recollection by a Vietnam veteran). Scanlon and Felton recruited crack talents from the mainstream like Joe Eszterhas from Ohio and Tim Cahill from Tennessee and Chet Flippo from Texas, names that would adorn *Rolling Stone* and other major American magazines for the next thirty years. What they had in common was ambition to burn and a set of insecurities that Jann Wenner could play on. "He must have perceived me properly," said Robin Green, who wrote on Dennis Hopper's drug-fueled orgies and the Mustang Ranch whorehouse in Reno (where she and Annie Leibovitz wore bikinis on assignment). "I was scared, I was inept socially, I was kind of straight. I became this ironic kind of hit man. He used me like that." (Wenner's unlikely assassin would go on to win Emmys for her writing on the *Sopranos* TV series on HBO.)

Joe Eszterhas started as a beat reporter at the *Cleveland Plain Dealer,* and when he first showed up at Third Street to buy back issues of *Rolling Stone*—in a bowl-cut hairdo and imitation-leather coat from Sears—he was taken for a narc. Paul Scanlon assigned him a Thompsonesque piece on a biker-bar shooting, after which Jann Wenner invited Eszterhas to join the staff in San Francisco in 1972. Eszterhas moved west with his wife, becoming a major soloist in Wenner's growing orchestra: the street guy who could worm inside the world of a corrupt narcotics officer or turn a minor news story on a man who died in a botched drug raid into stone-cold noir. "*Rolling Stone* was the first place where I worked where I didn't feel like some kind of insurgent against the people who read it," said Eszterhas. "I felt like Jann was my ally and the publication was my ally and I grew a terrific amount of feeling for it."

Eszterhas said Jann Wenner was not a "reader" per se, no man of deep literary interests. His editorial marks rarely ventured past the first page or two as his attention flagged on yet another magnum opus. Instead, Wenner had a lustful eye for ambition that rhymed with his own. (Only later would he learn that some of Eszterhas's gleam came from threading his reportage with fiction, which worked better when he got to Hollywood and wrote the screenplays for *Basic Instinct* and *Flashdance*.) The editorial meetings in the Raoul Duke Room were like group therapy, Wenner's men trying to divine his desires as he nervously chewed the cellophane from a fresh pack of Marlboros and nodded with the series of noncommittal, vaguely skeptical "uh-huh, uh-huh, uh-huhs"—until he grabbed his armrests, sat upright, and said, "Okay, do it."

A sure sign that Wenner liked a writer is that he would start flattering him with imitation. He regularly used Hunter Thompson's lingo in letters, signing off with Thompsonisms like *Selah* and *Cazart!*, slang Thompson co-opted from obscure sources. When Stanley Booth, the eccentric Memphis writer who wrote *The True Adventures of the Rolling Stones,* tempted Wenner with a Jerry Lee Lewis profile, Wenner replied by morphing into Stanley Booth, cribbing his style: "I could just sneak off and publish your latest letter, couldn't I, and trap you into an insane correspondence, to run in the letters column and get away with just sending you a little molasses, a free record, and a cut gram of cocaine for payment each time, couldn't I, if I was clever as a swamp fox." (Wenner told him in a telegram that *Rolling Stone* would print "whatever" and paid him for a story with a pound of weed procured by Laurel Gonsalves.)

Though Wenner continually asked writers to turn in shorter pieces and pare back their literary fulmination, he usually printed what they wrote. The pages of *Rolling Stone* were endless expanses of prose, page after page of the novelistic, the literary, the baroque, the indulgent, no shoe left undescribed down to the lace knots. Journalism was "the new Hollywood," as many were saying. It was a newly serious game, with big stakes, a horse race where everyone was running for the roses. Writing was rock and roll, and Wenner's journalists were pushing it hard— often too hard. Grover Lewis, a poet from Texas, summoned Faulkner and Steinbeck in his Grand Canyon of a story on the making of the classic 1971 film *The Last Picture Show,* a story that featured, in addition to director Peter Bogdanovich and actress Cybill Shepherd, the writer Grover Lewis. "In the darkness beyond the swath of headlights," he wrote, "the stringy mottes of mesquite trees and stagnant stock tanks and the Christmas-tree oil rigs flash past at 80 mph. Startled by the sight, I glimpse my bone-white hair and ravaged face in a window as I light a cigarette."

Point of view, the authorial "I," was central. As Wenner told a reporter in 1971, "There is no such thing as objectivity. It does not exist. Nobody is objective. No perceived event is objective, and any serious editor or writer will recognize that." (Or as he said of the *Columbia Journalism Review,* which published the scathing profile of Wenner, "So much for objectivity in journalism.")

Wenner's benchmark for the new subjective objectivity, of course, was Hunter Thompson. Though he was rarely in San Francisco, Thompson's Mojo Wire madness permeated the offices of *Rolling Stone.* Editors imitated Thompson's cranked-up personality, with cries of "Holy Jesus!" echoing down the hall every time someone stubbed a toe. In August 1973, when *Rolling Stone* converted to a new physical format, Wenner changed his byline to Jann S. Wenner, a clear homage to Hunter S. Thompson. "You just learned to have more fun with him," said David Felton, who took up smoking cigarettes with an FDR-style holder, "by being more of an asshole, in a way."

No one gunned for Thompson's status harder than Eszterhas, who began smoking a pipe and strapping a buck knife to his leg, hardly veiling his envy for Thompson. "That was tough to feel that," Eszterhas said. "Hunter was a god to all of us. The amount of attention his pieces got, the fan letters—I think Hunter was in a total separate category, but there was certainly a sense of competition with guys like Tim Cahill and David Felton and Ben Fong-Torres. We all felt that. We all wanted to be *Rolling Stone* stars. There was a very special cachet to being a *Rolling Stone* writer to begin with—especially the stuff that was on the covers."

The group of desks where Eszterhas and Felton worked was now dubbed Macho Village for the irascible and competitive men who jostled for cover bylines. When Robert Greenfield showed up from the London office, a longhair in dungarees, he was surprised to find the staff of *Rolling Stone* posturing like a fraternity of fighter pilots. "They all had *judgment,*" said Greenfield. "Ben Fong-Torres, Felton—they all considered themselves a step above many of the people they were writing about."

In 1973, a guerrilla documentary crew called TVTV interviewed Wenner and his big stars, Tom Wolfe and Hunter Thompson (who gamely popped a speed tablet for the cameras), and came away disgusted by the pretension inside Third Street. "I've talked to them high and low and I'll tell you this about *Rolling Stone*," said director Allen Rucker, standing in the parking lot below Wenner's office. "It's mystical. That's what Paul [Scanlon] said. It's a mystical place. It *is* mystical—boredom is mystery." (The film's co-director, Michael Shamberg, went on to produce *The Big Chill*.)

Behind all this mystery was a world of discontent, with Jann Wenner the subject of the staff's eternal complaint. Scanlon and Lewis regularly saddled up at Jerry's Inn down the block and bitched about his follies and excesses, bonding like abused family members. They called him "the fascist insect" (Joe Eszterhas), "Yarn Vendor" (David Dalton), and "the rotten little dwarf" (Hunter Thompson). In the press, current and ex-employees, including Ralph Gleason, aired their grievances over Wenner's ruthless personality ("He has real trouble with interpersonal relationships," reported Jerry Hopkins). Wenner had an especially toxic relationship with Grover Lewis, a man twelve years his senior who drank like a hardened novelist of the Hemingway school and resented Wenner's imperious youth ("It would be nice to think that he would die in the gutter," Lewis once said). The feeling was mutual: To get rid of him, Wenner gave Lewis a $40,000 book contract to write a biography of Texas governor John Connally and then canceled it once Lewis left town. Lewis sued him. "He sued Jann because he deserved to be sued," said Scanlon.

Three thousand miles of distance didn't soften his personality. When Wenner visited his New York bureau in 1973, he demanded that editor Stu Werbin go fetch him a club sandwich while Wenner commandeered his desk for the afternoon. Werbin (who first reported that a twenty-three-year-old Bruce Springsteen had signed to Columbia) was so angry he spat in Wenner's sandwich and delivered it to him. Later, Wenner asked Glenn O'Brien, whom he recruited from *Inter/View*, to fire Werbin and take over his job, but O'Brien refused. "I said, 'No, that was the last straw,'" recalled O'Brien.

But for his core group—Charlie Perry and Ben Fong-Torres and David Felton and Joe Eszterhas and Paul Scanlon—Wenner was a kind of paternal figure, the mercurial taskmaster whose peccadilloes became part of the fabric of their lives, which were wholly devoted to *Rolling Stone*. They were willing tools of his ambition. When David Felton failed to finish stories or slipped too far into a drug fog (he kept a canister of nitrous oxide next to his reclining dentist chair), Wenner would fire him and then hire him back later. He fired and rehired Felton three separate times. With the kind of drugged-out artist-writers Wenner was cultivating, second chances were necessary. "We gave him lots of reasons to write us off," said Felton, who became an alcoholic, as did Grover Lewis.

The staff of *Rolling Stone* grappled with the two irreconcilable sides of Jann S. Wenner: Jann No. 1, the seducer; and Jann No. 2, the betrayer. One minute Wenner was the pudgy princeling passing a joint, infatuated with every word from your mouth; the next a savage bully, asking your replacement to fire you. Charlie Perry said Wenner's two-sidedness was predictable in at least one regard: "Jann No. 2 has veto power."

"The closer people got to Jann, the more likely they were to get fired," observed Sarah Lazin, who worked for Wenner from 1971 to 1983. "People mistook that Jann was their friend. And that wasn't true. People around Jann were people who could do something for him."

"My sense of my value to the magazine was always at odds with the way Jann treated us," said Barbara Landau, formerly Downey, who started as a proofreader in 1972. "He was hard-ass. Very hard. He terrified the staff. Like going into the Colosseum with the lion."

"Jann, in those days, could be the warmest and most intimate, great friend," said Jon Landau, who after he divorced his first wife, Janet Maslin, married Downey, "and then he could turn on a dime. And everybody at one point or another would experience the negative. Today they'd probably call him bipolar. There was volatility and unpredictability. He was a master at going after people's vulnerabilities."

Landau was one of the few writers outside Hunter Thompson able to push back on Wenner. Landau was Wenner's critical standard-bearer and tuning fork, not just for rock criticism, but for the integrity of the newspaper as a whole. In 1973, Landau tore Wenner apart over the handling of an extensive interview with James Taylor and Carly Simon, written by Stu Werbin. In a letter, he described the crippling pressures they labored under to finish the story on deadline, spending late night hours closely editing the piece with Taylor and Simon themselves, who forked over a list of changes they wanted made and that Landau had wired to Wenner. The changes never got made, though Wenner had promised to make them.

> At 5:00 AM, I thought I was through. The last thing you told me Monday night was it was under control, you could handle it, would take care of the quotes and make sure that it looked right . . . How could you permit this level of incompetence to represent Rolling Stone? . . . [T]he masthead says you're the editor in chief. And aren't you the guy who lectured me about if you want the authority you have to take the responsibility? As long as you're running the show, you ought to be on the fucking case . . . I made the biggest mistake of all—I trusted you.

In response, Wenner blasted Landau's "arrogant and self-serving advice," which he said Landau delivered with a "reckless disregard for our friendship and at the peril of our professional relationship."

If his mercurial personality left bruised feelings and lifelong hatred, Wenner could hardly be bothered to care. "He never looks back," said Tom Wolfe. "I don't know how he does it, but I think he's pretty much immune to guilt." Wenner justified his cruelty as a business virtue, pointing to the mismanagement of the Beatles' Apple Corps as a cautionary tale. "The Beatles, when they started Apple, they couldn't say no; they didn't know how to fire anybody," Wenner said in 1973. "They had people working on payroll who had no business being there, old friends. They were pouring money out of there at $50,000 a week, you know, and they couldn't say no, you know, so they had to bring somebody who was, you know, a vicious bastard to say no and really had to overcompensate."

Wenner's temperament fostered a hermetic culture of ambition and fear—and, naturally, sexual tension. The staff socialized so little outside Third Street they became each other's only friends and lovers. The women's room was scrawled with graffiti about how certain male editors performed in bed. "Nobody on the outside would understand," said Bryn Bridenthal, Wenner's publicist, who started in 1971. "Everybody slept on their desks and had sex on their desks."

Marriages tended to break up when a new hire joined the staff. Robin Green was sleeping with the married David Felton; Jon Landau divorced Maslin and took up with editor Marianne Partridge before marrying copy editor Barbara Downey; Paul Scanlon was living with fact checker Sarah Lazin (in Sandy Bull's former house); the married Joe Eszterhas was sleeping with anyone who would sleep with him. Eszterhas claimed that he used Wenner's office as a trysting spot on weekends. "I had a girlfriend there, after hours," he said. "We would use his couch. [Wenner] comes back unexpectedly and when I come into the office—'Jann is looking for you right away!' I go back and he is really pissed. 'I let you use my office and I come back and, look, there's cum and coke and shit all over my desk.'" (Paul Scanlon insisted that this story was made up, in keeping with Eszterhas's penchant for fiction.)

The staff was not immune from Wenner's own adventuring either. "He fancied himself as a sort of polymorphous-perverse William Randolph Hearst," said Glenn O'Brien, who joined *Rolling Stone* in 1973 and quit after what he said were Wenner's unwanted advances. "He told me he had slept with everyone who had worked for him."

Though he tried for young men, Wenner said he slept with more women than men in the 1970s. "It may not be what I preferred," he said, "but that's what was available."

In letters, the Chicano lawyer Oscar Acosta facetiously addressed Wenner as "O Great Child God." But Wenner was only the boy his mother had made him, the wounded thirteen-year-old with the preposterous confidence and bottomless need for affirmation. By 1971, his mother was involved in a hedonistic self-improvement group led by an entrepreneur and swinger named Victor Baranco who published a magazine called *Aquarius*. Wenner said his mother "was close to him and talked about him all the time." Baranco recruited lost souls and spiritual seekers to live and work in his communal "More Houses," where residents rehabbed Baranco's real estate investments while paying him for "courses" on sex and the virtues of selfishness—having "more." As he prospered, Baranco started cruising around San Francisco like a would-be Jann Wenner, driving a purple Jaguar XKE with Wenner's mother in the passenger's seat, his long hair flapping in the wind. In an Oedipal rage, Jann Wenner attacked Baranco in the only way he knew how: He assigned writer Robin Green, his resident assassin, to profile him in *Rolling Stone* and "really expose him for the hustler he was," he said.

•

IN 1973, Jann Wenner was speaking to students at the University of Colorado about the success of *Rolling Stone* when a man bolted onstage and lobbed a pie into his face, declaring, "A present from the Rock Liberation Front!"

His face dripping whipped cream, Wenner asked plaintively, "Has anybody got a handkerchief?"

Wenner was compelled to explain to the audience the backstory of the Rock Liberation Front: an anticapitalist offshoot of the Yippies that came to include Jerry Rubin, A. J. Weberman, the Dylanologist famous for stealing and dissecting Bob Dylan's garbage, and John Lennon—Jann Wenner enemies all. Wenner compared the group to Lee Harvey Oswald: "They have no meaning to their own lives and finally seek it out by killing someone famous."

Afterward, the *Yipster Times* published an account of the pieing that added creative flourishes: "'Eat the rich!' cried [Sebastian] Cobot as he mushed the pie in the hip capitalist's baby face."

"Jann got scared," the paper reported, "and made a motion like he was gonna split, but froze in his tracks, figuring he was about to be shot."

Actually, Wenner sounded as if he were expecting it. Two years before, *Rolling Stone* had published an exposé on Yippie godfather Abbie Hoffman from a former associate who described in granular detail how Hoffman stole his book idea for *Steal This Book*, Hoffman's best-selling guide to fighting the "Pig Empire" of the establishment. The article's author, Izak Haber, a self-described "speed freak, male prostitute, chess champion, junkie, model," claimed Hoffman was a cynical opportunist who lived in capitalist splendor while exploiting idealistic naïfs like himself. Though Hoffman denied the story before publication, it comported closely with Wenner's personal view of Hoffman and his allies as hucksters. "I knew what the impact of this would be," said Wenner. "It was a full frontal attack on their integrity."

In the next issue, Wenner published letters from both Hoffman and his wife, the latter describing the financial trouble and jail time Hoffman suffered for his radicalism. "To be constantly harassed by cops, FBI, judges and the attorney general and then to read about . . . Abbie prancing around his fancy penthouse like Mick Jagger and Jann Wenner really makes me mad," she wrote. (Wenner, in a rare moment of guilt, said, "It makes me feel bad because of all the beatings he's had, the donations to Panthers. I'm sure he was sincere in his heart.") In a separate letter, Hoffman offered his own barbed attack on Wenner, pointing to his suspicious relationship with the chairman of the Xerox Corporation: "How about a similar piece on chief *Rolling Stone* stockholder Max Palevsky who doubles as chairman of the board of the Xerox Corporation. I'll bet he lives in a real shithouse just like us."

The idea of *Rolling Stone* as a front for the Xerox Corporation had taken hold in certain precincts of the underground. The *Yipster Times* ran a story called "The Day Rolling Stone Sold Out to Xerox," claiming Xerox paid off Wenner's debts in exchange for opposing antiwar demonstrations (an earlier report made the same postulation, subbing in Warner Communications). Wenner faced the accusation directly: "Max is chairman of our board of directors and, as it turns out, the largest single stockholder in Xerox. Maybe we control Xerox? Maybe the times they are a-changin'?"

But it was true that Wenner was steeping in Palevsky's influence. In late 1971, Palevsky took the Wenners on a Mediterranean cruise on a hired yacht, the SS *Lisboa,* where they lounged on the deck in sunglasses and Wenner went water-skiing off the coast of Sardinia in a red Speedo. Tanned and handsome, the Wenners set up a camera in their room to take a self-portrait on the bed, sexy siblings practically pinching themselves with delight. Wenner scored some pot for Palevsky's fifteen-year-old son, and Jane amused everyone by taking the ribbons off the Gucci and Hermès packages from Palevsky's shopping trips and sewing them into her blue jeans.

For a while, Jane Wenner had an office in Palevsky's Bel-Air home, where he kept his Rodins and Warhols, and Hunter Thompson squirreled himself away there to write on deadline. Palevsky was infatuated with Jane, the woman a friend once described as "an iridescent, jeweled spider. If you get stuck in her web, you don't want to leave."

For a while, Palevsky enjoyed the *Rolling Stone* ride, bringing a modicum of financial discipline to the company ledger and teaching Wenner how to run a proper business. Palevsky started another magazine called *L.A.* and funneled one of its scoops to *Rolling Stone:* a potential interview with D. B. Cooper, the man who hijacked a plane in 1971 and jumped out in a parachute with $200,000 in stolen cash. A mysterious source was promising to arrange the interview and a series of cloak-and-dagger high jinks ensued until Palevsky grew paranoid. "It was going to cost $25,000 in cash," recalled Wenner. "Max, on our behalf, got cold feet and said *Rolling Stone* shouldn't do this because the FBI is going to be after you, and the IRS, and you won't withstand all the pressure. Of course, it turned out to be a hoax."

But Wenner had tried Palevsky's patience. Palevsky found it infuriating that Wenner took his son to buy pot in Sardinia and that Wenner dined out on his access while flouting his financial oversight. Palevsky rolled his eyes at Wenner's proposal to build a massage room in the offices and rescinded Wenner's privileges to the Sherry-Netherland after Wenner and Earl McGrath threw a party for a hundred attendees. "He paid for it with Max's money," recalled McGrath. Meanwhile, according to Rinzler, he and Wenner once tried to make the company look more profitable by using a legal but dubious accounting maneuver that essentially allowed Wenner to credit unsold book inventory as revenue. Palevsky discovered what he called their "creative accounting." In 1972, after Wenner and Palevsky fought over how to calculate the value of Palevsky's stock holdings, a flurry of letters ensued until Palevsky told Wenner "any further action has to be between our lawyers."

The Xerox chairman eventually demanded Wenner put all of his shares into a blind trust controlled by Palevsky and a lawyer for a period of seven years, plus another 7 percent of the stock, or else Palevsky would resign as chairman of Straight Arrow Publishing. Wenner hated losing favor with his patron, a father figure who treated him like a good Jewish son and urged him to keep regular working hours and exercise. "I was distraught, because I was losing Max," said Wenner. "I went to Arthur [Rock], 'What can I do? I'm so upset.' I was crying. I didn't know what to do."

When Palevsky was hospitalized for a heart attack in 1973, Wenner directed Michael Rogers, who had published a story on the meditative effects of biofeedback, to take a modified electroencephalogram machine to Palevsky's hospital bedside in L.A. to help him recover. "I went back and [Jann] said, 'Did you give it to him? How'd he look?' I said, 'Jann, they wouldn't let me near him.'"

But Wenner had no intention of handing over control, and Wenner's controlling shares allowed him to maintain authority. Palevsky was furious. The final straw was Wenner's purchase of a three-story Victorian house on California Street in the rarefied neighborhood of Pacific Heights. According to Jane, Palevsky had offered to help finance a house, presumably to avoid Wenner dipping into the *Rolling Stone* coffers. According to Rinzler, Palevsky confronted Wenner about his "taking gobs of cash to buy his house in Pacific Heights and taking home original Steadman art and other *Rolling Stone* corporate assets. Jann pledged not to do it again, but did." (Wenner simply relisted the art as "personal assets" and kept Steadman's work in his house.)

As the relationship disintegrated, it was Jane Wenner who maintained the bond to the investor. When Palevsky organized a trip to Israel to tour a wing of the Israel Museum he'd underwritten, he wanted Jane to come, which meant bringing Jann as well. But Wenner said he was bored, so he and Jane escaped the Palevsky entourage for Tangier to hang out with novelist Paul Bowles, who was recently widowed. "We spent the next three days smoking hashish and eating in restaurants and hearing all about him and Jane Bowles, who had just died," said Wenner. "And met his boyfriend, Mrabet." (The artist Mohamed Mrabet.)

Palevsky resigned from the board of Straight Arrow in the summer of 1973. Ralph Gleason, who was equally fed up with Wenner, suggested they try a hostile takeover. Palevsky wasn't interested, because he didn't want to hurt Jane. "When I ask him, 'Why did you finally give up?'" said Jodie Evans, Palevsky's fourth wife, "he said, 'For Janie.' She came and had a talk with him. About letting go. I remember him wondering, 'Had Jann put her up to that?' If that was her, or if that was him."

Palevsky would maintain his investment until 1976, but his bitterness toward Jann Wenner never dissipated; he once told a reporter that Wenner had a "compulsion to kill his father." Wenner said Palevsky "blew apart every single relationship he ever had"—remember George

McGovern in 1972?—and he was only the latest. But over the years, Palevsky often asked aloud: Why did Jane stay with Jann Wenner?

"Max knew that Jann was gay," said Evans. "It was a mystery to him then why Janie was with him. Almost every time we got together, he would try to get Janie to explain. The mystery of Jann and Janie remained to the very end."

12

Whatever Gets You thru the Night

When Clive Davis was fired from Columbia Records, the Wenners were in Italy with Earl and Camilla McGrath, staying at Camilla's dazzling classical estate in the medieval city of Lucca. The Villa Reale di Marlia, bulging with Roman statues and priceless artworks, had once belonged to Napoleon's sister and was the site of fantastic decadence in the 1920s. As writer Ben Fong-Torres's in-progress profile of Clive Davis pivoted into an investigative story—which speculated on Davis's involvement in paying off radio stations with heroin trafficked by an organized crime syndicate—the Wenners went sightseeing in Rome and furniture shopping in Milan, acquiring two white modernist sofas for the new house at 2018 California Street, a three-story, four-bedroom Victorian they acquired in March 1973 for $127,000.

If the marriage of Jann and Jane Wenner was a mystery to some, for others it was completely obvious: They came together in their mutual desire for power and pleasure and style. "It was about superior entertainment," said Joey Townsend, the hippie daughter of Robert Townsend, the Avis Rent a Car CEO who wrote the only business book Wenner said he ever found useful: *Up the Organization: How to Stop the Corporation from Stifling People and Strangling Profits*. Townsend met the Wenners aboard the SS *Lisboa* as a guest of Max Palevsky's. "Epicureanism for that time," she said. "That's what that revolution was about."

The eyes of Wenner's writers now roved over the delicious details of celebrity interiors and fashion. The home of Columbia recording artist Barbra Streisand, according to *Rolling Stone* in 1971, was "massive, pin-neat, high-vaulted, gorged with Art Nouveau and Art Deco furnishings," and Streisand sauntered in wearing "matching denim jacket and flares with that unmistakable *de rigueur* patina of garments washed precisely once—the overall ensemble topped off by a bio-degradable denim sombrero." (That year, Wenner was observed by a gossip columnist wearing the same "Bob Dylan millionaire rock star look of denim jacket and bell-bottoms.")

After "Post-orbital Remorse," Wenner's next assignment for Tom Wolfe was an exposé about the mainstreaming of hippie antifashion as "Funky Chic," a 1974 analogue to "Radical Chic." "Today, in the age of Funky Chic égalité," wrote Wolfe, "fashion is a much more devious, sly and convoluted business than anything that was ever dreamed of at Versailles."

"Funky Chic" was as good a description of the Wenners' style as any, the casual mongrelizing of European jet set and California haute hippie. Jane curated California Street with the same care Wenner curated his pages, made it the backstage of *Rolling Stone,* a Victorian pleasure palace with rattan furniture and potted palm trees situated next to Wenner's Warhols and large bay windows overlooking the street ("They have a tree in their living room," marveled Mike Salisbury, the new art director). There was the 1961 Richard Diebenkorn painting Jane bought for $15,000, plus German lithographs given to them by Chris Stamp, the manager of the Who. There was a pinball machine and a Claes Oldenburg sculpture. There were mirrors, all over—mainly French, mostly eighteenth century. Inspired by the bathrooms she saw in the suites of expensive European hotels, Jane designed the bathroom upstairs, installing chaise longues, a wall-to-wall mirror bordered with Hollywood lights, and a Japanese-style steam room (with helpful advice, no doubt, from the *Rolling Stone* story on saunas in January 1973). Guests marveled at Jane Wenner's raven eye for refinement, whether a Tiffany floor lamp or an antique serving spoon.

Jane's epicureanism would reach levels of absurd refinement. "How did Jane suddenly know that she needed a Haitian laundress, because the Haitian laundresses really knew how to iron?" wondered Joey Townsend. "How did she know about ironing? She knew!" (The Wenners employed a Chinese couple as servants.) Herb Caen came to refer to Jane Wenner as "Bergdorf's by the Bay," but the secret source might have been Bloomingdale's in New York. As Jane told Wenner in a letter, "A walk thru the ground floor . . . and you are at once aware of what's current in Paris, Rome and [California]."

Flush with free wares from advertisers—*Rolling Stone* ran audio supplements featuring Frank Zappa and Ray Charles showing off their systems—Wenner outfitted California Street with a top-of-the-line McIntosh stereo and new Advent color-projection TV (on which Wenner and his pals watched the early episodes of *Saturday Night Live* in 1975). His underpaid staffers marveled at Wenner's audacious commitment to luxury. "I learned all about brand names from Jann," said writer Michael Rogers. "He got a beautiful gold Cartier lighter. He scratched it, the first day. And he took it out on [his secretary] Stephanie's desk, and said, 'This came scratched. Send it back.' 'Jann, it wasn't scratched.' 'No, it was already scratched.'" (Wenner later said he fired her for "bad judgment.")

The Wenners aimed to impress and it worked. When Jon Landau saw the house, he wrote to Wenner to say he was "blown back by the beauty." "You aren't ever going to be 'just folks,' but you're doing it in style," he said.

The house, the epicenter of the *Rolling Stone* social world, divided into two distinct spheres of influence: his and hers. After a guest climbed the twenty-four steps to the stained-glass double doors, the first room off a long hallway was the kitchen, which was Jane's domain. "She had this very hip sense of humor," recalled Craig Braun, who designed the cover of the Rolling Stones' *Sticky Fingers* album and fooled around with Jane in 1973. "She could prod people; she could provoke them. 'I know you fucked Richard Pryor!' she might say. She was a great manipulator. We were all high."

People were drawn to Jane's dewy looks and boyish sexuality but also to her keen-eyed judgment. She could take a person's measure while maintaining a tantalizing distance—a professional tease. People like Hunter Thompson and Max Palevsky found the effect irresistible.

Said Braun, "She was like Warhol in a way, a voyeur. She was very interested in talking about what people did or didn't do, sexually. She was obsessed with that. She was more open to talking about sexual escapades than doing them. She was coy. She had this beautiful face and boyish body, kind of ambisexual."

Wenner's luxe man cave was at the end of the hallway. As the Stones blared "It's Only Rock 'n Roll" from the state-of-the-art McIntosh, Wenner stood beneath his Warhols in suit pants and unbuttoned Brooks Brothers shirt, talking a mile a minute, too excited to finish a sentence. "Jann was always afraid he was going to miss something, some conversation," said Michael Douglas. "He's nodding to you, 'uh-huh, uh-huh,' but he's listening to two other conversations that are going on at the same time. He's got really a reporter's nose for that."

"If you captured his interest for a moment, it's really exhilarating," said Lynda Obst, wife of David, who called Wenner "the greatest spitball intellectual" she ever met.

Wenner made declarations on records and politics with the confidence of a man who stood atop a mountain, as if his access to celebrity and fame gave him expansive vision. "Even in a small circle he thought his opinion would have a ripple effect," observed Braun. "Almost like a silent parenthetical, 'You can quote me on this.'"

Wenner supplied guests with ample drugs, whether big rocks of cocaine from Laurel Gonsalves, who lived ten blocks away, or perhaps a bowl of unidentified pills. On the surface was the druggy ease of friendship, beneath it the torque of opportunism. The difference between an interview subject and a party guest was nil. Jane warned friends to be careful what they said around her husband, lest it appear in *Rolling Stone*. "Don't forget," she would say, "there's no such thing as gossip with Jann, or a secret. It's all news."

When John Gregory Dunne, husband of Joan Didion, wrote to tell Wenner about a movie he was cooking up for Diana Ross, he included an extensive postscript warning Wenner not to use it for Random Notes "or any other notes, or for Herb Caen, *Ramparts, Newsweek, Time,* the New York *Times* and/or any of the print or broadcast media, dinner parties, conventions or editorial conferences. Don't even tell Janie."

On the advice of his accounting firm, Wenner kept a detailed calendar of his guests to write off their visits as a business expense, logging the overnight stays of Carl Bernstein and Nora Ephron, Ahmet and Mica Ertegun, Marshall and Diane Chess, and of course his own employees Annie Leibovitz and Hunter Thompson. When the IRS questioned Wenner's use of the house as a tax deduction for Thompson, Wenner replied that it is "not only ordinary but necessary for many strategy meetings to be held after business hours which sometimes extend into the early morning hours."

The IRS had no idea how true it was. Daniel Ellsberg, riding the fame of the Pentagon Papers, roamed the halls in the nude between hours-long interview sessions with Wenner, who butchered his stream of consciousness monologues into an indulgent heap that ran in November of 1973 ("I made it even worse," said Wenner. "He was kind of an idiot savant, possessed by a mission, and you fell into it"). Bernstein and Ephron made out on the white Italian couch, after which Wenner assigned Ephron to review travel writer Jan Morris (who despite her displeasure with "Memoirs of a Transsexual: The Relentlessly Cheerful Jan Morris" later agreed to write for Wenner). As the nights progressed, the Wenners and their guests would drift upstairs to the steam room, where "everybody was kind of naked and adorable and ambisexual," recalled Lynda Obst, who went on to become a successful Hollywood producer (starting with *Flashdance* in 1983). "It was very kind of Virginia Woolf without the pretense. It was like everybody was attracted to everybody. Without it being gross. Without it being acquisitional. It was sensual." (It was in the sauna that Wenner attempted the occasional gay seduction after hours. "Have you ever made it with a guy?" he asked rock critic Dave Marsh, who was surprised less by the question than by how casually Wenner asked it: "This was like, 'Would you like another glass of wine?'")

All the while, Jane kept Jann on a silken leash. When his ego became too big, she whipped him with a wry put-down or poked at his weight, which seemed to balloon with his excesses. Jane called Wenner "Chubby Checker" and regularly put him on diets, including one involving sheep urine. "Jane had cleaned the house out of anything that was good to eat except frozen foods," recalled David Obst. "Jann, hungry beyond his comfort point, went to the freezer and actually ate the frozen foods without thawing them out and they expanded in his stomach and he had to go to the emergency room." (Herb Caen, who treated Jann Wenner like the gossip column version of a beach ball, reported that Wenner vacationed at a fat farm in Baja, Mexico, in 1976.)

California Street produced more folly than stories. In 1973, Maria Schneider, the star of the Bernardo Bertolucci film *Last Tango in Paris,* came to stay for a week, ostensibly to do an interview with Wenner, who was titillated by the infamous butter scene with Marlon Brando. Schneider had once stayed on Ord Court with the Wenners in 1970, a guest of her then lover Joey Townsend. For fun, the two wore matching T-shirts with the Wenners' address on it in case they got so high they became lost (they were spotted scoring barbiturates from Sandor Burstein and ended up in Herb Caen's column). This time, Wenner followed her around with a tape recorder on the pretense of an interview but in truth trying to sleep with her. "I had a crazy infatuation," he said. "I was really taken with her. I didn't know she was a lesbian. I just thought she was hot. But she wasn't interested in me."

Indeed, Schneider appeared to pursue Jane Wenner. "She and Jane are clearly together," recalled Harriet Fier, a *Rolling Stone* editor who saw them at a party that week. "They were on a couch. They were all over each other." Meanwhile, Wenner's "interview" tape was a long recording of the Wenners doing drugs with Schneider.

Though she was a frequent guest on California Street, Joan Didion never managed to write for Wenner, failing to finish her assignment to cover the Patty Hearst kidnapping trial in 1976. She did, however, use the Wenners' house as a setting in her 1977 novel, *A Book of Common Prayer,* referring to it as "the house on California Street" with incantatory repetition. The main character, Charlotte Douglas, whose marriage to a Berkeley lawyer is falling apart as their daughter becomes ensnared with Marxist revolutionaries, offered shades of Jane Wenner, an obsessive cleaner who spent hours vacuuming the floors of California Street. Jann Wenner wrote to Didion to tell her how much he loved the book, though he could not help but observe that "there is not a single happy, uplifting, lovable person in the novel."

•

JANN WENNER NOW STIPULATED in Annie Leibovitz's contract that in addition to her *Rolling Stone* work she was on call to the Wenners as the family photographer, a service she was expected to perform free of charge. Jann Wenner asked her to photograph him nearly every day and the photos quickly piled high: Jann Wenner at his typewriter, cigarette dangling from his lip; Jann Wenner, stoned and noodling on his red Gretsch guitar in the wee hours; Jann Wenner, pretending to read Erica Jong's *Fear of Flying* in Barbados; Jann Wenner, thumbs hooked through his orange *Rolling Stone* suspenders, grinning like a robber baron; Jann Wenner, smoking a cigarette poolside in Bel-Air; Jann Wenner, stoned and grinning, nose turned up in proud profile, gripping the lapels of a black leather jacket that Bruce Springsteen gave him for his thirtieth birthday.

The presence of the *Rolling Stone* fame maker gave Wenner the status of salon host and star in his own right. "It was like having the San Francisco version of Andy Warhol," said Leibovitz. "I served that purpose for them."

The Polaroid SX-70 instant camera first appeared in 1972, and Leibovitz used it both professionally and privately, generating piles of selfies, party shots, vanity portraits, "art shots," comic vamping, all the faces mottled in saturated chemical colors as they burned the nights to oblivion. Leibovitz used a flash to make overexposed paparazzo close-ups, filling square frames with Capote's full, fattened jowls or the cool, come-hither smile of Warren Beatty. On and on: Ken Kesey, Richard Pryor, Lily Tomlin, Carole King, Jimmy Buffett, Dick Avedon, Bob Neuwirth, Jane Fonda, Carl Bernstein, Ahmet Ertegun, Jac Holzman, Boz Scaggs, Jimmy Webb, Truman Capote, Paul Simon, Bill Graham. There were Polaroids of Wenner's guests admiring themselves in Polaroids and Polaroids of the Wenners arranging Polaroids across the dining room table. They scrawled in-jokes under their images: "Bump till you drop" under a blurred Annie Leibovitz; "50% of the stock" under Jane Wenner's face.

Of all her subjects, Jane Wenner was the one that most obsessed

Annie Leibovitz in that era. She snapped hundreds of images of her, daily, monthly, yearly. Jane, the sad-eyed lady in pigtails and kneesocks, reading magazines or tapping out a line of cocaine; Jane the waif, swallowed up in a rattan chair; Jane the chic dolly in striped French sailor shirts from Petit Bateau in Paris (her virtual uniform starting in the mid-1970s); Jane in a bikini, arms outstretched in homage to Jim Morrison, birdlike rib cage poking out; Jane, petulant and smoking, eyes half-lidded; Jane in rented bungalow in Barbados carving lines for Richard Pryor (who told Marshall Chess he had sex with her on the beach that night); Jane pursing her lips in the passenger's seat of Annie's Porsche as they zipped to Earl's house; and finally, Jane emerging from the bath, nude and smiling shyly as she dries her hair; Jane, topless, blue jeans unzipped.

When Jane tired of the *Rolling Stone* madness, Leibovitz caught that too—Jane curled up in the shadow of depression, her "blue periods," as her friend Peter Wolf called them, when she secluded herself in the house on California Street. When Hunter S. Thompson came knocking one too many times looking for cocaine at 3:00 a.m.—or to steal Jann Wenner's stereo as compensation for some unknown debt—she'd scream and kick him out, a woman on the verge of a nervous breakdown. She wanted credit for the success of *Rolling Stone,* but leaving the house was difficult, as was work. When she agreed to collaborate on an oral history for "everyone who graduated from the Sixties" (*The Sixties,* Random House, 1977), Jane couldn't muster the energy. "She had time on her hands, and it just festered," said Laurel Gonsalves, a frequent companion on California Street. "What do you do all day if you don't have something to do and you have this brain that's quite smart?"

Jane and Annie found refuge in each other, spending countless hours sharing drugs or poring over art and photography books in search of ideas. Jane would help conceive Leibovitz's pictures, then accompany her on photo shoots, acting as her civilizing hand. "The thing about Annie was, at that time, she was not a conventional beauty," said Jane, "or not even handsome, like she is today. She was always awkward. She always wore glasses."

When Leibovitz went on an assignment with Joe Eszterhas to shoot Paul Getty, the heir to the oil fortune whose kidnappers had cut his ear off and released him for a $3 million ransom, Jane commanded, "Honey, you've got to get a bra. You've got to get a bra now. This is, like, it." (Joe Eszterhas said Getty demanded $500 for the story and $2,000 for a photograph and Wenner paid.) "Jane never treated Annie as an employee," said Jim Messina, of Loggins and Messina, who used a Leibovitz photograph for their 1976 *Best of Friends* album cover. "She treated her like a partner."

What was plain to everyone was that this was some kind of love affair, at least for Leibovitz. "There is no question whatsoever that Annie was madly in love with Jane," Jann Wenner said. "And that went on for a long time."

Annie followed Jane with Nikon in hand, transfixed, as partygoers swirled around. "It's great to be in love," mused Leibovitz on her obsession with Jane. "If you're a photographer, it's more of a fixation." It was an article of faith among veteran *Rolling Stone* staffers that Annie and Jane were lovers. Leibovitz, who alluded to an affair in diaries in the late 1970s, was circumspect but hardly in denial: "You can have other people talk about it and it's fine." Jane said they weren't "lovers" per se, but something more ambiguous. "We were young; there were drugs involved, you know, late nights, who knows?" she said. "I mean, it was like—the idea that we were lovers, it's not—it doesn't have the same connotation."

In other words, things happened. Some staffers surmised a triangle involving Jann Wenner that went on for several years. "From the office angle, it was an obvious ménage à trois," said art director Roger Black, "and it became impossible to get between Jann and Annie and we didn't see too much of Jane, but we heard about her through Annie and we knew she had influence and maybe more common sense than Jann." (Wenner said he slept with Leibovitz; Jane said she didn't know about it: "Does a ménage mean all at once?")

Jane Wenner was the muse of *Rolling Stone*'s vision of celebrity—the glorification of pubescent bodies and semi-anorexic glamour, the model of the kind for louche 1970s indulgence and narcissism, with its dewy sadness and velveteen interiority. "You can't underestimate my sketching or my studying of Jane or Jann, how that feeds into taking pictures of people," Leibovitz said. "I got to see Jane in all kinds of configurations. I thought she was beautiful. I really enjoyed taking her picture. And it gave us something to do."

Her obsession had one other important virtue: It made Annie Leibovitz a vassal in the Wenners' growing court, financially in debt to Jann Wenner and romantically in debt to his wife. Given her obsession with Jane, Leibovitz didn't mind. "I found refuge in it, and they certainly didn't mind it," she said. "I became very, very close with them."

Said Jane, "There was always my friendship and love of Annie, but there was always the magazine. If I could rein her in, I would rein her in. Not in some horrible manipulative way—yes, it was manipulative, but somebody had to do it. It wasn't so much for the magazine, but for her. What the fuck are you doing? Why don't you have the pictures?"

As Leibovitz evolved as a photographer, Wenner built *Rolling Stone* around her talent, though more by momentum than by design. In 1973, when *Rolling Stone* changed to a larger format with color, Wenner recruited an art director recommended by Tom Wolfe: Mike Salisbury, a hotshot designer and photographer from L.A. Wenner hired Salisbury to inject a glossier, more commercial sensibility into his magazine, but to do it, he had to edge Bob Kingsbury out. Wenner was tired of his 1960s vision of *Rolling Stone*. When Kingsbury confronted Wenner about why Salisbury was getting paid more than he, Wenner told Kingsbury the new guy from L.A. was worth more. Outraged, Kingsbury quit, but his wife, Linda, Jane's sister, forced Kingsbury to apologize and asked Wenner to give him another job. Under pressure from the Schindelheim family, Wenner shuffled Kingsbury off to "special projects," but the wound was destined not to heal.

Salisbury, a dyed-in-the-wool Angeleno, found San Francisco provincial and boring, and he had a lot to learn about the oddly conservative and self-serious *Rolling Stone* folk. To him, it looked as if Wenner, in his sports jacket and jeans, were running a prep school newspaper. When he printed an illustration of Jerry Garcia as a corpulent cherub, by Robert Grossman, the editors were offended. "Boy," he said, "these people are super serious. The whole place took him seriously. I think there's two people in there that had a sense of humor."

From the start, Wenner asked Salisbury to help focus Annie Leibovitz, whose erratic working methods produced chronic headaches. Under Salisbury, *Rolling Stone* began pulling style elements from European magazines like *Nova,* a women's magazine from Britain, and *Twen,* a highly visual German publication, both of which poured sexuality and sophisticated culture writing into arid, formal spaces and ran photography to the page edge. This enraged the writers whose copy was being crowded out by pictures. But Wenner empowered Salisbury, who empowered Annie Leibovitz. It would take several months for her to make the cover of *Rolling Stone* again as Salisbury employed illustrators for cover images in the latter half of 1973, including a profile of Daniel Ellsberg as a Roman bust and a cowgirl riding a giant metallic dildo for the Steely Dan cover. Leibovitz's first full-color cover photograph arrived in April 1974, a portrait of Marvin Gaye in a knit cap and hiking boots sitting on top of Topanga Canyon at sunset. Leibovitz considered the image a failure—too dark, colors bleeding together—but it was also an epiphany in how she viewed color photos. The way color smeared on newsprint created a posterized effect—imagine 3-D without the glasses—which Leibovitz would use to reinvent herself as more than just a vérité photojournalist. It would mean using more studio techniques, strobe lighting and backdrops, and more stylized close-ups of faces to fill the cover of *Rolling Stone.* It would mean becoming a celebrity image maker for the new era.

•

IN THE SPRING OF 1973, Ahmet Ertegun, a forty-nine-year-old record business aristocrat with the half-lidded ease of a beat poet, met the twenty-seven-year-old Jann Wenner for lunch at a café on Broadway in San Francisco. He brought a young woman who he told Wenner was Geraldine Chaplin, the French-speaking daughter of Charlie Chaplin. For half an hour, a starstruck Wenner tried engaging her in broken French until Ertegun finally gave up the ruse with a laugh: She was just his assistant. Delighted by the prank, Ertegun would dine out on the story for the rest of his life. "He probably told that story in my presence twenty or thirty times," said Wenner. "He loved to laugh at his own jokes. You have to laugh along with them."

Son of a Turkish diplomat, Ertegun had expended his wellborn *oblige* collecting jazz LPs and frequenting blues clubs in Washington, D.C., in the 1940s. With money from his family, and the family dentist, Ertegun founded Atlantic Records in 1947, striking gold with Ray Charles in 1952. In horn-rims and goatee, Ertegun became the prince of hip in the music business, navigating the Mob-connected underworld as he brought forth Aretha Franklin and Otis Redding (who called him "Omelet"). He once flew in hookers for a record convention in Miami in which he and other record men, including Jerry Wexler, stood around a hotel bed watching a man have sex with a prostitute and placing bets on how long he would last (nineteen-year-old Marshall Chess was also present). "Somebody like Ahmet, in a three-piece suit, had the eloquence and the intelligence to kind of walk into some funky Harlem club, or walk into some hippie pad where Buffalo Springfield played, and say, 'Hey, baby,' and smoke a joint with him. Two weeks later, he signed them," said Peter Wolf of the J. Geils Band, whom Ertegun signed to Atlantic on the advice of Jon Landau.

Ertegun later became, for Wenner, a walking stylebook of personal sophistication. But early on, Jann Wenner underrated his significance. In the "Pinck on Wenner" tape, Danny Fields recounts Wenner's early encounter with Ertegun at a party the Atlantic chief threw on the Upper East Side. "All [Wenner] could do was talk about their second-rate paintings and the music was too loud, they were playing Stephen Stills's album too loud, people were tacky social climbers, and he and Paul [Morrissey] and Andy [Warhol] were the only groovy people there."

But their interests finally came together in Bette Midler, whom Ertegun invited Wenner to see at the Boarding House in 1973. The campy and outrageous belter sauntered down to Ertegun's table and serenaded him with "(Your Love Keeps Lifting Me) Higher and Higher" while Wenner watched in awe. Ertegun had Wenner's number: Midler started off performing in the Continental Baths, a gay trysting spot in the basement of the Ansonia hotel in New York that promised "the glory of ancient Rome" (and was later renamed Plato's Retreat). Her act as "the Divine Miss M" dovetailed with the faux androgyny of David Bowie and the New York Dolls—"mascara rock, sex and theater to the extremes, boring heterosexuality to the sidelines," as *Rolling Stone* described 1972. On this, Wenner was eager to tap the mood. For the Bette Midler story of February 1973—the first full-color image on the cover of *Rolling Stone,* illustration by Philip Hays—Wenner ran an attending story called "So You're Planning to Spend a Night at the Tubs?," written by an openly gay writer named Perry Deane Young. Young initially showed up on Third Street to propose an ambitious story in which he would travel to Vietnam to seek out missing friends (Wenner assigned it, but Joe Eszterhas killed it). But Perry also showed Wenner a story he'd written on the Continental Baths, which mentioned that Prince Egon von Furstenberg—a scion of the fabulously wealthy Agnelli family that owned the carmaker Fiat and the husband of fashion designer Diane von Furstenberg—cruised for sex there. "Jann was more than a little interested in the piece and took it," said Young.

Later that afternoon, Wenner met Young down the block at the Ritch Street Health Club, and they had a liaison. "For all these years, gay men have had these secret places to themselves in various capitals of the world," wrote Perry in *Rolling Stone.* "Dimly lit, unmarked doors opened onto a whole lifestyle that 'dared not speak its name,' that maybe never even wanted to talk because acceptance might have unmasked the mystery, the fun of it all."

While Perry was in town, *Rolling Stone* insiders filled him in on the Wenner lifestyle. "It was explained to me at the time that he and his wife had an arrangement," said Perry. "Having gone through the bullshit involved with being openly gay at that time, I can fully understand why anybody—especially anybody involved in business—would choose to be 'hidden.'"

By now, the Wenners were spending so much time in New York they started subletting a duplex on East Sixty-Sixth Street from Piedy Gimbel, a "political groupie" whom Wenner met through her then boyfriend, Dick Goodwin, a former Kennedy speechwriter. Wenner liked the location's rumored secret history: Gimbel supposedly slept with both John and Bobby Kennedy there in the 1960s (she denied it). From his new perch on the Upper East Side, Wenner could explore the convergence of uptown and downtown. Around this time, he premiered a column called New York Confidential, by writer Ed McCormack, who documented the "usual collection of sexes and sub-sexes" at Max's Kansas City, like Steve Paul, the gay club owner who managed the Winter brothers, Johnny and Edgar, and whom McCormack once described as navigating the space between "Woodstock Nation and Gramercy Park East."

In this new space, a minor press baron from San Francisco could casually float into high society with the drug dealers and the rough trade. "Jann, in a sense, was very lucky," said Dotson Rader. "It was in the '70s when the social categories collapsed. In the '70s, you'd go to a party at Leonard Bernstein's at the Dakota and you would see socialites, some of the Kennedys; you'd see the crème de la crème of New York society. And then you'd see musicians, artists, and then you'd see drug dealers and everybody, perfectly well mannered, but the social mix would've been unthinkable twenty years before. And suddenly, I think because the rich were frightened and were thinking, 'We better let the barbarians in before they tear the house down,' the walls came down. Forced tolerance is what it was. It also made it possible for Jann to move as quickly as he did."

Diane von Furstenberg, who designed her signature wrap dress in 1973, was introduced to Wenner by Craig Braun. "First time I saw him, he was a little fat guy with blue eyes, not particularly attractive," said Furstenberg. "He became attractive over the years. He was kind of judgmental. Provocative in his first opinion. So that he would get a reaction."

In 1973, *New York* magazine was preparing a story on the Furstenbergs, whose European marriage and mores were titillating Manhattan society, so Wenner assigned Rader to draw up a competing story for *Rolling Stone*. The resulting piece was a rare window into the secret world of polyamory in 1970s New York. "The only thing that matters in life is sex," declared Prince Egon, who when asked if he was a bisexual laughed and said, "Bisexual? That is funny! Hahaha. You talk like that is rare. Do you know any man our age, any man under thirty, do you know one who has not slept with a boy? No, you know none. There are none."

The Furstenbergs were catty and outrageous, baring their jeweled claws for the bourgeoisie. Diane von Furstenberg performed a savage impersonation of Jackie Kennedy Onassis and her "rolling Jackie-walk."

"Ohhh, don't you think . . . it's just faaaabulous!" Hahaha.

She laughed hoarsely, "I mean, really, the woman is stupid!" She slapped her hand against her thigh. "Did you see the nudes of Jackie? Hahaha. I have them here somewhere. The Italian editor who brought them, she thought she was so cunning, that American magazines would pay great prices to see Jackie naked . . . the pictures were so ugly. How can any woman look beautiful bending over naked to pick up a beach towel?"

Furstenberg illustrated, bending over and spreading her legs. "Haha. No, no, impossible! It all just hangs and spreads like that. It is so unattractive. Jackie is such a skinny woman."

Rader's story concludes with Egon, in skintight pants and wilting with ennui, being informed of a secret necrophilia bar where a cadaver hangs from the ceiling and drinks are $10: "God. Boring, yes? Life is so long."

Joe Eszterhas and Paul Scanlon rejected Rader's story, saying it was too far afield for *Rolling Stone* ("Unless you gave him stock options for it, let's kill it," said Eszterhas). Furstenberg wouldn't appear in the magazine until 1977, but the story was a delicious peek into a world of glamour and wealth that Wenner envied and adored and, within three years, would go marching like a glittering circus into Steve Rubell's Studio 54.

This was the era of the "New York marriage," in which gay men married for both friendship and social cover, including Leonard Bernstein and Felicia Montealegre, and Earl and Camilla McGrath. Egon called Diane his "best friend," which was not unlike Jann's feelings toward Jane. Theirs was a world where sex was as inconsequential as a handshake. "We thought we invented sexuality," said Furstenberg. "We were the generation between the pill and AIDS. It was just a form of expression."

The Wenners' marriage was nowhere near as open as that of Diane and Egon, but there was nonetheless a utility to their partnership. And nothing captured that utility better than their respective relationships to Simon and Garfunkel.

While Art Garfunkel was living in San Francisco in 1971 to record his first solo album, *Angel Clare,* he became Jann Wenner's friend and tennis partner. "One day we're in the locker room," Garfunkel said. "I'm spouting off about my quasi-political notions, my philosophy—I don't know Jann that well, he's never really shown his colors—and he says to me, 'Artie, you don't really believe that stuff, do you?'

"He pulled the rug out from under me," he said. "Just because I am selling a million records and sitting so pretty, Jann's not buying my philosophy easily."

This was also a flirtation. The nature of their friendship was "sexual understanding," said Garfunkel: a mutual interest in the open sexuality of the period. Wenner, he said, saw rock and roll through the prism of his homosexual libido. "My mind goes to Jackson Browne," said Garfunkel. "That was a cute rocker. Jackson Browne was a quintessential star for Jann Wenner to adore, praise, and push forward."

And so was Art Garfunkel, who appeared on the cover of *Rolling Stone* in October 1973. Wenner gave Ben Fong-Torres a list of questions to ask, inviting Garfunkel to air grievances with Paul Simon. Meanwhile, Wenner protected Garfunkel: After Fong-Torres interviewed him, Wenner let Garfunkel edit the manuscript and preview the photo shoot by Annie Leibovitz. Garfunkel thanked Wenner for "your deferral to my cover choice" and demanded the tapes and transcripts be destroyed. Fong-Torres was furious. He told Wenner he wished he'd removed his byline before publication. (In the next issue, Stephen Holden reviewed Garfunkel's album as an "opulent, if somewhat over-calculated, success.")

Conversely, Wenner's bias against Paul Simon was now conspicuous enough that Clive Davis, his champion at Columbia Records, was aggrieved that Wenner had failed to recognize his greatness, which he felt rivaled Bob Dylan's. "I always felt that *Rolling Stone* underestimated Paul Simon," said Davis. "There was not this serious enough evaluation of Paul Simon, so that was an issue at the time." (Told of Wenner's prehistory with Paul Simon, Davis grew heated: "You've now explained something that mystified me, because they were fucking putting him down.")

Jon Landau, a fan of Paul Simon's, was hot to interview him for *Rolling Stone* about his new self-titled solo record featuring "Me and Julio Down by the Schoolyard." But Simon was wary of Wenner and wanted assurances that he wouldn't use the interview in a book, as he had with John Lennon, without Paul Simon's express permission. Simon brought in his lawyer, an agreement was drawn up, and Simon gave Landau a thirteen-hour interview in his apartment on the Upper East Side. A year later, Wenner published Paul Simon's interview in *The "Rolling Stone" Interviews, Vol. 2.* Simon was livid and confronted Wenner at a party in New York, getting nose to nose with him in a doorway as Garfunkel looked on. "Artie, this guy is a no-goodnik," spat Simon. "Don't fall for him. He's taken my interviews and he is a wise ass. He never asked my permission!"

"And Jann would smile," recalled Garfunkel, "with that same likable smile as if, 'What can I say? My pants are down.' This is the first introduction to Jann as a mover and a groover. Got to make hay while the sun shines."

Two years later, however, Simon found something he did like about *Rolling Stone:* Jane Wenner. Their relationship blossomed during Jane's stays at the Gimbel duplex on East Sixty-Sixth Street. Suddenly Simon liked *Rolling Stone* again: In 1976, *Rolling Stone* published an engrossing cover story on Simon by Paul Cowan, titled "The Odysseus of Urban Melancholy," which featured photos of a bearded Simon riding in a limousine with "friends" on either side of him—one of whom is Jane Wenner, veiling her face. Annie Leibovitz took the pictures. In another published image, Jane is at the Manhattan hot spot Elaine's, sitting next to Simon at a table that also featured Lorne Michaels, Chevy Chase, and other cast members of NBC's *Saturday Night Live.* Jane gives a knowing smile. Something like a romance had blossomed between Simon and Jane Wenner. "Paul fell in love with her and actually asked her to leave me and go marry him," said Wenner. "Paul and I have always had a very prickly relationship. He's very, very full of himself, but he's a certifiable genius."

At the time, Simon was separating from wife Peggy Harper, whom he famously married after her divorce from his former manager Mort Lewis. Jane Wenner said she never slept with Simon and claimed surprise at his romantic overtures. "I thought we were buying furniture," said Jane. "I knew he had a crush on me. But I don't know. I guess a lot of people have crushes on me."

Said Leibovitz, "She knew exactly what she was doing. That was part of what she did. Jane wasn't going anywhere. Ever."

Garfunkel on Simon: "Nasty business. A married woman!"

Wenner on Simon: "Paul just looks at everything and judges it before he does one thing: What's in this for me? How does this affect Paul Simon? And he analyzes it very carefully. Is it good for Paul Simon? And he's extremely selfish that way."

Jane allowed Jann Wenner to have his cake and eat it, too. If a Max Palevsky or a Paul Simon tried squiring her away, Jane remained loyal to Jann Wenner, protecting his interests, which were hers as well. Meanwhile, she gave him implicit permission to enjoy extracurricular sex, as long as he kept it well hidden. She didn't want to hear about it, which Wenner considered permission. When she did get wind of it, Jane forgave him. "She didn't make me feel guilty; she let me off the hook every single time," said Wenner. "It hurt her, but she let me off the hook and it didn't change the relationship. And her explicit thing was 'Don't hurt me. I don't want to hear about this from other people; I don't want to be humiliated,' and she kind of winked and nodded and gave permission to it."

There was only one rule between them: Don't fall in love. "I was able to go have sex, the kind I liked, but there was no emotional content," said Wenner. "I wasn't risking betraying my love of Jane or our relationship. And this sexual thing—I could isolate that from the emotional content and not be betraying her fundamentally."

Jane Wenner knew as well as Jann that his homosexuality, had it been known, would curtail their social mobility. The gay vamping of *Rolling Stone* cover boys like Bowie and Jagger was all well and good, but it was "pretend libertine," observed Bette Midler, who traveled the fault line between the gay and the straight worlds in the 1970s. "Even though they pretended that all this was okay, those barriers were pretty high."

When an openly gay rock singer named Jobriath emerged in 1973, the headline in *Rolling Stone* was "Gay Rock Breaks All the Rules"—because it was the rule. "Today sexuality exudes from every pore in the body, instead of just the groin as it was in the Sixties," Jobriath told *Rolling Stone,* which praised his record. But after Jac Holzman of Elektra spent $500,000 to sign him, and his manager had a $22,000 nude statue of the singer made as a promotional stunt, Jobriath's career went nowhere. He died of AIDS in 1983.

With Jane's protection, Wenner said he never experienced his own homosexuality as a "conflict." "I could, in my own mind, be gay on the side and have relationships with guys without thinking it was of any consequence to my heterosexual identity," he said. "It didn't threaten my identity. I was quietly doing what I sometimes felt compelled to do without it interfering and it became a part of it and I was happy to hold on to that forever."

•

PAGE 61: Johnny Winter, the albino blues guitarist, naked on a bed with his tongue in the mouth of a female lover, her forested crotch aimed squarely for the camera.

The uncredited photograph was published by *Rolling Stone* alongside a review of Winter's 1974 album *Saints and Sinners.* "Winter's manic guitar is there in all its glory," ran the caption, quoting Jon Landau, who called the album "a fine rocker."

Winter famously scored a $600,000 record contract from Columbia in 1969 because of a rave write-up in *Rolling Stone.* But he was humiliated by this photograph, which, besides being a strange image to accompany a record review, upset his girlfriend. The issue got pulled from grocery stores. Johnny Winter knew the photographer and "beat the shit out of him," according to Susan Warford-Winter, the girlfriend in question, who later became his wife.

Jann Wenner had been threatened by unhappy rock stars before, most famously Buddy Miles, who showed up at the offices in 1973 after *Rolling Stone* said his album was boring and got into a physical altercation with Paul Scanlon while Wenner hightailed it. But now Wenner faced Winter's manager, Steve Paul, whom *Rolling Stone* had described as a "well-fed vampire." He had a more diabolical idea for revenge:

According to writer Paul Gambaccini, a friend of Steve Paul's, Winter's manager plotted to release a copy of the "Pinck on Wenner" tape and out Wenner as a homosexual. (Paul was gay and a friend of both Danny Fields and Tony Pinck.)

As fortune would have it, Wenner had just hired a brand-new managing editor from *Newsday* in New York: an albino named John Walsh. Walsh said he was unaware of the impending threat from Steve Paul, but he heard about Winter's fury and wrote an elaborate apology to both the guitarist and his girlfriend. "Being an albino myself," he wrote, "I've followed your career and think your latest album is your finest."

He signed off with "All white power."

The apology worked, and the Tony Pinck revelations remained underground.

In 1973, Wenner hired Walsh to streamline and professionalize *Rolling Stone*. Wenner was interested in the "name" writers Walsh could bring in, like David Halberstam. But the hire became an instant joke around the office: Jann Wenner had hired a legally blind albino to be managing editor.

Walsh moved west in October 1973 and lasted less than a year at *Rolling Stone,* but he built a vital institution inside Wenner's newspaper: a fact-checking department. When he arrived in the fall of 1973, Walsh noticed *Rolling Stone* didn't have a copy or research department, but it did have a lot of women with postgraduate degrees working in menial jobs. A women's lib movement had cropped up in the ranks of *Rolling Stone,* and the women—Marianne Partridge, Christine Doudna, Harriet Fier, Sarah Lazin, Cindy Ehrlich—formed a club to share their grievances. The leader was Partridge, whom Walsh hired as a copy chief after she was rejected for a job at PBS, told by her interviewer she was too frumpy for TV. Wenner said he kept tabs on their meetings through a spy in their ranks. But Walsh, a cultural outsider from a pro shop back east, saw how they served as de facto editors while Wenner's macho men, Paul Scanlon and Joe Eszterhas, failed to pull off their journalistic heroics on deadline and published embarrassing errors (when they weren't all getting drunk at Jerry's Inn down the block).

Rolling Stone was a notoriously sexist newspaper. Critic Paul Nelson famously snubbed Janis Joplin when he cast her as the "Judy Garland of Rock" and another critic called her an "imperious whore," a slight Joplin never forgave. Jon Landau also downgraded her. When John Burks tried calling her for details on her new band in 1970, she said, "I don't like the way your paper treated me and I don't see why I should do you any favors," and then hung up. "They were just always negative, always negative, always negative," Joplin said. "I really cried behind that, man . . . they shot me down, those shits."

Ellen Willis, a pioneering feminist and the first rock critic at *The New Yorker,* wrote to Ralph Gleason in 1970 saying she refused to write for *Rolling Stone* because it was "viciously anti-woman." "RS habitually refers to women as chicks and treats us as chicks, i.e. interchangeable cute fucking machines," she wrote, adding for good measure that Jann Wenner's bias against revolutionary politics fed the oppression of females: "To me, when a bunch of snotty upper-middle class white males start telling me that politics isn't where it's at, that is simply an attempt to defend their privileges. What they want is more bread and circuses; I like to have fun too, but what I really want is an end of my oppression."

Within two years, Partridge would become Wenner's most trusted editor and saw to it that Ellen Willis was published in *Rolling Stone*—starting with a story in August 1975 called "The Trial of Arline Hunt," about a rape victim who could not get justice. Willis also wrote a powerful feminist essay on Janis Joplin, proclaiming her second only to Bob Dylan in importance, in part for taking "advantage of changes in our notions of attractiveness; she herself changed them."

These women often had a different view of Wenner from his men. To Partridge, the pugnacious editor could seem vulnerable and shy—the little fanboy whose Mummy didn't love him. When the Wenners threw a New Year's Eve party in 1974, Wenner was dancing with Partridge to "Brown Sugar" when he stopped, grabbed her excitedly, and declared, "Oh my God! It's 1975 and I don't know what's going to be happening!"

But rock and roll was about men ("male supremacist," to quote Ellen Willis), and Wenner was more interested in men by default. When he published a special "men's issue" in 1975, with Muhammad Ali on the cover, a female staffer had to laugh: "Every issue of every magazine since magazines were *invented* has been a men's issue. And now you're trying to do one *on purpose*"—a line Michael Rogers published in his introduction. The men's issue also featured an essay on the pioneering gay magazine *The Advocate,* written under the pseudonym John Reid, who was Andrew Tobias, author of the gay memoir *The Best Little Boy in the World;* and a profile of a *Playgirl* photographer by Ed McCormack that began, "Eddie Bloom may be small and slightly built but he knows he has a very respectable schlong on him. Certified!"

Partridge said Wenner wasn't sexist per se. She liked to recall the moment she nervously pitched Ellen Willis's story on rape in an editorial meeting on Third Street. Joe Eszterhas snickered and said, "Why don't you just lean back and enjoy it and it wouldn't be a rape?" Wenner didn't laugh. He took the story seriously and assigned it, asking to meet Willis next time she was in town. He gave her a prominent cover line in August 1975. "I fell in love with Jann at that moment," Partridge later said.

"All he really cared about was who was gonna give him what he wanted," observed Harriet Fier, who started as a switchboard operator and rose to top editor in 1978. "Who was gonna get him where he wanted to go? And that he didn't actually see gender. It didn't matter."

But the empowerment was going to be a problem for some of Wenner's men, particularly Eszterhas, who, besides gaining a reputation for making up facts and plagiarizing from other writers, proclaimed his copy off-limits to women. (He left for Hollywood soon after.) And then there was the most macho and important of Wenner's fact-challenged man club, Hunter S. Thompson. "There are those who see Hunter's destructive tendencies as cute and then there are those who have to clean up," Sarah Lazin wrote in a memo to Wenner after finding a telephone smashed to bits, papers scattered, and several LPs missing. "If you could head him off toward some other pass, we'd appreciate it."

As the feminist revolution arrived at *Rolling Stone,* Hunter Thompson was already in decline. When Thompson came to San Francisco in the early 1970s, Wenner and his staff prepared for his arrival as if for a sitting president, work flow coming to a halt. "When you were with Hunter," said Wenner, "you felt like you were going to have the most fun you were ever going to have."

When *Campaign Trail '72* was published the following year, Wenner publicized it as a seminal book of American political writing. To finish on deadline, Alan Rinzler arranged for Thompson to hole up at the Seal Rock Inn, a motel near Golden Gate Park (which Thompson called the "Sealed Right In"), and coaxed him along with speed, acid, and Wild Turkey so Thompson could stitch his columns together into a coherent narrative. The effort almost broke Thompson. Feeling Wenner was exploiting his success while nickel-and-diming him on expenses, he didn't write anything interesting for *Rolling Stone* until late the next summer. Wenner realized that Thompson was in extremis. "I don't know why we could have thought that we could go ahead, without pause, with another year of the same," he wrote to him.

Thompson came out of his "decompression chamber" in September 1973 after writing a minor column on "the meaning of McGovern" that asked, "Where do we go from here?" Wenner declared the National Affairs Suite in Washington "re-opened and prepared for 'total coverage.'" But Thompson wasn't prepared and had no idea where he was going from there. In "Fear and Loathing at the Watergate," he gargled about the burglary at the Watergate but noted that it was "probably the most thoroughly and most professionally covered story in the history of American journalism . . . [T]here is not a hell of a lot of room for a Gonzo journalist to operate in that high-tuned atmosphere."

Wenner tried fanning his champion back to life, agreeing to Thompson's next big idea: a symposium of Democratic Party pooh-bahs in which *Rolling Stone* would unite the factions and forge a winning platform for the White House in 1976. Wenner and Thompson invited a bunch of young advisers—from the liberal and centrist wings of the party—to remote Elko, Nevada, where they holed up in the Stockmen's Motor Hotel. The plan was to review McGovern's loss in 1972 and then hash out a winning policy for 1976. Among the participants were Sandy Berger, Pat Caddell, and Adam Walinsky (who gave Thompson the Elko idea). Thompson handed out heavy-duty tire gauges used by long-haul truckers as a symbol of their street-fighting spirit, and Wenner tape-recorded the proceedings. They planned on turning the results into a manifesto, which Wenner would describe as an "attempt to fundamentally—and, if necessary, *radically*—change the whole organization of the government, the economic structures and the social circumstance, itself." Wenner gave Thompson a contract to write another election book for Straight Arrow Books, and they called the secret plan "C-76."

But the plan quickly dissolved as both men became distracted by diverging interests. In 1974, Thompson began a months-long college lecture tour, giving impromptu monologues for $20,000 a pop about his Fear and Loathing career, shadowed by groupies, mainly young men, who wanted to hear Thompson rip Richard Nixon and witness *Doctor* Hunter S. Thompson drink Wild Turkey by the bottle. He was happy to oblige. Soon his visits to *Rolling Stone* became a grand anticlimax. He would idle in Wenner's office or at the house on California Street, arguing about money and assignments while driven to distraction by Wenner's cocaine.

Thompson first tried cocaine when David Felton assigned him to review Sigmund Freud's *Cocaine Papers* in 1973. He initially dismissed the drug as expensive speed, but Felton mailed some to Woody Creek, and Thompson tried it and was quickly convinced. Cocaine became part of his writing life, which soon became a non-writing life. "From then on, he wouldn't do a story unless you included cocaine with the payment," said Felton. "And he dries up and couldn't write. I was there when he had huge fits of screaming because he couldn't write the next sentence. After he got into coke, every editor at some point broke into tears. He'd get maybe one paragraph an hour. And you had to write transitions, all this stuff. And then he would crash, and you had to edit everything, and you got no sleep for a week. It was very difficult for him. It turns your brain into cement."

The best you could hope for from Hunter Thompson was an amusing personal anecdote. Felton recalled Thompson pouring a gram on a mirror and cutting it into a swastika.

Thompson's frustration with his own writing morphed into a resentment of Jann Wenner's success. In the spring of 1974, Wenner began working as a political strategist to Bill Roth, a family friend from Marin County now running against Jerry Brown for the Democratic nomination for governor of California. Kent Brownridge, an advance man with the campaign who later joined *Rolling Stone,* recalled that Wenner "wanted to attack the oil companies, and he wanted to seize all the coastal property from the property owners and turn it into a bar." In a rambling letter to Thompson offering him a job as a correspondent in a new Washington bureau, Wenner bragged that Roth gave him a $700,000 media budget and that Roth's staff was now calling their fax machine a "Mojo wire."

The letter seemed to enrage Thompson, who returned it with snide comments scrawled all over it. Increasingly, Thompson saw loopholes and betrayals in Wenner's offers. He kept a running tally of his grievances, outraged that Wenner wanted repayment for a shot from Sandor Burstein (a "placebo," Thompson sneered) and accusing Wenner of talking smack behind his back. "Tell Jann to stop telling people that I'm going to die very soon," he wrote to Alan Rinzler; the remark "tends to bother Sandy," his wife. To placate him, Wenner tried offering Thompson stock options in Straight Arrow: five hundred shares at $12.50 a piece, the only caveat being that Wenner could buy them back at "market value" if Thompson was terminated. "This is a worthy offer to the assistant director of the mail room," Thompson spat, ending his reply with "fuck it."

Meanwhile, *Rolling Stone* was doing fine without Hunter Thompson. In January 1974, the newspaper scored an interview with the children of E. Howard Hunt, who was the White House "plumber" jailed, along with G. Gordon Liddy, for Watergate. When reporter Julia Cameron (future wife of director Martin Scorsese) announced she was from *Rolling Stone,* the long-haired son declared, "Far out!" The Hunt kids were the godchildren of William F. Buckley, a family friend who, they told *Rolling Stone,* fed their imprisoned father "distorted information" about their welfare. Mainly about their drug and sex habits. Buckley invited Wenner to lunch at the Four Seasons in New York to try persuading him to kill the story. He appealed to his sense of honor but also his vanity. He booked him on his public affairs TV show, *Firing Line*. But Wenner said he pressed Buckley on the fallout of Nixon's resignation: "I asked him, 'Do you believe in the Constitution as a governing document?' He said, 'I believe in America.' That's pretty fascist. Cryptofascist. 'No, I don't believe in the rule of law; I believe in the supremacy of America.' That was an insight for me."

Wenner sent Buckley an advance copy of *Rolling Stone,* with "Life

Without Father" inside, which prompted an outraged Buckley to cancel Wenner's TV appearance and rip him for publishing "the sickly and
internecine musings of two pathetic young people who are your pigeons,
my godchildren, and the poignant victims of a personal and public tragedy. Your failure to situate their story in the relevant contexts makes you,
in my judgment, a fraud as a journalist and, as a human being, a failure."

This was, of course, a great victory for Wenner. Certainly it impressed his newest quarry, former Kennedy administration speechwriter Dick Goodwin. Goodwin was a craggy Beltway operator with
bushy eyebrows and a cigar perpetually puffing in his mouth, an old
Democratic hand dining out on his career in the Kennedy and Johnson
administrations. He had broken up with Piedy Gimbel (who went on to
marry the director Sidney Lumet) and was now dating Doris Kearns,
ghostwriter of Lyndon Johnson's memoir, *The Vantage Point*. Warren
Hinckle once called Goodwin "the terrible-tempered Lord Fauntleroy
of the Camelot administration." Jann Wenner started writing to him in
1972, proposing a column in *Rolling Stone*. He invited him to Elko and
hired Goodwin because he thought he wrote some anti-Vietnam essays
in the Talk of the Town column in *The New Yorker*. They were written
by Jonathan Schell. Goodwin didn't disabuse him, and Wenner, in a
rush of excitement, told Goodwin he was prepared to spend $900,000
to make his mark in Washington. Politics, Wenner proclaimed, is the
rock and roll of the 1970s.

Goodwin grinned as Wenner gave him a six-month contract, a regular column called Politics, an expense account, a housing allowance in
D.C., a personal loan of $20,000, use of his white Mercedes while he
was in San Francisco, and tickets to see Bob Dylan. In late 1973, Wenner
published Goodwin's stentorian essay "The Obligation of the Congress
to Impeach the President," which was excerpted in *The Washington
Post,* injecting *Rolling Stone* directly into the chatter. The day *Rolling
Stone* opened its new Washington office at 1700 Pennsylvania Avenue,
Goodwin took Wenner on a grand tour of the monuments, including
the Lincoln Memorial, where he put his arm around Wenner's shoulder, squinted up at Lincoln, and declared the Gettysburg Address the
greatest piece of American political writing ever written. Wenner felt

himself standing on the pinnacle of history. "I was just swimming," said Wenner. "I was starstruck."

And then Goodwin gave Wenner the ultimate thrill: an introduction to Jackie Kennedy Onassis in the spring of 1974, in New York. Jackie Kennedy considered Wenner an ideal diplomat to bridge the generation gap between herself and John John and Caroline (the teenage children whose mid-1960s nanny inadvertently introduced Wenner to his first gay love). Onassis invited Wenner to stay at Ethel Kennedy's place in Hickory Hill, where the Kennedy children came bursting into his room to gawk at the editor of *Rolling Stone*. A dream! This put Dick Goodwin in good stead. As Nixon faced a televised drip of questions over Watergate, Wenner started cooking up a biweekly magazine for Goodwin called *Politics,* a reported tip sheet and opinion journal to rival *The New Republic.* Wenner drew up a proposal and assignment memos and let Goodwin hire his own deputy—Joe Klein, a twenty-seven-year-old reporter for *The Real Paper* in Boston. When Klein emerged from a taxi on July 2, 1974, he found himself at the gates of Ethel Kennedy's mansion, ushered in by a maid who announced his arrival at the foot of the pool. Goodwin was floating on an inflatable raft, smoking a Cuban cigar. "He looked at me and he said, 'Tax reform,'" said Klein. "And I said, 'Tax reform?' He said, 'If you really want to learn this town, you have to learn about how Congress works. They're marking up a tax reform package now, and I want you to watch them do it.'

"And I go, 'But the sucker is getting impeached!'"

Then Hunter Thompson showed up with a bagful of drugs and shared them with Klein and David Kennedy, son of the late Robert. Thompson was avoiding his latest deadline by dreaming up pranks, like delivering a truckload of rats to the White House lawn. The jukebox at Ethel's was filled with 45s by her boyfriend, crooner Andy Williams, and Thompson replaced them with Otis Redding records. The next week, Jackie Kennedy Onassis and Teddy Kennedy both called Ethel's house to find out what the hell was going on down at Hickory Hill, thus ending *Rolling Stone*'s access to the pool.

That summer, Goodwin invited Wenner and Thompson to his house in Maine for a weekend with Doris Kearns and Norman Mailer.

Thompson gave Wenner acid, and they drove all night from Massachusetts, making a tape recording of themselves screaming like monkeys. They arrived at dawn while everyone was asleep and put the tape recorder in the kitchen, volume all the way up, and ran.

It was a classic Thompson prank, but he was in a full-blown crisis, faced with a choice between his fame and his writing. Joe Klein advised him to write a novel, but Thompson gestured to the drugs and said, "Well, if I did that, I'd have to give *those* up." When Nixon resigned in August 1974, Wenner ordered John Walsh to get a column out of Thompson, come hell or high water. But Walsh couldn't do it. Instead, Wenner ran a photo spread by Annie Leibovitz, including her classic portrait of Dan Rather between stand-ups on CBS, and filled the cover with Richard Nixon's jowled face, which David Felton stamped, in a moment of inspiration, "The Quitter." (Soon after, Wenner fired Walsh.)

Things weren't going any better with Dick Goodwin, who was spending Wenner's money in rapid fashion, holding lavish dinner parties and demanding he be paid in cash to avoid taxes. Marianne Partridge, who edited Goodwin's columns, called them "Grappling with the Obvious." And Goodwin was laughing at all he was getting away with, encouraging Joe Klein to spend as much as possible and charge it to "the benevolent Mr. Stone." The same month Nixon resigned, Goodwin threw a dinner party for foreign-policy wonks, including future titan of American diplomacy Richard Holbrooke. Wenner showed up. While the experts jawed on the finer points of import-export, he sat on a stereo console and flipped through a copy of *Foreign Policy* magazine (edited by Holbrooke) and sized up his cigar-gnawing investment. The next day, Wenner called Klein to his new office at 1700 Pennsylvania Avenue and asked his thoughts on the dinner. The best idea to come out of the party, conceded Klein, concerned the production of shoes by overseas companies. Wenner agreed, and fired Klein. "I'd love to have you write for the magazine, but I got to send Goodwin a message," Wenner told him. "He's out of control. You're the message." (He hired him back on a contract basis a few months later.)

Jann Wenner refused to pay Goodwin's catering bill, and Goodwin offered to represent Ridgewells Catering in a lawsuit against Jann

Wenner. The fight blew over—Goodwin had an ironclad contract for six columns and was promising to recruit big writers like Seymour Hersh—but Wenner canceled *Politics* magazine and demanded Goodwin give back the company tape recorder, which Goodwin refused to do, claiming it was broken. Later, Wenner threatened to sue Goodwin for repayment of the $20,000 loan.

Wenner would say Hunter Thompson's postscript on Watergate— "The Scum Also Rises," from 1974—was one of the last decent things he wrote before his writing career died. Thompson's muse had climbed inside a helicopter and flown off the White House lawn. "Hunter always had to have an apocalypse going on, a demon, to energize him," said Wenner. "Somebody had to be the foil; somebody had to be the demon. And Nixon was his most constant lodestar demon." (Tom Wolfe told Wenner that covering politics ruined Thompson's talent.)

After Nixon, the relationship between Wenner and Thompson became a widening gyre of disappointment. In the fall of 1974, Wenner sent Thompson to Zaire to cover the "Rumble in the Jungle" boxing match between Muhammad Ali and George Foreman. But while Ali battered Foreman in the ring, Thompson dumped a bag of pot in the hotel swimming pool and floated around in it, missing the fight entirely. The bill came to thousands of dollars, and no story was produced.

A 1974 reader survey showed Thompson as the most popular writer Wenner published (Ben Fong-Torres second, Dick Goodwin last), and Thompson kept close tabs on *Rolling Stone*'s circulation numbers, mailing Wenner a memo citing *Rolling Stone*'s circulation of 2.9 million readers, more than *Esquire*'s. Thompson felt he helped make this happen, and he was right. The readers knew it, too, and demanded more. So Wenner kept trying, offering the assignment they'd been talking about since 1970: Vietnam. The United States was exiting Saigon in April 1975, the official end of the long and bloody war that defined the generation, and Thompson was gung ho. Wenner went to Woody Creek to conspire with Thompson, who would cross the border into Vietnam and directly into the apex of the war's denouement. But in the days leading up to his departure, Wenner mentioned offhand that he was shuttering Straight Arrow Books and killing the C-76 book, for which Thompson believed he was promised $75,000. Wenner said that Straight Arrow wasn't making money on eccentric titles like *A History of the Israeli Army (1870–1974)* and *The Queens' Vernacular: A Gay Lexicon,* and he was firing Alan Rinzler and instead partnering with New York publishing houses to produce *Rolling Stone* books.

At this, Thompson exploded:

> You came out here and laid a near-perfect con job on me while wallowing in an atmosphere of friendliness and hospitality that might be hard to revive on your next visit. The next time you feel like accusing ex-RS editors of "taking advantage," think back on your recent vacation out here . . . God's mercy on your ass when your time comes to explain yourself to the Lords of Karma (sp?), but in the meantime we should make some kind of legally & financially binding agreement as to my professional relationship with The Empire, however arthritic it may or may not be at this point . . . and if I wanted to get genuinely ugly on this point, I could look back on the bound copies of RS and find the RS pre-convention "coverage" on Chicago.

Thompson hit Jann Wenner where it hurt—his integrity. In a fit of pique, Wenner canceled Thompson's writing retainer, leaving his employment status ambiguous while Thompson was en route to Vietnam. Wenner also asked Tom Baker to draw up a life insurance policy on Thompson in case he died in Saigon. Was it proof that Wenner was determined to profit on Thompson or that he was trying to protect Thompson's family after suspending his contract? Wenner said the policy paid out to Thompson's family. Sandy Thompson said she had never heard of it, though she doubted Wenner would do something so underhanded. (Tom Baker wasn't so sure; he suspected it was tantamount to an investment scheme.)

In either case, a life insurance policy was probably smart. Thompson was ill-equipped to function in a theater of war—he later wrote that he brought ten hits of blotter acid with him, taped to the back of his press card—and after some misadventures wandering the streets of Saigon, he flew to Hong Kong, ostensibly to buy some surveillance equipment, and missed the iconic moment the last U.S. helicopter flew off the roof of an apartment building.

When Thompson came home, he believed that Wenner had, in effect, fired him and canceled his company health insurance along with his writing retainer and left his family in the lurch while he was in Vietnam. He was enraged. Wenner, acknowledging his actions, offered him an olive branch of sorts by sending him a copy of the letter Ralph Gleason sent to Wenner in 1968, which dressed him down for his various failings. *See,* Wenner seemed to say, *you're not alone.* Thompson shook his head: a Nixonian move, he said, like "sending an autographed transcript of one of his most damaging tapes to [White House lawyer] John Dean" (though he was impressed, he wrote, by "the integrity of Gleason's instincts"). Thompson agreed to take a new contract at *Rolling Stone,* but he told Wenner, "If I have any tax, medical or unemployment problems resulting from your capricious failure to clarify my situation, you can be goddamn sure they'll bounce back on you—in court, in person, and every other way that seems appropriate."

In case Wenner thought he was joking, Thompson gave interviews to the press declaring his past work for *Rolling Stone* "embarrassing" and demanding once again that his name be removed from the masthead. For a profile of Jann Wenner in *The Washington Post,* Thompson compared Wenner to William Randolph Hearst and Henry Luce—a publisher, he said, with more faith in logos than writers. Further, Thompson began circulating a rumor that would persist for years: that after shutting down Straight Arrow Books, Wenner secreted away the remaining five thousand copies of *Fear and Loathing: On the Campaign Trail '72,* presumably to profit from them later. (Thompson believed Wenner kept them in a warehouse in New Jersey.) Wenner would deny it for years, stung by Thompson's accusation. Infuriated with the public attacks, Wenner suggested that their working relationship might be over. "What *really* have I done to cheat you? Haggling? Fuck . . . that's been *your* trip, not mine, all along," he wrote. "I am sick and tired of the abuse, private even more than public, drained of my desire to work with you in the near future."

But the next year, fearing Thompson was cooperating for a negative profile of him, Wenner pleaded with Thompson to stop slagging him and return to the fold. "Let's put the misunderstandings and bitterness behind us and forget it," Wenner wrote. "Let's just end the quibbling that arose from the intense back-and-forth of the past, and return to the productive and enjoyable dealings of earlier years."

The reality was that Thompson was not able to return to those productive earlier times. His writing had dried up as his marriage to Sandy collapsed. Wenner, with mixed motives, kept up appearances, keeping him on the masthead, doling out assignments. He also used his likeness on a subscription card until Thompson threatened to sue him. In an unpublished interview, Wenner claimed he never made any money on Thompson. "He was always in debt to me," he said. "I lost money. I'm sure if you told it all, I lost a fortune. I mean, what did I ever make out of Hunter?"

But Wenner knew on some level what he owed to Thompson, and it was about more than just business. Thompson could belittle and humiliate Wenner for sport, steal his stereo, pound a dent in the hood of his Mercedes, turn every assignment into an expensive boondoggle, and let deadlines come and go, but Wenner would always endure it, even ask for more, hopelessly devoted to Hunter Thompson. Wenner would call Thompson his soul brother—"my Keith Richards." Their endless battles had a sadomasochistic feel, their tedious arguments over money an elaborate homoerotic smoke screen. Indeed, Thompson once said arguing with Wenner over money was "better than sex."

13

Love Will Keep Us Together

In June 1975, Cameron Crowe trudged up the twenty-four steps at California Street with jangling nerves. He was in trouble. Big trouble. Jann Wenner was upset with Crowe's cover story on Led Zeppelin and had asked him to fly from San Diego to discuss it. "It's like, wow, I'm actually being called to the principal's office, I fucked up," recalled Crowe. He was seventeen. "What wafted back to me was that Jann thought it was a puff piece."

Crowe joined *Rolling Stone* in 1973 after calling up Ben Fong-Torres with a story: He had tracked down Kris Kristofferson at a Mexican restaurant and learned about a new Bob Dylan recording, the soundtrack to the film *Pat Garrett and Billy the Kid,* in which Kristofferson played Billy. Fong-Torres put the item in Random Notes, uncredited, but offered Crowe assignments. His first bylined story was "Poor Poco: They Were the Next Big Thing Four Years Ago." When Fong-Torres discovered Crowe was sixteen, *Rolling Stone* immediately began advertising his age in Crowe's biographical blurb, a kind of public relations corrective to their accumulating reputation for dyspeptic and aging critics. "To me, it was fun," said Crowe. "It wasn't like I was being a hustler; I was just following bliss."

The critical apparatus of *Rolling Stone* was in turmoil in 1975. Wenner's writers didn't like music anymore. The late 1960s already looked like a bygone era, after which everything was cynical farce, show business, and greed masquerading as authenticity. Jon Landau had largely given up record reviews for film criticism. "I found myself withdrawing from the music and wondering whether or not I would ever be able to relate to it again," he wrote—in 1970. By 1975, *Rolling Stone* no longer pulled culture from the underground and put it aboveground; it was following big-budget industry stars from CBS and Warner Bros. and Elektra and Atlantic, companies that built rock and roll into a multimillion-dollar industry. Clive Davis had survived the Columbia scandal, written an exculpatory memoir called *Clive: Inside the Record Business,* created Arista Records, and launched Barry Manilow, a former piano accompanist for Bette Midler at the Continental Baths, into the stratosphere. Middle-of-the-road rock now ruled the increasingly powerful FM airwaves, and record companies spent hundreds of thousands of dollars to promote an artist in hopes of yielding millions in return. As the *Rolling Stone* cover line put it, "There's Gold in the Middle of the Road." The band was Loggins and Messina.

Wenner commissioned reports showing which covers sold and which didn't. *Rolling Stone* cost a few cents to print, but if *Rolling Stone* sold enough copies, the profit margins were high—best-selling artists were often best-selling covers. Wenner determined three things about poor-selling issues: Either "the personality involved is a minor one," or it had "little appeal on a sexual or vicarious identity basis." Wenner concluded that "editorial quality is not a reliable guide to covers." Cover stories by Joe Eszterhas were the worst-selling issues.

Consequently, the Carpenters, John Denver, Carly Simon, Donny Osmond, and even actor Peter Falk, star of NBC's *Columbo,* all made the cover of *Rolling Stone.* "That's the period where *Rolling Stone* really does turn into a promotional vehicle," said Greil Marcus. "Whether it's promoting a rock-and-roll performer, or a TV performer, or a movie star. It is promoting them. And it's symbiotic. You get this exclusive access, and you promote each other."

Wenner fired critic Lester Bangs in 1973 because he said his reviews were too negative. Bangs had declared that 1972 was "one of the stalest years in the history of popular music," but the last straw was his review of Bruce Springsteen's *Greetings from Asbury Park* in 1973: "He sort of catarrh-mumbles his ditties in a disgruntled mushmouth sorta like

Robbie Robertson on Quaaludes with Dylan barfing down the back of his neck."

Springsteen: "Hilarious review . . . I couldn't tell if it was positive or negative."

Unless critics were writing laudatory reviews of best-selling super-stars, Wenner generally considered them pains in the ass. "The fact that one of the two or three most popular sections of the magazine was record reviews drove him nuts," said critic Dave Marsh, who first wrote to Wenner in 1970 asking why he hated groups from Michigan and whether he was interested in seeing lithographs of John and Yoko "sucking and fucking."

Springsteen was, in many ways, the inflection point for the new era—a sign that rock and roll, perhaps, could be resuscitated. Jon Landau published his landmark essay in *The Real Paper* of Boston—where he regularly field-tested reviews before publishing them in *Rolling Stone*—describing how his faith was restored when he saw "the rock and roll future," Bruce Springsteen. Consequently, Springsteen tapped Landau to produce *Born to Run* and gave Dave Marsh, who lauded Springsteen in *Rolling Stone,* access to write a quickie bio, *Born to Run: The Bruce Springsteen Story,* the first of four books he would write about him. Both men became part of Springsteen's inner circle—Landau his intellec-tual mentor, Marsh his hagiographer, and Marsh's wife, Barbara Carr, business partners with Landau. (Maybe hoping to get in on the action, Wenner promised to personally write a Springsteen profile for *Rolling Stone* in 1976, but it never materialized.)

This all created quite an opening for Cameron Crowe, a fanboy far too young to judge Michigan groups or any other groups too harshly. *Rolling Stone* editors assigned Crowe to cover bands they all hated—Jethro Tull, Deep Purple—and to repair relationships with artists they offended, for example, the Allman Brothers, whom Grover Lewis made look like "a bunch of crackers getting high," said Crowe. "I was a kid in a toy store, like, 'I'll take Led Zeppelin, I'll take Deep Purple, I'll take Humble Pie, let me do it!'" said Crowe. "So I would stockpile these assignments, and then came Led Zeppelin."

As a rule, *Rolling Stone* critics hated Led Zeppelin. When Mike Salis-bury turned on *Physical Graffiti* one night in the office, they yelled at him to shut it off. Jimmy Page called Wenner out personally in the press. Led Zeppelin could sell records without *Rolling Stone,* he said, and declined its interview requests. But with the help of Joe Walsh, whom Crowe successfully profiled in 1974, Crowe convinced the band to do an interview in March 1975. Wenner gave Crowe some notes, including a barbed question about their "hippy dippy" lyrics. Crowe was careful not to ask it.

CROWE: Do you feel you have to top yourselves with each album?
PAGE: No. Otherwise I would have been totally destroyed by the reviews of our last album, wouldn't I? You see, this is the point. I just don't care. I don't care what critics and other people think.

Tim Cahill complained about the interview, telling Wenner that "despite the mail (which has been highly favorable), I personally thought the interview was soft, slushy, and sychophantic [*sic*]." The next thing you know, he said, the artists would ask for a "package deal" with Crowe, a guaranteed puff piece in exchange for access.

And so here was Crowe on California Street, frightened and a little perplexed by the Jann Wenner he was finally meeting: slumped in a chair, pale and unshaven, shirt unbuttoned, and cheeks streaked with tears. He held a half-empty bottle of vodka in his lap. Had Wenner really taken the Led Zeppelin story this badly?

No—Ralph Gleason was dead.

•

RALPH GLEASON HATED the commercialization of *Rolling Stone* as much as anyone. In his last letter to Wenner in April 1975, he called the cover with John Denver on it "the nadir of RS"—"unbelievable," he said. Gleason told Wenner he needed to rethink the magazine and start listening to people outside his increasingly rarefied bubble and rediscover the core mission. "Your instincts are great but you get seduced by something else," he wrote. "I'm not sure exactly what; sometimes I think you are a perpetual groupie: first music, then writers, then politics. But it gets in the way of your mind and destroys your perspective. For chrissakes, hire me as a consultant or something. But do something!"

Wenner had returned from an afternoon with Tom Hayden, the political activist and husband of Jane Fonda who was running for Senate in California, when he learned from Paul Scanlon that Ralph had had a heart attack. Wenner collapsed in grief. Gleason died that night. He was fifty-eight.

Gleason and Wenner hadn't gotten along well in years. Wenner's top staffers, Charlie Perry and Marianne Partridge, detested his columns as the endless opining of a geriatric cane waver for whom nobody was quite idealistic enough and who freaked out if editors touched a word of his columns. He often praised Wenner, saying *Rolling Stone* could not have happened without his zealous commitment, but he also criticized him for running Tom Wolfe and Hunter Thompson, whose work he didn't like, and publicly chided him for failing to run enough black artists, calling *Rolling Stone* a "white publication": "I don't think it's been fair to black music and by and large, *Rolling Stone* has not covered black music with either intelligence or space or effort and time."

This last part was true, and Wenner tried making up for it by running Gleason's epic profile of Duke Ellington in 1974, "Farewell to the Duke," which won a major award for music writing. But as Wenner outgrew Gleason, Gleason came to feel marginalized, hurt when Wenner didn't list his name in promotional advertisements for *Rolling Stone* and when he asked Gleason to stop writing about politics, calling his columns terrible "except in the rare instance where they are informed by unique vision or anger or election."

But the real fissure was over money. In the early 1970s, Gleason was living off a *Chronicle* pension and writing liner notes for Fantasy Records, the jazz reissue label. Wenner saw an opportunity to buy back his Straight Arrow shares and get Gleason to retire. Scared to do it himself, he tasked Alan Rinzler with the job. "Jann came to me and said, 'Ralph has to go,'" recounted Rinzler. "I went to Ralph and was supposed to say, 'Ralph, I know you need money.' I said, 'We're going to buy your stock back. For $3 per share.' It came to $10,000 to get rid of Ralph. He knew it wasn't fair. He said, 'If you want me to quit, I will, but I'm gonna write about it. I'm gonna write that *Rolling Stone* is losing its integrity.'"

Rinzler said they went up to $10 a share, which came to $50,000, which they agreed to pay out over time, said Rinzler, "to make sure he was going to keep his word and not write anything. Ralph was very bitter." His wife, Jeanie Gleason, who had treated Wenner like an adopted son, later expressed regret over the sale. When Rinzler ran into Gleason one afternoon in the mid-1970s, he told him to "punch Wenner in the nose for me."

Now Wenner was bawling with grief over Gleason's death. This was the Jann Wenner whom Cameron Crowe encountered. "Jann called me every night for a week, sobbing," said Denise Kaufman, who had remained close to Gleason, "and we would talk for hours." At his Irish wake in Berkeley, Wenner was a wreck—drunk, snorting cocaine, passing out on the couch—and had to be driven to the home of his former secretary to sleep it off. He had ignored Gleason's advice and cut him out, just as he had Alan Rinzler and Max Palevsky before him. In a letter to Rinzler, Wenner blamed his cruelty on "my own personal unhappiness and inherent difficulties in being able to handle human relations and sometimes even love." (Even his own mother felt slighted: When Wenner refused to publish a book she wrote in 1974, she told a newspaper, "His cup is full, but it doesn't runneth over.")

Wenner's health deteriorated in the weeks following Gleason's death. He grew pale, unkempt, bloated. In 1976, he said that in the fog of grief and overwork "I was at the point where I was really going to push a pencil through my hand. I mean, I almost did one day, push a pencil through my hand."

Gleason's son, Toby, had always felt jealous of Wenner for his father's affections. "I was his little baby; I was his boy," Wenner said of Gleason. "His own son was a nice boy, but kind of a fuckup, and I was living in Ralph's dream and doing things he wanted to do himself." But Wenner put Toby in charge of the memorial issue and treated him like his lieutenant. (He also gave him cocaine, which infuriated Jean Gleason.) Toby told Wenner his father would never want to be on the cover—not a *critic*—so Wenner acquiesced and put the Rolling Stones on instead. Wenner published a series of short elegies as a final Perspectives column, with recollections from Jerry Garcia, Dizzy Gillespie, John Hammond, Ken Kesey, Frank Sinatra, Miles Davis ("give me back my friend"), Lawrence Ferlinghetti, Paul Simon, and even John Lennon, who thanked Gleason for supporting his fight to retain his immigration status in the early 1970s. But the lead obituary was Wenner's own remembrance, the story of his history with Gleason, his inarticulate sadness smudged with emotion. He was the "eternally ungrateful" son. "He was a father to me," said Wenner. "He was number one, boss and most beautiful." He wept on the page.

Cameron Crowe was frightened to see a grown man crying. But in the twine of the moment, Wenner looked at Crowe and channeled the spirit of his mentor. "He told me a little bit of what Ralph meant to him," said Crowe, "and he segued into the privilege of the job and what it really means to be a journalist."

Wenner told him the Led Zeppelin interview was too wide-eyed and soft. He beckoned Crowe to his study, as Gleason had with Jann back in 1966, and advised him to read Joan Didion's 1968 profile of Jim Morrison for guidance on how a proper journalist dealt with a rock star. "We'll give you a break with this one," said Wenner, "but if you want to stay with us, you really have to dig deeper and learn your lesson and stand on the shoulders of the people who understand the gift they're being given."

•

THE COVER WAS THE SEVENTH for the Stones since *Beggars Banquet*. The black-and-white studio portrait by Annie Leibovitz cast the Glimmer Twins as shirtless gypsies, Jagger pouting and posturing, Richards looking as if his face were roasted for a Thanksgiving dinner. Leibovitz had badly wanted to cover the 1975 Rolling Stones tour, just like Robert Frank in 1972, but Wenner was reluctant to send her, fearing she would get sucked into the notorious drug vortex of the Stones caravan.

Keith was a full-blown heroin addict, but even Jagger was overdoing it, once falling unconscious on a couch in Marshall Chess's apartment at East Sixty-Ninth Street in New York in 1975. Recalled Diane Chess, "I was upstairs in the bedroom when I heard this slapping and Marshall yelling, 'Mick! Mick!' enough times for me to go see what was going on. He was blue, lips purple. And the poor, helpless, heavyset chauffeur just standing there almost made the whole thing comical." (While a panicked Marshall Chess tried giving Jagger mouth-to-mouth resuscitation, Ahmet Ertegun showed up with Peter Wolf and wife Faye Dunaway, who tried bringing order to the chaotic scene until Jagger could be rushed to the hospital in an ambulance. Jane Wenner called the next morning, fishing for details, but the whole thing was kept out of the press.)

Wenner believed Leibovitz was susceptible to this sort of excess. "And I was right, of course," he said. But he was overruled by Mick Jagger, who hired Leibovitz as the official Rolling Stones tour photographer for a few hundred dollars a week. As Richards recalled, "She was in our pay. Only because we liked the work that she had done with Jann and said, 'We need a really good photographer. You got a free pass to take any picture you like.'"

Leibovitz and Wenner were always fighting over money. Marianne Partridge once warned Wenner not to "nickel-and-dime" Leibovitz, and Wenner replied, "Are you crazy? I nickel-and-dimed my way to the top!" But Leibovitz was a star now, profiled in *People* magazine for her spiky images that stuck like burrs in the hide of the culture: Keith Richards passed out on junk ("You got to give it to Annie, she got me"); Salvador Dalí, cheek to cheek with Alice Cooper; Norman Mailer in a snorkel and mask, grizzled and drained of machismo. But stardom made Leibovitz more erratic than before. When a *People* photographer snapped pictures of her playing tennis with Michael Rogers, Leibovitz hurled her racket at the photographer: "Stop taking those fucking pictures!"

Wenner and Jagger were social friends now, connected by Earl McGrath, who became president of Rolling Stones Records after Chess got swallowed up by his own drug abuse. "Earl would have so many drink parties and get-togethers," recalled Jagger. "Jann and I would go to a lot of those. I was living in New York at the time."

But the trademark issue between *Rolling Stone* and the Rolling Stones was always in the background of any exchange, and occasionally in the foreground. Wenner warned Leibovitz not to share photos or negatives with Atlantic Records or the Rolling Stones "until I obtain a letter of agreement from each regarding their use." They belonged to *Rolling Stone,* not the Rolling Stones. Wenner and Jagger could joke about it until somebody wanted to put the combination of words "Rolling" and "Stone(s)" on, say, a brand of beer (as the Rolling Stones tried doing). According to several former business confidants of Wenner's, the editor and the singer worked out an informal agreement in the 1970s, reputedly on a cocktail napkin, though Jagger couldn't recall the details, and Wenner said it was an urban myth (one almost certainly spread by Wenner).

And now Mick Jagger was, in effect, taking Leibovitz as *his* concubine. And Wenner didn't just ask Leibovitz not to go; he tried pressuring her. "I can't guarantee you'll have a job when you get back here," he told her. But Wenner looked on the bright side: The Stones were covering her travel expenses and paying for her film stock, and Wenner could publish the Stones' photos. When the Rolling Stones appeared on the cover of *Rolling Stone* for the second time in 1975, it was a de facto Rolling Stones fan magazine, a reunion of the Trans-oceanic Comic Company of 1969. The only problem was the writers Dave Marsh and Jonathan Cott, who considered the tour bloated and cynical and the music not very good. So Jann Wenner came out of retirement to write the fan copy. Wenner hadn't conducted an interview since co-interviewing Jerry Garcia with Yale professor Charles Reich. After seeing the Stones at the Los Angeles Forum, Wenner declared it "possibly the best show ever." The Stones were "better as a band in 1975 than in any previous time."

"That's a conceited claim, stated in a conceited fashion, but I think it's true," wrote Wenner. "It is time to remove the curse of Altamont from this group, from rock & roll itself, from ourselves."

Meanwhile, Dave Marsh's story was an extended complaint about his endless hassles trying to score an interview ("I Call and Call and Call on Mick"). A week later Mick was doing lines off Wenner's table with a credit card.

Leibovitz said she was so naive in 1975 that she packed a tennis racket for the Stones tour. In a bit of foreshadowing, she photographed a line of twenty stitches on Mick's forearm after he accidentally ran it through a plate-glass window during rehearsals in Montauk. By the end of the tour, she would become more intimately familiar with hard drugs. (When asked if he'd shown Leibovitz a few tricks, Keith Richards replied, "Possibly she's got a good eye for tricks.")

"I did everything you're supposed to do when you go on tour with the Rolling Stones," she later wrote.

Indeed, she became consumed by the immensity of the experience but also began to think of herself, perhaps for the first time, as an Artist with a capital *A*. She would come to refer to a concert image of Jagger's spectral torso and writhing face as "the Francis Bacon" ("more grotesque than beautiful," she said). She beatified Jagger in a close-up, mid-concert, his eyes heavenward and face tenderized into the expression of Jesus Christ on the cross. Jann Wenner splashed this image across the cover of *Rolling Stone* in September 1975.

Leibovitz also captured Jagger alone in an elevator afterward, a white towel on his head and creviced face fallen in exhaustion. The intimacy of the image wasn't accidental: Annie and Mick had become lovers, an affair that began in Montauk and allegedly inspired the song "Memory Motel" from *Black and Blue*. Leibovitz listened to Jagger work on the song every night in hotels. And Jagger later told *Rolling Stone* the girl in the song was "actually a real, independent American girl." According to Jann Wenner, Jagger confessed to him that the girl whose "eyes were hazel" and nose was "slightly curved" was Annie Leibovitz.

Her experience with the Stones was destined to remind Annie Leibovitz of the high costs of her art. When the tour was over, she found herself in a studio in London surrounded by hundreds of wet prints of Mick Jagger's face, feeling trapped and alone. She missed moving Jane's furniture. Jann Wenner had been right. "I lost several years of my life," she said. "He wasn't wrong. I had no idea."

•

IN 1975, when Greil Marcus published the seminal *Mystery Train: Images of America in Rock 'n' Roll Music*, Ralph Gleason wrote to Wenner to say it was "the most important book on rock yet written" and urged him to "grab some of it ASAP. Have you read it?"

Wenner replied that he hadn't read it, but Marcus continued to have "an active distaste for RS, which inspires a similar feeling in me toward him."

But even in death, Gleason would end up helping Janno. Wenner used the memorial essays he commissioned for Gleason to patch up old wounds with people who loved Gleason but disliked Wenner. When Marcus sent Wenner his own remembrance of Gleason, Wenner wrote back to say, "Ralph would be happy if you and I finally got back together, and I mean to do this."

He brought Marcus back into the fold in 1975, giving him a regular column reviewing books, and Marcus also filed the occasional record review. His first for *Rolling Stone* since 1970 was of Bruce Springsteen's *Born to Run,* which Marcus called "a magnificent album that pays off on every bet ever placed on him."

Everywhere Jann Wenner went—every back stage, every cocktail party, every record industry function—he walked into a room charged with a backstory, stories told and untold in *Rolling Stone,* and not a little of it grievance and malice. As Mr. *Rolling Stone,* Wenner was held responsible for everything in his newspaper, good or bad. As Gleason had advised years before, Wenner could write twenty-five stories on an artist, and he or she would only remember the one bad one. *"Rolling Stone,* it was tough," said Lou Adler, who was angered by coverage of his mysterious kidnapping in 1976, which made light of the relatively paltry $25,000 ransom requested for his release and was accompanied by an unrelated studio portrait of Adler posing with a hunting rifle. "Journalism—his take on it is nothing's sacred. Here's the real story, or at least the real story as he sees it. So when I'm looking back on it, that's to be credited for. [But] I think more people disliked him than liked him."

The problem was *The Jann Wenner Method for Effective Operation of a Cool Newspaper.* The editor of *Rolling Stone* curled up in the lap of a celebrity one day, and then the editor of *Rolling Stone* spilled the star's guts in his magazine the next. "If he puts his arm around your back, there might be a dagger there," said Art Garfunkel. "You're not sure. Same way I feel about Paul Simon. These guys are too cute for my comfort."

Steve Miller, who broke through with *The Joker* in 1973, said Wenner offered to put him on the cover in 1976 and assigned Cameron Crowe to do the interview. Miller thought Crowe was too young to understand his "musical scope" and afterward Crowe circulated a snarky memo detailing their unpleasant encounter, ripping Miller as "the biggest ass-hole in the world." Wenner read the memo to Miller over the phone. "Jann says, 'I have a great idea—why don't we print it in the magazine and you can respond to it?'" recounted Miller. "Jann, fuck you." (Miller never made the cover of *Rolling Stone*.)

John Lennon once said "there are fuckers and fuckees," and Wenner, by dint of his barrel of ink, was destined to be a fucker. "I think to a certain degree, we're all starfuckers," said David Geffen. "In Jann's case, it was very important to him. He didn't seem to care or realize that if you think you're friends with people and write bad things about them, they're not gonna be okay with that. If you're gonna be my friend, along with that comes certain responsibility. He forgot that part. I know people that wanted to kill him!"

Geffen was one of them: When Wenner quoted him saying he had a good relationship with Bob Dylan, and then quoted Dylan in the same article saying he didn't like Geffen, Geffen arranged to have all the Warner Communications subsidiaries—Warner Bros., Atlantic, Elektra, and Asylum Records—pull their ads for three issues in 1974. Ex-Beatle George Harrison was furious at *Rolling Stone* for coverage of his 1974 solo tour, and his distaste put him in good company: John Lennon, Joni Mitchell, the Eagles, and, for a time, Bob Dylan.

Dylan held an active grudge against *Rolling Stone* over its publication of a Polaroid of his young daughter standing next to Tatum O'Neal in 1973. Wenner reasoned that the caption didn't identify the kid, but the nine-year-old O'Neal revealed her friend's identity in the interview: "Maria. Bobby Dylan's girl." Dylan claimed not to recall this incident but said, "I imagine if *Rolling Stone* published a photo of any of my kids, it would have disillusioned me about the magazine."

Dylan could not have been thrilled either with Jon Landau's review of his soundtrack album for *Pat Garrett and Billy the Kid:* "inept, amateurish and embarrassing," not to mention any number of Random Notes items about him. When Wenner came by Dylan's hotel after a 1974 show with the Band in Oakland, Robbie Robertson was eager to lay eyes on the big-time editor who had put the Band on the cover in 1968. "I don't know what *Rolling Stone* had just done, but they had written something on Bob that really pissed him off," Robertson recounted. "He comes in and Bob lit into him. While Bob is laying it on him, I recognized something in [Wenner's] face: This happens quite a bit."

Dylan gave an interview to Ben Fong-Torres but made him turn off his tape recorder and cornered him later to make sure he did it (Fong-Torres nonetheless contributed to a *Rolling Stone* paperback called *Knockin' on Dylan's Door: On the Road in '74*). A year later, a *Rolling Stone* writer named Larry "Ratso" Sloman befriended Dylan over a shared love of folksinger Phil Ochs (who was living in Sloman's apartment in New York) and gained his approval to cover the 1975–76 Rolling Thunder Revue tour, which featured a supergroup Dylan assembled to help support his *Desire* album and campaign for the freedom of Rubin "Hurricane" Carter, the incarcerated boxer whose 1974 memoir, *The Sixteenth Round*, inspired the Dylan song "Hurricane." Dylan made Sloman his *Rolling Stone* punching bag but also an outlet for his vituperative opinions. As it happened, Sloman was also upset with *Rolling Stone* after an editor added one too many fangs to an otherwise positive story on George Harrison. Sloman was so upset he sent Harrison the original unedited draft of the story, to which Harrison responded, according to Sloman, "I'm glad you sent me that article, Larry. I thought you were an asshole and then I realize that it was *Rolling Stone* that was the asshole."

Sloman produced two pieces about the Dylan tour in late 1975, but they would be his last for *Rolling Stone*. Sloman's second story was reworked by Chet Flippo to focus on complaints from fans that the concert venues were too crowded, the sound too muddy, and Dylan too greedy. According to Sloman's book *On the Road with Bob Dylan,* Jann Wenner came to the hotel where the Dylan entourage was staying in New York, a bottle of wine in hand, only to be attacked by Dylan's sidekick Bob Neuwirth, who "sliced him apart for the shitty way he hacked my second *Rolling Stone* piece into an attack on the tour."

Sloman remained on Dylan's tour to write the book, recording Dylan's complaint that *Rolling Stone* published "gossipy shit." "I can't get behind that magazine," he told Sloman, who sympathized:

"You wanna hear this, my fucking New York editor, you know what he asked me: 'Do you know who Dylan's sleeping with?' I said, 'What the fuck?' and he said, 'I know that Dylan's been sleeping with Ronee Blakely.'"

"Oh yeah?" Dylan sounds bored.

"I said 'Oh yeah? How do you know that?' and he said he heard it from someone on the tour. But he couldn't tell who, such bullshit."

"You know," Dylan gets animated, "those people who run that thing, those people who talk like that, they're the same people who got America into Vietnam, you know."

"Yeah, I guess they are. Except they're not as powerful."

Wenner said he finally reconciled with Bob Dylan at a party at Norman Mailer's apartment in Brooklyn Heights during the Rolling Thunder Revue tour. "We went over as their guests, and I just remember Bobby was sitting there holding court with a bunch of people, a circle of people around him," said Wenner. "I was on the other side of the room talking to Henry Grunwald" (the managing editor of *Time* magazine, who the year before had named Wenner one of the Top 200 "Faces for the Future" in America).

A friend of Neuwirth's approached Wenner and said Dylan wanted to see him. "I knew this was a moment," said Wenner. He said he walked over to Dylan and forewent the limp-fish handshake this time.

He was out to get me. I walked over and Bob said, "Well, sit down," pointing to the floor. I said, "Well, have somebody get me a chair." I knew going into this that this was staged. I knew he was pissed off that we hadn't done something having to do with Hurricane Carter or something, and I knew Bob could get loaded for it, the confrontation. Everybody knows about [Dylan's confrontations with the press] in *Don't Look Back,* but there was some specific thing. I said, "I'm going to play the game."

He had somebody come over with a chair. So right away, I've started to master the situation. I said, "No, I'm not going to be put on the floor." So I sat down. And right away he starts complaining about what *Rolling Stone* had done wrong to him, how he remembers when we first met, at the Berkeley Community Theatre, with Ralph Gleason, and I said, "Bob, we never met then; you gotta believe me, I would have remembered that." He said, "But you published that picture of my daughter, my child, in your issue." I said, "Bob, but, you know, that was in that article about Tatum O'Neal, and if you notice, in the picture, a little Polaroid of Tatum O'Neal, it says, 'Tatum O'Neal and her friend,' so you can't say that."

So then he starts on this thing about why we don't have Hurricane Carter on the cover of the magazine. I said, "Well, you don't have Hurricane Carter on the cover of your record." He said, "Well, but I have a single." I said, "Great, we'll run something inside the magazine about it, just like you've got a single on your album."

And that somehow got him. And the mood just shifted to friendly and easygoing.

Neither Sloman nor Bob Dylan remembered this confrontation ("a boring party at Norman Mailer's flat," Sloman recorded), but it loomed large in Wenner's mind. There would be other tellings of it, one in which Dylan threatened to start his own magazine and put *Rolling Stone* out of business. "Go ahead, start your own paper," Wenner allegedly shouted. "I'm a publisher. I'll beat you. I'll beat the shit out of you."

After Sloman left, *Rolling Stone* managed to get back on the tour by sending out the veteran jazz critic Nat Hentoff, whom the Dylan entourage welcomed. The image of Dylan that friends like Allen Ginsberg and Joan Baez painted for Hentoff was of a man who had changed over the years, from a "kid scrabbling for his turf" to a man who "has learned to share." And maybe Jann Wenner had learned his lesson as well: *Rolling Stone* named Bob Dylan, along with Bruce Springsteen, the Artists of the Year for 1975.

•

IN THE FALL OF 1975, Jann Wenner held a secret meeting at the house on California Street, calling in his editors and flying in correspondents from Washington. All of them climbed the twenty-four steps to Wenner's den and settled into the white Italian sofas with no idea why Wenner had called them there. With cigarettes lit and breaths collectively bated, they leaned in to hear Wenner's secret: "I've just heard that J. Edgar Hoover is gay. Can we get this story?"

They looked at each other with blank stares. "We all knew that J. Edgar Hoover was gay," recalled Joe Klein. "It was just shocking naïveté." (The idea was originally the brainchild of Truman Capote.)

Wenner's enthusiasm could produce moments of comedy, but the passion—along with the sheer volume of the notions he brought in from his nighttime ramblings—set him apart as an editor. Wenner would arrive at his Monday morning meetings in the Raoul Duke Room with pages and pages of ideas scribbled in notebooks, churned up from parties in L.A. and New York or the house on California Street. "Ninety percent of them were implausible or would have gotten us all sued," recalled Howard Kohn, an investigative reporter who joined *Rolling Stone* in 1974, "but the other 10 percent were amazing. The other 10 percent made up the bulk of the magazine."

The fall of Richard Nixon in 1974 ushered in an age of paranoia. Everyone now saw conspiracies, cover-ups, CIA spooks, and White House plumbers. After listening to Nixon's secret White House tapes for three weeks straight, Timothy Crouse wrote that he had succumbed to "Dingbat Paranoia," which "totally decimates the victim's faculties of skepticism and disbelief, leaving him helplessly in the grip of a conviction that the government is controlled by an unassailable coalition of Teamsters, hoods, millionaire fascists and the CIA." To this end, Wenner published CBS News correspondent Dan Rather's review of *All the President's Men;* Joe Eszterhas's lengthy interview with reporter Seymour Hersh about the My Lai Massacre; an essay arguing for the reopening of the JFK assassination case; and a deep dive into the secret foreign-policy agenda of Standard Oil.

Wenner was a social climber, but when it came to writers, he was not a snob. Two of the biggest stories of the 1970s were brought in by an unlikely pair of hippie journalists who'd been living in a commune in the Haight-Ashbury, Howard Kohn and David Weir. Kohn was a newspaper reporter from Ann Arbor who'd gone undercover for a year as a street junkie for the *Detroit Free Press* to try exposing a heroin ring inside the police department. Before the final story appeared, Kohn was fired over a bizarre incident in which he was kidnapped by a man trying to force Kohn to give up his sources. Kohn escaped and reported it to the police but failed to acknowledge that he carried an illegal gun with him and knew the kidnapper. Kohn hoped the newspaper wouldn't decommission his story for ethical reasons, but it did. His reputation in shambles, Kohn moved to San Francisco in 1973, and David Felton and Joe Eszterhas, no strangers to controversial journalism, vouched for him. Kohn's first assignment was an investigation into the death of a woman named Karen Silkwood, who was threatening to blow the whistle on a toxic nuclear plant in Oklahoma when she was killed in a mysterious car accident. The story, "Malignant Giant: The Nuclear Industry's Terrible Power and How It Silenced Karen Silkwood," produced more reader letters to *Rolling Stone* than any story before it. After readers started sending checks for the Silkwood family, Wenner agreed to match all donations and contribute $10,000 to the family's lawsuit against the plant, Kerr-McGee, which the Silkwoods claimed was negligent and had covered up her plutonium poisoning. (*Rolling Stone* would cover every hiccup of the story until the family won a civil lawsuit case in 1979.) "The fact that the Karen Silkwood lawsuit was successful is almost 100 percent due to Jann," said Kohn. "There would never have been a lawsuit carried forward."

In the summer of 1975, Kohn brought in his housemate David Weir, who had a line on a monster story. He'd found a source with deep first-hand knowledge of the entire backstory to the kidnapping of publishing heiress Patty Hearst by a group of Marxist revolutionaries calling themselves the Symbionese Liberation Army (SLA).

Hearst, a cosseted teenager who was the scion of the most famous journalistic dynasty in America, had been kidnapped from her apartment in Berkeley in February 1974. While her panicked family worked with the FBI, Hearst was spotted two months later participating in an armed bank robbery, now identifying herself as Tania, named for a Cuban revolutionary in Che Guevara's army. Nobody knew her whereabouts or whether she was pressured to join the group (she later said she experienced Stockholm syndrome after being raped and tortured), but the black-and-white image of the publishing heiress wearing a black beret and hoisting a machine gun at the Hibernia Bank in San Francisco became seared into the popular imagination—for some, a symbol of 1960s youth ideologies curdled into rank terrorism; for *Rolling Stone* readers, a pop hero. The media found the story irresistible and set up semipermanent encampments around the Hearst mansion in the suburb of Hillsborough, awaiting word from the family on the ongoing FBI investigation. The SLA strung the media along, issuing a demand that the Hearst family give free food to the poor of California, prompting the Hearsts to dole out $2 million in giveaways in hopes of getting their daughter back. In May 1974, six members of the SLA were killed in an FBI raid in Los Angeles, but Patty Hearst and her captors—William and Emily Harris—escaped, going from safe house to safe house to hide from the law.

David Weir had come to San Francisco from Michigan to help start a magazine with friends—*SunDance,* cofounded by investigative journalists Craig Pyes and Ken Kelley and supported by John Lennon as a rejoinder to Wenner's betrayal over the *Lennon Remembers* book. In the early 1970s, Weir circulated among the activist lawyers helping left-wing radicals resist subpoenas from the Nixon administration, which was on a witch hunt for people suspected of antigovernment activities (including, it turned out, John Lennon). One such lawyer led Weir to a client named Jack Scott, a sports activist who was under investigation by the FBI for being an SLA sympathizer. Indeed, Scott helped Patty Hearst and her captors/co-conspirators hide out at a farmhouse in Pennsylvania and was intimately familiar with the drama inside the group. He offered the story to Kohn and Weir in exchange for help publishing a book, which he hoped would make him rich. "He wasn't a professional journalist, and he needed collaborators to pull this off," said Weir. "So that was the deal. At some point it was agreed that *Rolling Stone* would be a perfect outlet to syndicate a chapter of that book when we were close to publication."

Wenner agreed to keep the story quiet until Scott's book was ready for publication or Patty Hearst was discovered, whichever came first. But four months later, Scott pulled out of the deal, deciding that his book didn't need the imprimatur of *Rolling Stone.* The breakup occurred just as a competitor in New York, *New Times,* was pursuing the same Patty Hearst story.

Rolling Stone's story was largely written, but Scott's decision had left it without a clear path forward. Weir worried that it was unethical to run the story without Scott; Kohn worried that his tainted reputation in Detroit would undermine their credibility.

Then, on September 18, 1975, Patty Hearst and the Harrises were discovered by the police in a hideout in San Francisco. After that, the imperatives of news, luckily for Wenner and *Rolling Stone,* overwhelmed all other issues. Wenner arranged to break the story on NBC's *Today Show* the following Monday morning and bought his reporters new suits and shoes to make them look like respectable journalists. He hired a Pinkerton security detail to pat down anybody coming and going from Third Street, partly out of paranoia, but mainly for showmanship. As the press, the FBI, and left-wing agitators circled, Wenner even hired a security detail for the printing plant in St. Louis. Lenny Weinglass and William Kunstler, lawyers representing the Harrises, Hearst's captors, accused the reporters of being shills for the FBI and arranged a conference call the Saturday morning before publication to pressure *Rolling Stone* to stop the presses. "They said, if you publish this, basically, we're going to shut you down," said Weir. "You're never going to publish anything in America, ever again."

For Wenner, the posturing was all part of the publicity machine. And he wasn't worried because he wasn't even present; he had corralled the entire *Rolling Stone* staff at the Ventana Inn, a lodge and resort in Big Sur, to shield them from growing media pressure and celebrate the biggest story in the history of his little rock-and-roll newspaper from San Francisco. When Kohn and Weir showed up, bedraggled and burned-out, they were greeted by a pandemonium of partying. Staffers had sex with each other, Ben Fong-Torres showed up with a pair of leather pants with a prosthetic cock (modeled on an Eldridge Cleaver fashion statement), and Wenner circulated the only printed copy of *Rolling Stone* featuring "Tania's World," the inside story of Hearst's months-long odyssey on the run with the SLA. Standing on a chair, he gave an emotional speech declaring that *Rolling Stone* had finally broken through and that he was paying for everybody's hotel rooms. Cheers! (Afterward, the proprietor of the inn expressed gratitude to Wenner but wondered why all the mirrors were off the walls and lying on desks.)

When Monday arrived, the offices of *Rolling Stone* were surrounded by every news outlet in the country. Hungover and sunburned, the staff peered out the windows at the insanity of cameras and boom mics below. While Wenner's publicist held a strategy meeting in the Raoul Duke Room, TV reporters forced their way into the building and up to the lobby, demanding interviews. Wenner hid in his office. By evening, the staff was popping champagne bottles to watch themselves on the evening news as death threats came pouring in from leftist groups accusing *Rolling Stone* of treachery. The FBI was humiliated at its own failures, and lawyers for the Harrises raged over Wenner's introduction to the story, which called their clients criminal thugs. (Lenny Weinglass had court-ordered subpoenas issued for both Kohn and Weir, sending both men into hiding for weeks until the ACLU came to their aid and the subpoenas were quashed.)

The Patty Hearst issue of *Rolling Stone* was the first to sell over a million copies. In the table of contents, Wenner wrote, "Apparently much of the so-called straight press has finally got it straight about who we are and what we're up to. Frankly, we've become pretty used to the confusion: 'Hey, what gives?' is the invariable question. 'Is *Rolling Stone* into music or politics or sociology or what?'

"What we're talking about, really, is not a generation but an event," wrote Wenner. "The greatest mass alteration of personal consciousness since the country began."

To exploit the attention, Wenner unfurled a new marketing campaign with quotations from celebrities and famous writers waxing positive about *Rolling Stone,* including Paul Newman, Dick Cavett, Julian Bond, Gay Talese, and, of course, Michael Douglas. *Rolling Stone*'s circulation ballooned to half a million readers in 1976.

Jann Wenner also used the story to gain entrée to a more exclusive social sphere: the Hearst family. The Hearst publishing empire had shadowed Wenner since he was a teenager. A few months before *Rolling Stone*'s Patty Hearst story, Wenner was asked in an interview if he'd ever visited the Hearst Castle in San Simeon, California. "I've always wanted to wait for the right time," he replied. "I've always wanted to be able to drive there and buy it." By the time the second installment of the Hearst story arrived—the two hundredth issue of *Rolling Stone*— Weir and Kohn had obtained the cooperation of Patty's father, Randy

Hearst, the fourth child of William Randolph, who agreed to pose for a cover portrait standing in front of a fireplace with a *Rolling Stone*–commissioned painting behind him: an homage to Andrew Wyeth's famous *Christina's World* with Patty Hearst as Christina.

Randy's nephew, the twenty-six-year-old William Randolph "Will" Hearst III, had provided the reporters with some of the family's inside account of the affair. Wenner first met Will Hearst in the early 1970s when Hearst tried getting him to write an op-ed for the *San Francisco Examiner*. It was Wenner who had helped funnel Hearst to his reporting duo so they could expand on the story of his kidnapped cousin. Will Hearst admired the journalism he read in *Rolling Stone,* so Wenner offered to help educate him. David Weir and investigative reporter Lowell Bergman, whom Wenner hired in 1976 to collaborate on an investigation into California governor Ronald Reagan, took Hearst to a storied newspaperman's bar called the M&M Tavern and got him drunk. In return, Hearst invited Wenner on a weekend trip to the family's thirty-thousand-acre private estate, San Simeon, in central California. Though Hearst Castle became a public park in the 1950s, the family had private access on holidays, and the Wenners joined Hearst for the bicentennial Fourth of July in 1976 to wander the grounds under the moonlight and swim in the vast Neptune Pool overlooking the Pacific Ocean, the whole thing gabled in Roman columns and marble statues of naked cherubs and frolicking muses. Hearst motored them around the property in a Jeep, shirtless and grinning. Wenner and Will set off firecrackers at night, prompting the police to show up for what they feared was a raid by leftist factions sympathetic to the SLA.

Wenner exposed Hearst to a piratical mode of publishing that hadn't existed in his family for a generation. "I had never been in the business where the owner could go to the cash register on a Friday night and say, 'Give me a grand,'" Hearst said. "Jann treated *Rolling Stone* magazine as if it were his store. He would just go to the accounting department and get it out of the petty cash fund."

For a time, Wenner and Hearst bonded over their youthful ambitions, with drugs the usual generational handshake ("Will has the lamp shade on tonight," his wife, Nan, would tell friends who called for him).

But Hearst was also taking copious notes. "I think I was picking his brain a lot more than he was picking mine," he said.

Wenner had more on his brain than Hearst imagined: In 1976, Wenner began conceiving a new magazine to expand his Straight Arrow empire, a camping and backpacking publication for the off-grid and back-to-the-landers that he would call *Outside*—with William Randolph Hearst III as editor.

14

Take It to the Limit

J ann Wenner for president.

In the mid-1970s, Wenner was spinning this fantasy with close confidants like Hunter Thompson and Howard Kohn. "He decided it was hipper to hang out with politicos than with rock 'n rollers," Hunter Thompson told *The Washington Post* in 1975. "There's no doubt that he wants to run for office. I mean, isn't that the ultimate power trip?"

Wenner generously offered to make Thompson either his press secretary or his secretary of state.

There was plenty of circumstantial evidence that Wenner was putting the pieces in place for a career in politics. While his closest lieutenants urged him to get back to the music, Wenner had a veteran speechwriter in Dick Goodwin and was publishing a D.C. gossip column called Capitol Chatter (written by Harriet "Hank" Phillippi, who was dating Richard Holbrooke and often used a mysterious source named Deep Thought). In 1975, he recruited a walking D.C. Rolodex named Anne Wexler, whom Wenner made his top publicist. Wexler had worked for both the Edmund Muskie and the George McGovern campaigns in 1972 and was married to a prominent Democrat who had run for Senate in Connecticut, Joseph Duffey. She not only promoted *Rolling Stone* in the press but held Beltway dinner parties for Wenner, selling his newspaper-magazine as a kind of biweekly youth lobby.

When reporters asked Wenner whether he was running for office—one day it was governor of California, the next senator—he said he was too young (only thirty) but left the door open with a politician's aplomb. In the meantime, Wenner was developing the outlines of a stump speech on the power of the youth vote, which doubled as a marketing assessment of his readership. "I think the vanguard of young people," he said in 1975, "is interested in restoration in the United States of integrity and truth as the operating method and way of life rather than hypocrisy."

Q: Are young people, then, more serious today?

A: Young people haven't lost their sense of humor. But it's certainly serious when you live in a country which has killed 50,000 of its own people in a senseless war and murdered easily two to five million in Indochina, that's damn serious business. And we've been trying—the young and the older people who have come around to a younger point of view— every goddamned way possible to stop this kind of thing. We've treated it with a sense of absurdity, with humor, skepticism, with anger, with violence, with pressure within the political process, pressure from outside the political process. We've even tried abandoning society altogether. Anything. At long last, some of it has started to work, I suppose. But youth are a little bit more realistic about how tough it is to change things. These are real problems in a real world that we are dealing with. And overall young people are less inclined toward the frivolous behavior of the 60s because of increasing gravity of the national situation.

Asked to name the figures the young most respected, Wenner rattled off Ralph Nader, Ken Kesey, Hunter Thompson, Bob Dylan, J. D. Salinger, Joseph Heller, Norman Mailer, Dustin Hoffman, Jack Nicholson, and Marlon Brando. All of them were in *Rolling Stone,* either as writers, subjects, sources, or as all three.

Wenner had never been, exactly, a revolutionary. He wanted to overthrow the establishment by *becoming* the establishment. The establishment, meanwhile, wanted a taste of the new fame and glamour that

Rolling Stone was charting. And Wenner's generation was now fully adult, forged in the fires of Watergate and Vietnam and receptive to political messaging by the Democratic Party. If rock and roll was the common tongue, maybe *Rolling Stone* could be a translation device. In 1976, when Wenner and Thompson were temporarily reconciled, Thompson pushed Wenner to support Georgia governor Jimmy Carter, inspired by the "king hell bastard of a speech" Carter gave in May 1974 at the University of Georgia Law School. Carter said that a "source of my understanding about what's right and wrong in this society is from a personal, very close friend of mine, a poet named Bob Dylan." In addition to the Democratic operatives they'd met through the Elko conference (like Pat Caddell, now Carter's pollster), Wenner's connection to the Carter campaign apparatus came through a financial donor from Macon, Georgia: Phil Walden, the head of Capricorn Records, Wenner's buddy from his Boz Scaggs days. Walden held a fund-raiser for Carter in 1975 attended by Bob Dylan, the Band, and Bill Graham. Walden's biggest acts, the Allman Brothers and the Marshall Tucker Band, helped raise $400,000 for his campaign with a live concert.

Wenner began planning a *Rolling Stone* party for Jimmy Carter during the Democratic National Convention in New York City. Wenner leaned on Anne Wexler—who was now both the associate publisher of *Rolling Stone* and the floor manager of the Carter convention—to help curate a guest list to celebrate Carter's campaign staff. Joe Klein, Wenner's man in Washington, recalled his discomfort with a "Carter for President" sticker on the front door of the *Rolling Stone* D.C. bureau, but Wenner had no such discomfort, renting a town house on East Sixty-Eighth Street, four blocks from his apartment, and casting his net wide: The guest list, in addition to the Carter staff, contained four hundred people, which virtually guaranteed an overcapacity crowd.

This would be the grand rollout of Wenner's fantasy fusion of celebrity and politics, and it would work all too well. In advance, Wenner published an illustration of Jimmy Carter on the cover of *Rolling Stone,* with a long and winding essay by Hunter Thompson, who opined that "the radicals and reformers of the Sixties promised peace, but they turned out to be nothing but incompetent troublemakers" who made possible both Watergate and the extended disaster of Vietnam. "By the time the 1976 presidential campaign got under way, the high ground was all in the middle of the road," he wrote.

As *Washington Post* gossip columnist Sally Quinn reported of the massive *Rolling Stone* Carter party in July 1976, the police shut down the street to accommodate the overflow of disgruntled partygoers who couldn't get through the clogged doorway. But what disgruntled partygoers: Lauren Bacall, Senator Gary Hart, Bella Abzug, Jane Fonda, Tom Hayden, Chevy Chase, Carl Bernstein, Nora Ephron, Paul Newman, Hunter Thompson—"and those were the people on the outside, who couldn't get in," reported Quinn. (Thompson grumbled that Wenner had stamped his Carter essay as an "endorsement" on the cover of *Rolling Stone;* Thompson wanted to maintain his pose as a "journalist.")

While Warren Beatty sat on the curb with the publisher and family owner of the *Washington Post,* Katharine Graham, "Wenner stood peering out the pane glass windows, at his guests outside, pushing and shoving, chanting his name in outrage. Then he would go back inside the room where the party was being held and give periodic reports as to who was being kept out. Jane Fonda, he reported to the guests inside, was unable to get in. In fact when last seen she was being crushed by two heavies who pushed her up against the marble column on her way in."

Lauren Bacall declared the whole affair "a terrible fuck up." Even the celebrated antiwar veteran Ron Kovic, whom *Rolling Stone* had profiled in 1973 with an iconic Annie Leibovitz image of the wheelchair-bound Kovic on the beach at sunset, was unable to wheel himself in. "I was spit on in Miami," he said, "and I can't even get into the *Rolling Stone* party."

Wenner's cousin Steve Simmons, a Carter campaign aide and later part of the administration, manned the door for Wenner. "I'm telling them, 'You can't come in right now; you gotta wait,'" he recalled. "It was a very wild thing, but I think it was a real tribute to Jann and how influential he had become."

In her column, Quinn articulated the general belief that Wenner was using the publicity as a stepping-stone for his own run for the Senate in California. "What's in it for Jann is the whole point of this party," said a *Rolling Stone* staffer. "He sold out. Now we all have a fix on where he is at."

Wenner got drunk that night, but the event was destined to be remembered more for its surfeit of boldfaced names than the logistical nightmare it actually was. And more so after what came next: That week, Wenner had a photographer with a portable studio set up in the basement of Madison Square Garden, the site of the convention, using a large-format camera to shoot images of major Democratic power brokers against a giant sheet of white butcher paper. The man behind the camera was famed fashion photographer Dick Avedon.

The absence of Leibovitz while she was touring with the Stones in 1975 gave Wenner the chance to experiment with new photographers, especially fashion and celebrity photographers, like Francesco Scavullo. Wenner initially approached Avedon about covering the 1976 presidential campaign, but Avedon, famed for his starkly glamorous images of Marilyn Monroe, Audrey Hepburn, Elizabeth Taylor, and the Kennedys, had a different idea: He would take a series of studio portraits of the political class in Washington, Republican and Democrat alike, for a yearbook of the American power structure. His photo editor would be his close friend Renata Adler, author of the 1976 cult novel *Speedboat*. Wenner rolled out the carpet for Avedon in San Francisco, chartering a prop plane so they could take in conceptual artist Christo's installation of a twenty-five-mile fabric fence that ran near Freeway 101 in Marin and Sonoma Counties. While they schemed, Annie Leibovitz hovered around and photographed Dick Avedon with her usual obsessive snapping. Wenner offered Avedon $25,000 for the job, plus $20,000 in expenses, a sum Leibovitz could only dream of. "Annie was awkward and competitive," recalled Wenner.

Avedon demanded total control of the feature, and Wenner gave it to him. With Anne Wexler's Rolodex and Avedon's fame, *Rolling Stone* procured access to Jimmy Carter, Gerald Ford, Henry Kissinger, Cesar Chavez, Daniel Patrick Moynihan, Jerry Brown, Katharine Graham, Bella Abzug, Nelson Rockefeller, Eugene McCarthy, Hubert Humphrey, George Herbert Walker Bush, Donald Rumsfeld, George McGovern, George Wallace, Lady Bird Johnson, Ralph Nader, Ted Kennedy, Ronald Reagan, and Jimmy Carter. (It also featured a portrait of W. Mark Felt, the man later revealed to be Deep Throat.)

"The Family 1976" was a landmark issue of *Rolling Stone,* an uncut expression of Wenner's devotion to the establishment, a fusion of the Who's Who directory and *People* magazine. The monument to the mostly white, mainly male mainstream was wedged between a Random Notes item about Bob Dylan talking to *TV Guide* and a review of a Beach Boys compilation by Greil Marcus. In addition, it featured one of *Rolling Stone*'s first auto advertisements—for the MG Midget—and an advertisement from *The New Yorker* with excerpts from Janet Malcolm's profile of Avedon and his "almost uncanny feeling for the zeitgeist."

Avedon proclaimed his work an attack on subjectivity in journalism, calling his images "visual facts," as stark as Roman busts. Wenner publicly disagreed with him, saying it was another kind of subjectivity. "The pictures tell you what power does to people," he said in 1976. "They tell you what success looks like." (Avedon excoriated Wenner for initially failing to credit Renata Adler as the editor of the feature and while reviewing the issue at the printing plant in St. Louis jammed his hotel key into the paper rolls and ruined the entire press run. "You don't fuck with me on something like a promise," he told Wenner.)

When Marianne Partridge saw the Avedon issue, she knew that *Rolling Stone* had crossed the Rubicon. "This is the end," she thought to herself. "This is the end of *Rolling Stone*." In 1976, Partridge was recruited by editor Clay Felker to join *The Village Voice*. She had been something like a den mother for Wenner, a reliable and talented right hand, and he was devastated by her departure. "I remember going into his office, and he was in tears, and he said, 'What are we gonna do now?'" recalled Joe Klein.

But the Avedon issue expanded Wenner's vision of what *Rolling Stone* could be. Imagine what he could do with this newfound access to the top levels of American politics. As the Republican National Convention in Kansas City loomed in August 1976, *Rolling Stone* put Gerald Ford's son Jack on the cover, prompted by the junior Ford's confession that he smoked marijuana and by his invitations to Andy Warhol and Bianca Jagger to visit the White House—not to mention a report that the square-jawed jock might have had a fling with Jagger. As he told Cameron Crowe, "I've been kinda waiting around, wondering when *Rolling Stone* would show up."

To cover the Republican convention, Wenner hired John Dean, the flamboyant Nixon lawyer who did jail time as the "master manipulator" behind the Watergate cover-up. Wenner knew Dean through David Obst, his book publishing partner in Rolling Stone Press and the super-agent rolling out Dean's 1976 tell-all memoir, *Blind Ambition*. When Wenner first went to meet Dean in Beverly Hills, Dean was wearing a caftan and mixing up margaritas, inviting him and Obst into the hot tub with his wife. "He'd already gone Hollywood," said Wenner. "It seemed like they might have been swingers. It was like a TV show. What happened to John Dean the lawyer for the president?" (Dean said he wasn't a swinger.)

Before he was hired to write for *Rolling Stone,* Wenner had assigned investigative reporter Lowell Bergman to write a profile of Dean. Bergman poked into Dean's dubious past with a powerful Washington law firm called Welch & Morgan, which had represented Howard Hughes, and discovered that before Nixon hired him, he'd been fired for "unethical conduct" and narrowly avoided being disbarred. (Jack Anderson originally broke the story for United Features Syndicate.) Wenner decided to show Bergman's manuscript to Dean, who told Wenner that if he published it Welch & Morgan would sue him and end up owning *Rolling Stone*. Wenner killed the story. Said Bergman, who later became a producer at *60 Minutes,* "Then the question becomes, which is unanswered in all of this, how did Dean get to be White House counsel? That seemed not to interest Jann."

Instead, Dean would cover the convention alongside Ralph Steadman, producing "Rituals of the Herd," an explicit homage to Hunter Thompson. When Dean told a Hare Krishna at the airport that he was from *Rolling Stone,* the man said, "I like that Fear and Loathing stuff you wrote. Hey, how'd you do all that writing with all those drugs, I mean, you were tripping a lot, weren't you?"

With every controversy he stirred, Wenner's sense of himself was expanding. *Jann Wenner for president.* Given the obstacles, it's remarkable how seriously the idea was being entertained. Wenner, after all, was a draft dodger with a "concomitant history of psychiatric treatment, suicidal ideation, homosexual and excessive heterosexual promiscuity, and heavy use of illegal drugs." Nonetheless, Wenner said that in the late 1970s Sidney Harman, the founder of Harman Kardon, the stereo maker and *Rolling Stone* advertiser, offered to back Wenner if he wanted to run for president of the United States. "He said he would fund me if I wanted to do it," recalled Wenner. "You never want to say no to people who think that because it enhances your mystery. And it's true, I did have quite a little political team there—[Dick] Goodwin, Anne Wexler, Hunter, the writers. I could have done it. I could have tried it. I don't think I could have gone very far."

"I didn't have the temperament for it," Wenner said. "I couldn't get up at six in the morning and shake hands outside a shoe factory."

•

JOE ARMSTRONG PULLED a lit cigarette from Jann Wenner's mouth. It was late one night at the house on California Street, and Wenner was passed out after a long night of partying. "If I had not been there, he could have set his house on fire," said Armstrong. "I thought to myself, 'I ended up saving that guy's life.'"

Armstrong had risen to become Wenner's most trusted business confidant, edging out Tom Baker to become publisher of *Rolling Stone*. When Wenner hired Rich Irvine, an executive from the Walt Disney Company, to run Straight Arrow, Armstrong viewed him as a rival and convinced Wenner to fire Irvine after less than a year (questioning why Wenner would hire a right-wing Republican in the first place). Now Armstrong regularly flew west to stay on California Street, his name filling up the guest register as he and Wenner mapped out the next step in his media-baron plan: moving *Rolling Stone* to New York City.

This had been in the conversation since at least 1974 as Wenner dreamed of ever greater professionalism. But Joe Armstrong, above all others, was Wenner's co-dreamer in the mid-1970s, convincing him that *Rolling Stone* could finally do what Laurel Gonsalves never bothered to try: take Madison Avenue by storm and rake in the lucrative ads from alcohol, cigarette, and auto manufacturers, the core industries that powered phone-book-heavy tomes like *Playboy* and *Esquire*. From 1974 to 1976, Armstrong would entirely repackage *Rolling Stone* as a mainstream magazine, rewriting the advertising script for the World War II–era executives who ran American agencies. In sales calls and public speeches—and trade advertisements featuring a sweet, smiling Joe Armstrong ("Joe wants for y'all to meet the '76 team")—the *Rolling Stone* adman promised to bridge the generation gap between Wenner's twenty-two-year-old readers and the blue-chip companies of America.

Joe Armstrong didn't do drugs, which made him a sober hedge against Wenner's excesses. "I often think *Rolling Stone* made it because I didn't take coke," he said. "I'd get there at 7:30 a.m. and leave at midnight."

Under Armstrong, *Rolling Stone* ran its first cigarette ads and finagled its first auto ad, from Ford Motor Company, Wenner's dream since he was rejected by Doyle Dane Bernbach. By 1977, *Rolling Stone* featured ads for the Ford Pinto, Dodge Van, Toyota Celica, Triumph Spitfire, MGB, Porsche 924, VW Dasher, Triumph TR7, MG Midget, VW Rabbit, Datsun 200SX, and Ford Mustang. The little newspaper from San Francisco became a fat newsprint magazine, doubling its ad revenue to $4.5 million between 1974 and 1976, more than *People* magazine.

Armstrong made sure everybody knew about these numbers and who was responsible for them. Wenner's new favorite partner worked the press like an orchestra, getting stories on *Rolling Stone* into *Business Week* and *The New York Times*. He and Wenner were regularly photographed for profiles, Wenner in his white Izod tennis shirt, Armstrong standing behind him in crisp suit and tie; or both of them in suits, Wenner tugging on his pin-striped vest like a baby press baron. They were dubbed "the Lennon and McCartney of publishing." "I felt like he was a soul buddy at one point," said Armstrong. "We loved the magazine, and that's all that I cared about. That's what we had in common, the magazine. At one point, I thought, 'Oh my gosh, this is fantastic, we're a team. And we're making this happen.' I remember saying to him, 'Jann, we could be the Time Inc. of our generation. We could end up building the Time Inc. for a whole new generation of Americans.'

"I believed in him," said Armstrong. "I also believed in him because I projected on him what I wanted him to be . . . He did his half, I did my half, and it ended up as a whole. That was what was great."

With Wenner's editorial antennae and Armstrong's relentless salesmanship, *Rolling Stone* would become one of two magazines to thrive in the decade of recession and oil crisis, the other being *People,* which

Time Inc. launched in 1974 with the express idea of publishing celebrity photographs and shorter articles. Under Armstrong's influence, the magazine was becoming shallower even as it became more intimate—which is to say, a more perfect representation of the fast-metastasizing culture of popular fame and power.

In addition to staking out new ad markets, Armstrong was flirting with editorial, encouraged by Jann Wenner. When Daniel Ellsberg came to San Francisco to be interviewed, Wenner brought Armstrong to their first breakfast meeting. "If you had a regular editor-publisher relationship, you kept them separate," Armstrong observed. "He didn't take anybody from the editorial department, but he took me."

Armstrong deepened his influence in 1976. At the time, singer Elton John wasn't speaking to *Rolling Stone,* unhappy with unflattering pictures by Annie Leibovitz and miffed by Jon Landau's review of *Captain Fantastic and the Brown Dirt Cowboy* (wherein he claimed John's music was "often devoid of noteworthy emotional content"). Rocket Record Company, the label operated by John's manager and lover, John Reid, pulled its advertisements from *Rolling Stone.* Armstrong befriended Reid at a record convention in Hollywood, Florida, and learned that Elton John felt "screwed" by *Rolling Stone.* "I went to try to mend the fences," said Armstrong.

Armstrong helped score an interview with Elton John for *Rolling Stone* on the eve of his 1976 record, *Blue Moves.* Elton John was not yet out as a gay man, but he wasn't hiding it either, wearing glittering coats, feather boas, and purple panty hose onstage. In *Playboy,* David Bowie had referred to him as "the Liberace, the token queen of rock and roll," which offended John. "That was a cunty thing to say from somebody like that," recalled John. "But then he's a cunt anyway. That was not necessary."

Elton John said he was ignorant of Wenner's sexuality (had he known, he said, "I could have mentored him; we could have gotten along like a house on fire"). But he remembered *Rolling Stone* writer Cliff Jahr approaching the subject of his bisexuality tentatively—until John gave him carte blanche to ask away. "I remember Cliff saying to me, 'I'm going to ask you a question, and if you don't want to answer the question, I'll turn the tape recorder off,'" said John. "I can't really believe nobody has asked me before. I've never kept it a secret; I've never gone out with women. You can keep the tape recorder rolling; it's not a big deal for me."

Wenner said he called Elton John before publication to make sure he wanted to come clean. "Are you sure you want to do this?" he recalled asking him. "I've got this interview in front of me, and it says you'd fuck anything, including a goat. I'm just double-checking. If you don't want to say this, we won't run it."

Actually, John said he drew the line at goats, and he hedged on his homosexuality, saying he was "bisexual": "There's nothing wrong with going to bed with somebody of your own sex. I think everybody's bisexual to a certain degree."

Wenner put Elton John on the cover in October 1976, and the confession made national news. The response from *Rolling Stone* readers was mainly positive, with the exception of a couple of readers offended by his homosexuality and disinterest in women ("The effect is shattering," wrote a female reader). Although Elton John's career survived the revelation—after a rough patch of a couple of years—he would not appear again on the cover of *Rolling Stone* for thirty-five years, a fact that John Reid, his manager, privately blamed on Wenner's ambivalence toward his own sexuality.

In 1975, a former *Life* magazine publisher named Jerry Hardy, whom Wenner appointed to his board of directors, mentioned to Wenner the possibility of exploring the outdoor equipment market of backpacks and tents, which was being covered by niche magazines like *Backpacker* and *Canoeing*. Perhaps they could roll up the market in one super magazine. With Hardy's backing, Armstrong field-tested the idea with an adventure supplement in *Rolling Stone*. Wenner assigned Michael Rogers to produce a special insert called "The Backpacker," which contained the seeds of their new venture. "Along with the hardware boom has come a whole new set of individuals anxious to try out their duds in the real woods, and the new technology has made it easier than ever before," he wrote.

This would become the basis for *Outside*. The project—a high-gloss magazine with a spare-no-expense rollout—would cost more than $1 million to launch. The original title was to be *Outdoors,* but the name was taken. Wenner said the title *Outside* came as an epiphany while driving around San Simeon in a Jeep with Will Hearst III ("Outside!"). Hearst initially resisted taking the role of editor and asked for a lower title, but Wenner replied, "You're the editor or there's no job offer." For the hands-on editing, Wenner recruited Terry McDonell, a refugee from Max Palevsky's magazine *L.A.* Meanwhile, Wenner made *Rolling Stone* cover boy Jack Ford assistant to the publisher—a celebrity dream that would attract instant press attention.

Inside the newspaper, there were growing questions about Joe Armstrong's relationship with Wenner, not least because of his outsized influence over editorial. Armstrong said he was only selling Wenner's "impact journalism," the core of *Rolling Stone*'s reputation. But to many top staffers, he seemed infatuated with Jann Wenner, eager to be his partner, perhaps something more. ("He was always extremely mysterious about his sexuality," said art director Roger Black, who, like Wenner, was in the closet at the time.) Others considered him a self-promoter who only wanted to see his name in print. Claeys Bahrenburg, the Detroit ad salesman, complained to Wenner that Armstrong spent more time dining out on *Rolling Stone* than creating ad revenue for it. But for a while, Wenner was equally infatuated with Armstrong, smitten with his good looks as well as the cash flow he produced, making him part of his inner circle and closely monitoring his social travels. After Armstrong went out to dinner with Carmella Scaggs one night, Wenner buttonholed him, asking angrily, "Did you fuck her?"

As the editor and the publisher grew closer, Armstrong began whispering the siren call of New York to Wenner. "Oh, I wish the whole company would move here," he told Wenner. "If we could all just be in one place." Wenner didn't have to be convinced. In late 1975, he purchased the Gimbel apartment at 137 East Sixty-Sixth Street, a duplex with a spiral staircase and floor-to-ceiling bookcases, for the bargain-basement price of $75,000. (When the Wenners were interviewed by the stuffy co-op board, Wenner told them, "I have the second most influential magazine in the country.") In the spring of 1976, Wenner wrote Armstrong a long memo on the "Big Picture" they were crafting together. The grand plan was to hit a paid circulation of 500,000—"then go higher!"—change the format of *Rolling Stone* to a stapled magazine ("make us a true magazine worth keeping lying around the house"), raise the newsstand price, expand circulation into new markets, penetrate hi-fi stores and retail chains like the Gap, create a prime-time network special on TV and advertise a 1-800 subscription offer, purchase an FM radio station, and execute a bold plan that Armstrong had recommended: buy back all the Straight Arrow stock from minority shareholders, consolidate power, and create a stock sharing program for top executives like Joe Armstrong. On top of this, Wenner recommended they shut down the Washington office, which was costing him $75,000 a year, and use the extra cash to hire big-name writers. "Begin to question our operations from the assumption that we should be *handsomely profitable* right now," wrote Wenner.

•

WENNER WAS ASLEEP on California Street when the phone rang and a man with a southern accent asked to speak to a "Mister Wayner."

"It's two o'clock in the morning," grumbled Wenner. "Who is this?"

It was a sheriff in the Louisiana bayou, and he had two of Wenner's employees in a jail cell. Their names, he reported, were Daniel Aykroyd and John Belushi. Wenner had assigned the rising stars of NBC's *Saturday Night Live* to write a travelogue of their misadventures driving a Ford Caprice Classic through the southern states with a *Rolling Stone* credit card and a custom-built $3,000 Nakamichi stereo installed in the back. But now, according to Sheriff Perez, the comedians had struck and possibly killed a man on the highway. "Oh no," said Wenner. "Is the man all right?"

> SHERIFF: Well, sir, he is in the hospital now. We don't know yet what will happen, but the man is in critical condition. These gentlemen were driving eighty miles an hour.
> WENNER: Oh, fuck! Where are they?
> SHERIFF: Mr. *Wayner,* I must also inform you that upon searching their vehicle we found what we suspect to be Class A

narcotics . . . Mr. *Wayner,* would you like to speak to either of these two men?

WENNER: Yes, I would. Let me find a pencil. Could you just tell me again what your jurisdiction is, and your phone number there?

The voice of Dan Aykroyd came on the line.

AYKROYD: Ahhh, Jann? Listen, man, we were on a two-lane road. This black guy ran out and hit the front of the car. It was real dark out and I couldn't see him. He bounced off the hood and went right over the car. He's in pretty bad shape. I'm really sorry, man.

WENNER: Fuck, Danny, this is going to be bad.

AYKROYD: Listen, Jann, they searched the car, and they found some stuff. See, John ran into some people at Carter headquarters in Atlanta, and . . .

WENNER: I understand. Don't talk about it on the phone, okay?

The entire conversation was a prank, with Belushi playing "Sheriff Perez" and a pal of Ackroyd's impersonating Ackroyd, who was asleep nearby. Wenner was horrified, and then delighted. A week later, Belushi and Aykroyd showed up on Third Street in San Francisco to write up the story Wenner assigned, a road-trip story called "New South Burn," which included the prank call. The piece was an homage to Hunter Thompson, whom the duo visited in Woody Creek before launching their trip. "It was totally inspired by Hunter," said Aykroyd. "We were gonzo apprentices."

Paul Scanlon read the resulting story and told Wenner it was "a towering monument to banality." "It could be that these guys are actors, not comedians, since their ability to transmute humor from the spoken to the written word seems nonexistent," he wrote.

But Wenner ran it anyway, giving it the subtitle "Two Famous Television Personalities, Both Personal Friends of the Editor, Risk Their Jobs, Their Reputations, Their Lives, and Your Patience."

If Jann Wenner had a North Star in New York, it was the "personal friends of the editor" at *Saturday Night Live,* especially the young Canadian TV producer who invented it, Lorne Michaels. Though Wenner missed the first episode of *Saturday Night Live* in 1975—unaware that it was produced by the man he met with Earl McGrath two years earlier—he was hooked by the fourth episode, when he saw the "Insecurities" skit featuring Gilda Radner and Candice Bergen having an informal and altogether realistic rap session about feminism. "When I'm with you, I feel unfeminine," Radner told Bergen, playing Bergen's willowy looks for uncomfortable laughs. "It didn't even feel like comedy for me," said Wenner. "It was so poignant you believed it." (In the same episode, comic Andy Kaufman did his "foreign man" act.)

Every Saturday night, Michaels's show declared itself with the blast of live rock and roll, the signature saxophone wail of Howard Shore. Here was ambition, talent, brains, and bracing social commentary beaming into Wenner's big-screen Advent on California Street like a dreamcast from his own DNA. In 1968, Michaels had changed his name from Lipowitz and moved to L.A. to become a comedy writer for *Laugh-In,* going on to a successful run as Lily Tomlin's head writer before selling his high-wire sketch comedy to NBC and planting his flag in the heart of New York at a time when the subways and streets of the city were only slightly less postapocalyptic than those depicted in the 1979 film *The Warriors.* "When we arrived, we were wearing Hawaiian shirts," Michaels said. "I didn't own a sweater. I had to go across the road to Saks to buy one, and I had to buy a jacket to come to work in, because you didn't need that in California. And so there was a sense of 'Oh, this is a more grown-up world.'"

The cast of *SNL* had the same cultural bloodlines as *Rolling Stone.* Belushi took a street beating during the Democratic convention in Chicago in 1968, and Aykroyd had sheltered American draft dodgers at college in Ottawa. The Blues Brothers, Belushi and Aykroyd's semiserious Chicago band, once opened for the Grateful Dead. In a coup, Michaels managed to reunite Simon and Garfunkel for the second episode of *SNL* in 1975, prompting coverage in *Rolling Stone.* Afterward, Wenner invited Michaels and *SNL* cast member Chevy Chase, whose depiction of Gerald Ford as a bumbling klutz was making him famous, to lunch at the hot eatery of the moment, Sign of the Dove, on the Upper East Side. "We all just hit it off great, and we were all the same age and all rebellious and breaking through the establishment," said Wenner, who assigned a writer named Tom Burke, who had previously profiled Wenner's Chadwick classmate Liza Minnelli, to write a story on the show. "The Post-prime-time Follies of NBC's Saturday Night," featuring photographs by the show's official photographer Edie Baskin, appeared in July 1976, on the cusp of Wenner's pivot to New York. "I remember there was talk of my being on the cover," recalled Michaels, but Wenner told him "his editors" had decided against it, "which means Jann decided that wasn't what he wanted."

"Listen," Chevy Chase told Tom Burke, "when you write about all this, don't be too hard on Lorne. He is, underneath, truly a teddy bear you wanta hug . . . Oh, Christ, what the fuck am I doing here, being interviewed? Listen, everything I said to you just now is a lie."

Wenner was transparently envious of Michaels. He'd been trying since the late 1960s to establish a beachhead on network television—starting with an ill-fated CBS venture with Porter Bibb in 1969—but he never found the right partners or idea. He was already making plans for a *Rolling Stone* TV special, modeled on what Wenner and his staffers were seeing on *Saturday Night Live,* and attempting to conscript John Belushi for a skit. "Lorne is a role model that is important to Jann," said Art Garfunkel. "Lorne is always up there with money and achievement."

Michaels remembered that it was Jane Wenner, the original Manhattan girl, who first charmed everybody at Elaine's, including his new friend Paul Simon and the rest of "the people that were infatuated with her," like John Belushi and John Head, an *SNL* talent scout with whom Jane had an affair in the late 1970s. It was Jane Wenner, Michaels said, who set the bar for the Californians in their social group, turning the Wenners' East Side duplex into a sophisticated stage set, complete with an indoor park bench and a potted magnolia tree. "Jane had elegance and style, the mirrors against the wall," he said. "The sparseness of that apartment and the style of it, which were elegant."

And Jann Wenner said it was Jane who ultimately catalyzed *Rolling Stone*'s move to New York. Her paranoia and anxiety had spiked to uncomfortable levels in the wake of the Patty Hearst episode. "San Francisco got very tricky at one point, because you had the Zodiac, the Zebra, and the SLA," she said. "It was too small. There were too many people that were just too closely removed from the SLA and the Mansons . . . there was something creepy happening at that point."

Jane felt isolated, and she bided her time with a photo editor named Joe Cleary, a comic hanger-on with big hair and a bigger mustache who occupied Jane while Wenner worked. To help sell *Rolling Stone* posters and T-shirts, Cleary designed an ad featuring a photograph of himself and Jane Wenner snuggling in the four-poster bed on California Street.

But Jane also felt that her husband, a man bestriding the boulevards of Washington and New York, was never properly feted in San Francisco. "I felt that they didn't treat Jann well there," she said. "Annie and I used to flip out because they had a stock picture at the *Chronicle* that wasn't Jann, and even though Jann was very important in San Francisco, they always printed it. It was Vincent [Fremont], who worked for Andy Warhol."

Meanwhile, Francis Ford Coppola was the new belle of San Francisco. The year before, Coppola, whose film company Zoetrope was fifteen minutes away from *Rolling Stone,* had bought a magazine called *City,* hiring Warren Hinckle as editor and Mike Salisbury as art director. Next, Annie Leibovitz began to hang out with the *City* staff, as did Hunter Thompson. Reviewing a prototype of *City,* Wenner wrote a letter to "Citizen Coppola" to give him a stern critique, chastising him for spending too much on writers and not enough on a decent editor:

> I am upset . . . by the incredible waste of money in a space where something worthy and long-lived could occur. "My Vietnam" is the perfect metaphor. Given such an insight, why are you still looking for the light at the end of the tunnel? Apocalypse now . . . or later?
>
> A million bucks and doomed to failure! Amazing. Yet, you could be supporting and bringing together the Bay Area's best local media talent as well as backing a magazine that would succeed.
>
> This is what pains me: Why blow it? If you really are going to get it on—with that million dollars and what not—then do it right and make it work.

He signed the letter "Citizen Wenner."

Wenner wasn't wrong: *City* went out of business after a year, and

Coppola left to direct *Apocalypse Now,* which he later screened for the Wenners.

Wenner once told *Town & Country* magazine that he would never take *Rolling Stone* out of San Francisco. Wasn't the Bay Area the very essence of *Rolling Stone,* its integrity, its history, its point of view? But Ralph Gleason was dead, and the success of the Patty Hearst story had rocketed Wenner to a bigger stage, where he could hear the blare of Howard Shore's sax. When *Rolling Stone* published a complete history of the Haight-Ashbury in 1975, by Charlie Perry, it was both an homage and a tombstone. The Hearsts were the last bit of glamour left in town, and Wenner had already done the backstroke in their pool, his visit captured for posterity by Garry Trudeau, who caricatured the scene in *Doonesbury.* Indeed, San Francisco was the Old World; New York was the New. Despite the recessionary gloom and high crime rate, New York slushed with ad dollars and teemed with Mailers and Wolfes and Ephrons who vied for choice checkered tables at Elaine's, the hub of intellectual and literary life operated by the rotund matron Elaine Kaufman. Wenner was halfway there, so why not go all the way?

But the move to New York was going to be a massive—and expensive—undertaking. Armstrong and Wenner hired a political advance man, Tony Podesta, former adviser to Gene McCarthy and brother of John Podesta, to coordinate the move, including finding apartments for the handful of staffers Wenner would move to the city. Wenner heralded his own arrival by signing a $330,000-a-year lease for four floors of the towering Art Deco building at 745 Fifth Avenue, with a sweeping view of the Plaza hotel and Central Park, right above F. A. O. Schwarz. Wenner likened it to the *Daily Planet,* a place fit for Superman and the proper monument to his ambition. When the move was announced at 625 Third Street, the San Francisco staff was mortified. "Everybody was crying; everybody was miserably unhappy," said Bryn Bridenthal, the publicist, who left to work for David Geffen.

Wenner began planning who would stay and who would not. David Felton was going east; Ben Fong-Torres was staying; Leibovitz was coming; David Weir was not. Howard Kohn said Weir was fired to pay "for Jann's limo." Meanwhile, Wenner moved Kohn and his wife to New

York and paid the rent on their apartment, a block from Richard Nixon's home.

The move seemed to have Joe Armstrong's fingerprints all over it. Staff memos were signed "Jann and Joe." When Wenner gathered his top lieutenants for a strategy meeting at Hilton Head, South Carolina, Roger Black brought a box of T-shirts featuring a picture of Wenner and Armstrong on the front. A story in *More* magazine, about the New York move, said that "no longer is *Rolling Stone* just Jann Wenner, it's Jann Wenner *and* Joe Armstrong."

But beneath the image of togetherness, things were already coming apart. In the spring of 1977, *Rolling Stone* was up for a National Magazine Award for "The Family 1976" by Dick Avedon. Armstrong was scheduled to appear at a table with Wenner to receive the award. Wenner said Armstrong had wanted "credit" for the Avedon issue. "He represented himself to the New York community that he was the editor of the magazine," claimed Wenner. Not long before, Wenner had asked Armstrong how he was going to feel when he was No. 2 in the company, no longer the Mr. *Rolling Stone* of New York City. The question had an ominous tone. Armstrong's moods had always waxed and waned with Wenner's affirmation but waned rapidly as Wenner appeared to sour on him.

Wenner made clear there was only room for one Mr. *Rolling Stone* and his name was Jann S. Wenner. Kent Brownridge, whom Wenner hired as a circulation manager in 1974, worked in the same Manhattan office with Armstrong and felt that Armstrong was "in love" with Wenner. "He thought he and Jann were going to be this married couple that owned and ran *Rolling Stone*," said Brownridge. "That wasn't Jann's plan at all."

That spring, Armstrong didn't show up at the magazine awards. "He called me and said, 'Where were you?'" recalled Armstrong, who adamantly denied ever wanting to fiddle with editorial or collect the award. "And I felt like we might win, I didn't care. I don't remember what I told him. But sometime right after that I said, 'I'm leaving.' He said, 'You can't leave without talking to me.'" (The Avedon issue won for visual excellence.)

The Wenner-Armstrong split had all the hallmarks of a lovers' breakup, with Armstrong the jilted one. Paul Scanlon would recall walking by the Isle of Capri restaurant on Third Avenue in Manhattan with Wenner's secretary and spying the two men in a heated, emotional argument. Each man would offer a different reason for the break: Wenner said Armstrong had oversold his business acumen and left the company's finances disorganized; Armstrong said he became disillusioned by Wenner's erratic behavior on cocaine, which revealed a decadent and unreliable character. But the bottom line was that Wenner wanted to walk through the doors Armstrong had opened for him—alone. "There was only room for one me and that was me," said Wenner. "I'm the one with the talent." (Afterward, he took the title of publisher on the *Rolling Stone* masthead and never relinquished it again.)

Armstrong never forgave Wenner. When Wenner began circulating rumors that Armstrong had left the business in disarray, Armstrong called him in a fury. "If you don't stop saying things about me that are not true," he said, "I'm going to start telling the truth about you."

Jann Wenner stopped talking about Joe Armstrong.

"I don't think he had the ability to be loyal to anybody," said Armstrong, who went on to work for *New York* magazine. "I don't know about who he loved, but obviously he didn't love his wife. And it's not the fact that I think he's in love with himself; I think he's deep down a very troubled person."

15

Big Shot

In the summer of 1977, Lorne Michaels and his star writer Michael O'Donoghue threw the first of what they called the "White Parties" at a rented mansion in East Hampton, the beach enclave on the far tip of Long Island. Along with Shelley Duvall and Paul Simon came Jann Wenner, newly minted resident of New York City, in pristine white clothes for the imagined parody of *The Great Gatsby*. While they all sipped Soiled Kimonos (two parts champagne, one part Japanese plum wine), a society reporter observed the editor of *Rolling Stone* as he "strolled about the spongy lawn in the fading afternoon sunlight."

This is how Jann Wenner wanted everything now: white, minimalist, clean, and wealthy. After Dick Avedon, white represented pure power for Wenner. In advance of his arrival, he commanded that every *Rolling Stone* cover subject be shot against a white background: the Bee Gees in white outfits, against a white background; Robert De Niro, smiling against white; the cast of *Stars Wars*—against white. Wenner loved it; others didn't: Annie Leibovitz resented being ordered to Avedon-ize her own work. "I thought it was a really stupid idea," said Leibovitz. "He had moved to New York, and he was coming to grips with 'How do you sell this thing?' It's stuff that I certainly didn't want to have to deal with. We had been running rampant for years [in San Francisco], and then somebody telling you, 'Now put these against white!'"

For *Rolling Stone*'s new office at 745 Fifth Avenue, Wenner asked designer Paul Segal to produce something clean and stark—and white, a virtual canvas against which Wenner could reframe *Rolling Stone*. "There is a lot of white here," wrote Paul Goldberger, the architecture critic, in *The New York Times*, "but one never senses an insistence on the sort of austere esthetic that is ruined by a cigarette butt or a vase of flowers. *Rolling Stone*'s editors brought a number of old oak tables from their San Francisco offices to use as desks, and they blend comfortably with Mr. Segal's white walls, glass-block partitions and gray carpets."

Rolling Stone's move to New York was viewed as a stroke of optimism after the city nearly went bankrupt in 1975 and sparked a business exodus from the crime-riddled metropolis. Its arrival made the evening news. "New York had been declared dead," said Wenner. "We came just at the moment of New York's rebirth, just as it started to 'explode. Because San Francisco had been the center for a decade. The '60s came from there. Not New York. But the '70s came to New York."

In the aborted story on Diane von Furstenberg from 1973, Dotson Rader had asked, "What does it mean to arrive in New York?" and quoted a high social mandarin as saying, "It means being seen at the right parties, having your name appear in the right columns, and being associated with the right people." In 1977, *Rolling Stone* paid homage to the right people and the right parties: an interview with Elaine Kaufman; a profile of fashion designer Diana Vreeland; a story on Princess Caroline of Monaco; a profile of *Taxi Driver* director Martin Scorsese. Furstenberg herself had an office in the same building as *Rolling Stone* and came by, jangling with jewelry, to peruse the *Rolling Stone* covers hanging on Wenner's white walls, remarking, "How many covers do you think I've slept with?"

Before Wenner showed up in New York, Lorne Michaels and Paul Simon had begun renting beach cottages in the Hamptons. The Wenners found an eighteenth-century shack on Further Lane, next to designer Ralph Lauren, whom Wenner impressed with a silver Ferrari he purchased from Jimmy Webb. "You'd pick up the newspapers on Sunday, go read the *Times*, and you'd see a picture of Ralph on the beach," said Wenner, "and you'd go to the beach and there'd be Ralph on the beach." The Wenners invited everyone to see their place, as Andy

Warhol would record in his diary in June 1977: "Jann Wenner had John Belushi at his place. Jann gave us a tour of the house. If he'd rented Montauk, he could have had something great, but I guess he and his wife Jane just wanted something 'adorable.'"

When Wenner asked superstar reporter Carl Bernstein to write about Cold War journalists who had secretly worked for the CIA, Bernstein demanded the same astronomical sum Wenner paid for his Hamptons rental, $28,000. Wenner paid. And why not? The sheer audacity—and the boldfaced name—created publicity, even if "The CIA and the Media" was a dud (and no revelation to Wenner, who appointed a former CIA agent, Putney Westerfield, a retired publisher of *Fortune,* to his board of directors in 1977).

Once Lorne Michaels and Jann Wenner began orbiting each other, the *SNL* influence on *Rolling Stone* took hold. "It became besotted with *SNL,*" said Greil Marcus. "It was like *SNL* was the new editor." In the late 1970s, viewers following *Saturday Night Live*'s guests, whether Steve Martin or Phoebe Snow, could soon find them in the pages of *Rolling Stone,* usually on the cover. Brian Wilson, Boz Scaggs, James Taylor, Santana, Ry Cooder, Joe Cocker—first through the *SNL* turnstile, then through the *Rolling Stone* turnstile, or vice versa.

Michaels and Wenner were the gatekeepers through which superstars of the moment passed, or rather, the two oversaw a new kind of moment, defined by young California émigrés heralding a New York zeitgeist. The Wenners were now regular invitees to Studio 3H at Rockefeller Center, showing up to watch classic skits like John Belushi's samurai impersonation and then joining the cast at after parties that lasted until dawn. When Wenner traveled to North Carolina with his advertising sales team to court tobacco companies, he invited Gilda Radner to help charm the executives. (On the flight south, she pretended to be the stewardess.) David Felton, the resident comedy expert at *Rolling Stone,* tried out-*SNL*-ing *SNL* with his cover story of Steve Martin in 1977, in which Martin wrote in parts of his own profile and Felton ran sentences up the side of the page.

In addition to the *SNL* influence, Wenner announced that he was "Elaine-izing" *Rolling Stone,* and Elaine Kaufman—who told *Rolling Stone* she once broke up a brawl between Norman Mailer and songwriter Jerry Leiber—announced a runoff between Wenner and Clay Felker, who lost control of *New York* magazine to Rupert Murdoch. "Felker would like to have Wenner's money, Wenner would like to have Felker's prestige," John Walsh told *More* magazine. (Their rivalry was later parodied to fantastic effect in *Murder at Elaine's,* the 1978 novel by Ron Rosenbaum in which a character named Jann Wenner takes a famed editor's prized table at the restaurant.) Wenner responded by hiring Clay Felker's girlfriend, Gail Sheehy, author of the 1976 best seller *Passages: Predictable Crises of Adult Life,* to write the inside story on Felker's battle with Murdoch, effectively winning the race. If critics questioned the objectivity of a story by Felker's girlfriend, and regular *Rolling Stone* readers were scratching their heads (Clay who?), Jann Wenner didn't care. What mattered was Wenner's publicist sending him a memo about the media buzz at a weekend party in the Hamptons featuring Eleanor Kennedy, Kurt Vonnegut, Truman Capote, and Dorothy Schiff, the owner and publisher of the *New York Post.*

They loved him, they really loved him. Or did they? New York would prove a giant X-ray machine on Jann Wenner. Garry Trudeau depicted "Yawn," as he now called him in *Doonesbury,* escorting Caroline Kennedy into Elaine's ("on a diamond-encrusted cart," snarled Hunter Thompson). In another strip, "Uncle Duke" asks him, "Well, what's your idea of a story these days? Drivel from John Dean? Photo essays of Princess Caroline? And how much did you pay John Belushi to pretend he's me?"

Wenner's chin now seemed well poised for an upper cut. In advance of the move to New York, Wenner was sliced to ribbons in a massive profile in *New Times,* an ostensible competitor to *Rolling Stone* operated by George Hirsch, who cofounded the New York City Marathon. The story, by thirty-one-year-old Robert Sam Anson, painted Wenner as erratic and cruel, a man snickering about the "blackness of my mystique" and dismissing former staffers as bitter has-beens. Wenner gave Anson a lengthy interview, only to freak out as he realized that ex-employees and partners, including Max Palevsky and Hunter Thompson, were raising knives for him. After it was published, Wenner drew up a laundry list of outraged corrections—he estimated 230 inaccuracies, including the quotation about his mystique—to serve as the basis for a lawsuit, citing the Supreme Court case of *Time, Inc. v. Firestone.*

In Wenner's estimation, Anson had depicted him as a caricature who "spends most of his time getting autographs, embezzling, in a drug frenzy, riding around in limousines and crying."

He was particularly aggrieved over the story of his reaction to the news of Janis Joplin's death in 1970. "Cancel her subscription," he reportedly told his secretary, who broke down crying. "Anson is twisting every possible shred of fact to paint me as an ugly, unsympathetic cold bastard," he wrote. "What will our readers think of RS when they read that my reaction to Joplin's death was 'cancel her subscription.' Many might cancel their subscriptions. This is an attempt to destroy the good will and credibility of the magazine with its readership."

In a BBC documentary about *Rolling Stone* in 1977, narrated by Harry Evans, editor of *The Sunday Times* of London, Anson went on camera to sum up his critique: Jann Wenner was now an establishment figure disconnected from his readers. "The genius of *Rolling Stone* has always been that it's Jann, that it's his magazine, that's *his person* in there," he said. "And now he's trying to guess on the basis of marketing surveys and what seems right to him and he no longer has this kind of feel, this instinctual feel, for where the culture is heading."

Wenner didn't disagree, except he knew exactly where it was headed: wherever Jann Wenner was going. "I think *Rolling Stone is* establishment," Wenner retorted. "I think that rock culture, youth culture, has become establishment in this country, and is the leading cultural establishment in this country right now . . . rock culture, and what we cover, has entered the mainstream, the mainstream has moved toward it, just as it's moved toward the mainstream."

In other words, Wenner never sold out; it was a swap.

Wenner never filed a lawsuit, and the Anson story stuck like a harpoon in his hide. Back in San Francisco, a bit of bathroom graffito— "Robert Sam Anson was here"—was scrawled on the wall as a reminder. Worse yet, Anson was staying in a house in the Hamptons next to Wenner in the summer of 1977. Though nearly everyone cooperated for the original story, many *Rolling Stone* staffers were upset with the result—even *they* thought it was a hatchet job—but in New York these same staffers were no less merciful, with one telling the local gossips, anonymously, that Wenner was a short Jew trying hopelessly to be accepted by Wasps. Wenner's insecurities seemed all too exposed. When *New York* magazine took a group portrait of Wenner and his staff for a story on the arrival of *Rolling Stone* in the city, Wenner kneed the back of Harriet Fier's leg—"Too tall," he hissed—in an effort to make her shorter. "I remember feeling sad for him," she said.

But he'd show them.

During the sweltering "Summer of Sam," when the city was rattled by serial killer David Berkowitz and paralyzed by a blackout, Wenner rented a gigantic mansion with an extraordinary lawn for a staff retreat in East Hampton, Long Island. To foster the New York spirit among his anxious refugees from San Francisco, Wenner gathered them on the floor as in a group therapy session while he tried leading a series of presentations from his different departments—until John Belushi came bounding in and declared, "Oh bullshit!" and performed an impromptu version of his samurai skit from *SNL*. When Wenner introduced his business team, who wore pastel-colored Izod shirts, and opened the floor for a debate on taking ads by the U.S. Army, the editorial staff groaned and were led screaming to the swimming pool by the art director for *Outside,* a large lesbian who had stripped naked. A blizzard of coke snorting ensued, Belushi slept with a *Rolling Stone* photo editor, and limos were sent back to Manhattan to raid the petty cash drawer and scrounge up more. (*Rolling Stone* later ran ads from the U.S. Army.)

That same afternoon, Wenner asked his New York business team to come to the house for individual meetings. They stood in line outside his bedroom door like "schoolchildren at an academy waiting to go see the principal," recalled Claeys Bahrenburg, the advertising director. Whispers of Wenner's ambiguous sexuality were already circulating, and paranoia set in that Wenner was trying to see which of his staffers would sleep with him. As one person emerged after an hour alone with him, recalled Bahrenburg, the other would ask, "Holy shit, did he try to do anything to you?"

"He was not even close to being out of the closet, but he was circling," said Bahrenburg. "He was exploring this stuff more publicly than he had been in the past. He was enjoying the power of it. He was omnipotent and had his employees brought in one by one, like slaves, sizing them up, seeing how stout they were."

That night, Wenner hosted a candlelit dinner party for his management team, including Will Hearst and Jack Ford. He arrived dressed in a khaki-colored military shirt, hefting a large wooden mallet—a gift from Belushi—and he pounded the table and declared, "I am Benito Mussolini!" "It was theater and he was loving it," said Bahrenburg, "absolutely loving it."

The first issue in New York was to be *about* New York, the cover of *Rolling Stone* featuring a suite of Andy Warhol screen prints of Bella Abzug, the colorful liberal who campaigned against Ed Koch to be the Democratic nominee for mayor of New York in 1977. A Socialist-Zionist, "Battling Bella" was a congresswoman from the Upper West Side who introduced a federal gay rights bill along with rival Koch in 1974. (To torture Wenner, Hunter Thompson used to pull a hat down over his ears and claim Wenner looked like Abzug, who always wore one.) It also featured a story called "The Plausible Gay," a profile of a colorful gay lawyer named Lenny Bloom (written by Vito Russo, author of *The Celluloid Closet*, the seminal book on gay Hollywood). The issue crackled with fresh (and sometimes pretentious) material, including a portfolio of paintings by the likes of Milton Glaser and John Cage ("49 Waltzes for the Five Boroughs"). Taken together, it was a pure expression of Wenner's social journey, but far afield from *Rolling Stone*'s rock-and-roll roots in San Francisco. Three days before it went to press, however, on August 16, 1977, Elvis Presley was found crumpled on the floor of his bathroom at Graceland, in Memphis, his bloated body full of liquid Demerol. When music editor Peter Herbst came into his office, Wenner was curled up in his swivel chair, crying. "It's a cover," he said. When Herbst started to reply, Wenner cut him off: "No, you don't know what I'm talking about—it's a *cover!*"

Death always had a dramatic and transformative effect on Wenner, dating back to the Kennedy assassination. "Jann loves death," Laurel Gonsalves once remarked. Wenner had seen Elvis in Las Vegas in 1969, and *Rolling Stone,* for all its critical fangs, had always been good to the King, treating him as above reproach. Even Jon Landau proclaimed Presley a great American artist in 1971. *Rolling Stone* instantly returned to the subject of rock and roll—indeed, the *essence* of rock and roll—at the very moment it was threatening to pivot away from it. The staff

assembled the entire issue in a frenetic five days, publishing newly discovered photographs of Elvis Presley from the 1950s. And seeing an
unusual opportunity, Wenner enlisted a rookie reporter to cover the
Presley funeral at Graceland. Her copy would require heavy editing,
but her byline was sterling: Caroline Kennedy. Aided by journalist
Pete Hamill, she gained access to Graceland before the funeral service,
allowing *Rolling Stone* a private and up-close look at the corpse. His
face was "swollen," Kennedy reported, "and his sideburns reached his
chin."

> "Would you like a Coke or a Seven-Up?" Priscilla offered as she
> walked into the living room, which was paneled in mahogany and
> decorated with fur-covered African shields and spears.

Wenner had been socializing with Jackie Onassis and her daughter since the mid-1970s, when he spent the greater part of an evening
trying to coax the teenage Caroline to the dance floor at a *Rolling
Stone* Christmas party. As soon as Wenner arrived in New York, he
was photographed squiring Kennedy, nineteen, to the star-studded
movie premiere of the Sydney Pollack film *Bobby Deerfield*. Wenner's
cat-that-got-away-with-the-cream smile was splashed across the New
York dailies, and Wenner had his PR man send him regular reports
on the coverage. Back in San Francisco, the *Chronicle* tried snubbing
Wenner by labeling him an "unidentified man" in the photo. Herb Caen
cackled with schadenfreude, writing up an item on it titled "Dead on
Arrival."

Wenner tried to get Jackie Onassis into *Rolling Stone* as well, asking her to interview Lillian Hellman, the storied and controversial
playwright. (She declined, but Wenner got Hellman to profile First
Lady Rosalynn Carter.) Wenner proudly toured Jackie through his new
offices at Fifth Avenue, propping his feet on the desk while she admired
his view of Central Park. *New York* magazine published an image of
Wenner, hair stylishly long and cigarette smoking in his fingers, while
he leaned in close to Jackie at a restaurant ("The Big Apple's current fun
couple"). At the time, Onassis was an editor at Doubleday, and Wenner
pitched her a *Rolling Stone* book on *Saturday Night Live*. After a night of

snorting cocaine, Wenner had a nosebleed during the meeting, prompting panicked waiters to rush to the table with towels. Wenner returned to the offices with an ice pack on his face, bragging to Harriet Fier, "I just bled all over Jackie—just like Jack!" (Onassis acquired the book.)

In his first few weeks in New York, Wenner looked like a man having more fun than anyone on earth. Over dinner at the Sherry-Netherland, a *Washington Post* reporter observed Wenner at his keyed-up pinnacle, knee bouncing up and down, chewing on a swizzle stick, flinging his long hair back reflexively. "A lot of people are jealous of my success," Wenner said. "I can't help it."

All the while, the writer noted, Wenner's eyes darted repeatedly to the restaurant door, "as if any minute now someone will glide through it, someone very, very important who will alter Wenner's life in some grave and wondrous fashion."

•

JACQUELINE KENNEDY ONASSIS NOTWITHSTANDING, Mick Jagger was still at the center of Wenner's pantheon—as he joked to the *Post* reporter, the true source of all his genius. They'd become some facsimile of actual friends. Jagger came by Wenner's apartment on East Sixty-Sixth Street to snort cocaine and have ragged, impromptu jam sessions with Wenner bashing out chords on his red Gretsch guitar. "It was terrible," said Wenner, "but it was fun. I was too obliterated to deal with it."

In May 1977, Charles M. Young, the magazine's first full-blooded punk devotee, who championed the Sex Pistols and dubbed himself "the Reverend" (in homage to his father, a Wisconsin minister), had taken over the Random Notes column and grown so disgusted by Wenner's continual demands for Jagger items that he assembled an entire column about Jagger, his name appearing in bold twenty-six times (not counting four photo captions), a response to the "rising tide of groupieism which has widely affected the journalistic community."

"Not only am I bored by reading about Mick Jagger," he quoted Daryl Hall of Hall & Oates saying, "I think even Mick Jagger is bored by reading about Mick Jagger."

Jann Wenner was amused by the column but agreed with Patti

Smith, who said, "I still have that element of the dizzy girl in me that likes that sort of junk."

The Wenners now vacationed with Mick and Bianca in Barbados, along with their mutual friend Annie Leibovitz. After dinner one night, Jagger and Leibovitz disappeared to the beach for a frolic and didn't return until after midnight. "He's got sand on his knees," recalled Wenner. "He's clearly been out fucking her. Bianca comes out with a pot of [ice] water—dumps it on his head."

Billy Joel said the song "Big Shot" was based on a dinner-table spat he witnessed between Mick and Bianca in L.A. in the early 1970s. "He was writing a song at the time and he kept singing it at the table," recalled Joel. "'I'm working so hard to keep you in luxury.'" (It was "Luxury" from 1974's *It's Only Rock 'n Roll*.) Random Notes kept close tabs on their volatile marriage, reporting the first rumblings of their breakup and finally the divorce in 1979. Another time on Barbados, the Wenners rented a house next to Stones bassist Bill Wyman, with whom they lunched every day. "He was the first one who told us Mick had the smallest penis in the world," recalled Wenner.

That did not make it into Random Notes.

Jane had never been especially fond of Jagger, regarding him as arrogant and cruel. She called him "the rude thing." And Jagger was not always happy to see the Wenners either, especially when Jann popped backstage unannounced before a concert. "If you make the mistake of intruding that space, he gets pissed off and says, 'Get out of here,'" said Wenner. "That's the only thing you have to do, is respect that space."

When Wenner first began conceiving a *Rolling Stone* TV special in 1976, he envisioned a Rolling Stones film being directed by Martin Scorsese or Stanley Kubrick. Now he wanted the band to perform a live concert on a private island. Wenner had contacted a TV producer named Steve Binder, who had produced two legendary programs for network television, Elvis Presley's 1968 *Comeback Special* and *The T.A.M.I. Show*, in which the Stones were famously blown off the stage by the kinetic James Brown. Binder convinced a CBS executive named Bud Grant to air a two-hour *Rolling Stone* show in prime time, and Wenner gave Binder a list of stars he wanted on the show, chief among them Mick Jagger. Binder met Jagger at his apartment in New York and was led in

Joe Armstrong, 1976.
(Morris Warman/Courtesy of Joe Armstrong)

Hunter S. Thompson, New York, 1977. *(Lynn Goldsmith)*

Jane Wenner (right) with Jean Stein and Woody Allen, May 1977.
(Getty Images)

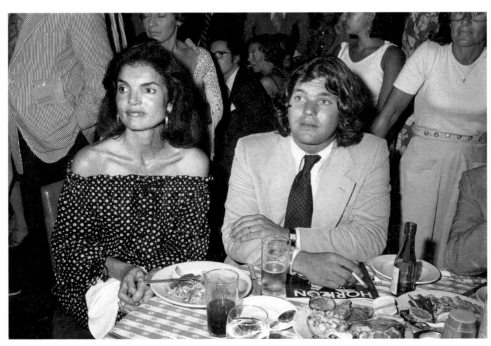

Jacqueline Kennedy Onassis and Jann Wenner attending a benefit to restore Grand Central Terminal held at the Oyster Bar, July 1977.
(Bettmann/Getty Images)

Jann Wenner in 1977. *(Jean Pigozzi)*

Jane and Annie, 1977. *(Jean Pigozzi)*

Wenner with Caroline Kennedy in 1977
after the premiere of the Sydney Pollack film
Bobby Deerfield. *(Ron Galella/Getty)*

Jann and John
Belushi, 1977.
(*Jean Pigozzi*)

Ahmet Ertegun and
Jane Wenner, 1977.
(*Jean Pigozzi*)

Wenner with
socialite Barbara
Allen at Studio 54,
1978. (*Anton Perich*)

Wenner jamming on his Gretsch, 1978.
(*Lynn Goldsmith*)

Jane Wenner and David Geffen, 1979.
(*Jean Pigozzi*)

Wenner at dinner with (to his left) Terry Southern, Jean Stein, and Stephen
Graham. (*Camilla McGrath*)

MED 08675 · JANUARY 22ND, 1981 · $1.50 UK80P

John Lennon and Yoko Ono. Photograph by Annie Leibovitz. *Rolling Stone*,
January 22, 1981. *(Courtesy of* Rolling Stone *magazine)*

Wenner and Lorne Michaels at the Simon and Garfunkel Central Park Concert party at the Savoy in New York, September 1981. *(Ron Galella/Getty)*

Hollywood agent Sue Mengers with Wenner outside the Ma Maison restaurant in Los Angeles, 1981. *(Ron Galella/Getty)*

Richard Gere in East Hampton with Jane Wenner, 1983. *(Jean Pigozzi)*

Wenner with John Travolta and Jamie Lee Curtis, his costars in the 1985 film *Perfect*. *(Fred W. McDarrah/Getty)*

Jann and Mick Jagger on vacation, 1985. *(Camilla McGrath)*

by his five-year-old daughter, Jade. Jagger asked what Binder wanted him to do on the TV show, and Binder said he replied, "Anything you want."

"He looks at me, and he shakes his head no," said Binder. "So I leave without Mick Jagger."

Jagger didn't remember the meeting but said his decision "sounds like a very good answer" because live TV performances were "a bad idea." Wenner said Binder had alienated Jagger by telling him he only wanted the Stones to perform old songs, nothing from their forthcoming record, *Some Girls*. "Mick said to me, 'How come you're not doing it with Lorne?' I didn't have a good answer for that."

But according to Binder, all of Wenner's top choices—Candice Bergen, Lily Tomlin, Mike Nichols and Elaine May, Richard Pryor, Jack Nicholson—either were booked or declined to appear. Even John Belushi, who initially agreed to do a skit, backed out, infuriating Wenner. "The minute I mention Jann Wenner and *Rolling Stone*, I got a no," Binder said. "I sensed that everybody had their issues with Jann, and he may have been their personal friends, and maybe they snorted coke together, but they weren't about to [do him a favor]."

Perhaps it was only Wenner's toxic relationship to Binder, which got off to a bad start when Wenner penciled a 24/7 limousine service into his contract, adding thousands of dollars to the CBS budget. Then, during a meeting in Binder's office in Los Angeles, Wenner idly tapped out a line of coke on Binder's desk and started snorting it. Infuriated, Binder got up and blew the powder into Wenner's lap, and Wenner stormed out of the office. The two didn't speak for the rest of the production.

At the time, Wenner had befriended the show's musical director, Jimmy Webb, a friend of Michael Douglas's. Wenner said their friendship marked the moment he realized that everybody he knew had cocaine and was doing as much as possible. "Jimmy had blow and we were doing it together and all of a sudden everybody had blow," he said, "and I just can't remember who didn't." (Steve Binder: "I think Jimmy had the potential to be the George Gershwin of his era. He was that talented. I think [drugs] destroyed him.")

From the start, CBS and *Rolling Stone* was a culture clash. Wenner assigned Ben Fong-Torres and David Felton, neither of whom had ever written for TV, to craft comedy skits and interstitial monologues to break up the rock-and-roll performances. Their work was immediately eviscerated by veteran network writers whose main job was to prevent *Rolling Stone* from offending viewers during prime time. After reviewing Bette Midler's act, CBS made clear that there would be "no tit holding, no crotch playing, no pulling up her dress at end to expose crotch . . . no 'thanks for coming, thanks for showing up, too' . . . no Jesus Christ references, no 'fucking Helen Reddy' . . . no god damn's."

Binder managed to recruit Steve Martin, on the brink of his break-through stand-up album, *A Wild and Crazy Guy,* and pair Gladys Knight with Art Garfunkel for a duet of "Bridge over Troubled Water," but the sensibility of a Las Vegas revue prevailed. Binder booked Ted Neeley, the star of *Jesus Christ Superstar,* to perform an elaborate Beatles dance medley called "A Decade in the Life," which included performers in foam strawberry suits and black leggings doing a psychedelic maypole dance as Neeley, dressed as Father Time, sang "Strawberry Fields Forever." The sequence also featured two men in rubber Nixon and Kissinger masks singing "I'm a Loser," inspired, no doubt, by a famous *SNL* skit of Aykroyd and Belushi praying in the Oval Office on the eve of impeachment. Binder said the Beatles sequence cost over $100,000 to shoot.

The opening bit featured Steve Martin groveling for the cover of *Rolling Stone* before "Jann Wenner," a stand-in with his back to the camera and a baritone voice dubbed in. After the real Jann Wenner appears, playing a hustling young staffer delivering photographs, the man playing Wenner turns around to reveal himself as . . . Donny Osmond. (In real life, Steve Martin got his *Rolling Stone* cover the following month.)

From there, the show went from the head-scratching to the downright embarrassing, the arguable nadir being Mike Love of the Beach Boys opining about transcendental meditation in an airless studio followed by L.A. police chief Ed Davis admitting he liked Joan Baez. When *Rolling Stone Magazine: The 10th Anniversary* aired in November 1977, the show lost ratings every half hour. The staff cringed in horror when they screened the show. In his review, Tom Shales of *The Washington Post* said it qualified as "a true fiasco fabuloso." Readers wrote in with scathing reviews—"And so it has come to this," said Susan from

Denver—and so did David Felton, whom Wenner allowed to publish a negative review of the show in *Rolling Stone*. He also published Felton's reply to reader complaints, wherein Felton blamed the "powers that be" at *Rolling Stone* (Jann Wenner) and noted that "they" could have pulled the plug on the special but it would have "forced its editor to give up his limousine service for a year." (Wenner, billed as the executive producer, regretted letting Felton slag the show in *Rolling Stone*.)

The TV show was originally meant to sell subscriptions to *Rolling Stone* through a 1-800 number, but it failed to produce any results. And then there was the ten-year-anniversary issue of *Rolling Stone,* a grand homage to the magazine's history that served as a kind of closure of the San Francisco years. "We try to capture the spirit of the times," Wenner orated in his introduction, which he signed, simply, J.S.W., "mindful always of the Rolling Stones lyric, 'Who wants yesterday's papers? Who wants yesterday's girl? Nobody in the world.'"

Well, some still did. The issue featured deeply solipsistic essays by Wenner's old hands—Chet Flippo, David Felton, Jon Landau, and Jonathan Cott—who opined with deep feeling about the lost worlds of the Beatles and the avatars of the 1960s spirit, against which the 1970s were one long disappointment (Landau: "The Thrill Is Gone"). But the issue was also the biggest Wenner had ever published, 176 pages long, lavish and exhausting, bloated with nostalgia and ads for baroque stereo systems, enormous speakers, sports cars, and low-tar cigarettes. "Is *Rolling Stone* still crazy after all these years?" asked the subscription ad.

At Wenner's behest, Roger Black designed a new *Rolling Stone* logo, shearing off Rick Griffin's curled, hippie ligatures for a curt, preppy one to match Wenner's arid new offices. The centerpiece was a fifty-page photo spread by Annie Leibovitz, with guidance from Bea Feitler, a talented art director from Brazil who designed the cover of the Rolling Stones' *Black and Blue* LP. Leibovitz wanted to reunite the Beatles for a portrait and shoot Bob Dylan, but none of them provided access. Instead, the two women spread Leibovitz's past photos across a floor in a rented studio and Feitler had an epiphany: They would publish them at odd angles in the magazine, as if dumped out of a shoe box. And so here they were: the light-meter reading of John Lennon from 1970; Brian Wilson, a Falstaffian figure in a bathrobe, coaxed out of hiding and absurdly holding a surfboard; Linda Ronstadt with her red-pantied derriere in the camera; Duane and Gregg Allman in matching aviator glasses, asleep on a tour bus; a fat Norman Mailer in swim trunks and scuba mask; Keith Moon cavorting in a room full of prostitutes; an ecstatic Bob Marley, celebratory dreads in the air (white background); Dolly Parton vamping in front of an oiled-up Arnold Schwarzenegger. (Afterward, Feitler would become a design director at *Rolling Stone* and Leibovitz's new lover.)

To help sell the issue, Wenner asked Leibovitz to pose for a full-page advertisement for Nikon that would appear on the first inside page. "It was the beginning of Jann trying to understand where the power in *Rolling Stone* lies, instead of just letting it run," Leibovitz said. "I remember being asked to pose for the ad. I turned it down, and they just got a woman to stand in with a camera; I realized they didn't need me. They just needed a woman with a camera." (Ad copy: "To me, photography is a new way of understanding others . . . and myself.")

The issue provided a skeleton key to the unrest behind the scenes. In his look back, David Felton joked about the long-standing tension between Wenner and his writers: "Sure, we're terrible to be with at parties; all we ever talk about is *Rolling Stone*—bitch, bitch, bitch, Jann this, Jann that. 'Bernstein got thirty grand? Jack Ford gets *what* for unloading trucks? Fuck Jann, man, and New York, too. Oh hi, Jann, you finally made it. Hey, great suit.'"

Felton even hinted at the private turmoil in Wenner's bubble. "We're not all stable, and we have trouble with personal relationships," Felton wrote.

Indeed, Wenner's most important and long-standing relationships were falling apart, including with Jane and Hunter Thompson. Through the Carter campaign, Hunter Thompson had rediscovered his southern roots and was blaring Lynyrd Skynyrd and Marshall Tucker. He was all the more disgusted therefore when he discovered that Wenner was, as he put it, "AC/DC." During the Democratic National Convention in 1976, Thompson observed Wenner in a hot tub with his arm around a young man. Thompson was rattled by the revelation. "That's the moment when Hunter started saying, 'What the hell? What is he?'" said Douglas Brinkley, the popular historian to whom Thompson confided the story in the 1990s. "Up until that point, it had never dawned on him."

This explained Thompson's send-up of Wenner in the anniversary issue. In a long, discursive essay on the mysterious disappearance and probable death of his old friend Oscar Acosta at the hands of Mexican drug dealers, Hunter Thompson aimed his gonzo rifle at Wenner, describing a picture in *Newsweek* of Caroline Kennedy "rolling Jann through the door of Elaine's on that custom-built, cut-glass dolly from Neiman-Marcus."

"Well I'll be fucked, that's Jann!" a friend tells Thompson, according to the story. "And look at the wonderful *smile* on him. Wow! And look what he's done to his hair . . . and those *teeth*. No wonder he moved to New York."

In New York, Wenner was exploring his sexuality more openly than in the past, socializing with Steve Rubell, the co-owner of Studio 54, and sexually ambiguous media executives like Geffen and Barry Diller, not to mention grade school classmate and gay icon Liza Minnelli. Harriet Fier claimed that during a stroll through Central Park one day in 1977, Wenner admitted that he preferred men to women. "He said he was crawling around Studio 54 and alluded to these back rooms and everybody had heard of them," she recalled. (Wenner denied he had this conversation with Fier, calling her a "fabulist.")

Jane Wenner believed Wenner was having an affair with Fier and harbored a smoldering animosity toward her (Wenner said he slept with Fier; Fier denied it). Jane was increasingly paranoid, feeling Wenner no longer needed his Manhattan wife now that he had finally planted his feet in New York. "I don't feel that at the time he appreciated me as much as he should have," Jane said. "It's complicated for him, because I was supplying something—whether he stopped to think about it—in his life that he didn't have."

Wenner blamed Annie Leibovitz for fanning Jane's dissatisfaction: "I know she was provoked by Annie saying you're not getting all the credit you deserve, because Annie felt she made such a contribution to her."

In the ten-year-anniversary issue, Wenner made a clear effort to assuage Jane, sprinkling her name around the issue and "belatedly" thanking her in his introduction for "ten incredible years of adventure." (Jane's name had appeared only once in *Rolling Stone* after 1968.) In a remembrance of Gleason, Wenner made clear, for the first time on record, that there were "three people who started *Rolling Stone*." But for a special section on the staff of *Rolling Stone,* alongside snapshots of Charlie Perry and Paul Scanlon was a picture of Jane Wenner by Annie Leibovitz—topless, with her back to the camera and a sexy look in her eyes. While the issue was being printed, Jane flipped through a dummy copy and discovered the caption underneath: "Editor's wife Jane Wenner as sex object."

The caption, coined by Jann Wenner, was a joke on the previous caption—"Chuck M. Young as Sex Pistol," a reference to his cover story on the Sex Pistols—but Jane Wenner was not amused. "She calls me screaming and yelling, 'You called me a sex object!'" Fier recounted. "I said, 'I, I—it's not me, I didn't do that.' I didn't give up Jann. Jane was furious and went raging to Jann to stop the presses. She forced the printers to try scrubbing off the text before the magazine continued printing."

It didn't quite work. The words were faded but legible in every issue: Jane Wenner was the house "sex symbol." "She wanted to be taken seriously," said Fier, "and that's not being taken seriously."

Afterward, there was a brief separation. Wenner moved into a hotel, and Jane sought Max Palevsky's counsel. Advised of the financial ramifications of a divorce, Wenner begged Jane to take him back. Afterward, Jane went to the Wenners' real estate lawyer Ben Needell, who took over the Wenners' personal affairs in 1978, to ask that her ownership be clarified in writing. To Needell's shock, the Wenners didn't have a shareholders' agreement between them, but he was loath to get between them now. Instead, he structured the company to effectively institutionalize Jane's position on the board of directors "so that Jane would never feel that she was going to end up with less power than she had," he said.

Afterward, Jane started showing up at the new offices of *Rolling Stone* and attended her first Straight Arrow board meeting. The word from on high was that Jane was now weighing in on matters of layout and design. *Did you hear that Jane picked out the color of this issue's logo?* But her involvement didn't last long, and she disappeared as quickly as she had appeared. In truth, nothing had really changed: Jann Wenner was still in charge. "It was, frankly, a bit of an illusion," said the Wenners' lawyer, "because [Jann] had 69 percent of the shares and he had all the votes. So it had a dual purpose: It gave Jann what he needed, and kept Jane where she had always been."

16

Stayin' Alive

Jann Wenner was pacing in a red T-shirt that said "Gonzo" across the chest.

Joni Mitchell glared at him from across the field.

Peter Cetera of Chicago, a band that *Rolling Stone* called "rock and roll Doc Severinsens," swung hard, hit a triple, and drove in the first run, putting the Eagles up 1–0.

Don Henley, in a polyester jersey that said "Bullshit" on it, cracked open a bottle of champagne.

The ticket stubs told the story: *Rolling Stone* Magazine vs. The Eagles, the Sunday afternoon of May 7, 1978. It was a supernova of 1970s spectacle, a "grudge match" of slow-pitch softball between the biggest rock-and-roll magazine and the biggest-selling rock-and-roll act, played out before five thousand spectators at Dedeaux Field at the University of Southern California in Los Angeles. A cheerleading team from Hollywood High School, hired by Wenner, danced on the sidelines. Chevy Chase and Daryl Hall rooted from the stands. Jerry Brown, governor of California and erstwhile boyfriend of Linda Ronstadt, showed up to give quotes to the press ("Of course the Eagles are going to win," he said). Jimmy Buffett, slated to be the umpire until he broke his leg in a previous game, followed the action via CB radio. Joe Smith, now head of Elektra-Asylum Records, announced the game over the PA system, asking the audience to rise for the national anthem and then blasting "Life in the Fast Lane" by the Eagles.

As any reader of *Rolling Stone* knew, Don Henley and Glenn Frey of the Eagles hated *Rolling Stone*. The music editor, Peter Herbst, who started in 1977, had described their live act as a bunch of "formless blobs" onstage who "flaunt no athletic grace—if anything, they loiter." Critics Dave Marsh and Paul Nelson considered them featherlight West Coast pap, as did Stephen Holden, who in a grudgingly positive review said they lacked a decent singer and that when they "attempt to communicate wild sexuality, they sound only boyishly enthused." Meanwhile, Chuck Young wrote up a snarky item in Random Notes making fun of the band's losses in intramural softball against a team led by Jimmy Buffett. Glenn Frey, whose competitive streak was legend, wrote in to correct the record and challenge *Rolling Stone* to a game: "Anytime you pencil-pushing desk jockeys want to put on your spikes, we'll kick your ass, too."

In Random Notes, Young replied that "Mr. Frey is apparently unaware that his own manager, Irving Azoff, supplied the information for the story."

Though the band's animosity was real, this was a canny PR stunt concocted by Wenner and Azoff, his newest friend and rival, who wore a mocking T-shirt to the game that asked, "Is Jann Wenner Tragically Hip?" An elfin man with large glasses and a Prince Valiant haircut, Azoff was known as Big Shorty. Standing only five feet three inches, he was arguably the most powerful figure in the record business, managing FM hit makers the Eagles, Jimmy Buffett, Steely Dan, and Boz Scaggs. He grew up in Danville, Illinois, and learned about the music business from his subscription to *Rolling Stone*. "I used to sit and read my *Rolling Stone* about David Geffen and Bill Graham, and to me, they were gods," he told the magazine. Azoff moved to L.A. with one of his first clients, Dan Fogelberg, and went to work for Geffen's company, which managed the Eagles. When Geffen sold his company to Warner Bros., Azoff took over the Eagles, formed Front Line Management, and sued Warner to get the Eagles' song publishing back, claiming Geffen had snookered them out of millions. "We started telling Irving our problems with the band, our producer, how we wanted our records not to be so clean and glassy and how we were getting the royal fuckin' screw job," Frey told Cameron Crowe in 1978. Geffen never forgave Azoff, whose name he spat in bitter disgust for the next forty years. But Wenner admired Azoff's success, and they soon became ski partners in Aspen. Wenner would take up residence at his ski lodge for weeks at a time as they mocked each other's height and status—"How's my favorite upstart?" Wenner wrote to Azoff. "Why are you richer than me?"—and did business in the pages of *Rolling Stone,* with Cameron Crowe the diplomatic go-between. Crowe wrote up friendly cover stories on Azoff's clients, and Azoff became Crowe's mentor, allowing the writer to hang out while he trash-talked and negotiated over a phone, as David Geffen used to do in the early 1970s. (Geffen once let Grover Lewis listen in while Joni Mitchell had an emotional meltdown over the phone; in the next call, Geffen booked her at the Greek Theatre.)

As always, Wenner's critics spoiled the fun by refusing to take the Eagles seriously, despite (or because of) their success. In 1977, Azoff promised Wenner the Eagles would perform at a "Welcome to New York" benefit concert at Grand Central Terminal that Wenner tried organizing with Jackie Onassis, but then Azoff had to rescind the offer: The Eagles didn't want to do Wenner any favors. And so the stands at Dedeaux Field bulged with gawkers eager to watch Wenner and *Rolling Stone* face the Eagles' wrath. The two parties had agreed to make it a charity game, with the loser donating $5,000 to UNICEF and the winner getting a page in *Rolling Stone* to crow about their win. If *Rolling Stone* won, the Eagles would submit to an interview. "We will regard any 'breakup' of the group as a sniveling excuse to get out of the game," Wenner joked to Azoff. Chuck Young called the Eagles "sissies," and the Eagles recruited a Los Angeles Kings hockey player as a bodyguard-cum-ringer. This was all great publicity. "They needed it more than we needed it," said Azoff, forty years later. "What I was trying to do was soften the relationship, which worked."

Jann Wenner wanted to win. He commanded his staff to practice every day in Central Park, marching them to the ball fields after work. When they heard the Eagles would use metal cleats, possibly to try injuring *Rolling Stone* writers with aggressive base slides, Wenner immediately bought $500 worth of metal cleats for his team and then argued that they were barred by United States Softball Association Slo-Pitch rules. There was a brief moment of hope that Hunter Thompson, the "sports editor" who inspired the team's name, might bring much-needed star power to their side, but the night before the game a group of staffers went to see him in a luxury hotel in L.A. and watched him snort a pile of cocaine while telling his life story to the producers of a new film, *Where the Buffalo Roam,* starring Bill Murray as Hunter Thompson. The papers would report that Thompson injured his hand punching an elevator door the night before, but Wenner said he just never showed up.

While the Eagles splashed champagne around their dugout, some of Wenner's knock-kneed staffers braced themselves with snorts of cocaine behind the dugout. Wenner pinned his hopes on shortstop Jim Dunning, his straitlaced new financial officer who had played high school ball and once talked to the Baltimore Orioles about going pro. Wenner had hired Dunning in 1977 to help streamline the books at *Rolling Stone* and streamline them Dunning did—discovering, only a few weeks before the Eagles game, that the magazine was almost broke.

Despite the sunny skies over Los Angeles, Wenner's world was in disharmony. When he hired Dunning, Wenner initially told him he had $2 million in the bank. But between the million-dollar launch of *Outside,* the spare-no-expenses office on Fifth Avenue, a $200,000 loan from Chemical Bank, and Wenner's profligate spending, including a giant party at the Museum of Modern Art featuring former president Gerald Ford, *Rolling Stone* lost $790,000 on $11 million in revenue in 1977. In 1978, it was on course to lose $1.8 million on $14 million in revenue—all of the money Wenner had in the bank. (Meanwhile, Wenner was telling *The Washington Post* the magazine made $38 million in advertising revenue alone in 1978.)

In addition, *Rolling Stone* faced a major lawsuit over a story by Howard Kohn, Wenner's man in center field. "Strange Bedfellows," published in May 1976, constructed a sweeping conspiracy of U.S. foreign policy connecting the CIA, Howard Hughes, the Mafia, the Kennedys, and Richard Nixon, including the alleged Watergate source, Deep Throat, whom Kohn pegged (falsely) as a D.C. public relations man named Robert Bennett. In Kohn's dubious construction, a publicly traded company called Resorts International, which at the time was trying to build its first gambling operation in Atlantic City (later, Donald Trump would become an investor), was a front for what Wenner called "the whole poisoned enchilada." Kohn's story, which originated with the J. Edgar Hoover–is–gay idea, and that Wenner called "one of the most ambitious and intricate pieces we have ever attempted," froze Resorts' bid for a casino license, prompting the company to file a lawsuit against Straight Arrow for $100 million. Wenner hired a libel lawyer named Victor Kovner, who concluded that the charges were an existential threat to *Rolling Stone*. "Had the case gone to trial, it would have been a very substantial judgment," he said. The lawsuit wouldn't be settled for another five years, when Wenner was forced to pay roughly $100,000 and publish a large retraction (in an issue featuring Prince on the cover). But the upshot at the time was that Wenner was headed for a financial ruin exceeding that of 1970. "The game was over," said Dunning. "Two million dollars was disappearing, and the question was, 'How are we going to survive?'"

And then the Eagles clobbered *Rolling Stone* 15–8.

Glenn Frey declared the victory "divine retribution," and Joni Mitchell, rooting for the Eagles from their VIP dugout, exulted in the win. She had recently called up writer Janet Maslin to scream about the negative review of *Don Juan's Reckless Daughter*. "I'm here as an enemy of *Rolling Stone*," Mitchell told an L.A. newspaper. "I have a personal grudge against mister Jann Wenner. He's very irresponsible. He doesn't even read his own rag, so why should anybody else? I'm so happy they lost."

Afterward, the two teams had a private party at Johnny Carson's favorite restaurant, Dan Tana's on Santa Monica Boulevard. At a candlelit booth, Peter Herbst faced off with Mitchell about *Rolling Stone*'s criticism, while Wenner went around the restaurant browbeating his staff to collect quotations for the next issue, some of which appeared in the June 15, 1978, issue of *Rolling Stone* alongside a bylined article by Glenn Frey and Don Henley. On page 25 of Wenner's paper, the Eagles called him "boy publisher" and noted that *Rolling Stone* liked the Eagles until they became successful "because we all know that success is inherently evil and we must be protected from it at all costs."

Cameron Crowe, who played right field, said he felt uneasy about the Eagles softball game for other reasons. Hadn't Jann Wenner told him to preserve his journalistic credibility? Would Joan Didion have played softball against Jim Morrison? "I felt it was blurring the line that had been so sculpted and held as precious and true," said Crowe. "It's the same thing that they were busting me about the Led Zeppelin piece, and other pieces, but they were doing the same freakin' thing."

But perhaps he was learning a larger lesson from observing Wenner and Azoff. After the Eagles game, Crowe wrote a glowing profile of Azoff describing his ruthless tactics on behalf of his clients and calling him "the American dream taken by the balls." The story detailed Azoff's push into Hollywood with the Universal Pictures film *FM,* starring comedian Martin Mull as a radio DJ and featuring concert sequences with Azoff clients like Jimmy Buffett. Within a year, Cameron Crowe would partner with Irving Azoff on a major motion picture of his own.

·

IN 1978, Jim Dunning saved *Rolling Stone* from financial ruin by procuring a $1.2 million loan. Michael Feltus, the vice president of Continental Illinois Bank, considered Jann Wenner "unstable," recalled Dunning, but was convinced that the magazine's readership of 600,000, should *Rolling Stone* go belly-up, was still a kind of asset, even if everything else was lost. The money would keep both *Rolling Stone* and *Outside* operating for a few more months. Wenner breathed a sigh of relief and continued skiing in Aspen.

And then there was a nuclear meltdown.

In March 1979, a nuclear reactor failure at the plant in Three Mile Island in Pennsylvania sent waves of panic across the Eastern Seaboard. At the time, Wenner was safely ensconced in Aspen with Michael Douglas and getting panicked calls from Jane, who was having a nervous breakdown watching the news on TV. With all the reporting Howard Kohn had done on the Karen Silkwood case, there was high anxiety—

and intense political energy—around the dangers of nuclear energy. Earlier that year, Wenner put his entire personal archive—every file, artifact, letter, and postcard he ever received—into a vault that could withstand a nuclear apocalypse.

Wenner told Jane to get on the next flight out of town with Laurel Gonsalves, and he directed Kent Brownridge, his business manager, to write up a memo outlining the emergency plan for the staff. In the event that New York was radiated, they would move the publishing operations to St. Louis, near the printer, and Brownridge would wire $20,000 to Jann Wenner, care of Irving Azoff's house in Aspen, Colorado. But more immediately, there was this: If any of the staff left the offices of 745 Fifth Avenue before the latest issue was finished, they wouldn't get paid. David Felton and Chuck Young were so petrified they got drunk, rented a car, and sped out of town. Harriet Fier, who started editing Wenner's paper in 1978, was furious with him. "We can all die in this nuclear holocaust, but he and his buddies are gonna be safe," she recalled. "I think at that point I soured on the whole notion that it was kind of 'us against them,' or 'we're in it together.'"

Incidentally, the latest cover of *Rolling Stone* was to feature actor Michael Douglas, who was starring in the movie *The China Syndrome*, about a fictional nuclear meltdown. Co-starring Jane Fonda and Jack Lemmon, the movie was released only twelve days before the Three Mile Island incident. Wenner ordered Fier to fax the pages of the story to him in Aspen. "I was putting Douglas on the cover, and Jann was faxing [back] Douglas's changes to the piece," recounted Fier. "I mean, it was a circus."

This was Michael Douglas's first *Rolling Stone* cover: Tie loosened, he held his baby son, Cameron, on his shoulder, like Jackson Browne and Joe Dallesandro before him.

Wenner's enthusiasms were now fully trained on Hollywood. Everybody was going Hollywood: *National Lampoon* magazine made *Animal House*, starring *SNL* star John Belushi; Lou Adler directed the Cheech and Chong pot movie *Up in Smoke*; and music industry powerhouse Robert Stigwood, manager of the Bee Gees, was producing music-powered spectacles like *Saturday Night Fever* and *Grease*. Over lunch at the Sherry-Netherland in 1978, Wenner met with the heads of Paramount—Barry Diller, Michael Eisner, and Jeffrey Katzenberg—and promised to deliver scripts from *Rolling Stone* writers, including Hunter S. Thompson. Wenner had met Diller through Diane von Furstenberg, who started dating the Paramount executive in 1975 following her separation from Prince Egon. Diller green-lighted a $150,000, three-picture deal with Paramount Studios, formally creating Jann S. Wenner Motion Pictures. He initially paired Wenner with Paramount vice president Jeffrey Katzenberg, but Wenner found him too boring to work with. "He's so square and tight and so driven and no real knowledge about movies," he said. "Maybe about the business, but not movies. And hanging out and having fun."

Instead, Wenner started working with Don Simpson, an executive under Michael Eisner who would go on to make blockbuster films with Jerry Bruckheimer in the 1980s, including *Flashdance,* from a script by Joe Eszterhas. For Simpson, a devotee of cocaine, Wenner was a man he could do business with. "I would say the studio, particularly Simpson, who was a wild man, was enormously enamored of Jann," recalled Jeff Berg, the Hollywood agent at ICM who negotiated Wenner's deal with Paramount and whom Wenner made a board member of Straight Arrow. "And I think for Don it became more of a social relationship than it did a professional one. And I think they did a lot of drugs."

Wenner began spending half his time in L.A., operating from a poolside cabana at the Beverly Hills Hotel or the home of Michael Douglas and taking meetings with directors Michael Mann and Oliver Stone to try to develop a drug-smuggling caper set in Key West, which he hoped against hope that Hunter Thompson would write. At the time, Thompson was living in Jimmy Buffett's house in Key West. The two were friends from Aspen, where Buffett and Irving Azoff and the Eagles partied and skied together. Both Mann and Stone wanted to make a dark, violent film, but Wenner resolutely did not. "I wanted to do the Jimmy Buffett–style pot-pirates movie," said Wenner.

For inspiration, Wenner held a *Rolling Stone* business conference in Key West in 1979, chartering a fishing boat with Hunter Thompson, Jim Dunning, and Harriet Fier to try witnessing real live drug smugglers coming in from Cuba. They dined on lobster, and Dunning climbed to the top of the crow's nest and became violently ill. Thompson fell asleep and the movie idea wasn't advanced, but Dunning said that before Thompson nodded off he did come up with a salable business idea: a Rolling Stone magazine for college students, which Wenner would launch that year as *Rolling Stone College Papers,* anointing his sister Kate Wenner the editor.

That same year, Wenner was partying with David Obst, his book partner on Rolling Stone Press, when the two arrived at an epiphany: Neither had any clue what young people were doing anymore. Both in their thirties, they were too rich and successful and disconnected to relate to teenage rock fans. But what if they could send a reporter back to high school to find out? Obst went looking for a writer and found the perfect candidate on Wenner's masthead: Cameron Crowe. He arranged a book deal with Random House and advanced Crowe enough money to spend a year hanging out around Clairemont High School in San Diego, California, infiltrating the lives of the young surfers and Led Zeppelin fans. Wenner immediately saw the project as a vehicle for Jann S. Wenner Motion Pictures. Though Wenner wasn't involved in the deal, Crowe was his employee and Obst his ostensible partner, so Wenner told Crowe he wanted to assign a screenwriter to do an adaptation of Cameron's work for his movie company. "So it went from being a pure effort to being an accessory of a film," recalled Crowe. "So suddenly this book that doesn't exist is now a movie, which felt weird to me. And then it became 'You do the research, and share your research with a screenwriter, and the book and the movie will come out at the same time.'"

Crowe, only twenty-two at the time, already knew something about how the game is played and had hired an agent from the powerful Creative Artists Agency to handle the book. Hoping to circumvent the agent, Wenner flew to the Los Angeles bureau of *Rolling Stone* to pressure Crowe into dealing only with him on the film. "There was a moment that we were face-to-face," said Crowe. "He was a little tense, and he said, 'We have to do this together,' and I remember he put his hand out and said, 'Shake my hand. Shake my hand. Shake my hand.'

"And I shook his hand," continued Crowe, "which I knew was a scary thing. All of a sudden I was funneling pages for a project that's going to turn into a movie. It was very weird. But my mistake was shaking Jann's hand, which I still regret to this day."

Crowe's new agent, Bob Bookman, called Wenner and told him Crowe was mistaken: There was no deal. Crowe said he tried calling Wenner to explain. "And Jann wouldn't speak to me," he said. "I tried to call Jann, and he would not take my call."

If Wenner was upset with Crowe for denying him the movie deal, he was even more galled when he found out who got the movie rights: Irving Azoff.

Crowe had profiled Azoff in *Rolling Stone* in the summer of 1978, an article that stopped just short of fawning, and the two had forged a friendship. When Azoff heard about the high school project, he called Crowe, and the two agreed that Azoff would produce it. Azoff used his roster of rock stars—the all-important soundtrack—to negotiate a deal with Universal Pictures to become the co-producer on the film. (*Fast Times at Ridgemont High* would feature songs by the Eagles and Joe Walsh.)

Azoff's intercession was particularly personal because, ever since the Eagles game, Jann Wenner and Irving Azoff had developed a mutually back-scratching friendship. Azoff regularly funneled his artists to *Rolling Stone,* and Azoff lent Wenner his ski house in Aspen, where Wenner partied with Hunter Thompson and Jack Nicholson (whose female personal assistant Wenner was having an affair with). Wenner solicited Azoff for advice on his film ideas, like a Paul Scanlon script about the Jefferson Starship, and joked about another film treatment "based around the life and times of a lively rock and roll newspaper, headed by this fascinating, young, brilliant, short genius." (As it happens, Wenner did consider turning Ron Rosenbaum's *Murder at Elaine's,* in which "Jann Wenner" figured as a character, into a film.)

Meanwhile, Wenner acted as Azoff's unofficial diplomat when Azoff ran afoul of Paramount, helping smooth out a fight between Azoff and Barry Diller over Azoff's next production, *Urban Cowboy,* featuring music by the Eagles and Joe Walsh (Azoff believed Diller tricked him into casting John Travolta, whom Azoff hated in the role of Bud Davis, the cowboy protagonist). Wenner also tried brokering peace between

Azoff and his archenemy, David Geffen, setting up a dinner at Morton's in Hollywood without telling either man. When Geffen showed up, he found himself dining not only with Wenner but also with Azoff and his wife. "He thought it was really comical," said Azoff. A heated argument over the Eagles ensued until Shelli Azoff let out an unholy scream. A slug was crawling across her salad. "And she shrieks and jumps up and David looks over at her plate," said Azoff, "and he's so intent on arguing with me he says, 'What's the big fucking deal? It's just a slug. Have them get you another salad!' and then turns right back to me and starts yelling again." (Geffen denied this dinner ever happened.)

The Crowe-Azoff partnership on *Fast Times* was spit in Wenner's eye. To head them off at the pass, Wenner instantly went into production on a competing high school project, offering $100,000 to Charles Young to infiltrate a high school in New Jersey and turn the resulting story into a film script. "So now it's Shakespearean," said Crowe. "I had a picture of Charles M. Young on my bulletin board because I wanted to be utterly focused on the fact that there was a competing project, and I was going to put everything I had into this because it was my only shot."

The relationship between Azoff and Wenner slowly deteriorated from there. Wenner's story is that he was renting Azoff's ski house for two weeks when Azoff unceremoniously kicked him out to make room for other guests, offending Wenner. Azoff told a different story: Wenner had been staying at his house when he and Azoff's brother used the kitchen stove to smoke hash and left the burner on, sparking a house fire. "I get this call from the Aspen Fire Department that your house is on fire," said Azoff. "Something had ignited and basically burned half the roof off the house. He won't remember that."

Indeed, Wenner said he didn't recall the incident. Irving Azoff, he said, is "almost a psychopathic liar. Where he employs a lie for sport. Every now and then I do something with Irving, and it always comes out fucked; he always lies about something."

Around 1980, Wenner began a concerted campaign of negative news on Azoff in *Rolling Stone,* running barbed items in Random Notes, including one quoting Azoff saying he "controlled" California governor Jerry Brown through his concert fund-raisers, and later publishing a business story alleging Azoff cut illegal deals to earn T-shirt revenue at concerts. "I'm sure I commissioned those, and I'm sure they were not commissioned as a friendly thing," said Wenner. "When I was angry at him, I used to call him R2-D2."

Certainly Wenner's failure to get a movie made in Hollywood— both Thompson and Fong-Torres had failed miserably—didn't help his feelings toward Azoff. Charles Young's version of the high school movie turned out to be so grim Wenner reportedly declared, "If this is the truth about American teenagers, I don't want to know it." As *Fast Times* was set to premiere in 1982, Azoff's lawyer sent Wenner a telegram threatening a libel lawsuit, claiming Wenner had issued a staff directive to "get Azoff." "Your staff called Mr. Azoff for a statement and he said, 'I refuse to comment on another of Jann Wenner's "kill pieces,"'" the lawyer wrote. "'We understand you intend to editorialize on Mr. Azoff's comment and print it.'"

Wenner's lawyer Victor Kovner was brought in and a lawsuit was averted, but *Rolling Stone* published nary a word about *Fast Times*, the quintessential youth movie of the 1980s that debuted a new generation of actors, including Nicolas Cage, and featured the breakout performance of Sean Penn. "Nobody has been Jann's friend straight through," said Azoff. "He's a difficult friend to keep 100 percent of the time, but once you're his friend, even if there's a falling-out, there's always the makeup."

Indeed, Cameron Crowe had managed to get back into Wenner's good graces, too, by conducting the first interview with Joni Mitchell since *Rolling Stone* had charted her various affairs. Wenner said he ran into Mitchell at a Christmas party at Gilda Radner's apartment and smoothed things over, winning her back for what *Rolling Stone* called "her first interview in ten years." But Crowe said the rapprochement came after he met Mitchell through a mutual friend and learned she admired his work. Mitchell had personally defended Crowe against *New York Times* critic John Rockwell, who told Mitchell in an exchange of letters that Crowe's work was puffy. Afterward, "Joni reached out personally to say, 'I'm going to do an interview, I will do it with you; if you want it to be for *Rolling Stone*, I will do it for *Rolling Stone*,'" recalled Crowe.

In July 1979, on the occasion of her collaborative album with Charles Mingus, Mitchell spoke freely to Crowe of her past relationships, her difficulties with love, her struggles with critics, and her history with Bob Dylan (when she first played him *Court and Spark,* he fell asleep). She also expressed her feelings about the magazine's attacks on her in 1972. "That hurt," she told Crowe, "but not nearly so much as when they began to tear apart *The Hissing of Summer Lawns.* Ignorantly." ("There are no tunes to speak of," wrote Stephen Holden in 1976.)

Crowe counted his Mitchell interview among the best he ever did for *Rolling Stone*. It was also one of his last before he left for a successful career in Hollywood, later directing *Almost Famous,* the nostalgic 2000 film based on his early life at *Rolling Stone,* in which he cast Jann Wenner in a walk-on part.

17

Shattered

John Belushi liked to do a private comedy bit for Jane Wenner that always made her laugh. In a high, musing voice, he would begin, "Jane, remember all those times I used to hang out at the house and do blow with Jann and tell him I was his best friend and how great he was?"

Jane would smile. She loved this one.

"And remember I was hanging out there every night and every day and acting like he was the greatest person in my life?" He would continue, drawing it out so he could land the punch line: "I really hated him. I was just using him the whole time to be on the cover of *Rolling Stone*."

Belushi, who appeared on the cover of *Rolling Stone* first in August 1978 and again in February 1979, was Jane's latest troubled soul. The comic was smitten with her. "She was very fond of John, it was clear, and seemed standoffish to me," recalled his wife, Judy Belushi. "She would call him and want to talk to him."

The lure was also drugs, and perhaps mainly drugs. The Wenners had an entertainment console permanently installed in the wall of their apartment on East Sixty-Sixth Street that was made by another of Jane Wenner's admirers, a handsome furniture designer named Dakota Jackson. Born to a family of magicians, Jackson gave his pieces a signature feature: hidden compartments. The $15,000 table had two partitions for storing cocaine—one for Jann, one for Jane—and a mirror that pulled out for snorting it. Lorne Michaels was so impressed he had Jackson make him a console.

The Wenners took cocaine for its effects but also because it drew people to them. In the late 1970s, the Wenners' apartment was the locus of a rolling party. The door was never locked, and anyone could walk in. Ballet star Mikhail Baryshnikov showed up with director Milos Forman and his new girlfriend, Joey Townsend; Hunter Thompson stopped by at midnight and blew lighter fluid across a match while Leibovitz snapped her Nikon ("Stop hanging out with all these groupies," Jane told Thompson, referring to his new girlfriend, Laila Nabulsi); Peter Wolf, a stone cold Jane Wenner groupie, arrived at 2:00 a.m. after Wenner finished doing blow with Bailey Gimbel, a teen heir to the Gimbel department store fortune; Richard Gere passed out on the couch after a pot brownie; Ahmet Ertegun, of Atlantic Records, stumbled in drunk to declare to Jane, "If you don't give me a blow job, I'm going to pull my advertising."

On the twenty-second floor at 745 Fifth Avenue, *Rolling Stone*'s camera room—a darkroom with a buzzer for entering and a revolving light-trap door—had become a de facto cocaine emporium, run by two employees who doubled as dealers. The room, a version of which had existed in San Francisco, was dubbed "the Capri Lounge" after the bar in the TV comedy *Mary Hartman, Mary Hartman.* Wenner was the biggest customer of all, but he also used grams of cocaine as bonuses for employees who pleased him. "The deal was," said Karen Mullarkey, Annie Leibovitz's photo editor in the late 1970s, "if I got Annie through a deadline, and everything worked out okay, I would come in and find a bindle, one of those little folding envelopes of coke, on my light box. That was a gift from Jann."

When Wenner threw parties at *Rolling Stone,* there were lines to the camera room, which Wenner manned like a velvet rope. "Anybody who came down there to buy drugs from them, they would take a Polaroid," recalled Wenner. "They would sit around, do a little blow, and they had a whole hall with like four hundred or five hundred Polaroids of all their visitors."

Here was a common image of Jann Wenner in most stories told

about him from the late 1970s: curled up in his swivel chair at the round table that Jane bought for him in 1968, snorting a line of coke and swigging straight from an open bottle of Polmos Wódka Wyborowa. This was the preferred cocktail of the jet set: vodka, which took the edge off the cocaine, which prompted more cocaine, which prompted more vodka.

Not surprisingly, Wenner developed a serious drinking problem. His erratic behavior was a constant concern to his staff, who wondered which Jann Wenner would show up on any given afternoon. Would he be jovial and bursting with novel ideas or edgy and glowering with rage? Chet Flippo once compared Wenner to "a shark swimming through water, nothing going on inside him except appetite." If he heard an office door slam, his Pavlovian response was to go find out who was doing cocaine without him. "Jann could get to the point where he could hear the door lock," said David Felton. "And he would knock. That was it, if he came in, it was gone."

His increasing detachment from *Rolling Stone* became such a joke that while on deadline in 1979 Harriet Fier and David Felton conspired to clear the staff from the office and leave only a tape recording of typewriters to mock their baggy-eyed editor, who was coming in later and later, if at all (Wenner didn't find it funny). Back in San Francisco, cocaine had seemed like another secret handshake of the counterculture. But with the move to New York, it had come to define his entire life, and it was corroding Wenner's judgment. On the eve of the move, Wenner had asked an advertising saleswoman to pick up an envelope for him at the airport in San Francisco and deliver it to him in New York. When she arrived, Wenner cut the package open and began snorting the contents in front of her. The woman was horrified. "I could have been arrested," she cried. "I could be in jail." (She quit soon after.)

By 1979, cocaine was so ubiquitous that Johnny Carson was cracking cocaine jokes in a monologue about his appearance on the cover of *Rolling Stone*. When bandleader Doc Severinsen told Carson he had a secret cure for Carson's cold, Carson replied, "Well, I'm not going to use the inhaler you use! Called the 'Colombian Contact.' Cold doesn't go away but you really don't care." Wenner said Jimmy Buffett taught him a valuable lesson: There was nothing worth saying after 2:00 a.m.

But that was often too early for Wenner. "If I heard the rumbling of the garbage trucks outside," he said, it was time to "go to bed."

Wenner would look back on his cocaine consumption with a touch of rare regret. "Your addiction is such that you start using it sooner and sooner during the day, or during the night, and you become a prisoner of it," he said. "It takes you over, and you start doing cocaine-related things. Talking too much. Overdoing it. At the beginning, you're not thinking you have to pull back. Nobody was abusing it that much; it was weekends. But then as it becomes more a part of your daily life, you start to show behavioral patterns that are upsetting to you and other people."

Cocaine was only one of the forces pulling things apart during Wenner's New York phase. The center of the rock-and-roll business was no longer holding. Until 1978, Wenner had carefully navigated, and shepherded, the ups and downs of the music industry. The rock-and-roll business peaked with *Frampton Comes Alive!,* which sold eight million copies for A&M Records and was named "Album of the Year" by *Rolling Stone.* Inspired, Wenner famously stopped the presses one night to change the Frampton cover to Francesco Scavullo's image of Frampton shirtless and willowy with a come-hither look in his eyes, which his staff rejected as too gay ("The Pretty Power Rocker," by Cameron Crowe). It cost him $15,000, and Frampton hated it, but Wenner didn't care: "It was one o'clock in the morning and we were all sitting around taking coke and I was getting crazier and crazier—'Oh yeah! Oh yeah!'—but one was a really good, provocative cover, and one was not."

Two years later, Frampton's bloated career cratered, and Robert Stigwood's *Saturday Night Fever* ignited the disco craze that effectively ended the reign of rock and roll. Wenner personally enjoyed disco—the soundtrack to Studio 54—and in the late 1970s he put Donna Summer, the Village People, and the Bee Gees on the cover. Stigwood invited Wenner to his home in Los Angeles to introduce him to Andy Gibb, who stood in the living room and sang along to his 1977 hit "I Just Want to Be Your Everything" for Wenner. Then the Bee Gees manager "took me upstairs by the shirt and tried to seduce me."

But disco didn't move copies, and Wenner and his critics gave it short shrift, bowing to their readers. In 1979, Timothy White painted a bruisingly comic portrait of the Bee Gees that singer Barry Gibb never forgave, despite the richly portentous portrait by Dick Avedon. Wenner's readership recoiled at the black and gay culture that animated disco, which now paraded through the airwaves like Prince Egon on a bender. Wenner "almost died when disco came out," said Claeys Bahrenburg. "Almost died. Every day it was strictly rock-and-roll white bands. He would no more put a black person on the cover than a man on the moon. The reality is that black people didn't sell."

Conversely, punk bands like the Ramones (ushered into the music business by Danny Fields) and the Talking Heads were remaking rock and roll downtown at CBGB in the East Village, but none had the popular traction needed to sell copies of *Rolling Stone*. This was made clear when Charles Young declared the Sex Pistols the most important band of 1977. Wenner was repulsed by *Never Mind the Bollocks, Here's the Sex Pistols,* but he put Sid Vicious on the cover anyway, only to have the issue sell poorly, thus ending the punk experiment. *Rolling Stone* critic Paul Nelson lavished praise on the Ramones, calling them "authentic American primitives," but noted that "the godheads of AM radio don't seem to be listening at all. Why? . . . Where's your sense of humor and adventure, America?"

Pincered between disco and punk, Wenner defaulted to what did sell: Hollywood celebrities and 1960s-era rock icons of the kind he had been putting on the cover since 1967. Indeed, the covers of *Rolling Stone* were increasingly coming out of Wenner's social calendar: the Wenners' old neighbor Boz Scaggs (February 1977); the former chairman of the Trans-oceanic Comic Company, Mick Jagger (June and September 1978); Jon Landau's new client, Bruce Springsteen (August 1978); Michael Douglas (April 1979); Lorne Michaels's *SNL* stars Gilda Radner (November 1978) and Dan Aykroyd and John Belushi (February 1979); and Jimmy Buffett, who Irving Azoff insisted get a cover in October 1979 if he was going to fork over the Eagles for the cover the following month. When a fantastic new group called the Pretenders made the cover in 1980, it was on the recommendation of Pete Townshend, whom

Wenner put on the cover two months later. "Pete Townshend told Jann they were going to be the next big thing," recalled Peter Herbst. "Jann said it's going to be a big deal and we're going to write an article about them." (He wanted Carl Bernstein to write it, but Herbst assigned it to the new editor of Random Notes, Kurt Loder.)

When Wenner's rare byline appeared in *Rolling Stone,* it was as the guardian of his favored icons, Bob Dylan or the Rolling Stones. In 1978, Wenner publicly confronted his own critics over the Stones album *Some Girls* and Dylan's *Street Legal,* calling out Greil Marcus, Paul Nelson, and Dave Marsh for their "weird hostility and bitterness," which he blamed on their need to "slay their figurative fathers and look for new heroes." Wenner defended the Stones against the critical consensus that the band had become a pale imitation of itself. Even Paul Nelson's ostensibly positive review of *Some Girls* was written as a series of backhanded compliments: "Where Mick Jagger and Keith Richards were once a pair of Humphrey Bogarts (or, in keeping with *Some Girls* imagery, Lauren Bacalls), they're now more like—who?—Warren Beatty and Robert Blake."

Wenner, in his sturdy defense, channeled Mick Jagger's thoughts on the matter, writing an imagined internal monologue that was equal parts insecurity and competitive piss. "Last year more than seventy albums went platinum, but our own LPs have been pretty lukewarm," Wenner wrote. "So, goddamn it, we find it a little embarrassing and painful to be taking a back seat again to Linda Ronstadt, Boz Scaggs, Peter Frampton and so on. Normally, we wouldn't give a shit, but these platinum artists are raking in royalties the likes of which we've never seen. Fuck the Eighties, we're old hands at this, so let's get it on."

As for Dylan, Wenner would concede in retrospect that *Street Legal* was "obviously not one of Bob's great albums," but at the time Wenner was starstruck by the venue in which he first heard it: sitting next to Bob Dylan at the recording studio. "Bob called me, asked me to come into the studio with him in [New York] and listen to it with him," he said. "It was really Bob implicitly lobbying for a good review." Wenner was happy to oblige and afterward procured the first *Rolling Stone* interview with Dylan since 1969, conducted by Jonathan Cott.

The Wenner byline returned the following year to defend Dylan's next album, *Slow Train Coming,* which marked Dylan's conversion to Christianity. Wenner called it "one of the finest albums Dylan has ever made. In time, it is possible that it might even be considered his greatest. The claim will not go down easily." Indeed it didn't: Harriet Fier said she tried stopping Wenner from publishing it, but Wenner overruled her. Publisher Claeys Bahrenburg recalled the intervention: "It was completely embarrassing and he would have people rewrite it and stuff, but he still insisted on doing it his way and people would say, 'Oh my God, he's going to publish it!'"

For his part, Bob Dylan said *Rolling Stone* reviews—including Wenner's defense—meant little to him. "*Slow Train Coming* was one of my strongest records, one of the biggest-selling ones right from the start," he said. "So if it wasn't for the reviewers that wrote for *Rolling Stone,* it connected with an entirely different group of people. Maybe Jann did go on record saying it was one of my finest records, and although I appreciated him doing that, it was more like a good cop/bad cop type of thing. That's all it meant to me."

Wenner would find Dylan's lack of appreciation upsetting, and he insisted that Dylan read every word written about him in *Rolling Stone.* "Bob will never, not until his deathbed, maybe not even then, confess that *Rolling Stone*'s coverage of him was important, or that anybody's was," said Wenner. "The fact is, he's read every goddamn fucking word that we've published on him, and brooded on it, too! At length!"

•

EVEN AFTER the John Lennon betrayal of 1971, Wenner continued to be part of the afterlife of the Beatles, the supreme center of his rock-and-roll canon.

In 1974, Wenner had received a mysterious cream-colored envelope in the mail, care of "Johann Weiner" and postmarked Los Angeles, California. Inside was a single Polaroid picture of John Lennon and Paul McCartney hanging out on a garden patio with friends: Linda McCartney, hoisting a pool stick; Keith Moon, in shorts and Roman sandals; and May Pang, Lennon's then lover, holding McCartney's daughter

Mary on her lap. On the white strip below the image, dated "Palm Sunday 1974," was the message "How do *you* sleep???!!!"

This was a reference to the John Lennon song from 1971's *Imagine,* a notorious attack on McCartney in which Lennon snipes, "The only thing you done was yesterday." Now the message was being repurposed to attack Jann Wenner. Wenner said he never understood the precise meaning of the picture, but it was obvious it was a bitter joke from the Beatle he betrayed. At the time, Paul and Linda McCartney had just appeared on the cover of *Rolling Stone,* while Lennon's latest album, *Mind Games,* was torched by Jon Landau for having "his worst writing yet."

What Wenner didn't know was that the Polaroid captured a pivotal moment in the history of the Beatles—the period when John and Paul managed a degree of détente after the acrimony of the breakup. It was also a portent of John Lennon's return to New York City.

For a while, neither Beatle was talking to *Rolling Stone,* a fact Wenner admitted to a group of students in Colorado in 1973: "Paul chose to have his own interview in *Life* magazine, which he edited himself. And it was very careful, it was pretentious and sententious and boring and *Life* magazine went out of business and then . . ." He paused to laugh. In the past, Wenner got to Paul through Linda, but the couple kept their distance from him. "We didn't really wanna hang with him," said McCartney. "We'd make fun of him."

McCartney had no idea that Wenner had alienated Lennon with the book and presumed he remained Lennon's top groupie. "I didn't feel like he was independent," he said. "When he was talking to me, I was sort of talking to someone who would report back to John. No doubt about it."

Rolling Stone regularly dinged McCartney in Random Notes, and Jon Landau ripped McCartney's second album, 1971's *Ram* (billed as Paul and Linda McCartney), as "the nadir in the decomposition of Sixties rock thus far . . . *Ram* is so incredibly inconsequential and so monumentally irrelevant . . . it is difficult to concentrate on, let alone dislike or even hate." This jibed with John Lennon's view of the record. On a postcard included with the *Imagine* LP, Lennon mocked the cover of McCartney's album—Paul holding the horns of a ram on his farm in

Scotland—with a picture of himself holding a pig. Wenner published the pig image alongside his introduction to *Lennon Remembers*.

Certainly *Rolling Stone* remained pro-Lennon and even managed a modest truce with him by supporting his battle with the Nixon administration, which tried and failed to deport Lennon for fomenting political disorder. Ralph Gleason was a fiery and vocal defender. When Lennon finally won his court case in 1975, he wrote a friendly note to *Rolling Stone* readers, saying "we couldn't have done it without you."

And McCartney eventually came around. After the first lineup of Wings dissolved in 1973, he needed critical applause for his new group, Paul McCartney and Wings, and Jann Wenner's *Rolling Stone* was at the peak of its powers, the industry turnstile through which one passed to sell records in America. When McCartney agreed to talk to writer Paul Gambaccini in London, Wenner submitted a laundry list of subjects he wanted him to cover, including "feud with Lennon," "why people dislike Linda," "could Linda make it without him?," "self image," and the "so it comes to this attitude against him."

McCartney finally cleared the air about Wenner's interview with Lennon, expressing the intense pain Lennon's words caused him. "Oh, I hated it," he told Gambaccini. "I sat down and really thought, I'm just nothin'. But then, well, kind of people who dug me like Linda said, 'No, you know that's not true, you're joking. He's got a grudge, man; the guy's trying to polish you off.' Gradually I started to think, great, that's not true . . . but at the time, I tell you, it hurt me. Whew. Deep."

McCartney said he didn't send the "Palm Sunday" Polaroid, but he recognized the moment. Not long before it was taken, Yoko Ono had come to see him at his farmhouse in Scotland to ask for help repairing her broken marriage to John. "She sat at our kitchen table, and she said, 'I'd like you to do me a favor,'" recalled McCartney. "'I'd like you to be the go-between between me and John. John's out in L.A., going crazy, and I will have him back. And I want you to tell him.'"

Lennon was in his "Lost Weekend" period, carousing with songwriter Harry Nilsson and famously getting evicted from the Troubadour for heckling the Smothers Brothers. He showed up at an Ann Peebles concert with a sanitary napkin taped to his forehead—an incident reported in *Rolling Stone* in February 1974:

[He] didn't leave the waitress a tip, and in response to her scowl, he said, "Do you know who I am?" "Yes," she said. "You're some asshole with a Kotex on your head." . . .

Meanwhile, Yoko consults an astrologer almost every day.

To keep a leash on Lennon, Ono had given her blessing for him to sleep with her personal assistant May Pang until he got through his period of wilding. Pang was referred to in *Rolling Stone* as a "friend" of Lennon's, but she was much more: McCartney called her "the voice of reason" who helped bring about a truce between Paul and John. (In the liner notes of Lennon's 1975 album *Rock 'n' Roll,* he would refer to her as "Mother Superior.") When the McCartneys showed up in Santa Monica, they were greeted by Nilsson and Keith Moon, who were hanging out in the house doing drugs. "John wasn't up yet, so I sat in the garden," said McCartney. "Harry Nilsson's opposite to me on this table in the sunshine. Harry says, 'Do you want any angel dust?' I said, 'I don't know, what is it?' He said, 'Well, it's an elephant tranquilizer.' I said, 'Is it fun?' He looks, and thinks, and says, 'No.' I said, 'Okay, I won't do it. Thanks for the offer.' That's how it was!"

When Lennon emerged, McCartney delivered Ono's message. "She's willing to have you back, if you want to go back," he recounted. "But you've got to go to New York, you've got to get your own place, you've got to court her, you've got to send flowers. You've got to do it all right, and then she'll take you back. And he did. That's how they got back together."

Afterward, Lennon moved back to New York to live with Ono on the seventh floor of the Dakota apartments on the Upper West Side of Manhattan, a Central Park stroll away from their former fanboy, Jann Wenner.

As the Polaroid suggested, McCartney and Lennon had worked out some of the divisions that Wenner's newspaper had exploited since the inception of *Rolling Stone.* At the time of the picture, rumors circulated of a Beatles reunion, with John's and Paul's lawyers trying to hammer out their financial wrinkles. John Eastman, McCartney's manager and Linda's brother, told *Rolling Stone* there was "fervent hope" of another musical collaboration.

The prospect of a reunited Beatles was a kind of holy grail for an era when everything the Beatles represented seemed to have been lost. As Jonathan Cott wrote in the ten-year-anniversary issue of *Rolling Stone,* the Beatles were the Platonic ideal of the 1960s from which all things had become unmoored, resulting in the "calculating, mean-spirited perspective of the Seventies."

"And they presented themselves to us," Cott continued, "not as Seventies 'geniuses' like Sonny Bono and Paul Williams—certified as such by inane and sentimental television talk-show hosts—but as members of a little tribe which provided an example of how each of us could become part of the necklace of Shiva in which every diamond reflects every other and is itself reflected."

Lennon and McCartney didn't respond to a televised offer by Lorne Michaels to reunite on *Saturday Night Live* in 1976, and McCartney responded to a BBC query that same year with a bit of verse that might have pleased Philip Larkin:

> *The Beatles split in '69,*
> *And since then they've been doing fine,*
> *And if you ask that question once more,*
> *I think I'll have to break your jaw.*

Meanwhile, John and Yoko went into seclusion with their new son, Sean, as Lennon became increasingly eccentric and Ono surrounded herself with dubious spiritual advisers. "They were being completely under the radar," said Wenner. "I got [to New York] and I didn't see them around. He was in his drug thing for a long time. You know, didn't go out. Maybe I couldn't have ended up being friends with him anyway because he was so nutty and they were so in their own world."

•

NOT LONG AFTER *Rolling Stone* moved to New York, Wenner had told Harriet Fier that after editing the magazine for ten long years, he was finished; she could take the next ten years. "I thought to myself, 'Not if I can help it,'" said Fier.

Art director Roger Black gave Wenner an ultimatum: pay him more money or return from his Hollywood adventures and edit the magazine again. Wenner refused both requests, and Black left in September 1978. Meanwhile, Wenner was giving finance man Jim Dunning greater and greater leverage over *Rolling Stone,* allowing him to fight editors for advertising space and police for "hard language" in the magazine. "I had to read everything in the magazine before it got published," said Dunning. "And I had the ability to say no to everything. [Wenner] gave me all the authority to say no to everything. That was what I was deep into."

Rolling Stone had moved very far away from its original vision of passionate bulletins from youth culture, which had fragmented into many pieces, with limited contact with one another. The magazine now used reader surveys to find the right "mix" of stories as rock-and-roll covers lost sales traction. How much could they pull back from music, move further into movie and TV stars, and redefine *Rolling Stone* as "general interest" before the magazine lost its definition? Factions formed inside the staff: the music people versus the general-interest people. "You had to be very targeted when you did [nonmusic]," said Dunning. "And you had to constantly move back to music to re-center everybody, because there was starting to be a blending of the cultures between music and entertainment and late night TV."

This was a matter of constant calibration, and often it was successful. *Rolling Stone* was corrupt until it wasn't, imperfect until it was. But after 1978, it was never again an *experiment* in American publishing, a thing that burned strictly to the rhythms of Jann Wenner's fascinations. Nearly all of the San Francisco staff were gone by the end of 1979, including David Felton. Some quit, some were fired, but others just outgrew *Rolling Stone,* feeling hamstrung by Wenner's controlling nature. "My God, we could have ruled the world," said Paul Gambaccini. "But Jann wasn't into ruling the world; he was into ruling *his* world."

There were new and great writers to replace them—like Timothy White, a talented and productive feature writer who interviewed everybody from the Bee Gees to Johnny Carson—but *Rolling Stone* was now a business formula, an uneasy détente between Wenner and his editorial staff rather than the cult of hip that it used to be in San Francisco. "To me, the whole scene felt unhappy," said Annie Leibovitz. "It wasn't exploratory any longer. I think everyone was living off of what *Rolling Stone* meant and was. Again, looking back at it, it's growing up. I don't know if *Rolling Stone* survived that move, on some level."

It was writer Abe Peck who summed up the staff's view of Wenner in that era: "He's a better editor than any of his business guys, and a better business guy than any of his editors."

To rally his troops, Wenner formed a pickup rock group called the Dry Heaves for the company Christmas party in 1979, hoping to impress guest Mick Jagger. Made up of Wenner and *Rolling Stone* writers Kurt Loder, Jon Pareles, Chuck Young, and Timothy White, they practiced relentlessly during a retreat on Shelter Island but remained a hapless if spirited band. At the party, Jagger told Wenner he should stick to writing. Ben Fong-Torres wrote a Bob Dylan parody for the occasion called "Gotta Suck Somebody," capturing the playful spirit of *Rolling Stone* in 1979 and the self-image of the staff as engaging in a series of demeaning transactions with power brokers.

> *You may know Paul Simon, you may know Elaine*
> *You may know Jann Wenner, you may even know Jane*
> *You may have home numbers for Ahmet and Clive*
> *You may know the cast of Saturday Night Live*
> *But you're gonna have to suck somebody.*

The irony was that for all his reputation as a rip-roaring capitalist, Wenner wasn't actually doing well financially. *Rolling Stone* was sagging under the weight of the million-dollar loan that Dunning negotiated, and the decline of the music business was eating into advertising revenue. In a risky gambit, Wenner tried raising the cover price while simultaneously expanding the circulation to 600,000 so he could charge advertisers more for a page in *Rolling Stone*. But the magazine sold erratically from issue to issue and barely broke even. The years 1979 and 1980 offered a narrow passage between profitability and decline. Wenner and Dunning concocted a plan to ask the record labels to sign long-term advertising deals to ensure predictable revenue, but record executives made clear they wanted more help marketing new artists than they were getting from *Rolling Stone*—and less criticism. "We tried to sell them on the idea that we were partners with the artists and not just tearing them apart," recalled Jim Dunning. "So there's that tension in that room at that meeting. You know, 'Come on, you guys criticize our stuff.'"

But even a lucrative schedule of ads from CBS wasn't enough to stave off the heavy losses from *Outside*. Despite reducing the frequency of the magazine, *Outside* was bleeding Straight Arrow and endangering the operating cash flow of *Rolling Stone*. When Wenner finally conceded defeat, Dunning negotiated a deal to sell *Outside* to Larry Burke, owner of Mariah Media in Chicago, for $700,000. Wenner had never had a personal interest in camping, but the loss of his first glossy magazine pained him. It was a Hearstian *empire* that he had wanted, but he was failing to build on the success of *Rolling Stone*. In Hollywood, he was spending more time partying with Don Simpson than making movies, and he had tried and failed to reboot the *Rolling Stone* TV show idea with Lorne Michaels in 1978 (to run after *Saturday Night Live* on NBC). In 1979, he briefly partnered with French publisher Daniel Filipacchi, who was trying to reanimate the 1960s picture magazine *Look*. With Filipacchi's backing, the plan was for Wenner to manage the magazine, with a $50,000 a month budget from Filipacchi and a cut of the profit. Wenner conceived of *Look* as a high-end publication featuring "actors, artists, musicians, writers, politicians, explorers, and adventurers and people of style and lifestyle." As he wrote in the prospectus, "The post-war baby of 1946 and 1947 and 1948 is now 33 years old. These are the new grownups, coming of age in America and our lives. This is what *Look* is for." His own publisher warned him that he was in danger of making *Rolling Stone* redundant. But Jann Wenner was shot out of a cannon: After he and the Frenchman toasted the deal over champagne, Wenner immediately went uptown to Elaine's to tell everybody he'd taken over *Look*. He rented an office, hired a staff of fifty, raided *Rolling Stone* for stories, and produced a single issue of the monthly photo magazine, with Clint Eastwood on the cover. Wenner wanted to prove something, and he imagined that *Look*'s instant success would give him greater leverage over Filipacchi's property. Instead, Filipacchi refused Wenner's demand for a better cut of the sales, and the revived *Look* magazine died after two issues.

Next, Wenner tried partnering with concert promoter Ron Delsener and a French aristocrat and art world figure named Francois de Menil, heir to the Schlumberger oil fortune, to start a rock-and-roll-themed dinner bar and concert hall called the Paramount, which would be like a Studio 54 for Wenner's social world and include "side rooms where you never knew what was going on," recalled Jim Dunning, whom Wenner tasked with executing the plan. Then Wenner offhandedly offended de Menil in the press—joking that he wore a sweater around his shoulders because nobody ever taught him how to put his arms through the sleeves—and the deal fizzled.

From afar, it looked as if Wenner's naked ambition were the only point to all this. In 1979, a magazine profile described him as "three people trying to get through a doorway at the same time." But none of the three Jann Wenners appeared to be the guy who started *Rolling Stone* in San Francisco in 1967:

Is the purveyor of the hip life, the voice from the other side of the Generation Gap, becoming bourgeois? Wenner scoffs. "I've been bourgeois forever. *Rolling Stone* is bourgeois. Its readers are bourgeois. All this counterculture, hippie stuff is—" Wenner spits out an obscenity. "That's all ended."

It was an image of a man so stripped of idealism his very existence seemed to contradict the authenticity of *Rolling Stone,* which, as Warren Hinckle had hissed back in 1977, was now "a deracinated journal still feeding off the table scraps of the 60s . . . there is no more spectacular narcissism than the media's staring into the fountain of youth at its own reflection."

Sometimes, it didn't like what it saw. Wenner refused to participate in the 1980 film *Where the Buffalo Roam,* based on Thompson's *Rolling Stone* article on Oscar Acosta and featuring Bill Murray as Hunter Thompson and an overweight actor named Bruno Kirby as Marty Lewis, editor of *Blast* magazine. It was a parody of Wenner described in the original script as "a short, pudgy, baby-faced kid in his early 20's. He is wearing neatly pressed jeans and a white, ruffled shirt." (To rub it in, the film was produced by Art Linson, Irving Azoff's partner in

Cameron Crowe's *Fast Times at Ridgemont High*.) Wenner was stung. He assigned David Felton to tear it limb from limb in *Rolling Stone*. Felton called it, accurately, "an embarrassing piece of hogwash utterly devoid of plot, form, movement, tension, humor, insight, logic or purpose. The cultural revolution of the Sixties is reduced to a Three Stooges routine." (Thompson agreed: "It sucks—a bad, dumb, low-level, low-rent script.")

Wenner was naive—perhaps willfully so—to the version of himself he saw in stories and movies. He chalked it up to jealousy and the sniping of bitter ex-employees. Hadn't he made them all famous? But only Wenner seemed to have survived the move to New York, while the rest fell apart. He said it was a matter of growing up—he didn't want to end up some old longhair living in Marin County. But for those who saw Wenner up close during these years, his drug and alcohol abuse could look like the actions of a man trying to kill the pain of his own disillusionment. He seemed miserable and alone. And as he became an object of ridicule—Jimmy Breslin said he had "the editorial ability found in a pair of shoes"—friends wondered how he withstood the attacks. "The most hideous things were written about him," recalled Lorne Michaels. "And you go, 'Wow, doesn't that kill you? Does it make you tougher?' He toughed it out, but it was so personal. The rage was so personal. You come up for air and people are just dumping shit on you. His thing started because he loved it, and then it morphed into something else. It's about passion and love and all that, and you find out that the closer you get to your heroes—and it's not that."

•

WHEN A BEARDED MAN in overalls showed up at East Sixty-Sixth Street one morning, Jane Wenner assumed it was the plumber arrived to fix the broken toilet.

"I'm from America," announced the man.

"Oh, great," she said. "The bathroom is that way."

"No, I'm from *America*," he said.

It was Gerry Beckley from the band America, whose visit Wenner hadn't mentioned to Jane.

The Wenners lived separate lives. If they were in the same room, they were fighting over cocaine—who stole whose. When they moved to New York, Jane had hoped to renew her life, get back in touch with her art, but instead she began to sink. By 1980, the twenty-four-hour party at East Sixty-Sixth Street had become too much, and according to Jann Wenner she developed an addiction to Quaaludes. Ensconced in her bedroom, she spent days at a time in bed as her body became shriveled and emaciated. The Wenners had a housekeeper who cut Jane's food and mashed up her vitamins. When Jane emerged in public, she sometimes wore three layers of clothing to make herself look more full-bodied. Jane said she wasn't addicted. She only "liked" Quaaludes, but her insularity and paranoia were self-evident. She would call lawyer Ben Needell regularly to ask if she still owned half of Straight Arrow. To socialize with her, friends would gather around her bed, sometimes bringing more drugs. "She was not functioning," said Art Garfunkel. "I got the feeling Jane was half herself, and Jann was fully himself."

"I just remember her up there in that duplex, never coming down," said Michael Douglas. "Just days and days."

Hunter Thompson called her "Queen of the Underground." When a workman came by to fix the thermostat and saw Jane curled up in bed in the afternoon, he exclaimed merrily, "Oh, Mrs. Wenner, you look like you're in baby Beech-Nut land!" That became the inside joke—Baby Beech-Nut Land. Her sister, Linda, said Jane had everything going for her but self-esteem. "She had all the opportunity but not the courage," she said, "and Jann brought her down in that way."

In the past, Jane had been part of Wenner's formula, her seductive charm softening the cruelty of his ambition. "Part of that cruelty played into Jane's strength," observed Skip Stein, an investment banker who was on *Rolling Stone*'s board of directors during this period. "He's going to be cruel to you and then she will rescue you, and then you stay under the tent. At the same time, it's creative, but it's chillingly lonely. That loneliness drove a lot of behavior."

During this time, Wenner conducted affairs with both men and women. In 1978, he had a "fling" with Caroline Kennedy during his separation from Jane (a couple of hot and heavy make-out sessions, he said). When Jackie Onassis heard about it, she froze Wenner from the Kennedy social orbit for two years. "It wasn't so much that he sailed into her private party, in her Fifth Avenue pad, acting offhand with

Fashionable Stimulants," wrote a Washington, D.C., gossip columnist. "It was that, as the evening wore on, he tried to Pounce on Caroline."

Wenner also slept with his own secretary, a gorgeous but drug-besotted woman named Iris Brown. When Jane discovered a stain on Wenner's office couch, Wenner begged for forgiveness and got it. "She was a masochist," said Wenner. "She was looking to be hurt. And she took years to get out of it."

Indeed, drugs were masking the deeper problem: The bargain of their marriage meant Wenner could never fully love her the way she loved him. "At some level, the homosexuality, my own sexuality, prevented me from having a fully realized, developed love for another person," said Wenner. "Not that it wasn't there; it was flawed. It wasn't as fulfilling, and you want that kind of fulfillment. And drugs were as destructive on our relationship as anything."

In the early days of New York, the businessmen of *Rolling Stone* would show up to the Wenners' cottage in the Hamptons for a weekend meeting at two in the afternoon and be shocked to see Jann, Jane, and Annie Leibovitz coming out of the bedroom together with drugs on open display. "We all conjectured that there were a lot of threesomes," said Claeys Bahrenburg, the advertising director.

But the once-powerful triangle of Jann and Jane and Annie was coming apart as they became consumed in their own private struggles. Leibovitz had declared they would all be "stars" when they moved to New York, but instead she found herself alone in a bleak and unforgiving cityscape. Most of the staff from San Francisco had been fired or left. "No one was really there for anyone else to help," she said. When art director Roger Black perused Leibovitz's contact sheets, they often showed her taking refuge in the beds of her subjects, both men and women. "If she could talk them into bed, they were in bed," Black said. "That was her MO. Boys and girls, it didn't matter. Sometimes it'd just be super intimate; sometimes there would be sex. Whatever it took. And it was fine."

Leibovitz said any relationships with subjects happened after the shoot—"the *photograph* was always the most important thing"—but her exploits were now a running joke at *Rolling Stone*. "We were going to send her to Cuba to interview Fidel Castro," recalled Laurel Gonsalves.

"The people were saying, 'Oh my God, she's gonna fuck Fidel Castro!'" (The story never happened.) Leibovitz said she didn't know she was gay, nor did she think of Wenner as gay. Sex, like drugs, was just another opportunity. "If you had Mick Jagger coming on to you or something, you just . . . whatever," she said. "It's too interesting. As I got older, I didn't have time for that stuff. But if it was presented in front of you, it seemed like 'of our time,' like drugs. To make a decision to go the other way . . ."

But Jane, once her ballast, was increasingly out of reach for Leibovitz, who was totally out of reach of herself. "When I had to break away, or get back into life, it was hard for me," said Leibovitz. "I only knew how to take pictures; I didn't know how to do anything else. I had to unravel myself. I was very caught up with over-taking drugs, too."

The result was that Leibovitz became more volatile and mean. "When she got home, all that frustration and anger of having to kind of demean herself on some level," said Black, "she tried to take it out on me and other people." At a birthday party arranged by Bea Feitler, Leibovitz showed up with a butcher knife and whacked the cake to pieces while the staff looked on in shock. Another time, she slashed apart one of Roger Black's layouts with a razor blade. Leibovitz once said she had a "love-hate" relationship with Wenner. He was controlling and paternalistic, but he looked out for her interests in his own way. "I remember the worst days," said Leibovitz, "one of the Eagles called him in the middle of the night and said, 'Annie used up the last of my crystal meth that I was writing with,' and Jann said, 'So, what do you want me to do about it?'"

Leibovitz was now under the watch of Karen Mullarkey, a photo editor who started at *Rolling Stone* in 1975 and became Leibovitz's steward and occasional cocaine partner. At six feet tall, Mullarkey towered over Jann Wenner. "Jann hated her," recalled Black. "She was a very headstrong Jewish lady from New York. She knew the whole story. And she didn't give a shit."

Mullarkey quit in late 1977, but she didn't go away. The following year, she encouraged Leibovitz to establish an independent studio away from the Fifth Avenue offices of *Rolling Stone* in order to take control of her career, especially the resale of her famous images, which Wenner had been managing since the mid-1970s and earning money from posters and calendars and T-shirts. But the first step was taking back Leibovitz's archive of photo negatives from a storage locker at *Rolling Stone*. On a day when Wenner was home sick with the shingles, Mullarkey and a lawyer working for Leibovitz devised a plan to hail three checkered cabs on the street outside *Rolling Stone,* sneak into the offices, load the trunks full of Leibovitz's boxes, and transport them back to Leibovitz's apartment at the Dakota. When he discovered what happened, Wenner was outraged. "He calls me at home and threatens to take me to court," Mullarkey recalled. "And he's going to sue me for stealing it. Never mentions suing Annie. He's going to sue me."

But Wenner was unprepared for Mullarkey's counterargument. "And I say to him, 'Sue me. Take me to court, then I get to testify,'" she said. "'Don't I get to testify about all the cocaine? And how you used to pay me in a bindle?' . . . It got real quiet on the other end."

Mullarkey found a French photo agent named Robert Pledge to represent Leibovitz and negotiate with Wenner, who was aggrieved that Leibovitz had cut him out. "Jann Wenner was really upset," said Pledge. "He thought it was highway robbery. It had to do with his own ignorance and misunderstanding of things."

It was a revelation to Leibovitz to learn that she owned her own negatives. "He was the one that made me realize I needed to protect my work," she said. "And I knew Jann would disagree with this. We never really had an agreement."

This was the moment Leibovitz began to slowly divorce the Wenners and *Rolling Stone*. Pledge would manage Leibovitz's work for the next four decades, but it would take five years for the relationship with the Wenners to fully unwind because Pledge had inherited a significant liability: Annie Leibovitz, the full-blown drug addict whose body was, more than once, unceremoniously dumped in front of a hospital by her dealer. Jane Wenner said she once found Leibovitz abandoned on a gurney in the hallway of the Metropolitan Hospital, skin turning purple, a camera bag full of cash by her side. Jane implored a doctor to save her, paying him to attend to Leibovitz immediately. (In a separate interview, Wenner said he was the one who "saved her life getting her out of a hallway," but Jane insisted it was her. "No, Jann was working," she said.)

Another time, after Leibovitz went missing for days, Mullarkey entered her apartment at the Dakota and discovered bloodstains splashed across the walls from needle jabs to the vein. A framed print of the Keith Richards image—the Stones guitarist passed out on smack—was lying on the floor next to the chair where Leibovitz shot up ("It was like a diorama," said Mullarkey). She called Leibovitz's parents, and for a while Leibovitz saw a cocaine specialist. "He just sat there taking notes," she said. "It was ridiculous. He went on to sue me for [not] being paid."

This was not the end of Leibovitz's career at *Rolling Stone,* but it was the beginning of the end. And looking back, Leibovitz concluded that Jann Wenner was the only one who had survived the move to New York from San Francisco. "I don't know how he did it," she said. "I mean, I'll still question why he moved to New York and felt like it had to be done there. I wondered what we could have been if we stayed put out there."

•

TO HIS FRIENDS in New York and Aspen and Hollywood, Jann Wenner was a wonder: the baby-boomer visionary whose singular will to power, rakish personality, fortitude for excess, and wild-man charm made him a force to be reckoned with. He was shameless but also unashamed. Even his cruelty, which Wenner openly discussed with Studs Terkel in the late 1970s—"I don't get too worked up about sometimes having to be mean to people"—was a marvel to behold. "There are a lot of people that you like just because of how terrible they are," observed Earl McGrath. "Not that he's terrible, but even when he's acting his worst, he's doing it with a certain verve. You can't help but admire—'I would never dream of doing that!' You can disapprove of him, but you're still amused."

Nobody captured this aspect of Jann Wenner better than the Wenners' new favorite photographer, Jean ("Johnny") Pigozzi, heir to a French car company called Simca, founded by his father, Henri. In 1970, Pigozzi came to the United States to study visual arts at Harvard, after which he gravitated to Hollywood, worked briefly at 20th Century Fox, and became a fixture in the celebrity jet set—an admirer and starfucker. Pigozzi first met Jane Wenner on a trip up the Nile to Egypt with Max Palevsky in 1976 and was smitten with her like everyone else. When Leibovitz helped curate a *Rolling Stone* spread called "12 Hot Photographers," she made Pigozzi a featured photographer, publishing his image of a row of Rolls-Royces parked outside the Beverly Hills Hotel. Pigozzi told *Rolling Stone* his obsessions were "gossip and toy rubber animals" and his fantasy for a photo series was a week with gossip columnist Rona Barrett in Hollywood. His friends, especially Mick Jagger, enjoyed Pigozzi's flattery and noblesse oblige, even more so his yacht and fabulous homes in France. For the Wenners' ten-year wedding anniversary in 1978, they flew to France with Lorne Michaels to see Bob Dylan at the Pavillon de Paris, staying at a Pigozzi family apartment overlooking the courtyard of the German embassy. Director Martin Scorsese and Robbie Robertson of the Band flew in from Italy with two models teetering on high heels, and a drug dealer in a white suit tapped out a vial of gray powder on the table. As Pigozzi recalled, Wenner and Michaels snorted the heroin, and "they were vomiting from the balcony of my apartment." (The next day, Wenner and Michaels visited the Chartres Cathedral, south of Paris, watching the light come through the stained-glass windows, still high.)

Wenner tried helping Pigozzi get a book off the ground called *Problems of Being Rich,* offering his book proposal to Jackie Onassis, who by then had welcomed Wenner back into her fold. Onassis was skeptical, especially after Pigozzi's last book failed to sell: *Pigozzi's Journal of the Seventies,* a softbound scrapbook featuring photographs of Pigozzi standing next to celebrities, his camera turned backward and aimed at his own face and that of his star quarry, whether Candice Bergen or Rod Stewart or Faye Dunaway or Martin Scorsese—a proto-selfie. Elsewhere, Pigozzi captured the New York demimonde in high-flash black and white: Paul Simon and Shelley Duvall in a Mercedes driven by Francois de Menil; Keith Richards in a limousine; Mick Jagger in a limousine; Carrie Fisher in a limousine with Lorne Michaels and "a successful, heavy newspaper editor" (Jann Wenner); and an unidentified man leaning close to John Belushi at a party (Wenner again). Jane, a favorite Pigozzi subject, said some of the pictures were taken at East Sixty-Sixth Street.

Jann Wenner wrote the introduction to Pigozzi's scrapbook. In clear, confident prose, he crystallized his thoughts on the decade that was coming to an end. It had been twelve years since Wenner began his journey on Brannan Street and gone blasting across the 1970s like a Roman candle. What did it all mean? What did it all add up to?

> What we are about to look at is a world that turns around the new jet-setting, where room service is a fact of daily life and where it is important to be rich, any way you can get there and any way you care to define it.
>
> People have mistakenly based their concept of the Seventies on the years '74, '75 and '76, a time in which it looked like nothing was happening. In fact, very little was happening and life was boring. (I believe that the Seventies didn't begin until 1977, and that the Sixties finally ended in 1974.) We can start to understand the years that really are the Seventies as a reaction to boredom: an attempt to substitute something, to divert ourselves, to get some amusement and distraction. The *real* Seventies was a period in which the post-Sixties search for meaning was found to be pointless and premature. It was a time of rejection of meaning, during which it is better to be somewhat foolish and famous and fun—rich, if you will—than mope around, bemused or blameful, about the accustomed quietude.

Here was Jann Wenner's magnum opus. The 1960s had been nothing but a lark. All that remained to do was count the money. When David Dalton, whose byline was last seen in *Rolling Stone* in 1974, visited Wenner in his offices, the editor was sitting at his desk "sorting bills. Hundreds, fifties, and twenties in piles," Dalton recalled. Pigozzi published a picture of Wenner, cigarette in his fingers, holding $100 bills against his starched oxford shirt (caption: "He loves paper"). As Wenner told Studs Terkel, "I wonder if the American Dream is as ugly as Hunter Thompson said it is."

In politics, there was little for Wenner or the *Rolling Stone* righteous to support. When Wenner threw a campaign party for Ted Kennedy's losing bid for the Democratic nomination against incumbent Jimmy Carter, it was a faint echo of the Carter campaign blowout of 1976. Party guest Walter Isaacson, then a twenty-eight-year-old writer for

Time magazine, summed it up: "Four years ago *Rolling Stone* was at its height. They'd hit politics and Gonzo journalism with Hunter Thompson, and people were waiting in the streets to get into the party. But now, how much can you write about new wave and punk, and whether or not the Bee Gees are going to be the new Beatles? It's hard to be serious about rock music. What *Rolling Stone* could do four years ago they can't do today."

Even Mick Jagger seemed resigned. As he told *Rolling Stone* in August 1980, "There is no future in rock and roll. It's only recycled past." And *Rolling Stone* proved his point in the same issue by publishing an interview with Tom Wolfe, who told the backstory to *The Right Stuff,* originally serialized in *Rolling Stone* in 1973, and discussed *The Electric Kool-Aid Acid Test,* which starred *Rolling Stone* contributor Ken Kesey and Wenner's college crush at Berkeley, Denise Kaufman.

Rock-and-roll music—"and the things and attitudes that music embraces"—had lost its grip on power, making Wenner's agenda uncertain. In 1981, Wenner would say that rock and roll, as a subject, had been "encroached upon" by the establishment, including network TV, which now covered Rolling Stones ticket sales on the evening news. "The territory we're in," said Wenner, "the thing that no one else is touching—rock, youth, drugs, a population shift, the whole consequence of the postwar baby boom, which everyone else ignored—now everyone is doing it."

But for every step he took from rock and roll, Wenner endangered the identity of his enterprise. The past was the past—until it wasn't. There was a sense of cultural depletion in the air as well as political purgatory. In advance of the 1980 election, *Rolling Stone* offered the tepid essay titled "Voting Without Retching: Beyond the Lesser of Two Evils" and carrying the tagline "What to Do If You Can't Stand Jimmy Carter or Ronald Reagan." On November 4, 1980, California Republican Ronald Reagan defeated Carter to become the fortieth president of the United States, promising to "Make America Great Again"—a national gut response to Carter's weak handling of an Iranian hostage crisis but also a moralistic rejoinder to the aimless decadence that Wenner wrote about in Pigozzi's book and the economic stagnation that was eating into *Rolling Stone*'s bottom line. The hammer was coming down on the 1960s, and Wenner's magazine had little to offer the afflicted: After the November election, the covers of *Rolling Stone* featured Mary Tyler Moore, for her role in Paramount Pictures' *Ordinary People,* and Michael Douglas and co-star Jill Clayburgh in the forgotten romantic comedy *It's My Turn* (cover line: "Soooo sexy"). The photo was by Annie Leibovitz (white background), the story by Jean Vallely, daughter-in-law of Katharine Graham. Surely Ralph Gleason was rolling in his grave.

For the coming year, Wenner wanted—needed—a complete relaunch of *Rolling Stone* for a new era. His plan was to complete the final conversion to the "slick" he had dreamed of since 1967, a traditionally shaped magazine with a staple binding and semigloss paper stock on which auto advertisers would pay a premium to display their wares. "The thrust of all manufacturing changes from 1967 to date—size, color, staple, paper quality, etc.—have been in this direction," Wenner wrote in a 1980 memo. "It will break down the remaining advertiser resistance to *Rolling Stone.*"

Wenner promised that Straight Arrow would be a $100 million company by 1985.

On Mick Jagger's advice, Wenner planned to return a hippie curl to the *R* in the *Rolling Stone* logo, starting with the first issue of 1981—an homage to its San Francisco roots, though also a faint echo of the Coors beer logo. In an equally symbolic act, Wenner would remove the Oxford border from the cover and let photographs run naked to the edges of the magazine. Inside, Wenner wanted to reshape *Rolling Stone* as a more upscale, general-interest magazine that no longer depended on music. Wenner told Harriet Fier if she could sell 400,000 copies on the newsstand for three issues in a row, she could put whomever she wanted on the cover with no interference from him or Jim Dunning. She couldn't do it, and Wenner fired her. Before she left, however, Fier recommended Wenner replace her with Terry McDonell, a former editor at *Outside.* A man of romantic machismo that would have made Grover Lewis proud, McDonell was living in Montana and finishing his novel, *California Bloodstock.* He told Wenner he thought *Rolling Stone* was a broken record, far too self-referential and predictable. "The bottom had fallen out of the music business," McDonell said. "It just wasn't very interesting. The Cars were the biggest band. The Police were on the cover and they didn't sell."

He would relegate music to the back of the magazine, remove the same old bylines from the covers, bring in heavy hitters like Larry McMurtry and Richard Price, and give *Rolling Stone* the muscular profile of *Esquire*. "It wasn't a new philosophy," said McDonell. But it seemed to reanimate Jann Wenner, who paid for McDonell to move to New York and start with the January 1981 issue of *Rolling Stone*.

On a mild evening in December, Jann Wenner sat at his desk on East Sixty-Sixth Street, satisfied with his place in the universe. He could see just over the horizon of the 1980s. Ronald Reagan promised to lower his taxes; that wasn't too bad. And problem child Annie Leibovitz had managed to turn in her latest assignment, though Wenner chose Dick Avedon's cover photo—Dolly Parton in a Santa suit—over hers. As usual, Jane Wenner was curled up in bed upstairs, the latest episode of *Lou Grant* blinking in the background with the sound shut off (the episode was about Grant's newspaper getting sued for libel). Maybe Jane was drawing. Maybe Jane was reading a magazine. It didn't matter. But sometime after 11:00 p.m., she casually peered up and saw a breaking news alert on the TV screen. She pressed a button to call downstairs. "Jann," came her disembodied voice through the apartment intercom, "put the TV on and see what's happening."

He flicked on the television. John Lennon was dead.

BOOK III

It's Only Rock and Roll

18

Get Back

After five years in the wilderness, John Lennon was finally coaxed out of hiding by David Geffen, who after selling Asylum Records and trying to become a Hollywood producer had decided to start another label because, as he told *Rolling Stone,* "the record business seems pretty fucked. People are doing it badly, and I think I can do it better." The second record issued by Geffen Records, after Donna Summer, was *Double Fantasy,* an intimate new album by John Lennon and Yoko Ono. It was Geffen who arranged for the couple to sit down with *Rolling Stone.* "I convinced Yoko that it was a good thing for *Double Fantasy,*" said Geffen. "She wanted the album to be number one."

Jann Wenner assigned the interview to Jonathan Cott, the Berkeley alum whose conversation style was as intellectually supple as it was astoundingly reverent. (Cott was one of Jane Wenner's most ardent devotees before depression overtook him and he underwent shock treatment in the 1990s.) This was Lennon's third interview for the release of *Double Fantasy,* and Jann Wenner wasn't happy that he had given *Playboy* the exclusive. In an unpublished portion of the interview, Lennon explained to Cott, "We would have done it in *Rolling Stone,* only [Wenner] shit on me with *Lennon Remembers* and put a book out after I asked him not to, but you know—so *Playboy* got it."

Lennon still remembered. But he was more sanguine now: This was strictly a transaction for selling records, with no pretense of friendship. "I know Jann is always looking for an angle, and when you listen to this, Jann, don't be dumb, because life goes on," he told Cott. "We have a product to sell, just the same as you've got a *Rolling Stone* to sell."

At one point, Cott told Lennon that Jann Wenner wanted to know what his apartment looked like at the Dakota. (Wenner had been tracking the couple's real estate since the 1960s. Reporting on the $100,000 sale of their twenty-seven-room mansion in Surrey, England, in 1969, *Rolling Stone* described everything they left behind, including a painted piano and various things Yoko Ono had sawed in half for art projects, like half a shoe.) At this, Lennon leaned into the microphone to talk to Wenner for the last time. He pronounced his name *Jan:*

> The carpet's the same, Jan, it's exactly the same carpet. Where it's got fretted and torn, we replaced it with a not as good one, because we can't get the same one. The white piano is the same one from the *Imagine* movie and the one that's in the white room, so it's basically white. Jan, it's just an apartment, not a house, alright? There's a TV in the bedroom, the same as I always have, and a record player and a tape deck. There's guitar and piano in most rooms, and that's about it, the only difference now is that there's a child and child's playroom and a lot of teddy bears and toys around the place, OK? So basically, it's the same as it was in Ascot, and Jan saw Ascot, and he can describe that. It's white.

Wenner assigned Annie Leibovitz to photograph Lennon, an homage to their original photo shoot, almost ten years to the day since the 1970 interview. Lennon received her with warmth. "It seems like old times," he told her. Leibovitz was overcome by emotion when she saw the cover of *Double Fantasy;* the image of John kissing Yoko on the lips, by Kishin Shinoyama, was a superb photograph, she said, similar to what she had wanted to do. Jann Wenner had only wanted John Lennon on the cover, but Lennon insisted Yoko be in the image or he wouldn't do it. "We're not selling Christ; we're selling our own product," he told Cott. "If they don't want the two of us, we're not interested." When

Leibovitz returned for a second session on Monday, December 8, 1980, Lennon virtually guaranteed that Wenner would go for it by taking his clothes off and lying on the floor with his body wrapped like a baby around Yoko Ono. Leibovitz had brought a drawing of this pose to show the couple—based "on a relaxed position that I'd had with someone," she said—and after she showed them a Polaroid of what they looked like, Lennon said she had captured their relationship exactly.

After Leibovitz left the Dakota, Lennon went to the Record Plant recording studio to listen to playbacks of a new Yoko Ono single, a disco track he wanted Geffen to promote called "Walking on Thin Ice." When John and Yoko returned home that evening, they were shadowed by a fan named Mark David Chapman, who had solicited an autograph from Lennon earlier that day and shook hands with five-year-old Sean. Chapman was a chubby fanboy obsessed with J. D. Salinger's *The Catcher in the Rye* and struggling with an overpowering desire to kill John Lennon. As Lennon entered the Dakota at 10:50 that Monday night, Chapman approached Lennon from behind with a .38 pistol in his fist. Expressionless, he got down, pointed the gun at John Lennon's back, and snapped off five bullets. Lennon lurched around, a horror-stricken look on his face, then crumpled to the ground, glasses shattered and blood pooling around his body.

•

TEN YEARS, six months, and 272 issues of *Rolling Stone* separated Jann Wenner and John Lennon from the movie theater in San Francisco, the day John Lennon wept seeing Paul McCartney sing from the roof of Apple Records. In the death of Lennon, the two irreconcilable halves of Jann Wenner met. Having drifted so far from the origins of his newspaper, he collapsed back into himself—back through the long, strange 1970s, back to the lotus flower of 1967, the nose and glasses that adorned the first issue of his young rock-and-roll newspaper. Shocked and grief-stricken, Wenner stayed up all night making phone calls to friends, trying to make sense of it like everyone else. He called David Geffen. He called Greil Marcus. He even called Jean Gleason, wife of Ralph. In the early hours of the next morning, he had his driver take him to the west side of Central Park, where he got out and mingled with other fans singing "Give Peace a Chance." According to Wenner, a reporter for the *Daily News* approached him and asked who he was. Wenner said he replied, "Just a fan."

Terry McDonell, editing his first issue as editor of *Rolling Stone,* argued with Wenner over whether to include detailed reporting on the killer. Wenner ordained that not a single word about Mark David Chapman would appear in the issue (it was emotionally "too hard," he told McDonell). Death seemed to expose Wenner entirely. "Every hour, Jann would just break into tears," said Howard Kohn, who returned from writing his book on Karen Silkwood to help with the issue.

The magazine still planned to use Leibovitz's photo. But the next day, Ono called *Rolling Stone* saying she wanted to see the image before it was published. When Leibovitz arrived at the Dakota, Ono was lying in bed, alone in the dark. "I brought it into her room," said Leibovitz. "And she said, 'Annie, just take this picture, just do what you want with it and go buy yourself a loft or a photo studio or something.' And I said, 'Thank you, but no, I'm not going to do that,' and we just made it the cover of *Rolling Stone. Life* magazine wanted to make it the cover, and I wouldn't sell it to them."

Afterward, Ono's lawyers tried stopping the release of the photo, but Ono intervened. They could use it, but only in *Rolling Stone.* And Jann Wenner agreed. That week, Wenner was a sought-after interview, and he gave only one, to Jane Pauley, co-host of NBC's *Today Show,* a social friend whom Wenner had assigned Frank Rich to profile. Wenner insisted on taping the interview in his office at *Rolling Stone.* He looked pasty and haggard, shirt open at the collar, eyes darting around nervously as he drank a Diet Sunkist. "The only way I can draw a parallel is when John Kennedy was shot in the same senseless fashion," said Wenner. "The Beatles and Jack Kennedy were intimately connected . . . Part of the reason the Beatles were so big is that after John Kennedy was shot, I mean, people's hopes were destroyed and the Beatles came along and replaced John Kennedy as a symbol of hope for young people in this country and around the world."

PAULEY: You knew him personally, what was he like?
WENNER: He was warm. He was very witty. Very funny. He had it

all, there was a lot of contradictions in him, but one thing he never was, he never hurt anybody. He wasn't a mean person in any way. He may have carried on, but he was never mean. Basically, I think, full of hope.

It was this interview, according to Wenner, that inspired Ono to reach out to him a few days after Leibovitz's visit. It was the first time they'd spoken since 1971. "Yoko called me," says Wenner, "and said she wanted to see me." Wenner took a town car to the Dakota, where a police line still ringed the sidewalks. He took the elevator to the seventh floor and found Ono sitting alone with Sean. "We start talking it all through," Wenner recalled. "She's telling me the story of what happened that night, constantly repeating it, reliving it. And she was talking about her and John and what they were planning to do. And at that time, [David] Geffen was a big figure in their life because he had just put out *Double Fantasy*. And so he was helping her with the business stuff, and I was helping her—you know, just listening. There's nothing to do except listen and be her friend."

The meeting, said Wenner, "had a huge impact on me. Huge." During his visit, Wenner promised Ono he would take care of her from there on out. And he would do it in the pages of *Rolling Stone*. For the first issue of the Reagan presidency, Wenner put the image of John Lennon wrapped around Yoko Ono on the cover without any text other than the logo. Every page was dedicated to John Lennon, with essays and remembrances from Greil Marcus and Mick Jagger. In the correspondence column was a reproduction of a typed letter from Yoko, in all caps, describing the very moment she told Sean that his father had been killed. "I took Sean to the spot where John lay after he was shot," she said. "Sean wanted to know why the person shot John if he liked John. I explained that he was probably a confused person."

"Now Daddy is part of God," she quoted Sean saying. "I guess when you die you become much more bigger because you're part of everything."

On the same page was an anguished letter from Diane von Furstenberg, who wondered what had happened to their once-hopeful generation. They had become decadent and disconnected from their 1960s idealism, relinquished their values to the reactionary political order that coincided with Lennon's death. "Some of us—the survivors— joined the establishment and became successful, but what kind of success?" she wrote. "Our selfish success achieved recognition and made money—plenty of it. Our stomachs got fuller, rounder, our apartments more comfortable, our children more spoiled. What happened to our goals to change the world? Did we fight in '68 for the Eighties to give us Ronald Reagan?"

Wenner's favorite piece was by Scott Spencer, author of the book *Endless Love*, which became the 1981 movie starring teen sex symbol Brooke Shields. Spencer's elegy echoed Wenner's allusion to John F. Kennedy. "It was, of course, like the Sixties again, waking up, hearing of his death," Spencer wrote. The back page of *Rolling Stone* featured a letter from Wenner, who wrote, "I feel older now. Something of being young has been ripped out of me—something I thought was far behind me." But Wenner's tribute to Lennon didn't end on the last page. Inside the seam of 1.5 million copies of the magazine, hidden in the binding where the pages were stapled together, Wenner published a private message to John Lennon reproduced from his own handwriting. His original words, written by Wenner in blue ink, were scrawled on an envelope for Jann S. Wenner Motion Pictures.

> I love you. I miss you. You're with God. I'll do what I said. "Yoko, hold on"—I'll make sure, I promise.
>
> XXX

The message could only be read with a magnifying glass. When Ono read it, she cried. But she also had to decide if Wenner's sentiment was genuine. They'd been down this road before. "That little writing did help," she said. "And I think you can take it in two ways. He's a very sharp, clever guy. He might have wanted to say that so I could notice it, or he really meant it. And I think he really meant it."

The January 22, 1981, issue of *Rolling Stone* was Jann Wenner's single greatest triumph as a magazine editor and a sculptor of rock legend.

It was an homage to a man but also to a time and to a generation. As a cultural marker, it was not only the official end of the Beatles, or even the possibility of the Beatles, but the end of the first life of *Rolling Stone*. Leibovitz said the cover image was the photograph she would be remembered for ("the photograph of my life," she called it). And Ono said Lennon's legend survived in part because of that issue of *Rolling Stone*. "I think that thing *Rolling Stone* did about John was rather truthful and daring," Ono said. "It was at the edge of whether it's going to be bad for him or good for him. But at the same time, it was good.

"There was no other magazine that did that," she said. "That's one of the reasons John's image survived. The strength of his image was the fact that he had both sides."

Another side, of course, was Yoko Ono. After the memorial issue, Wenner began policing the image of John Lennon in *Rolling Stone* like a zealous guardian. More than a mere dead rock star like Jim Morrison, whom Wenner mocked in 1981 with the infamous cover line "He's Hot, He's Sexy, and He's Dead," Wenner would turn John Lennon into a sacred figure and a political cause. In early 1981, he assigned Howard Kohn to write an investigative story on the National Rifle Association, called "Inside the Gun Lobby," which Wenner made into a statement by starting the story on the cover of the magazine with an inset image of John Lennon by Annie Leibovitz. The attempted assassination of President Ronald Reagan in March 1981 brought the gun-control issue fully to the forefront of the nation, and Wenner had hoped to make the Kohn article serve as the set piece for a new antigun lobby called the Foundation on Violence in America. The story was too inconclusive to be persuasive, and nobody talked about it. Nonetheless, Wenner began giving speeches expressing his heartbreak over the death of "my friend" John Lennon as he conscripted Barry Diller, Gil Friesen, and Michael Douglas to join his board of directors. He solicited money and advice from friends, sparking the usual transactions: Irving Azoff promised $10,000 and then dragged his feet sending a check; Carly Simon, on the cover of *Rolling Stone* in December 1981 (she called "begging me to be on the cover," according to Wenner), donated $10,000 two months later. Hunter Thompson snarled, "Why would we take up a collection to make the streets safe for you and Barry Diller? No wonder Terry [McDonell] looks at you 'kind of funny' if you hang around the office spouting this kind of flakey liberal bullshit."

In 1981, Wenner hired pollster Peter Hart to conduct a gun-control survey, but the results, which cost Wenner $75,000, again didn't provide a clear headline. It did, however, find that police officers were the most trusted messengers on handgun control. So Wenner hired Betsy Gotbaum, a Manhattan activist who was head of the New York Police Foundation, to run the group, which they renamed National Alliance Against Violence. Michael Douglas taped a PSA for police presentations, and Gotbaum held fund-raising galas and theater performances, starting with one by a young Whoopi Goldberg.

Wenner would spend four years trying to convert himself into a political organizer in the wake of John Lennon's death. But it was destined to be another boondoggle, as naive as it was well intentioned, though it earned him social cachet in Manhattan, bringing him into the orbit of Oscar de la Renta and the like. In the mid-1980s, Wenner clashed with Gotbaum over the direction of the group. The two fought bitterly and the group dissolved in acrimony over money.

In the interim, Wenner collaborated with Jackie Onassis to publish a book called *The Ballad of John and Yoko,* a compendium of interviews, essays, and reportage on the couple, including excerpts from *Lennon Remembers* and the *Rolling Stone* memorial issue. (May Pang was mentioned once, referred to as a "friend.") By this time, Ono had changed her mind about the use of the Leibovitz images, telling the photographer she wanted her late husband to "be remembered with the best possible photographs," according to Robert Pledge, Leibovitz's agent, and urged her to syndicate them. In the book's introduction, Wenner stated that Lennon was the most important Beatle—"not only the largest part of the foursome," he wrote, "but also something that could not be contained within the group; and finally, something that could not be contained within himself."

This was an echo of Ono's quotation from the 1971 *Rolling Stone* interview in which she said John's talent was held back by the Beatles. For the next several decades, Ono and Wenner would collaborate to make John Lennon the only Beatle who mattered. For *Rolling Stone,* it was the official position—Wenner's promise to Ono.

I'll do what I said.

This promise did not go unobserved. "Once John got murdered, he became the martyr, the Buddy Holly, the James Dean character," said Paul McCartney. "A revisionism started to go on, and Yoko certainly helped it. Now John was it. He was it in the Beatles. He was the force behind the Beatles; he'd done it all. I just booked the studio."

"Because of that climate," he said, "Jann was not sort of the favorite."

Ten months after Lennon's death, Wenner put Yoko Ono on the cover of *Rolling Stone* for her new solo LP (with Lennon's shattered glasses on the front) with a photo spread of Ono and Sean Lennon by Annie Leibovitz. "It was clear to me that this cover was personally very important to Jann, and Jane, too," said David Rosenthal, who edited the piece, "and it was the most precise attention he had paid to any cover package in some time."

The Wenners moved to the West Side of Manhattan in 1987, right around the corner from Ono, and became frequent dinner companions. They bonded over the subject that Lennon had shrewdly tweaked Wenner about in the 1980 interview: interior decorating. After Lennon's death, Ono became lovers with the couple's personal decorator, Sam Havadtoy, a Hungarian émigré who met John and Yoko when they were shopping for Egyptian furniture in a shop he ran with his partner on the Upper East Side of Manhattan. Havadtoy had a male lover before Ono, and he would have male lovers after her, but he became her companion for twenty years. The Wenners hired Havadtoy to decorate their new townhouse. Havadtoy said Wenner and Ono had a lot in common. "They're both crazy people," he said.

Havadtoy became part of the Wenners' lives, a sidekick to Jane as she bought expensive carpets and beds for every room. "Jane had a constant desire to have a bed everywhere, a daybed, a chaise," said Havadtoy, "and Jann didn't take to that so freely." Wenner would get mad when Havadtoy encouraged Jane to spend too much on carpets, but over dinner the Wenners learned the secrets of the Beatles kingdom from Ono, who would often suggest to Wenner that John Lennon was gay. "She's always hinted that there was some gay component to John," said Wenner, "but in a vague or generalized way, like, 'Isn't everybody gay?' Or, 'I always told John he was gay.'" (She also told McCartney this theory after Lennon died, which he didn't believe.)

Wenner became Ono's stalwart defender, her social walker, her mythologizer in chief. In the late 1980s, he even accompanied Ono to Moscow to meet Soviet leader Mikhail Gorbachev and later to Buckingham Palace for a private reception with the queen.

Ono and Jane Wenner also became friends. At Ono's fiftieth birthday party in 1983, she and Jane scandalized guests when they disappeared into the bathroom together. "Jane and I were so bored," said Ono. "We went to the bathroom and were in there for a long time, and when we came out, so many people were looking at us. Like, oh my God . . ."

Ono had an intimate view into the marriage of Jann and Jane. "I think that it is incredible that Jane survived in that relationship," she said. "She did. That is because Jane is a super-clever woman. But you see, I think it is unfair to say that she is a super-clever woman; she was also very honest. Very truthful, and an extremely emotional person.

"From Jann's point of view," she added, "it was like a sweet daughter or something."

In 1988, a writer named Albert Goldman published a massive biography called *The Lives of John Lennon,* which chipped away at the hagiography surrounding the Beatle to recast him as a closeted homosexual who was filled with rage and might have once beaten a man to death in Hamburg in the early 1960s. The book—which relied on twelve hundred interviews and was dedicated to Goldman's friend Max Palevsky—opened with a scene of Ono's drug dealer delivering her daily dose of heroin to the Dakota. Goldman's biography was widely attacked by friends and fans, including Paul McCartney, who protested that Lennon was not gay. Seven years earlier, Wenner had published a sizable excerpt of Goldman's previous biography of Elvis Presley, a lurid account of his excesses called "The Party Years." But now Wenner launched a frontal attack—"Imaginary Lennon: The True Story Behind Albert Goldman's Character Assassination of John Lennon," by David Fricke and Jeffrey Ressner—which attempted to discredit Goldman's sources, especially Ono's personal assistant, Fred Seaman, who had stolen Lennon's diaries from the Dakota and tried selling them to Wenner before being sued by Ono. The *Rolling Stone* story quoted Ono liberally. "It's as if somebody had just punched me 800 times," she said.

But Ono also perceived that the church of John Lennon would easily survive the assault. "In the big picture, it's a house of cards," she said about Goldman's book. "It's doomed to fail."

She was right. *Rolling Stone* followed up its story with a chorus of reader mail expressing horror and disgust at Goldman's book (though one reader pointed out that "both of you . . . end up capitalizing on the whole thing"). Wenner later published a comic illustration of Goldman in a year-end portfolio titled "Rogues Gallery," wherein a pallid-faced Goldman is depicted scribbling in his notebook over the skeletal remains of John Lennon in a coffin. Though the *Rolling Stone* debunking of *The Lives of John Lennon* was itself largely debunked by *Newsweek,* the book was indeed destined to be forgotten in the fog of biographies and remembrances. The memory of John Lennon, the working-class hero and 1960s icon, was an industry—in which Wenner was the central player—inspiring dozens of books between 1980 and 2017, including Jonathan Cott's *Days That I'll Remember: Spending Time with John Lennon and Yoko Ono* and reprints of Jann Wenner's *Lennon Remembers,* which in 2000 included a foreword by none other than Yoko Ono.

The death of John Lennon was the end of the Beatles, but it was the beginning of Jann Wenner as keeper of the rock-and-roll myth. The *Rolling Stone* version of history—in biweekly issues and *Rolling Stone*–branded picture books, anthologies, and televised anniversary specials—was carefully shaped by Jann Wenner. He was the fame maker but also the flame keeper. The success and power of *Rolling Stone* made him the de facto architect of rock's cosmology, but it was his attention to the *legends* that made him the indispensable man.

And for his efforts on behalf of John Lennon, Ono would knight Jann Wenner with the ultimate celebrity honor: She made him the godfather of John Lennon's son Sean.

19

We Don't Need Another Hero

Before John Lennon was shot, Wenner had considered selling *Rolling Stone* to publisher Bill Ziff, of Ziff Davis, who wanted to give control of the magazine to his rock-fan sons. In truth, Wenner didn't really want to sell, only to learn what he was worth: roughly $12 million. He savored the number and backed out.

After Lennon's death, Jim Dunning, who left for Wall Street in 1982, couldn't get Wenner interested in anything that didn't involve *Rolling Stone* magazine, not even an *Entertainment Tonight*–style TV program produced by Paramount and green-lighted by Barry Diller.

This new conservatism partly explains why Wenner had such a negative reaction when he met a former radio programmer with a glass eye named Bob Pittman, who had started a nascent cable TV outlet that aired nothing but music videos. Music Television was part of a cable operator called Warner-Amex, a joint venture between Warner Communications and American Express, and it had been launched with enormous fanfare. Over lunch at Mr. Chow's in 1982, Wenner and Pittman circled each other "like two dogs sniffing in the pen," recalled Jim Dunning. "I just thought it was bullshit," Wenner said. "I thought, 'Oh well, it's just another version of *American Bandstand.*'"

Whether Wenner understood it or not, MTV signaled a fundamental shift in how the record companies would market music, the dawn of the age of the music video as the driver of rock-and-roll image and success. Commercials as art forms—it was an ingenious stroke, and it would become a revolution not only in marketing but in music fandom. MTV wouldn't replace the cover of *Rolling Stone* as the quintessential rock-and-roll moment, but it would turn it into a victory lap rather than the main event. And the differing cultures and sensibilities of MTV and *Rolling Stone* would come to define a generational fault line. Wenner had abandoned much of the 1960s dream, but parts of it remained, and these parts anchored him in the past. "In our politically correct view of what rock and roll should be, and my view of what is hip and not hip, this is the worst!" Wenner recalled thinking. "This is really slicking it up, and I didn't care for it at all. On that basis, I had disdain for it and didn't want to see that vision of rock and roll proceed or succeed."

Wenner was far from the only skeptic. It was hard to see the future in 1981, and cable TV was populated with more losers than winners. But what Wenner really disliked about MTV wasn't the videos; it was that he didn't control it. Two months after MTV launched in August 1981, Wenner had asked a Warner-Amex executive named Ken Lerer to draw up a plan for a competing channel. He asked Lerer in a letter to "make some well-researched and well-thought out preliminary recommendations regarding your enthusiastic theorizing about a music cable service." Feeling Wenner misunderstood their conversations, Lerer wrote back to say he had no idea how to write a business plan and suggested Wenner go back to Pittman and "try to close a deal with Music television. It's going to be a tremendous success."

Said Lerer, "I think what I was writing to him, in a friendly way, is, 'Hey, schmuck, this is your business, and if you give it up, shame on you, because you should own it.'"

Within two years, MTV was one of the highest-rated cable channels on television, and Michael Jackson was the biggest star in the world with his MTV-driven *Thriller* album, produced by Quincy Jones. When Walter Yetnikoff of CBS tried to get Wenner to put Jackson on the cover for *Thriller,* Wenner said, "I rarely put R&B acts on the cover," and he didn't. (He had already put Jackson on the cover in 1971, when Jackson was twelve.) It would go down as a legendary failure of vision, but it was part of a conservative *Rolling Stone* worldview in which Kurt Loder regularly favored bands like Big Country and Dire Straits, whose musical DNA was in the 1970s, over MTV stars like Madonna and Human League. That worldview was also exceedingly white, as Miles Davis noted: "I like that magazine, but the last time I saw it they had all white guys in it. How about Kool and the Gang? Earth, Wind and Fire?"

But Wenner was content to defend his turf. In December 1981, he wrote one of his last stories of the decade, "Time Is on My Side," another ode to the Rolling Stones. The new bands, Wenner wrote, were "full of promise" but had yet to be "tested." "Rock and roll is here to stay," wrote Wenner, "if you want it. The Rolling Stones clearly want it, and—judging from the success of their tour—so do we all."

The occasion was the Stones' tour that became the movie *Let's Spend the Night Together,* directed by 1970s auteur Hal Ashby (*Harold and Maude*), which marked the last period of genuine relevance for the band. It was also around this time that Wenner and Jagger finally drew up a six-page legal agreement delineating the use of the trademark in licensing products and services with the words "Rolling" and "Stone(s)" in the name. "We would have had a conflict of interest if he wanted '*Rolling Stone* Magazine Perfume,'" explained Jagger, by way of example, "and you can see why that's unfair and that might impact us. That's where these things can go wrong."

For Wenner, the stone no longer rolled; it stood like a statue to a glorious past. Rock was ossifying into monumental cultural history and lucrative nostalgia. The radio genre "classic rock" first emerged in 1980, and the Hard Rock Cafe, a theme restaurant festooned with old guitars and shrunken stage outfits, began expanding into an international chain in 1982, setting the template for a 1960s memorabilia market. That same year, a cable TV entrepreneur named Bruce Brandwen, who produced Frank Sinatra performances for Jerry Lewis telethons, dreamed up the Rock and Roll Hall of Fame to celebrate the pioneers of the music as a pay-per-view program.

Clive Davis at Arista was alarmed that Wenner was abandoning the promotion of new artists, cautioning Wenner about "the R.S. trend away from music . . . It sure worries me." While Wenner trained the magazine on actors and old rock stars, he forbade any major story on

MTV, the elephant in his room, to be published in *Rolling Stone*. "Jann was concerned that MTV was going to hurt the magazine," said David Rosenthal, who replaced Terry McDonell as managing editor in 1983 after McDonell left for *Newsweek*. When Wenner finally bent, the story—"Inside MTV: The Selling Out of Rock and Roll"—was a frontal attack on the network, characterizing MTV as a shameless attempt to hit the "post-Woodstock generation's lurking G-spot."

"MTV is perfect for a generation never weaned from television," scolded journalist Steven Levy, who characterized music videos as shallow and even morally reprehensible:

> Sexual fantasies blend with toothless gossip about a rock community that really does not exist, having dissipated maybe a decade ago. It doesn't matter. There are no dissenting opinions or alternative views telecast on MTV. Profit-making television creates an unreal environment to get people into what is called "a consumer mode."

On the other hand, Wenner, in typical bipolar fashion, was not about to lose sight of any commercial G-spot. Before *Rolling Stone* published its MTV takedown, he realized it was more opportunity than enemy and had commanded his business managers to prepare an immediate and total makeover of *Rolling Stone* with the express purpose of exploiting MTV for "subscription deals, edit coverage, other tie-ins and so forth." "This is a golden, framed, window of opportunity, which will pass if we don't act soon," he wrote in April 1983. "Our credibility with record advertisers, newsstand sales, and edit success will all be greatly enhanced by proper use and understanding of the MTV breakthrough."

Within two years, every hit maker on MTV would appear on the cover of *Rolling Stone,* including Michael Jackson, Cyndi Lauper, Boy George, the Go-Go's, and Huey Lewis and the News. Far from losing out on "the MTV breakthrough," Wenner was going to exploit the new star factory for all it was worth, drafting behind MTV's momentum and collecting the music industry advertising that piled up in its wake.

In 1984, Pittman took Jann and Jane Wenner to the Quilted Giraffe, the most expensive restaurant in Manhattan, to discuss the obvious— a merger. The deal on offer was this: MTV would buy *Rolling Stone* in exchange for 25 percent of the company. Wenner enjoyed his meal. "I wsan't going to sell *Rolling Stone* to anybody," he said, adding ruefully, "the first of many bad strategic business decisions."

Pittman said that if Wenner had taken the MTV deal, "Jann would probably own about a third of MTV, which was worth more than *Rolling Stone*." But he understood why Wenner turned it down. "At that point in Jann's life, Jann was not a guy who spent a lot of time sucking up to anybody," he said. "So he was brutal and in your face."

By the mid-1980s, *Rolling Stone* would be making its own videos— subscription ads on MTV featuring late night bandleader Paul Shaffer and another with forgotten light-pop hit maker Richard Marx standing in neon lights and stage fog and talking about "the spirit of rock and roll": twenty-six issues for $17.95. "Maybe someday they'll even write an article about why rock stars have to stand in all this smoke," Marx cracked, coughing and waving away the fog with a copy of *Rolling Stone*.

•

AT DAVID GEFFEN'S FORTIETH BIRTHDAY at the Beverly Wilshire hotel in Hollywood, Wenner spent the evening commiserating with Diane von Furstenberg about his failed film career. Since 1978, Wenner had tried and tried to become a movie producer. He used to send Furstenberg's boyfriend Barry Diller long and rambling pitches seeking advice—What about *Alice in Wonderland* starring Gilda Radner? Or a Doors movie starring Matt Dillon (cover of *Rolling Stone*, 1982)?—but nothing panned out except copious partying with Don Simpson, the Paramount executive with whom Wenner once spent a weekend of heli-skiing and female prostitutes in Vancouver. (Simpson went on to success with *Flashdance* and *Top Gun,* then died of a drug overdose in 1996.) Wenner's closest shot at getting a movie made was a mistaken-identity script called *Going to the Chapel* ("a girl taxi driver and a young heir"), which was supposed to star Bette Midler. When her agent asked for too much money, Wenner tried getting Meryl Streep, but she also fell through. Sue Mengers, the sassy 1970s superagent, gave Wenner this advice: "So here's what we got to do: We'll get Penny Marshall to agree to it because she's renewing her contract with *Happy Days* at Paramount and she'll be forced to do it."

"And they wouldn't hear that either," lamented Wenner.

Furstenberg told him to give it up. "She took me aside," recalled Wenner, "and she said, 'Why are you doing this? There are fifty-five people around here who can produce movies; there's only one person who can do *Rolling Stone*. Do that. Stay with that.'"

Hollywood was Wenner's last stand after years of trying to expand himself beyond *Rolling Stone*, erratic misadventures that, like the anti-gun crusade, he later viewed as a big waste of time.

On March 5, 1982, John Belushi's naked body was discovered in a room of the Chateau Marmont in Los Angeles, dead from an over-dose of heroin and cocaine. The night before, he had been partying with Robert De Niro and Robin Williams until three in the morning. According to the female drug partner who was with him, his last words were "Just don't leave me alone."

She left shortly thereafter.

The post-1970s casualties were piling up. John Bonham of Led Zep-pelin. Lester Bangs. Mike Bloomfield. Art Garfunkel's girlfriend, the boyish cult actress Laurie Bird, who co-starred with Beach Boys' drum-mer Dennis Wilson in the 1971 film *Two-Lane Blacktop,* killed herself in Garfunkel's Manhattan apartment while he was acting in a movie being filmed in Europe. After Belushi, Dennis Wilson was next. On his way back from Belushi's funeral in Martha's Vineyard, Wenner fell ill to a gallbladder infection and was hospitalized. He had grown fat and unhealthy, bloated from alcohol and cocaine abuse, which exacerbated his psoriasis (and which Jane showed off to friends by pulling back his hair at a party to reveal his flaking scalp).

Wenner was deluged with get-well cards from celebrities like Jackie Onassis and Richard Gere ("I've reserved a racquetball court for Mon-day"). Wenner said it was Onassis who advised him to "avoid surgery." "I was there for two or three days and it suddenly cleared and I just walked out," he said.

Wenner would put all his get-well cards into a scrapbook he kept to collect party invitations, letters, photographs, and memorabilia. Over the years, these scrapbooks would become the physical evidence of the story Jann Wenner told about himself.

After Belushi's death, *Rolling Stone* published an oral history of the comedian's life. Carrie Fisher remembered Belushi locking her in a bathroom until she promised to cast him and Aykroyd in the next *Star Wars* sequel. Hunter Thompson declared, "John is welcome at my house, dead or alive." Dan Aykroyd refused to believe his partner had been a junkie—only a victim of a comedy experiment gone too far. "The Sixties and the Woodstock legacy applied a subcultural legitimacy to the consumption of drugs for both mind expansion and mind impairment," he told *Rolling Stone*. "John and, in fact, all of us from *Saturday Night Live* were participants in that new social phalanx. It was a touch of the hippie, the beatnik, the hipster that helped us to impart a weird, novel approach to our work." (He went on to suggest that something fishy had occurred because Belushi was afraid of needles and would, he said, never have shot himself up.)

After a drink at Elaine's, Wenner brought a draft of the Belushi story to Lorne Michaels's house, where Paul Simon read through it and discovered a gratuitous barb against Michaels from a former *SNL* writer. "How could you do this to your friend?" spat Simon. Recalled Michaels, "I was, in the meantime, dealing with John's family, the funeral, and all of that . . . Paul went, 'Jann, you're his friend, and you know this is not true, and this is a very vulnerable time for all of them, their friend just died.' Paul was pretty strong on my side. And Jann, that was it, he went and changed it."

But not without a fight: According to Wenner, he replied to Simon, "You're fucking thankless. After all these years, after all the wonderful reviews, you have never ever once said thank you. You are just an asshole!"

Wenner characterized the fight as two short, angry Jews yelling at each other. "And he stormed out of the place and drove back to his place in Montauk," said Wenner. "I was sorry. Next day, I called Paul and I apologized. It was kind of a breakthrough moment." (Simon declined to speak for this book.)

After the memorial issue, Wenner ran a more sordid account of Belushi's death at the Chateau Marmont, profiling the itinerant hanger-on who was with him before he died (she had started shooting smack while hanging out with the Rolling Stones). Belushi's mother, Agnes, wrote to excoriate Wenner, calling the story "a farce, a stab in the back." Wenner put the letter in his scrapbook.

Dan Aykroyd didn't hold the story against Wenner—"The guy died in an ignominious way, that's the truth"—but Wenner would later make a point of taking care of Belushi's widow, Judy. When Bob Woodward published *Wired,* the controversial 1984 biography detailing Belushi's drug addiction and penchant for cruelty, Wenner published a profile of Woodward by Lynn Hirschberg. Wenner allowed Judy Belushi, who felt betrayed by Woodward's bleak depiction of her late husband, to vet the story. "His theory was that Bob Woodward had gotten everything wrong and John Belushi was a terrific person and Bob didn't understand and was punishing Hollywood for his death," recounted Hirschberg, who was so "appalled" that she revealed Wenner's inside deal to Woodward, who leaked it to the press and howled that it was a sin against the "Holy Ghost" of journalism. (Hirschberg was horrified by her error, and Wenner punished her by making her profile Michael Douglas.)

The Wenners' marriage had also reached a crisis point. Jane Wenner was deep into pills, ensconced in her room, rarely venturing downstairs during Wenner's nightly bacchanals. When she did appear, in the last ragged hours of the party, it was to ask Jimmy Webb to sit at the piano and sing her favorite song, a ballad called "Just Like Always," a lament for a lost love.

> *Maybe someday I believe we'll forget*
> *I'll really learn to live again, I'll live without regret*

Wenner was desperate to get Jane, the muse of *Rolling Stone,* out of bed. And perhaps very desperate: According to Laurel Gonsalves, Jane showed her bruises she claimed were given to her by Jann. "The bruises on her thighs which Jane showed me were on a Polaroid, of course," she recounted. ("He might have grabbed me once," said Jane. "It was not Nicole Brown Simpson.") There were signs that Jane was suicidal. She left Wenner a note on March 28, 1980, bidding him take all her shares in Straight Arrow and give some family jewelry to her niece Megan.

(According to Wenner's calendar, he was in Aspen with David Geffen at the time.) Jackson Browne spent time with Jane during this period. "She was real messed up," he said. "I think she was making an attempt to commit suicide."

> WENNER: Yeah, she was really depressed. Potentially suicidal? Could be. Yeah. She was taking a lot of Quaaludes, which were depressants. She battled depression. She was very masochistic.
> JANE: Look, we had money, we had drugs available, and it was just the drama of drugs.

In 1982, Jane kicked Wenner out of the apartment on East Sixty-Sixth Street and consulted with a lawyer about a divorce. Neither Jann nor Jane could recall what sparked the separation, though Wenner said it was drug related. "Jackie [Onassis] was scheduled to come over with the kids and I had to call Jackie and say, 'I'm canceling dinner on you,'" he recalled.

It was during this period that Michael Douglas said he began to suspect Wenner had other sexual interests. "Let's just say I got a hint that there were other people involved in the marriage," he said. For a month, Wenner moved into an apartment in the West Village belonging to another *Rolling Stone* cover boy—Richard Gere, who first graced Wenner's magazine in March 1980 for Paramount Pictures' *American Gigolo* (cover line: "Stripped Down and Sexy") and again in 1982 for the cover story "Richard Gere Loosens Up," for Paramount's *An Officer and a Gentleman*. Wenner was infatuated with the actor, putting shirtless pictures of Gere from *People* magazine into his scrapbook. Chip Block, a member of *Rolling Stone*'s board of directors, recalled the two men in the back of a limousine on their way to see the 1981 film, *The Postman Always Rings Twice,* tittering over a much-ballyhooed sex scene showing Jack Nicholson's penis. "Jann and Richard were all about seeing if they could see a good view of Jack Nicholson's dick," recalled Block. "I didn't know exactly what to make of it."

At the time, Gere was dating Brazilian artist Sylvia Martins, but a rumor circulated that Gere and Wenner were having an affair, which overlapped with a malicious urban myth that Gere was once hospitalized for a kinky fetish involving a gerbil. Wenner said he was only subletting Gere's apartment while the actor shot a film. (Gere declined to speak for this book.) Wenner denied anything happened and said rumors of Gere's homosexuality derived from his role as a gay Holocaust victim in the 1979 Broadway play *Bent*. Asked if she ever confronted Wenner about the rumor, Jane said, "I probably did, I don't remember, all I know is he came back." Lawyer Ben Needell said Jane's divorce threat was never real and their reunion was inevitable: "I'm not sure anybody else could have dealt with either one of them."

Jane was not immune to affairs, but her motivations were different: to get Wenner's attention. "I would never let anyone get too close, because I was married and was in love with my husband," she said. "Was I aware of what Jann was doing? Not really. And when I asked, he wouldn't tell me."

But while Wenner was living in Gere's apartment, Jane was seen on the arm of David Geffen, who was infuriated with Wenner over a quotation he asked Wenner not to publish and that Wenner published anyway (when Geffen campaigned against music pirating on cassette tapes, Wenner published an old comment from Geffen saying he didn't care about it). Geffen accused Wenner of being in the pocket of the tape-manufacturing industry and vowed never to advertise in *Rolling Stone* again. "I never saw Jann as an ally," said Geffen. "It was too easy for Jann to tell you to go fuck yourself."

According to both Wenners, Geffen once told people he was having an affair with Jane. "He used to run around telling people he was sleeping with Jane," said Wenner. "But then [he] called up Jane and me and he apologized. 'I've been doing this and I've stopped. I was trying to be Mr. Macho.'"

Wenner took it personally. "But why my wife?" he wondered. "There were many people for him to try to humiliate in that little way, and he was trying to assert he wasn't gay." Recounted Jane, "His reaction was, 'Jane, you know I'm gay, I've always been gay. I was sitting around in a room with Artie Garfunkel and these people and I wanted to seem like, you know—so I said that.' He goes, 'You're not going to say anything, are you?'"

Wenner was reminded of the Paul Simon imbroglio—a supposed

friend pursuing Jane to hurt Jann Wenner. He ventured that these betrayals by Simon and Geffen had to do with "hatred among Jews. Maybe because I don't look Jewish, maybe they're pissed off. I'm just happier than both of them and have more fucking fun."

•

THE TENUOUS RELATIONSHIP BETWEEN Jann Wenner and Annie Leibovitz was now held together by the Brazilian art director Bea Feitler, the brilliant design consultant to *Rolling Stone* who imbued magazines like Gloria Steinem's *Ms.* with a pop sensibility. Under Feitler's tutelage, Leibovitz had come into her own as a portrait photographer, producing the stylized celebrity images she would come to be known for: Meryl Streep in geisha makeup; Liberace decked in furs and diamonds next to his chauffeur and lover, Scott Thorson; John Belushi and Dan Aykroyd as the Blues Brothers, faces painted blue (an image Leibovitz made to mock their self-importance and that Belushi hated so much he stopped speaking to her for six months). In addition to being creative partners, Leibovitz and Feitler were lovers. "When *Rolling Stone* moved to New York, Bea and Annie were sort of a secret," said Lloyd Ziff, a *Rolling Stone* photo editor in the mid-1970s. "I mean, it wasn't a secret from me, but nobody really talked about it."

But in April 1982, Feitler, a vivacious beauty with an infectious grin, died at age forty-four after a battle with cancer, a melanoma, leaving Leibovitz devastated and lost. Afterward, Leibovitz found it difficult to work without her teacher and muse. "I had no reason to work," she told David Felton. "Because she would really make the most mundane things seem as if they were very special and very exciting to do. She would whip me up."

Jann Wenner was still playing the role of aggrieved father to Leibovitz's hopeless teenager. She would bounce checks, and Wenner would refuse to send her royalties on her images until she paid off her debts. She still made brilliant images—the model Lauren Hutton, nude and covered in gooey mud—but she felt creatively uninspired without Feitler. Wenner and Leibovitz would disagree for the rest of their lives over what happened next. Wenner said her erratic behavior on drugs forced him to fire her. "I threw her out," he said. "I tried to get her to agree to a whole list of principles and things she would do. It was an uphill battle, and it was all costly. Her work was deteriorating. And we tried everything . . . it was a drug problem that exacerbated all her other problems. She was a junkie."

But Leibovitz said it was about money and control, not drugs. By then, she insisted, she'd gone to rehab in New Jersey and taken up jogging, encouraged by Feitler. And before her death, Feitler had redesigned the revival of *Vanity Fair* as a sophisticated pop-culture glossy, which offered Leibovitz more money and a new direction. Leibovitz said she offered to work for both magazines, but Wenner refused. It was *Rolling Stone* or nothing. "It wasn't about the drugs," she said. "[He] never said to me, 'You're all drugged out, let's call this a day.' He said, 'You can't be the photographer to both magazines.'" The Wenners felt betrayed. "I think they took it more personally than I did," she said, adding that the Wenners kept doing drugs long after she quit. "If it wasn't one drug with them, it was a different drug. Or drinking."

But Wenner never backed down from his version of events. When he repeated his drug claims for an *American Masters* documentary about Leibovitz for PBS in 2007, Leibovitz was so infuriated she exploded at the director, her sister Barbara Leibovitz, at a family gathering, tearfully complaining that she let Wenner talk too much.

Before she left, Jane Wenner helped Leibovitz put together a retrospective of her work called *Annie Leibovitz: Photographs,* a collection of her portraits of celebrities. It was a typically torturous experience for all involved—"Annie is once again on the warpath," Sarah Lazin wrote in a memo to Wenner—but it was a poignant capstone to a thirteen-year relationship that had made them all stars. The book was dedicated to Bea Feitler. Tom Wolfe wrote the introduction, calling the collection of images "a stiff whiff of the whole gloriously nutty era of Golden Funk."

But the era of Golden Funk had given way to something less funky—a harsh and deracinated new decade of money and celebrity. A critic, writing in 1983, noted that Leibovitz's late *Rolling Stone* work captured "the 60s generation gone to seed . . . Very few of her subjects are smiling; a far greater number seem diffident or exhausted." In December 1983, *Rolling Stone* ran a list of "the most overrated people in America," wherein the magazine separated the 1980s wheat from the 1970s chaff. Overrated were Jackson Browne, Gloria Steinem, Liza Minnelli, Quincy Jones (hot off producing *Thriller*), Joni Mitchell, Billy Joel, Linda Ronstadt, John Travolta, Nastassja Kinski (whose nude photos, published in *Rolling Stone,* Wenner hung in his office), and Andy Warhol, who ran into Wenner the week the article ran. "I said, 'Gee, Jann, you put down all your best friends in your article on "Overrated People,"'" he recorded in his diary. "And he said, 'Oh yeah, I made them take Gilda Radner off that list.' He didn't say a thing about me! And he's got a big pot belly and his hair is long again."

The story was the brainchild of David Rosenthal, a former *New York* magazine editor who brought a tabloid sensibility to *Rolling Stone* that came to embarrass Wenner. When he fired Rosenthal in the spring of 1984, replacing him with Bob Wallace, Wenner decided he needed to return to the values that had defined the magazine in the 1970s. Around the time of the Leibovitz book, Tom Wolfe told Wenner he wanted to write a social satire about life in the new go-go New York, modeled on Charles Dickens's nineteenth-century London, but he was suffering from writer's block. He hadn't published anything significant since *The Right Stuff* in 1979. Wenner suggested he take on biweekly deadlines to force himself to write his story about the fall of a wealthy stockbroker whose racially charged trial for vehicular manslaughter becomes a tragic media spectacle. Wenner suggested they publish it as an ongoing serial in *Rolling Stone.* "I knew that if I had to make a deadline, I could make a deadline," said Wolfe.

The Bonfire of the Vanities was Wolfe's fictional, ripped-from-the-headlines take on the divide between rich and poor at a time when the stock market was minting a new paradigm of social status, the Yuppie, in whose demographic profile Wolfe conceived his antihero, Sherman McCoy, a Wall Street trader and "Master of the Universe." McCoy's first appearance in the book is characterized by a description of his $3 million Park Avenue co-op—twelve-foot ceilings, marble floors, a walnut staircase. "It was the sort of apartment the mere thought of which ignites flames of greed and covetousness under people all over New York," wrote Wolfe, "and, for that matter, all over the world."

Wenner, who now wore pink shirts with suspenders, could relate to

Sherman McCoy, certainly more than to Wolfe's seamy journalist character, British tabloid reporter Peter Fallow, who according to Wenner was based on Anthony Haden-Guest. "We had such a laugh doing that," said Wenner. "We would curl up and giggle because he just nailed the guy."

Wolfe had hoped the first three chapters would buy him a month to write his next installment, but Wenner published them all at once, leaving Wolfe in a cold panic. "And talk about scrambling," said Wolfe. "I can remember this was one of the worst things I ever had to do." Wolfe spent the summer of 1984 in Southampton, not far from the Wenners' cottage, being tortured by a nearby church bell, the tolling of which reminded him of his deadline. "I would fall asleep at about ten in the evening, just from being so tired," he said. "And the next thing I knew, it was 'dong, dong,' and I would never go to sleep for the rest of the night."

Wenner published the first installment in July 1984, alongside profiles of MTV breakout stars the Thompson Twins and the Cars. Here was a complete vision of Wenner's 1980s *Rolling Stone:* one part MTV, one part 1960s *Rolling Stone,* a dash of left-wing polemic. In the same issue, the writer William Greider, Wenner's latest political columnist ("the conscience of *Rolling Stone* at the time," said Wenner), complained that "the party of the working class has turned its back on the poor"—a critique of the out-of-power Democrats clawing for influence in Ronald Reagan's Washington. *Bonfire,* for which Wolfe was paid nearly $200,000, ran for over twenty-six issues of *Rolling Stone* and acted like a kind of hedge against the pop culture that was actually selling *Rolling Stone.* Wolfe appeared inside covers featuring Prince and Madonna and Phil Collins, Cyndi Lauper and Bruce Springsteen (twice), and concluded in August 1985, abutting a story on Mel Gibson and Tina Turner in *Mad Max: Beyond Thunderdome.*

Wolfe once called Wenner his favorite editor. What he liked about him was that Wenner barely touched his copy. "I've never really seen him do any line editing," he said. "He would say, 'Okay, that's great,' or 'Do it over,' not giving much meaning in what he had to say. *We can't just change this around and just do it again!*"

Wenner said Wolfe's main problem was he didn't know how to end a story. "He was always ending abruptly," said Wenner. "They go on and on and on, and then in the last five chapters there's a rush to the ending."

Like "Post-orbital Remorse" in 1973, the series was a rough draft of a book. *The Bonfire of the Vanities,* wherein Wolfe declared Wenner "daring" for shoving him out on the high wire of *Rolling Stone* "without a safety net," was eventually published in 1987.

20

Purple Rain

I n 1985, Jann Wenner returned to Hollywood, but this time as a fictional character—his acting debut as Mark Roth, the editor of *Rolling Stone*.

The movie *Perfect,* starring John Travolta and Jamie Lee Curtis, was based on a *Rolling Stone* article by writer Aaron Latham called "Perfect! Coed Health Clubs Are the Singles Bars of the Eighties," which was something like Tom Wolfe's "Me Decade" reimagined for the aerobics craze. "If you perfect yourself, then you will be loved," wrote Latham of "Leslie," a woman remaking herself with plastic surgery and aerobics, "that is the important point. The reward for perfection is love. Perfect."

Deemed "overrated" two years before, Travolta was now playing a *Rolling Stone* reporter who falls in love with a sexy aerobics instructor played by Curtis. Jann Wenner was tapped to play a not-at-all-disguised version of himself (a role originally conceived for Richard Dreyfuss). Jane Wenner worried that he would make a fool of himself, but Travolta campaigned on his behalf, schmoozing her over dinner and inviting the Wenners to stay at his house in Isla Vista, California. For his screen test, Wenner moved into a penthouse at the Westwood Marquis in Hollywood, next door to Stevie Nicks, and the night before sought acting advice from Warren Beatty, who told him to talk slower, and from Michael Douglas, who told him to dial down his hand gestures.

Wenner bombed—"mugging," Travolta later said, "rolling his eyes"—but Travolta convinced director Jim Bridges to give him another shot and coached him to underact ("It's all in the eyes," he told him). Travolta was pleased with the results. He characterized Wenner's second screen test "one of the best I've ever seen . . . I've never seen a beast like this on celluloid before."

At least that's what he said in his "actor's notebook" that Wenner published in *Rolling Stone*.

Wenner's first day on the set was not fortuitous. Travolta's co-star in *Urban Cowboy,* actress Debra Winger, showed up at the Manhattan restaurant where they were shooting and started yelling at Wenner for bumping her from the cover of *Rolling Stone*. (She was supposed to appear alongside Richard Gere, her co-star in *An Officer and a Gentleman,* but Wenner only wanted Richard Gere.) Aaron Latham told writer Robert Draper she accused Wenner of "always fucking people in your magazine. You don't really fuck them—you just fuck them over. But you don't know the difference, do you?"

Recalled Wenner, "Debra Winger is a crazy bitch, and she's furious that Jim is using Jamie Lee Curtis instead of her after *Urban Cowboy* and all that. And she just takes off on me and says 'you can't act' and does everything she possibly can to upset me, an amateur actor on the first day."

Wenner was shaken but shot the scene anyway, with art imitating life as Carly Simon, playing herself, yelled about a negative story in *Rolling Stone*. The Mark Roth character was an accurate facsimile of Wenner, a peppy power broker who conducted rat-a-tat phone conversations with journalists while snapping the cuffs of his tuxedo for a society soiree. As one reviewer put it, "Wenner's fictional role is ruthless, bullying and totally inured to finer human feelings—Lou Grant in reverse—and *Rolling Stone* is shown as complicit in deception, muckraking and sabotaging innocent people's happiness."

Jane's concerns for Wenner's dignity were borne out in the final scene of *Perfect* when a decidedly chubby Wenner shimmied awkwardly in a roomful of aerobicized hard bodies, grinning like a delighted elf in a sleeveless *Rolling Stone* T-shirt. "I said, 'Jim, I just look too fat in this,'" recalled Wenner, "and he said, 'Jann, I told you three months ago and you had plenty of time.'" But one of Wenner's gifts was to be immune to embarrassment. This was a gang bang of self-promotion and celebrity hounding: The movie used the *Rolling Stone* logo's typeface to spell *Perfect,* was filmed on a set modeled to the last detail after the offices of *Rolling Stone,* and allowed Wenner to spend long days playing himself alongside a handsome actor with whom he was transparently infatuated. "He was out of Scientology during that period," recalled Wenner. "He was relaxed and adorable."

Bob Wallace recalled the staff's mortification at the movie screening. "Most of our jaws just dropped," he said. "It was so bad." He nonetheless put Travolta and Curtis on the cover of *Rolling Stone* in July 1985, featuring a profile of Jamie Lee Curtis; Travolta's "notebook" describing his studious attempts to impersonate a reporter; and an advertisement for a *"Perfect* Body Contest" in which the winner would receive a Bally fitness machine or the soundtrack of Thompson Twins and Wham! Travolta describes how he lingered around the offices of *Rolling Stone* for "research" and asked the staff to dish dirt on Jann Wenner: "They told me about Jann's insatiable appetite for food. 'He eats all day,' a New York accent said."

For a while, Wenner had high hopes for his future in film acting. While promoting the movie, he told *People* magazine, "Whatever movie [Travolta] does, I hope to be right there beside him." Afterward, rumors swirled that Wenner had an affair with John Travolta. Wenner denied it but said, "It occurred to me that he was completely gay because of the people around him," including director Jim Bridges. (After the movie, Travolta recommitted himself to Scientology, and Wenner said they rarely saw each other after that.)

When *Perfect* flopped at the box office, Wenner attempted to distance himself from the movie, offering this critique: "What I think is there's too much aerobics and not enough *Rolling Stone.* And the love story is not hot enough."

Wenner's film debut coincided with his acquisition of a new magazine—*US,* a celebrity biweekly started by the New York Times Company in 1977. Wenner's vision was a revival of his *Look* experiment from 1979. He advertised it as the "wide, wide world of what's hot," a full-color celebrity picture book that would eclipse *People,* which still published only black-and-white photography inside. The first issue under Wenner's management, with Cher on the cover ("an intimate *US* interview"), included a glowing capsule review of *Perfect* ("features some first-rate performances") and an introductory editorial note with a portrait of Wenner with his two Siberian huskies. The media world of Manhattan marveled at Wenner's naked self-promotion. "Should I say congratulations or let the buyer beware?" asked Bryant Gumbel of the *US* gambit in a snarky interview on NBC's *Today.* After needling Wenner about his performance in *Perfect,* Gumbel remarked that "somebody told me he's going to donate his ego to Harvard one day."

Wenner gave a pained smile.

At that same moment, the public-health catastrophe of AIDS had begun to lower the boom on the sexual revolution of the previous two decades, terrorizing gay men and ratcheting up homophobia in the culture. AIDS first appeared in *Rolling Stone* in 1983, when the magazine published "America's New Plague: Contagious Sexual Cancer," by B. D. Colen, which outlined the theories on how the disease spread, including the possibility of poor food handling. But already it was clear that the central driver was unprotected sex among gay men, "a phenomenon of the raunchy subculture in large cities, where bars and bathhouses are literal hotbeds of sexual promiscuity." A sidebar by writer Lindsy Van Gelder profiled two rock musician lovers, one of whom, Michael Callen, had AIDS. "AIDS raises the issue that everybody I know is struggling with," said his lover, Richard Dworkin, "the conflict between freedom and security." (Callen died in 1993, and the Callen-Lorde Community Health Center in Manhattan was dedicated to him.)

Wenner didn't remember the story. He said he first learned about AIDS in *The New York Times.* But starting in 1983, a *Rolling Stone* writer named David Black began a yearlong investigation that resulted in a massive two-part report on AIDS called "The Plague Years," exploring the scientific and sociological impact of the disease. The epidemic was ignored by the Reagan administration, seemingly on moral grounds, as the number of people dying of AIDS—which had originally been called GRID, "gay-related immunodeficiency"—doubled every nine months. The gay community in New York City was in a state of panic over the "mysterious wasting disease," organizing health and study groups to educate men on the dangers of the bathhouse culture and to lobby for research for a cure. Black articulated the stigma not only of the disease but of homosexuality in general. "The epidemic is not just the disease," wrote Black, "but the virulent reaction the fear of the disease can release in straights toward gays."

The report, originally assigned by David Rosenthal and brought to publication by editor Bob Wallace, won *Rolling Stone* a National Magazine Award. "Jann and his editors were as brave as I've ever known any editors and publishers to be," said Black. But Wenner seemed to absorb the success of the story with unusual detachment. "I remember walking into Jann's office," said Black. "He had a bunch of popcorn on his desk. 'Holy shit, you won!' I said, 'Holy shit, I did!' And I handed him [the award], which he put on a shelf and then he pushed the popcorn across the desk. 'You want some popcorn? Take the day off.'"

Jann Wenner said that AIDS had no "personal impact" on him. He knew almost no one who died of AIDS, he said, because his own gay activity was discreet and limited. He often heard about AIDS from Diane von Furstenberg because her friends were dying from it, but he only knew two people who contracted it: Jon Gould, a former ad salesman for *Rolling Stone* who became Andy Warhol's partner, and a *Rolling Stone* editor named Brant Mewborn, who had personally handled Tom Wolfe's copy for the *Bonfire of the Vanities* series. "I wasn't particularly promiscuous," Wenner said. "I was a practitioner of safe sex. It wasn't a thing that haunted me or bothered me. If you live in New York or a big city with a big gay population and you're promiscuous, it's probably frightening. I wasn't going out there doing that. The opportunities to have sex with guys were not that frequent. Generally, they were people you know. So you were in the reasonable comfort zone and you weren't engaging in any wild sex practice or dangerous stuff. It just wasn't my worry, because I didn't live that lifestyle.

"I was part of the straight world," he added. "Still am to this day."

Around the offices of *Rolling Stone,* Wenner was known for his jovial sexual harassment. He didn't discriminate between men and women; he liked them both. "He was hitting on every girl and every guy," said

Lynn Hirschberg. "He once grabbed me around the hips and said, 'Ten more pounds and you'll be perfect.' This was in front of everybody at a meeting and I wanted to die. It was like this schoolboy crap."

(After the dustup over the Belushi exposé, Michael Douglas told Hirschberg that both he and Wenner had slept with actress Kathleen Turner, Douglas's co-star in *Romancing the Stone,* a movie that featured Douglas discovering an old pile of *Rolling Stone*s in the cargo hold of a drug-smuggling plane. Wenner said he only "necked" with Turner.)

Wenner's nonchalance about AIDS came as a surprise to people who knew of his homosexuality. "He's lying to you," said Seymour Stein, the president of Sire Records who first recorded the Ramones. "He was frightened by it. We all fucking were." Kent Brownridge recalled bringing up AIDS with Wenner and seeing "fear in his eyes." Jane Wenner was equally concerned: "I know I used to ask him because I was worried about it. We *all* worried about AIDS. That is one of the reasons I could forgive in a way. Because to be that conflicted or to be able to deny it so much without saying, 'Look, I'—because I'm *sure* Jann loved me, you know. Don't you think?"

During this time, Wenner's drinking became more severe. He was notorious for keeping a bottle of vodka in the freezer of his office refrigerator and swilling from it during meetings. He was often ruddy-faced and stumbling around at parties. By 1986, when he turned forty years old, Wenner weighed nearly two hundred pounds and was diagnosed with diabetes, which he would have to manage through insulin injections for the rest of his life. This finally inspired him to get in shape, he said. "At the same time, I started reducing blow substantially because you just can't live that way," said Wenner. "I didn't like the way I was looking or feeling." (He started his diet with a regimen of fen-phen, which was later taken off the market for causing heart problems.)

Along with weight loss, Wenner became exceedingly interested in having kids again. He had long used babies as props to imbue celebrities like Jackson Browne and Michael Douglas with a touch of humanity on the cover of *Rolling Stone.* But he was also genuinely happy around children. At his core, Wenner yearned for the family he never had as a child. But the Wenners had been trying on and off since the mid-1970s to have a baby, and Jane's failure to get pregnant after a couple of years sparked rumors that Wenner was sterile. Others wondered whether they even had sex at all, such were their disconnected lives (a *Rolling Stone* circulation manager once advised, "Jann, you've got to fuck"). Meanwhile, the Wenners treated their niece Megan, daughter of Linda Kingsbury, like an adopted daughter, inviting her to live with them during summers in the Hamptons, paying the tuition for her private school education, and giving her signed autographs from her favorite pop stars. "When I saw him with Megan, I always knew he wanted to be a father," said Laurel Gonsalves. "He was always fabulous around kids."

Jane was more ambivalent. When Diane Chess, down on her luck after divorcing Marshall, showed up at East Sixty-Sixth Street and announced she was pregnant by a Latino street hustler, Wenner "lit up like a Christmas tree," recalled Diane Chess, wondering if he and Jane could adopt the child. Jane waved madly behind Wenner's back trying to get Chess to decline the offer. The next day, she paid for Chess's abortion.

Jane Wenner said her own history of abortions—and a miscarriage at age thirty-eight, the paternity of which she said was uncertain— might have hurt her ability to get pregnant. Wenner grew impatient and decided to adopt a child himself. He hired advance man Tony Podesta, who managed *Rolling Stone*'s move to New York in 1977, to fast-track an adoption. Podesta found one through a Chicago agency that specialized in procuring children from out-of-luck women in the rural South with few questions asked ("sharecropper babies," Wenner called them). After Wenner submitted a financial statement to the company for vetting, the owner asked, "Will you adopt me?" Soon enough, Wenner had a three-month-old boy born to a woman from Reno. He named him Alexander Zachary Wenner. "I could not have been more thrilled and happy," recalled Wenner. "I handed him to Jane and she said, 'No, you hold it.'"

Jane was unprepared for an infant. "Some people are very baby people," she said. "I'm not a very baby person."

This was Jann Wenner's baby, a boy he could craft into another version of himself. When Alex arrived in the Hamptons in May 1985, Wenner was so proud he immediately christened him in typical Wenner fashion, inviting celebrities Jack Nicholson and Dolly Parton, who were staying nearby, to come over and hold him. He asked Michael Douglas to be Alex's godfather. Johnny Pigozzi came over for the portraits. Soon after, Wenner decided that Alex looked enough like him that he changed the boy's middle name to Jann.

A magazine profile of Wenner in *GQ* in 1985—which opened with Wenner racing his Dino 308 GT4 Ferrari around the Hamptons at frightening speeds with Bob Dylan's *Empire Burlesque* blasting on the stereo—said of him,

> If there was an element missing in Wenner's life in the past, it was children. He is godfather to Joe Eszterhas's daughter and Jim Webb's son . . . fatherhood, maturity, and the times have had their effect on Jann Wenner. He says he has given up drugs and Elaine's. On nice nights these days he leaves the office at 7:30 and walks up Fifth to his brownstone in the East Sixties. If he's in the office in the mornings, he'll occasionally go home for lunch. In the evenings after the baby is in bed he and Jane have dinner together, then settle to watch TV. Wenner makes the occasional call to the coast, but he's generally in bed by 11:00.

The author was Graydon Carter, future editor of *Vanity Fair,* and the story was edited by Paul Scanlon, who had left *Rolling Stone* in 1979. It was the best magazine profile ever published about Jann Wenner, capturing the man and his contradictions to a T. "Out for a stroll up Fifth Avenue, he walks head up, elbows out, with the athletic, jaunty swagger of a pigeon-toed boulevardier," wrote Carter. "Lou Costello in a Giorgio Armani suit."

Afterward, Wenner, both offended and flattered, went to lunch with Carter at the Four Seasons to berate and befriend him. "He acted out by taking food off our plates," recalled Paul Scanlon.

And then a strange thing happened: Nine months after Alex arrived, Jane got pregnant with the Wenners' first biological son, Theodore Simon Wenner. In the glow of family life, the Wenners had rediscovered their intimacy. Jane stopped drinking, smoking, and doing drugs so that she could breast-feed her new baby. For a while, the Wenners seemed happy together, surrounding themselves with other celebrities with children, Michael Douglas and his son, Cameron, Yoko Ono and Sean, and documenting it all for new volumes of scrapbooks.

But then there was Alex, who would, as he grew older, come to comprehend his misfortune as the also-ran to his brother Theo. Far from becoming Jann Wenner Jr., he would become an unhappy child, the opposite of his father in almost every way imaginable.

•

BEFORE THE WORD "Yuppie" came into vogue, Tom Wolfe tried dubbing the 1980s the "Purple Decade." As he told *Rolling Stone* in 1987, "I said 'Purple' in the sense of royal purple, that in this decade people are going to become much more blatant in the pursuit of status than they were in the Seventies and the Sixties, when it was rather bad form to make your ambition naked—you had to cleverly cloak it."

Wenner had never cloaked anything, but the generational embrace of materialism and status worship had finally caught up to him, and he was about to get very, very rich. It began in 1985 when *Rolling Stone* achieved a goal Wenner had been talking about since the late 1960s: He grew the circulation to a million readers. *The New York Times* said Wenner's magazine "has reached the magical plateau where a good many advertisers interested in mass audiences will begin to take it seriously." The magazine got there through merciless attention to consumer research and focus groups that revealed the balance of celebrities and rock news readers wanted. "When people say *Rolling Stone* changed, it did, but what also changed was the pervasiveness of marketing," said Bob Wallace, who began as a fact-checker the week Ralph Gleason died. "That was really when marketing in general just really shifted into high gear. Focus groups, and all that bullshit."

Driving the rise in fortune was Kent Brownridge. A tall, bladelike man of Nixonian bearing and death-rattle-dry wit, Brownridge took over as business manager after Jim Dunning left for Wall Street. Brownridge had gone to high school with David Felton in Pasadena, California, and after meeting Wenner while working as an advance man for failed gubernatorial candidate Bill Roth in 1974 managed to work his way up from the circulation department to become Wenner's financial right hand. Brownridge had zero interest in rock and roll; he liked money, which made Wenner like him. More than that, he was in awe of Wenner. He considered him a genius and viewed his flares of cruelty and unvarnished greed as virtuous and even noble. For the next twenty years, Brownridge would become Wenner's chief hatchet man and consigliere—"the hand of the king," said Wenner. For magazine staffers, he was "Old Raisin Balls," legend for his bloodless cost cutting, interoffice skullduggery, press leaks, and unwavering commitment to Wenner's wealth and status. It was Brownridge who eliminated cocaine from the office because he saw it as a legal liability for the biggest customer of the Capri Lounge, Jann Wenner (who, despite publishing "How to Get Off Cocaine" in 1984, remained a stalwart user). Both flatterer and caretaker, Brownridge guarded the business like a Minotaur while Wenner was out having fun. He had observed Wenner long enough to know how to handle his irascible master. "My approach always was to not tell Jann, 'Jann, you can't do that,'" Brownridge explained. "You're not telling him his idea sucked. And you're not telling him he couldn't do something, because that would almost ensure that he would go ahead and try to do it."

According to Brownridge, *Rolling Stone* never made more than $500,000 in profit before 1983. But under his guidance, he said, it started taking in $10 million a year in pretax profits in 1986. As the money rolled in, Wenner's other business strategist, the real estate lawyer Ben Needell, a partner at the powerful Manhattan firm Skadden, Arps, gave Wenner the idea to trigger an "involuntary tender offer" that let Wenner buy back all the outside shares of Straight Arrow at "fair market value," whether the shareholders wanted to sell or not. A significant portion of the company was still owned by people other than Jann Wenner: former employees and family like Bob Kingsbury, Charlie Perry, Jean Gleason, and his stepmother, Dorothy, who had divorced his father, remarried jazz pianist Peter Clark, and changed her name to Dallas. The $11 million valuation on the tender offer was less than Ziff Davis offered for *Rolling Stone* in 1980, when it had a lower circulation. As Brownridge described it, "It was on a gray border of being fair, but it wasn't generous." Most shareholders took the money, unaware that *Rolling Stone* was about to double and triple in value. When the buyout was complete, Straight Arrow would belong almost entirely to Jann and Jane Wenner. Afterward, many of Wenner's oldest friends became embittered, including Wenner's stepmother. "It was right before he bought *US*," recalled Dallas Clark, formerly Dorothy Wenner. "He was getting rid of everybody. He knew he was going to be much more affluent. Jann is very greedy. He wants everything for his own. If he can't get it some other way, he'll steal it from you."

But there was one shareholder who decided to resist the buyout: their old friend Laurel Gonsalves, who lived upstairs from the Wenners at East Sixty-Sixth Street. After fourteen years at *Rolling Stone,* the former pot smuggler now owned 3.5 percent of the magazine. On the advice of Max Palevsky, Gonsalves had gone back to school to get an MBA from New York University and decided that Wenner's valuation of the company was preposterous. Wenner blithely suggested she use a clause in the shareholder's agreement to lodge a formal protest. But when she actually hired a lawyer and challenged the valuation, Wenner went ballistic. "He went into id mode," Gonsalves said. "'You are trying to take money from me and Jane!' I'll remember that to this day. It's all id. It was a zero-sum game. If I was going to get $2 million, that would be money that he and Jane didn't have."

The Wenners cut Gonsalves out of their lives, moved out of East Sixty-Sixth Street, leaving the Dakota Jackson cocaine-snorting table still mounted to the wall. "He even said stuff to me, trying to be cruel: 'You wouldn't have any friends if it weren't for *Rolling Stone,*'" said Gonsalves.

The lawsuit *Gonsalves* v. *Straight Arrow Publishers* would go on for a decade and conclude in an out-of-court settlement in which Wenner shelled out about $2 million, which included interest that began compounding in the 1970s. Ben Needell would argue that Gonsalves should have taken the first offer instead of wasting her money fighting in court. Gonsalves, who spent $1 million on legal fees, said Wenner paid double that to prevent her from getting the money, which was a satisfaction of its own.

After the buyback, Wenner launched a massive advertising campaign to fully exploit *Rolling Stone*'s circulation breakthrough. The "Perception/Reality" campaign was created by a small Minnesota agency that came recommended by the New York advertising giant Jay Chiat. Fallon McElligott Rice created a simple message: *Rolling Stone* readers weren't dope-smoking hippies living in teepees anymore, but rather status-seeking Yuppies like Jann Wenner who clawed for money and sports cars (Wenner knew this instinctually because he bought three in 1985). The ad campaign was a riff on one that Joe Armstrong had tried out in the 1970s. On the left panel stood a fringe-wearing hippie (perception); on the right, a briefcase-toting businessman (reality). Perception: a handful of dirty pennies; reality: an American Express card. In another, onetime youth culture presidential candidate George McGovern was juxtaposed with Ronald Reagan. This was Jann Wenner's true coming-out party, a celebration of the baby-boomer journey. "I think we came away looking so smart and cool," said Wenner. "People mistook why it was successful. It wasn't about rejecting who we were and changing. It celebrates who we were and is proud of who we were. Times change, and we evolved into who we were."

Wenner objected to just one of the ads: a peace sign contrasted with a Mercedes-Benz symbol. "The juxtaposition of two such symbols is guaranteed to be controversial and noticed," Wenner told the admen in a letter, but it insinuated that his readers no longer cared about peace. "What it says is selling out," he wrote, "abandoning positive values, moral drift, selfishness, blind ambition, and so forth.

"In the end," he concluded, "you are denigrating the very thing we're selling."

But in the end, Wenner decided to use the image anyway. The truth is that Wenner knew the core of his audience too well. They were young Reagan Democrats whose interest in left-wing politics paled next to their interest in Ford Mustangs. Internal research showed that *Rolling Stone*'s under-twenty-five readership voted two-to-one for Reagan in the 1984 presidential election while the over-thirty readers supported the Democratic candidate, Walter Mondale. Even as he helped campaign for Democrats like Alan Cranston, Wenner knew where the money was, and it wasn't in publishing anything about Alan Cranston and Fritz Hollings. As Brownridge told the *Times* in 1985, "You couldn't sell a political story if you pasted dollar bills around it."

(National affairs columnist William Greider, as erudite and insightful as he was, was never widely read. "We used to talk about that all the time," said David Rosenthal. "Is anybody fucking reading this thing?")

If critics sniped that Wenner was selling out, that was the point: Advertising revenue for *Rolling Stone* ballooned in 1986 and 1987. And now Wenner intended to live like a sultan. Brownridge said Wenner spent every dime he made as soon as it landed in his bank account, which drove an endless and exhaustive pursuit of advertising dollars from auto manufacturers and cigarette makers to keep pace with Wenner's yen for new luxuries. *Rolling Stone* was a lifestyle support system for Jann Wenner. After spending a quarter of a million dollars to renovate his East Sixty-Sixth Street duplex, the Wenners moved to the $4.2 million brownstone on West Seventieth Street, formerly owned by fashion designer Perry Ellis, and built a three-story Georgian manor in the Hamptons. Wenner employed a full-time driver for getting around Manhattan and hired a bevy of servants and nannies. But the sine qua non of status was the private jet. Wenner was first inspired by a trip aboard Malcolm Forbes's private plane, *Capitalist Tool,* which ferried him to a castle in France in the late 1980s. Wenner flew with the old-world crème de la crème like Henry Kissinger, Walter Cronkite, Douglas MacArthur's widow, Jean, and Jerry Zipkin, the gay socialite and best friend of Nancy Reagan. "I was one of the swells," marveled Wenner. One day Wenner was at a health spa in Arizona that he frequented with Michael Douglas and Yoko Ono when he decided to start skiing again as part of his health revival. When he couldn't get a flight to Aspen to see his ski instructor, Tim Mooney, Wenner chartered a private plane from Arizona and was on the slopes by mid-morning. "I said, 'Well, I'm going to ski, and I'm going to buy a plane to do this,'" he said. "Ben [Needell] came over and told me not to do it. As a business thing, it makes no sense, and I said I totally get that. I went ahead and bought it."

Wenner's Gulfstream II jet seated ten people and featured a dining table, four overstuffed couches, and a foldout bed. It cost $6 million. Wenner loved it so much he put the factory-issued model in his office on Fifth Avenue and dreamed of ways to take his *Rolling Stone* salon of celebrities and suitors to the air. "Then it became 'What can we do to fly this thing? Where can we go? How can I take it in the air?'" recalled Wenner. "I would just circle over LaGuardia to have lunch."

Soon enough he was taking groups of friends on trips to Bali, Hong Kong, and Morocco, across Europe and Africa. When the Berlin Wall fell in 1989, he assembled a traveling party to fly to Moscow. "I took Ahmet [Ertegun] and Fran Lebowitz," said Wenner. "Jane didn't come on that one, because she was pregnant"—with Edward Augustus "Gus" Wenner, her second biological son since the adoption of Alex in 1985. ("Joan Didion said 'Gus' sounded like a gas station attendant," said Jane Wenner.) Needell put the plane under a business subsidiary called Straight Arrow Transportation to write it off as a business expense, but Wenner said it was "90 percent personal." He kept a logbook, which doubled as a celebrity autograph book, and dubbed the plane the *Capitalist Fool,* after Malcolm Forbes's jet.

On the trip with Forbes in 1989, Wenner also hung out with Jay Leno, who showed him how to ride a motorcycle—clinging to his waist while Wenner blasted down the road on one of Leno's Harley-Davidsons—and advised Wenner to buy a Heritage Softail Classic. Soon enough he was motoring around with Bob Pittman of MTV, Woody Johnson of the Johnson & Johnson fortune, a Lehman Brothers banker, and a sporting goods tycoon, all trailed by Wenner's wine dealer from the Hamptons and a professional mechanic. Wenner had tried buying *Outside* back from Larry Burke, but Burke refused to sell, so Wenner launched *Men's Journal,* which explored adventure and lifestyle while selling gear and cars to male readers between the ages of eighteen and thirty-four. For the November/December 1992 issue, Wenner hired journalist Jon Krakauer to join him and his pals—"the Bridge Clubbers," they called themselves—on a four-thousand-mile cross-country motorcycle trip and write about it for *Men's Journal.* At first, Pittman balked at the idea. "Jann, we're doing this trip to get away; we don't wanna be in the public eye," he told him.

"Don't worry," Wenner replied, "it's my magazine."

The story—in which Wenner wore a leather jacket and bandanna and rode a Yamaha sports bike—came out much as Pittman had feared, "a bunch of rich guys on this motorcycle trip," he said. Krakauer splashed

Wenner and his men with the macho cologne of romantic overwriting. "You travel this fast only when the road is empty and its surface smooth as fifty-year-old cognac," wrote Krakauer, "but a high-speed run never fails to leave your clothes soiled with the stink of fear." After it was published, Wenner told *The New York Times,* "What my generation has been involved with is a search for quality and richness of experience. Although it comes out of a desire to understand the world, there is also a certain search for self in it."

Wenner's search for self was about the need for affirmation, which he found in exclusive experiences, expensive Ferraris, private jets, chartered yachts, and choice real estate in proximity to famous people. In 1992, he bought a hundred-acre ranch called Broadford Farm in Sun Valley, Idaho, and began spending his winters skiing with the local gentry, which would come to include Massachusetts senator John Kerry and actors Tom Hanks and his wife, Rita Wilson. Wenner's friends agreed he was the most aggressive skier they knew, and Wenner measured his winters by how many days he hit the slopes each season. His friend Don Simpson had highly produced ski videos made for Wenner's personal enjoyment. Caroline Kennedy called him "the Jimmy Buffett of winter."

(Broadford Farm was also where two workers whom Wenner hired to build his driveway discovered $23,000 in gold coins in the ground, the tale of which became a legendary *New Yorker* article. "We're going to be on the cover of *Rolling Stone!*" one of them exclaimed, after which their hapless infighting ended with Wenner's owning the coins and stowing them in a safe at *Rolling Stone*.)

Around the time that he bought the ski ranch, the contract on his Fifth Avenue office came up, and Wenner moved *Rolling Stone* to the office tower at 1290 Sixth Avenue, situated along the same vaunted corporate corridor as the Time-Life Building. He hired a high-end design firm to remake the former banking office into a sleek, luxurious hive of glassed-in offices decorated with expensively framed photographs of rock stars and museum-worthy memorabilia, like a Gibson SG smashed to bits by Pete Townshend and encased in see-through epoxy resin. The whole thing cost $7 million.

The new office marked a definitive culture change at *Rolling Stone*.

The glass-walled offices allowed Wenner to see whatever his employees were doing—they were no longer allowed to listen to music at high volume and had to keep their desks fastidious to avoid Wenner's wrath—while he hid away in his own back office lined with vacation photographs of his sailing trips with Mick Jagger and Richard Gere. *Rolling Stone* embodied the publishing establishment, fat with lucrative ads. And Wenner's gaudy lifestyle was an emblem of generational triumph.

Wenner's personal office, complete with a private kitchenette and spacious bathroom, allowed him to peruse the latest layouts of *Rolling Stone* at his old round table from San Francisco (now laminated to preserve Joe Eszterhas's old knife marks), a cold bottle of vodka in his hand, while he looked down on passersby on Sixth Avenue—from fifteen feet above ground level. The office was on the second floor of the forty-three-floor tower. Jann Wenner wanted not only to see but to be seen. "Look at these people come by, it's fascinating," he told Tom Wolfe. "I feel like I'm really in the public and I'm well off."

21

We Didn't Start the Fire

I n 1988, Edward Wenner died at age seventy after a wrench-
ing, months-long battle with cancer that Jann's sister Kate, a
producer at the ABC newsmagazine *20/20,* documented for
a private home movie. She interviewed her father as the three
Wenner children, including aging hippie Merlyn, huddled around him
and learned the lost secrets of the family like Ed's painful confession
that he watched his mother burn down the lingerie shop for insurance
money in the 1930s. By the 1980s, Ed Wenner had developed a successful business operating trailer parks and malls in Arizona and Southern
California. For years Wenner had maintained the dim view of his father
that his mother, Sim, had painted early on—the angry, distant man who
broke up their family. (When his father showed up in the dugout of the
Eagles versus *Rolling Stone* softball game at USC in 1978, Wenner barely
spoke to him.) But relations thawed in the 1980s, and his illness brought
them all back together. In Kate Wenner's movie, Wenner can be seen
curled up next to his ailing father in bed, looking like a little boy in a
business suit, kissing him on the cheek.

"My dad was dying, and I had spent a month with him out in L.A. in
the fall," Wenner recounted. "And my sisters were hanging out, and we
were spending a lot of time. We had been taking him around to doctors
and chemo and radiation therapy. We were visiting cancer specialists.

My sister Merlyn was researching everything to death, and I was chartering planes.

"I had spent a month out there in a center in Santa Monica. I was doing a diet thing. During the course of that month, Tom Cruise [cover of *Rolling Stone,* June 1986] had lent me his Harley-Davidson to get around, and I spent that month with my dad all the time. And I left at the end of the month, knowing it was going to be the last time with him."

He made a final visit before New Year's, after which he flew home to New York, where an airline official told him he had a phone call: "It was my sister. They were sitting on either side of the bed. And he wants to talk—his deathbed—I got on the phone and said, 'Good-bye. It's okay now.' And my sister said, at that point my father gave his last three breaths. He had been hanging on for that phone call, waiting to say good-bye. To hear a good-bye. As soon as he died, there was this electrical aura, this energy field, lifted off of him. They could see it. And I believe that. Because the body is electric. And it goes. And it just dissipates. He held on waiting for this phone call."

As his father was dying, Wenner had an emotional breakdown on vacation in St. Martin. Jackson Browne helped talk him through it, he said, marking the start of a genuine friendship with the rocker, who had appeared on the cover of *Rolling Stone* six times. (Later, however, it got fractious again when actress Daryl Hannah left Browne for John Kennedy Jr., after which Browne "was suspicious that I was in the middle of it," said Wenner. "That was an interesting dynamic.")

Midlife was upon the baby boomers, and nostalgia was in the air. In the Hamptons, the Wenners summered with their three kids and a host of servants and celebrities, including three-time *Rolling Stone* cover boy Billy Joel. In the 1970s, Joel had been a whipping boy for *Rolling Stone*— "For a while," said Joel, "it seemed like an editorial policy; they just kept finding ways to knock me"—but now they bonded over motorcycles and Gilbert and Sullivan and were known to sing selections from *H.M.S. Pinafore* at parties. Joel turned forty in 1989 and was trying to address a changing world in song when he called Wenner one afternoon. "I couldn't think of a title for it," recalled Joel. "I was at home and Jann was at the house and I threw a couple of titles at him. I was the pitcher, just throwing them at him: 'Walking Through the Fire'? No. 'Dancing Around the Fire'? No. Where am I going with this stupid thing? I think I threw out 'We Didn't Start the Fire,' and he said, 'Yes, I like that one,' and I wrote that down."

"We Didn't Start the Fire," a song so reviled that Joel himself later admitted it was terrible, was received by MTV viewers as the ultimate baby-boomer love letter to itself, a "Subterranean Homesick Blues" remade as glossy history, the kind of 1960s montage one saw on late night television ads for Time-Life picture books. And indeed, Joel said he fact-checked the song's rattle of historical events using a *Year in Pictures* anthology. "And I was pretty spot-on with the dates," he said.

As he told *Rolling Stone,* the boomers were ready to hand the whole mess off to "a whole new generation of people who are inheriting a world in crisis, and it's going to get interesting to see how they deal with it."

•

AS WENNER WAS CRISSCROSSING the country in his Gulfstream, things were shifting on the ground. Classic rock of the kind Wenner still loved to lionize, and the kinds of performers that MTV championed—Michael Jackson, Madonna, Prince—had long been reviled by a self-conscious underground. Punk and New Wave had never really gone away but had been organizing an entire counter-media of their own, whether *Maximum Rocknroll* or *New York Rocker.* In 1985, Bob Guccione Jr., son of the founder of *Penthouse* magazine, launched *Spin,* a music magazine that carved out a new youth market by doing something Wenner resolutely would never do: put alternative and college-rock bands like L7 and the Pixies on the cover rather than aging pop stars like Billy Joel. Out of the gate, Guccione declared *Rolling Stone* "arrogant, complacent and out of touch." *Spin* ran a monthly column about AIDS and published a blistering exposé on Bob Geldof and his Live Aid relief concerts, alleging that money intended for starving children in Ethiopia was being funneled to a dictator who used the money to buy weapons from the Soviet Union. By 1990, *Spin* had a circulation of a quarter million and had fully captured the leading edge of music in a way *Rolling Stone* hadn't since 1972. "I copied his idea, a generation later," said Guccione. "They were the first people to take rock and roll seriously when the culture did not. When I came along, rock and roll took itself too seriously and we did not. We made fun of rock and roll."

Wenner believed in his numbers more than anything that might be bubbling in the culture. He wrote an editorial in *Ad Age* claiming Generation X was just a subset of the baby boomers and listened to the same music, whether Rod Stewart or the Grateful Dead. And regardless, he had always seen competitors as cockroaches to be stamped out. Once, when Jane Wenner and Peter Wolf went to see their old high school in Harlem, with Annie Leibovitz along to take photographs, they saw two hip kids smoking weed and asked them what music magazine they read. "And the guy said, 'Oh, *Trouser Press,* for sure,'" recalled Wolf, referring to the underground magazine for punk and alternative records that published until the mid-1980s and became a series of critically acclaimed record guides. "I said, 'You think *Trouser Press* is better than *Rolling Stone?*' 'Ah, yeah, man, *Rolling Stone* sucks. *Trouser Press* is really fucking great.' So I remember, we went back, and we were having dinner, and Jane told the story to Jann. He rattled off the distribution of what *Trouser Press* is next to *Rolling Stone,* and blah, blah, blah. Then he threatens, in a half-joking way, 'I'm gonna buy *Trouser Press* just to put it outta fucking business!'

"It became the joke, and still is," said Wolf. "It was like, 'If you don't like it, take it to *Trouser Press.*' Which is long out of business."

One of the first major bands that *Spin* championed was U2, from Ireland, who were breaking through on MTV with the 1984 single "Pride (in the Name of Love)." When U2 made the cover of *Rolling Stone* in March 1985, Bono was put off by the grandiose cover shoot. "I remember arriving and it was like a movie set and I hated it," Bono recalled. "The scale of it looked worrisome. We were afraid of our own grandiosity, and we picked a fight with the photographer."

Word came down from Jann Wenner: Take it or leave it. Bono took it. The photographer, Rebecca Blake, said none of this happened, but Bono came away with a dim view of the magazine, especially when he saw John Travolta and Jamie Lee Curtis on the cover a few issues later. "We're going, 'This is not rock and roll,'" Bono said. "It's interesting that, in one sense, rock and roll gets owned by a kind of middle-class collegiate view of art having to be separate from commerce. But he's breaking with this, and he's taking some shit for it, including from me."

Spin would continue under Guccione until 1997, when he sold it for $43 million, and while it never hurt *Rolling Stone* financially, it was a constant reminder of the limited slice of American music Wenner's magazine was interested in and the distance it had traveled from its countercultural roots. *Rolling Stone* was the establishment standard-bearer whose power came from a Rolodex of 1960s luminaries, a proven brand name on Madison Avenue, and an audited circulation of one million readers for whom the name *Rolling Stone* rang out like a power chord of emotional associations: rebellion, celebrity, celebrity rebellion.

Whatever else was happening, the formula still worked. All Wenner had to do was underline the core story lines, over and over again. He was a kind of producer with his own cast of cultural characters, the same dozen stars he could turn to. For the twenty-year anniversary of *Rolling Stone,* Wenner partnered with ABC for a prime-time TV retrospective (co-produced by Lorne Michaels) and published a 310-page issue of *Rolling Stone* (featuring two Roman *X*s on the cover, an homage to Roger Black's ten-year-anniversary cover), which contained interviews with Bob Dylan, Mick Jagger, Keith Richards, Yoko Ono, Paul McCartney, George Harrison, Bruce Springsteen, and Pete Townshend. P. J. O'Rourke, a former *National Lampoon* editor and Hunter Thompson devotee whom Wenner hired to write comic dispatches from Lebanon and the Turks and Caicos, interviewed Hunter Thompson, with a picture by Annie Leibovitz of Thompson lounging on a motorcycle. For the occasion, Billy Joel performed a song called "Happy Birthday, *Rolling Stone,*" which Wenner ran in an ad on MTV along with taped well wishes from Yoko Ono, Van Halen, Cybill Shepherd, and Don Johnson. Wenner also gave Budweiser permission to use the *Rolling Stone* logo for an advertisement featuring a bottle of Budweiser on the cover of *Rolling Stone.* As Wenner told Bryant Gumbel on *Today,* "Rock is this great, wide river which constantly flows, and new ideas come in and go out."

By the end of the 1980s, MTV had fully revived the music business, helping *Rolling Stone* sell enormous numbers of magazines and cut lucrative licensing deals, including internationally based versions of the magazine, which now published in Australia and Italy. Wenner befriended the CEO of MTV, Tom Freston, a former clothing importer who had lived in Afghanistan in the 1970s and looked to *Rolling Stone* as a model for how to expand MTV into movies, politics, news. Under Freston, the channel recruited Kurt Loder, who had maligned MTV for years in the pages of *Rolling Stone,* to host a program called *The Week in Rock.*

The MTV–*Rolling Stone* axis mirrored the concentrated and all-powerful record industry. Kurt Cobain of Nirvana, who mocked baby boomers and wore a T-shirt that said "Corporate Magazines Still Suck" on the cover of *Rolling Stone* in 1992, became the martyr of lost rock-and-roll causes after he sold millions of albums for David Geffen's label and then shot himself in the head in heroin-ravaged despair.

The same year Cobain made the cover, MTV aired a twenty-fifth-anniversary special on *Rolling Stone,* featuring interviews by David Felton, who now worked for MTV as a writer on the Mike Judge animated series *Beavis and Butt-Head.* The special featured a scene where Hunter Thompson wires a framed studio portrait of Jann Wenner smiling in a sports jacket with explosives, props it against a wall, and blows it to pieces with a rifle. Thompson wanted to present the exploded portrait to Wenner as a gift during the twenty-fifth-anniversary party at the Four Seasons, but Wenner was scheduled to appear with Yoko Ono and told Thompson a bullet-ridden picture was in poor taste. Enraged, Thompson attempted to throw it out his hotel window. (Wenner eventually hung it outside the men's bathroom at *Rolling Stone.*)

While interviewing Wenner, Felton joked that they should conduct the conversation in the nude as he had with Michael Wadleigh, the director of the *Woodstock* movie, back in 1970. Felton brought up the "Perception/Reality" campaign and wondered if Wenner felt he had forfeited his idealism. After Felton left the room, Wenner darkened, expressing disgust with former employees like Felton who still clung to irrelevant 1960s notions like "selling out," saying they should "grow up."

"There's many people . . . like David who want things to stay in this kind of small world where they can be a big baby in a small playpen," said Wenner. "I didn't want to continue all that. So move along. And some people didn't make the transitions. That's the worst of it. The rest is all exciting and fun."

Jann and his adopted son, Alexander, 1985. *(Camilla McGrath)*

Sean Lennon (standing) and Cameron Douglas, son of Michael (right), with Alex Wenner, 1985. *(Camilla McGrath)*

Michael Douglas and Jann Wenner in East Hampton, 1986. *(Jean Pigozzi)*

Michael Douglas and Jane Wenner, 1986.
(Jean Pigozzi)

Wenner and Ahmet Ertegun, 1987.
(Ron Galella/Getty)

Hunter Thompson deplaning from Wenner's Gulfstream IV, 1993. *(Mark Seliger)*

Wenner and his writers—William Greider, P. J. O'Rourke, and Hunter Thompson—interviewing Bill Clinton at Doe's Eat Place in Little Rock, Arkansas, 1992. *(Mark Seliger)*

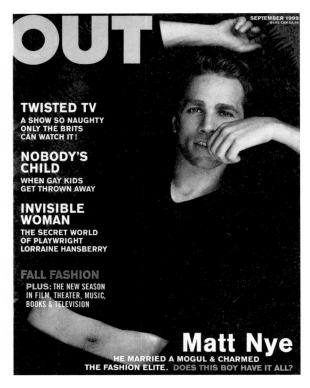

Matt Nye, cover of
Out magazine, 1999.
(Here Publishing Inc.)

Portrait of Jann Wenner, 2000.
(Mark Seliger)

Bonnie Fuller was named *Advertising Age*'s Editor of the Year in 2002 after reviving *Us Weekly*. *(Larry Busacca/Getty)*

In March 2004, Jann Wenner was inducted into the Rock and Roll Hall of Fame by Mick Jagger and Ahmet Ertegun. *(Kevin Kane/Getty)*

Wenner with his son Theo, 2009. *(Mark Seliger)*

Wenner interviewing President Barack Obama at the White House, 2010.
(Mark Seliger)

Bono, Jann Wenner, Mick Jagger, and Bruce Springsteen at the twenty-fifth anniversary of the Rock and Roll Hall of Fame, 2009. *(Mark Seliger)*

Jane Wenner in
Amagansett, 2016.
(Theo Wenner)

Jann Wenner and his son Gus, 2017. *(Jesse Dittmar)*

He stewed a minute more.

"He's a child," he muttered. "He's a baby. David, grow up. Stripping for the camera? Ho, ho, ho. What a dumb fucking joke."

It was ex-staffers like Felton who gave an earful to Robert Draper, author of the 1990 book *"Rolling Stone" Magazine: The Uncensored History,* which, while it censored Wenner's still-hidden sexuality, unleashed the dyspepsia of former employees for whom Wenner was a kind of antagonist to all that was once righteous about their magazine. Hunter Thompson cooperated for it. At first, Wenner tried winning Draper over by inviting him to dinner and an overnight stay at West Seventieth Street. Around midnight, Wenner invited Draper into his hot tub, but a paranoid Draper declined and retired to the guest room. In the final scene, Wenner gives Draper a brief interview in the Hamptons and while sipping a gin and tonic (brought to him by a servant) proclaims the past happily behind him. "I used to spend twenty-four hours a day at *Rolling Stone,*" Wenner said, but he was "not about to do that again."

When Wenner procured an advance copy of Draper's book, he was so upset he rescinded the use of photographs he initially granted to Draper.

Unlike his former employees, when Wenner looked back, it wasn't with sadness over what had been lost, the youthful dreams and passion. The rock-and-roll past was something that he'd had a hand in building, and something that, in a very literal sense, he still possessed. Over the years, Wenner had published his own version of history in *Rolling Stone* and through all manner of guidebooks and anthologies, including *The "Rolling Stone" Illustrated History of Rock & Roll, The "Rolling Stone" Interviews,* a *Rolling Stone* book on the 1960s, a *Rolling Stone* book on the 1970s, an anthology about Dylan, an anthology about John Lennon, and several *Rolling Stone* record guides, which inspired the star-rating system for records after the first one was published in 1980 (every review in the guide was written by Dave Marsh, saving *Rolling Stone* from having to depend on Jon Landau's critical excoriations of major records). Wenner's biases and machinations—his *success*—had made him the gatekeeper of the history of rock and roll. And the next step was to build an institution out of it—literally, an edifice—over which he could preside. And while he was often checked out of his own magazine, he was fashioning himself into the architect of rock's shining city on the hill: the Rock and Roll Hall of Fame.

It wasn't Jann Wenner who conceived the Hall of Fame, nor was it his co-founder, Ahmet Ertegun, though both were often credited as such. Rather, it began in 1982 with a cable TV entrepreneur named Bruce Brandwen. In the early 1980s, Brandwen conceived the Hall of Fame as a TV concert to honor rock-and-roll originators like James Brown and Elvis Presley, with an accompanying museum featuring guitars, stage outfits, and memorabilia. Brandwen and his pay-per-view company, Black Tie Network, first incorporated the Rock and Roll Hall of Fame (originally called the Kings and Queens of Rock and Roll until an ad man named Blake Lorick suggested the alternate title), converted it into a nonprofit, came up with the basic rules for induction, designed an award (a woman holding an LP over her head), and created a board of directors featuring Lesley Gore, the former teen idol, to operate it as a nonprofit. The Hall of Fame cut a five-year contract with Black Tie, with a pay-per-view show as the goal and main event. The only thing they lacked was the cooperation of the record industry.

In 1983, Brandwen and a lawyer named David Braun, whose client was Bob Dylan, set up a meeting with Ahmet Ertegun in hopes of recruiting him to run it. Ertegun was initially dismissive and declined to cooperate. But then he changed his mind two weeks later. "He said, 'Know something? I think it better if I am involved than if I am not involved,'" recalled Brandwen.

Ertegun agreed to join the advisory board of the Hall of Fame. He would recruit board members and bring in the artists, and Black Tie would underwrite the nonprofit foundation with 10 percent of the revenue from television and merchandising.

Wenner said it was the Hall of Fame's executive director, a young lawyer hired by Brandwen named Suzan Evans, who initially reached out to him, asking if he wanted to be on the committee that would nominate inductees. "I said I'm not interested in being on the nominating committee, but I'd be interested in being on the board itself," recalled Wenner. "And the Rock and Roll Hall of Fame was nothing, some concept for a TV show by a bunch of hucksters who copyrighted the name and called up Ahmet to be window dressing and to, you know, be the 'advisory board.'"

By this time, Wenner was a fixture in the social circle of record aristocrats who came out of the 1960s and 1970s. For the advisory board, Ertegun was bringing in all the venerable heavyweights, including famed Atlantic producer Jerry Wexler; Springsteen manager Jon Landau; entertainment lawyer Allen Grubman; Seymour Stein of Sire Records; and Bob Krasnow of Elektra. Most of them had long and woolly histories with each other, and with Jann Wenner. The record industry had always been a filthy business, full of exploitation, infighting, corruption, and payola, but the record labels had merged and consolidated under corporate umbrellas, and by this point Ertegun was more hood ornament at Atlantic Records than an active executive. But Wenner considered himself and Ertegun in a different class from the likes of, say, Seymour Stein or Allen Grubman, let alone Bruce Brandwen. They had all been social friends for years, partying in Los Angeles or Barbados or New York. Along with Mick Jagger and Earl McGrath, Barry Diller and Diane von Furstenberg, and of course Johnny Pigozzi, the Wenners and the Erteguns were dedicated to lives of wealth and taste and wielding power like cultural politicians. "That was a really influential and fun and intelligent group and we were all part of that," said Jagger. "It doesn't exist anymore, but our bond was the bond of the group. Of course, it's a bond of individuals, but it's also a bond of political views and cultural aims. And grievances. And laughter."

For years, Ertegun seemed to have Wenner under his thumb, treating him like his liege and making fun of him behind his back, and sometimes while he was in the room. "Oh and here's the new Wonder Boy," Ertegun would say archly. He never tired of telling the story of Charlie Chaplin's French "daughter." When Wenner asked Ertegun to give *Rolling Stone* a major interview on the fortieth anniversary of Atlantic Records, Ertegun turned him down. (He never gave a full interview to *Rolling Stone*.) But Ertegun saw opportunity in Wenner's energy, and also his deference. For the Hall of Fame, Ertegun would act as public ambassador while Wenner did most of the hustling. In exchange, Ertegun would become Wenner's mentor and style counselor and teach him the art of diplomacy—when to stop "hustling" (preferably after 8:00 p.m.) and when discretion is the better part of valor. "I think that Jann learned a lot from Ahmet: how to dress, where to have suits made, and how to behave socially and all that," said Johnny Pigozzi, their mutual friend. "And also, he was looking at Ahmet, who was taking cocaine and was screwing around and all that, and he said, 'Well, if Ahmet can do it, I can also do it.'"

"Ahmet had style, and, more important, he had access at the highest levels, and in that sense he was an inspiring figure," said Lorne Michaels, who also ran in Ertegun's social sphere, "but also Ahmet was completely ruthless, whereas Jann has some level of sentimentality, which he tries his best to disguise."

Once the record aristocrats signed up with Brandwen, a curious thing happened: nothing. For the next four years, the record men dragged their feet on an induction ceremony that Brandwen could film and broadcast. Indeed, their big idea was to procure some minor Elvis memorabilia from Priscilla Presley and set it up in a brownstone in Brooklyn. (It never happened.) But that changed in 1985 when emissaries from the city of Cleveland showed up with a detailed pitch about hosting a full-scale museum. This is when it occurred to Ahmet Ertegun and Jann Wenner that they might have something bigger on their hands than a cheap TV show. A committee was formed to consider bids from several major cities, including Philadelphia and Memphis, and after infighting between Jann Wenner and Bob Krasnow, who wanted the museum in New York, the board of directors finally agreed to accept the bid from Wenner's favorite, Cleveland, whose political officials had put together $65 million in donations and subsidies.

With a multimillion-dollar museum on the horizon, Ertegun and Wenner proceeded to organize the first Rock and Roll Hall of Fame induction ceremony to kick things off. It took place at the Waldorf Astoria in 1986, a $1,000-a-plate black-tie affair honoring Elvis Presley, Ray Charles, James Brown, Jerry Lee Lewis, Chuck Berry, Sam Cooke, Fats Domino, the Everly Brothers, Buddy Holly, and Little Richard. Wenner splashed it across the cover of *Rolling Stone*. The event was filmed but never broadcast. Nor was the next year's gala, honoring Aretha Franklin and Roy Orbison. The delay was probably tactical—to run out the five-year contract with Black Tie and take the Hall of Fame for themselves. Recalled Brandwen, "[Allen] Grubman kept saying, 'We're going to do it, give us time, give us time,' and when the five years expired, with no induction and no television, they said, 'Your five years are up; you've lost your rights.' Which was not atypical of how the music industry could operate."

The whole thing, said Brandwen, was a "beautifully crafted stall."

Wenner took credit for convincing the others to push Brandwen out. "I said, wait a minute, everybody, this is a great idea, let's do it right," Wenner said. "If you really want the cooperation of everybody, it's got to be nonprofit. I was persuasive on that point; everybody agreed on that, except for the TV people." (Technically, it was a nonprofit before Wenner became a board member.)

Consequently, Brandwen sued the Rock and Roll Hall of Fame Foundation for breach of contract in 1988. When a judge indicated that he might favor the defendants, Brandwen settled out of court, giving Ertegun and Wenner the Hall of Fame, lock, stock, and barrel. They fired Lesley Gore, who was never inducted, but kept the director, Suzan Evans, an efficient and willing administrator. "As soon as she saw the handwriting on the wall, which was day one, she switched to our side," said Ben Needell, Wenner's lawyer, who joined the board in 1985. "We did take it from [Brandwen]. It was easy."

Wenner would laugh to Kent Brownridge that they "fucked" Brandwen out of the Hall of Fame, but removing the Black Tie Network did what the record men intended: It gave the institution the nonprofit fig leaf it needed to shield against the moneygrubbing reputation of the music business itself. After all, men like Ahmet Ertegun had made millions off the artists they now intended to recruit for the Hall of Fame, especially the early R&B artists, some of whom were destitute after bad record deals in the 1950s and 1960s. Getting rid of Brandwen allowed the Hall of Fame to maintain that it was about Art with a capital *A:* an authentic form of American expression once considered trivial pap until Jann Wenner and *Rolling Stone* built a critical apparatus around it and helped Ahmet Ertegun and Joe Smith and Jac Holzman and David Geffen and Clive Davis and Mo Ostin and Lou Adler and Walter Yetnikoff get very, very rich selling rock and roll to the masses.

With Brandwen gone, the Rock and Roll Hall of Fame cut a deal with MTV and began broadcasting yearly, starting in the 1990s. And *Rolling Stone* became a full-scale public relations machine for the institution. The 1988 induction ceremony set the template, inducting Bob Dylan, the Beatles, and the Beach Boys, who were introduced by Mick Jagger, Bruce Springsteen, and Elton John, respectively. While co-hosts Ertegun and Wenner stood in the wings, Dylan spoke from a podium at the Waldorf Astoria about his devotion to Little Richard, who was in the audience, and expressed genuine gratitude for the honor. (Asked if the award really meant anything to him, Dylan said, "Yeah, sure it did.") An unwieldy but bracing jam session ensued, with Dylan, Jagger, Springsteen, George Harrison, Peter Wolf, and Billy Joel singing the Beatles' "I Saw Her Standing There." Ringo Starr played drums and late night TV bandleader Paul Shaffer thrummed the keytar, the faddish synthesizer-guitar hybrid. *Rolling Stone* produced a spread of party pictures in Random Notes, which described the audience as "music-industry Fortune 500."

Here was a vision of rock-and-roll Olympus that fans had dreamed about since 1969, back when a group of *Rolling Stone* editors, led by Greil Marcus, published a fake review of a Rolling Stones/Bob Dylan/Beatles supergroup called the Masked Marauders and even recorded a dubious LP to go with it, issued by Warner Bros. And once a couple of Beatles and Bob Dylan appeared with the Rolling Stones, there was no rock or pop star who did not want to be installed in that historic continuum. This was a public honor but also a media spectacle that could revive careers, kick up record sales, spark reissues (on the new format enlivening the coffers of the music companies, the CD), and burnish the reputation of forgotten artists like the Rascals or the Dave Clark Five. It would also stoke old rivalries, as when Mike Love of the Beach Boys ranted, during his acceptance speech, that Mick Jagger was "too chickenshit" to get onstage with him.

Inevitably, this was going to be a political process. Now a group of aging record men, every one of them white, with Ahmet Ertegun as chairman and Wenner as his loyal sidekick, nominated the artists in a backroom process that Jon Landau once advertised as purposefully "nontransparent," producing an induction ceremony and concert extravaganza for maximum media exposure on television. This was, for all intents and purposes, a rock-and-roll mafia. And for the next several years Ertegun and Wenner would be the dons of the Hall of Fame, the genteel hipster in goatee and spectacles and his plump partner in a three-piece suit, Mr. *Rolling Stone.*

After the opening of the museum in 1995, there was a seven-hour rock concert at Cleveland Municipal Stadium featuring Chuck Berry, Bob Dylan, Jerry Lee Lewis, Al Green, Aretha Franklin, Johnny Cash, Lou Reed, the Pretenders, the Kinks, Bruce Springsteen, Booker T. and the MGs, among others. The next day, architecture critic Herbert Muschamp reviewed the museum—a glass edifice designed by I. M. Pei, who had never listened to rock and roll—and noted its likeness to "Vladimir Tatlin's iconic Monument to the Third International, an unbuilt tribute to the founders of the Soviet state."

Wenner would call Ahmet Ertegun "the guiding moral and aesthetic sensibility" of the project, the one man who could "reconcile the formality and elegance of a museum with the rudeness and street stuff of an art form." "In the end," he told Robert Greenfield in his 2011 biography of Ertegun, "it was always, 'What does Ahmet think?' Because Ahmet had the vision."

But as Ertegun, a heavy drinker who was twenty-three years older than Wenner, began to recede from the limelight, Wenner became the primary face of the foundation and the force behind its success. He called himself "the principal driver of this whole thing." Indeed, he viewed the Rock and Roll Hall of Fame as part and parcel of his personal empire, an annex of *Rolling Stone.* "In a sense, it's owned by *Rolling Stone;* it's a creation of *Rolling Stone,*" said Wenner. "It's unfair to some people to say that. But that's what it is. It's my thing."

Suzan Evans, the onetime executive director who often found herself defending the integrity of the foundation against critics who charged that Wenner had his thumb on the scales of the induction process, was obliged to disagree, saying, "That's not how it started." Regardless, the Rock and Roll Hall of Fame, like *Rolling Stone* before it, made Jann Wenner the one-man *Pravda* of a deeply conservative rock-and-roll culture. As his friend Johnny Pigozzi put it, "He became like the pope of rock and roll, which was very, very important to him."

The official position of the Hall of Fame was that this was not true; Jann Wenner had no more power over who got inducted than any other committee member, even if a Jerry Wexler or a Seymour Stein privately complained. Wenner would nonetheless become the de facto bogeyman of rock, the gatekeeper whose deference to Mick Jagger defined his entire worldview. "In that sense, this is how successful Jann has been," said Dave Marsh, who served on the board from 1994 to 2016. "Jann Wenner is shorthand for the powers that be."

It was a reputation Wenner was happy to embrace. While rock bands whom he personally disliked were denied a place in the Hall of Fame for years, they watched as Jann Wenner was inducted in 2004 with the Lifetime Achievement in the Non-performer Category, with a surprise introduction by Mick Jagger, whose speech was co-written by Lorne Michaels: "This is a wonderful, heartfelt occasion, and I will treasure it, the memory of it, all the way to the airport." (As Cameron Crowe wrote to Wenner after, "Holy shit, Mick Jagger *opened* for you.")

Other rockers learned how to play the game. Bono, whose issues with rock and commerce evaporated around the time of U2's 1988 album *Rattle and Hum,* said his personal friendship with Wenner began at a Rock and Roll Hall of Fame event. He and his bandmates were watching Wenner give a speech and began making fun of him from the wings. "I said to the band, 'Shit, Jann Wenner has morphed into a Kennedy,'" he recalled. "He's a quiff. And his chin was jutting out and his teeth looked shiny and he was in a suit. And it was a long way from rock and roll.

"And he just turned—'I heard that,'" said Bono. "I thought, 'This guy's fucking sharp.'"

Bono would be the newest entrant in Wenner's pantheon, hosting Wenner at his home in the South of France and generously praising *Rolling Stone* onstage during a U2 concert in Detroit while Wenner hosted auto executives in a VIP suite (Bono did a meet-and-greet afterward and helped lock in fifty ad pages for Jann Wenner). Bono had already appeared on the cover sixteen times when he finally sat for a 16,613-word interview with Wenner himself in 2005, the same year U2 was inducted into the Hall of Fame, introduced by Bruce Springsteen (whom Bono had introduced at *his* induction in 1999). As with Mick Jagger and Bob

Dylan, Wenner allowed Bono to edit his own *Rolling Stone* interview. "It was an enchanting experience," Wenner wrote in his editorial. "The guy's a magician."

•

IT WASN'T JUST the underrated groups who disliked the opaque internal dynamics of the Hall of Fame. Even Paul McCartney felt Jann Wenner was back to his old tricks. McCartney didn't attend the Beatles' induction in 1988. But in the early 1990s, Wenner tried befriending him in the Hamptons, inviting Paul and Linda over to look at his new Picasso. Shortly after, McCartney got a call from Wenner. "He asked me, would I induct John into the Rock and Roll Hall of Fame," McCartney recounted. "I said, 'Yeah, sure.' I put the phone down, and thought, 'What about me?' The thing about John Lennon–McCartney is we were all equal."

When McCartney asked if he could be inducted too, Wenner said it wasn't up to him; there was a nominating committee, which now included onetime Elektra A&R man Danny Fields. "And it was like, 'Oh, no, we can't do that, we can't do that,'" said McCartney. "In all my dealings with him, it's never up to Jann. It's up to these 'other people' who are down the corridor somewhere. His thing just happens to have 'Owner, Editor' on the door, but *they're* responsible for things."

Indeed, the offices of the Rock and Roll Hall of Fame resided inside Wenner Media, which charged the foundation $80,000 a year for rent. According to Paul McCartney, Wenner told him that if he agreed to induct Lennon, the Hall of Fame would induct McCartney the following year. And so McCartney inducted John Lennon in 1994, reading an open letter to him that recounted the highlights of their lives together. "So now years on, here we are, all these people, assembled, to thank you for everything," said McCartney, looking skyward from the podium before a hushed room at the Waldorf Astoria. "This letter comes with love from your friend Paul. John Lennon, you made it. Tonight, you're in the Rock and Roll Hall of Fame. God bless you."

And then Axl Rose and Bruce Springsteen performed "Come Together" in a televised jam session on HBO.

The next year, McCartney discovered that he was not in fact being inducted into the Rock and Roll Hall of Fame. "I rang Jann and said, 'I'm getting all the papers; I don't appear to be in it. You fucking bastard,'" said McCartney. "We had a deal. A verbal contract that was not worth the paper it was written on. So that didn't endear me to him." (Wenner said he didn't remember making such a deal.)

Far from receding into the past, the history of rock and roll was a living drama, beholden to the same old *Rolling Stone* agenda, which was Jann Wenner's agenda. "It all added to this historical thing, that John was really *it* in the Beatles, and the other three weren't it, by implication," said McCartney. "To me, me and John writing, it was so equal. And sometimes it was not equal. Sometimes I was absolutely the one that got his ass out of bed. Which I don't go round saying. You won't find me saying, 'Oh, it was me!' You'll find other people saying, 'It was him! It was me!' I don't want to do that. I'm happy with half credit."

It would be another four years before Paul McCartney was inducted into the Rock and Roll Hall of Fame. In his unscripted and bittersweet acceptance speech, McCartney said he wished his wife, Linda, who had died of cancer the year before, could share in it. "She wanted this," he said, holding the award trophy in the air. In her stead, McCartney brought up his tearful daughter Stella, who wore a white T-shirt that carried a message for Jann Wenner and the board of the Rock and Roll Hall of Fame: "About Fucking Time!"

22

Nevermind

The first time Jann Wenner laid eyes on Bill Clinton, the Democratic candidate for president of the United States was standing in the driveway of the Governor's Mansion in Little Rock wearing a pair of Bermuda shorts. He was red-faced and screaming ferociously at an aide. "He just exploded," marveled Wenner.

Clinton disappeared into the house and returned wearing a suit for his *Rolling Stone* photo shoot. Now voluble and magnanimous, he asked Wenner for advice on his tie, then put his arm around him, struck a pose, and declared, "Leader of the free world."

In 1992, Clinton was hailed as the first baby-boomer candidate for the White House. He played saxophone on television and once tried marijuana (though he didn't cop to inhaling it), opposed the Vietnam War and campaigned for George McGovern, had an affinity for black culture, supported AIDS research, and even conscripted an environmentalist and former journalist for a vice presidential pick, Al Gore. For a theme song, the Clinton campaign used "Don't Stop" by Fleetwood Mac, whose first *Rolling Stone* cover was a bird's-eye view of the band half-naked in bed together, taken by Annie Leibovitz for a story by Cameron Crowe.

Wenner said Clinton wasn't exactly a rock-and-roll fan. "He liked Paul McCartney," he said. Wenner was also put off by Clinton's antidrug stance. And until the Democratic convention in New York in July 1992, Wenner had backed Jerry Brown, the 1970s-era California liberal who once dated Linda Ronstadt and now had his own 1-800 number to drum up support. During the primaries, Wenner endorsed Brown in *Rolling Stone,* writing that he "consistently stood for the values that matter most to our readers." In retrospect, Wenner would blame Sting, the former singer of the Police (cover of *Rolling Stone,* February 1991), and his fiancée, Trudie, for persuading him to back Brown. "We were talking about politics and commitments," Wenner recalled. "It was Sting or Trudie who forced me on the Jerry Brown thing."

At the convention in New York, Wenner hung out with Brown's campaign adviser, former *Rolling Stone* columnist Dick Goodwin, who was trying to convince Brown to throw his delegates to Clinton. A recalcitrant Brown refused and left the convention hall, but Wenner stuck around and used his convention pass to hover around the stage and eyeball Bill Clinton.

In the 1980s and 1990s, *Rolling Stone*'s political coverage was handled by William Greider, who had befriended Hunter Thompson while covering the 1972 presidential campaign for *The Washington Post* and started as Wenner's national affairs editor in 1981. Greider produced reliably left-wing and admirably detailed policy coverage of the Reagan years, but Wenner found "sunny Ronald Reagan" a low-yield target for his magazine, and besides, he benefited enormously from Reagan's tax policies. "Politics didn't get revived until Clinton," said Wenner. "The Clinton candidacy was a marker."

Wenner gained access to Clinton through George Stephanopoulos, the wunderkind strategist who was featured in *Rolling Stone* in 1989 for a roundup of young legislative comers called "The Hill Climbers." Wenner was also casually acquainted with Al Gore, who stopped by the offices of *Rolling Stone* with his wife, Tipper, to campaign for warning labels on rock albums with lyrics she deemed unfit for the ears of children (Wenner, the new family man, agreed with her). Gore was also a friend of Wenner's old pal John Warnecke, who during a period of personal decline first publicized the fact that Gore had tried marijuana in his twenties, causing Gore some political heartburn.

For his first meeting with Democratic nominee Clinton, Wenner decided to fly his entire political "team"—William Greider, Hunter Thompson, and P. J. O'Rourke—to Arkansas for a group interview. Thompson still published in *Rolling Stone* periodically, usually sweet-talked by the latest managing editor besotted with his legend and almost always against Wenner's advice; Wenner told them they would waste a lot of money and never get Thompson to write anything. But Harriet Fier managed to get Thompson to cover a Muhammad Ali boxing match in 1978; McDonell coaxed him into covering the sordid divorce trial of Roxanne Pulitzer in 1983; and in 1992, Bob Wallace got Thompson to write about Clarence Thomas in a story called "Fear and Loathing in Elko." Wenner had even salvaged Thompson's lost reporting from Saigon for "Dance of the Doomed," published in 1985. But Dr. Thompson was now a parody of his 1970s persona, usually drunk, coked up, gargling about Nixon, living off the legend that flatterers like McDonell imbibed as from a chalice in the Church of Jack Kerouac. His writing, while occasionally funny, was almost impenetrable to younger readers who hadn't been steeped in his highly personal vocabulary and endless self-reference. Thompson enjoyed having acolytes, who came to include actor Johnny Depp, read his own work to him aloud.

The relationship with Wenner remained volatile. Thompson needed Wenner for money, while Wenner maintained a sentimental affection for him, despite Thompson hosing him down with a fire extinguisher in his office for a camera crew to keep the myth of the "Good Old Days" alive. The myth, as Wenner knew, was what counted. Thompson began his 1992 story on the Clarence Thomas hearings as a wistful letter to Jann Wenner: "You have come a long way from the Bloodthirsty, Beady-eyed news Hawk that you were in days of yore. Maybe you should try reading something besides those goddamn motorcycle magazines—or one of these days you'll find hair growing in your palms."

The day of the Clinton interview, Thompson was sick with a cold and William Greider had to be rolled in a wheelchair to Wenner's jet for the trip to Little Rock. By the time they arrived at Doe's Eat Place, the café where they were to interview Clinton over tamales, Thompson was pouring sweat from doing too much cocaine (per Johnny Carson, "Colombian *Contact*"). Wenner, who by that point mostly abstained, took a sniff in solidarity. Thompson was unhappy with Bill Clinton's antidrug stance but showed up with a peace offering: a special saxophone reed like Charlie Parker once used, an unassailably poetic gift. Clinton blinked at it. "Clinton was like, 'Oh, thanks,'" recalled P. J. O'Rourke. "That hurt Hunter's feelings." Clinton kept his distance from Thompson, a fellow southerner whose bullshit detector he might have feared. While pontificating on crime, Clinton turned to Thompson, pointedly, and promised forty thousand more cops on the streets of America, decisively alienating Raoul Duke while also protecting his center-left flank from the lunatic fringe from Aspen. "Hunter did not like him," said Wenner. "I had to twist his arm into agreeing to endorse. He just didn't trust him; he thought he was slimy. And it turns out, Bill was not entirely aboveboard, not by a long shot."

Clinton spoke in long, complete paragraphs about policy, boring his interviewers stiff. Asked afterward what the benefit of the Clinton interview was to the magazine, O'Rourke said, "You have to have something to run in between the Guns N' Roses covers." But as transactions go, this was a natural: Clinton wanted the *Rolling Stone* stamp of youth approval, and Wenner wanted the ear of a president. To be sure, Wenner admired Clinton's steely ambition. After asking Clinton how he intended to overcome Republican resistance, Wenner told MTV in 1992 that Clinton replied, "Well, we're going to have to roll them."

"He didn't say negotiate," emphasized Wenner. "He didn't say peace, understand their side. He said, 'We're going to have to roll them.'"

•

BEFORE BILL CLINTON WAS ELECTED, Wenner told MTV he was heartened by Clinton's support of gay rights. "I don't know if it's literally a guarantee of the Democratic platform, but I think that's the point," said Wenner. "They put on gays at the convention, they've been wearing the red ribbons [for AIDS research] for a long time and giving sympathy to AIDS and so on like that. That's a big step ahead. Ten years ago, forget it, it wasn't part of the dialogue."

Clinton's first policy push—allowing gays to serve openly in the military—would not only fail, leading to the degrading "Don't Ask, Don't Tell" policy that lasted until 2010, but produce a powerful congressional backlash and throw the Clinton administration off course, ultimately empowering the new opposition leader, Speaker of the House Newt Gingrich. "This town is more conservative than I thought, more fixed. It's more change averse," Clinton told *Rolling Stone* in 1993, Wenner's first presidential interview.

When *Rolling Stone* editor Brant Mewborn became sick with AIDS, Wenner quietly paid for his hospital bills until he died in 1990. "He funded that guy and his family for some time without a whisper of it being known for anyone," said John Lagana, the company CFO in the 1990s. (His obituary in *Rolling Stone* didn't mention the cause of death, to shield his family.) But the AIDS crisis was making it harder and harder for the living to maintain denial. Sylvester, whose album Wenner had tried producing in 1971, died of AIDS in 1988. Cliff Jahr, to whom Elton John first confessed his sexuality, died in 1991, the same year Freddie Mercury succumbed. And Hunter Thompson's brother Jim died of AIDS in 1993. Meanwhile, a group called ACT UP (AIDS Coalition to Unleash Power) was pushing an aggressive agenda into the media world. It was ACT UP's first spokesman, Bob Rafsky, who pressured Bill Clinton to make AIDS part of the Democratic platform (Rafsky died of AIDS in 1993). In the late 1980s and early 1990s, a former gossip columnist and ACT UP executive named Michelangelo Signorile began reporting on closeted gay men in Hollywood and the media, effectively outing them in the pages of *Outweek*, a radical AIDS activism magazine. In his 1993 book, *Queer in America*, Signorile portrayed the "closets of power" (a phrase first coined by Taylor Branch in 1982) as a conspiracy in which gay publicists and gay newspaper columnists protected the careers of gay actors managed by gay agents and gay media barons—a self-enforcing closet that amplified homophobia. "The net result," wrote Signorile, "is to ensure that coming out of the closet remains a risky, dangerous, and dubious thing to do."

Signorile first revealed that Malcolm Forbes, who died in 1990, had been gay, and then he moved on to the living: In 1992, he pressured David Geffen, by accusing him of hypocrisy for profiting from Guns N' Roses' homophobic song lyrics and for distributing the work of comedian Andrew Dice Clay, who maligned gays as part of his retro stand-up act as "the Diceman." Geffen first tried admitting he was "bisexual" in *Vanity Fair* before fully embracing his gay identity with a speech before the AIDS Project Los Angeles, to which he became a major donor. Afterward, Geffen went into therapy to deal with his years-long denial.

Wenner, another cog in Signorile's closeted-celebrity industrial complex, believed identifying as gay meant being an "outcast," he said. Many of Jann Wenner's generation of gay men built their lives around their denial. Wenner claimed he didn't even know that his friend Barry Diller was gay back in the 1970s. When Diane von Furstenberg left Diller for a Brazilian man named Paulo in the early 1980s, Wenner said Diller would "commiserate" with him, asking Wenner, "What do I do?" "I wasn't even aware he was gay then," Wenner said. "He was deeply in love with Diane." ("I was trying to help him with his pain, and I tried to counsel him on it," Wenner added.) By the 1990s, however, Wenner knew Diller was gay because he was an occasional satellite to Diller's off-the-record social life, which overlapped with that of David Geffen. Wenner admired and deeply envied these men their power and money *while being gay*. In gossip circles, they were referred to as the "Velvet Mafia," whose ostensible members also included designer Calvin Klein and Hollywood agent Sandy Gallin. (In 1992, the humor magazine *Spy,* begun by Graydon Carter and Kurt Andersen, deemed them "Hollywood's powerful gay tong.") The men vacationed and socialized together, often on yachts staffed with handsome and available young men, a lifestyle not unlike that of Geffen's rock star clients back in the 1970s. The caustic humorist Fran Lebowitz sometimes joined them for comedy relief, arching her eyebrows when, for instance, Diller and Geffen fought over an advance copy of William Paley's memoir (they were both richer than he ever was, so what was the big deal?). Geffen said the term "Velvet Mafia" was a homophobic slur, but he also said that Jann Wenner was never a part of it. "Jann was not in that group," he said. "It didn't exist to begin with. But it was always Barry, me, and Sandy Gallin and Calvin Klein. Those were the four. It's so ridiculous. Velvet Mafia. It's a way of being homophobic."

As fun as it looked from afar, Wenner said he was always afraid of getting too close. "I didn't want to expose myself to that world, because then you'd be over," he said. "You'd come out of the closet then. That's something I didn't want to do."

For a while, Wenner remained discreet. Over the years, employees at *Rolling Stone* speculated on his flirtations with handsome male actors like Jason Priestley of *Beverly Hills, 90210* and Tom Cruise, motorcycle-riding pals who received favored treatment in Wenner's magazines, or his demand that his sales staff stay in a different hotel from him on advertising trips to Los Angeles (he stayed at the Peninsula Beverley Hills, the favored hotel of Barry Diller). But in 1993, Wenner finally began to break free from his former life—by falling in love with a man. It happened while the Wenners were on Christmas vacation in St. Bart's, the island retreat for the jet set, staying in a house formerly owned by the Rockefellers. Barry Diller's yacht was moored in the bay of the French Antilles, and Jann decided to go aboard—without Jane. (The boat, according to Wenner, was the SS *Lisboa,* the same one that Max Palevsky operated back in the 1970s.) That night Wenner became enraptured by a young fashion designer named Matt Nye, who was the companion of artist Ross Bleckner. With piercing blue eyes, a sturdy chin, and long blond locks, Nye was twenty-eight but looked even younger. "My," said Wenner, "he's very attractive."

Nye was far from naive. After he went to New York to study fashion, his striking looks quickly got him invited to parties where Andy Warhol and cocaine were present, a far cry from his suburban life growing up in Michigan, the youngest of ten children, born around the time Jann Wenner first tried LSD in 1965. His father, who changed the family's last name from Nienartowicz, managed a tool and die company. In high school, Nye was voted "Most Likely to Be Recast in a *Dynasty* Remake," and he studied biology at the University of Michigan, intending to go to medical school, but he thought better of it after meeting people in the theater department. He was working as a European fashion scout at Ralph Lauren when he was noticed by Calvin Klein at a party and became his boyfriend and a designer at Klein's company. Nye soon became part of the orbit of other gay moguls, like David Geffen.

After Wenner met him on the boat, Nye showed up at the beach near Wenner's house and began playing with his sons Gus and Theo and also met Jane. The following summer, Nye showed up at the Wenners' house in the Hamptons after giving Theo a ride home from a party.

With Jane none the wiser, Wenner asked Nye out on a date the next week. "We went out, had a dinner, and then it went rapidly from there," said Wenner.

Wenner was only the latest powerful man prepared to outfit Nye in expensive finery and ferry him around on a private plane. But Nye unleashed Jann Wenner's appetites like never before. For six months, they snuck around Manhattan for liaisons. At one point, Wenner asked Robbie Robertson, a board member of the Rock and Roll Hall of Fame, to suggest a suitable place for an inconspicuous meeting with an un-identified lover. Recounted Robertson, "He was talking under his breath on the phone, and he said to me, 'Is there a place downtown where I can go with a certain someone and not run into anyone we know?'"

Robertson was among the first to suspect the Wenner marriage was on the rocks. "I knew this was the beginning of the end," Robertson said.

Jane grew suspicious because Wenner was "being very odd," she said, "critical and nasty." Wenner would disappear for hours and come whistling home with a baguette under his arm. Still, Wenner had no intention of coming out of the closet. "I was having a great time," he said. "Every door was open. I had sex on the side when I wanted, very discreetly, I had a big successful life—you know, why would I possibly consider doing such a thing? It would be insane."

But Nye wasn't interested in living in the shadows, and Wenner said he was no longer happy living with Jane, whose depression and drug use he felt had diminished what was left of their relationship. "I became deeply unhappy that I couldn't be with him and longed to be with him," Wenner said of Nye. The two were sitting on a bench in Central Park the day Wenner proposed leaving Jane. "I said, 'If I jump over the river, are you going to be there to catch me?' and he said, 'Yes, I will be,'" recalled Wenner.

Three weeks later, Wenner said he let it "slip out" in front of Jane: He was leaving her for a man. It was Christmas Eve 1994. "It was en-tirely a gut decision, made in the moment, with no thought to conse-quences," Wenner said. "Like everything else I'd done, it was impulsive and guided by some sense of what's right and what's good for me. I'm not a person who plots things out and thinks things through and judges all the consequences. I do what makes me happy and feels good and makes other people happy. Just go. Just feel it. Go with it.

"People who write history," he continued, "want to find theories that explain everything, constructs to give things meaning, and there are those things, and they're meta ones, but they're not as linear, for me anyway. I'm sure Henry Luce thought through all this shit, but he's from an educated and religious background, so he was constructed that way."

Jane Wenner was stunned by Wenner's confession. "It was cruel" is all she could say about it. When Wenner left to go live in a hotel, she called Ben Needell at three in the morning while he was on vacation in Vermont, bawling and wondering if it could possibly be true. "Jann left me for a guy," she announced. "Why would he leave me?"

That spring, Wenner moved into an apartment rented to him by record executive Seymour Stein, who was familiar with Wenner's sexual interests. As word spread that Wenner left his wife for a man—first as a gossip item in *Advertising Age* and then in a British tabloid—a reporter for *The Wall Street Journal*, Patrick Reilly, began reporting a story on what the split would mean for the company, which had changed its name to Wenner Media from Straight Arrow. After all, Jane had a large stake in the company. Might a divorce tear the company apart and lead to a sale of *Rolling Stone*? Wenner was worried, too, if not about Jane and the ownership, then about what his outing would mean for business. "Jann was pretty freaked out," said Kent Brownridge. "He thought maybe he would lose his exalted business position and all the wealth he had and all the income he was enjoying at the time."

Wenner had a lot to protect: a $200 million company, a wife whom his friends loved, three sons on whom he doted, and the well-burnished persona of the ultimate baby boomer for whom the heterosexual high life was an almost religious devotion. The proof of his devotion was entrepreneurial: In 1993, he launched a magazine called *Family Life*, which he created with Nancy Evans, an editor he met through Jackie Onassis. ("A generation that once raised hell is now raising kids" went the promotional tag.) But now he was about to upend the public story line he had built for twenty-eight years. Reporter Patrick Reilly, a devotee of *Rolling Stone* in college, said the idea that Jann Wenner was gay simply did not compute. *Rolling Stone* was about "rock and roll machoism," he said. "Jann Wenner was, up to that point, a very cool, heterosexual guy. There was nothing gay about him. When the news came out, it was like, really? Of all the people in media who might be gay, Jann Wenner? The reaction was 'You've got to be kidding me.'"

If his story was about to shift, Wenner wanted a hand in authoring it. He dispatched Kent Brownridge and Ben Needell to work with Reilly and help shape the story that would appear in the *Journal*. Needell said he "accidentally" confirmed what Reilly already knew during a conference call: Jann Wenner was gay. "I assumed that everybody knew," he said with a shrug. And thus Reilly reported it on March 3, 1995: "Earlier this year, [Wenner] left the home he shared with his wife and three young children and began a relationship with a young male staffer at Calvin Klein."

And that was it: Jann Wenner was officially out of the closet. There was also the news that profits had declined at Wenner Media and the company was entertaining bids to sell one of its magazines—*Family Life*. The public narrative of it was almost too on the nose. The day the story ran, Wenner was scheduled to give a presentation to the board of an antigun group called CeaseFire, chaired by Michael Douglas and featuring Barry Diller, Tom Freston, and Sony chief Howard Stringer, among others. Awaiting Wenner's arrival at the conference room at Wenner Media on Sixth Avenue, the men all wondered what condition the publisher of *Rolling Stone* would be in. "Everyone in the room had read the article," recalled Freston.

Wenner arrived beaming and magnanimous. "Then a smiling Jann entered the conference room perfectly turned out in a striped shirt, tie, and banker's suspenders," said Freston. "I was like, 'Whoa, this ought to be something. Sure glad it ain't me up there.' He gave a tour de force, did not give an inch. He ruled the room."

The news of the Wenners' separation burned through their social sphere. Geffen called to hear all about it. Mick Jagger rang up to advise Wenner to avoid being a weekend dad. "It was kind of odd," said Jagger. "I didn't have an idea that that was going to happen." That same day, Wenner was scheduled to have lunch with Bette Midler, a longtime advocate for gay rights. The news surprised her and she was happy for Wenner, but her enthusiasm was tempered by a nagging sense that Wenner had betrayed his wife. "I think that was more disturbing to him than he talks about," she said. "I don't think he lets too much daylight in on that one. My sense of it is that it was very hard on her, and my heart went out to her. I'm going to say that, and I don't care if they never speak to me again; my heart went out to her."

The week after Wenner left his wife of twenty-six years, Johnny Pigozzi invited Jane on his yacht in the Mediterranean with Ahmet Ertegun and his wife, Mica, and Chris Blackwell of Island Records, where Jane spent the entire time crying her eyes out. "She was completely devastated," said Pigozzi. "She was crying all day long. I think it was huge. Because she was always madly in love with him. She's still in love with him."

The story made national news. *Newsweek* detailed Wenner's coming-out with a timeline of events, and *New York* magazine burrowed into the story for an exposé titled "Perception, Reality," which referred to Nye as "the boy toy of the Velvet Mafia." How could Jane have abided Wenner's homosexuality all those years? The cynical answer was money. Jane was utterly humiliated. "When I came out, Jane was going around saying she didn't know," said Wenner.

Indeed Jane insisted that she had been in denial all along. "But he never really *said* it, you know?" she said. "And there would be whispers, and every time I'd ask him about it, he said no, and so, you know, you turn a blind eye. I don't know." (Ben Needell, the family lawyer, said Jane mentioned Wenner's being gay to him "a dozen times over the years, before he met Matt.")

Many of the Wenners' longtime friends, like Earl and Camilla McGrath, blamed Wenner for breaking up a perfectly good marriage. "How can you do that?" Camilla asked him. "He lost some friends," Midler said. But Wenner was resolute: "They are from that old world, the European world, where anything goes. And great, I'm sure that worked for them. Ahmet and Mica loved each other deeply and Earl and Camilla loved each other, but it wasn't my world. I didn't want to be in that world of aristocratic relationships. I wanted to be completely who I wanted to be, and why live this lie? Why live a lie that ultimately humiliates the person you're with? And be this person who is openly fucking everyone in town, men or women? I don't want to do bad things, you know?"

•

SMACK IN THE MIDDLE of coming out, Wenner had decided to get back into journalism by interviewing Mick Jagger on the occasion of the Stones' twenty-second studio album, *Voodoo Lounge*. Over the course of a year, Wenner flew to meet Jagger in Palm Beach, Florida, in Montreal, Canada, and later in Cologne, Germany, engaging in casual chitchat about old records over meals and gossip. The interview was called "Mick Jagger Remembers." At one point, Wenner asked Jagger about the influence of homosexuality on his image.

> WENNER: When were you aware that you were this beauty, that
>   you had the power to attract both girls and boys?
> JAGGER: Oh, from the beginning.
> WENNER: The girls, and then the boys?
> JAGGER: Both, always.
> WENNER: In a sexual sense?
> JAGGER: I didn't really think about it. I mean, boys were a very
>   essential part of rock & roll. The girls were more onlookers . . .
>   I always felt the boys were more involved than the girls . . .
>   They want to be with you. Some might be attracted to you
>   without knowing it. The girls are more obviously reaching
>   out to you. In those days, guys didn't reach out, put their arms
>   around you and kiss you.

In Cologne, Germany, Wenner brought Matt Nye with him to meet his idol. Jagger said he never suspected Wenner was gay. "Jann's got a boyfriend," Jagger announced archly to his gay publicist, Tony King. "Mick wasn't old-fashioned about it," said King. "But for anybody, it's quite a transition when you're used to the wife all these years and then all of a sudden here comes a rather glamorous boyfriend."

This was a big moment. Wenner was keen to impress the boyfriend with his access to celebrity. Nye was nervous. "Jann went to go to

Mick's dressing room, and Matt wouldn't go," King continued. "And I said, 'Why won't you go?' And he said, 'I'm kind of embarrassed; I don't really want to go.' And I said, 'Don't be silly. Just go.' And he said, 'I haven't got the right clothes.' And I said, 'Listen, dear, go and tell your mum that you met Mick Jagger.' So he goes, 'All right.'"

The youth from Michigan was an object of desire for Wenner, a walking, talking status symbol among his friends. He had finally got the girl he desired and she was a man. But Matt would also become a genuine partner, the social ballast Wenner lost in Jane, who had lost herself to denial and drugs, in that order. For Wenner, there would be no denial with Nye. He was twenty-seven years old when he met Wenner, and though he didn't fall in love right away, he said Wenner grew on him. It would be hard to argue that Nye wasn't an opportunist. Jann and Jane Wenner, he observed, were narcissists with no emotional intelligence. "That's where I came in," he said. But he was also a pragmatic figure for Wenner. A healthy midwesterner with good horse sense, he was shy and retiring at parties, rolled his eyes at Jann's old rocker friends, gamely took up the role of step-whatever to Wenner's kids (who didn't understand who he was at first and disliked him), and replaced Jane as chief decorator ("He steals my style," said Jane). Wenner would support Nye's clothing design company, which Nye dropped after winning the Perry Ellis Award for Menswear in 1999. Wenner and Nye made each other laugh, gossiped about celebrities, made fun of Jane. (Nye declined to speak on the record for this book.)

Newly outed, Wenner began to study up in earnest on what it meant to be gay, calling editors like Adam Moss—whom he'd once pursued in the offices of *Rolling Stone* in the late 1970s, after Moss wrote a profile of a male hustler for *Rolling Stone College Papers*—to ask about life on the outside, and reading *A Boy's Own Story*, the classic coming-out tale by gay writer Edmund White, whom he invited to his office on Sixth Avenue. "And the very first thing he did was to tell me he was gay," said White, "and to show me a bikini picture of his boyfriend."

Wenner assigned White, who had written an essay on AIDS for *Rolling Stone* in 1985, to profile two of the biggest openly gay men in the music business, Elton John and David Geffen, for *Rolling Stone* and *US* magazine. Acting as Wenner's eyes and ears, White visited Geffen at his home in Malibu, where the mogul told him about a handsome straight man he met on the beach that day and intended on flying to Las Vegas for some fun. "That's their big thing, to fuck a straight man," recalled White. White's profiles didn't exactly earn Wenner plaudits. White made fun of Elton John's hair and interior decorating. Said John, "As a fellow gay man, we thought it would be a more positive piece. I thought he was a snotty queen who was a legend in his own lunchtime."

The gay world was no less complicated than the straight one. In the late 1990s, Wenner and Barry Diller got into a fight that involved Matt Nye and a yachting vacation that became so personal and heated that Diller, who ran the cable channel USA Network, pulled all of his advertising from *Rolling Stone* for three years. ("The state of our friendship hurts me a lot," Wenner later wrote to him. "Although we may see the facts differently, I offer my sincere apology to you for what I have done to offend you.")

Wenner's mother, Sim, who was living with a woman in Hawaii, said that Matt Nye "made a man" out of Jann Wenner. But in most ways the new Jann Wenner was the same as the old one. He struck no one as particularly gay—he still telegraphed the kind of sporting swagger familiar to readers of *Men's Journal*—but he drank less, tried to stop smoking, got his teeth capped, dyed his hair, trimmed his weight, and wore his shirt open like a rakish mogul. "Jann had a certain edge on him until he came out of the closet and that edge was gone," observed Bob Pittman. "Honesty always frees you."

But Wenner never apologized for his years of lying about his sexuality. In 1998, *Rolling Stone* published a special issue on the Bill Clinton and Monica Lewinsky imbroglio that was threatening Clinton's hold on the White House. Kenneth Starr's lurid report on Clinton's affair had become a referendum on the sexual revolution of the 1960s, but it hung as much on his lying under oath as it did the sexual details. To this, Wenner declared that "a lie about someone's sex life is one of those tolerated untruths."

Contrary to speculation, Jane did not immediately threaten the ownership of the company. Instead, she burrowed into denial and refused to deal with the breakup for several years. She commiserated with her best friends, the ex-wives of Harrison Ford and Lorne Michaels. She referred to Nye as "Soon-Yi." Ben Needell, the Wenner family lawyer, played go-between, taking Jane's anxious phone calls and gingerly getting her to sign off on Wenner's bonuses. If he mentioned the word "divorce," she lit into him: "Who said anything about divorce? There's no divorce! Did Jann talk about divorce?"

Jane rarely dated after Jann Wenner left her. She tried. Once with the son of a Greek shipping magnate. But ultimately she was too bound to Jann Wenner by *Rolling Stone* and their three sons. "I was so hurt by him," she said. "But I never was willing to abandon that relationship.

"He kept me close for years. That's probably why I never kind of moved on. Look, Jann was a very big personality, big shoes to fill, so to speak. I mean, he was smart, he was charming, he was cuckoo, he was—not cuckoo, but he was, like, dynamic and extremely smart and it's just . . . you don't have many relationships like that in your life."

The Wenners wouldn't divorce for seventeen years.

23

Bridges to Babylon

One day at a hotel in Montreal, Wenner and Jagger were taking a break from talking about *Sticky Fingers* for the "Mick Jagger Remembers" interview when the subject of the Internet came up. Wenner found the entire concept of the newfangled "World Wide Web" exceedingly dull. At the time, there were two major services, AOL and CompuServe, which struck deals with magazine companies to get "content" for their digital walled gardens. The web was accessible through painfully slow dial-up telephone connections, and most of it looked terrible. But Mick Jagger was an avid user, and he was awed by the ability to instantly get his soccer scores, read *The Daily Telegraph,* imbibe poetry and history, tour a virtual version of the Louvre, and, of course, trawl for unfiltered gossip through unofficial newsgroups.

Wenner wanted to hear more about that last point.

WENNER: Is it good?

JAGGER: It's a lot of people sitting in their offices on Friday, putting in—

WENNER: And feeding stuff into it? Oh, you mean it's open?

JAGGER: Well, it's open, you have to know where to look.

WENNER: But, I mean, it's not like a centralized service is gathering, is processing it and validating or not—

JAGGER: No, it's a news group.

WENNER:—it's just anybody can write from their little offices, saying, "I hate this fuck—"

JAGGER: Yeah, haha.

WENNER: Shit, that's dangerous.

JAGGER: [Laughs.]

WENNER: That's really—that's like the Xerox going around the office, it's a terrible thing.

He was laughing, but he was serious. And his attitude was not destined to change. When Jagger asked Wenner if he was putting *Rolling Stone* online, Wenner described a meeting with AOL in which co-founder Steve Case insulted him with a lowball offer. "The deal they were offering was just, like, pathetic," Wenner told Jagger. "I mean, it was, like, insulting."

JAGGER: Yeah, they just want to have it for nothing at that point.

WENNER: I said, "You know, Steve, you're a nice, bright—you know, but I haven't been offered a deal like that since I was 21 years old."

Case persisted, telling Wenner he needed to take a cheap deal with AOL to "get a learning curve" on the Internet; Wenner said he didn't want to overpay just to "learn." Finally, Case tried telling him he wasn't "hip."

JAGGER: [Laughs.]

WENNER: So I said, "You know, I'm not really—" haha, actually it was a little more arrogant than that. I said, "Steve, I've been deciding what's hip in this country for many years now."

Wenner made a one-year, $300,000 deal with CompuServe, the first of many partnerships that would earn him short-term cash but no long-term strategy. Wenner's attitude, which he expressed to Steve Case, was, "How about this: When it gets to be big, I'll hire your people."

Kent Brownridge saw clearly what the boss wanted and instead of having *Rolling Stone* invest in an Internet presence of its own decided to farm out the management of RollingStone.com to outside companies for cash payments up front. Let somebody else deal with it while Jann Wenner collected fees. He liked that deal. Even as the stock market pushed valuations of Internet companies to outrageous new heights, Wenner considered the prospects a black hole. He wasn't wrong. In the late 1990s, magazine publishers threw good money after bad trying to invent online analogues to their print magazines, little of it to any effect. As valuations rose, Wenner tried starting a print magazine called *Netbook,* which would refer people to the best websites and compete with *Wired* magazine.

But the disruptive power of the new medium had already begun to consume Wenner's business, from several directions. Before everyone's eyes, the Internet was destroying the music industry, the canary in the coal mine. The peer-to-peer file-sharing craze that started with Napster allowed people to trade music files online for free, fundamentally undermining CDs and eroding the income of record companies, which had only defensive and clunky answers to the Internet. "It wasn't like it wasn't in front of him," said Wenner's lawyer, Ben Needell. But Wenner said it was a gut thing; he simply liked print, the girl who brung him to the dance. He didn't even read RollingStone.com.

"The object is part of what I love," he said. "There's a level of importance to having [journalism] in a magazine still. You don't get that on the Internet; something important happens in print. It's been carefully edited and put together and a whole bunch of people are standing behind it, it takes money to put out there, and only the best people practice it."

Wenner didn't miss the tech boom entirely. In October 1999, his friend Gil Friesen, former head of A&M Records, offered Wenner shares of a new Internet company called Akamai Technologies, which hadn't existed fifteen months before. The day it went public, it shot up 458 percent over the asking price. Wenner was having lunch at the Four Seasons with Friesen, Hard Rock Cafe co-founder Peter Morton, and Tom Freston of MTV while he calculated the value of his investment on a piece of paper.

Suddenly, he leaped from the table and let out a whoop that stunned the walnut-paneled Grill Room. "And I'm just squealing, 'Yeah!'" recounted Wenner. "Go ask Julian [Niccolini, proprietor of the Four Seasons] about it. They remember it to this day. Nobody had ever screamed like that."

He made $35 million.

Around this time, Kent Brownridge convinced Wenner there was a gold mine right under his nose, and it had nothing to do with the Internet: *US* magazine. The celebrity monthly had never broken through and was losing $500,000 a year. But what if they took it weekly and went head-to-head with *People,* the most successful magazine in American history? Brownridge convinced Wenner they could bite off a share of *People*'s astonishing $627 million in yearly advertising revenue. This was about serving up a groaning smorgasbord of celebrity details but also about the grocery store "pockets" where tabloids sold like hotcakes at the checkout stands. It would require an enormous capital investment to break into the game—$50 million, they calculated—but Brownridge figured *US* could triple newsstand sales and pull in at least $10 million in three years. Brownridge started talking to outside investors, including Bain Capital, but Wenner demanded any outside group put up all the money for only 20 percent of the equity. Nobody would go for it, which meant Wenner would have to finance it himself. The Akamai windfall put him in a betting mood.

Editorially, Wenner wanted a degree of comfort and control, which is why he hired Terry McDonell to oversee his new celebrity tabloid. McDonell had edited most of Wenner's magazines, and the two vacationed together with their families. They once flew in Wenner's jet to see U2 in Dublin, and McDonell accompanied Wenner on a chartered yacht to pay a visit to Jackie Onassis in Martha's Vineyard. Neither had any idea how to run a celebrity weekly, but McDonell had once worked at *Newsweek,* which was good enough for Wenner, whose vision was decidedly straightforward: expensive photo shoots of actors, with interviews artfully arranged by the Hollywood publicity machines that managed them. Five months after the Akamai IPO, Wenner launched *Us Weekly* with outrageous fanfare, projecting he'd sell 500,000 newsstand copies a week and hit a guaranteed circulation of 1 million overnight.

The first issue, with Julia Roberts on the cover, sold less than half of what Wenner needed to break even. He was so shocked he refused to believe the magazine had even made it to the grocery stores. In a fury, he commanded Brownridge and two other sales staffers to take a week-long cross-country trip to check the racks where *Us Weekly* was sold to make sure it had been delivered. The magazines were there; they just weren't selling. Wenner panicked as weak sales figures came in, week after week. The venture lost $30 million in the first year. The press dubbed it "Wenner's folly" and "Wenner's Vietnam." "All of a sudden I was millions of dollars into this and my name was on the line," said Wenner.

Wenner was in a foul mood, and his employees scattered as he steamed around the offices. By 2001, *Rolling Stone* was underwriting the losses, and *Us Weekly* was threatening Wenner's lifestyle. And now Wenner wasn't the only voice in the equation: Jane Wenner didn't like the idea of funneling her profits to "Wenner's folly." To exert pressure, she hired a high-powered divorce attorney to scrupulously separate Wenner's personal expenses from his business expenses, shielding her own profits from his. The separation from Wenner had "really knocked her down, and she wanted serious revenge any way she could get it," recalled John Lagana, the chief financial officer for Wenner Media who regularly fielded calls from Jane during this period. Under duress, Wenner went looking for cash to buffer the losses. He turned to a friend from the old Paramount days, Michael Eisner, who was now the chief executive of a media empire, the Disney Company. Wenner offered Eisner a deal he couldn't refuse: For a mere $20 million, Disney could own half of *Us Weekly,* with a guarantee that if *Us Weekly* went under, Eisner would get $20 million worth of *Rolling Stone*. Eisner said it took him forty-five seconds to decide. "We had absolutely no risk," he said. "To this day, I can't believe he put the equity of his company up for grabs. It was just more proof that he knew what he was doing."

Kent Brownridge was skeptical of the sale, but lawyer Ben Needell argued that it was the equivalent of an interest-free loan and that the imprimatur of a corporate giant like Disney was worth its weight in gold with advertisers who might otherwise be shy about putting money into a "scandal mag." But the real trouble with *Us Weekly* wasn't advertisers; it was Terry McDonell. As Wenner conceded, "Terry didn't know dick about makeup, and obviously I didn't either. I should have, but I didn't."

McDonell had wanted to put the headline "The Weight Loss Hall of Fame" on the cover, and Wenner, who struggled with weight all his life, advised, "I don't like that, because it's ironic. It's a gag. But it doesn't get at all to the emotional quality of losing weight, and the shame. You're not getting to their emotional experience; you're making fun of them."

Ironically, it was *People*'s parent company, Time Inc., that delivered a stroke of fortune by recruiting McDonell to take over *Sports Illustrated*, leaving *Us Weekly* without an editor. Wenner said McDonell left "with my blessing," but he also refused to pay his retirement benefits, prompting McDonell to sue and get an out-of-court settlement. McDonell later wrote that "over the next 10 years, Jann was very friendly whenever we ran into each other, as if nothing had gone wrong between us." But Wenner said he withheld McDonell's money because McDonell owed him for a $100,000 personal loan. "What he's not willing to say is that he was reneging on his promissory note," said Wenner. "It was ungracious of him." But Wenner paid McDonell a high honor by comparing his version of events to a gonzo tale Hunter Thompson might cook up: "That's like Hunter telling me I canceled his life insurance." ("It was more complicated than that," McDonell said.)

It was Brownridge who recruited Bonnie Fuller, whose reputation as a crass and somewhat down-market but extremely talented editor—at *Marie Claire, Cosmopolitan,* and *Glamour*—preceded her. A fangirl from Toronto, she was, like Wenner, a celebrity hound who once edited a Canadian fashion magazine called *Flare*. Her vision for *Us Weekly* dispensed with old-school celebrity spreads and went straight for a remorseless celebrity exploitation that fused stories of weight loss and makeup with no-holds-barred gossip and paparazzi shots, a style imported from British tabloids like *Hello!* Fuller knew she was good, so when Wenner offered her a paltry $300,000 salary for the high-stakes job, she turned it down. If she was going to take on Wenner's failing magazine, she wanted $450,000 and a cut of the sales—ten cents a copy for every issue she sold over 450,000. She meant business. Wenner gave in; he needed her.

Almost instantly, Bonnie Fuller became Wenner's heat-seeking missile aimed directly for the zeitgeist, ushering in serialized tabloid stories of love affairs and breakups modeled on soap operas—starring Ben Affleck and Jennifer Lopez as "Bennifer"; Brad Pitt and Angelina Jolie as "Brangelina"—often produced in secret alliance with the stars themselves. This was the dawn of the reality TV era, in which a celebrity walked off the set of a big-budget Hollywood film or a multimillion-dollar world tour and into the pages of a tabloid docudrama about weight gain and dubious clothing choices. It was Fuller who invented the sections called "Stars—They're Just Like Us!" and "Who Wore It Best?," turning fashion into warfare and deploying armies of paparazzi to pursue celebrities as they picked up dog poop. She was hard driving but also expensive, taking a town car home to the suburbs after getting the magazine late to the printers. Like Wenner, she abhorred the Internet and didn't even bother turning on her computer; she hung her coat on it. In five weeks, *Us Weekly* was selling 500,000 copies a week.

At first, Wenner said he was embarrassed by *Us Weekly*. "I'm uncomfortable with the scandal, the prying, the paparazzi long lens," he said. "It took me a long while to get used to that. My friends, nobody likes that. In my crowd, no." Others said he loved it from the start. But unlike Wenner, Fuller saw the entire celebrity culture as fair game, including Wenner's pals. At *Glamour,* Fuller had made enemies of Catherine Zeta-Jones, partner to Michael Douglas, by publishing an unauthorized picture of Jones that was, Wenner said, promised to *Vogue.* At *Us Weekly,* Fuller published unflattering gossip about her and caused Michael Douglas to call up and complain. Wenner said he warned her to stand down and Fuller held off for a while, then went at her again. "She had it in for Catherine," said Wenner. "Bonnie had it in for anybody pretty or glamorous or happy. She was just one of the most unattractive people you've ever seen. There was just something about her face, one of those homely things where it's difficult to look at. And she had these dead eyes. Like a shark. Just dead. And that was her moral thing, too. She was just relentless."

As *Us Weekly* began succeeding, Wenner wanted to lay claim to it and began butting heads with Fuller over spending. People were talking about Bonnie Fuller and not Jann Wenner. Fuller's deputy, Janice Min, watched the two fight over picayune details like the design of the table of contents. "They were just going at it," said Min. "I was sitting there, looking at my feet—'This is super awkward.'"

Fuller lasted fifteen months before she was recruited to competitor *Star* magazine by David Pecker, owner of the *National Enquirer*. Wenner hired Min to take over, and she proceeded to turn Fuller's vision into an efficient and predictable formula that focused on the travails of a successful pantheon of celebrities. At the peak of Min's tenure, actor Tom Cruise was marrying Katie Holmes, a narrative ("TomKat") made for the tabloid trade wars. Privately, Min told people the marriage was a contractual arrangement that suggested Cruise had, in effect, hired a Hollywood beard, but Wenner told her, "Let's just believe it." This was a game of high-stakes negotiations with powerful publicists, who bid up stories and photographs by pitting *Us Weekly* against *InTouch* and *People*. When Holmes was pregnant with Cruise's baby, Wenner wanted exclusive photos, and Min proposed a $250,000 donation to a Scientology charity—the Citizens Commission for Human Rights, which "investigates psychiatric human rights abuses"—and guaranteed promotion of the Tom Cruise blockbuster *Mission: Impossible III*. "Doctors who've seen pictures of Katie estimate she'll give birth between March 15 and March 30," Min wrote to Wenner. "We should send this proposal ASAP, possibly even today."

Under Min, the circulation of *Us Weekly* reached an astounding 1.75 million by 2006, well beyond Kent Brownridge's initial business plan. Every Monday morning, Wenner would arrive at the office and immediately calculate his cut of the sales: $1.75 in profit per copy sold, multiplied by 550,000-plus copies, meant he made $1 million or more a week. Then he would tabulate the advertising, $95,000 a page. At its peak, *Us Weekly* was clearing almost $90 million a year in pure profit. It was raining money and Wenner reveled. Once, when the sales figures dipped a few thousand copies, he wrote a memo reminding Min how much she had lost him. "He could only visualize it as a loss," she said, "as money you took away from him because something didn't perform the way he wanted it to."

Us Weekly had conquered the culture. *People* was forced to reinvent itself, and now *Us Weekly* was fodder for skits on Lorne Michaels's *Saturday Night Live*—very satisfying. Wenner became fully engaged in the production, poring over images of handsome young actors like Zac Efron, who came by the offices to kiss the ring, and bid hundreds of thousands of dollars on baby and wedding photographs, paying off sources for intel, racing to beat *People* on news stories, whether about Angelina Jolie's adoption of an African child or Britney Spears's shaving her head during a bout of mental fragility. "We were scrappy and faster on our feet and more talented and attuned to the culture, and had better reporters," said Wenner. (*Us Weekly* once paid for a reporter to take flight lessons with Angelina Jolie's personal instructor to try shaking him down for details of her pregnancy.)

Wenner had blamed Brownridge for everything that went wrong, but now he took full credit for the turnaround. And in 2005, he decided he no longer needed Brownridge and fired him. Brownridge, who made plenty of money at Wenner Media, had begun spending weekends on a horse farm in Virginia, and after a dumb fight over a book publishing deal Wenner pushed him out. "He didn't like that people thought I was partly responsible for the success of *US* magazine," said Brownridge. "The richer Jann got, the more he thought he was smarter than everyone else, he was better than everyone. He was thinking he was right up there; he thought he was in the exclusive club of billionaires, and on paper he was getting close to that."

Said Wenner, "I had deluded myself that if I got rid of him, which I wanted to do and first articulated to myself five years before that, then I would not be able to go skiing."

Wenner upgraded his jet to a Gulfstream IV and rented a house on Martha's Vineyard so he could hang out with neighbor Larry David, the star of HBO's *Curb Your Enthusiasm;* there they campaigned for Senator John Kerry during the 2004 presidential election (David would make the cover of *Rolling Stone* in 2011). Wenner's supersized success supersized his cheapness. He rarely if ever offered to pay for lunch with friends at the Four Seasons.

The success of *Us Weekly* brought a degree of peace with Jane, who enjoyed the windfall—and the magazine, which she read religiously—as much as Wenner did, using the upgraded jet for her own trips. But she also continued to live in denial about Wenner's sexuality, viewing his relationship with Matt as a temporary folly rather than the decade-long partnership it had become. Over lunch at Michael's, a hot spot for the media elite, she once told Janice Min, "When this whole gay thing's over, we'll get back together."

Us Weekly decisively shifted the balance of power inside Wenner Media. Though his flagship magazine brought him respect, his new one produced triple the profit and had fully outed Jann Wenner's inner celebrity hound. Despite the occasional embarrassment, *Us Weekly* expressed a side of Wenner that *Rolling Stone* could never fully give voice to: the gay man who had struggled with his weight and imbibed gossip as hungrily as his female readership. "Jann works through his shame, but he does it publicly and through the pages of *Rolling Stone* and *Us Weekly*," said Gary Armstrong, the onetime chief marketing officer for Wenner Media and a gay man in whom Wenner confided. "Every really good issue is a therapy session."

Along with the therapy, Wenner was sure *Us Weekly* held endless profits. And in 2006, he decided he no longer wanted the Disney Company owning half of his golden cow. The stock market was cooking, Wenner was invested in exclusive hedge funds like Tom Steyer's Farallon Capital, and banks were lending at extremely low interest. Ben Needell, ever the real estate lawyer, liked wagering on borrowed money and convinced Wenner they should buy it back. With Wenner's blessing, Needell procured a $300 million loan.

For the next two years, Wenner would pay back nary a dime of the Disney loan, funneling all the profits directly into his lifestyle. "He just saw blue skies ahead," said Janice Min, whom Wenner gave a three-year contract for $3.25 million a year, with an annual bonus of $1 million. What Wenner did not yet know was that he had just made the worst business decision of his entire life.

·

THE WEEK OF SEPTEMBER 11, 2001, pop starlet Britney Spears appeared on the cover of *Rolling Stone* declaring, "Don't treat me like a little girl."

Jann Wenner was scheduled to have lunch with Michael Douglas at one o'clock on September 11. A few months earlier, his lawyer Ben Needell, of Skadden, Arps, had helped arrange the sale of the World

Trade Center to developer Larry Silverstein in a deal worth $3.2 billion. Now the towers were a raging inferno, thousands of innocent people were dead, and America's sense of security was vaporized. Wenner and Douglas sat at an outdoor café and talked about "how strange and bizarre the moment was," Wenner recalled.

Wenner arrived at the offices of *Rolling Stone* in full motorcycle leathers. His driver hadn't shown up for work. That week he oversaw a special issue featuring a photograph of his own American flag pin from childhood on the cover. In his editorial, Wenner criticized the warlike rhetoric of President George W. Bush (who was planning to "smoke 'em out") and argued that Islamic radicalism had to be understood as "an authentic political movement with widespread support and sympathy, grievances grounded in a legitimate historical record and extreme economic inequality. History tells us you can not end the rebellion without addressing its cause."

It was titled "A Pivot upon Which We Will View Our Future."

The post-9/11 wars in Afghanistan and Iraq would reanimate the 1960s political spirit of *Rolling Stone* in ways that Bill Clinton never did, but it was a fitful evolution and not one that came naturally to Wenner. The 1990s-era *Rolling Stone* had been culturally irrelevant but financially successful. Managing editors Sid Holt, and after him Bob Love, were talented caretakers who grew up inside *Rolling Stone* and ran Wenner's magazine as an advertising juggernaut defined as much by muscular journalism as by the art direction of Fred Woodward, who favored ripened images of shirtless and naked rock stars buried in cover lines and random lists of the latest buzz names—Nirvana, Christina Aguilera, Creed. Wenner preferred a simpler design, but he didn't argue with success. Indeed he'd grown somewhat detached from his magazine, with occasional strokes of editorial genius, like his advocacy for the "Fast-Food Nation" story by Eric Schlosser that became a book and a movie. Politically, Wenner was still an establishment Democrat, supporting Al Gore's run for the presidency in 2000 with a *Rolling Stone* cover story that made news because of Gore's unusually large crotch bulge in the photograph by Mark Seliger. Al Gore called Wenner and asked if the media controversy was a good or bad thing for him. "This can never be a bad thing," Wenner assured him. (Wenner hung the Gore cover directly outside his office.)

In the early years of the twenty-first century, Wenner was less threatened by George Bush than by the wild success of *Maxim*, a British-style "laddie" magazine produced by Felix Dennis, former editor of *Oz* back in the 1960s. A rude and rapacious capitalist who collected Rolls-Royces and hung out in Mustique in a white robe, Dennis went after *Rolling Stone* with a sharply edited pop music magazine called *Blender* that spoke to the Napster generation and clawed at Wenner's advertising base. In response, Wenner hired a British editor named Ed Needham, former editor of a *Maxim* knockoff called *FHM*, to aim *Rolling Stone* more squarely at male appetites with shorter articles, ample pictures of seminude women, and feature stories like a profile of a man who had a nine-and-a-half-inch penis. This was a version of *Rolling Stone* that Wenner began to regret, if for no other reason than that it didn't actually work. But it also threatened his reputation at a time when *Us Weekly* was defining his success in Manhattan. As Wenner once told his son Theo, "Put Hunter's name on my tombstone, not Brad Pitt's."

When Needham quit, Wenner elevated Will Dana, who came to *Rolling Stone* in 1996 and learned the contours of Wenner's ego needs, which defined interoffice politics. It was Dana who ran the political coverage during the 2004 election, who dialed up hard-hitting politics at *Rolling Stone* with more war-on-drugs stories, climate change investigations, and anti-Bush exposés—starting with Paul Alexander's blistering story on George W. Bush's lost years in the National Guard avoiding the Vietnam War. "Bush was the greatest thing that could have happened to *Rolling Stone*," said Dana.

Dana's editorship—Wenner called him the best editor in the history of *Rolling Stone*—heralded the arrival of Matt Taibbi, an irreverent, bomb-throwing writer who once ran a political humor magazine in Moscow called *The eXile* and published smart if juvenile reports that *Rolling Stone*, in a 1998 profile, called "the toughest, angriest, out-on-a-limb investigative journalism to come out of the new Russia." Dana recruited Taibbi during the 2004 presidential election and helped turn his Hunter Thompson homage into a voice of his own, starting with a story where Taibbi posed as a Bush campaign staffer in Florida for ten weeks and even collected a salary ("Bush Like Me"). "As a professional misanthrope," Taibbi wrote, "I believe that if you are going to hate a person, you ought to do it properly. You should go and live in his shoes for a while and see at the end of it how much you hate yourself."

Wenner's interest in politics was reanimated by the election as he helped organize fund-raising concerts (featuring the Eagles) for John Kerry, a social friend in Sun Valley whom Wenner interviewed and put on the cover of *Rolling Stone* in November 2004. "I don't think his actual policy ideas are that deeply held," Dana said of Wenner. "He's by no means a lefty. That instinct for who the powerful people are—he wants to be there. In his mind, he is somehow indispensable to that."

By the middle of the first decade of the new century, Wenner had achieved a kind of editorial parity in *Us Weekly* and *Rolling Stone* that truly reflected his personality—Jann Wenner the celebrity hound and Jann Wenner the muckraking publisher. He had it all: In 2006, he personally oversaw an issue of *Rolling Stone* naming George W. Bush "The Worst President in History," with an essay by Princeton historian Sean Wilentz; that same week, *Us Weekly* told the story of how actress Denise Richards left Charlie Sheen for Richie Sambora.

•

DR. HUNTER THOMPSON WAS a faltering drug addict whose cult legend was so potent that his celebrity sycophants—Johnny Depp, Sean Penn—managed to overlook the ravages of their hero's ongoing self-destruction. They could drink and shoot guns around the hallowed ground of Woody Creek and scrape off a little of the Thompson stardust and go home. Thompson was writing a column for John Walsh, editor at ESPN, but his embarrassing parodies of the 1970s-era snarl were cobbled together with help from fanboys who hung around and shared Thompson's drugs. Wenner hadn't given up trying to get him into *Rolling Stone*. When he assigned Thompson a story on Cuba in 2002, it was the full-time job of two employees to manage Raoul Duke (who referred to them as "cabana boys") and try squeezing a paragraph a week out of him. Sniffing at Thompson's bad prose, Wenner didn't publish anything and proclaimed Thompson a washup. "Hunter thought Jann was disparaging of him," recalled Laila Nabulsi, who dated Thompson from 1978 to 1984. "I think it really hurt Hunter's feelings. He said, 'Fuck him, I'm gonna go to *Vanity Fair.*' And that was a big slap to Jann. Because it wasn't about the money, although they paid better. It was, 'I don't want to hear this bullshit. He said too many things about me.'"

The difference between Thompson's real-life antagonism toward Wenner and the parodic antagonism of his writings had become blurred beyond recognition, but most people took his anger at face value. In 2004, Wenner decided to assign a writer named Rich Cohen to profile Thompson for *Rolling Stone* with the express intent of holding a mirror up to his tragic life. "Jann wanted a really tough profile of Hunter," recalled Will Dana. "He resolved he was going to show the world what a fuckup Hunter was. He wanted a piece that said Hunter is a huge degenerate junkie."

Thompson delivered the story on a platter. "He'd wake up and he'd have to start immediately doing [drugs]," recalled Cohen. "He was in a lot of pain. He couldn't move around very well. He was pissed off and he was angry at Jann. 'You're a messenger boy sent by grocery clerks! Why are you doing this? What are you doing here?'

"You did get a sense that his relationship with Jann wasn't very good," said Cohen. "He was angry at Jann about money and credit. He wasn't treated right; he was sort of forgotten."

Thompson could barely walk after an unsuccessful hip replacement and was consigned to a walker. Suffering intense pain, he started howling like a coyote at a restaurant one night in New Orleans while hanging out with Sean Penn and historian Douglas Brinkley during the filming of *All the King's Men.* Penn had flown Thompson down in his private jet because Thompson couldn't fly commercial with his drug supply. "He had a case of the blues," said Brinkley. "He would say things like 'This will be my last raw oyster feast.'"

On February 20, 2005, Cohen had just finished his profile of Thompson when he flipped on the radio and heard the news: Thompson had put a .45 to his head and pulled the trigger. Dead at sixty-seven.

Wenner presided over every last detail of the Thompson memorial issue, which took eleven straight days to assemble. "This morning I cried as I struck 'National Affairs Desk: Hunter S. Thompson' from the masthead—after 35 years," he wrote. "Once I had Hunter to myself, and now I don't have him at all. He was a careful, deliberate and calculating man, and his suicide was not careless, not an accident and not selfish."

He compared him to Mark Twain.

At Thompson's memorial in Woody Creek, Colorado—a multi-million-dollar bacchanal paid for by Johnny Depp—Wenner read from a letter Thompson had sent him a decade before. It wasn't how Thompson had left things with Wenner, but it was how Wenner wanted to remember their times together.

> My memory of those days is mainly of tremendous energy and talent and rare commitment running (almost) amok, but not quite. It was like being invited into a bonfire and finding that fire is actually your friend. Ho ho . . .
>
> But just how hot can you stand it, brother, before your love will crack?

Afterward, Wenner cut a book deal to publish an oral history of the writer's life and an anthology called *Fear and Loathing at "Rolling Stone."* Wenner assigned Corey Seymour, one of Thompson's "cabana boys," to conduct 130 interviews and stitch together the oral history. It took two years. Wenner was at odds with Thompson's last wife, Anita, who felt Wenner owed her special dispensation for her interview, which included details of his final moments, and after a fitful negotiation pulled out of the book altogether. But *Gonzo: The Life of Hunter S. Thompson,* published in 2007, was a worthy testament to Wenner's old friend and a highly successful publishing venture. It was also a distinctly Wennerian version of history that consigned Thompson's non–*Rolling Stone* life—his work for *Ramparts* and *Playboy*—to minority status. "He wanted to control the Hunter story after Hunter's death, and the book is a vehicle to do that," said Douglas Brinkley, who became the executor of Thompson's estate and a regular contributor to *Rolling Stone.*

Though the book was assembled and edited by Seymour, Wenner put his own name on it, prominently and before Seymour's. When Seymour went to Wenner's office to complain, Wenner shrugged and replied, "It's a 'droit du seigneur' thing." Seymour had to look up the French expression—the right of the king on the wedding night of any of his subjects to have sex with their bride.

"Who just got fucked here?" Seymour thought afterward. "Did I get fucked?"

Somewhere, Hunter Thompson cracked a thin-lipped smile.

•

BEFORE HE BECAME SO DRUNK that he fell onto a table at the four-star French restaurant Le Bernardin, Michael Douglas raised a toast to Jann S. Wenner. "So, for years, I thought Jann was just a compassionate, wonderful guy. Rather than a starfucker, you know?" said Douglas, sparking a roomful of laughter from the likes of Al Gore and Bruce Springsteen. "And, the reality is, as we sit here now, in 2006, Jann—he's booked baby, he is booked."

For his sixtieth birthday, in 2006, Wenner threw himself a lavish party starring his favorite celebrity royals: Yoko Ono, Robbie Robertson, Robin Williams, Bette Midler, Lorne Michaels, Senator John Kerry, Peter Wolf, and Larry David. (Jagger and Bono had other commitments.) The party hosts were, conspicuously, Jane Wenner and Matt Nye, who sat at separate tables. Douglas marveled at the "trapeze act" of Wenner's wife and his gay lover in the same room. A drunk Robin Williams, who was photographed by Dick Avedon for *Rolling Stone* in 1979, unleashed a lurid, semi-coherent tone poem that cast Jann and Matt as the stars of *Brokeback Mountain*. "Yes, before there was a cocksucker ranch, there was two gay men being rump wranglers way before everybody else. Yes, indeed," ranted Williams. "Look at sweet Matt, looking all that he is. Traveling that jizzum trail, and I know you have been. You a rump wrangler, and you know who you is! You a gay cowboy, and you know what you is!"

Al Gore tried pulling Williams down, but he was unstoppable, and then he pulled out some handcuffs for Wenner's birthday present. Sim Wenner, who had flown in from Hawaii, berated Williams for his homophobic remarks. But Jann Wenner loved it. Indeed he had never been happier—that is, until Bruce Springsteen got up and performed a song he wrote especially for Jann Wenner:

I got to know the man a little bit, by and by,
I've never seen so much innocence and cynicism walk side by side

I never guessed a man whose magazine once changed my life,
Would one day want to have a threesome with my wife.

The party cost $260,000.

After the death of Hunter Thompson, mortality was on Wenner's mind. *Rolling Stone* published an issue called "The Immortals: The 100 Greatest Artists of All Time," with the Beatles at the top, but they were proving all too mortal. James Brown (No. 7), Ray Charles (No. 10), Michael Jackson (No. 35), Johnny Cash (No. 31), Bo Diddley (No. 20), Jerry Garcia (Grateful Dead, No. 55). Obituaries were becoming the best column in *Rolling Stone,* and they were often personal losses: When Sandy Bull died of cancer in 2001, Wenner paid homage with a *Rolling Stone* obituary. And then came Ahmet Ertegun, who had proclaimed Wenner "one of the best friends I have ever had" at the sixtieth birthday bash and was hospitalized after falling on his head backstage at a Rolling Stones concert. "I went to sit at his bedside in the hospital a few times, and join [wife] Mica at her daily watch," Wenner recounted at Ertegun's memorial in Istanbul. "I was grateful to be able to talk to him, to whisper in his ear, although he could not hear me. It was amazing how strong and incredibly healthy he looked lying there. I asked Mica why he looked so good—and she said to me, 'Well, you know, he hasn't been drinking.'"

While Wenner's world was shifting with age and time, a large community of ex-employees continued to celebrate the anniversaries of *Rolling Stone.* Such were the memories that Wenner wasn't invited to the forty-year reunion in California in 2007. "We discussed if we wanted Jann to come," said Laurel Gonsalves, the organizer, "and we decided no. It was sort of the mice will play if the cat's away."

Wenner nonetheless sent a case of champagne with a letter that was read on a stage by Charlie Perry, who performed in the "No Talent Show" with his impersonation of Wenner conducting one of his famous "cocaine edits." "The major event was the AA meeting," recalled Joe Klein.

Anniversaries always made Wenner wistful, and restless. In the past, he entertained offers from Condé Nast, publisher of *Vanity Fair* and *The New Yorker,* which valued him at $500 million, and Felix Dennis, with whom he got drunk one night and tried to come to terms on a price. After Kent Brownridge agreed to testify on Wenner's behalf in a lawsuit brought by a former editor of *Men's Journal,* Michael Caruso, Brownridge tried parlaying the goodwill into a pitch to buy Wenner Media after the fortieth anniversary. Wenner turned him down, and Brownridge and a group of investors bought Felix Dennis's laddie magazines and went head-to-head with Wenner, poaching ten of his employees and infuriating him. (The company failed, and Brownridge went back to horses.)

But Wenner's temptation was put to the test with Hearst. The publishing behemoth whose legacy shadowed Wenner his entire life started by offering to buy a half interest in *Us Weekly* in 2006. At the time, Wenner's accountant valued *Us Weekly* at more than $750 million, and Wenner's lawyer figured the cash would buy back the Disney loan with a nice profit on top. But as negotiations evolved, Hearst upped the ante and offered to take a stake in the entire company, including *Rolling Stone.* This was a horse of a different color. At one point, Wenner's accountants were valuing the company at $1.1 billion. There was just one hitch: Hearst wanted Wenner to stay on as editor, while president Cathie Black took control of his business.

Jann Wenner could be a billionaire or he could be Mr. *Rolling Stone,* but he could not be both. As he often did, he turned to his lawyer to divine his emotions. *A billionaire.* Wenner rolled the numbers around in his mind. As Cathie Black recalled, "The deal was about to be made, and [Ben Needell] called the next morning: 'I just want to be very clear: This is Jann's decision, and he could change his mind at any second.'"

Wenner consulted David Geffen. Would he lose all his friends? Who was Jann Wenner without *Rolling Stone?* "I was like, 'Look, I sold four companies and I'm still me,'" recounted Geffen. "'You will still be you. People who are your friends are your friends, period. And the people you lose because you don't have this or that, they're not your friends.' But he never listened to that, anyway."

Wenner couldn't do it.

"My life is wrapped up in *Rolling Stone,* my career, what I do day to day, and I didn't want to jeopardize that," Wenner said.

And so he didn't. In 2008, the cool new Democrat Barack Obama was running on a promise of hope and change, and Jann Wenner was rolling in cash and busy expanding his life in other ways: making a new family. In 2005, after a decade with Wenner, Nye still had no stake in the empire, which Jane guarded jealously. When son Alex Wenner, semi-estranged from his parents but bound by a trust fund, decided to get married to his high school sweetheart, the Wenners opposed the marriage and forced his wife to sign a prenuptial agreement to shield the ownership from her. "There was no way they were going to let the possibility of my ownership getting into anyone else's hands," said Alex.

Nye was forty years old and ready for the kind of close-knit family he had come from. Children were also the surest way for Nye to be fathered into the fortune. The men arranged for a surrogate mother living in California to deliver a baby conceived from an egg donor picked out of a catalog, resulting in the birth of Noah Wenner in 2006. Wenner held a celebrity blessing ceremony with Bruce Springsteen and David Bowie, with whom Wenner had developed an informal book club over e-mail (Bowie: *Let the Great World Spin,* by Colum McCann). Sean Lennon and Bette Midler were the godparents. As Jon Landau recalled, "[Wenner] reads this letter by a guest who couldn't be there. It was a very lovely letter; it goes on for a while. It turns out it is Johnny Depp.

"Well, that's the Jann we all know and love, the groupie," Landau said. "Then he asked Bruce to serenade the baby. Bruce can handle anything, but he was put on the spot."

Next Wenner purchased a nineteenth-century manor in upstate New York called Teviot, a Gothic Revival built by a storied colonial family. It cost $5.8 million, and Nye oversaw reconstruction down to the lintels in addition to building a modernist pool house and guest bungalows. When Annie Leibovitz, who owned a retreat in nearby Rhinebeck, came by to survey Wenner's new estate and swim in the pool, she advised Wenner to chop down a stand of old-growth trees to improve his view of the Hudson River. Wenner had hundreds of trees chopped down without getting a permit, prompting complaints from local authorities.

Meanwhile, Wenner had begun work on a massive new business venture: an international chain of *Rolling Stone* hotels, starting with the *Rolling Stone* Hotel and Resort in Las Vegas. The hotel idea was the brainchild of a financier named Billy Tuchscher, to whom Wenner licensed the *Rolling Stone* name in exchange for a cut of the profits and editorial control over the plans. Before they could begin, however, there was a little problem: Mick Jagger. The old name issue was back. "One way we were going to get around it was to call it the *Rolling Stone*—in small letters 'magazine'—Hotel," recalled Tommy Cohen, Wenner's business consultant on the deal.

At first Wenner tried offering Jagger a residency in the rock club he was going to attach to the hotel. "You could be like Sinatra, appearing once a year," he told him. But Jagger didn't want a job, and they cut him in on the royalties. Architect Jon Jerde, designer of the Bellagio Hotel & Casino, was hired to draft an opulent mirrored tower to rock-and-roll excess, including a massive electronic billboard flashing the latest cover of *Rolling Stone,* a five-thousand-seat concert hall, a casino, a restaurant and a swimming pool shaped like a guitar. Wenner wanted to do a "Gonzo Club" and stage a musical version of *Fear and Loathing in Las Vegas,* complete with animatronic lizards of the sort Hunter Thompson hallucinated in the book. The groundbreaking was scheduled for late 2008.

On September 29, 2008, Metallica was set to appear on the cover of *Rolling Stone* with the headline "Louder, Faster, Stronger." That afternoon, the Dow Jones fell 778 points in a single day. The financial collapse sparked worldwide panic. An unsustainable real estate market engineered by Manhattan bankers who didn't have enough cash to cover their own bets was taking everybody down with it. While the government bailed the banks out, Wenner was ordering his accountant to extract him from hedge funds and pronto. He would lose millions before converting his money to government T-bills.

Advertisers snapped their purses shut. For the first time in years, Wenner was forced to trim his yearly bonus by several million dollars and lay people off. The hotel project evaporated. Wenner Media was worth a fraction of what Hearst offered him for *Us Weekly*. Instead, Wenner had a $300 million debt for the Disney buyback. Like the banks that once showered him with low-interest cash, Wenner had badly overleveraged himself and lived as if there were no tomorrow, and then tomorrow showed up like a motherfucker. The loan, it turned out, was Wenner's folly. "That was, easy, a half-billion-dollar mistake for me, that deal," Wenner said. "A half-billion dollars will change your life.

"That was the big coulda, woulda, shoulda," he said.

Now Wenner faced two nauseating trends: the slow and steady decline of the magazine business and the inevitable renegotiation of the $300 million loan on more onerous terms. The banks added interest, shackled Wenner's salary and bonuses, and took an automatic cut of his profits. This was necessarily going to redefine life. Within two years, Wenner would be forced to reduce the physical size of his magazine— among the largest on the newsstand, his pride and joy—to a pamphlet of its former self and relinquish the biggest and most expensive symbol of his status, the private jet. Now he could only gaze at the miniature Gulfstream models on the mantel at Sixth Avenue. He would have to fly commercial.

In retrospect, Wenner could tell himself that when the moment of truth arrived, he had valued something more than money. He knew who he was. He was Mr. *Rolling Stone*. This was a clarifying realization, though not a painless one. "I suppose I could have lived without an occupation and been very, very wealthy," Wenner mused. "And what does that get ya? It gets you a boat. I could be floating around on a boat."

24

Still Crazy After All These Years

A man in his sixties, Jann Wenner still liked to go backstage at Rolling Stones concerts, flip through Mick Jagger's costume rack, and squeeze into a pair of the singer's pants. "They don't quite fit me that well," he admitted. He described Jagger as "thin, but not tiny."

Wenner was still a groupie. He had scrapbooks lined with backstage passes and a Rock and Roll Hall of Fame autograph album signed by Tom Hanks and will.i.am. He had vacation photographs from the time he and Jagger went yachting in Panama with Johnny Pigozzi and ended up strumming the Stones' "No Expectations" around a campfire. He had a guitar signed by Paul McCartney and a painted portrait of himself by John Cougar Mellencamp that looked nothing like him. He had a keyboard from Bono, and he had Annie Leibovitz portraits of his family, which Wenner and Nye expanded again in 2008 with a set of twins named India and Jude (godparents: Gil Friesen, Bruce Springsteen, Patti Scialfa, Rita Wilson, Bono's wife, Ali Hewson, Robbie Robertson, Johnny Depp, etcetera).

Now Wenner thought of himself as the kindly uncle of rock and roll—celebrant of Springsteen, booster of Bono, arbiter of the latest Jagger-Richards tempest. When Keith Richards claimed in his 2010 memoir, *Life,* that Jagger had, among other failings, a small penis, Jagger was infuriated and went raging to Wenner. As it happened, Wenner had excerpted the book and put Richards on the cover, grinning. "He was, to use his own word, livid," Wenner said of Jagger. "He couldn't believe that Keith had done it. He had read an early version of the book, and he asked him to take out stuff. Keith took out some stuff but didn't take out a lot of it."

Wenner assigned Rich Cohen to interview Jagger off the record and inject his viewpoint into the *Rolling Stone* article about Richards's book, with readers none the wiser. "I gave him a lot of advice on what to do, which is: nothing," Wenner continued. "The more you respond, the more you make an issue of it. If you want to say anything, you say, 'Well, this is as reliable as the memoirs of William Burroughs.' But he was *fuuuuur-ious*. Furious, furious, furious. And until Keith apologized, he refused to get the band together for the last tour." (Richards, Wenner said, "is an egomaniac and a nasty guy, by the way.")

Rolling Stone—Wenner's life—had been a series of these kinds of transactions. Transactions weren't the same as friendships, but they were similar, especially when gilded by nostalgia. The rock stars collective stories, edited by Jann S. Wenner, helped sell millions of records and made them feel good about themselves. And in turn they made Jann Wenner feel good about himself. As he told an old friend from Chadwick, "You don't get to do what I've done if you are an asshole."

When Wenner produced and promoted the twenty-fifth-anniversary special of the Rock and Roll Hall of Fame, a four-hour concert broadcast on HBO, he cast his favorites—Mick, Bruce, and Bono—at the top of the bill and put the three of them together on the cover of *Rolling Stone*. It was a sales sheet for the TV show, but Wenner proclaimed the two-day concert, recorded at Madison Square Garden, among the greatest in the history of the art form, *The T.A.M.I. Show* notwithstanding. "It's only been a few days since the shows happened, but they already feel like a part of history," wrote Wenner in his editorial. "Not the history of textbooks and monuments, but the living, breathing history that lights you up with a sense of possibility and purpose."

The new story lines were the same as the old ones. When Bob Dylan was playing in Sun Valley one summer, he called up Wenner and spent the day on his ranch, jamming with Wenner's teenage son Gus. Afterward, Wenner conducted his first interview with Dylan since 1969. Once again, Dylan mocked him. "When was the last time you interviewed Cher?" he asked. But Wenner took the punches and Dylan softened, and pretty soon they were two old men looking back on the 1960s.

DYLAN: There was more free thinking then.

WENNER: Um hm.

DYLAN: You know, there wasn't such mass conformity as there is today.

WENNER: Um hm.

DYLAN: I mean, today a free-thinking person gets ridiculed.

WENNER: Um hm.

DYLAN: You know, back then they were just sort of ostracized and maybe avoided. But the popular, the consensus at the time— in this time we're *speaking* about—was a very mild form of entertainment. It was boring and uninteresting.

WENNER: Um hm.

DYLAN: And beneath that surface though there was this—there was an entirely different world.

WENNER: And you tapped that world?

DYLAN: Yeah, well, we *all* did. And some of us, some of us decided that we could live in this world, and others decided, well, they could visit it once in a while but it wasn't necessarily their thing.

WENNER: Um hm. So you lived in it.

DYLAN: I did.

WENNER: And allowed everybody else to visit it.

DYLAN: Yeah, I mean, you know—like the tourists.

And the tourists were still buying, year after year. Boxed sets. Reissues. Memoirs. Bigger and more expensive tours. It was only rock and roll, but they really did like it. And so did Jann Wenner, a lot. He commanded—demanded—the best backstage passes at concerts, and he harassed publicists until he got the highest level of access, the same as the artists themselves. When he went to a Bruce Springsteen concert and saw, from his exclusive VIP seating, Bono and members of U2 come in late and take empty seats near the stage, he was outraged and called Springsteen the next day to complain that he had somehow been denied the best seats. His grievance rolled down to manager Jon Landau. As it turned out, U2 had taken the only seats they could find. "You're a big fucking help," Landau told Wenner.

Springsteen and Wenner had an affectionate bond. "I don't know how other people describe Jann," said Springsteen, "but he's emotional. Pretty much wears it on his sleeve. Good friend." Springsteen began inviting Wenner and Nye on tours, resulting in ample publicity and a few comic misadventures. They all went shopping together at the luxury department store Barneys in New York. While Nye was modeling a shearling coat in the mirror, Springsteen came up from behind, cinched the belt around his waist, and drawled, "If you don't wear that thing, it's gonna wear you!" They later joined Springsteen on tour in South America, where they walked the streets of Rio at night and played a game of "Who would you fuck?" (Wenner declared Springsteen's taste in women "trashy.") These excursions earned Springsteen regular *Rolling Stone* covers and a permanent residency in Random Notes, and a degree of protection. When his wife, Patti, heard that a *Rolling Stone* reporter was poking around bars in Asbury Park asking about her and her husband, Wenner ordered the staff to stand down.

Similarly, he endeared himself to Bono, who considered the editor a kind of fan-therapist. "He gets me talking about things that I never talked about before with anybody," said Bono. "I start talking about my relationship with my father, and quenching or moaning and getting all Irish on his ass. And he says to me, at the end of it, he goes, 'I think your father deserves an apology. It sounds like you were a bit of a prick.' And I go, 'Really? I hadn't thought about that.'"

In 2014, Yoko Ono awarded Jann Wenner the LennonOno Grant for Peace, which she founded to honor people who did good deeds. Past recipients included Seymour Hersh and Lady Gaga. Ono said she gave it to Wenner because she heard that he was feeling blue. "Well, I heard he was sort of lamenting the fact that the young generation doesn't know him," Ono said. "But that happened to all of us, in a way. And I thought, 'I could do this for him.'"

She justified the prize this way: "I mean, everybody, including my assistants, when they heard that I'm giving it to Jann, said, 'What?' Because, you know, we're getting these high people . . . and Jann is a friend. So, many people think, 'Ah, she's doing that.' I don't care what people think."

It wasn't as if Wenner had praised her work in *Rolling Stone,* she reasoned: "He was never really good to my work. Sort of going over me to get Mick Jagger or whatever. So that's why I can give that award, you know?"

Jann Wenner still had a lifetime's worth of grudges and hurt feelings, the legacy of the passion he inspired. The band Kiss hated him for allegedly blocking them from the Rock and Roll Hall of Fame (in 1977, *Rolling Stone* depicted Gene Simmons as an unrepentant asshole in the classic "The Pagan Beasties of Teenage Rock"). Joni Mitchell threw a drink in Wenner's face at an awards ceremony and wrote a song called "Lead Balloon": "'Kiss my ass!' I said / and I threw my drink / Tequila trickling / down his business suit." (Jimmy Webb beat her to the punch with the Wenner-inspired "Friends to Burn," from 1993.) Jimmy Buffett was privately bummed that he couldn't get in the Rock and Roll Hall of Fame, and Steve Miller aired his grievances at his own induction ceremony. Wenner didn't mind. He was the center of the action and disliked a lot of these people. He especially disliked Jon Bon Jovi, who Wenner said campaigned unsuccessfully to get himself inducted into the Hall of Fame by enlisting billionaire investor Ron Perelman for muscle. "I don't think he's that important," said Wenner. "What does Bon Jovi mean in the history of music? Nothing."

But, of course, the value of a Hall of Fame induction had been declining as the institution dug deeper into music's back catalogs. And if the Hall of Fame was going to stay relevant, it needed fresh blood in the boardroom or at least to dispel the nasty rumors that Jann Wenner and Jon Landau were running everything. Tom Morello, the former guitarist for Rage Against the Machine who had become a sideman to Landau client Bruce Springsteen, joined the induction committee and pushed for Kiss. The band was finally inducted, and *Rolling Stone* put them on the cover for the first time. For his 2015 album of Frank Sinatra ballads, *Shadows in the Night*, Bob Dylan skipped *Rolling*

Stone and gave an exclusive interview to *AARP The Magazine*, a journal for retirees edited by former *Rolling Stone* editor Bob Love, and the year after that the Rock and Roll Hall of Fame inducted gangsta-rap group N.W.A, signaling a post-rock-and-roll mentality and perhaps a post-Wenner one as well.

The Internet age had almost vanquished Wenner's type, the old-school gatekeeper. A superstar like Kanye West didn't need *Rolling Stone*. He had once appeared on the cover—as Jesus Christ—but now he could edit, build, and market his own fame through Twitter and partnerships with streaming music services. When Wenner offered to put West on the cover again, the rapper demanded Wenner use his hand-selected cover image by rapper Tyler, the Creator and allow West to approve the headline and all the text inside the issue. When Wenner refused, West just tweeted a mock-up of a *Rolling Stone* cover to his twenty-seven million followers.

Wenner nonetheless remained an indefatigable curator of his year-book. He was the last of the big-time independent publishers, a cantankerous print barbarian who had chewed up and spat out bigger punks than Kanye West. He would not let the bastards get him down. When U2 released *Songs of Innocence* in 2014—with a botched marketing campaign in which iTunes users were forced to download it on their computers, prompting Bono to apologize—Wenner did not apologize for personally placing the record at the top of the year-end *Rolling Stone* list of best albums.

"My dictate," Jann Wenner said. "By fiat, buddy. That's that."

•

ONE FRIDAY NIGHT in December 2014, Jann Wenner was standing on the balcony of his manor overlooking the Hudson River and puffing tensely on an American Spirit cigarette. Something had gone terribly wrong. On the Internet, a media storm was brewing over a *Rolling Stone* exposé about a woman who was allegedly gang-raped at the University of Virginia. "A Rape on Campus" by Sabrina Rubin Erdely opened with a ghastly scene depicting an eighteen-year-old woman, "Jackie," getting thrown onto a glass table and assaulted by a group of fraternity brothers at Phi Kappa Psi.

There was a heavy person on top of her, spreading open her thighs, and another person kneeling on her hair, hands pinning down her arms, sharp shards digging into her back, and excited male voices rising all around her. When yet another hand clamped over her mouth, Jackie bit it, and the hand became a fist that punched her in the face. The men surrounding her began to laugh. For a hopeful moment Jackie wondered if this wasn't some collegiate prank. Perhaps at any second someone would flick on the lights and they'd return to the party.

"Grab its motherfucking leg," she heard a voice say. And that's when Jackie knew she was going to be raped.

When the story first hit, Wenner pointed to the news headlines as evidence that *Rolling Stone* was as relevant as ever—more so than his longtime rival Lorne Michaels at *Saturday Night Live*. "I haven't watched *SNL* for the longest period, for many years," Wenner said. "You don't even hear anything about it; it's lost it. People would say that about *Rolling Stone,* but I don't think that's true. We just stirred up another hornets' nest with the Virginia rape case, so we're still doing it."

But now a reporter at *The Washington Post* was picking the story apart as friends of the alleged victim cast doubt on her account of events. Simple fact-checking queries were proving that no fraternity party had occurred on the night in question. After Erdely confronted "Jackie," the troubled woman couldn't even identify her attacker correctly, and things were unraveling quickly.

The phone rang. Will Dana was in a cold panic and ready to retract the story. But Wenner wanted to hold firm and helped Dana draft what Wenner called an "adjustment." "We don't agree at this point that it discredits the entire story," he told Dana on the phone. "Because I'm not ready to give up. I think she—something happened to her."

After he hung up, Wenner explained, "Maybe she's just telling the truth, and she's just rattled and fucked-up. I mean, clearly something happened to her, clearly she was raped, I think."

The debacle would prove one of the biggest journalistic scandals in memory as *Rolling Stone* was eaten alive by critics who said the magazine's failures had undermined the cause of rape victims. On the advice of Matt Taibbi, Wenner asked the Columbia School of Journalism to conduct an independent audit of the story. Perhaps he could clear the air and stave off a libel lawsuit. The next week Wenner left for Sun Valley, where he skied for more than sixty days (he kept a running tally). He seemed to buffer himself from the reality of the situation. At one point, he circulated a link to a web parody imagining the UVA debacle as a Hunter Thompson story. It was called "Fear and Fabrication in Las Vegas."

LAS VEGAS—*Sports Illustrated* writer Raoul Duke's harrowing description of a drug-fueled trip to Las Vegas, detailed in a recent *Rolling Stone* two-part article, began to unravel Friday as interviews revealed doubts about significant elements of the account.

Meanwhile, Wenner's old friends—and two generations of *Rolling Stone* alumni—shook their heads in disbelief at the unraveling story. How could such a catastrophic error happen at *Rolling Stone,* a place that had prided itself on a strict fact-checking department since the days of the women's revolution of the mid-1970s? Wenner's reputation was in flames.

To this point, *Rolling Stone* had been experiencing a renaissance under editor Will Dana, who, along with an aggressive investigative editor named Eric Bates, returned the magazine to the map, starting with the explosive 2010 profile of General Stanley McChrystal by writer Michael Hastings. The story quoted the general's staff offhandedly impugning Joe Biden over the Obama administration's handling of the war in Afghanistan and led to McChrystal's ignominious resignation (a surprise to Wenner: He hadn't read the story before publication). Matt Taibbi had become a full-blown superstar for his brilliant eviscerations of the financial system. The idea of Goldman Sachs as a "great vampire squid wrapped around the face of humanity, relentlessly jamming its blood funnel into anything that smells like money," was lodged in the cultural firmament. (It also expressed Wenner's resentment at the banks, to whom he owed a lot of money.) But there were also creeping signs of desperation. In 2013, *Rolling Stone* lunged for the headlines again with a cover story on Boston bombing terrorist Dzhokhar

Tsarnaev. "Jahar's World" was an in-depth profile by Janet Reitman, but the cover image of the brooding youth, which Wenner had manipulated to make him look more like a rock star (over the objections of some of his staffers), caused a national furor over the ethics of giving a murderer the Jim Morrison treatment. Wenner reveled in the attention, even as retailers pulled the magazine from newsstands and *Rolling Stone* bled more than $3 million in advertising. (After initially agreeing to cooperate for a profile, Secretary of State John Kerry backed out to avoid offending his constituents in Boston.)

The risk taking was driven by Wenner's taste for old-fashioned controversy but also by growing competitive pressure. Pierre Omidyar, the billionaire founder of eBay, started poaching Wenner's staff for a new media company called First Look—starting with Matt Taibbi. The star columnist initially resisted a lucrative offer but then grew enraged when Wenner didn't repay his loyalty with a raise and left after all. Then First Look tried hiring away Wenner's art director and then a star feature writer—Sabrina Rubin Erdely, author of such stories as "The Catholic Church's Secret Sex-Crime Files" and "The Rape of Petty Officer Blumer." To stifle the raid, Wenner and Will Dana offered Erdely a writing contract worth $300,000 over two years, an impressive number in straitened times. (Taibbi, after disputes with First Look, returned to *Rolling Stone* in 2014.)

The UVA debacle was also preceded by a protracted period of cost cutting. As Wenner cut the editorial staff to a skeleton crew of what it was before 2008, he also reduced the use of the expensive outside legal firm that had vetted *Rolling Stone* for libel since the 1970s. He instead gave the job to in-house counsel Dana Rosen, who did all the corporate work. By the time the UVA story was being prepared for publication, Rosen was fed up with the workload and leaving for a new job, handing the libel work to an associate lawyer. The story that was originally slated to run that week was a profile of Robert Frank, the famed photographer who once documented the Stones tour in 1972 (and who, if you believed Truman Capote, captured the Stones' tour doctor having sex with a high school newspaper editor on a private plane). Two weeks before publication, however, Wenner killed the story, declaring the end of soft features in *Rolling Stone,* and ordered up Erdely's hard-hitting investigation instead. (The Robert Frank story was subsequently published in *The New York Times Magazine* as "The Man Who Saw America.")

In the scramble to publish, Will Dana said he operated under the assumption that Rosen had reviewed the manuscript for libel. She hadn't, and Dana barely knew the new lawyer, Natalie Krodel. Meanwhile, Dana was evidently unaware of Erdely's decision to steer clear of the men "Jackie" implicated in a rape, and he never inquired about it. Consequently, *Rolling Stone* would simply publish her account without contacting them. The practice of shielding a rape victim from undue trauma by her attackers was not unheard of, but *Rolling Stone* was convinced to forgo due diligence and had no way of knowing if the story was true, other than Jackie's own words and the advocacy of the reporter. *Rolling Stone*'s fact-checking department was still a largely female institution as well, which may have further blunted the skepticism of male editors reluctant to cast doubt on a female rape victim. Atop this rickety foundation, *Rolling Stone* rested a weighty narrative, publishing the name of the fraternity and painting an associate dean of the University of Virginia, Nicole Eramo, as insensitive to rape victims (and, indeed, a federal report later said she had, in certain cases, violated Title IX, the law requiring public institutions to respond to sexual assault claims). Wenner Media's associate lawyer was convinced the source was credible. Jann Wenner read the story and thought it was great. Indeed, he was so pleased he ordered a follow-up story on the bad reputation of the fraternity, Phi Kappa Psi.

All of this would have been eminently noble had it been correct. And it would take dozens of newspaper reports and a police investigation before Wenner finally admitted defeat. When the Columbia report was finished in the spring of 2015, Wenner read it and evinced surprise, as if he had no idea how bad it really was. He had just returned from Sun Valley. "How could you not confront the fucking guy you're accusing?" Wenner asked, incredulous. The report painted a grim portrait of baffling negligence. Wenner was ridiculed for continuing to blame "Jackie" rather than his own editorial system. He was blasted on Twitter and called out by Jon Stewart (cover of *Rolling Stone,* October 2004 and September 2011) for failing to fire everybody involved. "That kind of hit me in the gut," said Wenner.

Will Dana had offered to quit, but Wenner wouldn't hear of it. He was loyal to his staff, but he was also legally prudent. The next month, the former university dean filed a $7.5 million libel lawsuit against *Rolling Stone,* Wenner Media, and Sabrina Erdely, which was followed by a defamation suit from three Phi Kappa Psi members and later by a lawsuit for $25 million from the fraternity itself. Everything was actionable, and they had to stick together.

Wenner took a degree of comfort in his libel insurance, but he swerved between denial and confrontation. One minute he blamed the source, the next the writer, the next Will Dana. One minute he described himself as checked out of *Rolling Stone,* fading from relevance with his rock star buddies; the next he claimed he still controlled every aspect of the magazine down to the reader mail. "What a horrible thing to have happened," he said, sucking on his teeth, a thing he did when he was anxious. "The further it recedes on the horizon, the better I feel about it. Confronted with it on a day-to-day thing, it just makes me sick."

In the spring of 2016, Wenner gave a videotaped testimony in Manhattan for the Nicole Eramo trial. With his shirt rakishly open, he propped his feet on the table and declared that, excepting the botched rape anecdote, he stood by the article "personally, professionally, and on behalf of the magazine." Wenner seemed determined to isolate *Rolling Stone*'s bad reporting from the accurate parts of the story that maligned Eramo. Will Dana, he insisted, had overstepped his boundaries in fully retracting the story after the Columbia report (a claim that was untrue according to everybody involved). At one point, Wenner looked directly at the woman who was suing him and said, "I'm very, very sorry. Believe me, I've suffered as much as you have."

It turned out to be a costly line.

Afterward, Wenner needed a comeback. And in the fall of 2015, a big one landed in his lap: The actor Sean Penn called and said he had access to the man known as El Chapo, né Joaquín Guzmán Loera, leader of one of the biggest Mexican drug cartels. A Mexican actress named Kate del

Castillo had brokered access, and Penn could get *Rolling Stone* an exclusive interview. As part of the deal, Penn agreed to let El Chapo review and edit the story before publication as Wenner did with Mick Jagger. As Wenner later said, "It was a small thing to do in exchange for what we got."

The actress del Castillo said Penn duped her into collaborating for the interview—she thought it was just a friendly meet-and-greet—but the murderous drug lord was thrilled and called his time with Sean Penn "one of the best days of my life." When "El Chapo Speaks" was published in January 2016, it made the cover of *The New York Times,* because El Chapo was immediately captured by the Mexican government after it tracked him through his communiqués with the Penn entourage. Wenner's story was met with blowback from media critics accusing *Rolling Stone* of cutting an unseemly deal with a criminal thug and assigning the story to an actor whose lack of hard-hitting questions made it look like a giant publicity stunt by a self-aggrandizing celebrity. Back on his heels, Penn told *60 Minutes,* "My article has failed," and promptly went silent about El Chapo.

For Wenner, the whole imbroglio was a great coup, the return of the old razzle-dazzle. Print a famous drug dealer and the world will beat a path to your door. And for a while, it helped him forget that he had an outstanding bank debt of $100 million and $33 million in libel lawsuits with two highly public trials on the horizon.

•

ONE AFTERNOON Jann Wenner was smoking a cigarette on the veranda of a hotel near his country estate and recalling the salad days of the 1970s when Matt Nye showed up in his riding jodhpurs and surprised Wenner. "It's not smoking hour," Nye scolded, hands on hips. "Do we need to go back and see Virginia?"

Virginia was the therapist. Jann Wenner was busted.

NYE: Give me the cigarette. Give me it.
WENNER: No. C'mon . . .
NYE: Give it to me. Where is the pack of them? Give me the pack of cigarettes or we're seeing Virginia this week.

WENNER: No. Let me just have one.

NYE: No!

WENNER: Why?

NYE: How about you not have sex for the next week? Don't try to leave one in the pocket while you're fishing the whole pack out. You're such a—

WENNER: What are you doing here? Why, at this moment, do you show up? Where are the children?

NYE: They're with the pedophile tennis player . . .

WENNER: How can you come along just at that moment?

NYE: I can't believe you. I mean, do you want to be around when your children graduate at all?

When Nye left, Wenner ordered two plates of sausages and devoured them.

Nye was Jann Wenner's lifestyle editor, but he was also his caretaker. He tended to divide Wenner's old friends—moody, some said, an "odd duck"—but he did the lion's share of the child rearing, monitored Wenner's health, and forced his partner to go to therapy when he lost control of his appetites. Nye forgave him his trespasses, as when evidence of an affair ended up in the gossip columns. Nye also checked his ego, mocking him when he overheard Wenner bragging about his illustrious deeds: "You had to sacrifice yourself for the cause! It had nothing to do with your ego! It was all for *the cause!*"

"How was whipping horses?" Wenner snarled.

They were an old married couple.

After Jane came out of her problems in the late 1990s, she could not quit Jann Wenner. When gay marriage was legalized in New York State in 2011, Wenner had to carefully persuade her to give him a divorce before he could marry Nye. Wenner had had the company ownership rearranged to give the Wenner children a 28 percent stake, leaving Jane at 24 percent. But she got hers: Jane consulted with Ron Perelman and rattled Wenner's cage. "Ron Perelman has had five marriages and is a nasty son of a bitch," said Wenner. "He can be a real tough motherfucker. That probably got her a better deal than she might otherwise."

Jane got the house on West Seventieth Street and the estate in the Hamptons, plus the Picasso and her beloved Diebenkorn, now worth millions. Wenner was stung by the loss of the Hamptons home (even if Jane kept the initials "JSW" on the gate), but afterward he married Nye and built him a $12 million beach house in Montauk next to Ralph Lauren.

When this biography began, Wenner promised that Jane would claim more credit for the success of *Rolling Stone* than she actually deserved. But over time, he came around to the idea of giving her credit. And so did she. "I think Jann couldn't have done it without me," she said. "I would say it to his face and I'll say it to you. I don't care what he says. I do love him dearly. I will always love him till the day I die. I feel I worry about him. I know he worries about me. We're still so connected."

And so Jann Wenner had a family for each personality: on one arm, his ex-wife, Jane, and three sons; on the other, his husband and three children. He was the polymorphous paterfamilias. But they would all have to learn to live together to keep Jann Wenner whole. For a long while, his sons Theo and Gus despised Nye, following their mother's lead. Theo Wenner said it was Yoko Ono who smoothed tensions between Jann Wenner's two families when she gave him the peace award in 2014. At the ceremony in Iceland, Wenner casually thanked "the two loves of my life," Jane and Matt, while both sat in the audience. The comment somehow liberated Jane, at least temporarily. "He said it offhandedly," recalled Theo. "I felt her release years of tension. It was so simple, but it said so much and it just really made it clear to her in this beautiful way."

Perhaps nobody saw this whole menagerie as clearly as Alex Wenner, the adopted son who converted to Christianity, became a Brooklyn beer brewer, and produced four children. Tall, heavyset, bearded, and tattooed, he was the opposite of his father in every way, and the two had fought for years. Wenner wrinkled his nose at his son's interests—computers, heavy metal, fantasy books—and Alex internalized his father's disappointment. As a kid, he isolated himself from the celebrities who tromped through the household night and day. Good looks and style were important to the Wenners, and Alex's weight issues seemed to enrage Jann Wenner. "He just saw in me the things that he most hates about himself," said Alex. His father favored corporal punishment, but by the time he was thirteen, Alex had grown bigger than Wenner and confronted him. "There were punches thrown," said Alex. "And he backed up and that was like the very first moment I remember realizing, 'I'm actually looking down at him. Like, I'm bigger now, so this stops.'"

Alex was dispatched to boarding school and never came back. "I'm the one that doesn't exist," said Alex. "People meet me and they're like, 'Oh, Theo and Gus have a brother?'"

Wenner admitted that he struggled raising Alex, reacting poorly to his weight issues and his solitary pursuits. He was "not everything I would want in my son," he said. "But I accepted it and just tried my best to work with it . . . I think every oldest child suffers a little from the parents' learning experience. He chooses to be apart from the rest of the family, and I respect that."

If Alex shunned the privilege and entitlement, his brothers, Theo and Gus, embraced it as their natural birthright. Growing up, the Wenner boys were awakened by nannies, served breakfast by chefs, driven to school by chauffeurs, fed dinner by chefs, and put to bed at night by nannies. As a small child, Theo had once asked innocently, "Mommy and Daddy, did we buy Alex? How much did we pay for him?"

Over the years, Wenner tried bonding with his sons, once getting a matching tattoo of an Egyptian eye of Ra with Alex, who was covered in ink (including a Hunter Thompson fist emblem and script on his right wrist that read "All that is gold does not glitter," from *The Lord of the Rings*). In 2008, Wenner took his sons to Hawaii, where they ate magic mushrooms and wore sarongs and flowered crowns made by Alex's wife. Gus Wenner recalled how he and his father and Theo huddled together and observed Alex from afar, remarking that he was "different" from them. Wenner only saw Alex twice a year but always posted a picture on Instagram, the one social media outlet he understood. "I think a big thing for my dad is, more than anything else, he wants the good family photo," said Alex.

After prep school at Putney, Theo, broodingly handsome like his mother, studied photography at Bard College with Factory photographer Stephen Shore. After graduation he snapped his first *Rolling Stone* cover—Russell Brand, shirtless as Jim Morrison and insouciantly pulling his unbuttoned pants down. Theo dated actress Liv Tyler, daughter of Steven (cover of *Rolling Stone,* 1976), and roved around Manhattan with Miley Cyrus (whom he photographed, nude, for *Rolling Stone*— "Good Golly Miss Miley!"). Theo was closer to his mother, whose moodiness and formal sense of style he shared ("She's more gentle, and I guess I just kind of very much feel a deeper connection to that," he said), and while he did the occasional portrait for his father's magazine (Taylor Swift, Adele, Harry Styles), he also built an independent career away from *Rolling Stone*, mainly in high-end fashion photography, which paid better. He seemed to specialize in gorgeous women.

Wenner was proud that Theo looked so much like him, but Gus Wenner was the true doppelgänger, the leonine features of actor Joaquin Phoenix crossed with Jann Wenner circa 1972. "Gus is Jann," said Alex. "He's a mini-Jann." As a young teen, Gus innocently told his father, "Dad, isn't it great how you and I like all the same things? Tennis, skiing. Except I'm better at everything." The godson of Johnny Pigozzi (and Fran Lebowitz, until she was "deactivated," said Wenner), Gus walked into the Four Seasons as his dad did—as if he owned the place, swaggering in with ripped blue jeans and the baked-in confidence of the wellborn. When Paul McCartney appeared at a party in the Hamptons one summer and looked as if he might start playing the piano, all those present held their breath—until Gus Wenner walked in, made a beeline for McCartney, and announced himself the son of Jann Wenner.

Gus studied creative writing at Brown and like his father wrote a thinly veiled coming-of-age novel. It featured a character based on his father: "I remember vividly, at his center was a red necktie, pumping life into him like a car battery into a motor vehicle." After graduation, his plan was to wait for his classmate Scout Willis, daughter of actor Bruce, to graduate so they could do their band. After helping produce a song for Gus + Scout with Paul Shaffer of the *Late Night with David Letterman* band, and after editing his son's novel while on vacation in St. Bart's and putting it in the hands of Hunter Thompson's agent, Lynn Nesbit, Jann Wenner gently steered Gus to *Rolling Stone,* putting him under the tutelage of a technology executive named David Kang, who aimed Wenner's son at RollingStone.com. A quick study, the twenty-five-year-old started by firing a dozen staffers.

Jann Wenner had found his heir.

"People have always asked in the past, 'Was that weird being so young and inexperienced at firing people who are established?'" said Gus. "It was never, has never, won't ever be weird to me, because I believe so much in the cause. And there's so much on the line between what the brand represents, myself, and my family. The well-being of my family."

Once Wenner offered him the keys to the empire, Gus set about expanding the company into country music, video games, and ad-sponsored documentaries. He cut a $5 million deal with Google to convert his father's magazine covers into an online gallery for digital advertising. Tom Freston tutored him a bit. As Gus understood it, his biggest competitor was Vice, the edgy media company co-founded by Shane Smith, who like Wenner was a rude pirate who turned youth culture into a multibillion-dollar empire, aided by Freston and News Corp chief Rupert Murdoch. "It's not one man's editorial worldview," Gus observed of Shane Smith. "He's a deal maker. Don't get that mistaken. That, to me, is more what it's about now."

Not everybody thought having Gus take over the business was a great idea. David Geffen repeatedly advised Jane Wenner against pushing her son into a declining family business. "Janie will tell you, every time I see her, I say, 'I don't think it's a good idea for Gus to be working at the magazine,'" he said. "'Being the head of digital for *Rolling Stone* is an anchor. *Rolling Stone* doesn't matter. This isn't the best thing.' She won't hear it."

Certainly the challenges were formidable. With Wenner at his back, Gus spent a year negotiating a business deal to extract *Rolling Stone* from the clutches of the bank debt and lead it into some semblance of a digital future. In 2016 he sold a 49 percent stake in *Rolling Stone* to the scion of a wealthy Singapore family who paid $40 million for the worldwide rights to exploit the *Rolling Stone* brand overseas, especially in China. Six months later, the Wenners sold *Us Weekly* to longtime antagonist David Pecker, owner of *Star* and the *National Enquirer*, for $100 million and then sold *Men's Journal* to him three months later, finishing off the debt that had burdened the Wenners for a decade.

What was left was a half ownership in *Rolling Stone* and a well-trafficked website. Wenner began downsizing his personal life as well, liquidating his private art collection, including the original Ralph Steadman drawings for "Fear and Loathing in Las Vegas," which he sold for less than $1 million, and putting his Hudson valley and Montauk estates on the market. But if the empire was smaller and faced powerful digital headwinds from Google and Facebook (which his father once dismissed, in an interview with Charlie Rose, as a teenage fad), it was a fresh start for Gus Wenner, who promised his dad he would get the private jet back one day. Wenner was proud—a chip off the old block. Indeed Gus was eager to shove Dad aside and develop his own vision, including a redesign of the sacred logo. Father advised against such big changes, but Gus had his own ideas and said he wasn't afraid to overrule the old man. "It's not a problem," he said, sucking on a cigarette. "From a business perspective, I feel he's already let go. That's very much in my hands now."

Rolling Stone was always a business, but the magazine itself—what it stood for, how it felt, what it published—was something only Jann Wenner could do right. Everybody knew that. It was *his* magazine. What was *Rolling Stone* without Jann Wenner's thumb on the scales? Nobody was sure. Not even Gus Wenner. "It's a really good question," he said.

•

AFTER JANN WENNER LOST his first libel lawsuit over the botched rape story, jurists said his testimony had help tip the case to the plaintiff, to whom the judge awarded $3 million in damages.

Two days later, Donald Trump was elected president of the United States.

The day after the election, Wenner brought Gus along for his interview with Barack Obama in the White House. Obama and Wenner were world-weary. They always had a cordial if cool relationship. When the president stressed that America needed a "common set of facts" to cohere as a nation, Wenner suggested that the news media, as a business, might need a government subsidy to withstand the ravages of Facebook.

The solar eclipse of Donald Trump signaled the complete triumph of celebrity culture over every aspect of American life. A reality TV star with a casino and a Twitter feed. An egomaniac to rule them all. The message and the medium had merged. The message was fame, and fame was money, money was power, and power was just more fame, for ever and ever, amen.

Jann Wenner got it. *Rolling Stone* was among the first to take Trump seriously, publishing a profile—"Trump Seriously: On the Trail with the GOP's Tough Guy"—and putting him on the cover with a studio portrait by Mark Seliger, who had photographed Jimmy Kimmel and Pearl Jam. Afterward, Trump harrumphed that Wenner had twisted his quotations to make it look as if he said something sexist about GOP candidate Carly Fiorina ("Look at that face! Would anyone vote for that?"), and afterward Trump said, "The writer actually called me and said, 'I'm so upset, I wrote this great story, and Jann Wenner screwed it up.'"

In fact, Wenner had removed negative details from the story.

Wenner had a kind of grudging respect for Trump. Not for his politics, but for the way he bent the world to his ego. Jann Wenner's oldest and dearest friends—people who worked for him in the 1960s and after—could not help but notice the likeness between Trump and the Jann Wenner they knew. The crude egotism, the neediness, the total devotion to celebrity and power. Wenner and Trump were the same age and had met a couple of times at charity events in Manhattan. "I remember Jann saying to me, 'You kind of respect the guy. He works really hard,'" said Will Dana. "When I hear Trump talking, this sounds like Jann. High-functioning narcissists can be incredibly effective people."

When Wenner ordered up a *Rolling Stone* feature on Donald Trump and his "narcissistic personality disorder," the staff just had to shake their heads and laugh. Wenner took issue with the idea that he himself was a "clinical" narcissist: "Self-centered, egotistical . . . yes . . . but not beyond that." Wenner, of course, was a pioneer of the age of narcissism. He made his generation feel good about itself—righteous, independent, young. He also hung celebrities like sides of beef in his showroom window. The man adored fame. And so he saw the rise of Trump as he did everything else in life—as an opportunity. While Matt Taibbi railed about the "insane clown president" in *Rolling Stone,* Wenner was splashing very beautiful photos of Trump's "First Family" in *Us Weekly.* First Lady Melania Trump was another soap star in the weekly serial. "Because it was what everybody's curious about," Wenner reasoned. "Our sales almost doubled the three or four issues that we did that." (After several Trump issues, he sold the magazine to David Pecker, a strident Trump supporter.)

Meanwhile, Wenner was still busy editing—history. After he fired Will Dana, who he said was too traumatized by the UVA debacle to function anymore, Wenner amended his previous declaration: Jason Fine, his replacement, was now the best editor *Rolling Stone* ever had. *Rolling Stone* was fifty years old, and Wenner was rolling out special issues, a *Rolling Stone* coffee-table book, a four-hour *Rolling Stone* documentary on HBO co-directed by Alex Gibney. There would be an obligatory cameo by Cameron Crowe. Vintage footage of Hunter Thompson gnawing on his cigarette holder. Maybe Sir Mick would drop a royal quotation or two. Wenner loved it all. But the stress of the lawsuits and the downsizing of *Rolling Stone* had taken their toll, visibly aging Wenner. While he promoted his coffee-table book, the UVA episode shadowed him with painful regularity. And in June 2017, a week after he settled the suit with the fraternity for $1.65 million (a victory, all things considered), Wenner fell over while playing tennis with his son Noah and broke his hip—and then he had a heart attack. He would need a triple bypass operation *and* a hip replacement.

In the ambulance, Wenner had believed he was at "death's door." For days he had "insane visions" while on pain medications. But before surgery Bruce Springsteen dropped by the hospital for a three-hour visit and gave Wenner a mixtape—"a soundtrack for open-heart surgery." "There are a lot of silver linings," Wenner said. The whole episode, he concluded, was an opportunity "to take advantage of what you've learned about human nature and love—I've been given a chance to reboot a little."

In the preceding months, Wenner had expressed a certain fatalism about *Rolling Stone.* His friends and family noticed. It was a new thing. Wenner could not help but feel pangs of loss as he flipped through the back issues of his little rock-and-roll newspaper from San Francisco. "There's so much wonderful stuff in there that will never see the light of day," he lamented, "and it all coincides with digital, which is the most depressing thing, because it's the end of the magazine. The end of the big glory days of magazines."

The physical object—that's what he loved. When you held it in your hands, you held Jann Wenner's love letter to the culture, to himself. Every other week for fifty years. And now it was all but buried, part of the vast American archive. But nobody could say Jann Wenner hadn't given himself to it completely. He was an incorrigible egotist, but he made up for it with a life of impact. He had *mattered*. He broke things; he made things. A nude John Lennon curled around Yoko Ono—nobody would ever forget. An entire American cosmology of superstars and superstar journalists, stories, and myths, all fired in the kiln of his appetites and ambition. Millions had dreamed on his pages. Bruce Springsteen said *Rolling Stone* changed his life. Patti Smith found liberation in *Rolling Stone*. Bono embraced *Rolling Stone* when he finally embraced his own power. Stories begat stories and stars begat stars until Wenner's influence sprayed out like Roman candles across Max Palevsky's swimming pool as Hunter Thompson grinned behind Sandy Bull's Saigon-mirror shades.

Did Jann Wenner embody the vices or the virtues of his generation? Certainly the rock-and-roll hymnbook of the 1960s had promised something else. At one time, holding *Rolling Stone* was like holding a piece of hot shrapnel from the cultural explosion of the 1960s while it still glowed with feeling and meaning. An entire identity was coiled inside Rick Griffin's logo, the promise of never-ending provocation, never-ending progress. The rock-and-roll story lit the way. *Don't stop thinking about tomorrow.* But those visions had morphed into the Me Decade, and the Me Decade had turned into Me *Decades,* and finally the falcon could no longer hear the falconer, not even in the pages of *Rolling Stone*.

Well, it was just a story. A long, fine flash. This one began with John Lennon and ended with Donald Trump.

Wenner's hippie sister, Merlyn, once adorned her shower in Hawaii with healing crystals to shield herself from her mother's bad karma. She called her brother "one of the most feeling human beings that I've ever known. I know this sounds weird, especially after all you've heard." His sister Kate spent years on a memoir about Sim Wenner, raking over the past, investigating the root causes. In an interview before she died, Sim said her son was born "club fisted"—greedy, she said. She snarled at him from her assisted-living facility in Palo Alto. But before she died at age ninety-four, Wenner went to her bedside and held her hand and spoke soothingly to her unmoving body, a boy and his mother. At the memorial in Sausalito, Denise Kaufman read the Kaddish prayer along with the Wenner sisters, and Jann Wenner, in his remembrances, recalled Sim's long-ago words: "You're on your own, Buster Brown."

Jann Wenner had tried to become a great American media mogul on the order of William Randolph Hearst. For a while he was successful, but he didn't rate himself as a businessman now. He'd been too impulsive, fired too many people, took that loan. *Rolling Stone*—an idea so great it survived Janno's management. "I see myself primarily as an editor," said Wenner. "And that's what I have a real skill at. I've been more lucky and made more money than any other editor other than Hefner. Maybe Luce."

He related to the *Playboy* publisher. Now, there was a man who stamped the world with his personal vision of life. An individualist. A maverick. A lucky guy.

"He lived it," said Wenner. "He lived it."

•

BACK IN 1997, TOM Wolfe asked Wenner to read a draft of his second novel, *A Man in Full.* It was a social novel like *The Bonfire of the Vanities,* this time involving a racially charged rape case and featuring a real estate tycoon named Charles Croker. Wenner, whom Wolfe would thank in the book as the "generous genius" who helped shepherd his most famous works, told him he liked everything but the ending. "The kid, who was the protagonist, you know, was going to end up being nothing, just go back to being nobody," said Wenner. "I said, 'You just cannot do this to the person who is the hero of the book! You have to give him something. Have him come out to be good.'"

Editor Will Dana ended his career in infamy at *Rolling Stone,* but before that he witnessed Jann Wenner up close for twenty years. Brilliant, vulgar, courageous, cruel, that peculiar DNA twist of idealism and greed—god of two heads, gatekeeper of heaven. "I always think, with Jann, the question is, is he 51 percent good or 51 percent bad?" said Dana. "That's the big question. That's the big question, and no one knows."

He'd thought about this. Everyone had.

"But I basically think he's 51 percent good."

And maybe that was good enough.

Afterword

Jann Wenner asked me to write his biography in the fall of 2013. He sprang the idea over lunch at a restaurant in Rhinebeck, New York, not far from his Hudson valley estate. I was shocked and flattered: One of the great magazine editors of my lifetime was asking *me* to write his life story.

I grew up with a subscription to *Rolling Stone* and once posed for a fake *Rolling Stone* cover at Disney World when I was a teenager. I interned at *Rolling Stone* in 1995 (the same spring Wenner came out of the closet) and was formally introduced to Wenner in his Sixth Avenue office while working as a media reporter at *The Wall Street Journal* in 2005 (I marveled at his tales of hanging out with Bono and Mick Jagger). So it was the strangest of fortunes when I ran into him one day in a tiny upstate café while he was buying half a gallon of milk. His three young children were idling in the backseat of a Mercedes parked out front. He was gracious and interested in my work as a journalist and invited me to his house for a swim with his family. On subsequent social calls, he described shaking hands with Bob Dylan in 1969 and wearing Mick Jagger's pants, and spoke of a personal archive rife with historic treasures beyond imagining. I was wowed.

Still, I never asked to write his biography. Indeed, I was wary of Wenner because of his reputation in the business—mercurial, controlling, litigious. Two previous attempts at a biography ended unhappily, and I was warned by veteran media people to proceed with caution. It would end in tears, a former *Rolling Stone* editor warned, or worse. Thus began a protracted negotiation with Wenner in which he cajoled and charmed as I fretted and wrung my hands. Finally, we came to a crucial agreement—the biography would be independent, not "authorized" in the usual sense. He wanted the right to review the most deeply personal matters—namely, his sex life—but he would not attempt to limit my reporting or the scope of the *Rolling Stone* story. He would also give me endless hours of interview time and access to his trove of correspondence, documents, recordings, and photography, some five hundred boxes in all.

In other words, Jann Wenner did what Jann Wenner, at his very best, was known to do: He took a gamble on a writer. An independent biography meant he would expose himself to an objective assessment of his life and times, even if it meant taking a few lashes. And perhaps more than a few. But to his great credit as an editor—and further proof of his greatness—he freed me to research and report on his large and controversial story without interference. Jann Wenner did not read the manuscript of this book before publication.

For journalists of my generation, the names Hunter Thompson and Tom Wolfe are hallowed. A vintage copy of *The New Journalism,* edited by Wolfe and E. W. Johnson in 1973, has had pride of place on my bookshelf for years. Therefore, I felt duty-bound to convert my gratitude for Jann Wenner's generous access into the kind of no-holds-barred narrative journalism that Wenner was famous for publishing. To my mind, this was essentially Jann Wenner's last great assignment, and there was no way in hell I was going to screw it up.

Wenner, being Wenner, was intent on influencing the story at every turn, spinning away negative stories and gilding his deeds with ebullient bravado. He was especially intent on convincing me that the twenty-fifth-anniversary Rock and Roll Hall of Fame concert was among the best shows in history. It was a charm offensive the likes of which I had never seen: He gifted me with a boxed set of the complete mono recordings of the Beatles on vinyl (which, I will confess, I kept, in addition to a *Rolling Stone* beach towel); he mailed me pictures of himself with Bob Dylan and took me to see Bob Dylan at the Beacon Theatre in

2014, second row; he regularly forwarded me personal e-mails from Mick Jagger and Bono and Jackson Browne to demonstrate his outsized influence. At one point, Wenner suggested I look to a 2013 biography of Woodrow Wilson as the ideal model for this one. But that's Jann Wenner—a man of large visions and larger ambitions. I never worried that my reporting would hurt his feelings, only whether my own ambition could rhyme with his. I knew he would ask for nothing less from his own writers. Therefore, I could not be more grateful for his gamble.

Additionally, the true story of Jann Wenner would never have been possible without the express participation of Jane Wenner, whose candor, humor, and courage made this biography twice the book it would have been otherwise. It's true that there is no separating Jann from Jane; their symbiotic relationship was the core of the *Rolling Stone* story and therefore the core of this biography. I'm deeply grateful to her.

I could not begin to list the cast of hundreds who helped this story materialize, but I am particularly indebted to a group of lesser-known women whose honesty (and recall) provided an invaluable tuning fork for my understanding of the times described in this book: Denise Kaufman, Joey Townsend, Carmella Scaggs (RIP), Laurel Gonsalves, Diane Chess, Robin Green, Karen Mullarkey, Lynda Obst, Jodie Evans, Harriet Fier, and Barbara Landau.

A small army helped me compile the material, and I wish specifically to acknowledge the immense contributions of my ad hoc research team, Lisa Di Venuta, Matthew Giles, Sean Howe, and Acacia Nunes. They were my eyes and ears in an overwhelming landscape of information. I also wish to acknowledge the incomparable input of John Homans, the Thelonious Monk of magazine editors, whose wisdom and wit kept me straight and true. Many thanks to Peter Richardson and Peter O. Whitmer for their learned input. As well, I'm grateful for the trenchant advice of colleagues Gabe Sherman, Christopher Bonanos, Vanessa Grigoriadis, and Andrew Rice and for the enthusiastic counsel of excellent (and forgiving) friends: Tim Davis, Ian Davis, Douglas Stone, John Nathan, Paul La Farge, Herb Wilson, Franz Nicolay, Dan D'Oca, and Joshua Ferris.

Because this is my first book, I'd like to recognize the key influences of Joe Wilson, the teacher who sparked my interest in writing in twelfth grade; Barbara O'Dair, who plucked me from obscurity for a *Rolling Stone* internship in 1995; Adam Moss, in whose editorial Golden Age at *New York* magazine I was honored to take part; Kurt Andersen, a constant friend and advocate; John Adamian and Annie Gwynne-Vaughan, whose deep friendships have sustained me through the years; and the late, great Peter Kaplan, whose editorial spirit smiled mischievously over my shoulder during the writing of this book.

I am indebted also to the people who gave me the private space (and prolonged silence) required to complete this project: Andy and Nancy Hunt, in whose house I impersonated Martin Sheen in *Apocalypse Now* while laboring over the late chapters; the brothers of the Holy Cross Monastery in West Park, New York, in whose guesthouse I chronicled man's sins in supreme quietude; and especially the late Norma Nolan Santangelo, whose effervescent spirit, in addition to her condo, guided me over the finish line.

I offer a deep bow to my editor at Knopf, Jordan Pavlin, whose faith and enthusiasm fanned my sails to the very end; and PJ Mark, my agent and friend who has watched over my interests with both passion and moxie since we were just kids. Further, a special thanks to Bette Alexander and Ingrid Sterner at Knopf, who steamed and pressed my prose with great care; and to Bennett Ashley, general counsel at Janklow & Nesbit, who crafted the guidelines for how a biography of this scope could work independently.

I am also deeply grateful for the unwavering faith of my parents, Jerry and Carol Hagan, and my ever-supportive sisters, Allison and Audrey. Thank you.

And finally, this book would have been unimaginable without the love, inspiration, encouragement, and infinite patience of my wife, Samantha Hunt, and our three brave hearts, Rosa, Marie, and Juliet. This book is dedicated to them.

Notes

This biography was constructed from dozens of hours of interviews with Jann Wenner; from private letters, documents, memos, photographs, and recordings contained in Wenner's personal archive; and from over 240 original interviews with sources, nearly all of whom went on the record. These notes outline the primary sourcing for each chapter, though not every quotation, anecdote, and fact is referenced. All quotations are from my own interviews unless the construction of the sentence reads "once said" or "would say," in which case I have tried to include the original source here. To avoid redundancy, I do not include citations already noted in the text, but I have elaborated on some for clarity. I have taken pains to note where I have cited unpublished materials from a previous biographer, Lewis MacAdams, and transcripts of interviews conducted by other reporters, in particular Grover Lewis, Robert Sam Anson, Peter O. Whitmer, David Felton, and Corey Seymour.

PROLOGUE: GET BACK

The opening and closing scenes were reconstructed from interviews with Jann and Jane Wenner, Yoko Ono, Ed Ward, and John Burks, as well as office details gleaned from Jane Wilson, "Communicating via Straight Arrow," *West*, Nov. 22, 1970. Wenner's comment that he related to Miss Lonely in Bob Dylan's "Like a Rolling Stone" comes from an interview with Greil Marcus, *Like a Rolling Stone: Bob Dylan at the Crossroads* (New York: PublicAffairs, 2006). Sim Wenner's quotation about her son being "the most conservative" in the Wenner family comes from Tom Zito, "Citizen Wenner and 'Rolling Stone': A Sense of What Is to Be," *Washington Post*, Nov. 9, 1975. The typographical history of *The Sunday Ramparts,* and the origins of the Oxford border being imported by Marget Larsen, come from former *Rolling Stone* art director Mike Salisbury and are further described in Steven Bower, "How the Oxford Rule Led to *Rolling Stone*," *Print,* Feb. 11, 2016. The quotation from Tom Wolfe in 1987 is from an interview conducted by Brant Mewborn for the twenty-year-anniversary issue of *Rolling Stone,* No. 512.

1. ATLANTIS

My sources for the material on Wenner's early life were Jann Wenner, Sim Wenner, Kate Wenner, Merlyn Wenner, Steve Simmons, Dallas Clark, Andy Harmon, Bill Belding, Susan Pasternak, Terryl Stacy, Richard Black, Barry Baron, Susan Reid-Adams, Robbie Leeds, Susan Andrews, and Jane Kenner. All quotations from Ed Wenner come from *Time with My Father,* a film documentary made by Kate Wenner, produced in 1998, except the comment "A pain in the ass," which comes from a profile by Michael Bane published in *Hustler,* June 1980. Some childhood details are from unpublished material by Lewis MacAdams. For instance, Sim Wenner's description of her "homosexual gene" and Ed Wenner's twenty-five-page "Mother's Guide" describing the benefits of formula. The claim that Wenner could scramble an egg when he was three years old comes from Sim Wenner's *Back Away from the Stove.*

2. ARE YOU EXPERIENCED?

This material was derived from interviews and correspondence with Jann Wenner, Denise Kaufman, Linda Kingsbury, Toby Gleason, Greil Marcus, Bob Dylan, Michael Lydon, and Richard Black. The detail about Mick Jagger swinging a blue-checkered jacket over his head comes from Wenner's *Daily Californian* column, Something's Happening, 1966; the description of Wenner meeting Bob Weir comes from Wenner's profile of the Grateful Dead in *Sunday Ramparts,* Nov. 4–11, 1966. All of Ralph Gleason's observations on the San Francisco rock scene come from his book *The Jefferson Airplane and the San Francisco Sound* (courtesy of Paul Scanlon). Gleason's recollection of meeting Wenner comes from the hundredth issue of *Rolling Stone,* Jan. 20, 1972. Wenner's recollection of seeing Brian Jones emerging from a silver Rolls-Royce in London comes from Robert Draper's *"Rolling Stone" Magazine;* Wenner's purchase of a pair of striped bell-bottoms and a flowered belt is from Lewis MacAdams.

3. CALIFORNIA DREAMIN'

My sources for the material about mid-1960s San Francisco, *Ramparts,* and Monterey Pop were interviews and correspondence with Jann Wenner, Linda Kingsbury, Jane Wenner, Sandor Burstein, Herb Gold, Peter Richardson, John Muchmore, Peter Wolf, Jonathan Cott, Warren Hinckle, Lou Adler, Bob Neuwirth, Clive Davis, and Robin Gracey. The quotations from Ralph Gleason are from an interview for the WNET short film *TVTV Meets Rolling Stone* (1973), produced by Michael Shamberg and Allen Rucker. The quotations from Warren Hinckle come from his memoir, *If You Have a Lemon, Make Lemonade.* The references to Derek Taylor are taken from his memoir, *As Time Goes By.*

4. LIKE A ROLLING STONE

The sources for this chapter are interviews and correspondence with Jann Wenner, Art Garfunkel, Jerry Hopkins, Michael Lydon, Dan Parker, Baron Wolman, and

John Williams. Ralph Gleason's comment about Wenner's all-consuming devotion comes from a letter he wrote to Wenner in 1971. On the reputed comment that Wenner started *Rolling Stone* to meet John Lennon: Robert Draper reports that Wenner told people this, but I could not find an original citation. Wenner said it is apocryphal: "I honestly don't think I ever said it; it seems likely to come out of the anti-*RS*/Robert Draper vortex of demeaning my seriousness of purpose and ambition. Somebody made it up, sounds cute, but nobody ever heard me say it, because I didn't."

5. BORN TO RUN

The sources for this chapter were interviews and correspondence with Jann Wenner, Bruce Springsteen, Michael Lydon, Jane Wenner, Jon Landau, Jerry Hopkins, Robert Kingsbury, Linda Kingsbury, Lou Adler, David Crosby, Charlie Perry, Danny Fields, Art Garfunkel, Piedy Gimbel, Denise Kaufman, Paul McCartney, Ben Sidran, and Robin Gracey. The quotation from Eric Clapton describing his reaction to Jon Landau's review of Cream was referenced in Michael Schumacher, *Crossroads: The Life and Music of Eric Clapton* (New York: Hyperion, 1995). Townshend describes a druggy homosexual experience with Danny Fields in his memoir, *Who I Am*.

6. SYMPATHY FOR THE DEVIL

This chapter is derived from interviews and correspondence with Jann Wenner, Mick Jagger, Keith Richards, Georgia "Jo" Bergman, John Burks, Pete Townshend, Robin Gracey, Charles Fracchia, Clive Davis, Baron Wolman, Alan Rinzler, Alan Marcuson, Stephen Paley, Glyn Johns, Boz Scaggs, Carmella Scaggs, Bob Dylan, Greil Marcus, Marshall Chess, and Diane von Furstenberg. The anecdote about Wenner discovering employees of the Rolling Stones in his office was told to Robert Draper by then secretary Gretchen Horton, now deceased. Georgia Bergman supplied the detail about the Rolling Stones running up $140 in long-distance calls, citing her diary from the era. John Burks's comment to Wenner demanding the magazine "tell people what these fuckers did . . . like it was World War II" comes from Joel Selvin's *Altamont*.

7. BRIDGE OVER TROUBLED WATER

This chapter was constructed from interviews and correspondence with Jann Wenner, Ed Berkowitz, Jon Carroll, Craig Pyes, John Burks, Alan Rinzler, John Morthland, Ed Ward, Greil Marcus, Jac Holzman, Clive Davis, David Dalton, David Felton, Pete Townshend, Charlie Perry, and Bob Dylan. Some details of Wenner's remodeling of Third Street come from Robert Draper. For details on the 1968 Democratic National Convention, I relied on both Todd Gitlin's *Sixties* and Rick Perlstein's *Nixonland*. Abbie Hoffman's description of Berkeley as the "School for Advanced Toilet Training" comes from the *Berkeley Barb*, Sept. 10–16, 1971. Hunter Thompson recalled *Rolling Stone*'s coverage of the convention in an interview with David Felton for MTV's *25 Years of Rolling Stone* (1992). Jann Wenner was profiled by *New York* magazine reporter Carey Winfrey for the July 13, 1970, issue. Wenner said "psychic news" was also news in the *Buffalo Courier Express,* July 25, 1970. Wenner said he took the money from Independent News without signing the papers in an unedited interview with Robert Sam Anson in 1976. Wenner said he raised $200,000 in two weeks "without tying ourselves to anybody" in a speech to students at the University of Colorado, March 15, 1973. Bill Graham's comments about Wenner come from a transcription of a taped conversation that took place in the offices of *Rolling Stone* in 1972. "In the early days, Jann would sometimes put addenda into bylined articles," said Charlie Perry in Wilson, "Communicating via Straight Arrow." That top executives at CBS, Columbia's parent company, had cooperative ties to the CIA was reported by Abe Peck in *Uncovering the Sixties.* On a brick wall next to the office elevator on Third Street was scrawled "Smash 'Hip' Capitalism," per an unpublished profile of Jann Wenner by Grover Lewis, 1970. ("A lot of people say he's an asshole and blah, blah, blah": ibid.) John Burks's comment that Kent State and Cambodia were more concerning than news on Paul McCartney: Wilson, "Communicating via Straight Arrow."

8. TEMPTATION EYES

The John Lennon section of the chapter was constructed from interviews and correspondence with Jann Wenner, Yoko Ono, Paul McCartney, Jonathan Cott, Greil Marcus, Langdon Winner, Annie Leibovitz, and Alan Rinzler. The Hunter Thompson material comes from interviews and correspondence with Wenner, Douglas Brinkley, Ralph Steadman, Peter Whitmer, Peter Richardson, Warren Hinckle, Sandy Thompson, Timothy Crouse, Alan Rinzler, David Felton, and Garry Trudeau. The story of the "Thompson-Steadman report" comes from William McKeen's excellent biography, *Outlaw Journalist.* John Lombardi's comment that Thompson was "inventing vocabulary" during their meeting was recalled to Peter Whitmer in September 1991. Thompson making a "solemn promise to sell his soul to *Rolling Stone* . . . like a terminal heroin addict" comes from a written recollection by Ralph Steadman, courtesy of Steadman. The other sections derive from interviews with Bob Neuwirth, Candy Bull, Lynn Hodenfield, Arthur Rock, Lynda Palevsky, Laurel Gonsalves, Dick Kramlich, Tony Pinck, Danny Fields, Dotson Rader, Glenn O'Brien, Robin Gracey, Faye Hauser, Sandy Thompson, Charlie Perry, David Felton, Garry Trudeau, Andrew Bailey, Tim Ferris, Diane Chess, David Dalton, Susann Dalton, Ben Fong-Torres, Jane Wenner, and Robin Green. Jann Wenner quoted Bull saying, "Bright lights make you forget where you are" in *Sunday Ramparts,* April 1967. Details about Daphne Hellman come from Whitney Balliett, "Harp Lady," *New Yorker,* Dec. 24, 1990. Max Palevsky's comment that his Palm Springs diploma was a "testimony that we all made it through that night" comes from an interview with Peter Whitmer, Nov. 15, 1991.

9. STICKY FINGERS

This chapter was sourced from interviews and correspondence with Jann Wenner, Danny Fields, Robin Green, Annie Leibovitz, Robert Kingsbury, Linda Kingsbury, Bruce Mann, Michael Rogers, David Felton, Robert Greenfield, Marshall Chess, Keith Richards, Glenn O'Brien, Mick Jagger, Douglas Brinkley, Timothy Crouse, Pat Caddell, and Sandy Thompson. David Cassidy's quotations come from an interview with MTV for *25 Years of Rolling Stone*. Annie Leibovitz's recollection of seeing members of the Jefferson Airplane on a water bed smoking joints comes from an unpublished profile by Lewis MacAdams. Truman Capote would later say Wenner "thinks like a water moccasin": Judy Bachrach, *Washington Post,* Nov. 25, 1977. "Jagger is a master craftsman": Annie Leibovitz, *Shooting Stars* (San Francisco: Straight Arrow Books, 1973). Timothy Ferris's report on Mick Jagger's twenty-ninth birthday party is from "Gotham Satyricon: Chocolate Mousse at the End of the Road," *Rolling Stone,* Aug. 31, 1972. Wenner's quotation on "the rich and beautiful people" appeared in the Eye column of *Women's Wear Daily,* July 13, 1973. Wenner's claim that *Rolling Stone* was the "paper of record" for the 1972 campaign, more so than *The New York Times,* comes from *TVTV Meets Rolling Stone*.

10. CALIFORNIA

This chapter was sourced from interviews and correspondence with Jann Wenner, David Geffen, David Crosby, Jerry Hopkins, Charlie Perry, Jackson Browne, Ben Fong-Torres, Joe Smith, Annie Leibovitz, Earl McGrath, Brice Marden, Diane Chess, Eve Babitz, Lloyd Ziff, Michael Douglas, Joe Eszterhas, Bryn Bridenthal, and Laurel Gonsalves. David Geffen's recollections of Wenner offering him speed and his anger over a Clive Davis profile ("Fuckin' Jann Wenner") come from an unedited interview with Geffen by Grover Lewis. The fallout from Jackson Browne breaking up with Joni Mitchell comes from Sheila Weller's book *Girls Like Us.* Jann Wenner banning pot smoking in the office: Robert Draper.

11. THE COVER OF THE *ROLLING STONE*

My sources were interviews and correspondence with Jann Wenner, Timothy Crouse, Marshall Chess, Elton John, David Obst, Jane Wenner, Porter Bibb, Tom Baker, Joe Armstrong, Tom Wolfe, Michael Rogers, Jonathan Cott, Jerry Hopkins, Paul Scanlon, Robin Green, Bryn Bridenthal, Joe Eszterhas, David Felton, Glenn O'Brien, Jon Landau, Sarah Lazin, Barbara Landau, Jodie Evans, Lynda Obst, and Alan Rinzler. "Razzle-dazzle, night and day, coast to coast" comes from Alan Rinzler's recollections in "My Roller Coaster Years with Jann," *San Francisco Sunday Examiner and Chronicle,* May 29, 1977. His mother calling him "Citizen Wenner" was reported by Tom Zito in *Washington Post,* June 17, 1975. Clay Felker acknowledged that Wenner had "one of the best journalistic antennas in the United States" in *Blade Sunday Magazine,* Nov. 9, 1975. "The better they are, the less we pay them" comes from Wenner's speech at the University of Colorado in March 1973. Robert Palmer described accompanying Wenner while he shopped for Oriental rugs in *Blues and Chaos.* Jerry Hopkins's comment that Wenner "has real trouble with interpersonal relationships" was made to Connecticut Walker for "The Young Publishing Wizard of 'Rolling Stone,'" *Boston Globe,* Feb. 9, 1974. Max Palevsky told a reporter that Wenner had a "compulsion to kill his father" in Robert Sam Anson, "Citizen Wenner," *New Times,* Nov. 26, 1976.

12. WHATEVER GETS YOU THRU THE NIGHT

The sections on California Street and Annie Leibovitz come from interviews and correspondence with Jann and Jane Wenner, Annie Leibovitz, Joey Townsend, Mike Salisbury, Lloyd Ziff, Lynda Obst, David Obst, Laurel Gonsalves, Michael Rogers, Craig Braun, Harriet Fier, Dave Marsh, Jim Messina, Jenny Sullivan, Roger Black, and Peter Wolf. The detail about Wenner's "millionaire Bob Dylan" outfit comes from the Eye column in *Women's Wear Daily*, Aug. 9, 1971. The next section about Ahmet Ertegun and the New York scene derives from interviews with Peter Wolf, Bette Midler, Perry Deane Young, Dotson Rader, Diane von Furstenberg, Edmund White, Art Garfunkel, and Clive Davis. The concluding part on Hunter Thompson is sourced to Wenner, John Walsh, Susan Warford-Winter, Paul Gambaccini, Marianne Partridge, Harriet Fier, Sarah Lazin, Roger Black, Andrew Tobias, Alan Rinzler, Douglas Brinkley, David Felton, Kent Brownridge, Joe Klein, and Tom Baker. Thompson's recollection that he brought ten hits of blotter acid to Vietnam is from "Dance of the Doomed," *Rolling Stone*, May 9, 1985.

13. LOVE WILL KEEP US TOGETHER

My sources were interviews and correspondence with Jann Wenner, Cameron Crowe, Greil Marcus, Dave Marsh, Mike Salisbury, Charlie Perry, Alan Rinzler, Denise Kaufman, Toby Gleason, Annie Leibovitz, Mick Jagger, Marshall Chess, Diane Chess, Keith Richards, Ben Needell, John Lagana, Karen Mullarkey, Lou Adler, Art Garfunkel, David Geffen, Robbie Robertson, Bob Dylan, Larry Sloman, Bob Neuwirth, Joe Klein, Paul Scanlon, Howard Kohn, David Weir, Will Hearst, and Michael Rogers. The Jon Landau quotation "I found myself withdrawing from the music . . ." is from *It's Too Late to Stop Now*. Wenner promised to profile Springsteen in a letter to Joe Armstrong, 1976. In a letter to Alan Rinzler, Wenner reportedly discussed his inability to love: "My Roller Coaster Years with Jann." "I was at the point where I was really going to push a pencil through my hand": unedited interview with Robert Sam Anson, 1976. The other account of the Dylan confrontation at Mailer's apartment comes from Robert Sam Anson, *Gone Crazy and Back Again*.

14. TAKE IT TO THE LIMIT

The first section of this chapter, on Jann Wenner's political aspirations, derives from interviews and correspondence with Wenner, Joe Klein, Harriet "Hank" Phillippi, Joseph Duffey, Steve Simmons, Marianne Partridge, John Dean, and Lowell Bergman. Wenner's stump speech on the power of the youth vote comes from Mary Ann Dolan, *Washington Star*, April 14, 1975. Avedon proclaimed his work an attack on subjectivity in journalism in Susan Cheever Cowley, "Avedon's Faces of Power," *Newsweek*, Oct. 11, 1976. Avedon excoriated Wenner for initially failing to credit Renata Adler: David Ansen, "Avedon," *Newsweek*, Sept. 12, 1993. The sections on Joe Armstrong come from interviews and conversations with Wenner and Armstrong, as well as Claeys Bahrenburg, Roger Black, Elton John, Tony King, and Paul Gambaccini. Joe Armstrong provided invaluable archival material, including rare letters, photographs, and advertising materials. The section on *Saturday Night Live* and the move to New York City was constructed from interviews with Jann and Jane Wenner, Dan Aykroyd, Lorne Michaels, Art Garfunkel, Bryn Bridenthal, Howard Kohn, Kent Brownridge, and Paul Scanlon.

15. BIG SHOT

This chapter is sourced from interviews and correspondence with Jann and Jane Wenner, Annie Leibovitz, Jim Dunning, Diane von Furstenberg, Greil Marcus, Lorne Michaels, Bryn Bridenthal, Karen Mullarkey, Claeys Bahrenburg, Harriet Fier, Sarah Lazin, Laurel Gonsalves, Billy Joel, Mick Jagger, Steve Binder, Ben Fong-Torres, David Felton, Douglas Brinkley, and Ben Needell. The reporter who described Wenner at the "White Party" in the Hamptons was Jerry Parker for *Cosmopolitan,* July 1979. Wenner's estimation of 250 inaccuracies in Robert Sam Anson's *New Times* story comes from an interview Wenner gave to David Chamberlin, host of a cable access TV program called *Focus!* in Aspen, Colorado, 1977. The reporter who profiled Wenner at his keyed-up pinnacle was Judy Bachrach, "Rolling Stone, Ten (Light) Years Later," *Washington Post,* Nov. 25, 1977.

16. STAYIN' ALIVE

This chapter is sourced from interviews and correspondence with Jann Wenner, Peter Herbst, Irving Azoff, Cameron Crowe, Jim Dunning, Howard Kohn, Victor Kovner, Harriet Fier, Laurel Gonsalves, Jeff Berg, David Obst, Kent Brownridge, and David Geffen. Cameron Crowe's interview with Joni Mitchell was published in *Rolling Stone* on July 26, 1979.

17. SHATTERED

The section on cocaine and the decline of the music business comes from interviews and correspondence with Jann Wenner, Judy Belushi, Lynda Obst, Laila Nabulsi, Jane Wenner, Bailey Gimbel, Harriet Fier, Karen Mullarkey, David Felton, Claeys Bahrenburg, Peter Herbst, and Bob Dylan. The sources on the Beatles section are Paul McCartney, Greil Marcus, Paul Gambaccini, and Wenner. The nature of John Lennon's relationship with May Pang comes from her memoir, *Loving John,* written with Henry Edwards; and from Albert Goldman, *The Lives of John Lennon.* The latter sections, on the late 1970s lives of Annie Leibovitz and the Wenners, come from interviews with the subjects themselves in addition to Bahrenburg, Mullarkey, Roger Black, Jim Dunning, Robert Pledge, Lorne Michaels, Skip Stein, Chip Block, Laurel Gonsalves, Art Garfunkel, Michael Douglas, Dan Aykroyd, Johnny Pigozzi, Earl McGrath, Robbie Robertson, and Terry McDonell. Hunter Thompson's review of the 1980 film *Where the Buffalo Roam* ("It sucks—a bad, dumb, low-level, low-rent script") is from David Felton, "Hunter Thompson Cashed His Check," *Rolling Stone College Papers,* 1980. Wenner described himself as "bourgeois" to William G. Shepherd Jr. in *Avenue* magazine, Nov. 1979. The report on Wenner trying to "pounce" on Caroline Kennedy came from Diana McLellan's Ear column, *Atlanta Journal and Constitution,* March 5, 1978. Wenner openly discussed his cruelty with Studs Terkel in the book *American Dreams.*

18. GET BACK

This chapter was constructed from interviews and correspondence with Jann Wenner, David Geffen, Yoko Ono, Paul McCartney, Jane Wenner, Annie Leibovitz, Jonathan Cott, Robert Pledge, Terry McDonell, Howard Kohn, David Rosenthal, Sam Havadtoy, and Kent Brownridge. I also relied on details from *The Ballad of John and Yoko,* from the editors of *Rolling Stone;* Goldman's *Lives of John Lennon;* and an unedited transcript of an interview that Leibovitz gave to David Felton in February 1983 for the book *Annie Leibovitz: Photographs.*

19. WE DON'T NEED ANOTHER HERO

This chapter is sourced from interviews and correspondence with Jann Wenner, Jim Dunning, Harriet Fier, Kent Brownridge, Bob Pittman, David Rosenthal, Kenneth Lerer, John Branca, Mick Jagger, Dan Aykroyd, Lorne Michaels, Lynn Hirschberg, Jane Wenner, Laurel Gonsalves, Jackson Browne, Michael Douglas, Ben Needell, Chip Block, David Geffen, Annie Leibovitz, Robert Pledge, Sarah Lazin, and Tom Wolfe. John Belushi's last words, "Just don't leave me alone," were reported by Randall Sullivan in "The Last Days of John Belushi's Life: Wrong Time, Wrong Place, Wrong People," *Rolling Stone,* May 13, 1982. David Geffen pulled his advertising after *Rolling Stone* quoted him in Michael Schrage, "The War Against Home Taping," Sept. 16, 1982.

20. PURPLE RAIN

The section on the movie *Perfect* comes from interviews and correspondence with Jann Wenner, Bob Wallace, David Rosenthal, Jane Wenner, and Kent Brownridge. The quotation describing Wenner's fictional role as "ruthless, bullying and totally inured to finer human feelings" appeared in a profile by Mick Brown, *Sunday Times* (London), Aug. 18, 1985. The section on AIDS comes from interviews and correspondence with Wenner, B. D. Colen, Lindsy Van Gelder, David Black, David Rosenthal, Lynn Hirschberg, and Seymour Stein. The story of Wenner's family life is derived from interviews with Jann and Jane Wenner, Megan Kingsbury, Diane Chess, Alex Wenner, Kent Brownridge, and Paul Scanlon. The last section on Wenner getting rich comes from interviews and correspondence with Wenner, Brownridge, Ben Needell, Laurel Gonsalves, Dallas Clark, Pat Fallon, Bob Pittman, and Tom Wolfe. The article about the discovery of gold coins on Wenner's property was Tad Friend, "The Gold Diggers," *New Yorker,* March 31, 1999.

21. WE DIDN'T START THE FIRE

The first section of this chapter is sourced from interviews and correspondence with Jann Wenner and Kate Wenner, Billy Joel, Bob Guccione, Peter Wolf, Bono, Kent Brownridge, Tom Freston, and Robert Draper. Guccione's quotation that *Rolling Stone* was "arrogant, complacent and out of touch" comes from Jonathan Alter in *Newsweek,* July 17, 1985. The section on the Rock and Roll Hall of Fame comes from interviews with Wenner, Dave Marsh, Bruce Brandwen, Suzan Evans

Hochberg, Seymour Stein, Mick Jagger, Johnny Pigozzi, Kent Brownridge, Bono, and Paul McCartney. Jon Landau once said the nomination committee at the Rock and Roll Hall of Fame as purposefully "nontransparent": Janet Morrissey, "Battle of the Bands (and Egos) for the Rock Hall of Fame," *New York Times*, Dec. 3, 2011.

22. NEVERMIND

The Bill Clinton section of this chapter is sourced from interviews and correspondence with Jann Wenner, P. J. O'Rourke, and Corey Seymour. George Stephanopoulos was featured in Peter Osterlund, "The Hill Climbers," *Rolling Stone*, March 23, 1989. The "coming-out" section was constructed from conversations with Jann and Jane Wenner, Matt Nye, John Lagana, Michelangelo Signorile, Robbie Robertson, Johnny Pigozzi, Bette Midler, Kent Brownridge, Patrick Reilly, Ben Needell, Tom Freston, Mick Jagger, Chris Blackwell, Earl McGrath, Edmund White, Tony King, Elton John, David Geffen, Sim Wenner, and Bob Pittman. This quotation—"My," said Wenner, "he's very attractive"—was reported by Jeanie Russell Kasindorf for *New York*, March 13, 1995. Some biographical details about Nye come from Jode Jaffe, "Prince Charming," *Out*, Sept. 1999.

23. BRIDGES TO BABYLON

The section about *Us Weekly* is constructed from interviews and correspondence with Jann Wenner, Kent Brownridge, Tom Freston, Ben Needell, Terry McDonell, Bonnie Fuller, Janice Min, Bob Love, John Lagana, Michael Eisner, and Gary Armstrong. The next section, about the revival of *Rolling Stone*'s politics, is sourced from interviews and conversations with Bob Love, Will Dana, Eric Bates, Matt Taibbi, Sean Woods, and Jason Fine. The Hunter Thompson section comes from Will Dana, Rich Cohen, Douglas Brinkley, Laila Nabulsi, Corey Seymour, and Billy Tuchscher. The section on Wenner's life leading up to the 2008 economic crash comes from conversations and correspondence with Janice Min, Will Dana, Kent Brownridge, Ben Needell, Jon Landau, Gary Armstrong, Cathie Black, Billy Tuchscher, Tommy Cohen, Alex Wenner, and Laila Nabulsi. The story of Annie Leibovitz advising Wenner to chop down the trees is my own eyewitness account from 2013.

24. STILL CRAZY AFTER ALL THESE YEARS

The first section is sourced from interviews and conversations with Jann Wenner, Jon Landau, Bruce Springsteen, Matt Nye, Yoko Ono, Jane Buffett, and Bob Love. The Bob Dylan quotations come from the unedited transcript of an interview published in the fortieth-anniversary double issue of *Rolling Stone* on May 3–17, 2017. Wenner inspiring Joni Mitchell's "Lead Balloon" comes from Sheila Weller's *Girls Like Us*. The aborted *Rolling Stone* cover featuring Kanye West was tweeted by West on February 3, 2016, at 6:22 p.m. The section about the UVA scandal was constructed from an eyewitness encounter with Jann Wenner on the evening of Friday, December 5, 2014, in addition to interviews and correspondence with Will Dana, Sean Woods, Dana Rosen, Matt Taibbi, and Eric Bates, as well as reporting by T. Rees Shapiro of *The Washington Post* and the report assembled for the

Columbia Journalism School by Sheila Coronel, Steve Coll, and Derek Kravitz. The aborted profile of Secretary of State John Kerry after the Boston Bomber cover was originally assigned to me. The reporting on the El Chapo incident is derived from Robert Draper, "The Go-Between," *New Yorker,* March 21, 2016. The section on Wenner's family life was sourced from firsthand encounters and conversations with Matt Nye as well as interviews with Gus Wenner, Theo Wenner, Jane Wenner, Alex Wenner, Emily Wenner, Kent Brownridge, Jason Fine, and Tom Freston. The conclusion of the book was constructed from interviews with Jann Wenner, Will Dana, Sean Woods, Jason Fine, Matt Taibbi, Gus Wenner, Merlyn Wenner, Denise Kaufman, Sim Wenner, and Mary MacDonald.

Selected Bibliography

Anson, Robert Sam. *Gone Crazy and Back Again: The Rise and Fall of the "Rolling Stone" Generation*. Garden City, N.Y.: Doubleday, 1981.

Babitz, Eve. *Slow Days, Fast Company: The World, the Flesh, and L.A. Tales*. New York: Knopf, 1977.

Crouse, Timothy. *The Boys on the Bus*. New York: Random House, 1973.

Davis, Clive. *Clive: Inside the Record Business*. New York: Morrow, 1975.

Didion, Joan. *Slouching Towards Bethlehem*. New York: Farrar, Straus and Giroux, 1968.

———. *The White Album*. New York: Simon & Schuster, 1979.

Draper, Robert. *"Rolling Stone" Magazine: The Uncensored History*. New York: Doubleday, 1990.

Editors of Rolling Stone. *The Ballad of John and Yoko*. Garden City, N.Y.: Doubleday, 1982.

Fields, Danny. *Linda McCartney: A Portrait*. Los Angeles: Renaissance Books, 2000.

Fong-Torres, Ben. *Becoming Almost Famous: My Back Pages in Music, Writing, and Life*. San Francisco: Backbeat Books, 2006.

Gitlin, Todd. *The Sixties: Years of Hope, Days of Rage*. New York: Bantam Books, 1987.

Gleason, Ralph. *The Jefferson Airplane and the San Francisco Sound*. New York: Ballantine Books, 1969.

Goldman, Albert. *The Lives of John Lennon*. New York: Morrow, 1988.

Goodman, Fred. *The Mansion on the Hill: Dylan, Young, Geffen, Springsteen, and the Head-On Collision of Rock and Commerce*. New York: Times Books, 1997.

Greenfield, Robert. *The Last Sultan: The Life and Times of Ahmet Ertegun*. New York: Simon & Schuster, 2011.

Hinckle, Warren. *If You Have a Lemon, Make Lemonade*. New York: Putnam, 1974.

King, Tom. *The Operator: David Geffen Builds, Buys, and Sells the New Hollywood*. New York: Random House, 2000.

Landau, Jon. *It's Too Late to Stop Now: A Rock and Roll Journal*. San Francisco: Straight Arrow Books, 1972.

Leibovitz, Annie. *Annie Leibovitz at Work*. New York: Random House, 2008.

Lydon, Susan Gordon. *Take the Long Way Home: Memoirs of a Survivor.* New York: HarperCollins, 1993.

Marks, Craig, and Rob Tannenbaum. *I Want My MTV: The Uncensored Story of the Music Video Revolution.* New York: Dutton, 2011.

McDonell, Terry. *The Accidental Life: An Editor's Notes on Writing and Writers.* New York: Knopf, 2016.

McKeen, William. *Outlaw Journalist: The Life and Times of Hunter S. Thompson.* New York: W. W. Norton, 2008.

Palmer, Robert. *Blues and Chaos: The Music Writing of Robert Palmer.* New York: Scribner, 2009.

Pang, May, and Henry Edwards. *Loving John: The Untold Story.* New York: Warner Books, 1983.

Peck, Abe. *Uncovering the Sixties: The Life and Times of the Underground Press.* New York: Pantheon Books, 1985.

Perlstein, Rick. *Nixonland: The Rise of a President and the Fracturing of America.* New York: Scribner, 2008.

Richardson, Peter. *A Bomb in Every Issue: How the Short, Unruly Life of "Ramparts" Magazine Changed America.* New York: New Press, 2009.

Rosenbaum, Ron. *Murder at Elaine's: A Novel.* New York: Stonehill, 1978.

Selvin, Joel. *Altamont: The Rolling Stones, the Hells Angels, and the Inside Story of Rock's Darkest Day.* New York: Dey Street, 2016.

Seymour, Corey, and Jann Wenner. *Gonzo: The Life of Hunter S. Thompson.* New York: Little, Brown, 2007.

Signorile, Michelangelo. *Queer in America: Sex, the Media, and the Closets of Power.* New York: Random House, 1993.

Sloman, Larry "Ratso." *On the Road with Bob Dylan.* New York: Three Rivers Press, 2002.

Talbot, David. *Season of the Witch: Enchantment, Terror, and Deliverance in the City of Love.* New York: Free Press, 2012.

Taylor, Derek. *As Time Goes By.* San Francisco: Straight Arrow Books, 1973.

Terkel, Studs. *American Dreams: Lost and Found.* New York: Pantheon Books, 1980.

Thompson, Hunter S. *Fear and Loathing in America: The Brutal Odyssey of an Outlaw Journalist, 1968–1976.* Edited by Douglas Brinkley. New York: Simon & Schuster, 2000.

Townshend, Pete. *Who I Am.* New York: Harper, 2012.

Weller, Sheila. *Girls Like Us: Carole King, Joni Mitchell, Carly Simon—and the Journey of a Generation.* New York: Atria Books, 2008.

Wenner, Jann, ed. *Lennon Remembers: The "Rolling Stone" Interviews.* San Francisco: Straight Arrow Books, 1971.

Wenner, Kate. *Setting Fires.* New York: Scribner, 2000.

Wenner, Sim. *Back Away from the Stove.* Garden City, N.Y.: Doubleday, 1960.

———. *Daisy.* New York: Dell, 1961.

White, Edmund. *Arts and Letters.* San Francisco: Cleis Press, 2004.

Whitmer, Peter O. *When the Going Gets Weird: The Twisted Life and Times of Hunter S. Thompson: A Very Unauthorized Biography.* New York: Hyperion, 1993.

Wolfe, Tom. *The Electric Kool-Aid Acid Test.* New York: Farrar, Straus and Giroux, 1968.

Index

A NOTE ABOUT THE AUTHOR

JOE HAGAN has written for *New York, Rolling Stone, The Wall Street Journal,* and many other publications. He has published long-form profiles and investigative exposés of some of the most significant figures and subjects of our time, including Hillary Clinton (her first post-secretary-of-state interview), Karl Rove, the Bush family, Henry Kissinger, Dan Rather, Goldman Sachs, *The New York Times,* and Twitter. He lives in Tivoli, New York, with his wife and children.

A NOTE ON THE TYPE

This book was set in Hoefler Text, a family of fonts designed by
Jonathan Hoefler, who was born in 1970. First designed in 1991,
Hoefler Text was intended as an advancement on existing desk-
top computer typography, including as it does an exponentially
larger number of glyphs than previous fonts. In form, Hoefler
Text looks to the old-style fonts of the seventeenth century, but
it is wholly of its time, employing a precision and sophistication
only available to the late twentieth century.

Composed by North Market Street Graphics,
Lancaster, Pennsylvania

Printed and bound by Berryville Graphics,
Berryville, Virginia

Designed by Cassandra J. Pappas